THE GOVERNMENT OF ASSOCIATIONS

Selections from the Behavioral Sciences

edited by **WILLIAM A. GLASER** *and* **DAVID L. SILLS**

THE BEDMINSTER PRESS

CONTRIBUTORS

SETH ARSENIAN Professor of Psychology and Director of the Graduate Division, Springfield College. Author of *Bilingualism and Mental Development*. Co-author (with Francis MacKenzie) of *Counseling in the Y.M.C.A.*

NICHOLAS BABCHUK Associate Professor of Sociology, University of Nebraska.

ROBERT F. BALES Professor of Social Relations, Harvard University. Author of *Interaction Process Analysis*. Co-editor (with Paul Hare and Edgar F. Borgatta) of *Small Groups*.

ALEX BAVELAS Professor of Psychology, Stanford University.

WENDELL BELL Professor of Sociology, Yale University. Author of *Jamaican Leaders*. Co-author (with Richard J. Hill and Charles R. Wright) of *Public Leadership*.

ARTHUR BLUMBERG Associate Professor of Educational Psychology, Temple University.

DORWIN CARTWRIGHT Research Co-ordinator, Research Center for Group Dynamics, University of Michigan. Co-author (with Alvin Zander) of *Group Dynamics*.

ELIOT D. CHAPPLE Chief of the Behavior Laboratories of the Research Facility, Rockland State Hospital. Author of *Measuring Human Relations*. Co-author (with C. S. Coon) of *Principles of Anthropology*.

ORVIS COLLINS Associate Professor of Business Administration, Michigan State University. Co-author of *The American Federal Executive* and *The Enterprising Man*.

DONALD R. CRESSEY Dean of the College of Letters and Science and Professor of Sociology, University of California, Santa Barbara. Author of *Principles of Criminology* and *The Prison*.

KEITH DAVIS Professor of Business Administration, Arizona State University. Author of *Human Relations at Work*. Co-author (with Henry M. Cruickshank) of *Cases in Management*.

AMITAI ETZIONI Professor of Sociology and Research Associate in the Institute of War and Peace Studies, Columbia University. Author of *Modern Organizations* and *A Comparative Analysis of Complex Organizations*.

MARYANNE T. FORCE Instructor in Anthropology, University of Hawaii.

WILLIAM H. FORM Research Professor of Sociology, Michigan State University. Author of *Industry, Labor and Community*. Co-author (with Delbert C. Miller) of *Industrial Sociology*.

ORVOELL R. GALLAGHER Associate Professor of Anthropology, Skidmore College.

WILLIAM A. GLASER   Research Associate, Bureau of Applied Social Research, Columbia University. Author of *The Social Settings of Medical Care*. Co-author (with William McPhee and others) of *Public Opinion and Congressional Elections*.

C. WAYNE GORDON   Associate Professor of Sociology, Education, and Anthropology, University of California, Los Angeles. Author of *The Social System of the High School* and *Revolving Door*.

JOSEPH R. GUSFIELD   Professor of Sociology, University of Illinois. Author of *Symbolic Crusade*.

MURRAY HAUSKNECHT   Assistant Professor of Sociology, Hunter College, The City University of New York. Author of *The Joiners*.

CHARLES E. HENDRY   Director and Professor in the School of Social Work, University of Toronto. Author of *The Role of Groups in World Reconstruction*. Editor of *A Decade of Group Work*.

HERBERT H. HYMAN   Professor of Sociology, Columbia University. Author of *Political Socialization* and *Survey Design and Analysis*.

R. WALLACE JONES, JR.   Associate Director of the Center of Alcohol Studies, Rutgers University. Co-author (with S. D. Bacon) of *The Relationship between the Alcoholic Beverage Control Law and the Problems of Alcohol*.

BUFORD H. JUNKER   Chairman of the Social Science Department of the Southeast Junior College, Chicago City Junior College. Author of *Field Work*. Co-author (with W. Lloyd Warner and W. A. Adams) of *Color and Human Nature*.

C. WENDELL KING   Professor of Sociology and Anthropology, University of Massachusetts. Author of *Social Movements in the United States*.

PAUL R. LAWRENCE   Professor of Organizational Behavior, School of Business, Harvard University. Co-author of *Organizational Behavior and Administration* and *Administering Changes*.

RENSIS LIKERT   Director of the Institute for Social Research and Professor of Psychology and Sociology, University of Michigan. Author of *New Patterns of Management*. Co-editor (with Samuel P. Hayes, Jr.) of *Some Applications of Behavioral Research*.

SEYMOUR MARTIN LIPSET   Professor of Sociology, Harvard University. Author of *Political Man* and *Agrarian Socialism*.

MHYRA S. MINNIS   Associate Professor of Sociology, Texas Technological College.

EDWARD NORBECK   Chairman of the Department of Anthropology, Rice University. Author of *Takashima: A Japanese Fishing Community* and *Religion in Primitive Society*.

CHARLES P. PERROW   Associate Professor of Sociology, University of Pittsburgh. Co-author of *Organization for Treatment* and *Study on the Non-Segregated Hospitalization of Alcoholic Patients in a General Hospital*.

JOHN M. PFIFFNER   Professor Emeritus of Public Administration, University of Southern California. Co-author of *Public Administration* and *Supervision of Personnel*.

MARTIN REIN   Associate Professor of Social Work and Social Research, Bryn Mawr College.

ARNOLD M. ROSE   Professor of Sociology, University of Minnesota. Author of *Sociology* and *Human Behavior and Social Processes*.

MURRAY G. ROSS   President of York University. Author of *New Universities in the Modern World* and *Community Organization*.

PETER H. ROSSI   Director of the National Opinion Research Center, University of Chicago. Author of *Why Families Move* and *The Politics of Urban Renewal*.

LEONARD R. SAYLES   Professor of Business Administration, Columbia University. Author of *Individualism and Big Business* and *Managerial Behavior*.

JOHN R. SEELEY   Professor of Sociology, Brandeis University. Co-author of *Community Chest* and *Crestwood Heights*.

HANAN C. SELVIN   Chairman of the Department of Sociology, University of Rochester. Author of *The Effects of Leadership*.

PHILIP SELZNICK   Chairman of the Department of Sociology, University of California, Berkeley. Author of *TVA and the Grass Roots* and *Leadership in Administration*.

FRANK P. SHERWOOD   Professor of Public Administration, University of Southern California. Author of *Management Approach to Budgeting* and *The Mayor and the Fire Chief*.

VIOLET M. SIEDER   Associate Professor, The Florence Heller School for Advanced Studies in Social Welfare, Brandeis University. Author of *Community Organization for Rehabilitation*.

DAVID L. SILLS   Research Associate, Bureau of Applied Social Research, Columbia University. Editor of the *International Encyclopedia of the Social Sciences*. Author of *The Volunteers*.

HERBERT A. SIMON   Professor of Administration and Psychology, Carnegie Institute of Technology. Author of *Administrative Behavior*. Co-author (with James G. March) of *Organizations*.

WILLIAM SPINRAD   Associate Professor of Sociology, Paterson State College.

GEORGE STRAUSS   Professor of Business Administration and Research Economist in the Institute of Industrial Relations, University of California, Berkeley. Author of *Unions in the Building Trades*. Co-author (with Leonard R. Sayles) of *The Local Union*.

JAMES D. THOMPSON   Professor of Business Administration and of Sociology, Indiana University. Author of *Organizations in Action*. Co-editor of *Comparative Studies in Administration*.

VICTOR A. THOMPSON   Professor of Political Science, Syracuse University. Author of *Modern Organization*. Co-author (with Herbert A. Simon and Donald W. Smithburg) of *Public Administration*.

MARY B. TREUDLEY   Professor Emeritus of Sociology, Wellesley College. Author of *Prelude to the Future: The First Hundred Years of Hiram College*.

JOHN E. TSOUDEROS   Senator in the Parliament of Greece. Author of *Agricultural Cooperatives in Greece* and *Regional Development*.

CHARLES R. WRIGHT   Associate Professor of Sociology, University of California, Los Angeles. Author of *Mass Communication*. Co-author (with Wendell Bell and Richard J. Hill) of *Public Leadership*.

Voluntary associations are a familiar and essential part of modern society, but few books have been written about them. There are some interesting but essentially journalistic descriptions of the role of voluntary associations in American life; there are some training manuals prepared for the use of professional and volunteer leaders; and there are some sociological analyses of individual voluntary associations. Some of the selections in this book of readings are drawn from this handful of sociological studies.

A full-scale analysis of the organization, activities, and accomplishments of voluntary associations is sorely needed; preparing it would be a formidable undertaking; and in the end it would probably be of interest primarily to behavioral scientists. We have attempted to achieve a more modest goal by preparing this book of readings; it is our hope that it will find an audience both within and beyond the audience of behavioral scientists.

PURPOSE

The book consists of 47 selections from books, journals, and research reports in the behavioral sciences. Twenty-seven of the 50 contributors are sociologists; six are political scientists; five are psychologists; and four each are from the fields of anthropology, business administration, and social work. By design, none of them is primarily a professional in the field of national organizations, for the book has been planned to report research results rather than the experience of informed insiders.

The behavioral sciences are a new grouping of fields that have traditionally belonged to the social sciences. Since the grouping is new, the boundaries are not firm, but it is widely agreed that the behavioral sciences include at their center those portions of sociology, anthropology, psychology, and political science that study human behavior at first hand, i.e., by observing and interviewing people. In that sense they differ from the other social sciences, which for the most part study human behavior at second hand—through the analysis of census data, artifacts, economic statistics, government documents, and the written record of mankind. The name is newer than the methods, and its creation a decade ago seems to have had a healthy influence on the social sciences. It is difficult to say whether it is cause or effect, but the past decade has certainly witnessed an increased level of collaboration both within the social sciences and between the social sciences and such related disciplines as education, genetics, law, and psychiatry.*

The behavioral sciences attempt to describe and explain human behavior; their concern is with how people *do* behave rather than with how they *should* behave. Accordingly, most of the selections in this book are reports of empirical research, rather than directives for action. Occasionally behavioral scientists do make recommendations, and a few practical advisory essays are included. We have tried to recognize our responsibility to those readers who want or need translations from research reports into prescriptions for action: we have selected materials that seem to us to have rather obvious implications for professional and volunteer leaders; we have given the selections titles and arranged them into parts and chapters that help

* The interested reader should consult Bernard Berelson and Gary A. Steiner, *Human Behavior: An Inventory of Scientific Findings* (New York: Harcourt, Brace & World, 1964) for a review of the fields, methods, and findings of the behavioral sciences.

to point out their relevance; and we have inserted introductory and transitional paragraphs (in italics) to guide the reader from one selection to another and to point out possible applications to a situation he might face.*

AUDIENCE

We have tried to attract two different audiences, and we have tried to avoid including materials that are readily available to each. First, we hope that the book will be useful to leaders, board members, working volunteers, and staff members of voluntary associations. But it is not primarily a manual of practical advice; readers can find elsewhere many valuable books of this nature. For example, the Association Press has published a number of useful guides to the management of voluntary associations, such as Harleigh B. Trecker, *New Understandings of Administration* (New York: Association Press, 1961). Nor is it in any sense a reference book, such as the *Encyclopedia of Associations* (Detroit: Gale Research Company, 4th edition, 1965), which lists the basic descriptive information about 12,900 national voluntary associations in the United States.

Second, we think that the book will be useful to behavioral scientists and social workers—both students and professionals—who are interested specifically in voluntary associations. This audience has a number of excellent collections of essays in organizational sociology available to it—e.g., Robert K. Merton et al. (editors), *Reader in Bureaucracy* (Glencoe, Ill.: The Free Press, 1952); Amitai Etzioni (editor), *Complex Organizations* (New York: Holt, Rinehart and Winston, Inc., 1961); and James G. March (editor), *Handbook of Organizations* (Chicago: Rand McNally and Co., 1965). These collections, however, are largely devoted to discussions of government, business, and industrial organizations.

SCOPE

The scope of this volume is best defined by its title and its table of contents. We have called it *The Government of Associations* in order to stress an important difference between voluntary associations and business and industrial firms: leadership in voluntary associations is to a much greater extent based upon the consent of the participants. Voluntary associations are in a very real sense private governments, and we hope that the title will serve as a reminder of this important aspect.

We have tried to present a representative selection of the research literature about organizations; we hope we have selected the best; and we have tried to represent a wide range of points of view. Whenever possible, we chose reports on voluntary associations. But since not enough research has been carried out exclusively on voluntary associations, some selections concern other private organizations—business firms, trade unions, and factories. Since many characteristics and problems are inherent in organizational structure, translation of these findings into findings that pertain to voluntary associations should not prove difficult.

ACKNOWLEDGMENTS

This book is one product of a program in leadership development sponsored by the Council of National Organizations for Adult Education (CNO), an organization of national organizations that seeks both to provide materials and to sponsor conferences on the organizational and educational aspects of volutary associations. It was prepared under the auspices of the Bureau of Applied Social Research, Columbia University, with a supporting grant from the Fund for Adult Education, which was administered by the CNO.

* Portions of most selections, and many footnotes, have been deleted when they did not seem useful to the readers of this book.

The editors are grateful to the officers of the Fund and of the CNO for their support, and particularly to an advisory committee chaired by Evelyn Christiansen of the Young Women's Christian Association. At the final stages of preparation, George Beebe, President of the CNO, provided welcome assistance in making arrangements for publication.

Our grateful thanks go to the authors and publishers who gave us permission to reprint the selections in this book; we hope that the authors are not too dismayed by the titles we have given their selections and by the deletions we felt were necessary to suit the purposes of the book. Formal acknowledgments and bibliographical citations are given at the beginning of each selection.

We also wish to thank Fred Abrahams of the Bureau for his assistance in searching the literature of the behavioral sciences and in nominating selections for inclusion; Madeline Simonson of the Bureau for her skillful handling of administrative details; and Nelson Glover and Ivan Merber of the Bureau for their conscientious typing of a complicated manuscript. Blaise Zito of SDZ Associates redrew all of the figures, carefully following the details in the original drawings. Shirley Diamond prepared the index. Diane Olsen of the Bedminster Press guided the manuscript from typescript to published book. The co-editors, however, are jointly responsible for whatever errors and shortcomings the book contains.

WILLIAM A. GLASER
DAVID L. SILLS

New York City
March 1966

CONTENTS

PART ONE
VOLUNTARY ASSOCIATIONS:
AN OVERVIEW

1 THE SOCIAL ORIGINS OF VOLUNTARY ASSOCIATIONS

Every association obtains both its originating stimuli and its continuous support from a larger social system. Therefore, whether a certain type of association can exist at all and the particular form that it takes depend on the nature of the society. Some societies have few voluntary associations of any kind, and those that exist have limited power. As observers have noted for over a century, America long has had many influential voluntary associations.

In order for voluntary associations to flourish, a society must have certain characteristics. There must be a tradition of limited central power and of performance of social functions by numerous smaller units; voluntary associations will not be created if everyone assumes that the state or the church should solve every social problem. The government must not have a tradition of closely controlling and manipulating private organizations. The country's religion and national philosophy must to some extent preach the duties of the community and of community elites to help the less fortunate. The religion and national philosophy must be optimistic, so that it is assumed that the plight of the unfortunate or of society as a whole can improve. The upper and middle classes must have enough time and money to spare for association activity. These broad social conditions exist in some countries—particularly in the United Kingdom, Scandinavia, the Netherlands, and the United States—and have resulted in a strong tradition of voluntary service association activity. In many other countries, the social conditions are largely absent and associations are few and weak. This book is largely concerned with the American situation. Chapter 5 presents two selections that describe the structure and function of voluntary associations in two other countries—Japan and France.

The types of voluntary association existing at a particular time depend on the problems, personnel, and resources generated by the contemporaneous social environment. Changes in the society will produce changes in the number, types, and organization of its voluntary associations. The first selection, by Violet Sieder, describes how the history of voluntary associations of the social service type in America has been affected by the evolution of American society.* Changing social conditions have produced new problems, thus creating occasions for new voluntary associations and causing old ones to change their goals. Changes in the class structure have altered sources of voluntary personnel and funds. Crises have produced sudden shortages of personnel and funds and have created opportunities for new contributors, such as female volunteers, who remained active thereafter. As technical expertise developed in American life, as association work became more complex, and as the leisure class, full-time volunteer disappeared, the leadership of associations became professionalized. While social change was altering the volunteer, it introduced into the associations a new type of member, thereby creating new organizational problems of relationships. As Sieder notes, social changes are continuing—such as the movement of the upper classes to suburbs far away from their lower class clienteles—and therefore associations are continuing to change in response. Sieder's paper devotes special attention to the volunteer and voluntary associations in social welfare activities, but social change affects other associations similarly.

---

* For a similar social history of voluntary association in a Canadian city, see Aileen D. Ross, "Organized Philanthropy in an Urban Community," *Canadian Journal of* *Economics and Political Science*, Volume XVIII, Number 4 (November 1952), pp. 474-486.

THE HISTORICAL ORIGINS OF THE AMERICAN VOLUNTEER*
Violet M. Sieder

The numbers and personal characteristics of volunteers has varied drastically from one period of history to another, and between one field of service and another in the same period of history. In general, it can be said that the age, sex, income level, social status, and organizational affiliation of volunteers at given times in history were directly related to social, economic, and political conditions and to such exigencies as war, depression, prosperity, or periods of heavy immigration and population mobility.

Central to any examination of the changing role of the volunteer is the complementary and changing function of the paid staff member. Although this differs between fields, it is safe to say that there has been a significant reversal of roles in most fields. In the early days the volunteers employed staff to undertake routine activities, reserving the "treatment function" to themselves. Today the professions of social work, nursing, recreation, and allied fields are reexamining their functions to factor out those activities not requiring expert knowledge gained through specialized training and are employing paid aides or seeking volunteer help for these tasks. Where treatment begins and ends is a moot question, with modern practice conceding that this function can be a shared one if sufficient controls are established. In fact, a partnership approach can even enhance treatment in many situations . . .

The broad outlines of historical development of social services will show movement from independent and fortuitous activity on behalf of helpless members of the community to the institutionalization and professionalization of services in which the volunteer becomes a supervised and defined part of an organized approach to meeting human needs.

In the Colonial period the natural hazards to living made necessary a code which placed emphasis on industriousness and thrift and which equated poverty and moral weakness with sin. We can trace our attitudes toward the rights and responsibilities of individuals in a democracy to these early days when a premium was placed upon independence and self-help, and when success was attributed to hard work, thrift, and shrewdness, while failure was an individual fault for which society was not responsible. Individual problems were handled in Puritan times by the clergy and in Colonial times through discussion at the town meeting for those with "legal settlement."

* Pages 40-58, "The Citizen Volunteer in Historical Perspective," by Violet M. Sieder, from *The Citizen Volunteer*, edited by Nathan E. Cohen. Copyright © 1960 by The National Council of Jewish Women. Reprinted with the permission of the author and Harper & Row, Publishers.

The overseer of the poor was introduced after the English pattern in the early 1700's to handle the indentured immigrants so as to protect the town against the poor and destitute. The employable youth and adults were auctioned to farmers and other poor were sent to almshouses.

It was not until after the Revolution and the coming of the industrial revolution that social work institutions were created to correct "social evils." In the period from 1820 to 1860 the population was swollen by four million immigrants and a high birth rate. The population began to shift from rural areas to cities in response to industrial growth and increasing demands for labor. Women, children, and immigrants provided a source of new workers which changed patterns in the home and created social problems for the community. These problems, in turn, awakened the moral conscience of the country and resulted in efforts to reform both the individual and the society of which he was a part.

The reformers, the volunteers of their day, belonged to the new social class of industrialists and bankers most of whom were influenced by their religious Protestant background and laissez-faire economic theory to undertake "good works" on behalf of the "shameful poor." It is not surprising, then, that the wealthy men who organized and served as friendly visitors for the association for the Improvement of the Poor in New York City in 1843 placed emphasis on moralizing and teaching the individual, even though this period followed a severe depression. Emphasis was placed on the "wise giving" of charity so as to prevent "sliding into pauperism." This was achieved by influencing morals through religious principle, teaching the virtue of industriousness, and setting a good example through superior character. As this responsibility became burdensome, paid agents were employed to do the routine fact finding and to handle relief payments, since the giving of money was considered secondary to the influencing of behavior. The prestige role was carried by the wealthy, educated, hard working upper class male volunteer. To be "idle rich" was as reprehensible as to be poor, for laziness was the sin.

The Charity Organization Society was introduced in Buffalo following another severe depression in 1873, to examine and coordinate the giving of charity. Agencies grew out of the personal interests of wealthy individuals, inspired by local concerns or by growing national movements. Loring Brace had initiated the Children's Aid Society in 1853 to place "vagrant boys and girls" with families in rural districts.

YMCA's were organized in this same period to care for rural youth coming to the city by providing a home away from home under good moral influence. The young men in these associations undertook volunteer activities as part of their Protestant evangelical mission. Homes for unmarried mothers were established by various religious groups. The Independent Order of B'nai B'rith was organized in 1843 as a mutual aid society for German Jews. Most Jewish benevolent societies prior to 1850 were related to synagogues, and gave help to immigrants, transients, and the local poor in the congregation. At about this same time, in 1845, the Society of Saint Vincent de Paul was founded in the United States as an association of Catholic laymen who volunteered their services "to promote the spiritual welfare of members through works of charity, material and spiritual." This it accomplished by giving personal service through home visits to give advice, encouragement, and financial aid to the poor and the sick.

The Civil War further developed the institutionalization of charity as people were encouraged to support agencies rather than to give personal charity. This period has great significance for women volunteers, for as men were unavailable for war relief tasks, women were emancipated for charitable work and they took over the hitherto male friendly visitor and other roles.

Public agencies in this same period also claimed the attention of the volunteers as the more progressive states in the 1860's established welfare boards, and local departments recruited visiting committees to stir the indifference of church members to terrible conditions in institutions for the poor. However, public aid was generally neglected as private charities flourished. Although concern was felt over children held in poor houses, the horror of these institutions was justified as a deterrent to poverty out of dread to be sent there.

When the Charity Organization Society of New York City was organized in 1882, there were 194 private agencies giving relief on an uncoordinated basis. To assure care for the "worthy poor" the society's volunteers carried out investigations of applicants, established a central registration system to avoid duplication, and encouraged inter-agency cooperation. The city was divided into districts, each with an advisory committee. Paid agents investigated the need for aid, the district committee determined the course of treatment, and the volunteer gave the treatment. It was theorized that the friendly visitor could influence the poor family by virtue of his superior class. The friendly visitors of the Charity Organization Societies of this period offered a combination of detective and moral influence whose objective was to overcome weakness of character, intellect, or body necessary to establish individual independence. During the eighties and nineties paid workers replaced the volunteers because not enough able and willing wealthy ladies and gentlemen were able to give time.

This system changed as Mary Richmond of Philadelphia and Zilpha Smith of Boston distinguished between pauperism and poverty, and recognized that poverty had multiple cases. Poverty was recognized as a social as well as an individual problem. Social investigation was undertaken to determine how, not whether, to give treatment. Social work was born as a profession at the turn of the century when emphasis was placed on the "helping process." The paid workers, as trained observers, gathered data pointing to poverty as an abnormal condition requiring fundamental changes in income, housing, employment practices, health conditions, education, and recreation. As a result of this more scientific approach, it became clear that increased giving by the wealthy was not enough to solve the problem.

The emphasis on social justice became the core of the settlement house movement, initiated in 1880 in the United States by Jane Addams at Hull House in Chicago. The pioneer workers were young people from middle- and upper-class families who escaped sheltered homes to experience the reciprocal advantage of associating with people from different economic and social backgrounds. The program centered in clubs and groups, although the settlements pioneered any needed activity not carried on by others. Activities ranged from playgrounds and kindergartens to baths and social reform. Slum dwellers were neighbors to be liked and respected. Then, as now, settlement philosophy was to help people to work together to meet their own needs. Emphasis was upon social reforms rather than individual improvement. Although settlement houses have continued through the years to depend on large numbers of volunteers, they, like other welfare agencies, began to employ staff for administering the program.

This growing group of paid workers in charitable organizations began early in the twentieth century to develop a profession of social work. There followed years of self-conscious preoccupation with defining a philosophy and developing methods and techniques. In the struggle for recognition and status, the paid worker often felt threatened by the volunteer who until recently had carried the responsibility. Agencies, too, sought status through the employment of trained personnel.

At this crucial period in the history of volunteers, two women's organizations, The National Council of Jewish Women and the Association of Junior Leagues of America, were born, both of which have made significant the role of the trained volunteer and at the same time enhanced the value of the trained paid worker. This they did through active participation, as formally organized groups of volunteers, in the philanthropic enterprises of the community, often creating and demonstrating needed but nonexistent services. Since "lady bountifuls" were being relegated to the administrative volunteer responsibilities of board and committee work involving policy making, financing, and interpretation of services, the ladies sometimes organized and operated their own charities, in which they could directly serve people in need. Young women in both organizations were being trained for community leadership by gaining first hand knowledge and experience in social service, recognizing that they would later carry important responsibilities as board members.

Founded in 1893 by Mrs. Hannah G. Solomon of Chicago, the National Council of Jewish Women has as its purpose religious education and philanthropy. From the first, Council recognized and emphasized the importance of "scientific" training for social service of both volunteer and paid personnel. Although scholarship programs have been developed for the training of professional social workers, volunteers have always carried important roles. In 1894 a junior section was established (since discontinued) "to give young women an experience in democratic institutions" and became one of the first youth organizations in the United States. Council early established a policy of undertaking programs not offered by other organizations, and then turning over a demonstrated service to other public or voluntary groups better equipped to handle them on a broader basis. Thus Council sections in a number of cities pioneered neighborhood centers, day nurseries, free dispensaries, and work with prisoners.

The Association of Junior Leagues of America was founded some years later, in 1921, with emphasis on volunteer service to community agencies and education for citizenship. It was an exclusive membership organization for young ladies in the socially and economically prestigeful families to whom the community looked for support and leadership for health and welfare programs. Social service on a voluntary basis was a condition of membership, and although the organization offered the attractions of social functions and social status, it served as a vehicle for exposing sheltered young women to social problems and for training them in methods for dealing with such situations. Many outstanding leaders of international, national, and local agencies owe their start to this important volunteer organization.

With the great improvement in economic conditions in the early 1900's, social reformers saw in abundance an opportunity to alleviate inadequate living standards through a redistribution of wealth. As the concern of people from all classes of society turned to the effect of low wages, child labor, and poor working conditions on breeding poverty, new sources of citizen participation joined the ranks of social reform. Thus the working man expressed himself through labor unions, which together with religious groups, consumers leagues, federations of women's clubs and other organizations joined forces with settlement houses and charities aid societies to promote child labor legislation in spite of opposition from the National Association of Manufacturers. The National Child Labor Committee, and its promotion of the United States Children's Bureau established in the Department of Commerce and Labor in 1912, was a direct result of citizen volunteer efforts directed at prevention of social ills.

Public opinion was mobilized through the White House Conference on the Care of Dependent Children in 1909, the first of a series of decennial conferences held on problems of children ever since. Concern for infant deaths and births, children's education, living, working, and health conditions now become a federal government responsibility. Thus the accepted democratic value of the importance of human life over money making and goods was reaffirmed.

Volunteers found new opportunities for service in the recreation-informal education agencies organized for boys and girls early in the twentieth century. Boys Clubs (1906), Boy Scouts (1910), Camp Fire Girls (1910), Girl Scouts (1912), Pathfinders of America (1914), the National Jewish Welfare Board (1917) all depended, as did the settlements, YMCA and YWCA before them, on citizen volunteers. Most of these agencies were dedicated to an ideology which guided the nature of their program activities and the selection and training of their volunteers. It is significant that these organizations, which built strong membership and volunteer identification, prospered and grew. Citizen involvement made for general understanding, acceptance, and support of programs dedicated to citizenship, homemaking, and other widely held middle-class American values.

Although there was a growing consciousness of the need for training, volunteers and paid staff were exposed to the same institutes given by the new schools of social work and social science departments of universities. It was not until Mary Richmond's book *Social Diagnosis* was published in 1917 that social work, particularly case work, began to identify itself as a profession. In this same year, the National Social Workers Exchange was established to bring together opportunities in the field of social work and available paid and volunteer workers. This organization was the forerunner of both the social work professional associations and the volunteer bureaus of later days.

In fact, the responsibilities of the Exchange for standard setting and professional concerns were taken over by the newly created American Association of Social Workers in 1921, while the Joint Vocational Service in 1922 carried the counseling and placement service.

As Nathan Cohen observes, "Mixed motives were undoubtedly involved in the striving for professional status in this period. For some it represented social status, for others it represented a way of drawing a line between the volunteer and the paid worker, and for a small group, conscious of the emergence of a unique methodology, it represented the recognition of a 'functionally specific technical competence'." [1]

As groups of citizens organized agencies to meet the many specific needs which their interest and awareness dictated, the community was bewildered by the complexity of the pattern of services and annoyed by the many demands for contributions to good causes. Not only were there agencies dedicated to family and child welfare, recreation and informal education, health and hospitals, mental health, and prison reform, but these in turn were under the auspices of various religious groups, nonsectarian bodies, and public departments. To "bring order out of chaos" and to protect the giver's dollar there were important developments in the field of social planning which created new roles for the volunteer.

From the organization of the first council of social agencies in Pittsburgh in 1908 and the first federated fund raising and planning body in Cleveland in 1913, the concepts of coordination and integration of services, joint planning by agencies for new services, and federated efforts at voluntary fund raising and distribution of the welfare dollar gained impetus. The board members of agencies and other influential citizen leaders became heavily involved in these new movements. The fund raising bodies attracted the top business and industrial leaders who were the backbone of the so-called "givers' revolt." Their wives, professional leaders from medicine, law, education, clergy, and other liberals were more strongly drawn to the cause of social planning. As the primary responsibility for fund raising shifted from the agency board to the community chest or fund, the membership of agency boards became more of a broad cross section of the community. Agencies now were responsible for their services to a broader community of givers, and the control of wealthy individuals and families of "pet charities" gave way to rotating board members who had to be more sensitive to public reaction.

This field of community organization came into prominence as it was called upon to mobilize community support for the social services necessary to the

prosecution of World War I. In 1918, the second year of our participation in the war, two national organizations were born: the American Association for Community Funds and Councils of America, Inc., and the United War Activities Fund. The latter brought together seven national agencies to establish a joint national budget, and to assign quotas to be raised by local war chests. This movement substantially increased amounts raised and the numbers of contributors, and expanded the twenty pre-war chests to 300 war chests. Thus for the first time national board members and business leaders engaged in a national planning effort affecting local community services on a coordinated basis.

The National Travelers Aid Association, Inc. was born in 1917, to meet the needs of people uprooted by war. Its work, carried out primarily by volunteers serving in railroad and bus stations, and more recently in airports, aided people moving within or coming to the United States. This agency played a significant role in World War II when the demands of war industries necessitated tremendous mobility on the part of large numbers of families.

World War I witnessed another major development in the expansion of volunteer service under the American National Red Cross, organized first in 1881. Charged with serving as liaison between the men in service and their families at home, the Home Service Bureau was developed to carry out this responsibility in more than 3,000 communities. Volunteers who were local chapter chairmen and their assistants were given training and performed services for a group of clients new to social agencies, since the problem was not necessarily economic need. Although some of the professional service was contracted by the Red Cross with local family and public agencies, much of the work was carried on by local volunteers.

The prosperous years between World War I and the depression of the thirties was characterized by increasing professional self-awareness, and attention to agency standards of service. In the traditional family and child welfare agencies, volunteers were being excluded from direct contact with the "client" and were relegated to clerical tasks or to service on boards and committees. Agencies strove toward professionalization of staff and high standards of service as a more important goal than the extension of services. Public agencies, the source of general relief, were directed by public officials often with the guidance of citizens boards, commissions, or committees. Volunteers served as institution visitors and as program assistants under both public and voluntary auspice.

The disastrous depression years of the thirties served to consolidate the experience of volunteers and to set and raise standards of volunteer work. Principally responsible for clarifying the role of the volun-

---

[1] Nathan E. Cohen, *Social Work in the American Tradition* (New York: Henry Holt–Dryden Press, 1958), p. 138.

teer were such national organizations as the Association of Junior Leagues of America, The National Council of Jewish Women, The Family Welfare Association of America (now the Family Service Association of America), and the National League for Public Health Nursing (now incorporated in the National League for Nursing, Inc.). Specific opportunities for volunteers in the health and welfare field were defined, and principles and techniques for recruiting, training, and supervising were worked out. The National Committee on Volunteers in Social Work, organized in 1933 as an independent group but with relationship to the National Conference of Social Work, brought together social workers and volunteers to stimulate and improve volunteer service. This was accomplished locally through the organization of volunteer bureaus, most of which formed a part of or were affiliated with the local council of social agencies. The volunteer bureau's function was to counsel and refer potential volunteers to the various health, recreation, and welfare agencies, both public and voluntary.

The depression days brought an important realignment of the responsibilities of public and voluntary agencies. Out of the pressures on time and funds came the principle that mass needs, be they relief or recreation, should be met by public agencies administering public funds. Voluntary agencies were to offer the intensive, specialized service needed by specific groups of individuals, and/or to demonstrate and initiate new services. This principle inevitably affected the opportunities for volunteer service. Since the public relief-giving agencies were employing large numbers of persons as investigators and clerical workers who otherwise would become clients, they offered little room for direct service volunteers.

Another factor affecting volunteer work in agencies at this time was the inclusion of social workers in trade unions. In the public field, the American Federation of Government Employees, organized in 1932, and the American Federation of State, County, and Municipal Employees, organized in 1936, both affiliates of the AFL, had social work members from government agencies. In 1937, several national unions with significant numbers of social work members were organized which emerged in 1946 to form the United Public Workers of America, affiliated with the CIO. The United Office and Professional Workers, through its National Social Service Division, coordinated the efforts of locals of the Social Service Employees Union serving social workers in the voluntary field. One concern of these unions was to protect employment opportunities for social workers and other paid personnel against replacement by volunteers. Social welfare had now become "big business" with thousands of workers in the ranks. Volunteers contin-

ued to serve the recreation and informal education agencies, the hospitals and health agencies, and through church and civic groups to man such auxiliary services as clothing collections.

The advances made in defining the role of the volunteer in the depression years were tested and further refined during World War II. With the creation of the Office of Civilian Defense, the independent Committee on Volunteers in Social Work was disbanded. By December of 1943, the OCD estimated there were 4,300 civilian defense volunteer offices with responsibility for manning the protective services and community war services. Under the latter category came most services in the social welfare field which were called upon to expand or to extend services to meet the needs of youth, women, old folks, and handicapped workers pressed into wartime employment. Disruption of home life placed heavy demands on day care, recreation, counseling, and other services for which volunteers were in urgent demand. Small communities previously without social work established services staffed largely by volunteers to meet pressing needs.

The United Service Organizations (USO),[2] made up of six national agencies, was created to meet warborn needs of the armed forces and workers in defense industries. Through its local Councils, the USO gave leadership to organizing volunteer service.

Wartime records show that eleven million volunteers served in a variety of volunteer capacities in many types of welfare agencies. More important, they demonstrated the values of broadening the base of citizen participation from volunteers drawn in the prewar years from the upper and middle classes to men, women, and children from all walks of life, regardless of race, creed, color, or economic status. Teenagers, retired people, members of organized labor, civic organizations, professional groups, all joined as volunteers and continue to serve. Some agencies, too, got their first exposure to volunteers during wartime personnel shortages, and have since continued or expanded opportunities for volunteer service.

Anticipating the termination of the OCD, the Association of Junior Leagues of America, and Community Chests and Councils of America, Inc., in 1944 jointly sponsored a study of postwar possibilities for local centralized services bureaus. The problem of maintaining the contributions of volunteers in peacetime, when they were no longer motivated by meeting the wartime crisis with patriotic service, was a central concern. It clearly called for national leadership, and

2 Made up of National Jewish Welfare Board, National Catholic Community Service, National Travellers Aid Association, Salvation Army, National Council of Young Men's Christian Associations, and the National Board of the Young Women's Christian Association.

the Advisory Committee on Volunteer Service, established by Community Chests and Councils of America, Inc., in 1944, assumed this responsibility. This became, in 1945, the Advisory Committee on Citizen Participation, jointly sponsored by the National Social Welfare Assembly.

It was responsible for organizing, in 1951, an Association of Volunteer Bureaus which holds annual workshops and institutes, and works on common problems. Out of these deliberations has come a shift in emphasis for volunteer bureaus from recruiting, interviewing, and referring volunteers to agencies, to consultation with agency staff and volunteer committees on principles, methods, and procedures best calculated to achieve a mutually rewarding experience for the volunteer and the agency. The agency continues to have the ultimate responsibility for selecting the individual volunteer, and for his training and supervision. The bureaus, however, have been able to advise agencies, on the basis of wide experience with many agencies, on both suitable activities, agency structure, and potential sources for recruitment. Volunteer bureaus have also consulted with civic organizations, labor unions, church groups, student groups, and other clubs in developing group volunteer projects. These include such diverse activities as planning parties or other entertainment for institutions and hospitals, making clothes, repairing toys, giving blood, clerical tasks, and public interpretation of agency programs. The exposure of large membership groups to the work of social agencies has done much to gain support and understanding for health and welfare work. These membership organizations have served as an important channel for recruitment of volunteers with special interests or skills, as for instance, a garden club to work with mental patients in growing flowers, an advertising women's club to help plan a foster home recruitment program, college students to paint and repair settlement house club rooms. In fact, it is the rare civic or citizen organization today which does not have an identification with one or more welfare projects in the international, national, and local communities of which they are a part.

In addition to direct service in agencies, increasing numbers of volunteers with special knowledge and skill have served on agency study and project committees. Their work is reflected in changes in agency policy and program in line with their findings and recommendations. Frequently such committees draw upon members of professions other than social work, such as lawyers, doctors, clergy, city planners, educators, psychologists, nurses and engineers.

Outstanding local volunteer leaders are drafted to serve on national agency boards and committees. Persons with local planning experience in community welfare councils, community funds, and federations are frequently called upon to serve national planning agencies as volunteers. Professional social workers also serve as volunteers in agencies for whom they are not employed, particularly their local council or fund. Needless to say, many social workers carry volunteer responsibilities in the National Association of Social Workers and its local chapters. They also work for Leagues of Women Voters, parent-teacher associations, boards of education and other related civic activities.

The post-World War II period brought new problems as well as the need for many adjustments. As was anticipated, this was a period of letdown for many volunteers. The end of crisis brought a release of tension and a sense of fatigue, and large numbers of volunteers deserted the agencies which had come to depend upon them. Some women turned their volunteer-gained knowledge and experience to gainful employment when patriotism no longer dictated a personal sacrifice of time.

The war-created problems of delinquency, need for day care, planning for refugees, and adjustments of new Americans did not disappear. In fact, the postwar period soon became the Cold War period. The Federal Civil Defense Administration set up by executive order of the President, was officially established by the Federal Civil Defense Act of 1950. Responsibility for civil defense was placed in the several states with the federal government providing coordination and guidance. Although FCDA set up a Volunteer Enrollment and Utilization Division in its Training and Education Office, which became a part of the Volunteer Manpower Office in 1951, this office was abolished in 1953. There has since been no counterpart to the Civilian Defense Volunteer Office of the old OCD. Rather, manpower needs of defense are expected to be met through existing governmental agencies, private industry, and health and welfare agencies except for those services for which there is no peacetime counterpart. Under this plan, volunteer bureaus worked cooperatively with the civil defense organization by recruiting and training volunteers for existing agencies which offered services keyed to the civil defense program.

The Cold War also brought a decentralization of industry, creating numerous new communities in former small towns or rural areas. These communities, made up primarily of young families, lacked the basic services of public health, hospitals, and education—to say nothing of recreation and family counseling. A new national organization, the United Community Defense Services, made up of fifteen national agencies, moved into the breach in 1950. New patterns of service were created by local leaders with the help of experts from national voluntary agencies and federal departments. Volunteer leaders had to be recruited even before paid staff was employed to guide their efforts. The tradition of citizen participation was put to severe tests, as persons with leadership experience in former home towns, and others new to volunteer work, went to work on community problems. The co-operation of organized labor, industry, public officials, and health and welfare agencies facilitated the process by submerging special interests to the common good.

Rapid changes were occurring in the life of big cities which drastically affected old patterns of volunteer service. Growing suburban areas drained off many city volunteers from the middle and upper income groups who busied themselves with interest in their new communities. Big cities, left with a population of the old, the very rich, and the poor, and large percentages of migrant Negro, rural white, and Puerto Ricans, were presented with new and extremely difficult problems of volunteer staffing. Although board members who worked in the city and lived in the suburbs continued to be willing to serve on an administrative and policy level, many experienced service volunteers were lost to the city agencies. New methods of recruiting, training, and assigning jobs had to be developed to teach the employed worker, the union member, the retired person, and the large corps of college and high school students. A large reserve of potential volunteers still exists among housewives with leisure, but this field remains uncultivated in most instances.

Without the experienced volunteers in the more economically privileged classes to work for and with people served by the agencies, these institutions, particularly the recreation and informal education agencies, have rediscovered the strengths in helping people to help themselves. Through block organizations and neighborhood and area councils, the citizen was put to work at identifying and solving his own problems through fact finding studies, planning, and social action. Tackling such problems as playgrounds, law enforcement, housing, intergroup tensions, and adult education, these local organizations more recently have been fostered and worked with by voluntary and public agencies which are promoting urban renewal. Once again, the role of the volunteer and the role of the professional are being defined, but this time in relation to community organization and city planning. The citizen volunteer leader works as decision maker and spokesman with public officials, legislative bodies, and public and voluntary appropriating bodies on behalf of his community. The professional offers expert knowledge on substantive matters and on methods of study and action. The strength of neighborhood planning rests on opportunities for joint action with similar organizations in other parts

of the city and metropolitan areas through associations of neighborhood councils, and backing and support from community-wide coordinating and planning bodies. Central community welfare councils in more than fifty cities in the United States are offering community organization staff service to neighborhood and area planning councils.

In spite of this rich heritage of experience, the essentiality of volunteers has only begun to be realized. Thanks to automation and improved methods of production, more goods are available for more people, although the working day and working week have been shortened. As August Heckscher, Director of the Twentieth Century Fund, notes in his 1956 annual report: "Two decades hence the five day work week is almost certain to have been reduced to four. Vacations have been lengthened, and meanwhile at both ends of the life span—youth and age—the period uncommitted to a regular occupation has been extended." This increased leisure time offers new opportunities to engage in cultural and civic activities; but these, in turn, call for expanded programs and leadership to meet the new demands upon them.

To complicate matters, health and welfare agencies are caught in a period of staff shortages as the small crop of depression babies reaches employment age and must be shared by all the professions, as well as by business and industry. The number of people to serve is greater than ever, thanks to the increased birth rate of the war years and increasing longevity made possible through scientific and medical knowledge.

This dilemma has been recognized by national agencies which are beginning to plan individually and collectively to meet it. The first line of defense is a reassessment of how the volunteer is being used in relation to professional staff and paid aides. The basic question is, where can the volunteer carry more and where should he carry less responsibility for agency programs? A few current developments are cited to illustrate this trend.

The Education–Recreation Conference of the National Social Welfare Assembly appointed a committee to study the problem of staff shortages. A first stage of this exploration resulted in the publication, in May 1958, of "Leaders and Leisure" followed by an all-day workshop in January of 1959 of representatives of national agency boards, staffs, and volunteers. This study showed that for four national recreation-educational agencies, the number of full time paid staff increased from 11,297 in 1950 to 12,843 in 1956. However, in this same period part time paid workers increased from 59,983 in 1950 to 77,625 in 1956; and most dramatic of all, the number of volunteers increased from 86,459 in 1950 to 164,998 in 1956. In terms of percentages of personnel, full time paid leaders decreased from 7 per cent to 5 per cent, part time leaders from 37 per cent to 30 per cent, while the number of volunteers increased from 56 per cent to 65 per cent. Two of these four agencies reported a decrease in actual numbers of full time paid leaders from 1950 to 1956. In 1956, six national recreation agencies reported that their positions for paid staff were 20 per cent vacant. Although most of those agencies had carefully delineated job descriptions and personnel policies for paid staff, little had been done to define or guide volunteer work in spite of its growing importance. The Assembly's Education–Recreation Conference is now charged with responsibility for further study and development of plans to meet this problem of staff shortages. This is to include an examination of the changing function of volunteers.

The family welfare field, with its emphasis on professional case work service, has traditionally used few volunteers. When the Family Service Association of America held an overflow session on direct service volunteers at its 1959 Biennial Conference, it became apparent that the tide had turned. Experience was cited by agency directors to show that volunteers do indeed have a unique and important contribution to make to the treatment process, and that they can free the professional worker from tasks auxiliary to the core of his practice. The problem of staff shortages proved to be an important consideration here, too.

In the health field, the National League for Nursing, Inc. has activated a Committee on Community Participation with responsibility for stimulating greater participation by citizens and civic organizations in advancing the standards and coverage of nursing care in local communities.

The American Public Welfare Association has developed a manual on organization and work with boards in public agencies and has endorsed the value of citizen participation on public agency boards and as service volunteers. A growing corps of friendly visitors to Old Age Assistance recipients, and the chronically ill, offer a much needed service to lonely people.

The Council on Social Work Education has held two workshops on the responsibility of schools of social work for preparation of students to work with volunteers; one in Los Angeles in 1945, and a second in Philadelphia in 1959. Reports from various schools indicate awareness of the importance of such training, but there is unevenness in coverage between fields and between schools. Community organization and group work courses contain more specific content, while case workers get little exposure. Attention in some schools is being focused on exposure of students to work with boards, committees, and direct service volunteers in their field work experience. There seems to be a general need for specific teaching materials and curriculum planning, to cover professional philosophy and attitudes toward volunteers as well as methods for working with them.

SUMMARY

The volunteer in health, recreation-informal education, and welfare agencies has been playing a changing role, but at each stage it has been essential. The activities of volunteers have been dictated by social, economic, and political considerations of the times, but a constant factor has been the motivation of citizens to change the lot of their fellow men for the better. From the Colonial period, when individual charity was directly administered, to the institutionalization of welfare with paid staff and structured programs, the volunteer has maintained his responsibility of stewardship.

At first an upper-class male activity, later the prerogative of society matrons, volunteers now represent a cross section of society. Motivated first by a desire to save souls from the degradation of poverty, volunteers learned the causes of social evils and promoted reforms. Then came the period of self-fulfillment and perfection of skills through training. Once again the volunteer is deriving satisfaction from identification with the community, and is playing a greater part in public social policy.

The individual volunteer long tended to identify directly with a favored agency. The volunteer bureau widened opportunities for matching skills with needed service. More recently, organizations such as service clubs, women's clubs, church organizations, labor unions and professional associations have enlisted their members in group projects or individual service.

The scope of welfare activities in which volunteers engage has completed a cycle: starting with reform programs embodying relief, housing, sanitation, and employment practices; moving through a period which narrowed welfare activities to those engaged in by the growing social work and health profession and practiced primarily in family and child welfare, recreation and informal education, and health agencies; and now expanded to services which include preventive health services, urban renewal, chronic illness and rehabilitation, international social welfare, and community planning.

Today's welfare planning was preceded by sociological studies of communities, such as the Pittsburgh study in 1909, and a preoccupation under charity organization societies with "neating-up" welfare services through integration and coordination. Today's volunteer must plan with the help of social science projective tools and the knowledge of social workers about social problems and their solutions for the design and development of new programs for the future. Faced with such tremendous problems as mental illness, chronic illness, juvenile delinquency, and growing numbers of aging and children, community planning has acquired a high priority on the volunteer's time. It no longer can be considered an adjunct to agency administration, but is, rather, an important function requiring the combined skills of many professions and interests, and projected to national and international dimensions as well as to the local community.

The volunteer shares with the paid staff the dilemma of trying to perfect quality by controlling numbers served; and, on the other hand, trying to reach the vast numbers of persons needing assistance. This problem is further complicated by existing and potential staff shortages in the years ahead. A reassessment of the professional's job in relation to his specific skills must be made in relation both to employment of paid aides, and the enlistment of volunteers. The time has come for concentrated attention upon perfecting methods for selecting, supervising, and generally integrating volunteers into our health and welfare agency programs as an essential part of the service. Only then can the welfare organizations of this country hope to tap the tremendous potential reserve of manpower available and necessary to meet the growing needs. In the face of international crisis and the battle for minds, this reorientation of social values becomes an imperative of our times.

BIBLIOGRAPHY

Brenner, Robert H. *From the Depths—The Discovery of Poverty in the United States* (New York: New York University Press, 1956).

Cohen, Nathan E. *Social Work in the American Tradition* (New York: Henry Holt-Dryden Press, 1958).

Goldman, Mrs. Maurice L. *The First Years: A History of the National Council of Jewish Women 1893-1943* (New York: National Council of Jewish Women, 1943).

National Council of Jewish Women, Inc. *Council Pioneer, 1893-1955: A History of the Vanguard of Social Advance*, 1955.

Sieder, Violet M. "Volunteers," *Encyclopedia of Social Work.* (New York: National Association of Social Workers, 1965). Volume 15, pp. 830-837.

Stein, Herman D. "Jewish Social Work in the United States," *1956 American Jewish Year Book* (Philadelphia: Jewish Publication Society of America, 1956), pp. 85-86.

Voluntary associations are not only affected by social change—as Violet Sieder points out—they are also instruments for bringing about social change.* Associations that are so influential as to bring about a fundamental change in the nature of society are relatively rare—but the history of Western society is studded with examples. When an association is this influential it is invariably merely an organizational expression of a much broader social movement.

Many societies generate social movements, and many voluntary associations were created by and are sustained by social movements. According to C. Wendell King's definition, a social movement is "a group venture extending beyond a local community or a single event and involving a systematic effort to inaugurate changes in thought, behavior, and social relationships." Some social movements are revolutionary, others seek only to reform selected parts of the society, others seek to resist changes proposed by revolutionary or reformist movements. Usually a movement begins as a small group of enthusiasts who sense a deficiency or hostile challenge in the society, propose remedies, and feel a common impulse for action. Dramatic leaders soon arise, and like-minded followers are attracted from many communities. The selection by King describes the careers typically experienced by social movements. Many voluntary associations have originated during the "organizational phase" of King's cycle.

---

* For a discussion of these two aspects of associations, see David L. Sills, "Voluntary Associations: Instruments and Objects of Change," *Human Organization*, Volume 18, No. 1 (July 1959), pp. 17-21.

CAREER PATTERNS OF SOCIAL MOVEMENTS*

C. Wendell King

INCIPIENT PHASE

There is no reliable way as yet to predict whether a specific undertaking will eventually develop into a full-blown social movement. At the time of inception, most such undertakings are almost formless and frequently confused in purpose. Many show little promise of growth, sometimes because they have only local appeal or because their goals are so immediate and specific. Others show greater likelihood of evolving into movements because of the potentially wide appeal of their aims, the capacities of the founders, or the social and psychological needs which they meet. The difficulty in prediction stems largely from the dynamic nature of movements and their goals. Thus an incipient undertaking whose ends indicate the least likelihood of sustaining a genuine movement may nevertheless flourish because these ends are altered from time to time—or what seems a beginning with real promise may abort because a more effective organization with similar purposes appears on the scene. This is to say that "independent variables" are a potential source of embarrassment for the person who forecasts that this or that sign of social ferment is a movement in the making . . .

The incipient phase, then, is one which is only recognized and defined in retrospect. It begins when the individual or individuals chiefly responsible for the inception of a movement become conscious of this possibility. The point of origin, however, is less important than the immediate social consequences of the innovator's inspiration. The initial period extends through the time when a small nucleus of followers comes to share the leader's ideas and enthusiasm. Throughout this period, the organization of the movement is almost always simple (though its elaboration may already be envisaged by some members). Initial members necessarily constitute a primary group marked by face-to-face informal relationships, and generally there is no more differentiation of statuses than the inevitable distinction between the founder and his coterie. Refined status differences rarely emerge at this early stage. The beginnings of Christian Science exemplify well the rather nebulous quality of the incipient phase. Though some of the early disciples were held in greater esteem than others by both Mrs. Eddy and their associates, statuses were fluid and ill-defined among the followers. Tactics remained relatively unformulated; about the only goal explicitly recognized was the spreading of the Christian Science gospel and the conversion of outsiders to the faith.

Although some writers claim that the birth of a movement is necessarily attended by a charismatic leader† (and his talents are undoubtedly helpful), cases can be found where, despite the absence of such leaders, movements have entered the world quite successfully. Contrariwise, his presence is no guarantee of success. The fact is that movements have been born through the efforts of some very ordinary people whose qualifications for leadership seem to have been chiefly enthusiasm and industry. Such a person was Oliver Kelley, founder of the Granger Movement and as unlike a charismatic leader as could be found. Indeed, when the national offices of the Grange were decided upon, he assumed the secretaryship rather than the presidency. Tireless and self-sacrificing though his efforts were, there is no evidence that he was a dominant policy-maker or in any way occupied a charismatic status.

During this first phase, goals are likely to be general and regarded by at least some members as immediately attainable; other ideological elements remain nebulous and tactics crude or unformulated. Loyalty is usually intense and group cohesion strong, reenforced by personal contacts between founder and disciples and by the emotional momentum generated through participation in a new undertaking. The magnetic founder of the American movement for birth control, Margaret Sanger, describes her early cohorts in this way: "When they remained they found work, work, work, and little recognition, reward, or gratitude. Those who desired honor or recompense, or who measured their interest by this yardstick are no longer here." At the same time, intimacy can also give rise to conflicts, and internal dissension is as possible now as in later stages. Limited size, experience, and resources make for vulnerability to opposing or competing groups. These and other hazards are especially formidable during incipience; hence a high mortality rate for young movements.

† [Inspired by the writings of the German sociologist Max Weber, many modern social scientists distinguish among three types of leadership. A "charismatic leader" is one who inspires followers by exhibiting magical powers, heroism, or other unusual gifts. A "legal leader" exercises domination by administering rational and well-known general principles that members of the group accept. Followers obey the law rather than obeying the specific individual who administers it. A "traditional leader" is the occupant of an inherited status that is customarily obeyed by the group. His orders follow ideas hallowed by long usage. Victor A. Thompson's essay on bureaucracy, reprinted in Chapter 8 of this book, analyzes these three types of leadership in organizational settings.—Eds.]

ORGANIZATIONAL PHASE

As the plans and ideas which originally existed only on paper or in the minds of founder and followers develop into systematic activities and a more definite organization, the movement enters its second phase. The transition takes place gradually, one phase blending into the next.

Organization becomes more and more complex as division of labor is made more specific. Though they are often untrained and part-time amateurs, functionaries are increasingly specialized in their activities and their offices are dignified by distinctive titles. Through the process of shuffling and re-shuffling of statuses, the outline of a hierarchy begins to emerge.

With respect to leadership types, generalization should be as cautious as in the case of the incipient phase. If the movement is founded by a charismatic leader, he may continue to head it throughout the organizational stage too. On the other hand, leadership may have evolved to the legal type. Elaboration of the hierarchy does not necessarily require a marked increase in the number of followers, for numerical growth may occur chiefly after such elaboration. The appearance of branches or chapters, however, as excrescences of the original group must wait upon membership expansion sufficient to support them. If the movement is a coordinated one, channels of communication and control are simultaneously developed to connect the local units with the central headquarters and perhaps with each other. The informality of the incipient stage is thus gradually lost, except among the local rank-and-file members. The Ku Klux Klan, for instance, achieved organization more rapidly than do most movements. The little group of Confederate veterans who founded it improvised much of the bizarre regalia and the equally bizarre offices which became the trademarks of the Klan. Soon the Southern countryside was flecked with white-robed, hooded night riders led by their Grand Dragons, Titans and Cyclops. With rapid growth in membership, state, county and community units appeared very early, all federated within an "Invisible Empire" which encompassed the entire South.

Ideological elements as well as structure undergo modification and rearrangement during the organizational phase. For example, in those movements where ceremony is emphasized, rituals will now be well worked out if they were not blueprinted previously; rarely are they developed or radically altered later on. Original goals are reappraised: some are now defined as ultimate rather than immediate possibilities, others discarded altogether in favor of quite different objectives. Since values and goals from the incipient phase are mainly of a general kind, they are now supplemented by more specific aims and values—espe-

cially if efforts at conversion have not been fruitful. The movement called Moral Rearmament illustrates this process of modification, for its original and rather nebulous goals of absolute purity, honesty, love and unselfishness were eventually overshadowed by emphasis on such objectives as industrial peace in the domestic sphere and pacifism in international relations.

Often neglected during the first phase, norms for behavior now become specified and so too their supporting sanctions. Proselytive tactics frequently change as trial and error proves some to be more effective than others; gradually they become more systematic and less a matter of improvisation or whim. Tactics of agitation are changed for the same reason and also for the sake of conforming with alterations in ultimate and immediate goals. Clearly, this stage of development is not only organizational but reorganizational as well.

In the organizational stage, a movement remains vulnerable to both external and internal threats to its survival. By altering goals and tactics with an eye to combating opponents or competitors, external hazards may be overcome. But the very steps necessary for success in that direction may at the same time alienate the faithful or create internal dissension. Rapid growth at this stage carries inherent dangers as new members bring into the movement new points of view; the reservoir of potential functionaries swells and competition for status achievement is intensified; local units may seek greater autonomy and local leaders greater recognition; the apostate becomes an increasing possibility and with him a major internal cleavage. Then too, many who join under impulse, in a flush of enthusiasm, may easily become disenchanted—especially if immediate satisfactions are not strong or if there is scant evidence of progress toward the attainment of goals. The Birth Control movement in the United States experienced these growing pains in the 1920's when internal differences of opinion arose over financial policies, the recruitment of members, and the role of birth-control clinics; consequently the founder and the Birth Control League she had helped build went separate ways, each to make a new beginning.

STABLE PHASE

The organizational phase does not persist indefinitely in long-lived movements (although no undertaking can evolve into a full-fledged social movement without first attaining this stage). Any venture remaining in an extreme state of ferment dissipates its energies, so to speak, to the point of exhaustion: hence, some degree of stabilization is eventually required.

Another reason for stabilization is that movements

are one refuge for those members of a mass society who are in search of security, unequivocal values, and definite—even dogmatic—answers to their questions. The hope of finding meaning and direction for at least some part of their lives makes people converts. If, instead, normlessness and shifting goals are encountered, the hopeful convert may soon become a disgruntled deserter. Thus, some movements experience a high turnover in membership which can weaken group cohesion even though the total number of members does not decline.

These are some of the circumstances that guarantee that movements which persist beyond their days of organization and fermentation undergo a process of stabilization. Here stability does not refer either to the position of the movement in the greater society or to its numerical membership; it refers rather to an *internal* development during which the unsettled, organizational phase gives way to clarification and stabilization of the component elements of the movement. Goals are no longer shifting nor values transitory; tactics and other activities, no longer hit or miss, are now prescribed. Perspiration replaces inspiration as the basis of accomplishment. This is not to equate stability with a static condition, for ossification can be as fatal as continued instability. But the movement must attain enough equilibrium so that people can perceive clearly its aspirations and how it plans to realize them. The Grange affords an interesting case of a movement which, in its stable phase, returned to some of the original goals it discarded during the process of organization; at the same time the militancy and radicalism of its organizational phase was sloughed off, and—apart from agricultural problems —the movement in recent decades has generally favored the status quo.

Organization, as well as ideology and tactics, becomes more clearcut and orderly. A charismatic leader may postpone or limit stabilization, but with the end of such leadership the stable phase becomes imminent and inevitable. Principles for selecting the topmost leader or functionary must be formulated; other positions of authority and prestige must be given an air of legitimacy; and this process of routinization involves "transition from a charismatic staff . . . to one which is adapted to everyday conditions." [1] For example, the death of Mary Baker Eddy left Christian Science relatively unshaken, for she had herself instituted a complex and effective bureaucracy—headed by a self-perpetuating board of directors—to carry on the movement which had acquired its original momentum at her hands.

Unlike the earlier phases, stabilization requires a distinctive type of leadership, the legal as contrasted with the charismatic. The relationship of this leadership type to ideological elements is clear: legal authority involves a belief in the "legality" or rules and the right of those elevated to authority under such rules to issue orders. Conformity is largely obedience to legal commands, to an impersonal order, and not to an exalted or adored individual. Officers are organized as a bureaucratic hierarchy, each under the supervision of another on a higher level. Administrative functionaries are usually appointed, though the top level functionaries may hold office through election, designation, or even appropriation. The sphere and function of each office are clearly defined and the candidates are chosen presumably because they are technically qualified. Mere enthusiasm is not as sufficient an asset as it was in earlier stages. The officials are not bound to the legal chief as they were to the charismatic leader; they are personally free, apart from their impersonal official obligations. With such bureaucracy the performance of daily activities and operations can be routinized for maximum efficiency; internal stabilization of the movement as a whole is achieved.

[1] Max Weber, *The Theory of Social and Economic Organization* (New York: Oxford University Press, 1947), p. 371. [First published in 1922.—Eds.]

The relationships between voluntary associations and social movements are diverse. Some associations, such as historical study groups or certain associations for pursuing the self-interest of employees, may never have been directly connected with any social movement. Some associations are prominent in social movements and may have been the charismatic leader's specially-created instrument. Some may have been created during the early stages of a social movement, experiencing all its ups and downs. Others may have been created long after the movement has become routinized, and thus did not experience any of the organizational strains that might have resulted in earlier stages.

If a voluntary association arose during the organizational phase of a social movement, its leadership faces certain problems depending on the current stage of the cycle. Some of the problems may be inferred from King's typology. If the movement is just entering its organizational phase, it may still contain the charismatic leaders and zealous followers recruited during the incipient phase. They can instill the association with enthusiasm and attract considerable public attention, but they may complicate the attempts of any newly recruited professionals to routinize organizational procedures and financing. Because of their innovating enthusiasm, they may try to involve the association in new policies and, as described later in this book, changes of goal place great strains on the structure and personnel of associations. The enthusiasts may attempt suddenly to expand existing association activities and engage in new ones, both costing far more than the association's current income. While the professional seeks organizational stability, the enthusiasts may indulge in disputes about the goals and true spirit of the association. While the professional seeks favorable public relations that will ensure the association necessary funds and the cooperation of other organizations, the charismatic leader (being by nature a controversial and perhaps flamboyant personality) may attract to himself and to the association considerable criticism. During the organizational phase, the leadership of a voluntary association may have to cope with a considerable turnover in membership and in donors, and much of its energy must be devoted to recruiting and keeping both. The movement may have an expansionist and optimistic spirit, and the association leadership will be motivated both by its own attitudes and by membership demands to seek rapid increases in budget, membership, organization, and clientele; mere stability may damage morale, arouse internal disputes, and invite the formation of rival associations claiming to speak for the movement.

If the movement is well along in the stable phase, the leadership of the association will have quite different experiences. The early zealots will be gone, the charismatic leader no more than a hazy figure in association lore and a portrait in the board room. Such associations are easy to administer, but the leadership's problem (as shown in Chapter 11) is to prevent both employees and volunteers from becoming preoccupied with the organization's affairs to the neglect of its goals. Once beset by too many enthusiasts, the leader may find too few; once barraged by too many ideas for new policies and tactics, the leader may find that too few new ideas are advanced to cope with the changing social problems in the association's environment. The employees and voluntary membership may become complacent at having achieved part of the association's original goals and may relax their efforts short of complete success. The social problem may persist at a level that no longer critically disturbs society, while the association's containment actions give enough apparent justification for its continued existence. The association may come to rely on regular volunteers and on regular financial donors and thus, for organizational survival, it may become identified with certain groups and organizations in the society. Meanwhile, new social movements and new voluntary associations directed at publicized new social problems may be attracting the zealous volunteers, new financial donors, and public attention.

An example of the connections between a social movement and a voluntary association is the Planned Parenthood Federation of America, described in the selection by Martin Rein. The movement began at a strategic time in American history and thus was destined to grow: urbanization and the declining economic value of children were creating a desire for smaller families; the health, comfort, and employment of women were being given priority over traditional child-bearing roles. Numerous persons were becoming interested in birth control policy, but a charismatic leader electrified and personified the movement. Effective action was not possible without organization, but the various associations experienced dissension over goals, received alternating inspiration and harassment from the charismatic leader, and occasionally lapsed into a preoccupation with organizational procedure at the expense of goal fulfillment and vitality. The association itself experienced an organizational evolution from an early period of leadership by the charismatic leader and lay upper class volunteers to a later period of leadership by professional managers and physicians. As American society changed, the association's functions and structure changed. As the social demand changed from the prevention of unplanned large families to the creation of planned medium-sized families, the goals of the association had to change from contraception to family planning. As public taboos eased and as public interest increased, the association grew in activity and structure; but as contraceptive information became well known and available through medical channels, the association suffered the penalty of success and entered a period of temporary decline.

Since Martin Rein carried out his research, the Planned Parenthood Federation has entered new fields, reorganized itself, and grown in size. It merged with the World Population Emergency Campaign, thus increasing its concern for the world-wide population problem. In its domestic services, the Federation has become involved in many programs designed to assist low-income groups. Consequently, the adoption of new goals and structural reorganization have helped the organization to solve its dilemma.

THE TRANSITION FROM SOCIAL MOVEMENT TO ORGANIZATION*
Martin Rein

At the turn of the century Margaret Sanger, a visiting nurse on New York's lower East Side, observed with compassion and deep concern the endless cycle of problems created among her patients by large families, poor health and severely limited economic resources.

Time after time she treated women critically ill after having attempted crude, self-induced abortions. Such primitive and dangerous measures were anathema to Mrs. Sanger. The answer to the problem of controlling family size, she felt, must rest in medical contraception. To promulgate information on "birth control and procedure," which phrase she coined, Mrs. Sanger in 1912 launched a social movement that ultimately attracted national attention and affected public attitudes and social legislation.

The early history of the birth-control movement

* From Martin Rein, "An Organizational Analysis of a National Agency's Local Affiliates in Their Community Contexts: A Study of the Planned Parenthood Federation of America," an unpublished dissertation for the Doctor of Philosophy in the Florence Heller Graduate School for Advanced Studies in Social Welfare, Brandeis University, Waltham, Massachusetts, 1961. Reprinted with the permission of the author and the Florence Heller Graduate School.

was largely a chronicle of Mrs. Sanger's vigorous struggle to educate a public still constrained by Victorian reticence; to eradicate taboos; to establish contraceptive clinics; and to induce states to alter laws prohibiting or, at best, severely limiting circulation of birth-control information.

As part of a long range educational program Mrs. Sanger began publication, in 1914, of a monthly magazine, *The Woman Rebel*, whose maiden issue contained an article called "The Prevention of Contraception." The effort earned its originator not a heroine's acclaim but a Federal indictment. The specific charge was violation of the Comstock Law, an 1873 enactment forbidding, among other things, using the mails to distribute lewd and obscene literature. Though the law made no mention of contraception, its provisions were easily stretched to cover Mrs. Sanger's offense.

Forsaking, for the moment the field of battle, Margaret Sanger retreated to Europe to prepare for her trial—to which she seems to have looked forward as an opportunity to air her views on a public platform. It was perhaps with a certain amount of disappointment that the determined crusader saw her trial repeatedly delayed and the charges finally dropped.

The arena was not vacant during Mrs. Sanger's absence. In 1915, with the support of ardent feminists and Suffragettes, the National Birth Control League, the first national organization advocating birth control, was formed under the leadership of May Ware Dennett . . .

Mrs. Sanger, who saw herself as the agitator, not the organizer, as the rebel resisting the shackles of formal structure, shunned the League and declined to lend its early struggles her considerable support. On her return from Europe, before the wave of publicity that had followed her arrest had entirely dissipated, Margaret Sanger embarked on a tour of the United States to spread her gospel. Her perorations before women's groups in nineteen cities resulted in eight Birth Control Leagues being formed—in St. Paul, Minneapolis, Milwaukee, Detroit, Seattle, Spokane and Cleveland. Of these fruits of her labor Mrs. Sanger says:

> Not wishing to tie myself down to committees and organizations, so I could be free to organize and agitate, I referred all of these groups to the National Birth Control League, and hoped for the best.[1]

The function of these early Leagues is not entirely clear. In Mrs. Sanger's cryptic terms, they were "doing educational and practical work for the movement." Probably they served little actual purpose beyond providing occasions for their members to meet and serving as a reservoir of potential support for their progenitor, who was, by this time, ready for her next step.

In her talks with women across the United States, Mrs. Sanger—who had directed her appeal primarily toward the leaders of society in the communities she had visited—had sounded out her audiences on the advisability of establishing free clinics to dispense contraceptive information. Convinced by their responses that her idea had support, she opened, in the Brownsville section of Brooklyn, the nation's first birth-control clinic. The establishment, for whose opening Mrs. Sanger had taken pains to insure adequate publicity, was promptly raided and its founder arrested and charged with violating Section 1145 of the New York State Penal Law, which prohibited the distribution of contraceptives and birth-control information.

The society women whose sympathies Mrs. Sanger had courted rallied around their martyred champion. A reporter described the scene at the Sanger trial, which opened on January 29, 1917, as "more suggestive of a '400' social event than a criminal prosecution." [2] . . .

[1] Margaret Sanger, *My Fight for Birth Control* (New York: Farrar and Rinehart, 1931), p. 144.
[2] Quoted in Lawrence Lader, *The Margaret Sanger Story and the Fight for Birth Control* (Garden City, N.Y.: Doubleday and Company, 1955), p. 127.

Mrs. Sanger was convicted and sentenced to thirty days in Queens County Penitentiary. Judge Crane of the New York Court of Appeals upheld the conviction, but added an *obiter dictum* that Section 1145 was "broad enough to protect the physician who in good faith gives such help or advice to a married person to cure or prevent disease." This opinion Mrs. Sanger cited five years later as legal authority to establish the nation's first permanent birth-control dispensary—the Clinical Research Bureau, now the Margaret Sanger clinic.

ORGANIZATION AND SCHISM

With May Ware Dennett's death in 1919 the Voluntary Planned Parenthood League, outgrowth and successor to the National Birth Control League, dissolved, leaving no national organization to coordinate the work of the numerous local leagues. Mrs. Sanger, who had differed sharply with Mrs. Dennett on the best way to approach the problem of disseminating contraceptive information, in 1920 convened a conference of social and professional leaders to form a national birth-control organization. From the National Birth Control Conference evolved, in 1921, the American Birth Control League, which immediately elected Margaret Sanger president . . . The American Birth Control League served local leagues as a national clearing house, supplying them information, advice and, in some instances, moral support.

Mrs. Sanger felt that the best means to educate the public on scientific birth control procedures was through medically supervised clinics, and hoped in time to see contraceptive services offered in hospitals and public health agencies. As a start she applied, in the name of the League, to the New York State Board of Charities, for a license to operate a dispensary. Informed that the League's articles of incorporation did not authorize it to conduct a dispensary, she, with League backing, incorporated the Clinical Research Bureau as a separate organization. Partly because of Mrs. Sanger's own orientation as a nurse, partly because of a desire for respectability and prestige, and partly because of judicial interpretations like Judge Crane's, which decreed that physicians were exempt from the provisions of statutes forbidding dissemination of birth-control information, doctors were from the outset the Bureau's central professionals. The organization's purpose was not simply to distribute existing knowledge on contraception, but also, as its name implies, to develop new knowledge through research.

Forbidden, as a medical institution, to advertise, the Bureau was quartered in the same building as the League. Women who came to the League for advice were referred to the clinic for service. The Research

Bureau's success led local leagues to follow suit, until by 1930 fifty-five birth-control clinics were operating in twelve states.

THE CHANGING AMERICA

Changes in the structure of American society, particularly swift-paced in the years just following the first World War, had served to dispel some of the hostility engendered by Mrs. Sanger's earliest efforts, and to make the public much more receptive to her aspirations . . . In the wave of idealism that continued for a time after the war ended the principle of woman suffrage, already law in many states, was incorporated into the Federal constitution. The battle for the emancipation of women appeared to be won. Altered mores, the need to supplement family incomes in the face of a new inflation, mechanical aids to housework, and, perhaps, an exhilarated sense of their liberation all combined to send women in great numbers out of their homes into business and industrial worlds. The working woman could not be burdened with caring for a large family . . .

This was an age of ferment and agitation for social reform. Muckrakers deplored child labor, slums, political corruption and white slavery. And Eugene Debs, in 1920, led his Socialist Party to its highest plurality in a presidential election. Assured that prosperity would never end, the people began to prepare for a better tomorrow. The birth-control movement, like other social programs of its day, was in part a product of the general surge of social consciousness that swelled throughout the country. Margaret Sanger herself campaigned actively for Debs, and wrote a column, "What Every Girl Should Know," for the *Call*, a leading Socialist newspaper.

THE ANTI-ORGANIZATION WOMAN

In 1928 Margaret Sanger, beleaguered by the intricacies of an increasingly complex administrative machinery, withdrew from the American Birth Control League. Outlining the reasons for the rift, Lader says:

> They had fallen back into the conservative pattern of an organization that had tasted partial victory and was willing to settle for that. The executive board wanted only safety. Instead of the expansion that lay ahead, they wanted only to consolidate the gains of the past. Instead of faith and action they had substituted a new doctrine—the "doctrine of accountability." . . . All this machinery of "accountability" had the obvious purpose of checking the daring, the impulsive quality of her own leadership. Some of her critics had called it a "one-woman movement." . . . The league had become a creature of routine and red tape. The conservative bloc, trained in the rigid school of the League of Women Voters, had brought the doctrinaire and highly stratified approach of that organization to birth control. But this was a revolutionary movement . . . The members of the conservative bloc wanted to place the movement in the hands of women of leisure and

position, young women of the Junior League, who would take on birth control as a social responsibility, as one of their expected duties along with settlement home and welfare work . . . Even the conservative bloc's financial policy reflected this shift to quiet decorum. They instituted five- and ten-dollar membership, giving them the advantage of a planned budget. . . . Mrs. Sanger had made even finances a part of the ever changing pattern of struggle and development. Each new objective she made a campaign in itself.[3]

Though Mrs. Sanger did not mind the "theoretical" part of the organization passing into other hands, she insisted on retaining control of the Clinical Research Bureau. Resuming Mrs. Dennett's fight for legislation to permit free dissemination of birth-control information, shortly after leaving the League Mrs. Sanger organized the National Committee on Federal Legislation for Birth Control. (Though such legislation has not yet evolved, a 1936 judicial decision liberalized the Comstock Law to the extent "that contraceptives imported for a lawful purpose did not come within the restrictions of the Federal Statutes." [4]

EXPANSION AND MERGER

During the late 1920's and early 1930's the Clinical Research Bureau and the American Birth Control League operated as two separate and independent national organizations committed to common goals: to establish and maintain clinics and clinical services to gain acceptance from the medical profession; and to promote inclusion of birth-control clinics in public-health and welfare programs. The two organizations to a large extent duplicated each other's functions and competed for local league affiliations. Some local leagues belonged to both.

The two nationals retained their separate identities for eleven years, until 1939. The League recognized —after hiring a professional fund-raising organization to study its difficulties in attracting contributions —that it needed the appeal of Mrs. Sanger's name in order to survive.[5] On January 19, 1939, the American Birth Control League and the Clinical Research Bureau merged to form the Birth Control Federation of America. It was at this time that the Bureau was renamed the Margaret Sanger Clinic. Three years later the Federation changed its name to the present Planned Parenthood Federation of America.

The League and the Bureau brought to the new Federation several essential differences in emphasis and focus: (1) the Bureau accorded its affiliates more direct financial assistance than did the League; (2) the Bureau, stressing its program's medical aspects, employed two full-time doctors on its field staff,

---

3   Lader, *op. cit.*, pp. 249-251.
4   *Ibid.*, p. 433.
5   *Ibid.*, p. 309.

while the League was looking forward to replacing its graduate nurses with social workers, who would stress organizational development over medical acceptance; (3) the League emphasized collection, evaluation and distribution of existing birth-control information, while the Bureau as we have seen, stressed development of new knowledge; (4) the Bureau's stated objective was to serve "all mothers regardless of financial condition" while the League's was to reach "the medically and economically indigent" (this is a difference in degree, not in goals, since the Bureau also favored bringing contraception to the poor); (5) the Bureau, perhaps because it enjoyed the support of Mrs. Sanger's wealthy husband, was less concerned with financial problems than the League, which hoped to establish a country-wide fund-raising campaign for birth control; (6) the Bureau placed more emphasis than the League on working to induce public-health agencies to incorporate birth-control services into their programs.

The newly merged organization, like its predecessors, is, as the name implies, a federated—that is, decentralized—structure comprising numerous local leagues, each one of which "retains its sovereignty, its freedom and its independence." [6] Differing from a corporate, or centralized, organization, in which policy making authority would reside in the national body whose decisions would be binding on its branches, the Federation serves mainly as a coordinating and research agency and an advisory body for local leagues. Through such means as regional conferences and field-staff services it creates some common identification among its autonomous affiliates.

Throughout the movement's history the leadership of the national birth-control organization has been weak. For one thing, Mrs. Sanger, as we have seen, has never been sufficiently interested in the problems or organization to attempt to build strong relationships with the local affiliates. For another, the local leagues are usually dominated by their communities' social leaders, who tend to be "high-spirited . . . with forthright opinions and a willingness to battle for them . . ." [7] Yet another factor militating against any degree of firm policy control from the national level has been the local groups' need to adapt to wide variations in community conditions affecting their operations—variations that a uniform policy could not accommodate.

The merger of the League and the Bureau brought together forces dedicated to differing organizational philosophies. The Bureau's board, which did not include representatives from local affiliates, hoped to develop within the new Federation a subcenter of power that could present a united front, particularly in times of crisis. The League board, which did provide for democratic representation of local leagues, opposed creating a structure which would place policy-making authority in the hands of the national organization . . .

The Bureau, favoring approaching contraception as a medical problem, worked directly with local clinics, shunning the organizational machinery of intermediary state leagues. Its primary appeal was naturally to local affiliates likewise medically oriented. The Bureau's policy of encouraging local groups to integrate with and transfer their services to public health organizations whenever possible inclined the local agencies to work independently of the national body, and to chiefly adapt their operations to community conditions.

The League, on the other hand, preferred to work through state leagues, rather than to make direct contact with local agencies. Thus to the local league the national organization was little more than a remote body with whom it was only loosely identified. The League's major policy emphasis was not on the medical aspects of the over-all goals, but on the organizational procedures necessary to attain them. Its program was focused primarily on abetting the state leagues to create small, stable local units and on strengthening fund-raising procedures. The League did not suggest working to get its program assimilated into public agencies, but rather urged laying the groundwork for strong, self-sufficient local leagues. To further its organizational objectives the league replaced the nurses on its field staff with social service workers. Its whole operation was aimed at creating an administrative machinery to give continuing direction to social-reform movement, birth control.

The Bureau was admirably structured for just the sort of messianic leadership Mrs. Sanger chose to give it. The emphasis on integrating birth-control services into public agency programs made it less concerned than the League with preserving and consolidating gains already won, which in turn made it more responsive to situational changes and more ready to take a stand on controversial issues. It reflected its founder's interest in creating an instrument for social reform, rather than a self-perpetuating institution. Mrs. Sanger's, and consequently the Bureau's, search was for "an organizational structure and personnel that would not smother the fire of the movement but would help it spread." [8]

[6] D. Kenneth Rose and George A. Hasting, "Summarized Factual Report with Analysis and Conclusion to the Joint Committee Representing the American Birth Control League and the Birth Control Clinical Research Bureau, in the Interest of Co-ordination" (mimeographed report), October 3, 1938, p. 7.

[7] Rilma Buckman, "Social Engineering: A Study of the Birth Control Movement," *Social Forces*, Volume 22, Number 4 (May 1944), pp. 420-428.

[8] *Ibid.*, p. 425.

In the years immediately preceding the merger of the two organizations American society had again undergone rather sweeping structural changes. The euphoric ferment of the twenties had passed into the paralyzing despair of the thirties—a period of so little hope that the country's political leadership identified combating public fear as its paramount goal. Social theorists were deeply anxious about the sharp decline in the nation's birth rate, which fell in 1933 to only 16.6 new babies per thousand people . . .

These years of general pessimism saw the birth-control movement in its fullest bloom. In 1939, the year of its creation, the American Birth Control Federation employed eight full-time field workers; today Planned Parenthood has three. In 1936 the Clinical Research Bureau served more than 6000 new patients; in 1959 the Margaret Sanger Clinic served 2700. The League and the Bureau together, at the time of their merger, comprised 417 local units; today only ninety-four local agencies are affiliated with the Federation. Of these, the national organization has recently severed connections with two whose operations failed to meet Federation standards. A third has just been placed on a year's probation and will be disaffiliated if it fails to improve its program to meet certain stipulated conditions.

TRANSITION AND DECLINE

Organizationally, the newly formed Birth Control Federation at first attempted to retain the League's emphasis on working through state leagues rather than on establishing direct contact with the local units. By 1942 the number of state leagues had increased from the fourteen in existence at the time of the merger to thirty-two. But despite this initial increase in their number, state leagues today are virtually defunct organizations. With fewer local affiliates the Federation has had less and less need for state coordination. The local agencies, in turn, as their finances have waned, have found it increasingly difficult to pay membership dues to both national and state organizations. Hence, though some states have made efforts to keep the leagues going on a voluntary basis, it appears obvious that the state league is a superannuated body . . .

Into the League's state administrative machinery the Federation attempted to incorporate the Bureau's stronger medical dimension. Efforts to persuade hospitals and public-health agencies to offer contraceptive services were also strengthened and expanded. In 1937 North Carolina became the first state to add such services, to its state maternal-health program. Six other Southern states followed suit within the next decade. Between 1940 and 1944 the number of local public-health clinics offering birth-control programs increased from 139 to 251. The number of contraceptive clinics affiliated with hospitals declined during the same period from 110 to sixty-five. From 1944 to 1949 the number of clinics in public health departments remained the same, while the number of hospital clinics dropped to fifty-two . . . Recently Planned Parenthood's national leadership has launched a program, called the "Big Push," in the hope of increasing the extent of integration into hospitals and public-health agencies. The Federation urges its affiliates to work closely with health and welfare agencies in local communities. Since public reactions to contraceptive programs are strongly influenced by political and religious considerations, it would seem likely that only a definite reversal of the Roman Catholic position on birth control could effect the sort of integration Planned Parenthood hopes to achieve.

Doctors associated with local affiliates had begun to stress family planning rather than birth control, and to promote a series of such auxiliary medical services as infertility clinics and cancer-detection programs. Reflecting its medical orientation, the Federation in 1942, as we have noted, changed its name to the Planned Parenthood Federation of America, and in 1945 established in the Margaret Sanger Clinic a fertility clinic to serve childless couples. Stone and Hines, associates of the Margaret Sanger Clinic, writing in 1949, projected the logical results of these efforts:

> The planned parenthood center of tomorrow will deal with all aspects of family planning. It will serve not merely as a clinic for information on conception control and fertility, but as a family guidance center for the skilled and sympathetic consideration of the many problems of marriage and family living.[9]

Planned Parenthood's co-operation with the medical profession continues strong. In 1959 local affiliates made a total of 21,572 referrals, of which 52.4 per cent went to health agencies and medical laboratories and an additional 35.5 per cent to private physicians.[10]

A 1945 report from the Federation staff made no mention of the medical research program so strongly advocated by the Bureau.[11] In 1959 the activity was discontinued because many commercial drughouses were also sponsoring research in this area. The Federation has, however, continued to do clinical testing of new contraceptive methods including the birth-

9 A. Stone and N. E. Hines, *Planned Parenthood: A Practical Guide to Birth Control Methods* (New York: Viking Press, 1958), p. 199.
10 These figures were computed from annual report forms submitted by all local affiliates to the national Federation.
11 "Yardstick: A Report to the Executive Committee of the Planned Parenthood Federation of America from the Federation Staff" (mimeographed), September 20, 1945.

control pill, whose discovery climaxed research begun under a pilot grant from Planned Parenthood to Dr. Gregory Pincus, then at Clark University. There is some indication that a program of research into the social aspects of contraception will take the place of the abandoned medical program.

PATIENTS AND PURSESTRINGS

The period since the beginning of the second World War has been marked by reductions in fund-raising income and in the total number of clinics, and by fluctuations in the total number of clients served. In 1941, before the war had begun, 222 clinics reported more than 49,000 new patients. Three years later, 306 clinics reported approximately 38,000 new patients.[12] A 1949 report lists 158 extramural clinics (clinics located outside health departments or hospitals), reporting 46,300 new patients.[13] This report states further that statistics on extramural services are "generally regarded as . . . the best indication of the acceptance of birth control."

The Federation's great expenditures in 1941 hit an all-time high of $241,700. By 1944 they had fallen to $170,600. The Federation's chief sources of funds are a campaign in metropolitan New York and dues from local affiliates and state leagues. Income from affiliates' dues rose from $1500 in 1941 to more than $5,900 in 1945. But income from the Federation's own fund-raising campaign declined sharply from $235,000 to $163,300 in the same period. The Federation's 1959 operating expenses of $340,000 indicate a reversal of the downward trend of the 1940's.

Throughout the war years and those immediately following, Mrs. Sanger continued to lend impetus to the birth control movement. Her nationwide lecture tours whose influence in terms of forming new leagues is not measurable—attracted wide attention and, in many communities, met firmly entrenched Catholic opposition . . .

After World War II, when most national voluntary health agencies, led by the fledgling National Foundation for Infantile Paralysis, entered an era or booming growth and expansion, Planned Parenthood began a period of steady decline. The despair of the 30's had given way to a wartime boom and a prosperity that continued into the postwar years. The number of marriage increased, and young couples, in Lerner's words, "grew old fashioned about babies and family size just when everyone was expecting them to be very modern and very cynical."[14] The birth rate rose from 16.6 per thousand in 1933 to 25.8 per thousand in 1947. In recent years family size, too, appears to be growing larger. A 1960 report states: "Women born in 1931-37 expected to have 3.2, which is substantially more than the 2.4 children produced by mothers who had completed their child-bearing by 1950."[15]

Increased prosperity, broader sex education in schools and colleges, greater freedom to deal with birth control in the popular press, and repeal or relaxation of prohibitive legislation in many states are only a few of many factors that have combined to make the free clinic a less vital source of birth-control information than it was in the 30's. Many families who might, in different circumstances, have made use of clinic services now consult their own physicians or seek information from other sources. To maintain the dwindling clinic caseloads some Planned Parenthood leaders have suggested broadening the range of services offered, while others have urged directing the Federation's major appeal to new client groups.

[12] *Ibid.*, p. 4. These reports provide the only figures available on the total number of clients served, but their accuracy is open to a certain amount of question, since the definition of and procedure for recording "new patients" was not uniform. Year-to-year differences in totals may result from variations in the recording procedures.

[13] "Report on Contraception and Fertility Clinics" (New York: Medical Department, Planned Parenthood Federation of America, 1949), p. 1.

[14] Max Lerner, *America as a Civilization* (New York: Simon and Schuster, 1957), p. 117.

[15] Reuben Hill, "The American Family Today," in Eli Ginzberg (editor), *The Nation's Children* (New York: Columbia University Press, 1960), pp. 88f.

When confronted with many separate facts, we try to categorize them into a few groups as an aid to thought and communication. Since voluntary associations are so numerous, various classifications have been developed. Leaders of voluntary associations are accustomed to see listings based on the official memberships (i.e., "veterans," "women," "youth," and other types), based on the official goals (i.e., "religious," "civic," "fraternal"), based on quantitative characteristics such as size of budget, etc.

Social scientists often use classifications that refer to the social structures and the social processes they study. Therefore, when thinking about voluntary associations, they may use categories quite different from the administrative classifications customarily used by persons in association affairs. Sherwood Fox, for example, noted the functions performed by some 5,000 voluntary associations, and developed a classification based upon the distinction between majoral, minoral, *and* medial *organizations. Majoral associations are those that serve the interests of the major institutions of society. Business, professional, scientific, educational, labor, and agricultural associations belong in this category. Minoral associations serve the interests of significant minorities in the population: women's clubs, fraternal groups, hobby clubs, and various ethnic associations are all examples. Finally, medial associations mediate between major segments of the population. Social welfare organizations mediate between the community and the underprivileged population, veterans' groups mediate between war veterans and the Government; and voluntary health associations mediate between research scientists and the public, as well as between individuals suffering from a disease or disorder and the medical profession.* David L. Sills developed the typology of "corporate-type" and "federation-type" to analyze problems of organizational structure and control in national organizations.† This typology is similar to the familiar distinction between "episcopal" and "congregational" churches.*

The selection by C. Wayne Gordon and Nicholas Babchuk illustrates some of the variables that sociologists use in classifying associations. Their typology is constructed from three dimensions often used in sociological thinking: whether membership is open or restricted; whether membership confers social prestige on members; and the functions that the association performs for its members.‡

Parenthetically, the idea of social function will reappear often in this book, since it is one of the central ideas of contemporary sociology. The function of a social institution is the effect that institution has on a larger social system. Or, one may say that an institution performs certain functions for the personnel who occupy positions in the social structure. Gordon and Babchuk use the concept of function in the second sense, by describing the functions that organizations perform for their members. As they say, the functions of an organization may or may not correspond to its stated aims, which may be most salient at first inspection and may seem like the most obvious way to describe an organization.§ Sometimes an association's

---

* Sherwood D. Fox, "Voluntary Associations and Social Structure," unpublished Ph.D. dissertation, Harvard University, 1953, pp. 59-68.
† David L. Sills, *The Volunteers* (Glencoe: The Free Press, 1957), pp. 3-8.
‡ For a summary of the typologies of organizations in the sociological literature, see Peter Blau and W. Richard Scott, *Formal Organizations* (San Francisco: Chandler Publishing Company, 1962), pp. 40-57.
§ Functions that are not recognized or intended by the people involved are called "latent" functions. Consciously understood and intended functions are called "manifest." Examples of both appear in the following selection and in later chapters of this book.

unacknowledged social functions may be a more informative way to describe it than its stated aims. Later selections will give other examples of the functions that associations perform for other institutions in the social system.

A TYPOLOGY OF VOLUNTARY ASSOCIATIONS*

C. Wayne Gordon and Nicholas Babchuk

This paper proposes a theory of voluntary associations in the form of a typology. The central ideas developed are those which bear on the various functions or organizations as these relate to association . . .

AIMS, FUNCTIONS, AND MEMBERSHIP

Examinations of voluntary association make apparent the significance of the group's aim in relation to its criteria for the selection of its members. The stated aims of the organization may be misleading insofar as these reveal the organization's function. Equally pertinent is the relationship between criteria of membership and function. For example, the D.A.R. is a voluntary association, but to join, it is necessary to be an adult female who can trace familial lineage to a participant in the American Revolution. Here, ancestry, indicating long association with old American stock, is an important limiting factor; in many organizations membership criteria are almost wholly ascriptive.† Thus the criteria of membership may or may not bear on the alleged functions of the organization. Relatively exclusive membership may be viewed as more of a desideratum by the persons belonging to the organization than their concern with its stated objectives.

The membership criteria, the activities, and its stated objectives, as these relate to the functions of the organization, warrant analysis. Here this analysis takes the form of study of specific cases.

Davis and the Gardners in *Deep South* found membership in the Historical Club to be composed primarily of upper-class women.[1] The stated concern of the Club was to honor the local past through an annual community celebration called "Historical Week." Although membership in the Club was limited to upper-class women, upper-middle class women interested in the organization could participate in a limited supportive non-membership capacity. Such women carried on many of the same activities as those engaged in by the members during Historical Week, namely, by serving as guides for tours, opening their homes as rooming houses for visitors, serving meals (although for a price), acting as costumed assistant hostesses, and otherwise participating in pageants recreating and honoring the past.

In short, many of the activities of interested upper-middle class women paralleled the activities of the actual members. This strongly suggests little or no difference between the activities and the "proper attitudes" of the participating members and non-members. The alleged aims of the organization were advanced by both. A discrepancy between the alleged aim of the Club, as revealed in activity and stated purpose, and the purpose or function of the group, as shown by examination of membership attributes, is further indicated. Hence the function of this organization is not to be found in its stated objectives but in its status conferring function made possible by membership selection based on prestigeful and highly limited ascriptive qualities.

An organizational prototype standing in almost direct contrast to the Historical Club in membership criteria and status conferring function is the YMCA. The membership consists of males within a wide age range. It is difficult to focus sharply on a single aim or over-all objective of this Association. A local affiliate states the objectives as follows: ". . . to improve the spiritual, mental, social and physical condition of people and to associate them in a world-wide fellowship united by a common loyalty to the principles of Jesus Christ for the purpose of building a Christian personality and a Christian society."[2] Membership in the Association, with the minor exception of fees and the informally operative tie with religion is open. Members may engage in a wide range of activities directly related to interest. The extent to which an individual participates in one or more specific groups (assuming the usual qualification such as age), as well as the intensity of his participation, are purely voluntary. There is a direct relationship between the

* From C. Wayne Gordon and Nicholas Babchuk, "A Typology of Voluntary Associations," *American Sociological Review*, Volume 24, Number 2 (February 1959), pp. 22-29. Reprinted with the permission of the authors and the publisher, the American Sociological Association.

† ["Ascription" is the classification of an individual by some inborn characteristic, such as ancestry, sex, or ethnic group. It is the opposite of "achievement." Later selections in this book describe the ascribed and achieved statuses in the social structure that affect the government of voluntary associations.—Eds.]

[1] Allison Davis, Burleigh B. Gardner, and Mary R. Gardner, *Deep South* (Chicago: The University of Chicago Press, 1941), pp. 194-195.

[2] From the Constitution and By-Laws of the YMCA, Rochester, New York.

stated aims or objectives of the interest group and the activities in which the person engages.

The openness of membership in the YMCA stands in direct contrast to the limitations on membership in the Historical Club. A parallel contrast is apparent. While membership in the Historical Club confers high status on the individual, this is not the case with the YMCA. At the same time, however, the activities in both the Y and the Historical Club do not *per se*, confer status upon the individual.

Another type of voluntary association is illustrated by the Boy Scouts of America. The membership consists of males within a specified age range. The aims of the Scouts, as outlined in their manual, are as follows: "The purpose of this corporation shall be to promote, through organization, and cooperation with other agencies, the ability of boys to do things for themselves and others, to train them in scoutcraft, and to teach them patriotism, courage, self-reliance, and kindred virtues, using the methods which are now in common use by boy scouts."[3] This association is "democratic" insofar as the criteria of class, religion, ethnicity, and race bear on membership qualification. The activities are uniform for all members and successive steps in achievement depend upon results graded by objective standards of evaluation which are consistent with the officially stated standards. Hence the function of the organization, on the whole, coincides with the stated objectives.

INSTRUMENTAL AND EXPRESSIVE ASSOCIATIONS

The discussion of formal voluntary association thus far has examined the basis for membership selection in relation to the status defining the function of the organization. An additional basis for distinguishing between types of associations is to be found in their stated objectives. Certain groups do not exist primarily to furnish activities for members as an end in itself, but serve as social influence organizations designed to maintain or to create some normative condition or change. Such groups exist in order to attain goals that lie outside of the organizations themselves.* The NAACP, the League of Women voters, and a Neighborhood Improvement Council represent this type. Here these organizations are called *instrumental* groups.

A highly visible example of an instrumental group

---

[3] *Boy Scouts of America: The Official Handbook for Boys* (New York: Doubleday, Page, 1916), p. viii.
* [The authors do not define "expressive" as explicitly as they define "instrumental." An expressive organization is one whose activities aim at the immediate gratifications of the participants, rather than the pursuit of some goal that occurs subsequently in time and perhaps outside the organization itself.—Eds.]

is the NAACP. The expressed goals are indicated in the name of the organization itself: National Association for the Advancement of Colored People. Its explicitly stated purposes are:

1. To educate America to accord full rights and opportunities to Negroes.
2. To fight injustice in the courts when based on race prejudice.
3. To pass protective legislation in state and nation and to defeat discriminatory bills.
4. To secure the vote for Negroes and teach its proper use.
5. To stimulate the cultural life of Negroes.
6. To stop lynching.

Membership is unqualified for adults. Participation can be nominal or active; the activities of members are consistent with the stated objectives of the organization. These objectives are highly consistent with the Judaic-Christian and democratic traditions, but various segments of the population disagree on the specific means which should be used by the NAACP for accomplishing the stated aims. Thus, while the objectives of the organization are esteemed by many, the formal group itself may rank low relative to other organizations. This is true despite the fact that the NAACP may be credited, in part, for bringing about change consonant with its stated purposes. (The low evaluation of an organization such as the NAACP by a significant proportion of the population may be attributed to the low rank held by many of its members and leaders in major status systems, either ethnic or racial.)

Another instrumental organization is the League of Women Voters. Membership is allegedly open to any interested adult female. The purpose of the League is "to promote political responsibility through informed and active participation of citizens in government." It is studiously non-partisan and confines itself to issues in government (on which the League often takes a stand after extended research) and to the qualifications of candidates for office. Membership activities are directly consistent with the aims as stated. The League stands for diffuse and widely held goals relating to an active and enlightened citizenry. Both the purposes and the means for their implementation are highly approved by most persons familiar with the organization.

The dichotomy of organizations of expressive and instrumental types is an over-simplification since some associations seem to manifest both functions. (Below, a third possibility, the instrumental-expressive, is introduced.) For example, it is possible that a national veterans' organization may operate to a great extent on an expressive level locally but on an instrumental level nationally. The apparent expressive character of any organization is consistent with the view in organization theory that activities and sentiments tend to develop above and beyond the requirements of the formal system. Hence, whatever the purpose of the organization, it will incorporate expressive characteristics for its maintenance and provide a framework for personal gratification. Although an instrumental organization might meet the expressive needs of its members, its principal requirement is that it focus on activity and goals that are outside the organization itself.

GUIDING CRITERIA

Several assumptions about the relationship between the members and organizational activities have been introduced. These assumptions can now be reformulated as concepts for the classification of associations. These concepts are: accessibility of membership, the status defining capacity of the organization, and the categorization of organizational functions as instrumental or expressive.

DEGREE OF ACCESSIBILITY

Organizations may be divided into two classes, those with high and those with low accessibility. Associations with almost completely unqualified membership, seeking very large numbers, represent an extreme form of the highly accessible organization. Such an organization is the New York Association for the United Nations. Some groups with relatively unlimited membership use as a selective principle some gross ascriptive attribute such as age or sex. Examples of these associations are the Boy Scouts and the YMCA. A somewhat more selective organization, though one which purports to seek members by stating minimum membership requirements, is the League of Women Voters; in addition to the gross ascriptive qualifications of age and sex, the League is highly "self-conscious" about its recruitment policies as a result of informal control of membership: it is predominantly an organization for college women.

Labor unions like the CIO and veterans' groups such as the American Legion add to the gross ascriptive membership qualifications membership in some other organization, either present or past.

Associations of low accessibility are of two major types. First, there are organizations whose membership is limited by the highly selective criterion of achievement or talent or both. For example, the criterion for active membership in the American Sociological Society is a Ph.D. or its equivalent—most professional societies would fall into this category. Second, there are those groups whose membership is qualified by formally ascriptive qualities limited through a de-

vice such as kinship, illustrated by the D.A.R. Ascription may be related to social class, ethnicity, race, or all three, which operate informally to limit membership. The Historical Club as reported in *Deep South* is a case where membership is limited by ascription of a highly valued but scarce attribute which few people in the community possess. It does not follow that scarcity necessarily results in high evaluation. The membership of an American-Armenian club, for example, is limited by ascription of a relatively lowly valued but scarce attribute which few people in a community may possess. Therefore, the present distinction is based not on ascription or scarcity but on the evaluation of the ascribed attribute.

STATUS CONFERRING CAPACITY

By "status conferring" we have reference to the capacity of an organization to bestow prestige or to be associated with prestige which accrues to its members. The assumption is made that organizations can be arranged in a rank system and the evaluation on which the ranking is based is related in part to the accessibility dimension considered above. . . . Certain activities are highly valued in our society and it often follows that organizations promoting such activities are also highly valued or seriously considered. Thus the League of Women Voters lends considerable support to the activities related to good government and "enlightened" voting. Further, the approach by which the League gives support to voting activity is also highly approved. Here is an illustration of how both ends and the means employed to achieve them are relevant in the evaluation of an organization and its members.

There are various ways in which an organization, its membership, or both may relate to activity. The right to engage in organizational activities can be based on prior ascription or achievement qualifications, either or both of which may be formally or informally operative. Thus the status of the American Medical Association may derive in part from the achievement of its members prior to entering the organization. The prestige of the Historical Club may be the consequence of social class position of the members, not the activities of the club itself.

The status conferring capacity of an organization is often related to the ethnic and racial composition of its membership. The status of ethnic and racial organizations often depends on the place of the group in the ethnic or racial ranking systems. Ethnicity and race of membership, then, are sources of organizational status. These ranking systems also operate independently of the activities of organizations as they bear on evaluation.

Many organizations do not confer prestige on their members through their activity outside the organization. The activities may be engaged in fairly equally by all of the members so that no prestige results from the competitive achievement within the organization. This is generally the case in the YMCA.

Status may accrue to an individual on the basis of achievement in activities within an organizational context. Eagle Scouts and Thirty-Second Degree Masons, for example, receive recognition and status within their own organizations and in society at large.

The status significance of an organization for its members may depend upon the relationship of its activities to objectives which lie outside the organization and the effectiveness of their implementation. These activities and objectives, as well as the means of attaining them, may be highly approved or disapproved, as illustrated, once again, in the work of the League of Women Voters—in contrast with the activities of, say, the Ku Klux Klan.

FUNCTION

Generically, organizations may be classified according to their functions for members. One major type provides the framework for immediate and continuing gratification to the individual, exemplified by a "senior citizens" club, the Boys' Club, and such special interest groups as bowling, chess, and checkers associations. These groups perform a function primarily for the individual participants through activities confined and self-contained within the organization itself. More specifically, they provide the opportunity for carrying on activities, such as recreation, of direct interest to the participants or help to provide satisfactions of personal fellowship. Also included in this category are honorific or status conferring organizations. This type of organization has been designated as expressive. In the main, the orientation of the group is not to the attainment of a goal anticipated for the future but to the organized flow of gratifications in the present.

In contrast, the major function and orientation of the instrumental organization are related to activities which take place outside the organization. It seeks to maintain a condition or to bring about change which transcends its immediate membership. Examples of associations of this type are Americans for Democratic Action, the Young Republican Club, the Ku Klux Klan, and the League of Women Voters. Members identify with the group, at least in part, because of its commitment to goals which do not contribute directly to their own personal and immediate satisfactions. Of course, this tendency does not preclude the possibility of "expressive functions" being found in the instrumental type of organization.

Standing between predominantly instrumental and expressive associations are those groups that incorporate both functions self-consciously. A case in point is the American Legion. At the national level the Legion has registered lobbyists and a legislative program officially endorsed by its members, but at the local level it functions primarily as a club for convivial activities. In the present scheme, such organizations are designated as instrumental-expressive. Members identify with the organization both for the fellowship it provides and for the special objectives it seeks.

THE TYPOLOGY

In the foregoing discussion, various elements bearing on a theory of voluntary association have been considered, namely, accessibility, status defining capacity, and the instrumental, instrumental-expressive, and expressive functions of organizations . . . [A typology based on these variables] may be used as a basis for a sociological classification of voluntary organizations. It also suggests criteria for ranking organizations . . . The typology also can be employed as a heuristic device for generating hypotheses, as the following tentative formulations suggest:

Organizations with low accessibility of membership as a result of ascriptive criteria which are highly evaluated will provide high status for their members.

If membership is highly accessible and the organization espouses and implements widely held and esteemed values, it will be highly ranked.

If the means by which an organization implements its goals are controversial, it will rank lower than one in which this is not the case.

If an organization, through its activities, is capable of implementing its stated goals, it will tend to rank higher than one which is not capable of implementing its goals.

If an organization which is highly accessible exists only to provide immediate satisfactions through activities for its members, it will rank low.

There is a direct relationship between organizational talent or training requirements for membership, or both, and its rank.

Organizations with low accessibility of membership as a result of negatively evaluated ascriptive criteria will be ranked low.

The typology as a classificatory scheme has utility in the analysis of relationships between specific variables as these relate to organization. Status, accessibility, and function become analytic when considered in connection with age, sex, nativity, education, and so forth. An examination of an old-age organization (in our research on associations in a zone of transition in a city) is illustrative. Information derived from interviews of 52 persons, a random sample of a membership of over 300, revealed that these individuals (mean age of 75 years) were primarily engaged in expressive activities within the organization. In addition to their affiliation with the organization studied, these persons held memberships in 41 different associations. The latter were primarily of the expressive type, consisting of social clubs, recreational clubs, golden-age groups, and hobby clubs. Thirty-seven persons in the sample belonged to three or more associations, and over 80 per cent of the memberships were in the expressive-association category. The extreme age of this group makes it an interesting case of the expressive organization. According to the present scheme, this old-age association would be classed as having low status and low accessibility relative to the entire adult population.

An interesting parallel is to be drawn from associations of children. Clearly, children characteristically do not form or maintain instrumental-type groups. Nor do children's groups, with few exceptions, have high status. Children and the very old are very likely to belong to expressive groups.

SUMMARY

This paper has discussed a number of concepts pertinent to the analysis of voluntary associations. A typology of voluntary associations has been developed employing and interrelating the degree of accessibility of membership, the status conferring capacity, and the classification of groups as instrumental, instrumental-expressive, and expressive, as these relate to the functions of organizations. The usefulness of this scheme for generating hypotheses has been suggested and demonstrated.

PART TWO

VOLUNTARY ASSOCIATIONS AND THEIR ENVIRONMENT

3 SOCIAL INFLUENCES UPON THE MEMBERSHIP

Every organization fits into its surrounding social environment. Every society consists of a system of positions or "social statuses," and each individual occupies several statuses. For example, he is a man, a Roman Catholic, a citizen of a certain community, a father, and many other things; someone else may be a woman, a Congregationalist, a wife, a mother-in-law, a member of the upper class, etc. Among other supports, each organization recruits personnel from the social statuses in the society. The existence and success of any voluntary association depend on whether particular categories in the population are willing to supply volunteers and financial contributors in sufficient numbers. Much of the social research about voluntary associations has concerned the recruitment of volunteers from various social statuses.

Any activity is performed differentially by people of different statuses. For example, newspaper readers usually have better education, better occupations, and higher incomes than nonreaders; more men, married people, upper class persons, and white people can be found among those voting in elections than among nonvoters. Such differences among social statuses also govern recruitment into voluntary associations, as shown in the selection by Charles R. Wright and Herbert H. Hyman. According to the surveys of the American population they report, membership in associations varies with race, religion, social class, community, living conditions, family status, etc. In addition they describe some differences between members and nonmembers that might be influenced by the social stimuli experienced during participation: compared to nonmembers, members are more interested in politics, they vote more often, and they contribute more to charity. These findings duplicate those in many other surveys.* Chapter 12 of this book presents some of the research describing how individuals decide to become volunteers.

WHO BELONGS TO VOLUNTARY ASSOCIATIONS?†

Charles R. Wright and Herbert H. Hyman

The bulk of the analysis to be presented is based on two national probability samples of the adult, non-institutionalized population of the United States, over 21 years of age. The first sample contains 2,809 men and women, and the second 2,379. The studies were conducted in the years 1953 and 1955. In addition to the national data, findings on voluntary association membership were available for representative samples from [National Opinion Research Center] studies of the following localities: a large metropolitan area (New York metropolitan area represented by a probability sample of 1,053 cases drawn in 1951); a medium sized Western metropolis (Denver represented by a probability sample of 920 cases obtained in the spring of 1949); a small city and surrounding county (Findley and Hancock County, Ohio, represented by 535 cases drawn in May, 1952). The local findings on magnitude of membership and its social distribution are not presented in detail, although, where confirmation or contradiction occurs, some brief reference will be made. They will be used to examine hypotheses about particular variables, however, which are not demonstrable on a national scale.

* A comprehensive review of this research appears in Murray Hausknecht, *The Joiners* (New York: The Bedminster Press, 1962), chs. II-IV, VI.
† From Charles R. Wright and Herbert H. Hyman, "Voluntary Association Memberships of American Adults," *American Sociological Review*, Volume 23, Number 3 (June 1958), pp. 284-294. Reprinted with the permission of the authors and the publisher, the American Sociological Association.

MEMBERSHIPS OF AMERICANS

Data from the national surveys confirm the conclusions drawn by previous researchers based on local studies, which showed that a sizable group of Americans are not members of any voluntary associations and that only a minority belong to more than one such organization. Table 1 presents data from two surveys, one of which inquired about the voluntary association membership of *any* member of the family, the other survey pertained to activities of the respondent himself. Calculated either way, voluntary association membership is not a major characteristic of Americans. Nearly half of the families (47 per cent) and almost two-thirds of the respondents (64 per cent) belong to no voluntary associations. About a third of the families (31 per cent) and a fifth of the respondents belong to only one such organization. Only about a fifth of the families (21 per cent) and a sixth of the respondents (16 per cent) belong to two or more organizations. These findings hardly warrant the impression that Americans are a nation of joiners.[1]

TABLE 1

Membership in voluntary associations for two national cross-sections of American adults, 1953 and 1955

Number of voluntary associations	Percentage of *families* whose members belong to organizations as indicated (1953)[a]	Percentage of *adults* who were themselves members of the organizations, as indicated (1955)[b]
None	47	64
One	31	20
Two	12	9
Three	5	4
Four or more	4	3
Unknown	1	0
	100%	100%
Total	(2,809)	(2,379)

[a] "Does anyone in the family belong to any sort of club, lodge, fraternal order, or union with ten or more members in it?" If yes, "What organization? Any other?" *Source:* NORC Survey 335.
[b] Union membership is *not* included in these data because the interviewing on organization membership during this part of the survey concerned associations other than union. The question was, "Do you happen to belong to any groups or organizations in the community here? If yes, "Which ones? Any other?" *Source:* NORC Survey 367.

Data on the types of organizations to which Americans belong are also revealing. In the 1953 survey, which contained an account of organizations to which any family member belonged, only two (unions and fraternal or secret societies) have relatively large memberships, 23 per cent and 19 per cent respectively. Next in order are neighborhood-ethnic-special interest groups (8 per cent), veterans' organizations (7 per cent), civic organizations (5 per cent), church

[1] . . . Of course, this is not to dispute the fact that from a *comparative* point of view, Americans may be more prone to such membership than other national groups.

sponsored organizations (3 per cent), youth organizations (2 per cent), and professional and learned societies (2 per cent). These findings provide national perspective on the data recorded by former studies of local populations, such as the Detroit Area Study, in which unions and fraternal organizations also accounted for more of the citizens' voluntary memberships than any other type of association.[2]

RACIAL AND RELIGIOUS SUBGROUPS

Table 2 presents figures on the membership patterns for two types of subgroups within American society: racial and religious. Comparison of Negro and white respondents shows that voluntary association membership is somewhat more characteristic of whites than Negroes. Less than half (46 per cent) of the white families and 63 per cent of the white respondents belong to no associations in contrast to 60 per cent of the Negro families and 73 per cent of the Negro adults. And nearly a quarter (23 per cent) of the white families belong to two or more organizations in contrast to only 11 per cent of the Negro families.

Differences in rates of membership also distinguish

TABLE 2

Voluntary association memberships of racial and religious subgroups based on national samples

(A) Family data (1953)

	Per cent of families whose members belong to:			
	No organization	One	Two or more	N (100%)
Race[a]				
Negro	60	29	11	279
White	46	31	23	2,472
Religion[b]				
Jewish	31	37	32	99
Catholic	44	34	22	579
Protestant	49	30	21	1,992

Source: NORC Survey 335.

(B) Respondent data (1955)

	Per cent of respondents who belong to:			
	No organization	One	Two or more	N (100%)
Race[c]				
Negro	73	18	9	229
White	63	20	17	2,139
Religion[d]				
Jewish	45	25	30	71
Protestant	63	20	17	1,701
Catholic	69	17	14	519

[a] Figures exclude 58 cases of other races or of unknown race.
[b] Figures exclude 139 cases who report some other religion or none at all.
[c] Figures exclude 11 cases of other races.
[d] Figures exclude 88 cases who report some other religion or none at all.
Source: NORC Survey 367.

[2] Morris Axelrod, "Urban Structure and Social Participation," *American Sociological Review*, Volume 21, Number 1 (February 1956), pp. 13-18.

the major religious subgroups of the population. Whether measured on a family or individual basis, the highest rate of membership is found among the Jews. On a family basis, the next highest participants in voluntary associations are the Catholics (56 per cent), and the least active are the Protestants (51 per cent). Data on individual memberships, however, are different, with a higher percentage of Protestants than Catholics belonging to any organizations.

Interesting comparisons with national data on memberships of religious subgroups are available from the local studies of New York City and Denver. In both cities the ordering of memberships agrees with the national sample on individual memberships: the rate of membership is highest for Jews, next for Protestants and lowest for Catholics. In New York, 64 per cent of the Jewish respondents reported membership in at least one voluntary association, 54 per cent of the Protestants and 37 per cent of the Catholics. In Denver, the membership rates were 77 per cent for Jews, 65 per cent for Protestants and 55 per cent for

Catholics. Thus the Catholic membership rates in these urban settings appear lower than those of the Jews and Protestants, as in the 1955 national survey.

SOCIAL STRATIFICATION AND MEMBERSHIP

On the local level, several studies have demonstrated a relationship between the social status of the respondent, as measured by a variety of indices, and membership in voluntary associations. These studies generally agree that there is an increase in the percentage of memberships in formal associations the higher the status of the respondents. . . .

Data from the national samples support the correlation between social status and membership. Table 3 presents data on the membership of the 1955 sample classified by five indices of social status: family income, education of respondent, interviewer's rating of family's level of living, occupation of head of household, and home ownership. Whichever index of status

TABLE 3

Indices of stratification and voluntary association membership, 1955[a]

	No organization	One organization	Two or more	No. of cases (100%)
A. Income level				
Under $2,000	76	17	7	385
2,000-2,999	71	17	12	304
3,000-3,999	71	18	11	379
4,000-4,999	65	21	14	450
5,000-7,499	57	22	21	524
7,500 and over	43	22	30	328
B. Education				
0-6 years	83	12	5	348
7-8 years	73	17	10	522
9-11 years	67	20	13	495
12 years	57	23	20	610
1-3 yrs. of college	46	24	30	232
4 yrs. college or more	39	25	36	170
C. Level of living (Interviewer's rating)				
Very low	92	7	1	125
Below average	81	14	5	580
Average	61	22	17	1,318
Above average	43	25	32	288
Very high	18	18	64	44
D. Occupation				
Professional	47	24	29	259
Prop., mgrs., officials	47	24	29	294
Farm owners	58	28	14	265
Clerical and sales	59	21	20	240
Skilled labor	68	19	13	447
Semi-skilled labor	77	14	9	492
Service	73	18	9	142
Non-farm labor	79	16	5	155
Farm labor	87	13	0	54
Retired, unemployed	77	11	12	35
E. Home ownership				
Owns home	57	22	21	1,407
Rents	75	16	9	968

[a] Data exclude union membership.
Source: NORC Survey 367.

is used, an appreciably higher percentage of persons in higher status positions belong to voluntary associations than do persons of lower status. For example, fully 76 per cent of the respondents whose family income falls below 2,000 dollars do not belong to any organizations in contrast to only 48 per cent of those whose income is 7,500 dollars or more. Furthermore, there is an increase in the percentage of persons who belong to *several* organizations as social status increases. For example, only 7 per cent of the lowest income group belong to two or more associations in contrast to 30 per cent of the highest income group. Similar findings are obtained from inspection of the data on education, level of living, occupation, and home ownership, as examination of Table 3 reveals.[3]

One set of findings warrant special mention. The pattern of voluntary association membership among different occupational levels indicates even less participation among blue collar workers than had been noted in previous local studies. For example, from 68 to 87 per cent of the blue collar workers belong to no organizations (not counting union membership), in contrast to 59 per cent of the white collar workers and 47 per cent of the businessmen and professionals. The higher rate of voluntary association membership among businessmen and professionals is clearly documented by the national data, which show that 29 per cent of the members of these two occupational categories belong to two or more organizations, in contrast with only 5 to 13 per cent of the blue collar workers. . . .

[3] Data from the 1953 sample on family participation in voluntary associations generally corroborated the findings presented above and hence are not reproduced here. In addition, several of the local studies contain data in support of the relationships described. For example, home ownership data were available in Denver and provided an opportunity to examine the influence of this factor within an urban setting. Here, as on the national level, home owners were more likely to be members than were renters, 67 per cent versus 59 per cent respectively. And in New York, families employing domestic help were more likely to be members than those without help, 73 per cent versus 45 per cent.

URBANIZATION AND VOLUNTARY ASSOCIATION MEMBERSHIP

Voluntary associations customarily have been identified as characteristic of the urban way of life, and membership in such associations has been assumed to be more common for city residents than rural people. Recent observers, however, have noted that the spread of urbanization in America is reducing such differences between city and country. . . . Nevertheless, we have lacked specific information on the differential rates of voluntary association membership of residents of various sized communities. A breakdown of national survey data provides considerable information on this question.

From the 1953 national survey it is possible to determine the number of associational affiliations of family members living in counties of varying degrees of urbanization, taking the size of the largest city in the county as a crude index of its degree of urbanism. Three types of counties can be examined: (1) highly urbanized counties, those with at least one city of 50,000 population or more; (2) moderately urbanized, with at least one city of 10,000 to 50,000 population; and (3) least urbanized, having no city of 10,000 or more. Examination of the memberships of residents of these three types of counties reveals that only 57 per cent of the families who live in highly urbanized counties have members in at least one voluntary association, 53 per cent of those in moderately urbanized counties, and 41 per cent of those living in the least urbanized or predominantly rural counties. Thus some correlation appears between the degree of urbanization and voluntary association membership, although the difference between the most urban and least urban counties is not great.

But the type of county is only a crude index of the social atmosphere within which the citizen lives. Within each county, for example, there are areas of more *and* less urban nature. Therefore a finer breakdown is desirable in order to determine more precisely the relationship between urbanism and mem-

TABLE 4

Urbanism and voluntary association membership, 1953

Per cent of families whose members belong to:	Place of residence								
	Metropolitan counties (with city of 50,000 or more)			Other urbanized counties (with city of 10-50,000)			Primarily rural counties (have no town of 10,000)		
	Urban Residence	Rural Non-farm	Rural Farm	Urban	Rural Non-farm	Rural Farm	Urban	Rural Non-farm	Rural Farm
No organization	42	40	67	46	46	53	54	52	70
One organization	33	37	21	36	34	28	27	24	21
Two or more organizations	25	23	12	18	20	19	19	24	9
Total	100% (1,394)	100% (193)	100% (48)	100% (294)	100% (115)	100% (134)	100% (110)	100% (264)	100% (252)

Source: NORC Survey 335.

bership in voluntary associations. Table 4 presents data on membership according to urban, rural non-farm, and rural farm residences within each type of county.

Several interesting findings emerge. First it appears that, with one exception (rural non-farm residents in moderately urbanized counties) the relationship between urbanization of county and membership in voluntary associations persists. That is, more of the residents of highly urbanized counties belong to organizations than do persons living in similar types of neighborhoods but in less urbanized counties. For example, only 42 per cent of the urbanites in highly urbanized counties belong to no organization, in contrast with 46 per cent of the urbanites in moderately urbanized counties, and 54 per cent in the least urbanized.

Secondly, within each type of county rural farm residence is more closely associated with non-membership than is either rural non-farm or urban residence. For example, within highly urbanized counties 67 per cent of the rural farm residents belong to no voluntary association, in contrast to only 40 per cent of the rural non-farm residents and 42 per cent of the urbanites . . .

SOME SITUATIONAL DETERMINANTS OF MEMBERSHIP

In this section some data from the Denver survey are examined to clarify certain situational factors which might be presumed to affect urban participation in voluntary associations. Specifically, data are presented on the effect of length of residence in the community, length of residence at the same address, type of residence (for example, single family dwelling versus apartment), travel time to work, and family status (for example, single, married with children or without children). The presumed influence of such factors is illustrated by the hypothesis that long-time residents in the community or in the neighborhood are more likely to be involved in formal organizations. Or, persons living in apartments might be expected to participate less in voluntary associations than those living in single family dwellings. Persons who spend less time commuting to work, it may be argued, should have more time to devote to organizations and therefore should show a higher incidence of membership. Similarly, single men and women, who are unencumbered by children, might have more spare time and hence be more apt to belong to voluntary groups. Table 5 presents data which fail to support several of these arguments.

None of the residential factors shows a systematic relationship with the incidence of affiliation with voluntary associations. For example, persons born in

TABLE 5

Some situational determinants of voluntary association membership: evidence from Denver survey

	Percentage of each type who belong to voluntary associations	No. of cases in base
A. Residential history		
Born in Denver or lived there at least 20 yrs.	65	504
Lived in Denver less than 20 years	62	404
Lived in Denver at present address over 20 years	63	200
Lived at present address for 5 to 20 years	67	346
Lived at present address less than 5 years	60	358
B. Residential mobility		
Moved to Denver from place of under 2,500 population	61	272
Moved from place of 2,500 to 25,000 population	60	205
Moved from place larger than 25,000	64	281
C. Type of residence		
Single family house rented	57	81
Multiple family dwelling rented	59	165
Apartment building, rented	60	117
Owned, all types of dwelling	67	512
D. Travel time to work		
45 minutes or more daily	60	81
35-44 minutes	70	185
30-34 minutes	64	256
25-29 minutes	66	192
Less than 25 minutes	57	205
E. Family status		
Men: Not married	66	79
Married, no children under 18 yrs. old	74	182
Married, with children under 18 yrs. old	82	162
Women: Not married	51	149
Married, no children under 18 yrs. old	53	174
Married, with children under 18 yrs. old	56	174

Source: Denver Community Survey, NORC-12B.

Denver are hardly more likely to belong to voluntary associations than those who have arrived recently.[4]

4   These data are consistent with those obtained in Hancock County, Ohio where 51 per cent of the persons who had resided in the county for 20 years or more were members of voluntary associations, 57 per cent of the 10-19 year residents were members, 58 per cent of the 5-8 year members, and 57 per cent of the persons living there less than five years. The survey was conducted in May 1952. On the other hand, Zimmer, in a study of married men in a mid-western community of 20,000, found that membership in formal organizations increased directly with length of time in the community. Zimmer's relationship persisted within age, occupational and educational control categories. See Basil Zimmer, "Participation of Migrants in Urban Structures," *American Sociological Review*, Volume 20 (April, 1955), pp. 218-224. And a recent study in Spokane, Washington indicates a relationship between mobility and voluntary association membership; see Howard Freeman, Edwin Novak and Leo Reeder, "Correlates of Membership in Voluntary Associations," *American Sociological Review*, Volume 22 (October, 1957), pp. 528-533.

Apartment dwellers are slightly more likely to be voluntary association members than persons renting houses. Commuters who spend more than 45 minutes getting to work are about as likely to belong to organizations as are those people who have to travel only 25 minutes or less.

Only two of these situational factors—home ownership and family status—seem related to voluntary association membership. Home ownership as a determinent of membership, as brought out above, is related to social stratification. The data on family status show that married persons are more likely to be members of organizations than single persons; and that men and women with children are more likely to be members than childless couples. One might hypothesize that children—and perhaps the expectation of children—draw adults into participation in the voluntary associations in the urban community. This finding corroborates that of Janowitz in his study of Chicago residents in which he notes that neighborhood involvement often centers around activities connected with the rearing of children in a metropolis. As Janowitz remarks, on the neighborhood level, "children are not only the best neighbors in the community but they lead their parents to neighborhood community participation and orientation." [5]

CIVIC INVOLVEMENT OF VOLUNTARY ASSOCIATION MEMBERSHIP

In this final section, data from the Denver Survey are presented which demonstrate psychological and behavioral differences between citizens who are members and those who are not members of formal organizations. Admittedly the data do not indicate that such differences can be attributed solely to the respondents' patterns of associational membership. Clearly several factors already established as correlates of membership (for example, high socioeconomic status, occupation, place of residence) may also account for differences in political interest, voting and charitable acts of members and non-members. The authors feel, however, that comparison of members and non-members without controlling these associated factors is proper insofar as the purpose is solely to *describe* the differences between persons who are or are not members of voluntary associations, regardless of the ultimate causes of such differences. Hence Table 6 presents simple comparisons between the formally organized and unorganized, concerning their interest in political topics, voting records, and contributions to charity.

Several measures of interest in public affairs (including presidential elections, unemployment, labor

[5] Morris Janowitz, *The Community Press in an Urban Setting* (Glencoe, Ill.: The Free Press, 1952), p. 124.

TABLE 6

Political interests and behavior associated with voluntary association membership: evidence from Denver survey, 1949

	Persons who were members of:	
	No organizations	One or more organizations
A. Per cent who said they take "a great deal" of interest in:		
Presidential elections	73	84
Unemployment in the U.S.	53	57
The Denver public schools	33	50
City planning in Denver	31	50
Labor relations	31	45
The situation of Denver Negroes	23	35
B. Per cent who voted in each of the following elections:		
1944 Presidential	36	40
1946 Congressional	27	36
1947 City charter	15	24
1948 Primary	24	34
C. Per cent who report making a contribution to the Community Chest in Denver	56%	72%
Total cases	335	585

Source: Denver Community Survey, NORC-12B.

relations, minority problems, public schools, and city planning) indicate that persons belonging to voluntary associations are more concerned with such topics than are non-members. For example, fully 84 per cent of the Denverites who belonged to any voluntary association said they took a great deal of interest in presidential elections, in contrast with only 73 per cent of the non-members. And members were more likely than non-members to be interested in city planning, 50 per cent to 31 per cent respectively.

Political interest is backed by participation in the political process, insofar as participation is measured by voting. Data on behavior in four elections—the 1944 Presidential, 1946 Congressional, 1947 City Charter, and 1948 Primary—indicate in every instance a greater percentage of voting among Denverites who were members of voluntary associations than among non-members.

Finally, in the non-political sphere of community life, charity, 72 per cent of the persons belonging to associations reported having made a contribution to the Community Chest in Denver, in contrast to 56 per cent of the non-members. . . .

SUMMARY

A secondary analysis of two national and several local surveys provides evidence on the topics: the pattern of membership in voluntary associations of Americans in general and of such specific subgroups as class and religion; some possible determinants of membership, for example, socio-economic status; and certain correlates of membership which relate to civic participation, for example, interest in public issues and voting.

The major findings are listed below in abbreviated form. In each case, the major source of data, that is, national or local survey, is indicated in parenthesis. Subject to the qualifications noted above, the major findings are:

(1) Voluntary association membership is not characteristic of the majority of Americans (National).

(2) A relatively small percentage of Americans belong to two or more voluntary associations (National).

(3) Membership is more characteristic of the white than Negro population (National).

(4) Membership is more characteristic of Jewish than Protestant persons, and of Protestant than Catholics (National).

(5) Membership is directly related to socio-economic status, as measured by level of income, occupation, home ownership, interviewer's rating of level of living, and education (National).

(6) Membership is more characteristic of urban and rural non-farm residents than of rural farm residents (National).

(7) Membership does not appear to be related to a variety of situational factors, for example, length of residence in the community, length of residence at the same address, type of dwelling unit, commuting time to work (Denver).

(8) Membership is related to family status, being higher for couples with children than without (Denver).

(9) Membership is accompanied by a greater interest in such public affairs as unemployment problems, city planning, and public schools (Denver).

(10) Membership is associated with voting in Presidential, Congressional and local elections (Denver).

(11) Membership is associated with support for local charities (Denver).

Wright and Hyman summarize the social variables that affect entry into voluntary associations and relate these characteristics to membership in particular types of associations. Each organization has a certain public image and certain needs. Therefore, each attracts people disproportionately from groups in the population that favor its goals and structure; each prefers to recruit people from those groups that will help realize its aims; and each fails to attract or may even repel persons with incompatible personal traits. In the next selection, Murray Hausknecht summarizes a national American survey (the NORC survey of 1953 also used by Wright and Hyman) and identifies the types of voluntary association joined by people of different social status. He also suggests some reasons for the group differences in membership reported in his own and in the Wright–Hyman selection.

A voluntary association, like every other organization, secures more of its members from certain social categories than from others. This is most true of associations formally tied to a particular social status: for example, the League of Women Voters has a membership of women; sectarian associations get members from the religious group. But in practice, voluntary associations that aim at universal membership may also draw their members primarily from certain groups in the population. Thus, a leader should identify the traditional connections between his association and particular groups in the public, in order to deepen his understanding of his internal organizational tasks and in order to assess the probable costs and gains of new membership drives. However open it may be, an association may be unable to recruit persons from social groups that have not customarily joined it. A select membership may hamper an association's attempt to project a universal and representative public image.

MEMBERSHIP IN DIFFERENT TYPES OF ASSOCIATIONS*

Murray Hausknecht

Table 1 gives us an over-all view of the kinds of associations to which individuals belong and the percentage of individuals belonging to each type. The rank order of these types from those with the highest percentages of members to those with the least is: civic and service; lodges and fraternal; church and religious; social and recreational; veterans, military, patriotic; economic, occupational, professional; cultural, educational, alumni; political and pressure.

Membership in both civic and service associations and political organizations may be taken as symbolic of a "community orientation." But Table 1 shows that while one type has the highest rank order the other has the lowest. If the functions of voluntary association membership are to link the individual to the community and to play a role in determining attitudes and patterns of behavior in the community, this lack of membership in political organizations is significant. It indicates that his behavior in the community will not be overtly "political"; i.e., his attention will not be explicitly directed at the power structure of the community and he will not see the latter as being immediately relevant to his own situation within the community. Since most of the organizations categorized under the rubrics "civic" and service" and "political and pressure" are oriented to the community as a whole, we can put the matter somewhat differently by saying that the distribution of membership between these two kinds of voluntary associations reflects a traditional American suspicion of using political power for achieving community ends.

TABLE I

Distribution of voluntary association members by type of association

Type of association	Per cent belonging*
Veterans, military, patriotic	14%
Civic and service	38
Political and pressure	4
Lodges and fraternal	31
Church and religious	25
Economic, occupational, professional	9
Cultural, educational, alumni	4
Social and recreational	16
	(853)

* Percentages do not add up to 100% since any individual may belong to more than one type of association.

* From Murray Hausknecht, *The Joiners* (Totowa, N. J.: The Bedminster Press, 1962), pp. 71-82. Reprinted with the permission of the author and the publisher.

SEX ROLES AND VOLUNTARY ASSOCIATIONS

Voluntary associations are built about specific activities and interests, therefore any differences which appear between men and women in terms of the organization to which they belong will reflect cultural definitions of what is appropriate for men and women respectively. Thus, it is not surprising that Table 2, in which the independent variable is sex, shows that more men belong to veterans, military, and patriotic associations than do women. But it is also possible to see that the greater membership of men in lodges and fraternal societies—63 per cent of the membership is male and 37 per cent female—can be explained in the same terms. One of the manifest functions of these organizations is to provide cheap life insurance, burial benefits, etc., and these are functions congruent with the man's family roles.

TABLE 2

Distribution of voluntary association members by type of association and sex

Type of association	Men		Women		
Veterans	22%	68%	9%	32%	(120)
Civic	34	39	46	61	(322)
Political	3	33	6	67	(36)
Lodges	44	63	23	37	(265)
Church	13	23	39	77	(214)
Economic	13	63	7	37	(76)
Cultural	2	22	6	78	(32)
Social	14	39	20	61	(139)
		(377)		(422)	

* When the percentages are read across toward the base figures in parenthesis in the right hand column they represent the distribution of the sexes within each type of association. When the table is read down the columns toward the base figures in the last row the figures represent the percentage of individuals of each sex belonging to each type of association.

On the other hand, it is possible to argue that some associations are organized about activities and ends which are culturally defined as appropriate for both sexes. Yet when we examine membership in one type of association which theoretically should exemplify this, church and religious groups, we find that 77 per cent of the members are women and 23 per cent are men. This means that there is an implicit definition of religion and associated activities as being part of the "women's world." There is an interesting consistency to this "cultural logic" in light of the fact that women outnumber men in civic and service organizations. Most of the organizations comprising this category have functions which might be termed as "succorance," "supportive," or, more invidiously, "do-goodism"—all implying behavior more congruent with the orientations traditionally associated with the roles of wife and mother. And this, of course, is also congruent with the meaning of activity associated with religion, e.g., the contemporary notion of "charitable works." The greater number of men belonging to civic and service organizations than to church-related groups is probably accounted for by the fact that the former category of associations also contain organizations functional for occupations and careers, e.g., Lions, Kiwanis, etc.

It would seem, then, that the type of organizations to which one belongs is in part determined by the imperatives associated with the sex role.

AGE, SOCIAL INTEGRATION, AND ASSOCIATIONS

Table 3, summarizing the age distribution in different types of associations, points up some interesting differences among the age groups. First, in the civic and service organizations there is a greater percentage of young people than old people; 37 per cent of the membership is between 21 and 34 years of age

TABLE 3

Distribution of voluntary association members by type of association and age*

Type of association	21-34	35-54	55 and over	
Veterans	15%	13%	16%	
	29%	41%	30%	(118)
Civic	49	42	20	
	37	52	11	(308)
Political	4	3	5	
	27	38	35	(34)
Lodges	20	32	40	
	18	48	34	(260)
Church	20	25	31	
	22	45	33	(210)
Economic	9	7	9	
	31	40	29	(65)
Cultural	4	4	3	
	29	52	19	(31)
Social	21	14	14	
	32	48	20	(156)
	(234)	(384)	(221)	

* When the percentages are read across toward the base figures in parentheses in the right hand column they represent the distribution of the age groups within each type of association. When the table is read down the column toward the base figures in the last row the numbers represent the percentage of individuals in each age group belonging to each type of association.

and only about 10 per cent is 55 or more. However, the opposite occurs among those belonging to lodges and fraternal societies: 18 per cent of the membership falls into the youngest age group and 34 per cent into the oldest. . . .

The high proportion of young individuals in the civic and service organizations is probably related to the instrumental functions membership in these associations have for occupations and careers. It should be noted that of all those between the ages of 21 and 34 *only 9 percent are 21-24* years old. This means that the overwhelming majority of the youngest age group are in an age bracket, 25-34 years of age, in which they are begining to assume full-fledged adult family and occupational roles, i.e., becoming fully integrated into the society. Thus, membership in these associations not only has the aforementioned instrumental functions but is symbolic of the individual's new status in the community. By the same token the sharp drop in the percentage in the oldest group reflects the decreasing saliency of these instrumental functions for those already established in a career or those whose careers have already ended, and is symbolic of the gradual loss of integration with the society characteristic of old age in contemporary America. . . .

The functions of associations are related to sex roles as well as age. When the sample is divided into two age groups, less than 35 and over 35, 6 per cent of the membership of church related organizations is composed of young men and 17 per cent of young women. The bulk of the membership is drawn from the older sections of the population, since in these organizations the rest of the membership is made up of 59 per cent older women and 18 per cent older men. On the other hand, there is a tendency for the older men and women to self-select different kinds of associations. Of the membership in lodges and fraternal societies 52 per cent are older men as over against 30 per cent of older women; this is a reversal of the distribution of the sexes in church-related organizations. If it is true that sex roles play some part in determining voluntary association membership, this continuing separation of activities apparent among older persons may signify something more than mere force of convention. Belonging to an association congruent with one's sex role may help the individual to maintain an identification as male or female at a point in life when retirement from occupational and family roles weakens such an identification.

THE RACES AND ORGANIZATIONS

The comparison of whites and Negroes in Table 4 shows some expected patterns and at least one that is a surprise. Given the facts of prejudice and discrimination, it is to be expected that 15 per cent of the whites and only 4 per cent of the Negroes are members of veterans, military, and patriotic associations, and that 17 per cent of the white and 9 per cent of the minority group belong to associations of a social and recreational nature. Also, in view of the traditionally important role of the church in the Negro community, it is not surprising that 35 per cent of the Negroes belong to church-related associations and 24 per cent of the whites belong to groups of this kind. How central such organizations are in the Negro community can be seen from the fact that more Negroes belong to these than to any of the others, while among whites such organizations rank in third place. On the other hand, while 38 per cent of the whites belong to civic and service associations, almost a third of the Negroes, 31 per cent, also belong to such organizations. If we assume that the bulk of these organizations are all-Negro in membership and have as their "clientele" members of the Negro community, this would indicate that there is a considerable degree of "community orientation" among Negroes.

TABLE 4

Membership in types of associations: by race

Type of association	Whites	Negroes
Veterans	15%	4%
Civic	38	31
Political	3	13
Lodges	31	28
Church	24	35
Economic	9	4
Cultural	4	1
Social	17	9
	(785)	(68)

The one unexpected result in Table 4 concerns the rates of membership in political and pressure groups: While 3 per cent of the whites belong to these associations, 13 per cent of the Negroes are members. Normally, we would expect no difference between the races or, if differences did appear, for them to run in the opposite direction. Obviously, given the small number of Negroes upon which the percentages are based, too much cannot be made of this finding, and any conclusions must be highly tentative. So, for example, it is entirely reasonable to assume that the entire Negro sample represented in Table 4 is middle class, and that the 13 per cent who are members of political and pressure groups are all members of one organization, The National Association for the Advancement of Colored People. But in view of the fact that only 4 per cent of the entire sample belong to organizations of this sort (Table 1), the possibility that over 10 per cent of all Negro voluntary association members may belong to organizations like the NAACP tells us something interesting and important about the Negro community in the United States at the present moment. Our figures may be one indication of a growing self-consciousness in the Negro community . . .

RELIGION, MINORITY STATUS, AND ORGANIZATIONS

Table 5 indicates three areas of difference in the membership patterns of Catholics and Protestants. There is a slight tendency for more Catholics to join veterans, patriotic, and military associations than Protestants: 19 per cent of the Catholics belong to such organizations and 13 per cent of the Protestants join them. Secondly, 39 per cent of the Protestants join civic and service associations and 32 per cent of the Catholics are members. Finally, more Protestants than Catholics also join economic, occupational, and professional organizations—11 per cent of the Protestants and 4 per cent of the Catholics.

TABLE 5

Distribution of voluntary association members by type of association and religion*

Type of association	Protestant	Catholic	Jewish	
Veterans	13%	19%	8%	
	70%	27%	3%	(116)
Civic	39	32	19	
	78	16	6	(313)
Political	4	3	13	
	70	15	15	(34)
Lodges	30	29	54	
	74	18	8	(256)
Church	25	26	33	
	74	20	6	(210)
Economic	11	4	3	
	91	8	1	(73)
Cultural	4	3	3	
	84	13	3	(30)
Social	17	18	8	
	76	22	2	(135)
	(624)	(160)	(39)	

* When the percentages are read across toward the base figures in parentheses in the right hand column they represent the distribution of the religions within each type of association. When the table is read down the columns toward the base figures in the last row the numbers represent the percentage of individuals of each religion belonging to each type of association.

These results are extremely suggestive, and they may throw more light on our previous findings on the low rate of Catholic voluntary association membership. One result of a long history of prejudice and discrimination would be the growth of an "avoidance pattern" among members of a minority group; that is, to withdraw from interaction with others and restrict interaction to fellow members of the same group. Therefore, prejudice and its consequences would result in a decline in the rate of participation in the life of the community as a whole. This tendency is further reenforced by a strong central institution like the Catholic Church which by its structure and belief system promotes a high level of group cohesion.

The figures of Table 5 are congruent with this hypothesis. We note, first, that Catholics participate less than Protestants in civic and service associations. These are precisely the organizations which link the individual to the community, and they also represent, as it were, the common ground upon which the diverse groups in the community meet and interact with one another. That relatively few Catholics belong to economic, occupational, and professional organizations is probably accounted for, in part, by the fact that fewer Catholics are middle class. But the size of the Catholic middle class cannot wholly account for the difference, since we have previously found that within each class Catholics still had a lower rate than Protestants, particularly in the middle class.

The differences between Catholics and Protestants with respect to membership in veterans, military, and patriotic organizations seemingly contradicts the hypothesis, but at least two points must be kept in mind. First, many organizations falling into the category have a wholly Catholic membership, e.g., the Catholic War Veterans. Second, many organizations like the American Legion post, for example, draws its members from a residential neighborhood which is apt to be ethnically and religiously homogeneous, and therefore the Catholic legionnaire is more apt to be interacting with other Catholic legionnaires than with veterans representative of other groups in the society.

The proposition that minority group members have a lower rate of membership in voluntary associations because of prejudice and the "avoidance pattern" is obviously contradicted by the membership rate of the Jews. However, there are three factors present which would tend to make this group a deviate one. First, there is no functional equivalent of the Catholic Church serving to reinforce and maintain a distinct religious identity and a foundation for group cohesion. Second, the group has developed a tradition of voluntary association membership as a result of its history. Finally, the educational level of the group and its rate of social mobility have probably been greater than that of Catholics, and these are factors correlated with high rates of voluntary association membership.

POLITICAL IDENTIFICATION AND ORGANIZATIONS

In previous comparisons of Democrats, Republicans, and Independents we usually found differences among these groups. But as we can see from Table 6 there is, with two exceptions, no difference among them in terms of the kinds of organizations they join. About one-fourth of the Democrats and Republicans belong to church and religious organizations—27 per cent and 26 per cent respectively—only 17 per cent of the Independents belong to groups of this type.

TABLE 6

Distribution of voluntary association members by type of association and political party identification*

Type of association	Democrat		Republican		Independent		
Veterans		14%		15%		16%	
	46%		36%		18%		(120)
Civic		37		40		34	
	46		35		17		(321)
Political		5		4		2	
	60		31		9		(35)
Lodges		30		31		34	
	46		34		18		(264)
Church		27		26		17	
	51		36		11		(211)
Economic		8		10		11	
	43		27		20		(76)
Cultural		3		4		4	
	37		37		20		(32)
Social		16		16		16	
	46		34		17		(138)
	(402)		(286)		(140)		

* When the percentages are read across toward the base figures in the right hand column they represent the distribution of party identification groups within each type of association. When the table is read down the columns toward the base figures in the last row the numbers represent the percentage of individuals in each political identification category belonging to each type of association.

Given the American political system, one must talk rather gingerly of the relationship between political parties and "ideology"; that is, one must be cautious in making inferences about "commitment to an ideology" from the mere fact of identification or non-identification with a political party. Nonetheless, if we use the term "ideology" somewhat loosely, we can say that for some, if not all, identification with a political party does imply an "ideological commitment" and identification with a group or stratum in the society. Similarly, membership in a voluntary association with religious affiliations implies some commitment to a religious belief system and identification with a specific social group. One possible meaning of Table 6, then is that those describing themselves as Independents in terms of political party identification tend to be consistent, i.e., they are individuals not only relatively uncommitted to a political ideology but to a religious belief system as well. In short, they may be defined as a relatively alienated and apathetic group in the society. Thus their low rate of membership in voluntary associations of any kind can be seen as both a consequence and a symbol of this alienation.

The other item of interest in this table concerns the membership of political and pressure groups. Of the entire sample 48 per cent of the respondents identified themselves as Democrats, 26 per cent as Republicans, and 19 per cent called themselves "Independents." In all types of associations Republicans tend to be over-represented, and more Republicans than Democrats are members of associations. Yet 60 per cent of the membership of political and pressure groups are Democrats and 31 per cent are Republicans. There are two possible explanations for this. On the one hand, if we take into account that there are more Democrats in the working class than Republicans, this may represent the last vestiges of the Democratic political machines' connections with the urban working class. On the other hand, it may be the result of an interest, awakened during that period, which is more likely to continue among Democrats than Republicans.

URBANIZATION AND ORGANIZATIONS

Table 7 presents the picture of membership in various organizations by size of community, and it is apparent that differences between communities emerge in four areas of associational activity. First, residents of less urbanized areas tend to have a higher rate of membership in veterans, military, and patriotic associations than do people living in more urbanized communities. In each of the two metropolitan areas 11 per cent and 12 per cent of the respondents belong to these organizations, while in the more urbanized counties 17 per cent belong to them and 19 per cent join in the least urbanized areas. This suggests that the experience of having served in the armed forces, i.e., of living for a period of time in a radically different environment from that of a small town, is a special experience for people in less organized areas which may distinguish them both in their own eyes and the eyes of others. Also, it may be another expression of that "integral association between military institutions and rural society." [1]

Membership in organizations of the civic and service types declines among those living in less urban-

TABLE 7

Membership in types of association: by size of community

Type of association	Metropolitan area over one million	Metropolitan area less than one million	County largest town 10-50,000	County no town as large as 10,000
Veterans	11%	12%	17%	19%
Civic	43	38	25	29
Political	5	6	5	*
Lodges	30	34	28	31
Church	27	20	30	23
Economic	5	8	11	14
Cultural	3	4	4	4
Social	14	18	18	16
	(238)	(232)	(178)	(177)

* Less than 1%.

[1] Morris Janowitz, *The Professional Soldier: A Social and Political Portrait* (Glencoe, Ill.: The Free Press, 1960), p. 85.

ized areas. In the most heavily populated areas 43 per cent of the respondents join these organizations, and in the smaller metropolitan areas 38 per cent join them. Among those living in the more urbanized and less urbanized counties 25 per cent and 29 per cent respectively are members of civic and service associations. This pattern is congruent with the notion that voluntary associations, especially those of this type, are more important in metropolitan regions. On the other hand, it is more difficult to account for the inconsistency in the results for membership in church and religious associations. Here we find 27 per cent of those in the largest metropolitan areas belong to them, and this rate declines to 20 per cent in the smaller metropolitan areas. But 30 per cent of those living in the more urbanized counties join church-related organizations while 23 per cent of those living in the less urbanized areas belong to them.

Finally, we note that there are differences in the membership rates in economic, occupational, and professional associations. In the metropolitan areas 5 per cent and 8 per cent respectively of the respondents join them, but 11 per cent and 14 per cent respectively of those living in the relatively less urbanized areas are members of these organizations. In the less urbanized regions individuals who would be more apt to be members of organizations of this type, professionals and small businessmen, would not only be a smaller stratum in the community but represent perceptively distinctive orientations and styles of life. Their tendency to belong to associations organized about their occupational and economic interests may be symptomatic of a latent conflict with the rest of the community, especially within the more rural areas.

Within communities differences in membership patterns between owners and renters emerge in two areas of activity. Among home owners 40 per cent belong to civic and service associations, while 33 per cent of the renters join these organizations. Obviously, this may be the result of class differences between the two groups. However, we may also postulate that the economic investment represented by home ownership would motivate a higher level of interest in organizations oriented to "the welfare of the community." Furthermore, the membership rate of owners in this type of association is congruent with our previous hypothesis about the significance of home ownership. We have said that renters are likely to be more mobile individuals and less integrated into the community, and conversely, owners a more stable group. The difference in the extent of integration into the community each group represents is symbolized by the different rates of membership in civic and service organizations.

Of those belonging to church related organizations there is a slight tendency for owners to have a higher rate than renters: 27 per cent of the owners belong and 21 per cent of the renters are members of such associations. Since owners are likely to be older than renters, and older individuals have a higher rate of membership in associations of this type, the difference between owners and renters probably reflects the more fundamental age difference.

SOCIO-ECONOMIC STATUS AND ORGANIZATIONS

We now turn our attention to the effects of class status upon membership in voluntary associations. Table 8 summarizes the relationship between income, as an index of socio-economic status, and types of associations. Perhaps the most interesting datum in this table is the rate of membership in civic and service organizations: as income increases the membership rate in this type of organization also increases. The difference between the extremes is striking; 59 per cent of the members of these organizations have an income of at least $5000, and 9 per cent earn less than $3000.

Table 9 shows, as with income, a correlation between education and membership in civic and service organizations, but here there is an interesting variation. Among those belonging to these associations 10 per cent fall into the lowest educational level and 39 per cent into the highest. However, the majority of the members, 51 per cent, are those with only a high school education. A similar pattern is apparent in the membership of lodges and fraternal associations: 27 per cent of the membership has only an elementary school education; 48 per cent has a high school education; and exactly a quarter of the membership has attended college. This pattern is found again in the membership of church and religious associations, veterans groups, and among those belonging to social and recreational associations. These findings suggest that education is associated with a particular kind of orientation. A higher rate of membership in civic and service associations combined with a lower rate of membership in the other types seems to point to a more "cosmopolitan" orientation among the college educated as opposed to a more "local" orientation among the less well educated.

TABLE 8

Distribution of voluntary association members by type of association and income*

Type of association	Under $3,000	$3,000–$4,999	$5,000 and over	
Veterans	14%	18%	12%	
	22%	40%	38% 47%	(120)
Civic	16	38	47	
	9	32	59	(319)
Political	4	3	5	
	22	22	56	(36)
Lodges	13	23	32	
	10	35	55	(233)
Church	36	24	21	
	31	31	38	(213)
Economic	10	7	10	
	24	24	52	(76)
Cultural	3	5	3	
	16	42	42	(31)
Social	13	19	16	
	17	36	47	(139)
	(181)	(269)	(397)	

TABLE 9

Distribution of voluntary association members by type of association and education*

Type of association	Elementary school	High school	College	
Veterans	14%	16%	11%	
	22%	57%	21%	(120)
Civic	16	39	51	
	10	51	39	(322)
Political	3	4	7	
	16	42	42	(36)
Lodges	36	30	28	
	27	48	25	(265)
Church	28	26	21	
	26	51	23	(214)
Economic	12	6	12	
	29	35.5	35.5	(76)
Cultural	3	2	7	
	19	31	50	(32)
Social	13	18	17	
	19	54	27	(139)
	(198)	(426)	(229)	

* When the percentages are read across toward the base figures in parentheses in the right hand column they represent the distribution of income groups within each type of association. When the table is read down the columns toward the base figures in the last row the numbers represent the percentage of individuals in each income group belonging to each type of association.

* When the percentages are read across toward the base figures in parentheses in the right hand column they represent the distribution of education categories within each type of association. When the table is read down the columns toward the base figures in the last row the numbers represent the percentage of individuals in each education category belonging to each type of association.

This same pattern is also apparently in membership rates for lodges and fraternal societies. Among the members of these organizations 10 per cent are in the lowest income bracket and 55 per cent in the highest. The rate of membership of the individuals in the upper income levels in these organizations as well as the civic and service ones is probably associated with the instrumental functions such organizations have for occupational and career ends.

The statistics of membership by occupational status are consistent with our previous findings for income and education. Thus, the higher status occupational groups have a higher rate of membership in church-related associations than those at the lowest occupational levels. The occupational group with the highest percentage of members in veterans groups and social and recreational organizations are the skilled workers.

Taking our findings on socio-economic status as a

whole, the most suggestive are those on membership in civic and service organizations. We already know that middle class individuals have a higher rate of membership in all kinds of voluntary associations than working class individuals. To the extent that voluntary associations serve as mechanisms for linking the members of an industrial society to its institutions, one significant conclusion of our over-all findings is that members of the working class are less likely to be "integrated into the society." Our present results serve to underline and emphasize this conclusion. Not only are working class individuals less likely to be members of voluntary associations but, of those who are, relatively few are affiliated with those organizations which most directly link the individual and the community or have as their main orientation that of the community rather than more particularistic interests.

The membership rate of the working class is obviously related to educational level, but it is important to see that this is only one part of a complex process. A low level of education means a low level of interest in and knowledge of the uses of voluntary associations, and therefore the low rate of membership. But this rate, especially as it applies to membership in civic and service organizations, has the further consequence of maintaining the low level of interest and knowledge of institutionalized means of achieving individual and group ends, i.e., voluntary associations. As a consequence, in conflict situations working class interests cannot be achieved, and this may result in a sense of alienation among members of this class. This sense of alienation, in turn, would result in a reinforcement of initial lack of interest and knowledge of the use of voluntary associations.

Most reports of surveys of association membership are based upon individual characteristics. Each characteristic—age, family status, place of residence, etc.—is correlated with the individual's membership and rates of membership are computed for various categories of the population. But of course every individual is a combination of several social and personal characteristics. Therefore, the researcher seeks to learn how certain configurations of characteristics affect membership. In other words, he is not only interested in how income, sex, family status, and education separately correlate with membership, but he is interested in how the total way of life of married middle class men (for example) affects their inclination and ability to join associations.

In their selection, Wendell Bell and Maryanne Force show how sets of characteristics fit together to produce patterns of membership in association. Since their research aims differ from the previous selections by Wright and Hyman and Hausknecht, their methods differ. The previously excerpted surveys generalized about the characteristics of individuals and used national samples representative of the American population. Since Bell and Force were interested in how the social environment interrelated with the individual's characteristics, they first selected a sample of neighborhoods on the basis of census data, and then they sampled individuals within each type of district. The following selection uses more complex statistical analysis methods than the previous ones, since it aims to weigh the relative importance of the variables in producing the outcome.* We reproduce most of the article, since it is a good example of sampling strategy and multivariate analysis in social research. Parenthetically, another virtue of the selec-

---

* The authors use chi-square (X^2), a statistical test designed to estimate whether a relationship in the data could have occurred by chance. $P < .01$ means that the relationship could have occurred by chance in fewer than 1% of all possible samples of such data; $P < .05$ means that the relationship could have occurred by chance in fewer than 5% of all samples. Such low probabilities suggest that the relationship in the data analyzed by the authors does represent a real fact and is not an eccentric characteristic of their one sample alone.

tion is that it shows how the same social and motivational determinants affect both membership in an association and participation by the membership in organizational affairs. For simplicity, we have discussed membership and participation in separate chapters of the book, but they can be viewed as a continuous process.

THE INFLUENCE OF THE NEIGHBORHOOD*

Wendell Bell and Maryanne T. Force

This paper reports part of a study of social participation conducted in San Francisco in the spring of 1953. The investigation rested upon two main notions:

First, that the major social roles which an individual occupies regulate the amount and nature of his participation in society. For example, if one knew a person's economic, family, and ethnic status, his age and sex, his aspirations or expectations regarding the roles he might achieve, and his status history with respect to these types of statuses, one should be able to predict closely that person's participation in the various activities of society.

Second, that the social type of neighborhood in which an urbanite lives is an efficient indicator of his social participation and may be a significant factor in its own right in shaping his social participation. It has been contended, for example, that social differences between the populations of urban neighborhoods can be conveniently summarized into differences of economic level, family characteristics, and ethnicity. It is our hypothesis that neighborhood populations having different configurations with respect to these three variables will have different patterns of social participation. . . .

DESCRIPTION OF THE SAMPLE

SELECTION OF THE NEIGHBORHOODS

Using the census tract scores given in *Social Area Analysis*[1] four census tracts were selected in San Francisco in which to conduct the study of social participation. The identifying place names, census tract designations, and index scores for the four tracts selected are given in Table 1. It was decided to hold ethnicity constant as far as possible, so all four of the tracts selected contain relatively few non-whites and few members of foreign-born groups, as indicated by their relatively low scores on the index of ethnicity.

* From Wendell Bell and Maryanne T. Force, "Urban Neighborhood Types and Participation in Formal Associations," *American Sociological Review*, Volume 21, Number 21, Number 1 (February 1956), pp. 25-34. Revised by the authors and reprinted with the permission of the authors and the publisher, the American Sociological Association.
[1] Eshref Shevky and Wendell Bell, *Social Area Analysis* (Stanford: Stanford University Press, 1955).

TABLE I

Identifying place names, census tract designations, and index scores for the four study tracts[*]

Index	Mission (N-8)	Pacific Heights (B-6)	Outer Mission (M-6)	St. Francis Wood (O-7)
Socioeconomic status[†]	46	96	43	92
Familism[‡]	28	9	67	70
Ethnicity[§]	14	7	20	6

[*] Index scores can vary approximately from 0 to 100.
[†] Composed of measures of occupation and education.
[‡] Composed of measures of fertility, women not in the labor force, and single family detached dwelling units.
[§] Per cent of persons in the census tract who are nonwhite or foreign born white from Southern and Eastern Europe, Asia, and French Canada.

Census tracts N-8 (located in the Mission district) and M-6 (located in the Outer Mission district) have low scores on the index of socioeconomic status relative to the scores of the other census tracts in the San Francisco Bay Region. The Mission population, however, is a rooming-house district with a relatively low score on the index of familism, having a low fertility ratio, many women in the labor force, and few single-family detached dwellings. The population of Outer Mission was a relatively high score on the index of familism and is characterized by high fertility ratios, few women in the labor force, and many single-family detached dwellings. Census tract B-6 is in the Pacific Heights district and is a high-rent apartment house area, having a relatively high socioeconomic level, but a low score on familism. Census tract O-7 contains the district known as St. Francis Wood and, like Pacific Heights, contains a population having high socioeconomic status, but like Outer Mission is a single family home area characterized by a high score on familism.

SELECTION OF THE RESPONDENTS

A probability area sample was selected for each of the study census tracts. First, a complete list of dwelling units in each of the tracts was compiled by means of standard block listing procedures. Second, a sampling interval (k) was established for each tract, and a sample of dwellings drawn by taking a random number from 1 to k and selecting every k the dwelling unit thereafter. Third, within each sample dwelling one male over the age of 21 was selected as the respondent, thus eliminating from this study social participation differences resulting from the differential requirements of the roles of the two sexes. Dwellings containing no males over age 21 were removed from the sample, and in those which contained two or more males over age 21 one male was selected randomly from a respondent selection table provided on each interview schedule. In order to assure randomness in the sample no substitutions were allowed. . . .

AMOUNT OF PARTICIPATION BY NEIGHBORHOOD

NUMBER OF FORMAL GROUP MEMBERSHIPS

One measure of formal group participation used in many previous studies and employed in this study is the sheer number of memberships in formal associations. Table 2 contains the per cent of persons in each neighborhood who belong to a certain number of formal organizations.* From Table 2 it can be seen that in each of the different neighborhoods more than 76 per cent of the men belong to at least one formal group. This finding is comparable to the findings of other studies of formal group membership in urban areas. . . . However, these figures indicate considerably higher membership in one or more formal associations than is given in some other studies of formal participation among urban dwellers, especially among those men who are blue-collar workers.

Although the data shown in Table 2 support the contention that the formal association is widespread throughout diverse social groupings in an urban envi-

ronment, only about a third or less of the men in every neighborhood, except St. Francis Wood, belong to three or more formal associations.

Comparing the tracts with respect to the number of formal group memberships, we find that the high socioeconomic status tracts contain relatively more men who belong to a greater number of formal associations than do the low socioeconomic status tracts. The largest percentage (66.1 per cent) of men belonging to three or more associations is in St. Francis Wood, and the next largest percentage (35.6 per cent) is in Pacific Heights. The two low socioeconomic level neighborhoods at each level of familism have significantly (P<.01) lower percentages of men who report that they belong to three or more associations with 16.8 per cent so reporting in Mission and 12.9 per cent so reporting in Outer Mission.

Differences between neighborhoods having different levels of family life, holding socioeconomic status constant, are not consistent, although at the high socioeconomic level St. Francis Wood, being high on familism, has a much larger percentage of men who belong to three or more associations than does Pacific Heights, the low familism neighborhood. Pacific Heights also contains a larger percentage of men who belong to no associations than does St. Francis Wood.

ATTENDANCE AT FORMAL GROUP MEETINGS

The mere number of memberships does not give adequate information regarding the amount of participation in formal associations, since membership in some cases may be only nominal. Table 3 contains the frequency of attendance at all formal association meetings for these men who report belonging to at least one such organization.

In St. Francis Wood only 5.8 per cent, in Mission 12.1 per cent, in Pacific Heights 14.1 per cent, and in Outer Mission 17.5 per cent of the members of formal

TABLE 2

Per cent of men having membership in a certain number of formal associations

Number of groups	Low familism Low socioecon. (Mission)	Low familism High socioecon. (Pacific Heights)	High familism Low socioecon. (Outer Mission)	High familism High socioecon. (St. Francis Wood)
Seven or more	2%	11%	0%	19%
Six	0	3	0	4
Five	1	3	1	12
Four	2	7	3	14
Three	12	11	9	17
Two	22	23	22	14
One	38	20	45	13
None	23	22	19	7
Not ascertained	0	0	1	0
Total	100%	100%	100%	100%
Number of cases	(172)	(191)	(170)	(168)

* [In this selection, "formal associations" are defined to exclude churches, government agencies, and business firms. They include church-connected associations and trade unions.–Eds.]

TABLE 3

Per cent of formal association members who attend a specified number of meetings

Frequency of attendance	Low familism Low socioecon. (Mission)	Low familism High socioecon. (Pacific Heights)	High familism Low socioecon. (Outer Mission)	High familism High socioecon. (St. Francis Wood)
More than once a week	8%	31%	7%	27%
About once a week	8	15	11	14
A few times a month	29	18	16	23
About once a month	18	7	16	6
A few times a year	19	12	25	20
About once a year	6	3	7	4
Never	12	14	17	6
Not ascertained	0	0	1	0
Total	100%	100%	100%	100%
Number of members	(132)	(149)	(137)	(156)

groups do not attend meetings. Thus, the vast majority of the members in each of the neighborhoods, in excess of 82 per cent, attend at least one meeting a year. . . .

When the members in the four neighborhoods are compared with respect to the frequency of formal association attendance, marked differences between neighborhoods appear. Again, the greatest amount of formal participation occurs among the persons who live in the high socioeconomic status neighborhoods. Men living in St. Francis Wood and Pacific Heights who belong to formal associations attend more frequently than those living in Mission and Outer Mission. In Pacific Heights 30.9 per cent of the members attend meetings more than once a week compared to only 8.3 per cent in Mission ($P < .01$); in St. Francis Wood 26.7 per cent of the members attend meetings more than once a week compared to only 6.6 per cent in Outer Mission ($P < .01$).

Considering those men who belong to formal associations but who attend only about once a year or less, it may be noted that Pacific Heights, the high socioeconomic, low familism neighborhood, has almost as large a percentage of men who are relatively isolated from social contacts in formal groups as the two low socioeconomic status neighborhoods. Since Pacific Heights, Mission, and Outer Mission are the neighborhoods with the largest percentages of men who do not belong to formal groups, it is evident that sizeable segments of the population in these three neighborhoods are socially isolated from this form of participation. This is consistent with the general conclusion of Komarovsky who says with respect to formal group participation that a large segment of the population, particularly the lower social and economic level ". . . is cut off from channels of power, information, growth, and a sense of participation in purposive social action." [2] We would add to this generalization that even on the higher socioeconomic levels a significant segment of those men living in neighborhoods low in family life are similarly isolated.

OFFICE HOLDING IN FORMAL ASSOCIATIONS

Generally, holding positions of leadership in a formal association denotes more active participation in the group than not holding positions of leadership. Thus, a third measure of formal association participation used in this study, and one which indicates the relative power position of the individual within the association, is whether or not the individual holds office in the formal associations to which he belongs. Table 4 contains a summary presentation of this material. Consistent with our other findings, the high so-

cioeconomic status neighborhoods contain a larger percentage of members who hold office in a formal association than do the low socioeconomic status neighborhoods at each level of familism. Pacific Heights (24.5 per cent) contains a larger percentage than Mission (13.0 per cent) ($P < .05$), and St. Francis Wood (34.8 per cent) contains a larger percentage than Outer Mission (11.6 per cent) ($P < .01$).

TABLE 4

Per cent of formal association members who hold offices

Holds office	Low familism Low socioecon. (Mission)	Low familism High socioecon. (Pacific Heights)	High familism Low socioecon. (Outer Mission)	High familism High socioecon. (St. Francis Wood)
Yes	13%	24%	11%	35%
No	86	75	88	65
Not ascertained	1	1	1	0
Total	100%	100%	100%	100%
Number of cases	(131)	(151)	(138)	(155)

Although no difference appears between the two low socioeconomic status neighborhoods, the relative number of office holders is somewhat higher in St. Francis Wood (high socioeconomic status and high familism) than it is in Pacific Heights (high socioeconomic status and low familism). Our findings consistently show that the higher socioeconomic status neighborhoods contain relatively more men who belong to formal associations, more members who frequently attend meetings, and more members who hold office in formal associations when compared with neighborhoods of a lower socioeconomic level.

The differences by familism are not so large nor so consistent, although at the high socioeconomic status level, the neighborhood lower on familism contains a higher percentage of men who are socially isolated with respect to formal association participation by all three measures of participation used here than the neighborhood higher on familism contains.

INDIVIDUAL AND NEIGHBORING CHARACTERISTICS

EDUCATION, OCCUPATION, AND INCOME

Thus far in the analysis the discussion has been limited to the formal association participation of men as that behavior is related to the social type of neighborhood in which the men live. In effect, we have been assigning to each man his neighborhood scores for socioeconomic status and familism, and relating his formal association behavior to these scores. The neighborhoods are, however, not completely homoge-

2 Mirra Komarovsky, "The Voluntary Associations of Urban Dwellers," *American Sociological Review*, Volume 11, Number 6 (December 1946), p. 698.

neous with respect to economic and family characteristics; that is, each man by some measure of his own individual socioeconomic status or family life does not necessarily have a score which equals the average for his neighborhood. A neighborhood's score has been referred to as a unit variable, and an individual's own score as a personal variable. In this section we wish to explore further the relationship between economic position and formal association by tabulating these two types of variables simultaneously.

Since the most significant and consistent findings concern socioeconomic status and not familism, the study neighborhoods have been grouped so that the two low socioeconomic status neighborhoods, Mission and Outer Mission, are together, and the two high socioeconomic status neighborhoods, Pacific Heights and St. Francis Wood, are together. Education, occupation, and annual family income were taken as measures of personal socioeconomic status. As is shown in Table 5, the high socioeconomic status neighborhoods contain relatively more men wih higher education, with white collar occupations, and with higher incomes; and the low socioeconomic status neighborhoods contain relatively more men

with lower education, blue collar occupations, and lower incomes. There is, however, a small percentage of men living in the high socioeconomic status neighborhoods who have either relatively low education, blue collar jobs, or relatively low incomes, that is, who would be classified as low socioeconomic status on the basis of personal variables even though they are living in high socioeconomic status neighborhoods, Similarly, there are in the low socioeconomic status neighborhoods small percentages of men who would be classified as high socioeconomic status on the basis of their personal ratings on education, occupation, and income. The question arises whether differences in amount of formal association participation between high and low socioeconomic status neighborhoods, an aspect of the social context within which men live, still exist when controls are introduced for personal socioeconomic status.

Table 6 shows the per cent of men who attend formal association meetings frequently by the average

TABLE 5

Per cent of men having selected socioeconomic characteristics by neighborhood

Socioeconomic characteristics	Neighborhood Characteristics	
	Low socioecon. status (Mission and Outer Mission)	High socioecon. status (Pacific Heights and St. Francis Wood)
Education		
Some college or more	10%	50%
Completed high school only	24	26
Some high school	24	13
Grade school or less	42	11
Not ascertained	0	0
Total	100%	100%
Number of cases	(342)	(359)
Occupation		
Profs., mgrs., props., and offs.	13%	67%
Sales, clerical, and kindred workers	8	21
Craftsmen, foremen, and operatives	57	9
Service workers and laborers	22	3
Not ascertained	0	0
Total	100%	100%
Number of cases	(342)	(359)
Income		
$10,000 and over	2%	41%
6,000-9,999	18	29
3,000-5,999	65	21
0-2,999	14	5
Not ascertained	1	4
Total	100%	100%
Number of cases	(342)	(359)

TABLE 6

*Per cent of men who attend formal association meetings frequently by neighborhood and individual socioeconomic characteristics**

Individual socioeconomic characteristics	Neighborhood Characteristics	
	Low socioecon. status (Mission and Outer Mission) Per cent	High socioecon. status (Pacific Heights and St. Francis Wood) Per cent
Education		
Some college or more	27 (33)	46 (181)
Completed high school only	15 (83)	28 (92)
Some high school	17 (81)	30 (46)
Grade school or less	8 (144)	23 (39)
Occupation		
Profs., mgrs., props., and offs.	33 (43)	43 (241)
Sales, clerical, and kindred workers	21 (29)	26 (76)
Craftsmen, foremen, and operatives	9 (194)	23 (31)
Service workers and laborers	11 (74)	33 (9)
Income		
$10,000 and over	0 (4)	53 (148)
6,000-9,999	17 (65)	29 (103)
3,000-5,999	13 (222)	20 (75)
0-2,999	13 (48)	16 (19)

* Men were classified frequent attenders if they attended meetings 37 or more times per year. The total number of cases on which the percentages is based is given in parentheses in each case.

socioeconomic status of the neighborhood and by the respondent's own education, occupation, and family income. Comparing the percentages *within each neighborhood*, the general tendency is for relatively more frequent attenders to have higher education, white collar occupations, and higher incomes. This, of course, is consistent with the findings of many studies which have related such measures to formal association participation.

Of particular interest here, however, is the comparison of amount of formal association participation between neighborhoods, holding personal education, occupation, and income constant. For example, a larger percentage of the men who have been to college are frequent attenders in the high socioeconomic status neighborhoods than in the low socioeconomic status neighborhoods. This is also true of the men in the less educated categories. At each of the educational levels the men living in the higher socioeconomic status neighborhoods are more likely to be frequent attenders than are the men living in the lower socioeconomic status neighborhoods ($\Sigma_x^2 = 15.78$, $P < .01$).

Although not statistically significant, a similar tendency can be seen when personal occupation and income are held constant. Men with high occupations are more likely to be frequent attenders if they live in the high socioeconomic status neighborhoods. The same is true for the other occupational groups. For example, men who are service workers and laborers are more likely to be frequent attenders if they live in the high socioeconomic status neighborhoods. A similar tendency occurs between the two neighborhoods when comparing men who have similar incomes. Those who live in the high socioeconomic status neighborhoods are somewhat more likely than those who live in the low socioeconomic status neighborhoods to be frequent attenders at formal association meetings. Thus, differences in formal association participation still exist when comparing the low with the high socioeconomic status neighborhoods, even when certain measures of personal socioeconomic status are controlled.

There seem to be at least two explanations for these findings. First, the neighborhood characteristics may be an index to the self image of the individual, and second, the type of neighborhood in which a person lives may itself be a factor in the kinds of pressures which are brought upon the individual to participate in formal associations.

In the first instance the lower socioeconomic status persons who live in high socioeconomic status neighborhoods and the higher socioeconomic status persons who live in low socioeconomic status neighborhoods may be the "deviants" who are found in many stratification studies; that is, they may be those whose objective class position does not seem congruent with their own placement of themselves. The socioeconomic characteristics of the neighborhoods in which they live, however, may give important objective clues regarding their group identification and, thereby, give indications of certain kinds of behavioral and and attitudinal correlates.

The second case would involve the effect of the neighborhood in determining the role expectations of the individual after the individual became a part of the neighborhood. For example, persons living in high socioeconomic status neighborhoods may come under much greater pressures to participate in certain types of associations than do persons living in low socioeconomic status neighborhoods. Neighborhood improvement associations, civic groups, welfare and charitable organizations, etc., are more likely to have members from high than from low socioeconomic status neighborhoods.

FAMILY CHARACTERISTICS

Within each of the four neighborhoods the number of formal association memberships, as well as the frequency of attendance at formal association meetings, was tabulated against marital status, age of children, employment status of wife, and type of dwelling (single family detached vs. two or more family dwelling). Although other writers report relationships between formal association participation and these variables, we find no consistent trends when making comparisons within each of the neighborhoods.

AGE DIFFERENCES

Many writers have investigated the relationship between age and formal association participation. Axelrod, for example, in his Detroit study finds that formal association membership starts out relatively low in early adulthood, reaches a peak in the forties, and then declines to a new low by the sixties. He also finds this same pattern for the very active participants.[3] Goldhamer found that when participation is measured by frequency of attendance, the young men tend to exceed the older and that participation tends to decline in the oldest age group (fifty and over).[4] From his study of persons aged 65 and over living in a California community of retired people, McKain noted that formal association participation declined with advanced years; about 50 per cent of those over age 65 reported that they gave less time to associations than they did when they were 50 years of age,

[3] Morris Axelrod, *A Study of Formal and Informal Group Participation in a Large Urban Community* (Ann Arbor: unpublished dissertation for the Ph.D. at the University of Michigan, 1953).
[4] Herbert Goldhamer, *Some Factors Affecting Participation in Voluntary Associations* (Chicago: unpublished dissertation for the Ph.D. at the University of Chicago, 1942).

only 1 per cent said that their social activities had increased.[5] These findings have been interpreted by some as indicating a structural relationship between the adult life cycle and formal association participation: ties with formal associations prevent many formal associations in the twenties; consolidation of occupational position, a home and a family lead the individual to join associations in the thirties; formal associations become an end in themselves in the forties and occupy more time; children grown to adulthood, retirement, and loss of physical stamina and vigor result in less and less formal association participation at the older age groups.

Annual formal association attendance by age is given in Table 7 for each of the four study neighborhoods in San Francisco. These data require a revision of the above view, and constitute some evidence of the degree of difference in life styles of segments of the population at different levels of socioeconomic status. In each of the high socioeconomic status neighborhoods *the per cent of men who are active participants increases with increasing age*. No such relationship, however, occurs between age and formal association participation among the men who live in the low socioeconomic status neighborhoods. On the contrary, in these neighborhoods the smallest percentage of men who attend meetings "seldom or never" is in the middle age group and the largest percentage, who are thus "socially isolated," is in the older age group. Thus, the relationship between age and formal association participation in the low socioeconomic status neighborhoods approximates that found by most other writers, but we find an entirely different pattern in the high socioeconomic status neighborhoods. . . .

In addition (see Table 7) the reported relationships between participation to some of the social types of neighborhoods in which men live and to certain social roles which men occupy. A brief review of the findings follows:

1. Although the four urban neighborhoods studied were widely divergent with respect to socioeconomic level and extent of family life, over three-fourths of the men hold membership in at least one formal group, and a relatively small percentage of these are inactive.

2. Men living in the high socioeconomic status neighborhoods belong to the greater number of associations, attend more frequently, and hold office more than men living in low socioeconomic status neighborhoods.

3. Comparing the two high socioeconomic status neighborhoods, the neighborhood low on familism, contains relatively more men who belong to no formal associations, who never attend meetings if they do belong and who do not hold office than does the neighborhood high on familism. No such relationship appears when comparing the two low socioeconomic status neighborhoods.

4. Within each of the neighborhoods persons of higher socioeconomic status, as indicated by their own individual educational level, income, and occupation, generally have a greater amount of associational participation than do individuals of lower socioeconomic status. Holding individual socioeconomic status constant, persons living in the high socioeconomic status neighborhoods still have more associational participation than those living in the low socioeconomic status neighborhoods. Thus, the socioeconomic characteristics of the neighborhood population as a unit may be an important indicator of the socioeconomic reference group for those living in the neighborhood, and may define a set of general societal expectations with respect to associational behavior for the residents.

TABLE 7

*Annual formal association attendance by neighborhood and age**

| | Age | | |
Neighborhood	21-39	40-59	60 and over
Low familism, low socioecon. (Mission) Attendances per year:			
37 or more	19%	7%	16%
5-36	34	55	11
0-4	47	38	73
Total	100%	100%	100%
	(53)	(82)	(37)
Low familism, high socioecon. (Pacific Heights) Attendances per year:			
37 or more	28%	36%	44%
5-36	33	19	17
0-4	39	45	39
Total	100%	100%	100%
	(46)	(87)	(57)
High familism, low socioecon. (Outer Mission) Attendances per year:			
37 or more	10%	17%	17%
5-36	30	37	17
0-4	60	46	66
Total	100%	100%	100%
	(67)	(72)	(30)
High familism, high socioecon. (St. Francis Wood) Attendances per year:			
37 or more	21%	38%	53%
5-36	54	33	25
0-4	25	29	22
Total	100%	100%	100%
	(28)	(108)	(32)

* The numbers on which the percentages are based are given in parenthesis.

5 Walter C. McKain, Jr., *The Social Participation of Old People in a California Retirement Community* (Cambridge: unpublished dissertation for the Ph.D. at Harvard University, 1947).

5. It was reported that family characteristics of individuals within each of the neighborhoods, such as a respondents' marital status, children's ages, wife's employment status, etc., showed no consistent relationship to formal association participation.

6. Finally, the relationship between age roles and associational participation depends upon socioeconomic level. In the high socioeconomic status neighborhoods the percentage of frequent attenders increases with increasing age, but in the low socioeconomic status neighborhoods no such trend exists. In fact, in the latter type of neighborhoods the relationship between age and participation tended to follow the pattern most often reported in other studies with the older aged persons being the most isolated and the middle aged persons the least isolated.

The selection by Hausknecht reports that different kinds of people gravitate into different kinds of voluntary associations. Some people cross the boundaries, but each association tends to have a certain public image and a particular membership. Each association may thus become identified with a particular sector of a society, if that society is divided on bases of social class, religion, and ethnicity. In her selection, Mhyra Minnis describes how social differentiation in an American city produces differentiation and prestige stratification among the voluntary associations. A serious problem for a leader of an association experiencing unintended exclusiveness is to recognize such a trend early enough, in order to widen recruitment and thus maintain a public image appropriate to the community-wide goals the organization may have.

THE INFLUENCE OF THE SOCIAL STRUCTURE*

Mhyra S. Minnis

The study reported here is an empirical investigation of women's secondary or voluntary associations in New Haven, Connecticut, a city of some 160,000 population. The primary focus of the research is on the relationship of these organizations, considered by racial, religious, ethnic, and social prestige factors, to the social structure of the city. The latter, including the differentiation of the population according to race, ethnic origin, religion, occupation, and ecology, is shown to affect or underlie the differentiation of women's organizations. The study is limited to formally organized clubs, within the city's limits, and to those having an adult (18 years of age and over) membership. Various methods were employed to gather material on these associations, including:

(1) Basic orientation interviews with thirty-five individuals of different socio-economic levels who were familiar with the structure of organizations in the community.

(2) Participant observation and lectures at meetings of women's clubs.

(3) Compilation and classification of a master list of women's clubs through interviews, correspondence with national women's organizations, city directories, the *New Haven Social Register*, histories of the city, literature from the organizations, a detailed newspaper clipping file for over one year, and conferences with the "Society" editors of the newspapers.

(4) A questionnaire to over 400 presidents of women's organizations, covering the histories of the clubs, purposes, their classification according to type, membership, activities, services, and the value of the organization to the community and to the members themselves.

(5) The use of "raters" to initiate or corroborate the social prestige ranking of organizations. Protestant organizations were rated by the president of a federation of Protestant church auxiliaries; Catholic

* From Mhyra S. Minnis, "Cleavage in Women's Organizations," *American Sociological Review*, Volume 18, Number 1 (February 1953), pp. 47-53. Reprinted with the permission of the author and the publisher, the American Sociological Association.

organizations by two presidents of Catholic clubs; Jewish organizations by the head of the Jewish federation of clubs; and Negro organizations by presidents of Negro clubs. The newspaper society editors rated all of the clubs in the sample that was later drawn.

It was possible to identify 379 women's clubs in New Haven, comprising the universe of organizations in this study. From the questionnaires, a representative sample of 177 organizations was obtained. The data from both the universe and sample of organizations were analyzed and evaluated, although the sample was used as the basic source for the statistical analysis. . . .

RACIAL CLEAVAGE

The study revealed that the sharpest line of cleavage is by race. Of the 177 organizations comprising the sample, at least 90 per cent are racially exclusive. When the type of organization is considered, the two main racial divisions present a culturally varied pattern. Organizations with an all-white membership include all types. There is, however, a preponderance of social, service, auxiliary to fraternal orders, and college alumnae types among them. On the other hand, among the Negro organizations religious clubs and church auxiliaries are the most common.

Racial background of members is found to affect organizational formation even where the services and purposes, or charters, of the organizations aim at similar educational, occupational, professional, or social goals. To illustrate such racial separation in New Haven we cite the following specific organizations:

> Business and Professional Women's Club
> Negro Business and Professional Women's Club
> Ladies' Auxiliary to the Elks (white)
> Ladies' Auxiliary to the Elks (Negro)
> King's Daughters of the City Mission (white)
> King's Daughters of Loyal Workers Circle (Negro)

Some racial intermixture, 8 per cent of the sample, occurs structurally, depending upon the type of organization. This is found in auxiliaries to churches or to veterans' organizations in the lower social prestige ranks. Also some functional type of intermixture occurs with reference to services rendered by administrative officers—as is the case of the Negro youth-serving Twentieth Century Club of Hannah Gray Home—but these are from white to Negro and are not reciprocal.

Within the large racial divisions, social prestige acts as a further divisive force (Table 1 below). The white organizations predominate in Ranks II and III, the mixed in Ranks II and III, and the Negro organizations in Ranks III and V. No Negro organizations meet the criteria of Rank I.

RELIGIOUS CLEAVAGE

While racial cleavage in women's organizations is the sharpest, religious cleavage is the most pervasive. In the first place, 76 per cent of the organizations in the sample are religiously exclusive. The study reveals a basic tripartite division among the Protestants, Catholics, and Jews—the main faiths of the city. Only 24 per cent of the organizations allow religious intermixture in membership. This occurs in college alumnae associations and auxiliaries to veterans' organizations, although, in a few cases, even veterans' clubs separate according to religion. Religious cleavage is found in The Council of Church Women (Protestant), The Council of Catholic Women, The Council of Jewish Women, Ladies' Auxiliary of New Haven Veterans of Foreign Wars, and Sergeant Fishman Auxiliary of Jewish War Veterans, among others.

Division according to religion is also found to take place even when the type of association and the services rendered to the community are not of a religious nature. To illustrate, among the Protestant organizations 44, or 60 per cent, are not religious as to charter, services or activities. This is also true of 20, or 74 per cent, of Catholic organizations, and of 15, or 79 per cent, of the Jewish organizations.

Within the large religious divisions, further differentiation of clubs occurs according to race, ethnic origin, and social prestige. Which of these three divisive factors is the most significant depends upon the particular religious denomination. Specifically, within the Protestant grouping, race is the most basic, with social prestige and ethnic background playing secondary roles. Racial cleavage is strong in the Protestant organizations even when the type of club and services rendered are identical. To cite a few examples: there are two literary clubs, one white, one Negro; two Junior Leagues, one white, one Negro; two literary societies, one white, one Negro; and two garden clubs, one white, one Negro. All eight clubs are Protestant, upper socio-economic organizations within their particular racial division. Similar cleavage is found among the lower socio-economic Protestant organizations such as auxiliaries to churches, each association being connected with a separate white church or a Negro church. It is significant that all the Rank I organizations in the sample are white and seven of the eight are Protestant.

Among the Catholic organizations, on the other hand, cleavage affects the formation of clubs first along ethnic lines and secondarily according to social prestige. Racial differentiation is, of course, not important since Negroes are mainly Protestant. We thus discovered that the 27 Catholic organizations in the sample are the most widely distributed according to ethnic divisions, falling into five categories, with the

Italian clubs comprising the largest ethnic unit.

Among the Jewish organizations, social prestige proved to be the predominant element of cleavage. It plays a very influential role whether type of organization or services rendered are considered. Within this large Jewish religious division a further subdivision became apparent in relation to auxiliaries to synagogues—Reform, Conservative, and Orthodox. The Reform congregation represents the group of highest prestige both within the city and in women's organizations; the Conservative is the most powerful numerically and, perhaps, economically; and the Orthodox, with less economic power and prestige, the lowest in ranking. Specifically, Jewish religious cleavage, with attendant social prestige differentiation, occurs in Temple Mishkan Israel Women's Organization, Reform, Rank II; B'nai Jacob Sisterhood, Conservative, Rank III; B'nai Israel Synagogue Ladies' Auxiliary, Orthodox, Rank V; among others. The structure of Jewish women's organizations is representative of the Jewish community in New Haven.

ETHNIC CLEAVAGE

Ethnic origin is a contributory element of cleavage in the structure of women's organizations, being, however, neither as sharp as that of race nor as pervasive as that of religion. The study revealed, nonetheless, that more than half of the women's organizations are structured along ethnically differentiated lines. We cite a few selected examples of such cleavage: Polish Falcons, Svithiod Lodge No. 122 (Scandinavian), Freden Lodge Danish Sisterhood (Jewish), Center Garden Club, Daughters of American Revolution (Old American Stock), Saint Mother Cabrini Society (Italian).

The largest group of organizations by ethnic affiliation in New Haven is that of the "American" (native born though frequently of recent immigrant origin), second, the Old American, while the Italian and Jewish organizations tied for third place. A detailed analysis of the types of organizations which characterized the eleven different ethnic units in the sample disclosed an interesting and varied pattern. The three dominant types are found to be:

Auxiliaries to churches—characteristic of the Old American, "American," and the unspecified ethnic units.
Service—characteristic of the Jewish, Greek, Irish, Scandinavian, Polish and German ethnic units.
Social—characteristic of the Italian and mixed ethnic units.

The study revealed further that, within the ethnically differentiated units, social prestige acts as a separating element and promotes still other subdivisional patterns. The Old American, "American," and Jewish

ethnic units are distributed in the broadest range as to social prestige levels. Furthermore, in the large ethnic units, i.e., those including many organizations, social prestige is especially apparent. In short, ethnic factors play a contributory but significant role in determining sub-patterns within the large religious divisions; social prestige, in turn, creates further differentiated grouping within the ethnic units.

SOCIAL PRESTIGE CLEAVAGE

Social prestige is found to be a permeating or dominating element of cleavage within the three other basic divisional patterns in the structure of women's organizations. When this study began there was an attempt to relate women's organizations to the concept of social class, as this term is generally understood in the sociological field. A careful analysis of the questionnaires revealed, however, that such a treatment was not feasible because many large clubs and numerous auxiliaries to churches were cross-class in membership. We discovered further that women's organizations represent a gradation or continuum from one class to another and that sharp delimitations are difficult to make. After a careful analysis of the organizations by means of the combined criteria of (1) residential area, (2) occupation of husband or, if single, of women members, (3) education, and (4) the social prestige or reputation of the organization,[1] a hierarchical classification of wom-

---

[1] The fourth criterion, not unrelated to the other three, was derived from a *particular combination or cluster of club characteristics* such as: type of organization; religion, race, and ethnic origin of the members; date of founding; how membership is secured; place of meeting; type, space, and frequency of newspaper publicity. These characteristics are a function of or vary with social prestige rank. There is a gradation as to the significance of these evaluative factors, some bearing directly upon social prestige, others being merely contributory.

Indications of social prestige (utilizing the universe of organizations) were also found in: (1) Literature sent by the organizations to the investigator. The lower socio-economic organizations did not send literature relating to their constitutions, projects, and functions, presumably because they did not have such printed material. The socio-economic clubs, however, sent printed booklets, mimeographed forms, or pamphlets, depending upon their organizational wealth, size, and affiliation. (2) The names of organizations are a further cue to social prestige rank. For illustration, "Ladies Aid Society," "Tent," "Corps Number . . . . ," "Sunshine Club," and "Sew and Sew Mothers' Club" are names characteristic of Rank V organizations. Such names as "Nest, Number . . . . ," "Degree of . . . . ," and "Auxiliary of Post Number . . . . " are characteristic of Rank IV or III organizations. "Federation of . . . . ," "Branch of . . . . ," and "Section of . . . . " are often used by Rank II organizations. Simple names are found in Rank I, such as "Saturday Morning Club," and "The Thursday Club." (3) Titles of address are a further index of social prestige ranking. The presidents of upper socio-economic organizations give their husbands' first names, as Mrs. John Smith; whereas members of the lower socio-economic clubs use their own first names, as

en's organizations by prestige ranks, numbered I through V, was worked out. To be sure, these ranks tend to overlap with the general sociological concept of social class. It is felt, however, that such a social prestige stratification makes possible a broader, more applicable, and less confusing evaluation of women's organizations and is sociologically meaningful. A brief characterization of each rank follows.

THE PRESTIGE HIERARCHY OF WOMEN'S ORGANIZATIONS

RANK I

The majority of the members in these organizations live in the suburbs or in the highest residential rent-areas in the city.[2] The husbands are industrialists, business executives, professionals, and members of the Yale faculty. About three-quarters of the women are college graduates. The social rank of these organizations is the highest in the city. There are eight such organizations, or 4.5 per cent of the sample. These are roughly comparable to the upper social class.

Racially, of course, there are only white members in these clubs. Ethnically, they are predominantly of Old American stock; religiously, Protestant. An illustration is "Our Society," the oldest women's club in New Haven. There have been four generations of Eli Whitneys and Daggetts, influential and "old families" of New Haven, in Our Society. Membership is limited to 130, and one becomes a member, with only a very

few exceptions, by being the daughter of a member. The club shuns publicity but the members are proud of the "uniqueness" of the club's place in the community. Our Society has been referred to in newspapers as "the sacrosanct" and "the very top drawer" women's organization. Examples of other clubs in this rank are: the North End Club, the Junior League of New Haven, the Badminton Club, and the Garden Club of New Haven.

RANK II

The majority of the members in these organizations live in the first and second highest residential rent-areas of the city. The husbands are professionals, large business proprietors, and white-collar workers. About three-quarters of the members are college graduates. The organizations rank second highest in the city social rank. There are 41 such organizations, or 23.2 per cent of the sample. These are roughly comparable to the upper-middle social class.

A few specific examples of Rank II clubs are: the Auxiliary to the Hospital of St. Raphael, the Soroptimist, the Daughters of Patriots, the Daughters of the American Revolution, the Catholic Charity League, the American Association of University Women, and auxiliaries to the Church of the Redeemer, the United Church on the Green, and Temple Mishkan Israel. There is only one Negro club in this rank, a college alumnae type.

RANK III

The members of these organizations are widely scattered in the city, covering residential areas that range from the first to the fourth class. The majority of the members, however, excepting Negroes, live in the second and third best residential areas. Occupationally, the husbands of the members are predominantly white-collar workers, with a few professionals, and some small business proprietors and skilled workers. About three-fifths of the women are high school graduates and two-fifths are college graduates. In social

---

Mrs. Bertha Smith. An exception is provided by presidents of professional and business clubs who include their first names and often continue the use of "Miss" after marriage.

[2] An interesting ecological pattern emerges from the analysis of the questionnaire returns as to membership residence, indicating that the upper socio-economic organizations draws members primarily from the suburbs; the middle-class clubs have members from the suburbs and the better residential areas within the city; and the lower socio-economic clubs draw solely from within the city limits, especially areas adjoining factories, stores, and railroads.

TABLE I

Characteristics of women's organizations by social prestige rank

| Prestige rank | Organizations | | Race | | | | Religion | | | | | |
	Number	Per cent	White	Negro	Mixed	Unspecified	Protestant	Catholic	Jewish	Greek Orthodox	Mixed	Unspecified
Rank I	8	4.5	8	—	—	—	7	—	—	—	1	—
Rank II	41	23.2	38	1	2	—	16	2	2	—	15	6
Rank III	77	43.5	61	6	7	3	29	8	13	1	19	7
Rank IV	29	16.3	23	1	5	—	13	11	2	—	3	—
Rank V	22	12.5	15	7	—	—	9	6	2	—	5	—
Total	177	—	145	15	14	3	74	27	19	1	43	13
Per cent	—	100.0	81.9	8.4	7.9	1.8	41.8	15.3	10.8	0.6	24.1	7.4

rank these organizations are third highest. There are 77 organizations in this rank, or 43.5 per cent of the sample. These are roughly comparable to a large cross-section of the middle social class.

Rank III includes such organizations as the New Haven Women's Club, the Council of Catholic Women, the League of Women Voters, the Swedish Junior League, and Auxiliaries to the American Legion and to the Congregational and Methodist Churches.

RANK IV

On the whole, the members of these organizations live in scattered residential areas, ranging from the second to the fifth highest in the city. This wide spread is again due to the Negro organizations whose members live predominantly in class five areas. The majority of the members who are white live predominantly in third and fourth class residential areas. Occupationally, the husbands of the members are factory workers, with some white-collar employees, a few skilled workers, and some tradesmen. The educational level of the women in this rank is predominantly that of high school graduates; more specifically, about two-thirds graduated from high school, three per cent from college, and the rest from elementary school. These organizations rank fourth in social esteem. There are 29 such organizations, or 16.4 per cent of the sample. These are roughly comparable to the lower-middle social class.

Illustrations of this rank are organizations such as: The Polish Falcons, Society Regional Marchegiana, and auxiliaries to Disabled War Veterans, to St. Luke's Church, to Howard Avenue Methodist Church (Negro), and to fraternal orders.

RANK V

The majority of the members in these organizations live in the lowest socio-economic residential areas, ranging from the fourth through the sixth or lowest class in the city. The occupations of the husbands are predominantly those of mill and factory workers and manual laborers. There are also some tradesmen and domestic employees. Like Rank IV, the members of these organizations also are in educational attainment about two-thirds high school graduates, one-third elementary, and none college trained. Two organizations, however, claimed three members who attended college but did not graduate. Social esteem of these organizations is the fifth, or lowest, in the city. There are 22 such organizations, or 12.5 per cent of the sample. These are roughly comparable to the lower social class. The investigator believes that the lower-lower social class is not represented in women's organizations.[3]

Illustrative of this rank are the following organizations: the Mothers' Club of the YWCA, the Salvation Army Home League, the J. R. and Joliffee Union, and the Ladies' Aid of the African Zion Church. The largest percentage of Negro clubs is found in this rank.

CONCLUSION

The present study has revealed the relationship between the structure of women's secondary associations, according to racial, religious, ethnic, and social prestige factors, and the social structure of the city. The cleavage existing in the social structure of a city—as seen ecologically, occupationally, racially, religiously, and ethnically—is reflected in or may be regarded as a cause of the differentiation of women's organizations. Race appears to be the sharpest form

[3] Contrary to assertions made in other studies of participation in formal organizations by social class . . . , this investigation revealed that women in the lower-middle and upper-lower social classes do join organizations. These are usually small, neighborhood, social clubs or small auxiliaries to churches. The researcher feels that some of the small Italian, other foreign-born, and Negro clubs were not discovered because they are not publicized, thus excluding some organizations in the lower economic strata. . . . However, in line with these other studies, the present research indicates that the largest number of women's organizations are to be found in what would be comparable to the upper-middle social class.

TABLE I

Characteristics of women's organization by social prestige rank (Continued)

| | Ethnic | | | | | | | | | | |
Prestige rank	Irish	Greek	Italian	Polish	Scandinavian	German	Old American	Jewish	American	Mixed	Unspecified
Rank I	—	—	—	—	—	—	8	—	—	—	—
Rank II	1	—	—	—	—	—	11	2	15	7	5
Rank III	—	1	7	1	3	—	9	13	30	7	6
Rank IV	1	—	6	1	—	1	1	2	13	2	2
Rank V	—	—	6	—	—	—	—	2	9	1	4
Total	2	1	19	2	3	1	29	19	67	17	17
Per cent	1.1	0.6	10.8	1.1	1.6	0.6	16.4	10.8	37.8	9.6	9.6

of cleavage; religion the most pervasive; ethnic differences contributory; and social prestige a dominant or permeable element.

Women's organizations are not formed according to a simple pattern of functional differentiation and diversity of membership interests but are born and exist in a complex pattern of interlocking strands of cleavage. To illustrate with a single summary example this complexity of organizational cleavage, with overlapping factors of race, religion, ethnic origin, and social prestige, we may cite the existence of no less than seven Junior Leagues in New Haven—Junior League of New Haven (Protestant), Catholic Junior League, Junior Community League (Negro), B'nai Brith Junior League (Jewish), Swedish Junior League, Italian Junior League, and Polish Junior League.

In general, our findings indicate that, within the basic pattern of racial cleavage, religion may become a divisive element; that, within the religiously separated organizational groupings, ethnic differences become significant; and that, within racial, religious, or ethnic divisions, social prestige may create still further subdivisions. Thus, the diversity of population groups in the complex social structure of a city is reproduced in the intricate patterns of cleavage in women's organizations.

An organization generally affects society when it fulfills its stated goals; in addition, it generally performs certain latent functions for the social system, often fulfilling ends far removed from its official goals. Since sociologists are always interested in discovering how social arrangements have functions neither intended nor noticed by the participants, there is considerable interest in the various latent functions performed by formal organizations.

In the first selection, Arnold M. Rose describes certain ways that voluntary associations create social conditions and individual attitudes appropriate to American democratic government and American society. According to Rose, social power is thereby distributed among many autonomous groups and leaders; a monopoly of power is impossible; individual citizens gain experience in organizational technique and parliamentary procedure; support for existing institutions is encouraged; and mechanisms are created for locating problems, recording opinions, and inducing social reforms. At the same time that they are pursuing their official goals, voluntary associations also perform important latent functions for American society.

SOME FUNCTIONS OF VOLUNTARY ASSOCIATIONS*

Arnold M. Rose

Voluntary associations—at least those that are organized to accomplish some goal outside the direct satisfaction of expressive needs of the members—play a major role in American democracy. More specifically, the hypothesis is that the voluntary associations have three important functions in supporting political democracy in the United States:

1. Through the voluntary association the ordinary citizen can acquire as much power in the community or the nation as his free time, ability, and inclinations permit him to, without actually going into the government service, provided he accepts the competition for power of other like-minded citizens. A consideration of the varied activities of the "social improvement" and "social influence" types of associations would support this. Political power, or influence, in the United States is not concentrated in the government but is distributed over as many citizens, working through their associations, as want to take the responsibility for power. As Goldhamer says: "It is precisely this function of expressing and enforcing the wishes of its members that has characterized the activities of many American organizations. In this

way these organizations appear to revive once more, in varying degrees, the participation of citizens in the governmental process."[1]

2. Those who thus participate become aware of how processes function in their society; they learn how things are done in at least the limited sphere in which they operate. The voluntary association informs its members on matters occurring in the society at large that affect the association's purpose. This does not make the members satisfied in the sense that they always like what they learn, but it makes them satisfied in the sense that they understand some of the complex social mechanisms that control them. As society grows more and more complex, the average citizen is usually less and less able to understand the devious controls within it, and this creates dissatisfaction. The voluntary association provides him an avenue for understanding some of the controls and thus a degree of social satisfaction. By working in voluntary associations, he also learns exactly what is wrong with the power structure of the society, and this gives him something definite to work toward, rather than leaving him with a vague and delusive feeling that

* From Arnold M. Rose, *Theory and Method in the Social Sciences*, pp. 50-51 and 68-71. Copyright © 1954, The University of Minnesota. Reprinted with the permission of the author and the publisher, The University of Minnesota Press.

1 Herbert Goldhamer, *Some Factors Affecting Participation in Voluntary Associations* (Chicago: unpublished dissertation for the Ph.D. at the University of Chicago, 1942).

because "something" is wrong, only a complete revolution can change it.

In like measure, the opportunity to engage in something creative, even if only in a hobby association, provides a compensation for the deadening effect of working on a simple, repetitive task on the modern production line. The association which does most about this is the trade-union, which seems to the worker to provide him with a significant measure of control over his working conditions, to give him the leisure time outside the factory to engage in many creative activities formerly not available to him because of lack of time, and even to provide him directly with some recreations, "social reform" activities, and other "creative" opportunities. Many intellectuals overlook the fact that there are many compensations for, controls over, and satisfactory adjustments to, the monotony of work on the factory production line. Not the least of these is participation in voluntary associations. The present difficulty—which has certainly not been solved in the United States—is that many people do not take advantage of their oportunities, because they do not see that their need for understanding the "mysterious" social mechanisms and their need for creative activity can be satisfied by participation in the associations. While they are constantly propagandized to join, the propaganda is far from being always successful.

3. The voluntary associations offer a powerful mechanism of social change; they are an important factor in making the United States what European observers call "dynamic." As soon as a felt need for some social change arises, one or more voluntary associations immediately spring up to try to secure the change. Not only do they operate directly on the problem, but their attention to it also makes the government concerned about the problem, as a democratic government has to pay attention to the interests of alert voters. It may take decades to effect the change completely, but movement toward that change is likely to occur in gradual steps all along the way. Sometimes the change is never completely achieved because the needs behind it disappear or are converted into other needs, but it would be hard to find a need for a specific social change that existed as long ago as a hundred years in the United States and that still exists today substantially unsatisfied. The associations and the other mechanisms of change are thus usually successful in the long run.

A final word about this often ignored aspect of American social life: The voluntary association is characteristically a voluntary activity, and to make it anything but voluntary would destroy its basic functions as listed above. It is true that informal community pressures occasionally push people into associations that they have no desire to join. Such people, with the exception of the few who change their minds once they are in the association, are seldom satisfied with, or effective workers in, the association. They do not share the power, understand it, or effect social change. They are the "paper" members, from whom dues cannot be collected, and they almost invariably drop out of the association.

This leads us to a broader observation: There is no value in participation *per se;* it is only when the individual spontaneously feels the need for participation that it does him or the society as a whole any good. This implies, further, that the effective voluntary association is one in which not only membership is voluntary but the type of activity is also voluntary, in that the members choose their goals and the means for obtaining the goals. Few things would do more harm to associations than to give them a coordinated goal and an identical means of action. In other words, pluralism is a necessary component of voluntarism in democracy.

Even worse than to force participation would be to encourage the individual to participate in a group activity which could not possibly have any effect, because the sources of power in the society were beyond the influence of that association's activity. If, say, all political power were lodged in a government, and the individual citizens were encouraged to be active in associations that were not allowed to influence that government, the individual's frustrations and lack of understanding of the power processes would be compounded. Fortunately for the United States, participation in associations is voluntary and the associations are able to compete for their share of real power in the society.

*Voluntary associations often help Americans to become adjusted to new residential neighborhoods; in so doing, they contribute to the integration of the community—an important social function in a country with much geographical mobility.**

Voluntary associations help assimilate the foreign immigrant as well as the native-born person who has moved his residence. Such mechanisms of assimilation and social unity are indispensable to countries of high immigration such as America. Mary B. Treudley, in the next selection, describes how social clubs in the Greek community of Boston facilitate individual members' adjustments to American life. These clubs provide a good example of the latent function performed by a social mechanism for the larger social system: the clubs' manifest aims are to preserve Greek culture and to furnish recreation among fellow immigrants; their latent function for the American social system is to facilitate the assimilation of new members.†

THE TRANSFORMATION OF PEASANTS INTO CITIZENS‡
Mary B. Treudley

Formal organization is an important instrument in the transformation of peasants into citizens of a modern state.

While autonomy is permitted in clique formations, it is the formal voluntary associations that are important in the remolding of personality. Only groups as devoted to peasant visiting patterns as the Italians can long preserve rural types of interactions in the urban environment in which their New-World lives are spent. One of the major steps which the ethnic individual takes in developing an American personality is the transference of a large part of his leisure time from the clique to the club. More specifically in this case, a Greek starts to become an American when he stops frequenting a coffee shop and is initiated into a lodge. In the Greek American organizations which occupy his time, he becomes accustomed to the election of officers, the collection of dues, the writing of minutes, the making of motions and their debate in formal fashion. Gradually both he and the group to which he belongs learn to use formal organizations as an instrument for achieving common ends . . .

Greek Americans have proved to be as great "joiners" as any of the older American stocks. They have set up a bewildering array of associations. These fall into eight categories. The first are the organizations essential to the maintenance of the church. An illustration is the Greek afternoon school, where children are taught the language and traditions of Greece, so that they may feel at home in the nationalistic church. The League of Orthodox Youth has been newly formed to encourage loyalty to the church among young people. The second are mutual-aid societies. As a matter of fact, though several of the men's organizations possess mutual aid features, none is limited to that purpose today. This type of primitive insurance is dying out, as even first-generation men learn to lay aside their peasant fear of impersonal relations and to replace mutual assistance among friends with commercial contracts written by strangers. The third are charitable societies, such as the Philoptokos, whose membership is drawn largely from the older women of the church. Charity is not confined to such societies, but is exercised in one form or another by almost every Greek organization. The fourth are regional societies—Pan-Arcadian, Pan-Cretan, Pan-Laconian—whose chief purpose seems now to be the enrichment of their particular section of Greece through philanthropic gifts. The fifth are prestige organizations, like the Ahepa (American Hellenic Educational Progressive Association), the G.A.P.A. (Greek-American Progressive Association), and the Helicon, which stress Americanism and success, as measured by education, income, and the active promotion of the general welfare. The sixth are auxiliaries for adolescents, like the Maids of Athens, the Daughters of Penelope and the Sons of Pericles, sponsored by Ahepa. The seventh, like the Pythagoras Musical Society, have no other purpose then to preserve Greek culture and to stimulate its development in America. The eighth are branches of American or-

* For an able research report documenting this point, see Eugene Litwak, "Voluntary Associations and Neighborhood Cohesion," *American Sociological Review*, Volume 26, Number 2 (April 1961), pp. 258-271.
† Two sociologists have noted that Israeli formal organizations also have performed the same latent assimilative functions: Elihu Katz and S. N. Eisenstadt, "Some Sociological Observations on the Response of Israeli Organizations to New Immigrants," *Administrative Science Quarterly*, Volume 5, Number 1 (June 1960), pp. 113-133.
‡ From Mary B. Treudley, "Voluntary Associations and the Americanization Process," *American Sociological Review*, Volume 14, Number 1 (February 1949), pp. 44-53. Reprinted with the permission of the author and the publisher, the American Sociological Association.

ganizations, such as various veterans' associations, ethnic political clubs, and the like.

FUNCTIONS OF AUTONOMOUS ORGANIZATIONS

The classification just given is derived from the stated purposes of the various organizations. The functions that they serve for their members are not formulated in their constitutions or by-laws, but have to be inferred from casual comments or from observed behavior. People may use the same organization to satisfy widely differing needs and desires. The analysis that follows disregards the individual and presents only services performed for large sections of the ethnic group. It deals chiefly with the social rather than the psychological needs of people . . .

I. CUSHIONING THE SHOCK OF TRANSITION

In the first place, these organizations cushion the shock of the transition from a simple village society to a complex urban one by creating a semblance of the earlier social setting. They provide a time and place for seeing familiar faces and hearing the language of one's childhood. While they are formally organized, the informal aspects are much more important to the older generation than are the avowed purposes. Many individuals, for example, maintain membership in the Cathedral, even though they also belong to some other Greek Orthodox or American Protestant church, so that they can keep in touch with their friends and up to date on the current gossip.

Another of the cushioning effects is that of supporting essential aspects of the Greek personality as long as they are retained. A peasant, thrown alone into America society, would have the feeling of being *spurlos versenkt* if he could not continue to talk and act, laugh and make merry, or mourn his dead in company with others in ways to which he was accustomed. The more complex personalities developed by upper-class European culture often feel more lost in the American environment, where no one seems to speak their language. Personality disorganization . . . is prevented for most individuals by the sense of still being in familiar surroundings and remaining themselves unchanged.

Still another of the cushioning effects comes from the fact that the organization itself is undergoing Americanization. Since it is autonomous, the leaders, who are usually moving more rapidly than the rest, can adjust the tempo of change to suit the majority. Even those most resistant to American influence often assume American personality characteristics in imitation of their more assimilated compatriots, but so gradually and unconsciously as to be unaware of their own development.

2. MAINTAINING INTERACTION AMONG GREEK AMERICANS

A second major function of these organizations is to hold together individuals who no longer share enough common experience and understanding to be bound by informal ties. Successful members, immersed in American activities and relationships, would find it difficult to maintain informal ties within the ethnic community. Only in a formal setting are they brought into association with the less successful of the group. Without the societies, leadership would be drawn away from the community more quickly than it is.

Dispersion through the class structure is paralleled by dispersion in physical space. The Greek Americans are ecologically widely scattered throughout metropolitan Boston. They have no colony, such as the Italians have maintained in the North End and which is useful to them in at least two ways. Such segregation permits a locality grouping, which maintains primary relationships among its residents. The North End is also a center to which dispersed Italians may return, to visit their friends in residence or to meet those from other sections of the city. The Greeks have no such geographic base for their informal relationships, once they have graduated from the coffee shops. It is chiefly the Cathedral that provides them with the physical space essential to all face-to-face interactions, while the associations supply the occasions for their meeting with their friends.

3. MAKING ETHNIC SOCIAL STRUCTURE OVERT

A third major function of these organizations is to make apparent the social structure of the community. People need the sense of belonging to a society and of knowing their own relative position in that society . . . Mere residence in a given community does not entitle a man to membership in the local group. His conduct also must meet certain minimum standards. There was no indication of such blacklisting of outcastes by the Boston Greeks. What they did instead was to evaluate the relative weight to be attached to position in Greece and success in the United States, and thus to develop a measure by which status is accorded here.

Besides satisfying the need for an ordering of relationships, these formal organizations make more explicit the climbing systems within the Greek community. They also serve to reward the successful climbers. Helicon, for example, is open only to those who hold college degrees. The importance attached to membership is evidenced by the resentment felt, both within and outside the club, against the occasional person who slips in without a sheepskin. Membership either in Ahepa or G.A.P.A. is a testimonial to one's solid worth and achievement. Even for the less successful, there are satisfactions to be derived from the public recognition of those who have surpassed them. They can identify themselves with these "race heroes," sharing vicariously in their distinction. They can also use the prestige group as role models, picking up useful hints on how to get ahead. Since rising in the ethnic structure and becoming more American are almost synonymous, the minority group offers incentives to its members to take on the personality patterns of which the majority approves.

4. SOLVING PROBLEMS ARISING FROM AMERICANIZATION

A fourth major function of these formal organizations is the solving of the specific problems of a group in transition from a European peasant society to an American urban one. Associations are formed to relieve the group of certain types of anxiety or distress. One problem is the support of the needy. An ethnic group, until its complete Americanization, continues to feel a special responsibility for dependent compatriots. To compensate for traditional community provisions for their care, charitable societies have been formed, to which are transferred the obligations once carried by the Greek village. Another problem grows out of the fact that American culture minimizes the duty of children to support their parents. The first generation learn quickly that they must make some other provision for their old age, and do so through setting up mutual benefit associations. Collective action, in both cases, eases the burden for the individual.

Still another problem becomes acute as the second generation moves through adolescence. Childhood arouses no particular anxiety in the Greek American community. Children are allowed to mingle freely with those of every nationality background in public schools and on public playgrounds. But when they reach the dating age, the parents become disturbed lest they marry non-Greeks. They realize, for the most part, that traditional match-making is inappropriate to the American scene, but they do not approve of American courtship patterns. They resort, instead, to the formal organization of young people of the same age and opposite sex, to provide a setting in which their sons will come to know the daughters of their friends and "fall in love," as is the odd American custom. The younger generation tend to accept this transitional pattern with little opposition, for they too prefer a marital partner of their own nationality. For the non-conformists, at least among the boys, there are real alternatives and some possibility of marriage outside the ethnic circle.

5. PRACTICING AMERICAN BEHAVIOR IN AN ETHNIC SETTING

A fifth major function of these autonomous organizations is that they permit the practice of American behavior at various levels of sophistication. Americanization is both hastened and made easy by allowing the ethnic individual to practice behaving in terms of his new personality among his own kind, where he is not overwhelmed by a sense of inferiority, before he is called upon to play similar roles in the presence of alien and possibly unfriendly observers. Unaware of how carefully American culture has patterned the transformation from European into American personality, the individual undergoing the process feels that he is achieving new social skills by his own volition. His growth seems voluntary, and in a very real sense it is, for there are alternatives among which he has the right to choose. That his range of choice is not as great as he believes it to be is a delusion which he shares with most of mankind.

Most interesting to observe, in many ways, are the charitable societies of older women of the first generation. No group could be more awkward and self-conscious at first in their handling of unfamiliar forms of interaction. But since they are all in the same situation, the tension occasioned by acting in strange ways is pleasantly exciting rather than emotionally upsetting. With surprising speed some among them acquire enough skill to provide adequate leadership for the rest.

Formal organizations also permit outstanding members of the ethnic group to practice still more difficult leadership techniques. They learn to handle typical American problems, involving complex cooperative effort, such as securing members and keeping them active, raising and disbursing money, and arriving at joint decisions acceptable to all factions. Some individuals were found who had graduated from Greek-American societies, moved on to full-time participation in non-ethnic associations, and, after prolonged training in organizational behavior patterns, had returned to take top positions in organizations in which they had once been subordinates. As a result of their outgroup experiences, they have incorporated more firmly in their own personalities American upper-class characteristics. At the same time, their greater sophistication leads to the wider diffusion of more complex interactional patterns among the whole ethnic community.

6. MAKING GROUP CHOICES BETWEEN CULTURE PATTERNS

The problems associated with double loyalty have not presented to the Greek Americans the tragic dilemma which faced German Americans during the first

World War and Japanese Americans in the second world conflict. While conflict in allegiance is not an issue, every ethnic individual is forced to consider over and over again his relation to Greek and to American culture. "Shall we dance Greek or American?", is one way in which adolescents phrase the basic question of culture conflict. In the home it becomes the decision between a Greek broadcast and the reporting of a big-league game. Innumerable choices of this type determine the rate of speed with which individuals doff their old habits and become "new men."

While the important decisions of an ethnic group are made informally, the various associations translate into words the consensus of the moment. They record the fact that attitudes toward Greece are ceasing to be traditional and inarticulate. Their formal discussions of the plight of their native land help their members to think and feel as Americans about its problems. They act in American terms, petitioning the President and Congress to adopt the policy of their preference. The decision to build a hospital in Arcadia or a school in Crete, a typical American action, grows out of informal talk but requires ratification by a responsible group before contracts can be let and materials and workmen assembled. A church leadership as sensitive to public opinion as is the Greek Orthodox marks fairly quickly each new stage reached on the journey from Greece to the United States.

USE OF NON-ETHNIC ASSOCIATIONS

The ethnic individual, once he has attained a certain degree of Americanism, is not limited to his own nationality societies. Both inter-ethnic and non-ethnic organizations are open to him. The International Institute is a good illustration of the first type. He is not required on entry to lay aside his ethnic personality, but he does have to make some adjustments to outgroups. Patterns that are less Greek are provided for his use, on the assumption that he will in time become a full-fledged participant in American society. Settlement houses make similar allowance for groups who want to retain for the time being as much as possible of their ancestral culture.

For the person who is ready to act on American terms only, there are still other voluntary associations. Women have a narrower choice than men, but they may join the Parent-Teachers Association or the League of Women Voters. Men are often forced to join the proper business or professional organizations, while fraternal societies compete for their membership. In time, some individuals are ready to separate themselves completely from the Greek community. They sever their connections with the Greek Orthodox Church and become either Protestants or Catholics. They retain a sentimental affection for their native land. Their children may study Greek in college. But they are too busy with their new American activities to find time for their old Greek friends. The church is particularly concerned with the question as to whether such complete alienation from the community is inevitable with increasing assimilation. Its future depends on whether the essential characteristics of Greek Orthodoxy can be maintained by a priesthood and a membership who have become fully American.

Every society has a system of stratification according to social class, income level, ethnicity, and other criteria of evaluation. Chapter 3 cited examples of how the class and ethnic composition of a community brings about a differentiation among its voluntary associations. One latent function of associations is to reinforce and elaborate the various social differentials existing in the community by creating new symbols of ranking.

The selection by William H. Form describes an example of voluntary associations contributing to the establishment of a new class structure. A new community was created without antecedent social class inequalities and with the official aim of avoiding their development. Several voluntary associations arose to perform necessary social tasks, such as recreation and welfare. The associations unintentionally became the mechanisms for differentiating among higher and lower members of the community: the as-

sociations made some persons leaders while others were followers; some associations became exclusive clubs for a new elite while membership in others became a sign of lower prestige.

VOLUNTARY ASSOCIATIONS IN A PLANNED COMMUNITY*

William H. Form

Greenbelt, Maryland, is a planned suburb [of Washington], built in 1937 by the federal government on the model of a "garden city" . . . [The physical and social architects of Greenbelt envisioned a minimum amount of stratification.] Through the Farm Security Agency they tried to create conditions which would operate against the formation of "classes" and class antagonisms.[1] The main techniques they employed to insure this were: (a) the application of certain "rules" to guide the selection of Greenbelt residents, so that they would be socially and economically similar; (b) the establishment of a local economic and social life that would be popularly controlled and operated along cooperative principles; (c) the chartering of a city-manager form of self-government which (was supposed) to encourage active and responsible citizenship; and (d) the provision of a self-sufficient organizational program to satisfy most of the needs and interests of the townspeople.

Other conditions operated against stratification. Since the town was inhabited almost overnight by people who were for the most part strangers to one another, the task of building its total social organization had to proceed afresh. No old families, no settled groups could erect social barriers against newcomers.

Status stratification could not be readily based on economic grounds for at least three reasons: (a) only families of similar economic resources, roughly "lower middle class," were chosen as resident;[2] (b) all economic services in the town were organized along strict cooperative lines;[3] the cooperative prin-

ciples proposed by the Government for the stores were encouraged to spread into non-economic organizations;[4] and (c) status or economic segregation could not occur on the basis of ecology because of the planned nature of the town.[5]

Other factors tended to reduce stratification. Most important of these was the rather homogeneous occupational composition of the heads of families. Three quarters of them were white collar workers employed largely by the federal government. The remaining were manual workers employed by the federal government and private enterprise.[6] All of the resident population was white and only 2.5 per cent was foreign born. Thus the town of 880 families in 1942 was rather homogeneous in income, occupation, education, age, nativity, quality of housing, and economic structure.

Determining the existence and shape of the status structure necessitated a rather involved method, the explanation of which cannot be given in detail here for lack of space. In general the method was largely concerned with the discovery of the existence, varieties, and direction of deference behavior. The author had an excellent opportunity to witness deference behavior, for he lived in Greenbelt as a participant observer for two and one-half years. Other methods were employed that in general corroborated the re-

* From William H. Form, "Stratification in a Planned Community," *American Sociological Review*, Volume 10, Number 5 (October 1945), pp. 605-613. Reprinted with the permission of the author and the publisher, the American Sociological Association.

[1] A non-stratification ideology permeated the early government literature about Greenbelt. See *Greenbelt Towns*, pamphlet of the Resettlement Administration, Washington, D.C., 1936.

[2] The mean annual family income for families at the date of entry into Greenbelt was $1535; S.D., $240. The Administration at first ruled that anyone or any family making over $2200 per year had to move from Greenbelt. In 1939 almost ninety per cent of the family incomes were between $1200 and $2000. Since rentals were staggered according to size of family, the differences in effective income were very small. Sixty-eight per cent of the families at entry had savings under fifty dollars, apart from insurance, while almost one-half had debts under fifty dollars. Property ownership was negligible.

[3] There are no production industries in Greenbelt. All of the gainfully employed, except employees of the local

stores and local government, work outside of Greenbelt. Apart from the seven stores, the Credit Union, Health Association, and the nursery school are also cooperatively run.

[4] A campaign for engendering the "cooperative spirit" and widespread participation was actively promoted from the beginning. Even a Community Church was sponsored to de-emphasize denominational differences.

[5] All dwelling units from bachelor apartments to seven-room houses meet approximately the same housing standards. Determination of residence is not a matter of choice, for houses are assigned by a federal officer on the basis of size of family and the presence of unoccupied units. In 1942 one thousand "defense" homes were built around Greenbelt which did not come up to the housing and architectural standards of the original settlement. The newer areas housed a more heterogeneous group of servicemen and "defense-manual" workers.

[6] Eighty per cent of all workers were employed by the federal government. Occupationally, 23.4% of all the workers were either manual or domestic workers; 8.1%, professional and semi-professional; 4.1%, petty managers and officials; 0.9%, entrepreneurs; 63.5%, clerical and kindred workers. Almost three-quarters of the total were salaried employees. Except for a few professionals, the incomes of the occupations did not vary widely.

sults observed from participant observation.[7] First we attempted to outline the status structure and then we sought to induct the principles along which it was based.

When the town was opened for occupancy, a rash of social and organizational activity was evident. Participation in the numerous mushroom organizations that were arising was the main attention-getting device. Rivalry for leadership in these organizations was rather intense, and the circulation of their officers high. At first, almost every adult belonged to a committee or was an officer. In four years, the process of social selection operated slowly until the town had developed a definite status structure. Some individuals dropped out of the status struggle entirely, some were concerned only with their status in a particular group, while others competed for status on a town-wide level. Often a person's rank in a group did not coincide with his status in the town as a whole. This study is limited to "generalized status." A brief social-psychological description of the eight main status groups that evolved in Greenbelt follows.

SOCIAL CLASSES IN GREENBELT

(1) At the top of the status scale are the officials selected by the federal government to oversee the town. They include the Community Manager, his assistant, the Family Selection Agent, and several other officials. These people receive deference in all public and semi-public meetings. That they maintain distance is evidenced by the fact that they address others by their first names, although they are addressed by their surnames. Even though the officials live in the town, they retain a bureaucratic perspective by referring to the town as "the project."

The prestige of this group rests upon a number of factors. Due to a curious government arrangement, its members are local as well as federal officials. For example, the community manager, who is appointed by the federal agency, is also selected as town manager by the locally elected town council. As town manager, he appoints other local officials, who may be on the federal payroll.

The officials are at the top of the political-power pyramid. They frequently provide the initiative in local action. Their endorsement of pet local projects is usually necessary before these may be materialized. This does not mean, however, that local officials have

no power at all. Local power seems to be shared with and subservient to federal authority.

The officials keep in the public view constantly. Their names are published frequently and conspicuously in the local weekly, *The Greenbelt Cooperator*. Many of the organizations continually seek their sponsorship and approval. Despite this pressure, the officials and their families do not participate actively in many organizations or even in their neighborhoods. However, when they do participate, their influence is weighty.

The officials constitute not only a political elite, but also an economic and educational elite. Their income and education is considerably higher than that of the townspeople. Needless to say, the homes of the officials are more luxuriously furnished, and residents consider it an honor to enter them. The officials constitute a tightly-woven ingroup. They know one another rather intimately. This is not the case for the next lower group, to which the doctors, college professors, school principals, dentist, mayor, pastor, priest, and some school teachers belong. Since such people are highly esteemed in most communities, it is not surprising that they are accorded respect in Greenbelt.

(2) The members of status group II are aware of their high status. They acknowledge deference with nonchalance but also with expectation. On the whole, they do not identify themselves psychologically or politically with the town's official family. They maintain a self-satisfied social and organizational independence. However, when they do evince the slightest interest in any organization, they are immediately selected as important committee heads or as officers.[8] For such participation they receive extra deference. Their advice is not ignored irrespective of their competency to give it. This accounts for part of the instability of some of the town's organizations. This group is also an economic elite.

(3) About thirty of the town's "leaders" comprise status group three. They are members of the town-council, the head managers of the co-operatives, the editor of the local weekly, the board of directors of the co-operatives, and the presidents of the larger organizations such as the American Legion and the Athletic Association. This group is not as occupationally homogeneous as the others. Its members are, rather, specialists in participation; those who "have the interests in the community at heart," those who receive psychological gains from being consulted, those who think that they control the "destiny" of the town. They claim honor by virtue of the "service" they render, even though much of their efforts are directed toward

---

7 [The author bases his ranking of people on responses during interviews with Greenbelt residents. Persons were asked to rank occupations according to prestige, they were asked "what kind of people do you look up to," and they responded to other questions. In the following paragraphs Form describes the people who were ranked at different levels in his opinion survey.–Eds.]

8 There is no recorded instance of a member of this group being defeated in any organization when a candidate for a first term of office.

entrenching themselves against slates of would-be officers.

The "leaders" constitute a self-conscious group, that constantly tends to be atomized into cliques that show intense mutual antagonisms. To remain a "leader" one must maintain a democratic façade and, above all, continue participation on the neighborhood as well as on the organizational levels.

The "leaders" have some official contacts with the two upper status groups.[9] These relations with the "powerful" and the professionals are not only considered pleasant, but helpful in the quest for prestige. The "leaders" continually try to personalize these contacts, while the upper two status groups try to maintain distance.

The wives of the three upper status groups are bound by intimate and sympathetic social ties. They have abandoned the democratic façade of their husbands and have created a "social" organization with closure rules. The Women's Club is the only organization in Greenbelt in which one becomes a member only by invitation.

(4) About sixty-five people make up status group four. Its members may be dubbed, "strainers and apprentices." They are the officers of the special-interest groups, the heads of important committees of the larger organizations, and the petty governmental officials. The latter receive recognition because of their association with the high federal officials; the former because of their services. Both groups often claim more recognition than they receive. They are ambitious for higher posts and the recognition accorded status group three. Although the latter does recruit most of its members from status group four, many others fail to achieve upward mobility. It is understandable that the personnel of the "strainer group" is changing continually.

The marginal characteristics of the group are displayed in various ways. Its members regard their roles with more seriousness than do others. At the public meetings they are visibly active, straining and intense. When given the floor they speak loud and long, displaying remarkably complete knowledge of the business, past and present. They become past masters at parliamentary tactics, using them to obtain attention as well as their ends. For this reason, they are often regarded as "obstructionists."

The members of the four upper status groups are known to one another and to the townspeople at large. This is not the case for the lower status groups. In the lower strata the principles of status ranking operate along more categoric lines. If little is known about a person, his prestige tends to be determined by his occupation, which does not remain a secret long in this occupation-conscious settlement. For example, non-participating professional people receive more recognition than manual workers who participate in one or two minor organizations, but not more recognition than officers of large organizations who are clerical workers.

(5) The fifth status group is the largest. It is composed of the "ordinary" clerical worker who is affiliated with one or two organizations. Although he receives no special recognition, neither is he the object of "negative prestige." He is the person who crowds the meeting rooms whenever a "crisis" occurs, but who stops participating when the excitement dissolves. Some of these were "leaders" who lost in their struggle for status, or who redirected their energies along job-advancement channels.

(6) The status of "manual workers," unless they participate actively in town affairs, is lower than that of the "ordinary clerical workers." Since the average incomes of the groups are quite similar, one may infer that the status differences are largely occupational. The manual workers, however, hesitate to admit their status inferiority. . . .

(7) Status group seven consists of the town's maintenance laborers, those who cut the lawns, collect trash, drive trucks, keep the town clean, and make minor repairs. At first they consisted of about ninety people, who in general received lower incomes than the town's average. These laborers are known to many townspeople, for they are seen about the town doing their work. Curt salutations constitute practically the total contact of this stratum with the others. Most Greenbelters do not even bother to ascribe them "peculiar" characteristics. They are ignored not only on account of their low occupational status, but also because they do not even constitute a nuisance value in the competition for status. Local laborers attend meetings, but rarely participate actively. They do not have or seek to have any psychological or political affinity with other manual workers in the town. The laborers claim status superiority only over a small number of Negroes who provide janitorial services. This is a small status "gain," inasmuch as Negroes are not allowed to live in Greenbelt.

(8) The people of Hebraic faith occupy a peculiar position in the status structure. The seven per cent of the population that claimed Judaism as a faith participated more actively than the general population from the very beginning. Their influence was most heavily felt in those organizations that had ideological perspectives such as the co-operatives.

At first, prejudice against the Jews remained either latent or unorganized. They were appointed and elected to the highest offices. This happened because

---

9 For example, the councilmen must work with the federal officials; the board of directors of the Health Association with the doctors, the P.T.A. officers with the teachers, and so forth.

the town needed good organizers, and the Jews were willing to exert themselves in leadership positions. An organizational structure was not already existent to operate in a closure fashion against any group. Also, the Jews were not accused of pursuing uniform ideological paths.

As competition for officers became more acute, the factor of religious affiliation was increasingly interjected into campaign issues. The Jews were accused of "sticking together" and "monopolizing offices." If the participation or occupational status of a Jewish person is unknown, he is usually assigned status somewhere below the fourth status group. If the two factors are known, he is accorded slightly lower status than a gentile with the same socio-economic characteristics. Thus, although Jewish physicians have high status, there is no doubt that they would receive even higher status were they gentiles.

SOURCES OF CLASS DISTINCTION

Despite the fact that a non-stratified society was envisioned for Greenbelt, we found that actually a rather complex status structure did appear within a few years. It was based primarily on organizational participation and secondarily on occupation. If we could, in turn, find what factors these rested on, we would arrive at a more exact picture of the principles of status stratification operating in Greenbelt. Since participation was more important than occupation, it was first necessary to measure it in some way, and then find the factors that made for high participation.

Membership or affiliation in organizations is admittedly a crude index of participation; but leadership and officerships are more valid criteria. We used both to measure participation. We found that the results as measured by affiliation supported those obtained by analyzing the leaders or officers.

The examination of affiliational data is taken up first. Membership data for 1942 were gathered for all organizations, excluding the local churches and the Washington organizations. The affiliation profiles of the heads of families were analyzed for such factors as age, duration of residence in Greenbelt, income and income changes, religion, education, occupation, occupational mobility, and occupation of father.

Almost three-tenths of the heads of families in Greenbelt were affiliated with no organization; i.e., they refused or were not permitted to enter the areas of status competition. Seven-tenths were affiliated in at least one organization, and forty-five per cent belonged to two or more organizations. The affiliation profiles of the wives almost exactly paralleled those of their husbands.

What socio-economic factors, if any, were related to affiliations? Affiliation and income were slightly and positively related at all times. Age and affiliation were also positively related, although age and income correlated only $+0.1$. A rank correlation of income and education, on the other hand, was significantly positive, $+.618 \pm .145$. Those who remained in Greenbelt longer seemed to have higher incomes than the newer entrants. As late as March, 1942, occupational differences in regard to affiliation did not appear to be significant. By late 1943 we found that the semi-professionals and the petty administrators and officials were participating more heavily than others. They had been the "higher clerks" (auditors, technical aids, etc.) before 1942. Thus, we may conclude that those who were members of more organizations, or roughly those who were selected for higher status, were slightly older, better educated, and longer residents of the town. Also, they had experienced more occupational and income ascent than the average earner. Any particular factor seemed insufficient to assure status, but when combined with length of residence, the probability of receiving status increased.

We suggested that 115 officers of the town's organizations had high status. Apart from having status within certain groups, they participated in more organizations than the population as a whole.[10] An analysis of some of their socio-economic attributes might further clarify the factors that were important in the acquisition of social honor.

A statistical comparison of the officers for 1942 with the general adult population for the date *when all entered Greenbelt* indicated no statistically significant differences for such factors as age, income, occupation, and perhaps education. Some differences between officers and general population did appear, although we were unable to detect their full significance. For example, no future officer on entering Greenbelt classified himself as having "no religion" or "no religious affiliation," whereas six per cent of the town's population fell into these categories. The officers were overrepresented as Protestants and Jews and underrepresented as Catholics; more of the former than of the latter.

Perhaps more important than the religious differences were the differences in occupational distribution of the fathers of both groups. The officers' fathers were represented in larger proportion in the semi-professional, proprietary, and managerial occupations, while the fathers of the non-officers were more concentrated in the manual and clerical occupations. This evidence suggests that the officers may have been reared in slightly higher socio-economic circumstances than the population as a whole.

Other differences appeared. Officers tended to be

[10] The mean number of organizations to which officers belonged was 3.7, as contrasted to 1.6 for the heads of families and their wives.

residents of the town for longer periods than the general population. They also had slightly larger families than average. The direct positive relation found between size of family and number of affiliations might have been expected, for parents joined associations that were organized to acquaint them with the needs of their children.

Although no significant differences were noted between officers and non-officers for some factors at entry, this situation did not persist after four years of residence in the town. This was especially the case for income and occupation. On the date of entry, no statistically significant difference between the groups was found for income. This situation was altered by June, 1943. The others were then receiving a mean income of $2,755, as compared with $2,655 for the heads of all families including the officers.

This difference was reflected in part in the changed occupational profiles of the two groups. At date of entry no large differences were present. By 1943, the officers were represented in significantly larger proportions in managerial, sub-administrative, and administrative occupations. They also had larger proportions in professional, semiprofessional, and "higher" clerical jobs. The parent population had larger segments engaged in manual, technical, and "ordinary" clerical operations. The differential changes in income and occupation suggests that officers were those that showed on entry larger chances of income and occupational upward mobility.

The development of formal organizations has fundamental effects on the structure of power in a community. In his report on a study of a Midwestern community, Peter H. Rossi describes how many innovations and public actions are performed not by the city government but by a coalition of private business firms and voluntary associations. Many social needs are met by a system of private government that has more flexible resources, more vigor, and sometimes better leaders than the official government. Rossi also describes the functions that participation in voluntary associations performs for the private business firm. The business organization needs to give proof of its solicitude for the community, to test the leadership potential of its junior executives, to develop social contacts between its transient executives and the permanent citizens, and to gain business allies and customers. Participation in voluntary associations enables the business firm to contribute to its official community goals, but participation also performs certain latent functions for the company.

VOLUNTARY ASSOCIATIONS IN AN INDUSTRIAL CITY*

Peter H. Rossi

The most striking characteristic of contemporary cities, compared with the American community in the nineteenth century, is the relative drop in the importance of local government, not only in its relation to state and federal governments but also in its relation to local voluntary associations. To understand what is happening within a contemporary community an investigator cannot confine himself to the official table of organization for municipal government but must add to it a host of voluntary associations which act on behalf of the community and which together with the formal structure of local government form the basic organizational framework of the local community.

There is no doubt that this is the age of the "community project." Significant community enterprises are often initiated outside the framework of local government, and are aided and abetted by a proliferation of civic associations and citizen committees.

* From Peter H. Rossi, "The Organizational Structure of an American Community," in Amitai Etzioni (editor), *Complex Organizations: A Sociological Reader* (New York: Holt, Rinehart and Winston, 1961), pp. 301-311. Reprinted with the permission of the author and the holder of the copyright, the National Opinion Research Center.

In many communities the mayor and city council often appear to be dragging their heels while organized "prominent" citizens exhort the community to push toward progress. The voluntary associations, ranging from the more permanent varieties—the Community Chest, Chamber of Commerce, and service clubs—to the *ad hoc* Citizens' Committees, have taken over many of the functions of initiating social change and marshaling community support for changes that are formally allocated to local government, and to political parties. Although it is often true that voluntary associations eventually must move local authorities, the initial spark and a great part of the task of mobilizing public opinion have been performed for these authorities in advance.

Another striking characteristic of the American community of today, in contrast to that of the past, is the status gap between the personnel of local government and the local elites of wealth, intellect, and status. The local echelons of the party organizations and the elective offices of municipal, county, and even state governments are manned by persons whose social positions are often many levels below the denizens of the Country Club, Rotary Club, and the Chamber of Commerce. The City Fathers and the county commissioners are recruited, at best, from among local lawyers of somewhat uncertain income and miscellaneous clientele, and more likely from among small proprietors or professional politicians. Money, status, and intellect seem to be in one place and political control in another. Such anomalies lead to the hypothesis that somewhere there are strings by means of which local government is guided from without.

How things "get done" has therefore become more and more problematical as the lack of articulation grows between the political elite and the industrial, commercial, and professional elites. It is hard to believe that the corner grocer who is elected mayor can govern in his own right in a community with branch factories of several national firms, a local elite of considerable wealth, and several large commercial establishments.

As a consequence of this separation in status and resources, the organizational structure of the American community consists of the formally constituted local government and its agencies, supplemented by a number of organizations which are concerned with the local community but which have no standing in the official table of organization. The number of such supplementary organizations and their vigor vary from community to community, but they all share several characteristics in common. First, such community organizations are the focus of the community activities of the elite of wealth and status. Second, such organizations are not responsible to a constitu-

ency broadly defined, as is local government, but are run as private preserves. Finally, these unofficial community organizations serve to redress the local imbalance of power by giving to the elite of status and wealth important sectors of community life to control.

A FUNCTIONAL ANALYSIS OF THE COMMUNITY PARTICIPATION ACTIVITIES OF BUSINESSES

The rationale advanced by Mediana's[1] businessmen for participating in community activities is the impact of such activities on workers and customers. Typically, a manager of the local branch of a large corporation would state that his workers expected him to play an important role in the community and that they rewarded such participation by loyalty to the firm. However, as we shall see later on, industrial workers scarcely knew of the participation of managers and concentrated their expectations of business firms primarily on the bread-and-butter topics of wages and layoffs. The incongruity between managerial rationale and workers' concerns raises the question anew why there is such a strong drive toward participation among the businessmen of this community.

A fruitful way of looking at participation in the community by business is to examine it from the perspective of what functions it serves for business. In this connection, we must look beyond the manifest or surface motivations to view the community organizations as a system performing various types of functions for the participating organizations and individuals.

Perhaps the most obvious function served by clubs and other community organizations is to provide a framework for social life, opportunities for interaction and for gregarious pleasures. Many respondents, particularly those who had experienced mobility from community to community, remarked how the clubs provided opportunities to meet and become acquainted with persons on roughly the same status level.

Secondly, participation provides a context in which businessmen may build up the right of access to one another and to community leaders. At the same time, community leaders can have easy access to those who control the economic institutions of the community. Most business managers are on a first-name basis with one another and with city and county officials. The number of times these "contacts" are employed is considerable. During many of the interviews, tele-

[1] Mediana is a pseudonym for a Midwest industrial city of about 45,000 population. The data were collected through personal interviews with about fifty businessmen and community leaders, supplemented by fifteen interviews with a "sample" of the general population.

phone calls were received by respondents from other businessmen and community leaders concerning "favors" or other actions facilitating the conduct of business. As one city official put it,

> If a new firm comes in and remains completely aloof (from civic affairs) there would be no effort from the city to make their load lighter.

Asked how the city might make a firm's load lighter, he replied,

> Of course, for a firm coming in, the city can do a hell of a lot. There is one firm in this town that is only paying a dollar a year for water. Or, you might rent them city property at a nominal rate. Now, Power Parts and American Ceramics: we helped them out on their parking problem. (City Solicitor)

Mediana Bell commercial managers have excellent access to officials of the city government and to the local newspaper. The number of items on Bell activities appearing in the newspaper is quite large, a function, we believe, of the excellent relationships between the local manager and the editor of the newspaper.

Although the traffic in favors among businessmen and between businessmen and community leaders is not a traffic in heavy goods, it does constitute a steady flow of a considerable magnitude. The stream of favors is a lubricant, making the conduct of business in Mediana much easier than it would be if every request had to go through official channels and be subject to bureaucratic scrutiny.

Community participation also builds a bridge between the locals and the itinerant managers of business enterprises. The locals, who can command popular support by virtue of their personal reputations and higher degrees of notoriety, occupy the posts of leadership in the local government and in whatever civic organizations rest on mass support. It is in the civic organizations that the business-manager outsiders establish contact with the local leaders and obtain their support in actions involving the general population.

Finally, the community participation system provides a means of ordering firms and individuals who have no intrinsic ordering relationships among themselves. Most of the firms in Mediana are not competing with one another but with firms located elsewhere. Business managers do not compete with one another in their career lines, which are located primarily within the industries of which their firms are parts. In the absence of any enduring economic traffic among firms and individuals, the status of units within both groups is quite ambiguous. The community participation activities provide a means of ordering firms according to a unitary criterion. Indeed, the reputation of a firm in Mediana among members of the business community—an important reference group for businessmen—is to a large part determined by the extent to which its managers participate in community affairs. Note that this explanation also provides an understanding of why firms and their managers are not allowed to participate beyond what is their proper level—or, at least, they are not given credit for such participation. This is an ordering device for separating firms which are alike in size and wealth, not for producing anomalies.

As a device for allocating prestige among businessmen, community participation furnishes the major outside-of-plant method of cashing in on one's success and achievements. It is particularly important for the top men in each of the industrial plants, the remainder of whose firms are located at some distance. For these persons success in community organizations represents on-the-spot prestige returns. It is significant that for the telephone company, especially the plant and traffic departments, where company loyalty is much greater on the managerial level, and where career opportunities within the company are so plentiful, community participation does not seem to be as important a source of gratification.

One consequence of the development of community participation as a ranking device is to give to the professional community organization manager (e.g., the Chamber of Commerce manager or the United Fund manager) the function of prestige broker. He serves as the information center, relaying to each businessman how he stands vis-à-vis the others. Indeed, the Mediana United Fund manager has managed thoroughly to convince the telephone company personnel that they are much lower on the totem pole of United Fund contributions than they actually are. Since the success of the managers of community organizations depend on the extent to which they are able to rally the financial and manpower support of the business community to their organizations, a clever man has a powerful weapon at his command.

This analysis implies that the primary audience in front of whom the roles of community participation are played consists of the members of the business community. This, of course, is not the only audience. To some degree what a firm's management does becomes known to the workers in the plant and to the public at large. A firm which has a good reputation in this respect probably benefits by being able to recruit workers and to obtain a favorable acceptance, generally. But the process by which the activity of a firm becomes known is slow and somewhat tricky. The things which are best known about firms by the general public are not those which necessarily mean the most to the business community. For example, the outstanding company in public esteem is Ajax Steel, whose employees' park (an impressive place indeed) was often referred to as its major contribution to the community. The busy committee life of the Chamber or the clubs receives some mention in the newspaper, but, like announcements of birth, deaths, and marriages, such notices seem to be read mainly by those most closely concerned. Indeed, it would almost appear that the general public is about a decade behind in its perception of various firms' activities.

The analysis of community participation presented here receives additional support when we consider the types of activities in which businessmen prefer to participate. The desirable forms of participation in the eyes of Mediana's business community are those which are clearly acceptable to the community as disinterested and which meet with no overt opposition. Participating in political affairs is acceptable only when the element of hostility and possible opposition are moved from the scene, preferably in advance. Hence, the preference is for the "citizens' committee" form of organization, a citizens' committee being ordinarily composed of representatives from all segments of the community which might possibly raise some opposition. Thus, in Mediana, the citizens' committee which sponsored the school bond issue drives was headed by a Protestant, a Catholic and a Jew.

BUSINESS AND COMMUNITY LEADERSHIP

The managers of the "average" business enterprise are at least members of the Chamber and one or more of the clubs. The firm contributes to the various fund drives and allows the solicitation of contributions from its employees. Some of the firms provide "leadership"—this is to say, its managers take on more than rank-and-file duties, perhaps setting up drives or becoming members of the various boards of the civic organizations. Even more important is the type of leadership which goes beyond office holding to supply some kind of initiative and momentum to community projects.

The leaders of Mediana—both officeholders and "hot rods"—come from two sources. Locals provide a good proportion of the leadership. Particularly political office, which involves popular appeal, is almost the exclusive province of this group. For a local it often does not matter what his occupation is as long as he is in business. A local, in other words, can rise to leadership position on his personal merits, whatever they might be.

Not so for the recent arrival, however. His rise to leadership seems more dependent on his job and his firm. The new manager of a large plant can find himself a place in the local firmament much more easily than the new manager of a small enterprise. All he need do is give in to the invitations he will receive.

While leadership is open to the larger outsider firms, it is not expected that leadership necessarily is forthcoming. However, for the managers of locally owned large enterprises, leadership is definitely expected. Hence the common complaint in our interviews concerning the failure of the owners of American Ceramics to provide leadership for the community.

These considerations all lead to the conclusion that it is difficult for the manager of a small branch of an outside firm to make any significant impact on Mediana's civic life. Mediana Bell, which fits into this category, can rise only to the second level of leadership, because it is neither local nor large. Indeed, the personnel of Mediana Bell tie in most closely with the second level of command in large industries (e.g., personnel director, general foreman, and the like), or on the level of the small retail merchants.

Among the various management levels within a particular firm, each finds its own niche in the organizational structure. In Mediana, all persons on the top two or three levels within a firm are in the Chamber of Commerce: usually it is mainly the top man who is active enough to get on the Board of Directors.

There is a rank order to the service clubs as well. The personnel of Mediana Bell demonstrate this rather nicely: the District Commercial Manager is in Rotary, the Local Commercial Manager is in Kiwanis, and the Plant and Traffic Chiefs are in lower-ranking clubs like Sertoma and Optimists. There is a saying in Mediana to the effect that Rotary owns the town, Kiwanis runs it, and the Jaycees do all the leg work. . . .

COMMUNITY EXPECTATIONS AND ENTERPRISES

If the participation of business in community affairs is as we have interpreted it, a matter of conforming to company policy and to the prevailing patterns of life in the business community, then we should be able to detect the existence of commonly agreed-upon expectations concerning the roles to be played by business. Such is indeed the case.

I. EXPECTATIONS BY NONBUSINESS LEADERS

Perhaps the main expectation concerns financial contributions to the organization. Here expectations vary according to the size and prosperity of the business operation. The larger and more prosperous the operation, the more it is expected to give, and to help the civic organization to obtain funds from other businesses.

In addition, businesses are expected to supply personnel to man committees, and to do all the work that constitutes a "project." A "cooperating" firm is defined as one which is liberal in assigning one or another from its staff to do community "duties." . . .

Community leaders hope that each firm lives up to the expectations they hold of it. However, the highest rewards do not go to firms which fulfill only these expectations. Additional credit goes to firms whose participation is performed in proper *style*. Grudging and reluctant fulfillment of expectations, even if it is complete, is not regarded as highly as partial fulfillment accomplished in a spontaneous and generous mood.

Perhaps the best way to define this style element is to give a few examples: the two companies which received especially commendatory remarks from the United Fund manager were Mediana Power and Power Parts. Mediana Power's manager was praised because he had worked out a method, by cooperating with the Utility Workers' Union, of getting around the Power Company's stricture against pay-roll deductions for the United Fund. Union representatives and company personnel men stationed themselves at the pay office on pay day and solicited contributions from the Power Company employees.

Power Parts received special praise because of its policy of permitting its workers to work up to four hours overtime at time-and-a-half, the wages so earned to be contributed to the United Fund. The overtime is worked on a particular day each year, specially designated as "Good Neighbor Day." Power Parts gives to its participating workers special stickers for their cars and for the windows of their homes as visible indicators of contributions as "Good Neighbors."

2. BUSINESS COMMUNITY EXPECTATIONS

The business managers in Mediana have somewhat less firm expectations concerning the participation of other business enterprises in the community. Perhaps the common theme which ran through all the interviews was that these men expected other business managers to "do their share." In fact, this attitude came out quite clearly in the way in which they talked about their own companies. Perhaps the most frequent response was, "We do our share."

Specifically, a "proper share" means participating in the following activities: a company should have a number of memberships on the Chamber of Commerce, the number being proportionate to the size of the company's operations in Mediana. The company should make a reasonable corporate contributions to the United Fund and to the special drives. It should allow the fund solicitors to have access to its workers, and to allow a pay-roll deduction plan for United Fund gifts and pledges to other fund drives. The company should send some of its managerial personnel into the various service clubs and its younger executives into the Jaycees. Some member of the firm should be in the Country Club. It is not expected that a company should strive for leadership in the civic organizations or in other community activities. However, if some member of the company does provide leadership, it redounds to the benefit of the company. . . .

3. EXPECTATIONS HELD BY THE GENERAL PUBLIC

Perhaps the weakest expectations concerning participation along the lines desired by the business community in Mediana are held by the few members of the general public whom we interviewed. For the general public, the world of community organization is a newspaper phenomenon—that is, something about which the newspaper generally prints articles but which has relatively little connection with their everyday life. The typical respondent was more concerned with the community problems amenable to political treatment than with those amenable to treatment through the voluntary organizations. Typically, the average citizen was concerned with community problems like parking, street conditions, the pollution of Mediana's rivers, and the provision of adequate recreation for children. Business community projects are usually on a "higher" plane, concerned with less "concrete" matters.

When asked what should be the obligations of a business to the city where it is located, twelve of the fifteen respondents indicated that a primary obligation of a business was to pay "adequate" or "just" or "decent" wages. This obligation to maintain a reasonable wage policy was the most important one in the minds of our respondents. Another nine referred to "working conditions," indicating that it is the obligations of an industry to provide conditions of work which are not dangerous to life or limb and have some amenities. The typical respondent would refer both to wages and working conditions as areas in which businesses had their primary obligations. Four indicated that businesses should not be "anti-labor"— that is, they should have an accommodative attitude toward labor unions. Three referred to the permanency of the plant, indicating that the industry should "stay in Mediana." Another three spoke of contributions to fund drives. Two referred to "contributions to community progress," meaning largely aiding the town to obtain additional industries. Finally, one each referred to "becoming part of the town" and to keeping their plants looking well. . . .

5 VOLUNTARY ASSOCIATIONS IN OTHER SOCIETIES

The types of organizations described in this book, their structure, and their social functions are for the most part American. Organizational life may be quite different in societies with different personnel and economic sources of support, with different needs, and with alternative methods of satisfying the needs that exist. Nothing can better underscore the close mutual dependence of American voluntary associations and American society than comparisons with other countries.

The selections by Edward Norbeck and Orvoell R. Gallagher describe the patterns of voluntary associations in two countries—Japan and France—and compare these patterns with those in America. In addition, Norbeck summarizes the main findings by social scientists about voluntary associations in other societies. Both authors attempt to generalize about the relations between voluntary associations and the social environment from the following standpoints: how particular social activities generate voluntary associations, how particular social classes support and use associations, the functions performed by associations for the entire society and for particular classes, and the effects of social change upon associations. Both Japan and France reveal similarities with and differences from the United States, and each also differs from the other.

RURAL JAPAN*

Edward Norbeck

Postwar publications by sociologists and anthropologists have provided us with valuable information and illuminating interpretations concerning social changes in rural Japan. A major point of emphasis in these writings has been kinship, the Japanese family and other kin groups, and ritual kinship modeled after familial relations. Only the briefest examination of demographic data on Japan points clearly to trends of change that must have had strong influence on kin groups and kin relations. Recent population statistics may be cited in illustration. The average size of the family throughout the nation dropped from 4.97 members in 1955 to 4.53 in 1960. During this interval of five years the national population increased 4.6 per cent, but most of the increase occurred in cities and industrial prefectures. Twenty-six of the forty-six prefectures suffered a decline in population. These statistics represent the continuation and acceleration of trends established long ago, and they suggest extensive changes at both family and community levels.

Published accounts have provided us with some information on the nature of the social changes that these statistics suggest. The principal events reported may be summarized as a decline in the size and functional importance of kin groups, a weakening of the bonds of kin-like personal ties with unrelated community members, and a change in patterns of authority, making kin groups and communities less strongly hierarchical. Principal factors influential in bringing about the changes have usually been cited as improved economic conditions of the nation as a whole connected with increased industrialization and world trade, improved technology in farming and fishing, the postwar land reform, and the emergence of increased growth of many impersonal institutions that provide economic and social security.

But social change in rural Japan does not end with the alterations outlined above. An additional and important development that has received far less attention is the growth of associations based upon common interests, the kind of social groups that we have often called "voluntary associations." Both native and foreign scholars of Japan have generally considered common-interest associations in highly specific or fragmented ways. No systematic attempt has been made to describe and classify them, to present an in-

* From Edward Norbeck, "Common Interest Associations in Rural Japan," in Robert J. Smith and Richard K. Beardsley (editors), *Japanese Culture: Its Development and Character* (Chicago: Aldine Publishing Company, 1962), pp. 73-83. Reprinted with the permission of the author, the editors, and the holder of the copyright, the Wenner-Gren Foundation for Anthropological Research.

terpretation of their functional roles, or to compare them cross-culturally. This paper hopes to make a first step in this direction.

As a type of social group, the common-interest association is ancient in Japan.[1] One of its early forms was undoubtedly age graded associations, which appear to have been most common in southerly and coastal regions. Japanese scholars have presented historic evidence of the revamping of old age-graded associations into modern groups, such as the Seinendan (Youths' Association), sponsored in modern times by the Japanese government.

It seems reasonable to expect great antiquity for communal associations concerned with irrigation. We know from archeological evidence that wet rice cultivation was established in Japan more than two thousand years ago, and we can assume that its intensive cultivation required the co-operation of many persons to build and maintain substantial systems of irrigation. The necessary cooperation may have come through kin groups, especially when the population of Japan was small. If modern theorizing on this subject is sound, however, we may think that common residence was the more important factor in determining the composition of communal work groups associated with agriculture. Formal and informal groups concerned with planting rice, harvesting crops, and other agricultural tasks and community enterprises requiring the combined efforts of many people are also old in Japan.[2]

Whatever the history of the numerous individual associations found in rural Japan today, it is safe to say that their roots as a class are ancient. In his discussion of the role of agriculture in the Tokugawa era (1600-1868) in the formation of modern Japan, Smith writes at length of "the decline of cooperative groups." [3] His discussion must be understood as referring to a decrease in the size of the farm family and the decline of co-operative fictive kin groups. Human co-operation by no means declined during Tokugawa times, but it did take other forms.

Hoynden's account of the co-operative movement in Japan, although it concerns chiefly associations connected with credit, production, distribution, and other economic matters, contains information that is relevant here. He discusses the great antiquity of co-operative groups in Japan, and describes the nation as being one of the most highly developed in the world in all types of co-operatives except consumer's co-operatives, which are less well developed than in countries of the West.[4] The circumstances of which Smith writes, intensive market agriculture based on techniques that favored cultivation of small holdings by small family groups, very likely encouraged the growth of non-kin associations as well as paved the way for the later industrialization of the nation. Small land holdings may be seen as a factor disfavoring extensive co-operation among kin but favoring co-operation in the form of common-interest associations. Among other social effects, the small size of Japanese farms has made the actively cooperating kin group small and has made loans through banks impossible. Farmers' credit co-operatives first arose in the fourteenth century, before Tokugawa times, and have now had a history in Japan of six centuries.

Smith's account of agricultural and social developments that aided the later industrialization of Japan concerns chiefly southwestern Japan, which led the nation in economic change and growth. It is noteworthy that the late Tokugawa and early Meiji eras (the mid-nineteenth century) appear to be the time of emergence of communal associations in small face-to-face living communities (*buraku*) of northeastern Japan, an area that until very recent times lagged behind southwestern Japan in cultural innovations. These were *buraku* associations, concerned with the control and maintenance of local paths and roads, with community forest lands, and with various other matters of communal interest. The name often given to these associations in northeastern Japan, *keiyaku-kō*, is literally translated "contract associations." The middle of the nineteenth century is also a period that saw the rapid growth in urban Japan of co-operative associations concerned with finance, production, and marketing. The greatest growth of formal common-interest groups of all kinds has come in the twentieth century. This is a subject to which we will return in considering the functional role of the modern associations.

TYPES OF JAPANESE COMMON-INTEREST ASSOCIATIONS

An examination of reports on modern rural communities of Japan displays marked uniformity in the types of common-interest associations described. Although full data are lacking, it seems fairly certain that rural settlements everywhere follow a common pattern that varies principally in accordance with the occupations that villagers follow (i.e., farming, fishing, dairying, seri-culture, forestry, and the life). Local ecological

1 See Yoshio Hoynden, *Cooperative Movement in Japan* (Toyko: Maruzen Company, 1958), Volume I: Marusuke Konno, "Wakamono-gumi, Musume-gumi" (Youth Associations, Girls' Associations), in Kunio Yanagita (editor), *Kaison seikatsu no kenkyu* (Tokyo: Nihon Minzokugakkai, 1939); Edward Norbeck, "Age-Grading in Japan," *American Anthropologist*, Volume 55 (1953), pp. 373-384; Kiyoko Segawa, "Dorei Shuzoku no tsuite," *Minzokugaku Kenkyu*, Volume 12 (1947), pp. 46-51.
2 Hoynden, *op. cit.*
3 Thomas C. Smith, *The Agrarian Origins of Modern Japan* (Stanford: Stanford University Press, 1959).
4 Hoynden, *op. cit.*, Preface and Chapter I.

features also exert influence on associations. In communities that offer little employment for young men, for example, the youths' associations are poorly developed by default because the young men migrate to industrial areas.

Customarily, the number of associations to which *buraku* members belong ranges between fifteen and twenty-five. Membership in them depends upon sex, age, occupation, and other special interests. The list appearing below of the associations in a rice-raising *buraku* in Miyagi Prefecture in 1959 may be taken as representative.[5]

> Agricultural Co-operative Association (I)
> Youths' Division, Agricultural Co-operative Association (I)
> Women's Division, Agricultural Co-operative Association (I)
> Daruma 4-H Club (young men) (I)
> Angel 4-H Club (young women) (I)
> Irrigation Association (I)
> Parent-Teacher Association (I)
> Children's Association (E)
> Crime Prevention Association (I)
> Fire Prevention Association (I)
> Young People's Association (I-E)
> *Buraku Association (I)
> *Funeral Association (in groups of 10-12 households) (I)
> *Neighborhood Association (several small groups) (I)
> *Irrigation Association (independent grouping concerned with a small water supply used by a part of the community) (I)
> *Tax Association (to remind members of dates payments are due and to facilitate payment of the numerous taxes. Several small groups; all households do not belong) (I)
> *Yama-no-kamisama Kō (religious society, brides and young mothers) (E)
> *Zoshin Kō (religious society, men) (E)
> *Kannon Kō (religious society, women) (E)
> *Nembutsu Kō (religious society, women) (E)
> (I) = Instrumental; (E) = Expressive; (I-E) = Instrumental-Expressive. See discussion that follows. Classifications (I) and (E), as made here, imply that associations are principally rather than wholly instrumental or expressive. The lone association marked (I-E) seems about equally instrumental and expressive. *Independent *buraku* associations. All others are segments, usually *buraku* sub-divisions, of larger organizations.

Gordon and Babchuk's reformulation of Arnold Rose's typology of voluntary associations, although apparently based principally upon data from the United States, lends itself fairly well to the Japanese scene.[6] Based upon an interpretation of their functions, this classification places associations into three categories: *instrumental*, those "designed to maintain

[5] Edward Norbeck, "Postwar Cultural Change and Continuity in Northeastern Japan," *American Anthropologist*, Volume 63 (1961), pp. 297-321.
[6] C. Wayne Gordon and Nicholas Babchuk, "A Typology of Voluntary Associations." [Reprinted in Chapter 2 of this volume.–Eds.]

or create some normative condition or change" which "focus on activity and goals that are outside the organization itself"; *expressive*, those providing "continuing gratification" to the individual through "activities confined and self-contained with the organization itself"; and *instrumental-expressive*, those combining the goals and functions of the two foregoing types. Lack of space prohibits any detailed discussion of the aims and functions of most of the Japanese associations listed above, but these may generally be inferred from the titles.

We would accept the Gordon–Babchuk typology with two reservations. The first, a minor point that Gordon and Babchuk also note, is that instrumental associations probably always have some element of "expression"; that is, they may give personal satisfaction to individuals in varying degrees in ways that are not directly connected with the goals of the associations. The second reservation is more serious. We question the suitability of the word "voluntary," as have others before us in more general discussions of the nature of associations. Many of the Japanese associations on the *buraku* level are branches of larger organizations. They were established under pressure from the national government and receive strong encouragement from the prefectural and national governments. During World War II, co-operative associations connected with occupations, and women's and youths' associations, were nationalized, and membership in them was virtually obligatory. No legal provisions today require membership in any *buraku* association, whether instrumental or expressive, but social and economic pressures serve, for most people, to make membership in a large part of the groups obligatory. On the local level, membership in associations is not by ascription. One joins them, but membership often comes close to being ascribed. These circumstances are, of course, not unique to Japan. We wonder, for example, whether participation in such organizations as the Parent–Teacher Association may aptly be called voluntary in the United States or Europe.

FUNCTIONAL ASPECTS

Certain roles of the Japanese associations seem self-evident from their titles: they provide individual satisfaction through recreation, education, and religious acts or they attempt to reach educational, economic, civil, or moral goals. Using the concept of function in another sense, we may say that they are also in considerable measure substitutes for kinship and personal ties. In the Japanese rural community, intra-*buraku* social relations have come increasingly to stress non-kin associations that have ties to neighboring communities and the nation as a whole. It is through them that much of the economic and social life of the *buraku* is conducted, and, increasingly, community solidarity is expressed through identification with the associations. Referring to northeastern Japan and other regions where associations were slower to develop than in southwestern Japan, it is probable that solidarity within the *buraku* and with neighboring communities has increased in postwar years as a result of their growth.

Most important in the respects discussed above are the occupational co-operatives, particularly the farmers' co-operative association, which probably exists in every agricultural community of Japan. This organization is the medium through which machinery, tools, fertilizer, other farm supplies, and education in new techniques of horticulture are obtained; it is the only important agency for obtaining loans of money, the principal repository for cash savings of its members, and the customary agency for the sale of crops. The farmers' co-operative, expectably, has great power. It may be described as a mechanism by which communal action is made to serve effectively for individual or familial ends.

In pointing out the great importance of agricultural co-operatives in Japan, Hoynden goes so far as to state that rural communities in Japan are formed around them. He calls the agricultural co-operatives multipurpose and lists as their major functions: credit, marketing, purchasing, guidance in farming, mutual relief, medical services, and management and finance.[7] Under the provisions of the Agricultural Co-operative Law, enacted shortly after the end of World War II, activities in which these co-operatives may engage are:

a) Loaning funds necessary for the business or livelihood of members.
b) Acceptance of deposits from members.
c) Supply of articles necessary for the business or livelihood of the members, or installation of common facilities.
d) Facilities relating to co-operation in agriculture or the promotion of the efficiency of agricultural labor.
e) Reclamation, improvement or administration of agricultural land or establishment or administration of irrigation facilities.
f) Transportation, processing, storage or sale of articles produced by members.
g) Facilities relating to village industry.
h) Facilities for mutual relief from loss or damage.
i) Facilities for the improvement of village life and culture.
j) Facilities for the education of members to improve their knowledge of agricultural technique and the business of the cooperative, and for the provision of general information to the members.
k) Conclusion of collective bargains for the improvement of the economic position of members.
1) Such business as is incidental to any one of the preceding items.

Since the agricultural co-operatives do in fact engage in all or most of these activities, their importance in community life goes far beyond affairs connected with agricultural technology and economics. Many co-operatives also provide recreation and promote cultural activities by sponsoring or subsidizing movies, concerts, lectures on many subjects, and instruction in dietetics and other matters of domestic life. Some have established public halls for recreation and instruction and provide electric washing machines, barbers, and bathhouses. An especially common facility provided to members is a wire broadcasting system that transmits to the homes of members programs of various kinds, news, weather reports, educational addresses, and entertainment. These broadcasting systems often incorporate telephones. The majority of the agricultural co-operatives have women's divisions. A recent trend toward the formation of young men's divisions is also apparent. These divisions are perhaps better called auxiliaries, since their objectives appear to stress recreation, instruction in non-agricultural spheres, and civil affairs more than they do matters directly connected with agriculture.

It is clear that agricultural and other co-operatives of Japan that are concerned primarily with technological and economic matters have been strongly influenced by Western models. Some of the other Japanese associations we have listed (i.e., Parent-Teacher Associations, 4-H Club) appear from their names to be foreign-derived and were in fact established by Occupation directives. The whole fabric of Japanese rural associations nevertheless follows a Japanese pattern, historical aspects of which we have already discussed. In even the most backward areas of rural Japan, a tradition of communal action in at least certain spheres of life has long co-existed with hierarchically ordered social groupings based on the model of the family. It is useful to note again circumstances in northeastern Japan, where, until the postwar land reform, most of the land and other property was in the hands of a few individuals. The bulk of the rural population consisted of tenant farmers or people having access to lands through ties of kinship and fictive kinship. Communal associations developed first in connection with religion and such vital community affairs as did not present economic threats to those in power. Once the great landowners were removed from power by the land reform, the way was clear for rapid development of associations. Altered economic and social circumstances in fact gave strong encouragement to their development. The growth of the foreign-derived or foreign-influenced Japanese associ-

7 Hoynden, *op. cit.*, p. iii; Hoynden, *Agricultural and Fishery Cooperative in Japan* (Tokyo: Azuma Shobo Co., 1960).

ations seems thus to follow an indigenous pattern. Policy-makers in the Japanese government, having an established model before them, used native and foreign models of the association to provide an effective and inexpensive channel for reaching and controlling its population during the years that Japan prepared for and actively waged war. Following World War II, additional foreign models reached the Japanese through officials of the American Occupation.

Under the circumstances of modern life in Japan, which discourages elaborate ramifications of kinship and personalized bonds, the nature of common-interest associations offers a number of obvious advantages. Associations are malleable, adjusting to changing conditions with less difficulty than do kin groups. They may be formed, altered, or dissolved to meet changing circumstances, and their presence or absence affects or disrupts family and community membership in no important way. They may be regarded in one sense as a transitional social device, well suited to a rapidly changing society. Their growth has marked a transition from heavy Japanese reliance upon kinship and personal ties, and they themselves have served as one of the instruments of transition. The shift from former conditions that gave greater emphasis to kinship and social relations channeled through a hierarchical ordering of individual community members has not been socially disturbing because it represents a shift of emphasis rather than drastic innovation.

Part of the strength of the modern common-interest associations in rural Japan may arise from the lack of kin. Although still large in comparison with the urban family, the farming family of Japan has shrunk in size and continues to shrink. The rural community, economically based on tiny farms that cannot support, and, during most of the year, do not require a large labor force, generally has no place for any of the mature young males except eldest sons or such younger sons as may substitute for them. It has no place for adult females except those who marry stay-at-home males, and many women marry outside the *buraku* of their birth. It is, then, often difficult to maintain a substantial body of kin within one's own community, or even within range close enough so that frequent contact may be maintained.

CROSS-CULTURAL COMPARISON

Research on common-interest associations has rarely been comprehensive or systematic for any nation. We have, however, a number of reports dealing with associations in the United States and Great Britain[8]

and a growing number of pertinent writings on other foreign countries. Assuming that the foregoing interpretations of Japanese conditions are sound, let us compare the Japanese rural associations briefly with similar social groups among certain other nations of the world.

In the United States voluntary associations are primarily urban. We have been told in various ways that the lack of widely embracive kin ties, the impersonality of city life, and the waning influence of the church has led the people to turn to these associations to satisfy sociopsychological needs. At one time we were told that the United States was the land of "joiners," but sociological surveys seem to have revealed that membership in associations is confined mostly to the middle class and, although common enough, is not so prevalent as once thought. The American lower class is said to rely more heavily for these "needs" upon the family and kinship.[9]

Circumstances reported for England resemble those in the United States. Reports on France, however, differ somewhat, and differ from one another. Rose states that associations, especially those seeking to exert "social influence," are relatively rare, and he points to functional equivalents: the French family, trade unions, and the extensive use of parks and cafés for social interaction.[10] Gallagher holds that associations are not rare in France and describes them as being mostly urban, connected with occupations, and found among the "rootless bourgeoisie *radicale*." He states further that the French government has repressed various kinds of associations.[11] A study of rural Ukrainian immigrants to France describes a luxuriant growth of voluntary associations of all types and states that the social life of these people centers on them.[12] We may note that this group of Ukrainian Frenchmen might also be called rootless, since its core is composed of nuclear families migrating from the Ukraine from 1921 to 1939, which, in their new environment, lack any substantial number of kin. Again the associations here may be classed as urban,

8 Gordon and Babchuk, *op. cit.*; David Glass (editor), *Social Mobility in Britain* (Glencoe, Ill.: The Free Press, 1954).

9 Charles R. Wright and Herbert H. Hyman, "Voluntary Association Memberships of American Adults" [Reprinted in Chapter 3 of this volume.—Eds.]. Floyd Dotson, "Patterns of Voluntary Association Among Urban Working Class Families," *American Sociological Review*, Volume 16 (1951), pp. 687-693; Howard Freeman, Edwin Novak, and Leo G. Reeder, "Correlates of Membership in Voluntary Associations," *American Sociological Review*, Volume 22 (1957), pp. 528-533.

10 Arnold M. Rose, *Theory and Method in the Social Sciences* (Minneapolis, Minn.: University of Minnesota Press, 1954), Chapter IV.

11 Orvoell Gallagher, "Voluntary Associations." [Reprinted as the next selection in this volume.—Eds.]

12 Robert T. Anderson and Gallatin Anderson, "Voluntary Associations Among Ukrainians in France," *Anthropological Quarterly*, Volume 35, Number 4 (October 1962), pp. 158-168.

since the community is composed of industrial workers living on the outskirts of Paris.

An account of a suburb of Copenhagen reports the development of an abundance of voluntary associations since the end of the nineteenth century in connection with urbanization.[13] In Italy, development of voluntary associations is described as poor, especially in southern Italy, where an ethos of "amoral familism" is said to inhibit them.[14]

Writings on Negro Africa report the recent growth of voluntary associations among former tribesmen in various of the new industrial cities. Many, but not all, of these associations follow European models, and their growth is characteristically interpreted as resulting from urbanization. Little states that two conditions are required for their growth in Africa: a socially heterogeneous, unstable urban population composed largely of immigrants and "adaptability of native institutions to urban conditions."[15] (At least some development of comparable social groups is found in many of the tribal societies from which the modern Negro urban residents come.)

A brief account of voluntary associations in Guadalajara, Mexico, states that associations are poorly represented among the working class, where kin ties perform the functions filled in various other places by associations.[16] A similarly brief account on Korea discusses the past and present abundance of associations closely resembling those of pre-industrial Japan.[17] I am aware of no other substantial accounts useful for comparison. (Considerable has been written, of course, on common-interest associations in primitive society and on commercial co-operatives in Europe and various former colonies of European nations.)

If we examine these various writings to see what they hold in common, two ideas appear prominently. One is that the associations serve as a substitute for or functional equivalent of kinship and other personalized ties under conditions that make social relations

based upon these latter considerations inefficient, difficult, or impossible. The second commonly recurrent idea outlines the conditions; that is, the associations are said to be a phenomenon connected with urbanization.

Now let us examine the Japanese associations from these standpoints. An interpretation of the role of the Japanese groups as a partial substitute for kinship seems reasonable. . . . This statement does not seem to imply that common-interest associations are everywhere necessarily or inevitably correlated with the weakening of kin ties. It seems however, to be a pattern that many societies can and do easily take when the maintenance of close or ramified kin ties becomes difficult. Perhaps there is merit in the idea . . . that the blossoming of the associations has been greatest and fastest in industrialized societies that provide long-established models, such as age-graded groups, co-operative work groups associated with irrigation, and the like.

The theory that associations are products of urbanization and find their greatest development in the socially heterogeneous and depersonalized city does not seem at first glance to fit the Japanese scene. Unfortunately, quantitative data on the cities of Japan are not available, but it is my strong impression that common-interest associations find far greater development in its rural areas. This statement does not, however, necessarily indicate a lack of correlation between urbanization and common-interest associations in Japan. The question hinges on the definition of urbanization. Japan is certainly urbanized in at least the sense that it has become heavily industrialized and more and more of its population is concentrated in large cities. Japan's cities may also be described as socially heterogeneous and impersonal. In the rural world, a continuing process of amalgamation of formerly independent small communities into towns and cities has left only a relatively few politically independent small villages in all Japan. The rural *buraku*, although still physically isolated from neighboring communities, small and large, is in increasing contact with them. Many farming communities are now in fact administratively parts of cities, and their members participate more than formerly in urban affairs. The growth of the industrial city has had far-reaching effects. With each succeeding year, as techniques of agriculture, animal husbandry, and fishing have grown more efficient, the work of the farmer and fisherman has accordingly become more specialized. As a specialist, the rural resident may be regarded as a highly integrated part of a complex, co-operative national economic and political scheme. The term "peasant," with its connotation of emotional attachment to a fixed way of life, self-sufficiency, subsistence economy, and sharp segregation from other seg-

13 Robert T. Anderson and Gallatin Anderson, "Voluntary Associations and Urbanization, a Diachronic Analysis," *American Journal of Sociology*, Volume 65, Number 3, November 1959, pp. 265-273.

14 David L. Sills, "Voluntary Associations: Instruments and Objects of Change," *Human Organization*, Volume 18 (1959), p. 19.

15 Kenneth Little, "The Role of the Voluntary Association in West African Urbanization," *American Anthropologist*, Volume 59 (1957), p. 594. [For further description of African voluntary associations, see Immanuel Wallerstein, "Voluntary Associations," in James S. Coleman and Carl G. Rosberg, Jr. (eds.), *Political Parties and National Integration in Tropical Africa* (Berkeley and Los Angeles: University of California Press, 1964), pp. 318-399.—Eds.]

16 Floyd Dotson, "A Note on Participation in Voluntary Associations in a Mexican City" *American Sociological Review*, Volume 18 (1953), pp. 380-386.

17 Eugene I. Knez, "Ke Mutual Aid Groups: Persistence and Change," *Korean Report*, Volume I (1961), pp. 17-20.

ments of the total society, no longer seems suitable for the Japanese farmer. It does not seem inappropriate to think that most of Japan has become urbanized.

We may note various other characteristics of the common-interest associations of rural Japan. Unlike circumstances in the United States and various countries of Europe, membership in Japan in the associations under discussion is, of course, linked almost entirely with what must be called the working class. Various reports on the United States and Europe hold that ties of kinship are the most intimate among members of the working class, those who least frequently join associations. Kinship surely remains important to the rural resident of Japan, more important than either "true" or ritual kinship in Japanese cities. As we have noted, however, common-interest associations appear to have their greatest development in the country, where the bonds of kinship are also the more pervasive. Japan, then, differs in this respect not only from Europe but also from Africa, where membership in associations is strong among urban workmen as a surrogate for kinship.

I wish to call attention again to the farmers' co-operative associations of Japan. No close counterpart appears to exist in other countries. As we have noted, the roles in community life of this association cover a very broad range and are extremely important to the welfare of the people. It is not surprising that this association shows a tendency to engulf other, sometimes older, associations as auxiliaries. I noted this trend in several communities of Miyagi Prefecture in 1959,[18] and I have the impression that it is a national tendency wherever the farmers' co-operative is economically powerful (i.e., where farm lands are highly productive.)

We may note also that there is virtually no development in rural Japan of associations attempting to exert "social influence" except those encouraged by the government. (The farmers' co-operatives may form something of an exception. Although such activities fall outside their stated and primary objectives, these powerful associations seem well suited for use in influencing opinion in political matters. The extent to which they actually engage in political activities is unclear and needs investigation.) Governmental control over associations during the third and fourth decades of this century and until the end of World War II was very strict. With the exception of suppression of Communist activities, however, present-day governmental policies do not appear actively to discourage the formation of associations aiming toward social change. Perhaps the shadow of the past continues to inhibit the independent emergence of associations with goals of social reform.

The study of common-interest associations in Japan has bearing upon another subject that has concerned social theorists. Since the seventeenth century, Western social philosophers have linked associations and the growth of democracy, holding that associations serve the important function of encouraging greater involvement of their members in the affairs of the general society. We have no convenient yardstick for judging quantitatively the democratization of rural Japan, but many observers in addition to myself have stated more or less impressionistically that familial and other social relations have become more democratic since World War II. It is certain that through the medium of the common-interest association participation in local community affairs is greater than in former times. Moreover, since many associations are sub-divisions of national networks and are therefore linked to outside communities and the nation as a whole, the association has also brought about greater participation in the affairs of the total society. We may note also that members of the Japanese associations, as representatives of their households, ideally have equal voices in determining policy and deciding issues. But these circumstances do not necessarily imply democracy. Common-interest associations were well developed in Japan before and during its war years, a period that can hardly be looked upon as democratic. Certain of them at this time served in fact as important media for strict governmental control of the people, a function that they seem not to have served in most other nations. Perhaps in some measure they continue to serve in this capacity today in a less rigid fashion. Such diverse governmentally sponsored activities as instruction in contraception, education in the metrical system of weights and measures (adopted in 1959), and a movement to shorten the length of traditional festival seasons continue to flow from the government through various of the nationalized associations. The actual role in Japan of the common-interest associations as a democratizing force remains unclear, and thus far it has hardly received scholarly mention.

As these remarks indicate, much remains to be done before we can offer an assured interpretation or even an adequate description of common-interest associations in Japan. We need in particular information on circumstances in Japan's cities, and, for both rural and urban areas, information on the internal organization of the associations, motives for participation in them, trends of change, and knowledge of their relationships to governmental bureaus, kin groups, fictive kin groups and other segments of society, and to the society as a whole.

[18] "Postwar Cultural Change and Continuity in Northeastern Japan," *American Anthropologist*, Volume 63 (1961), pp. 297-321.

FRANCE*

Orvoell R. Gallagher

Based on his research in France, Arnold M. Rose has recently suggested several hypotheses concerning the bases and functions of voluntary associations.[1] Although in general agreement with much of what Rose has to say about the role of associations in French culture, this writer would like to comment both upon Rose's basic data and upon certain of the conclusions deriving from these data. This writer's comments are based upon his own field work in two French communities.

Rose defines the voluntary association as a group of people who, "finding they have a certain interest (or purpose) in common, agree to meet and act together in order to try and satisfy that purpose." Voluntary associations are divided into two broad types, the "expressive" association, one that expresses or satisfies the self-interests of members, and the "social influence" association, one facing or directed outward and aiming at achieving social improvement, social welfare, or other philanthropic goal in the larger society. Both types of association are viewed by Rose as products of urbanization and heterogeneity which satisfy such social-psychological needs as "self-expression" and the "satisfaction of interests through collective action"—needs, Rose points out, which have historically been satisfied by community, church, and family.

Because of the relatively weak or loose social structure in the United States, Americans have turned to voluntary associations to satisfy these social-psychological needs, and Rose cites a number of community studies (Yankee City, Middletown, Detroit, etc.) to support this observation. Comments on the Americans as "joiners" by such foreign observers as Lord Bryce, de Tocqueville, and Myrdal are also quoted. Rose notes that the association in America not only gives the individual a sense of belonging, but it also plays a role in mediating change in a highly mobile society.

In France, however, Rose sees the voluntary association as playing a quite different role. Voluntary associations are, he claims, relatively rare in France. Such associations as exist, especially the "social influence" association, play a more minor role in France than in the United States. The basic social and psychological functions that associations play in the United States

are, therefore, he claims, probably assumed in France by other types of social institutions.

Data are presented to support the above statements. The results of a market research study by a French polling group are cited. These indicate that "only 41 per cent of French adults belong to any kind of association." The Auxerre (an urban community in Burgundy) study by French sociologists Bettelheim and Frère is quoted (although the quote does not entirely support Rose's theses as to the quantity of associations) to indicate the relative unimportance of associations in a French provincial town. In Auxerre, according to Bettelheim and Frère:

> Associations are numerous and varied but are generally not very important . . . . these associations have not developed an *espirit de corps* among their members . . . . they do not play any particular role in social cohesion. Their main role is to provide occasions for meeting or for presenting information to persons who, without the associations, would live in almost complete isolation.[2]

Two other studies are mentioned, a Unesco study of Vienne and a depopulation study in Brittany. Both offer mostly negative evidence as to the minor role of associations in these French communities. Finally, Rose states that it is his "impression" from talks with French sociologists that voluntary associations play "but a small role, both in the functioning of the community or nation and in the lives of the average citizen."

Assuming the minor role of voluntary associations in France, Rose goes on to develop the historical reasons why associations have developed differently in France from the course of development in the United States. Of most importance, he feels, is that French governments have consistently repressed associations as representing possible revolutionary or subversive forces. There has also been some concern—probably with the Catholic Church in mind—that associations make for hoarding wealth and consequent evasion of taxation. Further, the central government through its bureaucracy has commonly performed many of the functions which in the United States have been left to local governments or to private citizens. French governments have, even when permitting associations, severely restricted the amount of money they may collect and disperse. Finally, other reasons such as the Catholic practice of encouraging individuals to associate within the church and under the guidance of the clergy rather than in independent organizations may also be of importance.

* From Orvoell R. Gallagher, "Voluntary Associations in France," *Social Forces*, Volume 36 (1957), 153-160. Reprinted with the permission of the author and the publisher, The University of North Carolina Press.
[1] Arnold M. Rose, *Theory and Method in the Social Sciences*, (Minneapolis: University of Minnesota Press, 1954), pp. 50-115.

[2] *Ibid.*, p. 75.

These data are convincing and Rose's hypotheses important if verified by field material from French communities. The essential questions are: (1) Are voluntary associations in France as few in number as Rose's data suggest? (2) Do voluntary associations play a relatively minor role in French life? (3) Do other institutions (such as church, community, family, café, etc.) assume in France the social-psychological functions which Rose claims are filled by voluntary associations in the United States? One of the communities to be discussed is a rural commune with a population of about 800 inhabitants; the other is an urban community with an estimated 50,000 inhabitants. Both communities are located in central France.

Below are listed the types and members of voluntary associations in each of the two communities. The

TABLE I

Voluntary associations in a rural and an urban community in France

	Number of associations	
Occupational associations	Rural	Urban
Agricultural, employer associations, artisan, trade union organizations, professional societies, etc.	6	120
Athletic associations		
Aero club, hunting-fishing clubs, horse racing, ski clubs, various football, cycling clubs, etc.	4	20
Cultural associations		
Academy, writers, artists, clubs, museum, cinema, symphony clubs, etc.	1	10
Political associations		
Various political parties	—	6
Fraternal and social clubs		
Terrace club, Rotary, camera club, stamp club, various *amicales*	—	20
Veterans' associations		
Various organizations of both World Wars, special campaigns, Africa, Near East, Indo-China, etc.	2	25
Others		
Associations of parents, former students, religious, family associations, orphanage associations, etc.	2	25
Total	15	226

categories used are approximately those of the 1951 market-research survey of the *Service de Sondages et Statistiques* quoted by Rose. My own data refer primarily to the quantity of associations in each community, the type of Frenchmen who belong to particular kinds of associations, and the role of the association in the larger society. The number of associations in the rural community is believed to be substantially correct; in the urban community it may be presumed that the total number of voluntary associations would run well above three hundred.[3]

[3] Data from the urban community are based on the associational affiliation of about 150 individuals. In the

THE RURAL COMMUNITY

The above data on voluntary associations in the rural community give firm support to Rose's hypotheses. Not only are associations few in number, but they seldom play a vital role in community life. The few existing associations are all "expressive" associations and could, in this writer's opinion, be eliminated from community life without much effect on the daily lives of the inhabitants. Even affiliation in a political party is uncommon. Candidates of the various political parties enter the community briefly before each election, but, while the meetings are "events" and fairly well attended, the great majority of the inhabitants continue to vote for personal favorites without regard to party affiliation. Only the two veterans' organizations (the "real" soldiers of World War I and the "prisoners" and "workers" of World War II) manage to work up any degree of *esprit de corps* and this is probably as much a reflection of age antagonism as of the goals of either organization.

For the majority of the inhabitants, it would appear, therefore, as Rose claims, that community, family, and church (at least for the women), and the café (for the men) do serve as the functional equivalents of voluntary associations. The daily round of rural life is such that everyone knows not only everyone else but almost everything about everyone. Men meet more or less regularly in one of the three cafés; women meet when they shop, go to market, or around the church door after mass. The various individual *rites de passage* tend to be communal as well as familial ceremonies. Such religious and national holidays as *Toussaint* (All Saints' Day) and Easter, and the national holidays on May 8, July 14, and November 11, when individuals return to the *foyer* to unite around the tombs and memories of the dead, also make for community and family solidarity.

Full participation in these rural institutions tends, however, to be restricted to those inhabitants who have a permanent stake in the community. Nearly 30 per cent of the 800 inhabitants earn their livelihoods at irregular farm and domestic work, lack property, and have few kin in the community. Propertyless in a culture which places high value on the ownership of property, members of this rural proletariat participate relatively little in community life.

This isolation has, however, a sound social basis, for social relations in this rural community are built upon and maintained through the possession of property. Lacking property, individuals are more likely to

rural community data were got informally and through participation. The categories are obviously not all neat fits. For example, the Communist Party sponsors four or five veterans' organizations, which might more properly be placed under "political associations."

live together as man and wife without going through the traditional civil and religious ceremonies, for marriage is a traditional time for property arrangements to be settled. Children of the propertyless tend to scatter in search of jobs and are less likely to retain ties with parents than is true of the children of the propertied. These factors make it difficult to maintain the rites and rituals associated with family life and give few stimuli for the establishment of a stable kin system.

As a result, participation in community life is limited, too, for social relationships are normally based on reciprocity. One invites because one has been invited, and one does not ordinarily attend the *rites de passage* of others unless they have attended yours. Even in the men's club, the café, there is little reciprocal drinking, between the propertied and the non-propertied Frenchmen. Though ruralites by census declaration, the rural propertyless Frenchman has actually little share in those virtues assumed inherent in rural life. Moreover, members of this rural proletariat have the fewest affiliations with voluntary associations of all socio-economic groups in the community. In other words, their "social-psychological" needs must be assumed to go unsatisfied, for these needs are met neither through the traditional institutions of community, church, and family, nor through membership in voluntary associations.

THE URBAN COMMUNITY

Formerly a walled feudal town, the urban community was made administrative center of its department in 1791, and it has grown steadily since that time to a present day population of nearly 50,000. Today, it is the banking, marketing, and general trade center of its rural hinterland as well as political seat of the department government. Economically, the community has remained in the pre-capitalistic era, for the family-type enterprise, whether factory, corner store, or artisan's shop, is still the predominant form of economic organization. These enterprises are inherited, guarded preciously, and transmitted to descendants as a sacred trust.

The community's principal enterprises are still in the hands of several dozen old families, the descendants of the founders of the enterprises. During the past two or three decades, a number of Paris-owned corporations have established branch factories and retail stores in the community. The factories are not yet in direct competition with the enterprises of the community's bourgeoisie (though they do compete with similar enterprises elsewhere), but the more recently established "department stores" are competing directly with the community's shopkeepers and artisans.

Because class is relevant to membership in voluntary associations, reference is pertinent here to the community's class system. Five classes may be defined: the nobility, the bourgeoisie, and the bourgeoisie *radicale*, the petty bourgeoisie, and the proletariat. Although many of the rural communities in the department still have a resident noble family, the nobility do not play a role of economic or political importance in the community under discussion. The bourgeoisie, however, are the town's top families, the owners of the community's principal economic enterprises, and they have a very high social and political prestige in the community. The bourgeoisie *radicale* are professionals or individuals of first generation wealth, career rather than family or lineage oriented. A typical member of the bourgeoisie *radicale* would be a doctor, an upper level bureaucrat, or the manager or skilled personnel employed by an outsider corporation.

The petty bourgeoisie are, as the name implies, the small merchants or shopkeepers and artisans. The majority of their stores and trades are inherited, and the majority of the enterprises are run by members of a family. The proletariat, numerically the most important class, is made up of the great mass of unpropertied and usually unskilled workers.

The number of voluntary associations in this urban community is impressive even when compared with American communities. As in Yankee City, individuals of different social classes in the French community do not belong to the same number of associations nor to the same associations.[4] Though the chart below blurs some overlapping of association membership, it does present a reasonably accurate picture of the concentration of different classes in particular associations. Though concentrated in rural areas outside the urban community under discussion, the nobility are included for purposes of comparison.

Nobility	horse society, agricultural organizations
Bourgeoisie	horse society, agricultural organizations, the "academy," museum society, Catholic charitable organizations, the Terrace Club
Bourgeoisie radicale	employer and professional associations, the Rotary Club, ski, aero, camera, cinema, and symphony societies
Petty bourgeoisie	trade and artisan associations and defense groups, sport clubs (cycling, football, etc.)
Proletariat	veterans organizations, political parties, trade unions

4   899 associations were "discovered" in Yankee City by Warner and his associates, but analysis was made of only 357. W. L. Warner and P. S. Lunt, *The Social Life of a Modern Community* (New Haven: Yale University Press, 1941), Volume I, p. 320.

The concentration by class is evident. The bourgeoisie is concentrated in religious, social and cultural associations; the bourgeoisie *radicale* in professional associations and social clubs. As the Terrace Club might be claimed as symbolic of the bourgeoisie, the Rotary Club is typically the organization of the well-to-do and mobile bourgeoisie *radicale*. Appropriately, the Terrace Club was founded nearly a century ago by the ancestors of current members of the club. Though the bourgeoisie participate little directly in economic or political organizations, this observer noted that the officials of most important economic organizations in the community were linked by economic or kin ties with important bourgeoisie families.

Though there exist many associations with memberships typically [composed of] tradesmen or artisans or working class, proportionately fewer individuals from these classes belong to associations. Many tradesmen and artisans have recently joined one of the two organizations formed to combat the corporation-owned department stores, but roughly half of the tradesmen and artisans belong to only one association or to none at all.

As in the rural community, members of the urban proletariat appear to have fewest associational affiliations of all the classes. Workers may be passive members of a veterans' organization, of a political party, or of a trade union, but the majority of workers do not even belong to a trade union, the association which might be assumed to be typically working class. Because trade union leaders will not give out their membership figures, it is impossible to obtain membership data, but, by averaging the best estimates from varying sources (government, union, and employers), it is probably accurate to state that not more than 40 to 45 percent of the community's workers belong to trade unions.

Because the number and kind of voluntary associations the individual joins are related to class status, the poll by the French polling group, quoted by Rose, which showed that only "41 percent of French adults" belong to one or more associations is not very significant.[5] This writer knew, for example, of no individuals of the three upper classes who did not have at least two associational affiliations, but there are plenty of working class and petty bourgeoisie men and women in the urban community without any associational memberships at all.

Associations are evidently fewer in number in France than in comparable urban centers of the United States. This is, however, less a measure of the importance of associations than a reflection of difference in function. Because of the relatively rigid French social structure, voluntary associations play less a mobility and integrative role than a defense or maintenance role. The community's present structure is not one to require a large number of associations; it is a stable structure with little mobility.[6]

The role of the association as a defense mechanism can be illustrated by a series of events which occurred during the writer's stay in the community. A new agricultural *syndicat* was organized following the end of World War II. Founded by Socialists and Communists, this organization aimed at improving the lot of the small peasant by applying trade union techniques (i.e., strikes, boycotts, etc.). In general, the department's large farmers were not associated with the new organization during its formative days. However, as the new *syndicat* grew more powerful and influential, the well-to-do farmers "got together," as a rural squire put it, "and decided that we could not allow the leaders of this organization to speak for agriculture." The large farmers joined the organization, put up their own popular candidates to run against Socialist or Communist district representatives, and had control of the *syndicat* within a year. Though satisfied with the old established agricultural organizations, which they controlled, the large landowners joined and assumed the leadership in yet another agricultural association in order to maintain their leadership in agricultural circles, a leadership threatened by a new, aggressive, and uncontrolled organization.

The great majority of associations in this urban community are obviously special interest or group defense organizations, or what Rose has called "expressive" associations. "Social influence" associations do, however, exist. There are at least 25 organizations specifically devoted to "improvement" or "welfare." These range from associations of former students or parents, aid-to-mothers and aid-to-families societies, to a protection of animals organization. Many, it is true, do not appear to go very deep nor involve the participation of very many individuals, but regular meetings are held, and members do have activities aimed at improving or assisting other individuals.

---

5 These proportions would appear to fit American urban communities, too. Komarovsky's study suggests that approximately 60 per cent of working-class Americans lack any organized group affiliation. As in the United States, it is Frenchmen of the middle class and upper socioeconomic levels who organize and join. Mirra Komarovsky, "The Voluntary Associations of Urban Dwellers," *American Sociological Review* (December, 1946) pp. 686-98. Similarly, Barber's study of associations in the United States reveals that "almost without exception . . . joiners were more numerous in the upper classes than in the lower classes." B. Barber, Mass Apathy and Voluntary Participation in the United States, unpublished PhD dissertation, Harvard University, 1948, quoted by M. Weinberg and O. E. Shabat (eds.), *Society and Man* (Englewood Cliffs: Prentice Hall, 1956), p. 32.

6 For example, when a member of an old established family was asked about forming another social club, his reply was: "Why have another club. We already have the Terrace Club."

This relative lack of participation is probably not unique to urban France, and it would be of interest to learn to what extent urban Americans are really involved (other than through financial contribution) in improvement and welfare organizations.

Welfare and improvement goals may, however, be sponsored by the "expressive" voluntary associations in this French community. Veterans' organizations raise funds to aid needy veterans and their families; the Rotary, like its mother organization in the United States, encourages community "improvements" and sends financial aid to disaster areas in Europe. Many of the purely athletic or social-cultural associations assist children to go to summer camps. A list of organizations directly concerned with "welfare" or "improvement" does not, therefore, give a complete list of associations participating in "social influence" activities.

There is perhaps a different value orientation among individuals belonging to French welfare associations. The welfare or improvement type of association in this French urban community does not conceive its function to be the "raising up" of the distressed so much as the mere temporary alleviation of immediate distress. This would seem to reflect, as Rose states, that government is expected to provide most welfare services, but also it may reflect the values of the French upper classes. Class statuses are taken for granted as being just and proper, and apparently, the French upper classes feel little guilt about the statuses of the mass of workers. For example, in this community, the bourgeoisie feel that by their rejection of the Church and the adoption of either Communism or Socialism, the workers have forfeited their right to assistance. The workers, according to the bourgeoisie, "drink and smoke their wages away anyway." Not only is there little "use" helping the workers, but these attitudes can be conveniently extended to justify low wages, for "higher wages would simply go into the hands of the café owners."

The term "extended family" and certain of the religious data used by Rose, it is felt, give an incomplete view. In tracing the decline of the "historic institutions" in France, Rose uses the term "extended family." This is defined as "the conjugal family (father, mother and children) plus any other relatives (grandparents, uncles, aunts, cousins) who live with them or are in close contact with them." The term has been used and misused often enough by both anthropologists and sociologists, but as used by Rose, it is so vague and inclusive as to be meaningless. This writer knows of both urban and rural proletariat families which have been "extended" to include miscellaneous kin or of tradesmen and professional men who have "extended" their families to include aged parents and often other relatives.

This type of residential grouping is, however, quite different from the lineage type of grouping in which a son inherits his father's trade, business, or farm and lives and works under the guidance and control of his father until the property is transferred. Both types of extension are common in both urban and rural France, but the relationships involved (authority, security, affection) are quite different. The "extended" family in its original sense is still the family type of the property-oriented nobility, bourgeoisie, petty bourgeoisie and peasantry; the non-propertied French family, urban and rural, may include miscellaneous kin, but it tends to lack structural continuity.

This writer is also skeptical about the utility of Rose's data on "religious influence" as taken from surveys by French public opinion groups and from French sociologists. These data, it is claimed, indicate that the Catholic church "does not have much hold over a majority of the French today." The survey quoted was based on respondents' answers to such questions as "belief in God" and "attendance at mass." At stake is the question of how accurately such a survey measures the "hold" of the Church on individual Frenchmen.

In the rural community discussed above, it was extremely rare that this writer could count more than five male heads at Sunday mass. Additionally, since 1946, over 25 percent of the population had consistently voted Communist. Though the question "belief in God" was not subjected to polling, this writer knows from personal experience that a very large proportion of the male population would deny such belief. However, in this rural community, only one individual had ever been buried without benefit of church rites (and even the Communists say this was to have been "buried like a dog"); no one has failed to take his First Communion, and Communists and non-Communists alike send their children faithfully to classes in religious instruction given by the parish priest. The questions "attendance at mass habitually" or the "last two Sundays" would not adequately measure the "hold" of the Church in a community where, even though (except at Toussaint and Easter) males rarely enter the church, everyone is confirmed, baptized, married and buried by the Church.

A similar conformity to the rites of the Church is common in the urban community. As in most regions of France, males are conspicuously few at Sunday mass. Probably fewer urban Frenchmen conform to the rites than in the rural community, but most children take their First Communion and the wives of local Communists go to mass almost as faithfully as those of the local bourgeoisie. A priest told me that "last week" he had taken the confession of the wife of the departmental leader of the Communist Party— "who would come himself, if he dared." As an index of religious influence, questions as to belief in God or attendance at mass are not accurate measurements of the "hold" of the Church in contemporary France.

CONCLUSION

Rose's main thesis is, as we have seen, that community, church, and family have traditionally satisfied the needs of "fellowship, security and an explanation of and influence on the forces controlling the social world." Following the Industrial Revolution and the consequent decline of these institutions, equivalent institutions were required. Because of governmental repression of associational forms of organization in France, the French, it is claimed, have turned to such substitute institutions as the café, the trade union, political parties, the conjugal family, and public parks.

The writer is not concerned with the validity of the postulated social-psychological needs, but simply to what extent data from his own studies in urban and rural French communities fit Rose's statements on the role of the association in France. Because both communities are located in a particular region of France, no claim is made that they are representative of all France.

The two communities evidently differ sharply in the sheer quantity of associations. As the same social classes can be distinguished in the rural community as in the urban community, social class in itself is not the significant variable. That the urban community has more associations than the rural community must be, therefore, in large part a function of the sheer numbers of inhabitants.

In the urban community the relationship between social class and associational affiliation is very close. This relationship does not exist in the rural community because there are too few middle- and upper-class Frenchmen to form organized groups. In the urban community, however, each class tends to have its unique special interest association as well as associations in which the members of each class engage in more or less exclusive social, fraternal, cultural or athletic activities.

The urban community can count close to 300 voluntary associations. While this number is not comparable to the quantity of associations in American urban communities, 300 associations are an impressive number of organizations for a provincial town. This number does not, moreover, seem compatible with Rose's statement that associations are not numerous in France. It is apparently true that there are proportionately more "expressive" than "reform" or "welfare" associations in France. This is related, as Rose suggests, to the French tradition of looking to government for action in matters concerning public health and welfare. Perhaps of equal importance, however, is the rigidity of French social structure. If the two communities known to this writer are at all representative, the French upper classes tend to take for granted the fixity of statuses of the lower classes and feel little compulsion to welfare or improvement activities.

It might be argued that French social structure has not required the upper classes to maintain a large number of associations. Perhaps the majority of existing economic associations are oriented towards protecting or maintaining special interests. If a new or competing association arises, the present leaders in the community attempt to neutralize, or, on last resort, join and "take over" such an association. The association in the United States may be a mechanism for integrating or mediating change, but in the French community, associations appear to be oriented toward the prevention of change.

That community, church, and family have "declined," necessitating equivalent institutions, seems to need at least some qualifications. Among the propertied classes in both the urban and rural community attachment to the traditional institutions remains strong. The nobility, the bourgeoisie, the petty bourgeoisie, and the peasantry still adhere in large part to the community, the church, and to the "extended" family. It is among the growing proletariat and the career-oriented and rootless bourgeoisie *radicale* that the historic institutions are weakest. Among the latter, the association would seem to play a role nearly equivalent to that among the middle classes in the United States. Among the proletariat, some workers have substituted Communist or Socialist party or the trade union, but the majority seem to have found no equivalent other than the café. It is perhaps worth noting that the need for equivalents is greatest among the workers, the class which has fewest associations.

PART THREE

THE NATURE OF LEADERSHIP

Leadership can be viewed either as a personal attribute of the individual leader or as a social relationship between leaders and followers. The selection by Murray Ross and Charles Hendry summarizes the various ways of conceiving leadership in everyday conversation and in the research by social scientists. They classify the research literature into studies of the personal traits of leaders, studies of leadership as a role in a group, and studies of leadership as a response to a situation. They conclude that a fully adequate description of leadership must synthesize the three viewpoints. This scheme applies to the leader of a voluntary association as it does to any other leader: each of his acts is a function of his personality traits, the expectations and structure of his organization, and the pressures and opportunities of the immediate situation.

THE TRAIT, GROUP, AND SITUATIONAL THEORIES*

Murray G. Ross and Charles E. Hendry

For present purposes three broad classifications will be used in examining conceptions of leadership. The more closely one studies these viewpoints, the more apparent it becomes that they overlap. Indeed, it is when this overlapping is denied or ignored that difficulty arises. It is the conviction and contention of the authors that any truly adequate conception of leadership involves elements from all three conceptions. Attempts to separate and insulate such interdependent elements are as futile as they are arbitrary. Leadership is an interactional phenomenon, and it is this view that constitutes the thesis of this book.

LEADERSHIP AS TRAITS WITHIN THE INDIVIDUAL LEADER

It was inevitable that the earliest studies of leadership should concentrate on the leader as a person. For centuries leadership was in the nature of an inheritance. Leaders were born, not made. Leadership was thought of as being a monopoly of the aristocracy. With the overthrow of the feudal nobility and the rise of equalitarian democracy, the emergence of a new leadership demonstrated that leaders are made, not born. Leadership, it appeared, could be learned. Whichever way one regarded leadership, however, "the conditions which permitted an individual to become or remain a leader were often assumed to be qualities of the individual." [1] This gradually took the

form of a theory, the "great man" theory of leadership, which stated that it was men of a distinctive stamp, predestined by their possession of unusual traits, who led events and molded situations. Impressionistic studies, based largely on biographical documents, gradually gave way to more sophisticated investigation of leaders in action. The study of the personality of leaders became a phase of the dominant preoccupation of psychologists. Between the two World Wars countless studies were made to discover personality traits uniquely and invariably associated with leadership. Some sought a unitary leadership trait capable of characterizing leaders wherever found. Others looked for a constellation of traits constituting general leadership capacity. Still others hoped to uncover traits whether of temperament, disposition, or aptitude that would prove invariably to be associated with certain occupations involving leadership functions.

A goodly number of reviews have been undertaken of the many studies made in this search for leadership traits. One of the best-known, earlier surveys of leadership trait studies, made by Bird in 1940,[2] found seventy-nine traits mentioned in twenty different studies, only 5 per cent of which were common to four or more investigations. The most comprehensive and the most recent survey was made by Stogdill in 1948.[3] The more commonly identified, so-called "leadership traits" reported by Stogdill include the following: (1) physical and constitutional factors:

* From Murray G. Ross and Charles E. Hendry, *New Understandings of Leadership* (New York: The Association Press, 1957), pp. 17-32. Reprinted with the permission of the authors and publisher.

1 Alvin W. Gouldner (editor), *Studies in Leadership* (New York: Harper & Brothers, 1950), p. 21.

2 Charles Bird, *Social Psychology* (New York: Appleton-Century-Crofts, 1940).

3 R. M. Stogdill, "Personal Factors Associated with Leadership," *Journal of Psychology*, Volume 25 (1948), pp. 35-71.

height; weight; physique; energy; health; appearance; (2) intelligence; (3) self-confidence; (4) sociability; (5) will (initiative, persistence, ambition); (6) dominance; and (7) surgency (i.e., talkativeness, cheerfulness, geniality, enthusiasm, expressiveness, alertness, and originality).

The most discerning examination of the relation between these personality traits and leadership demonstrates a complete failure to find any consistent pattern of traits which will characterize leaders.[4] Gouldner provides an excellent discussion of the inadequacies of the trait approach.[5] He points out that traits are seldom listed in any order of importance. Frequently traits mentioned in a single list are not mutually exclusive. Traits associated with achieving leadership are not separated from those associated with maintaining leadership. One is not informed whether, and which, leadership traits exist before and which develop after leadership is assumed. In addition, one is reminded that the same "trait" will function differently in personalities which are differently organized.

Contrary to the guiding assumptions underlying traits studies, there would clearly seem to be no one leadership type of personality. On the other hand, and this is strongly confirmed by a quite recent study reported by Borgatta, Bales, and Couch in which they undertook to test four hypotheses relating to "the great man theory of leadership," [6] there is considerable evidence to suggest that "member personalities do make a difference to group performance, and there is every reason to believe that they do affect that aspect of the group's behavior to which the leadership concept applies." [7] Deficiencies in research methodology —inadequate means of measuring basic personality dimensions, failure to concentrate on a large enough sample of similar groups, and unwillingness to focus on particular leadership roles—according to Gibb, may well account for the failure to establish a definitive relation between personality and leadership.

Gouldner suggests that one of the possible reasons why personality traits common to different leaders have not emerged is that so many of the studies made along these lines have employed an erroneous concept of "traits." All too frequently personality or psychological traits have been spoken of as if they were similar to physical traits, that is, relatively permanent and consistent in their manifestations. This obviously is not the case. Clearly some more adequate concept is needed. Gouldner suggests that the psychoanalytical concept of "character trait," meaning a "deep-going, persisting motivation—to some degree unconscious—which may produce variable behavior, but variable within limits," may be helpful. "Traits so conceived are not so likely to undergo significant modification due to role or group needs in adult groups." [8] One of the most illuminating expositions of this basic approach is to be found in the experimental work of Fritz Redl, much of which is built upon these theoretical foundations.

Redl's approach combines a highly sensitive awareness of group and situational dynamics along with a penetrating analysis of the personality and interpersonal patterns of group members.[9] It is for this reason that Redl cannot be confined exclusively in this first "theory" category. Because he feels that the term "leader" is no longer appropriate, he uses the term "central person" not in conventional terms, as a "strong" personality, but rather as one with "group psychological flexibility," enabling such a person to serve as a dynamic focus around whom group formative processes, particularly those producing group integration, take place. Ten types of central persons and group-integrative situations are proposed by Redl. These are:

1. *The "Patriarchical Sovereign"*: here the group is integrated because they incorporate the super-ego, or conscience, of the central person into their own. Wanting his approval, they adopt his standards of right and wrong. They thereby come to hold similar values and are able to orient themselves to each other.

2. *The "Leader"*: In this situation the group is integrated because the individuals want to *be like* the central person, rather than because they accept the values for which he stands. They accept his authority because he sympathizes with their urges, or possibly illicit goals. Wanting to be like him establishes a common bond among the members, which furthers integration.

3. *The "Tyrant"*: Here, too, as in the "patriarch," the group is integrated because they accept the values of the central person. Unlike the first type, however, they do so out of fear, rather than love. The ends are similar, but the individual's motivation is different.

4. *The "Love Object"*: The central person is not idealized; the members do not accept his values, nor do they aspire to be like him. The group is integrated because they love the same person.

5. *The "Object of Aggression"*: The situation is similar to number 4, except that the central person

4 Cecil A. Gibb, "Leadership," in Gardner Lindzey (editor), *Handbook of Social Psychology* (Cambridge, Mass.: Addison-Wesley Publishing Company, 1954), Volume II, p. 889.
5 Gouldner, *op. cit.*, pp. 23-49.
6 Edgar F. Borgatta, Robert F. Bales, and Arthur S. Couch, "Some Findings Relevant to the Great Man Theory of Leadership," *American Sociological Review*, Volume 19, Number 6 (December 1954), pp. 755-759.
7 Gibb, *op. cit.*, p. 889.

8 Gouldner, *op. cit.*, pp. 40-41.
9 Fritz Redl, "Group Emotion and Leadership," *Psychiatry*, Volume V, Number 4 (November 1942), pp. 573-596.

integrates the group because he is the common object of their *aggression*, rather than their love.

6. *The "Organizer"*: Neither love, hatred nor fear of the central person is the basis of group integration in this case. By facilitating the members' satisfaction of "forbidden pleasures" the central person minimizes their inner conflicts and guilt feelings. Because the organizer "services" those of the group's common ends which are non-legitimate, he becomes a focus for integration.

7. *The "Seducer"*: Integration is enhanced when the central person commits an "initiatory act," satisfying the socially disapproved ends of the individuals around him. These individuals ordinarily may be inhibited from pursuing these ends by their super-ego. By doing it *first*, the "seducer" enables the others to engage in the forbidden action openly by providing them with some justification for their own behavior and thereby minimizing their guilt feelings. (As later indicated, some of the success of the fascist agitator is understandable, in that light.)

8. *The "Hero"*: Contrary to the "seducer," the "hero" integrates the group by encouraging the manifestation of socially approved action. The "hero's" initiatory act is courageous, enabling other individuals to cast off their anxieties, and permitting them to take a stand in favor of approved values.

9. *The "Bad Influence"*: While similar to the "seducer," there is in this case no initiatory act integrating the group. The "bad influence" is one not inhibited or blocked by his conscience, in the same way that others are. Those of his drives which are socially forbidden do not meet the resistance of a formidable super-ego. He simply pursues these ends without conflict and "infects" the others so that they may do likewise without guilt. Since they have a common mode of solving their internal conflict, the individual's relationships with each other may be integrated.

10. *The "Good Example"*: Similar to the "bad influence," this central person integrates the group by encouraging the opposite kind of solution to their conflicts. The "good example's" lack of conflict leads *him* in the direction of the socially approved ends. The *conscience* of the others is reinforced by his actions.

As we review this "trait theory" of leadership it will be noted that the dominant tendency is to assume that leadership is something that resides in an individual, something that he brings to a group, and something presumably that is capable, under almost any circumstances, of producing the same results in different groups and in different situations. There can be little doubt that to perform leadership functions a person must bring with him, as part of his personality and character structure, qualities of being and capacities for doing that connect with what others bring to the group and to the situation. The importance of what such a person is and does is not denied. What is crucial in operative terms is whether what he brings meshes with what others bring to the group, whether in fact the psychological gears mesh, and in meshing produce the leadership energy required by the group. It is because Redl sees this so clearly that our reference to his analysis of the "central person" provides a particularly fitting transition to a consideration of the second major conception of leadership—leadership as a function of the group.

LEADERSHIP AS A FUNCTION OF THE GROUP

Just as it was natural, under the circumstances that obtained earlier in the century, for students of leadership to concentrate on the personality traits of leaders in general, so it was natural, as the problem of leadership became redefined, to direct attention to leadership traits in specific groups. The greater the concentration on actual groups and on groups in action, the greater became the need to observe behavior, to isolate leadership acts, and to describe interaction between leaders and nonleaders. Soon it became evident that "for most groups the interindividual relationships *within* a single group are determined by the structure of the group to a considerable degree rather than by the personality of the individuals." [10] Leadership becomes defined more as a structure, less as a person.

This transition in conceptualization is not unrelated to research method. If to lead is to engage in leadership acts, then it becomes necessary to devise techniques to observe, describe, and categorize such behavior. And this is precisely what was done.

Attempts first were made to develop categories of leadership behavior by examining the behavior of quite outstanding leaders. In some studies, members of air squadrons were asked to identify persons with whom they preferred to fly and to say why, also to recall and to describe incidents in which Air Force officers had behaved effectively or ineffectively. Related research has been undertaken in experimental groups organized under university supervision to observe the behavior of persons designated to function as leaders and to compare it with that of persons who emerged as leaders in similar groups where no leader was appointed. Steadily, as theoretical and technical research approaches have been improved, there has been a corresponding refinement in the determination of the dimensions of leader behavior. Of special inter-

[10] David Krech and Richard S. Crutchfield, *Theory and Problems of Social Psychology* (New York: McGraw-Hill Book Company, 1948), p. 401.

est in this respect is the work of Hemphill and his associates at Ohio State University, also Cattell at the University of Illinois. At present Hemphill is completing a comprehensive memorandum on "A Proposed Theory of Leadership in Small Groups." His efforts are being directed toward theory construction and research methodology in the study of leadership phenomena. Hemphill's definition, "To lead is to engage in an act that initiates a structure in the interaction as part of the process of solving a mutual problem," gives some indication of his approach to the problem. Cattell seems to go even further when he asserts that "all group functions are leadership functions." According to this view one would rarely, if ever, properly speak of "the leader" of a group. A more precise terminology would seem to be "the leadership structure of a group." [11]

Cartwright and Zander summarize the general point of view here represented quite clearly:

> Research conducted within this orientation does not attempt to find certain invariant traits of leaders. Rather, it seeks to discover what actions are required by groups under various conditions if they are to achieve their objectives, and how different group members take part in these group actions. Leadership is viewed as the performance of those acts which help the group achieve its objective. Such acts may be termed group functions . . . In principle, leadership may be performed by one or many members of the group.[12]

Among the many group functions that have been isolated, two appear to be basic in their relation to leadership: (1) goal achievement and (2) group maintenance. Hemphill and his colleagues Halpin and Winer[13] have postulated nine "dimensions of leader behavior": initiation, membership, representation, integration, organization, domination, communication, recognition, and production. These in turn have been subjected to measurement through the use of Leader-Behavior-Description scales in an attempt to discover dimensions that may have general validity. These studies begin by defining leadership tentatively as "behavior of an individual when he is directing the activities of a group toward a shared goal." This is quite similar to the view expressed by Cartwright and Zander of leadership as "the performance of those acts which help the group achieve its objective." They go on to suggest, more specifically, that "leadership consists of such acts by group members

as those which aid in setting group goals, moving the group toward its goals, improving the quality of the interactions among the members, building the cohesiveness of the group, or making resources available to the group.[14]

Members of the group when performing leadership functions play many different roles. Various inventories of leadership roles have been suggested. Probably the listing developed by Krech and Crutchfield is the most comprehensive. They list the following, thirteen in all: executive, planner, policy maker, expert, external group representative, controller of internal relationships, purveyor of rewards and punishments, arbitrator and mediator, and examplar, also symbol, surrogate, father figure, and scapegoat. Redl, writing in the psychoanalytic tradition, and whose theoretical orientation belongs essentially in the "group function" category, proposes a rather different formulation relating mainly to the group's formation, maintenance, and disruption. He conceives of these functions as operating through such mechanisms as identification, cathexis, guilt reduction, impulse control, and incorporation of superego. Gouldner has made an interesting suggestion which belongs in this context. He proposes the study of a new unit of leadership.

> . . . when investigating the personalities of leaders, we are perhaps overly influenced by an individualist bias. It may be that for certain purposes a useful unit of examination would be all the leaders of the group, treated as an entity, rather than the individual leader.[15]

Quite a similar view has been expressed by Thelen in writing about "The Leadership Team." Thelen observes:

> On the whole, in the thinking of students of leadership, the ideal of the one-man leader, the paterfamilias, is on the way out. There is some doubt that the monolithic leader, working out his lonely destiny entirely by himself, ever actually existed [16] . . .

In essence the view represented in this second conception of leadership is that it is in the nature of a group property. Leadership resides not primarily and certainly not exclusively in an individual leader. Rather, leadership is viewed as a function of group structure. We would do well, if we follow this line of analysis, to speak of the leadership structure of a group and not of the leader or the leaders of a group. To formulate and to achieve its goals and at the same time to maintain itself as a well-integrated and effective group, many different functions and roles

11 Raymond B. Cattell, "Determining Syntality Dimensions as a Basis for Morale and Leadership Measurement," in Harold Guetzkow (editor), *Groups, Leadership and Men* (Pittsburgh: Carnegie Press, 1951), pp. 16-27.
12 Dorwin Cartwright and Alvin Zander (editors), *Group Dynamics, Research and Theory* (Evanston, Ill.: Row, Peterson & Company, 1953), p. 538.
13 A. W. Halpin and B. J. Winer, *The Leadership Behavior of the Airplane Commander* (Columbus: Ohio State University Research Foundation, 1952).

14 Cartwright and Zander, *op. cit.,* p. 538.
15 Gouldner, *op. cit.,* p. 45.
16 Herbert A. Thelen, *Dynamics of Groups at Work* (Chicago: University of Chicago Press, 1954).

must be performed, and these get lodged with different persons in terms of how individuals and the group perceive the needs of the group and the usefulness of given individual members at different times.

One can readily see that this "group property" conception of leadership adds a new and important dimension to our understanding of the phenomena of leadership. In doing so, however, let it be noted that it does not deny or discard the view that what individuals bring with them to the group is basic. Individuals constitute essential elements and set certain limits to the development of the leadership structure. Let it also be noted that the group itself as a group sets limits, and particularly so as circumstances and settings change through time. It is for this reason, therefore, that we turn now to a third view of leadership—leadership as a function of the situation.

LEADERSHIP AS A FUNCTION OF THE SITUATION

Dissatisfaction with the trait approach has given rise not only to an examination of group functions and their relation to leadership, but also to the situation in which the group is located.

> A. J. Murphy, emphasizing the relative fluidity of leadership traits, points out that the "self-confidence" of a work leader may disappear if his group is placed in a parlor situation. Or that a leader noted for his "dominance" may become "shy" when placed in a situation in which his *skills* are not useful. Thus not only must the *group* in which the leader operates be considered, but also the *situation* which the group encounters.[17]

The situational approach to the study of leadership, according to Gibb, involves four elements:

> The situation includes: (i) the structure of interpersonal relations within a group, (ii) group or syntality characteristics such as those defined by the group dimensions already discussed, (iii) characteristics of the total culture in which the group exists and from which group members have been drawn, and (iv) the physical conditions and the task with which the group is confronted [18] . . .

After discussing several experiments in which the same groups were observed working on six different tasks: a reasoning task, an intellectual construction task, a clerical task, a discussion task, a motor cooperation task, and a mechanical assembly task, Gibb suggests:

> The important suggestion appears to be that a group member achieves the status of a group leader for the time being in proportion as he participates in group activities and demonstrates his capacity for

contributing more than others to the group achievement of the group goal. It is known that the situation is especially liable to change through changes in goals, changes in syntality, changes in interpersonal relations, the entrance of new members and the departure of others, pressures from other groups, and so on. Since individual personality characteristics are, by contrast, very stable, it is to be expected that group leadership, if unrestricted by the conscious hierarchical structuration of the group, will be fluid and will pass from one member to another along the line of those particular personality traits which, by virtue of the situation and its demands, become, for the time being, traits of leadership. This is why the leader in one situation is not necessarily the leader, even of the same group, in another different situation.[19]

NEW TRENDS IN LEADERSHIP THEORY

For a considerable period now the trait theory of leadership has been unfashionable. The pendulum of research and theory on leadership has swung, as we have seen, to the opposite pole, an emphasis on situation or field theory. We are beginning, however, to see a swing back of the pendulum, and strangely enough some of the effective impetus is originating with the situationists themselves . . . Studies being made by social scientists who work on the explicit assumption that "leadership is always relative to the situation" (situationist) or that "leadership is the product of interpersonal interaction and not of the attributes residing within persons" (sociometrist) are turning up findings which make it extremely difficult to deny the operation and the importance of certain personality characteristics. Intelligence and psychosexual factors are specifically placed in this category by Brown.[20] Gouldner concludes, on the basis of a careful review of the evidence, that "perhaps the most which may be said is that lower than (group) average intelligence inhibits access to leadership, but higher than average intelligence is no guarantee of leadership." [21]

Despite her own contrary predilections, the sociometrist Jennings reports finding certain constant characteristics of persons in leadership roles.

> In a population so large as that of the test-community, the varieties of leadership are manifold. Nevertheless, in *personality a number of characteristics of leaders stand out as common attributes.* Each leader "improves" from the point of view of the membership, through one method or the other, the social milieu. Each widens the social field for participation of others (and indirectly her own social space) by ingratiating them into activities, introducing new activities, and by fostering tolerance on the part of one member towards another. Each leader shows a feeling for when to censure and when to

---

17 Gouldner, *op. cit.*, p. 27.
18 Gibb, *op. cit.*, p. 27.

19 *Ibid.*, p. 902.
20 J. F. Brown, *Psychology and the Social Order* (New York: McGraw-Hill Book Company, 1936), p. 347.
21 Gouldner, *op. cit.*, p. 33.

praise . . . No leader is invariably a "pleasant" person . . . instead each is definite in her stand and will fight for what she considers "right" . . . each leader appears to succeed in controlling her own moods at least to the extent of not inflicting negative feelings of depression or anxiety upon others. Each appears to hold her own counsel and not to confide her personal worries except to a selected friend or two . . . Each appears able to establish rapport quickly and effectively with a wide range of other personalities . . . Each appears to possess to a greater or less degree unusual capacity to identify with others[22]. . .

A SYNTHESIS OF THE THEORIES

Each of the three theories of leadership discussed briefly above has a good deal to support it. Yet none of them, taken separately, provides an adequate theory of leadership. One may accept the validity of the reasoning inherent in each, and yet not be satisfied that any one provides a complete theory of leadership.

Surely an adequate theory of leadership involves at least all three of these concepts. The leader undoubtedly has some special traits or characteristics which

distinguish him from other members of the group regardless of the task or the structure of the group. Similarly, the task on which the group is engaged certainly affects the type of leader chosen or selected and the behavior of that leader. Further, it is both reasonable and consistent with experience to claim that more than one person may perform leadership functions in the sense that many in the group may contribute to goal achievement and that leadership is, to this extent, a "group property." This suggests that leadership is a shifting and dynamic concept that is not adequately explained or described by any one of these theories.

We may ask further whether the combination of these three theories, which are not, of course, mutually exclusive, would provide a sufficient description of leadership. This would imply that while there are a variety of leadership functions, the selection or election of a central person to perform some of these functions is dependent upon the nature of the task, the character of the group, the qualities of the members of the group, and the relations of group members.

[22] Helen Hall Jennings, *Leadership and Isolation* (New York: Longmans, Green & Company, 1943), pp. 203-204.

Most discussions of the merits and demerits of various styles of leadership are based on common sense impressions of how they succeeded in a few settings familiar to the author. Social scientists have attempted to test some of these impressions by means of laboratory experiments or systematic observations. Their goal has been to discover the effects of various types of leadership upon different kinds of groups. Since they are most convenient to study, chiefly small groups have been examined until now, although some are real-life units in larger organizations such as factories and the armed forces.

The selection by Hanan C. Selvin summarizes the results of several studies by sociologists and social psychologists. Some of the research was done by controlled experiments with human subjects in laboratories in schools or colleges, other studies were performed by means of social scientists' observations in real life settings. The reader can find detailed descriptions of the research technique in the original sources. Two themes recur in the studies summarized by Selvin: work will not be accomplished without initiative by the leader, but morale, personal relations, and even work itself will be damaged by inept autocratic control. The problem for the leader of a voluntary association, like that of any leader, is to achieve the combination of initiative and humane consideration that is best for his circumstances.

FIVE STUDIES OF THE EFFECTS OF LEADERSHIP STYLE*

Hanan C. Selvin

AUTOCRATIC, DEMOCRATIC, AND LAISSEZ-FAIRE LEADERSHIP: THE IOWA STUDIES[1]

Probably the most widely known investigations of leadership, the work of Kurt Lewin and his colleagues at the University of Iowa during the 1930's may be said to have launched the empirical study of leadership. Unlike many pioneer studies, their procedures and analyses can still serve as models of scientific research. In the most elaborate of their researches, four hobby clubs were organized among selected ten-year-old boys, who were as similar as possible in relevant physical, social, and intellectual characteristics. The adult leader of each group, a collaborator of the experimenters, was instructed to behave in an autocratic, a democratic, or a laissez-faire manner, and the behavior of the boys was carefully observed and recorded.

Ingenious and precise experimental controls made it possible to attribute the differences in the boys' behavior to the prescribed actions of the leaders rather than to such factors as the personalities of the leaders or events external to the experimental groups. Typical of the differences noted were a greater amount of aggressiveness in the autocratic groups, both in reacting to the leader and in interacting with the other boys, and greater attention to "group-minded" suggestions and "work-minded" conversations in the laissez-faire and democratic groups. Laissez-faire and democratic leadership also turned out to differ significantly: a lower level of psychological involvement in the laissez-faire groups resulted in less work and poorer work than in the democratic groups.

"DOMINATIVE" AND "INTEGRATIVE" TEACHERS: THE ANDERSON STUDIES[2]

These studies may be considered a replication of the Lewin experiments in a real-life situation, with naturally-occurring variations in leadership rather than experimentally-manipulated group atmospheres. Carefully trained observers characterized the behavior of teachers and their pupils in several classrooms

1 The most recent of the several reports of this study is Ralph K. White and Ronald O. Lippitt, *Autocracy and Democracy* (New York: Harper & Brothers, 1960).

2 Harold H. Anderson et al., "Studies of Teachers' Classroom Personalities," *Applied Psychology Monographs* (Stanford: Stanford University Press, 1945 and 1946, Numbers 6, 8, and 11.)

94 | *Nature of leadership*

as either "dominative" or "socially integrative." From the descriptions given, dominative behavior by the teacher seems to be similar to the autocratic leadership of the Iowa investigations, and integrative behavior to resemble democratic leadership. The principal finding was that integrative behavior by the teacher leaders to integrative and procedure behavior by the pupils and that dominative teachers correspondingly have a high proportion of dominative and unproductive behavior in their classrooms.

As in the Lewin experiments, Anderson and his colleagues took pains to show that these effects were not peculiar to the particular teachers and students who were studied. Since the actions of the teachers could not be experimentally manipulated, the researchers undertook an elaborate series of replications; the initial results were confirmed in different grades of the same school, in different types of schools (departmental and nondepartmental), and for the same pupils when they changed from one teacher to another. The extent to which these researches complement those of Lewin is all the more noteworthy in view of the apparent lack of familiarity with the Iowa studies in Anderson's group; at least, there is no mention of the Iowa experiments in Anderson's three monographs.[3]

PARTICIPATORY AND SUPERVISORY LEADERSHIP: PRESTON AND HEINTZ[4]

Following the Lewin tradition of experimental groups, Preston and Heintz adopted two important innovations. (1) Instead of an adult leader chosen by the experimenters, the leaders were elected by the members of each group and were subsequently instructed in the appropriate experimental behavior. (2) The dependent variable was the group's ability to achieve consensus on the ranking of twelve potential Presidential candidates, rather than the individual activities of the boys in the Iowa investigations. Only two kinds of leadership were considered. "Participatory" leaders took an active part in the process of group decision, making sure that all topics were discussed with as little prejudice as possible and encouraging contributions from all members of their groups. The responsibility of "supervisory" leaders was limited to "seeing that the work was done with reasonable expedition." They were instructed to bring the group back to its task if necessary, but otherwise not to guide the discussion or to stimulate activity among the members.

Participatory leadership resembles the democratic group atmosphere of the Iowa studies, and supervisory leadership the laissez-faire atmosphere. Many replications of the original experiment confirmed the principal findings: members of groups with participatory leadership were more likely to change their opinions to agree with consensus of the group, and they were also more satisfied with the consensus than were the members of supervisory groups.[5]

SUPERVISION AND PRODUCTIVITY: THE MICHIGAN STUDIES[6]

The Survey Research Center of the University of Michigan had studied the relationships between the actions of first-line supervisors and the behavior of the workers under them in a variety of settings—the home office of an insurance company, section gangs of a railroad, agencies of the federal government, and different kinds of factories. The general procedure was to classify each work group as "high productivity" or "low productivity" and to relate these differences to the behavior of the supervisors.

High-production supervisors differed from low-production supervisors in three principal ways: (1) They spent more time in planning, supervision, and other kinds of leader behavior and less time in working alongside their subordinates at the same tasks. (2) Although they behaved more like leaders than did the low-production supervisors, the greater freedom they accorded to their subordinates resulted in higher morale in the work groups, as well as higher productivity—although high morale and high productivity did not go together consistently. (3) High-production supervisors were more likely to be "employee-oriented" and less likely to be "production-oriented." They tried to create a "supportive personal relationship" between themselves and the members of their work groups; they took a greater interest in their subordinates and were more understanding and less punitive.

These findings confirm and extend the Lewin conclusions. Productive and satisfying work conditions are most likely to result from leader behavior that combines effective coordination, a large measure of individual freedom in routine decisions, and respect for the dignity of the individual—all characteristic of

Another study of the effects of teachers' behavior on their pupils found results comparable to those of Anderson. Morris L. Cogan, "Theory and Design of a Study of Teacher–Pupil Interaction," *Harvard Educational Review*, Volume 26 (1956), pp. 315-342.
[4] Malcolm G. Preston and Roy K. Heintz, "Effects of Participatory vs. Supervisory Leadership on Group Judgment," *Journal of Abnormal and Social Psychology*, Volume XLIV (1949), pp. 345-355.

[5] Another replication with a different type of group is reported in A. Paul Hare, "Small Group Discussions with Participatory and Supervisory Leadership," *Journal of Abnormal and Social Psychology*, Volume XLVIII (1953), pp. 273-275.
[6] Robert L. Kahn and Daniel Katz, "Leadership Practices in Relation to Productivity and Morale," in Dorwin Cartwright and Alvin Zander (eds.), *Group Dynamics* (Evanston, Ill.: Row, Peterson & Company, 1953), pp. 612-618.

"democratic" leadership rather than "laissez-faire" or "autocratic" leadership.[7]

MULTIDIMENSIONAL DESCRIPTIONS OF LEADER BEHAVIOR: THE OHIO STATE STUDIES[8]

In 1945 the Personnel Research Board of the Ohio State University began a ten-year program of research on leadership. Among the major tasks of the program was the identification of basic dimensions for describing the behavior of leaders in business, educational, and military organizations. Several sets of dimensions were identified at one time or another in this series of studies; here the most relevant dimensions are those identified by Halpin and Winer in a study of aircraft commanders, as rated by the members of their crews.[9] In all, four dimensions were found, but only two of these, "Consideration" and "Initiating Structure," are empirically important. Consideration is associated with "behavior indicative of friendship, mutual trust, respect, and warmth in the relationship between the aircraft commander and his crew." It is negatively associated with "authoritarian and impersonal" behavior by the commander. Initiating Structure measures the extent to which the aircraft commander "organizes and defines the relationship between himself and the members of his crew." [10] Most succinctly expressed, scores on these two composite variables represent the "human relations" and the "get the work out" dimensions.[11]

Dimensions of leader behavior similar to Consideration and Initiating Structure have been found in each of the other studies discussed in this chapter. There is one important difference, however. The Ohio State researchers did not set forth these dimensions *a priori*. They began with nine tentative dimensions of leadership, for each of which ten to twenty specific indicators were developed. For example, one of the nine dimensions was "Membership," which is measured by "the frequency with which a leader mixes with the group, stresses informal interaction between himself and members, or interchanges personal services with members." [12] It turned out, however, that these nine dimensions were not statistically independent, but could be represented rather well by the two major dimensions of Consideration and Initiating Structure defined above.

Another significant departure of the Ohio State studies was the recognition that these two dimensions do not refer to types of leaders, but rather to types of behavior. Any one leader may have a high score on Consideration and a high score on Initiating Structure, a low score on both dimensions, or any other combination of scores. This typology of leader behavior turns out to be significantly associated with the behavior of the followers. In Halpin's study of air crews,[13] high performance and high morale among members of the crew were more likely when the commander had high scores on both Consideration and Initiating Structure than for any other pattern of scores, a result theoretically similar to those found in the other studies discussed above, but based on a more careful analysis of the nature of leadership behavior.[14]

[7] Argyle and his collaborators have summarized the literature on social factors affecting productivity and have carried out a study that replicates the Michigan investigations of supervision and productivity. Michael Argyle, Godfrey Gardner, and Frank Cioffi, "The Measurement of Supervisory Methods," *Human Relations*, Volume X (1957), pp. 295-313; and "Supervisory Methods Related to Productivity, Absenteeism, and Labor Turnover," *Human Relations*, Volume XI (1958), pp. 23-40.

[8] Ralph M. Stogdill and Alvin E. Coons (editors), *Leader Behavior: Its Description and Measurement* (Columbus: Bureau of Business Research, The Ohio State University, 1957).

[9] Andrew W. Halpin and B. James Winer, "A Factorial Study of the Leader Behavior Descriptions," in Stogdill and Coons, *op. cit.*, pp. 39-51.

[10] *Ibid.*, p. 42.

[11] Carroll L. Shartle, *Executive Performance and Leadership* (Englewood Cliffs, N.J.: Prentice-Hall Inc., 1956), p. 120.

[12] John K. Hemphill and Alvin E. Coons, "Development of the Leader Behavior Description Questionnaire," in Stogdill and Coons, *op. cit.*, pp. 6-38, at p. 11.

[13] Andrew W. Halpin, "The Leader Behavior and Effectiveness of Aircraft Commanders," in Stogdill and Coons, *op. cit.*, pp. 52-64.

[14] [The results reported in *The Effects of Leadership* further corroborate and extend these findings.—Eds.]

When reading Selvin's selection and the next one by Rensis Likert, it should be kept in mind that the generalizations set forth may be respecified in the future. In social research, propositions are developed in several stages: the first studies find that a rule often is true; then exceptions are noted in some *circumstances; finally, more systematic research attempts to identify the conditions under which a generalization is true. The same sequence will probably be followed in research about the effects of leadership styles on work groups. Selvin and Likert summarize the early studies demonstrating the efficacy of democratic leadership. However, some social scientists recently have noted that the recommended leadership style does not have the same desired effects in all work groups.* On the basis of research and practical experience, some management consultants have suggested that more authoritarian leadership styles may be successful under some conditions.† Future research probably will be directed at the effects produced by each type of leadership in each type of situation.*

The Institute for Social Research of the University of Michigan has done numerous studies of the effects of different styles of leadership upon work groups. The selection by Rensis Likert, extracted from his book summarizing the Institute's research, presents some main conclusions. The effects of leadership style upon work output are quite complicated and depend on numerous other organizational conditions. But employee morale, absenteeism, job turnover, waste, and other employee actions fundamental to organizational costs depend on human relationships. Leaders can improve employee satisfaction and reduce costs by the supportive and consultative techniques mentioned by Likert. (His entire book is recommended for further details about the Institute's research and about leadership techniques that do and do not produce beneficial results. Most of his data are drawn from the Institute's studies of industry, but Chapter 10 of his book summarizes research about the effects of leadership styles and organizational structure upon the performance of local chapters of the League of Women Voters).

When reading the Likert selection, two distinctions should be remembered. First, one must distinguish between employee productivity and other employee behavior important to the organization, such as morale and absenteeism. As Likert's book and other research show, a particular leadership style can affect employee morale independently of any effect on work output. Both are important to the organization's performance and profit-and-loss position, but they do not correlate perfectly. Most of Likert's recommendations about leadership pertain to the improvement of employee satisfaction.

A second distinction is that between the leadership of an organization and the leadership of a work group within an organization. Likert is summarizing research about work groups. Consultative and participative methods would have to be modified and the leadership would exercise more initiative in top-level management. In large organizations whose leaders and employees have diverging commitments and interests, considerable authority must be exercised from the top in setting goals and institutional policies, supervising production, and maintaining efficiency. But if humane supervisory relationships can improve employee satisfaction and cut costs, as Likert says, then they should be practiced in work groups.

* For example, Harold Wilensky, "Human Relations in the Workplace: An Appraisal of Some Recent Research," in Conrad Arensberg et al., *Research in Industrial Human Relations* (New York: Harper & Brothers, 1957), pp. 31-36.

† For example, Robert N. McMurry, "The Case for Benevolent Autocracy," *Harvard Business Review*, Volume 36, Number 1 (January-February 1958), pp. 82-90.

LEADERSHIP STYLES AND EMPLOYEE PERFORMANCE*

Rensis Likert

The research findings summarized [in Likert's book] show that the high-producing managers, much more often than the low-producing managers, have built the personnel in their units or departments into highly effective organizations. These operations are characterized by favorable, cooperative attitudes and high levels of job satisfaction on the part of the members of the organization.

Although the research findings show that this general pattern is *more often* characteristic of the operations of the high-producing managers than the low, the results do *not* show that *all* high-producing managers adhere to this pattern. Technically competent, job-centered, insensitive, and tough management can achieve relatively high productivity. The evidence clearly indicates that if this kind of supervision is coupled with the use of tight controls on the part of the line organization, impressive productivity can be achieved. Members of units whose supervisors use these high-pressure methods, however, are more likely to be among those which have the least favorable attitudes toward their work and their supervisors and are likely to display excessive waste, scrap loss, and turnover. In general, these are the work groups which show the greatest hostility and resentment toward management, the least confidence and trust in their supervisors, the largest number of grievances that go to arbitration, and the greatest frequency of slowdowns, work stoppages, and similar difficulties.

It is important also to recognize that the research findings . . . do *not* support the conclusion that *every* organization in which there are high levels of confidence and trust, favorable attitudes, and high levels of job satisfaction will be highly productive. Even though a manager may have built his department into an organization with these qualities, his department will not achieve high productivity unless his leadership and the decision-making processes used by the organization result in the establishment of high performance goals by the members for themselves. High performance goals as well as favorable attitudes must be present if an organization is to achieve a high degree of productivity.

The behavior of the high-producing managers, in drawing upon more motivational forces and using them so that they yield favorable attitudes, points to a fundamental deficiency in the traditional theories of management. These theories are based on an inadequate motivational assumption. They assume that people work only or primarily for economic returns. More specifically, these theories assume that buying a man's time gives the employer control of the subordinate's behavior. Management textbooks emphasize authority and control as the foundation of administration. They either take for granted the power to control or they hold that "the relationship of employer and employee in an enterprise is a contractual obligation entailing the right to command and the duty to obey." . . .

Research findings indicate that the general pattern of operations of the highest-producing managers tends to differ from that of the managers of mediocre and low-producing units by more often showing the following characteristics:

(1) A preponderance of favorable attitudes on the part of each member of the organization toward all the other members, toward superiors, toward the work, toward the organization—toward all aspects of the job. These favorable attitudes toward others reflect a high level of mutual confidence trust throughout the organization. The favorable attitudes toward the organization and the work are not those of easy complacency, but are the attitudes of identification with the organization and its objective and a high sense of involvement in achieving them. As a consequence, the performance goals are high and dissatisfaction may occur whenever achievement falls short of the goals set.

(2) This highly motivated, cooperative orientation toward the organization and its objectives is achieved by harnessing effectively all the major motivational forces which can exercise significant influence in an organizational setting and which, potentially, can be accompanied by cooperative and favorable attitudes. Reliance is not placed solely or fundamentally on the economic motive of buying a man's time and using control and authority as the organizing and coordinating principle of the organization. On the contrary, the following motives are all used fully and in such a way that they function in a cumulative and reinforcing manner and yield favorable attitudes:

(a) The ego motives. These are referred to throughout [Likert's] volume as the desire to achieve and maintain a sense of personal worth and importance. This desire manifests itself in many forms, depending upon the norms and values of the persons and groups involved. Thus, it is responsible for such motivational forces as the desire for growth and significant achievement in terms of one's own values and goals, i.e.,

* From *New Patterns of Management* by Rensis Likert, pp. 58-60 and 98-101. Copyright © 1961, McGraw-Hill Book Company. Used by permission of the author and the publisher.

self-fulfillment, as well as the desire for status, recognition, approval, acceptance, and power and the desire to undertake significant and important tasks.

(b) The security motives.

(c) Curiosity, creativity, and the desire for new experiences.

(d) The economic motives.

By tapping all the motives which yield favorable and cooperative attitudes, maximum motivation oriented toward realizing the organization's goals as well as the needs of each member of the organization is achieved. The substantial decrements in motivational forces which occur when powerful motives are pulling in opposite directions are thereby avoided. These conflicting forces exist, of course, when hostile and resentful attitudes are present.

(3) The organization consists of a tightly knit, effectively functioning social system. This social system is made up of interlocking work groups with a high degree of group loyalty among the members and favorable attitudes and trust between superiors and subordinates. Sensitivity to others and relatively high levels of skill in personal interaction and the functioning of groups are also present. These skills permit effective participation in decisions on common problems. Participation is used, for example, to establish organizational objectives which are a satisfactory integration of the needs and desires of all members of the organization and of persons functionally related to it. High levels of reciprocal influence occur, and high levels of total coordinated influence are achieved in the organization. Communication is efficient and effective. There is a flow from one part of the organization to another of all the relevant information important for each decision and action. The leadership in the organization has developed what might well be called a highly effective social system for interaction and mutual influence.

(4) Measurements of organizational performance are used primarily for self-guidance rather than for superimposed control. To tap the motives which bring cooperative and favorable rather than hostile attitudes, participation and involvement in decisions is a habitual part of the leadership processes. This kind of decision-making, of course, calls for the full sharing of available measurements and information. Moreover, as it becomes evident in the decision-making process that additional information or measurements are needed, steps are taken to obtain them.

In achieving operations which are more often characterized by the above pattern of highly cooperative, well-coordinated activity, the highest producing managers use all the technical resources of the classical theories of management, such as time-and-motion study, budgeting, and financial controls. They use these resources at least as completely as do the low-producing managers, but in quite different ways. This difference in use arises from the difference in the motives which the high-producing, in contrast to the low-producing, managers believe are important in influencing human behavior.

The low-producing managers, in keeping with traditional practice, feel that the way to motivate and direct behavior is to exercise control through authority. Jobs are organized, methods are prescribed, standards are set, performance goals and budgets are established. Compliance with them is sought through the use of hierarchical and economic pressures.

The highest-producing managers feel, generally, that this manner of functioning does not produce the best results, that the resentment created by direct exercise of authority tends to limit its effectiveness. They have learned that better results can be achieved when a different motivational process is employed. As suggested above, they strive to use all those major motives which have the potentiality of yielding favorable and cooperative attitudes in such a way that favorable attitudes are, in fact, elicited and the motivational forces are mutually reinforcing. Motivational forces stemming from the economic motive are not then blunted by such other motivations as group goals which restrict the quantity or quality of output. The full strength of all economic, ego, and other motives is generated and put to use.

Widespread use of participation is one of the more important approaches employed by the high-producing managers in their efforts to get full benefit from the technical resources of the classical theories of management coupled with high levels of reinforcing motivation. This use of participation applies to all aspects of the job and work, as, for example, in setting work goals and budgets, controlling costs, organizing the work, etc.

In these and comparable ways, the high-producing managers make full use of the technical resources of the classical theories of management. They use these resources in such a manner, however, that favorable and cooperative attitudes are created and all members of the organization endeavor to pull concertedly toward commonly accepted goals which they have helped to establish.

This brief description of the pattern of management which is more often characteristic of the high-producing than of the low-producing managers points to what appears to be a critical difference. The high-producing managers have developed their organizations into highly coordinated, highly motivated, cooperative social systems. Under their leadership, the different motivational forces in each member of the organization have coalesced into a strong force aimed at accomplishing the mutually established objectives of the organization. This general pattern of highly motivated, cooperative members seems to be a central characteristic of the newer management system being developed by the highest-producing managers.

How do these high-producing managers build organizations which display this central characteristic? Is there any general approach or underlying principle which they rely upon in building highly motivated organizations? There seems to be. . . . The research findings show, for example, that those supervisors and managers whose pattern of leadership yields consistently favorable attitudes more often think of employees as "human beings rather than just as persons to get the work done." Consistently, in study after study, the data show that treating people as "human beings" rather than as "cogs in a machine" is a variable highly related to the attitudes and motivation of the subordinate at every level in the organization.

The superiors who have the most favorable and cooperative attitudes in their work groups display the following characteristics:

(1) The attitude and behavior of the superior toward the subordinate as a person, *as perceived by the subordinate*, is as follows:

(a) He is supportive, friendly, and helpful rather than hostile. He is kind but firm, never threatening, genuinely interested in the well-being of subordinates and endeavors to treat people in a sensitive, considerate way. He is just, if not generous. He endeavors to serve the best interests of his employees as well as of the company.

(b) He shows confidence in the integrity, ability, and motivations of subordinates rather than suspicion and distrust.

(c) His confidence in subordinates leads him to have high expectations as to their level of performance. With confidence that he will not be disappointed, he expects much, not little. (This, again, is fundamentally a supportive rather than a critical or hostile relationship.)

(d) He sees that each subordinate is well trained for his particular job. He endeavors also to help subordinates be promoted by training them for jobs at the next level. This involves giving them relevant experience and coaching whenever the opportunity offers.

(e) He coaches and assists employees whose performance is below standard. In the case of a subordinate who is clearly misplaced and unable to do his job satisfactorily, he endeavors to find a position well suited to that employee's abilities and arranges to have the employee transferred to it.

(2) The behavior of the superior in directing the work is characterized by such activity as:

(a) Planning and scheduling the work to be done, training subordinates, supplying them with material and tools, initiating work activity, etc.

(b) Providing adequate technical competence, particularly in those situations where the work has not been highly standardized.

(3) The leader develops his subordinates into a working team with high group loyalty by using participation and other kinds of group-leadership practices. . . .

PART FOUR

PROBLEMS OF GOVERNMENT

Everyone realizes that daily life places the individual in a variety of relationships with others. Often one thinks of an organization as a simple and clear-cut structure, following the relationships mapped by an organizational chart. But when behavioral scientists have studied organizations, they have found in them the same complex of relationships as in other phases of daily life. In their selection, John M. Pfiffner and Frank P. Sherwood describe the various relationships existing simultaneously in the same organization. They conclude by summarizing the essential properties of formal organizations in general.

THE PROCESS OF INTERACTION*

John M. Pfiffner and Frank P. Sherwood

The formal structure of an organization represents as closely as possible the deliberate intention of its framers for the processes of interaction that will take place among its members. In the typical work organization this takes the form of a definition of task specialties, and their arrangement in levels of authority with clearly defined lines of communication from one level to the next.

It must be recognized, however, that the actual processes of interaction among the individuals represented in the formal plan cannot adequately be described solely in terms of its planned lines of interaction. Coexisting with the formal structure are myriad other ways of interacting for persons in the organization; these can be analyzed according to various theories of group behavior, but it must not be forgotten that in reality they never function so distinctively, and all are intermixed together in an organization which also follows to a large extent its formal structure.

These modifying processes must be studied one at a time; a good way to do so without forgetting their "togetherness" is to consider each as a transparent "overlay" pattern superimposed on the basic formal organizational pattern. The totality of these overlays might be so complex as to be nearly opaque, but it will still be a closer approach to reality than the bare organization chart so typically used to diagram a large group structure.

Five such overlay patterns will be considered here; many more or less might be chosen from the kinds of studies that have been made, but these five might well be considered basic:

— The sociometric network
— The system of functional contacts
— The grid of decision-making centers
— The pattern of power
— Channels of communication[1]

The idea that these processes are overlays upon the conventional job-task pyramid does not require that the latter take a subordinate position, although much of the research in organization might give this impression. The overlay approach aims to be realistic in recognizing that organization also consists of a wide variety of contacts that involve communication, sociometry, goal centered functionalism, decision-making, and personal power. Let us consider this complex of processes one at a time.

THE JOB-TASK PYRAMID
(See Chart 1)

The job-task pyramid constitutes the basis from which all departures are measured. It is the official version of the organization as the people in the organization believe that it is and should be. It would be correct to say that in most production organizations today, whether private or public, this official version of the organization-as-it-should-be reflects the view of those in the top echelons of the job-task pyramid. The actual operating organizations may differ in some respects from the formal organization; this

* From John M. Pfiffner and Frank P. Sherwood, *Administrative Organization*, pp. 18-30. © 1960. Reprinted by permission of the authors and Prentice-Hall, Inc., Englewood Cliffs, N. J. The editors are indebted to the authors and publisher for permission to use several selections from this book, which we consider the best available summary of the recent literature on administration.

1 For much of the conceptual underpinnings of this chapter we are indebted to John T. Dorsey, Jr., "A Communication Model for Administration," *Administrative Science Quarterly*, Volume 2 (December 1957), pp. 307-324. While Dorsey would seem to view communication as the central component of administration, we would put it on a level with others dealt with here.

difference can be expressed by showing the manner in which the other networks vary from the job-task hierarchy.

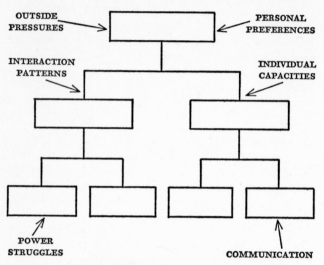

CHART I. *The typical job pyramid of authority and some of its interacting processes.*

JOB-TASK HIERARCHY AS FOUNDATION

Variations of the other networks from the job-task hierarchy should not be taken as an indication that the latter is being undermined or has no acceptance in the organization. It is well recognized in practice that there is an operating organization that varies from the chart with the full knowledge of those in authority. Day-to-day and hour-to-hour adjustments must be made, and there is no need to revise the chart for each of these. Nevertheless, the job-task hierarchy as depicted by the organization manual does set forth the grid of official authority as viewed by those in the organization. Without it the other networks would simply not exist.

THE SOCIOMETRIC OVERLAY
(See Chart 2)

In any organization there is a set of relationships among people which is purely social in nature; it exists because of a net feeling of attraction or rejection. This pattern of person-to-person contacts is called sociometric because it is revealed in the kind of group testing that was given that name by its originator, J. L. Moreno. Some investigators have felt that individual attitudes lending themselves to sociometric measurement include as many as the following:

1. The *prescribed* relations, which are identical with the official or formal organization.

2. The *perceived* relations, which consist of people's interpretation of the meaning of the official network.

3. The *actual* relations are those interactions which in fact take place among persons.

4. The *desired* relations are people's preferences regarding interactions they want with other persons.

5. The *rejected* relations are the relationships with other people which are not wanted.

It is, however, the last two categories that are primarily sociological in nature, and it is these that will be considered sociometric here. Desired and rejected relationships are fairly easy to ascertain with statistical reliability, and are found to be very responsive to the other dynamics of the group. Ohio State studies of naval leadership have effectively utilized sociometric charts (sociograms—graphic representations of social relations) superimposed on the traditional job-task charts.[2]

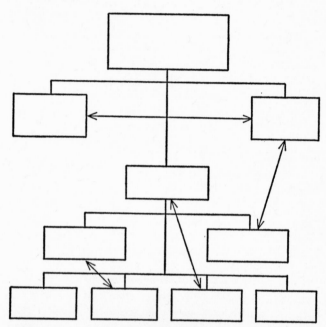

CHART 2. *Social overlay—the special friendships in the organization.* ("I'll talk to my friend George in Purchasing. He'll know what to do.")

THE FUNCTIONAL OVERLAY
(See Chart 3)

There is in the organization a network of functional contacts that is important to and yet different from the formal authority structure. Functional contacts occur most typically where specialized information is needed; through them the staff or other specialist, the intellectual "leader," exerts his influence upon operations without direct responsibility for the work itself. This relationship, something like that between a professional man and his client, is a phenomenon of the

[2] Ralph M. Stogdill, *Leadership and Structure of Personal Interaction* (Columbus: Ohio State University, Bureau of Business Research, Monograph No. 84, 1957), p. 10.

twentieth century, and more markedly of the mid-century period.

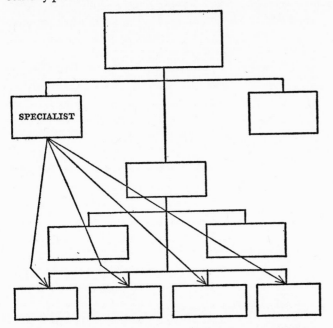

CHART 3. *Functional overlay—the direct relationships between the specialist assistant and the operating departments. ("You have to see Personnel for approval to take that training course.")*

Frederick Taylor was so perceptive as to understand the importance of the network of functional contacts in a management institution. Taylor called these functional contacts "functional supervision"; this term upset many theorists who worshipped the concept of clear cut supervisor-subordinate authority relationships.[3]

While Taylor's original concept of multiple supervision was rejected as a theoretical instrument at the time, it is still true that most organizations exhibit a system of functional supervision. Many charts of formal authority structures, such as those of the military, also show functional contacts through such devices as broken connecting lines.

THE DECISION OVERLAY
(See Chart 4)

Simon maintains that the best way to analyze an organization is to find out where the decisions are made and by whom.[4] It can perhaps be assumed that normally in an organization the decision pattern follows the structure of the formal hierarchy, that is, the job-

task pyramid. However, the power and authority network, together with the functional network, may cut across hierarchical channels. It is in this sense that they take on the configuration of a grid or network. Thus the network pattern of approach is helpful, not in undermining the concept of hierarchy but in conveying the picture of actual practice. It modifies the harsh overtones of hierarchy by pointing out that actual organizations permit a great many cross-contacts.

NETWORK OF INFLUENCE

It might be more correct to say that there is a network of influence, not a network of decision. This, of course, depends upon one's definition of decision-making and if one insists upon there being a clear cut choice between alternatives by a person in authority,

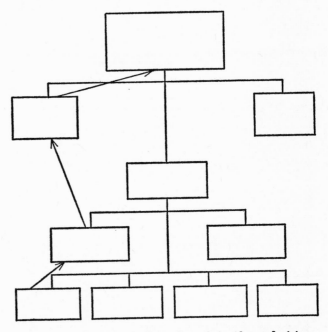

CHART 4. *Decision overlay—flow of significant decisions in the organization. ("Don't worry about Joe. He doesn't concern himself about this. Our next step is to go topside.")*

then decision-making usually follows clear hierarchical paths and channels. However, if we think in terms of a decision *process* rather than a decision *point*, the sense of interaction and influence is more appropriately conveyed. In this connection it is helpful to refer to Mary Parker Follett's concept of order giving in which she says "an order, command, is a step in a process, a moment in the movement of interweaving experience. We should guard against thinking this step a larger part of the whole process than it really is."[5]

3 A collection of excerpts from the literature of the early scientific management movement relating to staff specialization and functionalism is contained in Albert Lepawsky, *Administration* (New York: Alfred A. Knopf, Inc., 1949), pp. 299-306.

4 Herbert A. Simon, *Administrative Behavior* (New York: The Macmillan Company, Second edition, 1947), p. xix.

5 Henry C. Metcalf and L. Urwick, editors, *Dynamic Administration: The Collected Papers of Mary Parker Follett* (New York: Harper and Brothers, 1940), p. 49.

THE POWER OVERLAY (See Chart 5)

Any discussion of power as a factor in organizational dynamics rather quickly encounters difficulties of definition and terminology. Since this is a subject upon which there will be considerable discussion at a later point in this book [reprinted in Chapter 9 of this volume.—Eds.], let it be noted here that many of these problems arise from a confusion of the terms *power* and *authority*. They are not necessarily synonymous; yet there has been a tendency to look at the organization chart, note the various status levels, and to assume that power increases as one rises in the pyramid. Much of this attitude is based on old concepts of authority as they are found in jurisprudence. Within this framework there is an assump-

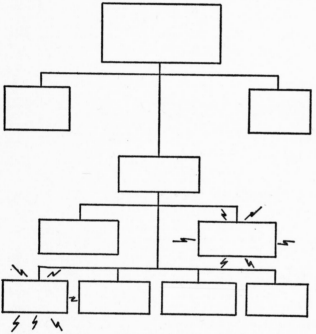

CHART 5. *Power overlay—centers of power in the organization. ("Before you go further, you had better clear that with Jack in Production Planning.")*

tion that a rule laid down by a political superior who is ultimately sovereign can be enforced by the imposition of sanctions. Translated into the terminology of management institutions, this means that authority, and hence power, rests with those at the top echelons of the job-task pyramid.

POWER NO LONGER VIEWED AS SYNONYMOUS WITH AUTHORITY

However there has been a considerable rebellion against this narrow view of the power factor in organization environment. Almost everyone who has had any experience in a management institution has encountered a situation where the boss's secretary, or

his assistant, or the executive officer, is the "person to see." For a great variety of reasons, these people may be effective decision-makers in the situation. Thus power is really personal; it is political; and it may or may not be legitimate in that it has been authorized by formal law or has achieved hierarchical legitimization. Involving a person-to-person relationship, power exists when one has the ability to influence someone to behave in a particular way or to make decisions. As a result the mapping of power centers would seldom follow the pattern of a typical hierarchy.

MANAGEMENT INSTITUTIONS ARE POLITICAL

It seems desirable to emphasize that management institutions are political in nature and that the basis of politics is power. While the use of the adjective "political" may be jarring to students of business administration who regard politics and government as being synonymous, the fact remains that business organizations are also political to an important degree. The maneuvering for proxies to gain control of an industrial corporation is certainly a political act and the same is true of struggles on the part of individuals to "build empires," or the use of artifice to gain the ear of the president.

The important consideration from the standpoint of organization theory is that there is a network or grid of personal power centers, though sometimes latent and not expressed. They may or may not coincide with the official structure of authority. Power is not institutionalized in the sense that one can look in the organization manual and find out where it resides. As a matter of fact one might find it in unsuspected places. The person of comparatively low status may be a power center because he has been around so long that only he knows the intricate rules and the regulations well enough to make immediate decisions.

THE COMMUNICATION OVERLAY (See Chart 6)

Perhaps nowhere is the inter-relationship of the various overlays more clearly to be seen than in communication. As will be observed at countless points in this book [see the selection reprinted in Chapter 10 of this volume—Eds.] the information process is central to organizational system. It affects control and decision-making, influence and power, interpersonal relationships, and leadership, to name only a few facets. Dorsey, in making a case for the significance of communications, says that "power consists of the extent to which a given communication influences the generation and flow of later communications. Points in the patterned flow where this occurs . . . are positions of power . . ." [6] Furthermore, the communi-

[6] Dorsey, *op. cit.*, p. 310.

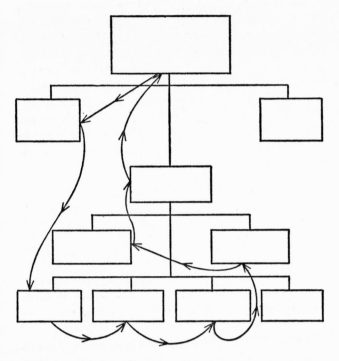

CHART 6. *Communications overlay—the route of tele-phone calls on a particular matter. ("If we had to go through channels, we never would get anything done around here!")*

cation net "consists physically of a complex of *decision centers* and *channels* which seek, receive, transmit, subdivide, classify, store, select, recall, recombine and retransmit *information*."[7] This net consists not only of the technical information apparatus, but also of the human nervous systems of the people who make up the organization.

It is important to recognize that communication is itself a clearly identifiable facet of behavior. Redfield tells, for example, of the consultant who "starts his studies in the mail room, for, by plotting the lines of actual communication, he can sometimes build a more accurate organization chart than the one that hangs on the wall in the president's office."[8] Such a chart is, of course, one of communications. And it may tell a great deal more about how life is really lived in an organization than the formal authority picture. Thus an important and useful means of taking a look at an organization is to ask the question, "Who talks to whom about what?"

Answers to the question will often reveal that patterns of communication are at variance with official prescriptions. That is something the consultant mentioned in the previous paragraph frequently found. Furthermore there have been enough experiments with small groups to give great strength to the proposition that "the mere existence of a hierarchy sets up

restraints against communication between levels."[9] Gardner has pointed out that factory production reports on productivity are sometimes rigged in order to give higher echelons the type of information which will make them happy.[10] Such blockages and distortions are certainly frequent enough to force us to recognize that the communications overlay represents an important dimension of organization analysis.

ORGANIZATION DEFINED

. . . First, it may be observed that the state of being organized does occur in every relationship. Some individuals can order their time more effectively than others. Certainly the mother of five small ones who still has time for the church, P.T.A. and bridge is "organized." Yet such individuals are not the focus of interest in this book; this suggests, therefore, an important point of reference: *size*. We are concerned with entities of scale; and these may roughly be identified as those associations of people which are too large to permit immediate, face-to-face leadership by a single individual. A *group* may gather around a table; some *organizations* couldn't crowd into Yankee Stadium.

COMPLEXITY

A second element in the development of our definition is complexity. Task specialization, as has already been noted, represents one of the most significant factors in twentieth century management. It is doubtful that a really *simple* organization exists today.

CONSCIOUS RATIONALITY

There is an assumption of conscious rationality implicit in the study of organization. To be sure, the overlays indicate clearly that this goal of rationality is not always achieved, but it is nevertheless there. Argyris has called it the "most basic property of formal organization";[11] he has quoted Herbert Simon approvingly:

> "Organizations are formed with the intention and design of accomplishing goals; and the people who work in organizations believe, at least part of the time, that they are striving toward these same goals. We must not lose sight of the fact that, however far organizations may depart from the traditional description, . . . most behavior in organizations is *intendedly rational* behavior. By intended rationality I mean the kind of adjustment of behavior to goals

[7] *Ibid.*, p. 317.
[8] Charles Redfield, *Communication in Management* (Chicago: University of Chicago Press, 1953), p. 7.

[9] Burleigh B. Gardner and David G. Moore, *Human Relations in Industry* (Homewood, Ill.: Richard D. Irwin, Inc., Third edition, 1955), pp. 213ff.
[10] Leon Festinger, "Informal Social Communication," in Dorwin Cartwright and Alvin Zander, *Group Dynamics* (Evanston, Ill.: Row Peterson, 1953), p. 201.
[11] Chris Argyris, *Personality and Organization* (New York: Harper & Brothers, 1957), p. 54.

of which humans are capable—a very incomplete and imperfect adjustment, to be sure, but one which nevertheless does accomplish purposes and does carry out programs." [12]

PRESENCE OF PURPOSE

Finally, the significance of rationality to organization theory suggests a fourth major point, the need for a purpose. Relatively artificial accumulations of people exist to accomplish something, even though it may be so mundane as survival. As these purposes grow dim, the prospects of rationality decline; and if they disappear, the chances are that the consciously-created organization will also cease to exist. It is important to

remember that the need for purpose perhaps exists only in organizations rooted in rationality. Smaller social groups, such as families, are held together by emotional, kinship ties; and who can say what lies behind the phenomenal organization of parts of the animal kingdom?

THE DEFINITION

On the basis of these assumptions (and their limitations), a definition may be attempted of organization as it will be used in this book:

> "Organization is the pattern of ways in which large numbers of people, too many to have intimate face-to-face contact with all others, and engaged in a complexity of tasks, relate themselves to each other in the conscious, systematic establishment and accomplishment of mutually agreed purposes."

[12] Quoted by Argyris from Herbert A. Simon, "Recent Advances in Organization Theory", *Research Frontiers in Politics and Government* (Washington: The Brookings Institution, 1955), p. 30.

Many organizations are bureaucratically and hierarchically constructed. In his selection, Victor A. Thompson summarizes contemporary sociological thinking about the nature of bureaucratic organization. The characteristics of bureaucracy include the arrangement of work into a series of specialized jobs, appointment of job-holders according to merit, impersonal evaluation of new members according to specialized training and skilled performance, promotion through a hierarchy according to merit, rewards through pay, privileges differentiated by rank, strict controls over subordinates, and responsibility to superiors in the chain of command.

While many organizations are bureaucratically organized throughout, voluntary associations generally are not, because of the presence of so many volunteers. Volunteers' motivations are more spontaneous and less pecuniary, their qualifications are more general, their careers in associational activities are briefer and more changeable, they are less responsive to discipline, and so on.

Nevertheless, an understanding of the nature of bureaucracy is important for leaders of voluntary asociations. Bureaucratic tendencies appear in any formal organization, and possibly every voluntary association acquires more bureaucratic characteristics and procedures with the passage of time.* Some departments of voluntary associations may be manned entirely by full-time salaried staffs and may operate in bureaucratic ways. Leaders of voluntary associations often must deal with business firms, government agencies, and other outside organizations that are full-blown bureaucracies, and therefore leaders must understand the orientations, duties, and career opportunities that bureaucrats are likely to have.

* For example, the gradual and still incomplete bureaucratization of American trade unions—which began as informal associations—is described in Harold L. Wilensky, *Intellectuals in Trade Unions* (Glencoe: The Free Press, 1956), pp. 243-258.

THE CONCEPT OF BUREAUCRACY*

Victor A. Thompson

The great German sociologist, Max Weber, was the first to attempt a systematic theory of bureaucratic organization. His views remain important to us not only because of his enormous influence on American social scientists, but also because of the continuing validity of much of his analysis.

Weber pictured an evolution of organizational forms in terms of the kind of authority relations within them.[1] At one extreme is a simple, relatively nonspecialized kind of organization in which followers give almost unqualified obedience to a leader endowed with "charisma"—presumed unusual, generally magical powers. Such organization was primitive in the sense that it was based upon belief in magic. Since their prerogatives depended upon their leader's charisma, his immediate staff felt insecure and sought a firmer legitimation of these prerogatives. Their fears came to a head at the time of succession in the leadership. Routinization of methods used to obtain a successor and thus to secure staff prerogatives resulted in the traditionalistic form of organization. Monarchy would be an example.

Weber conceived of the world as becoming progressively rationalized and demystified, with corresponding change in organizational forms. Both charismatic and traditional authority become harder to maintain, and a new, rationalized, legalistic kind of authority and structure emerged. He called this kind of organization "bureaucracy."

Weber believed in a cycle of change from charismatic to traditionalistic and bureaucratic forms of organization against a background of increasing rationalization. Charisma disrupts and is antithetical to the process of rationalization. Charismatic leadership is needed when existing routines cannot cope with growing problems or crises. The charismatic personality emerges and overshadows routine and procedure.

Weber specified a list of criteria for the fully developed bureaucratic form, including technical training of officials, merit appointments, fixed salaries and pensions, assured careers, the separation of organizational rights and duties from the private life of the employee, and a fixed and definite division of work into distinct officers or jobs. He noted that all offices were arranged in a clear hierarchy of subordination and superordination, that members of the organiza-

tion were subject to strict and systematic control and discipline, and that a rationalized set of rules and regulations tied the whole organization together. He said that it should make no difference how these rules and regulations were adopted, whether they were autocratically imposed or adopted by consent. He also said that obedience to commands should be prompt, automatic, unquestioning.

He noted that the principal general social consequences of this organizational form were a tendency toward social leveling, resulting from the attempt to get the broadest possible basis for recruitment of technical competence; a tendency toward plutocracy, resulting from an interest in the greatest possible length of technical training; and the dominance of a spirit of formalistic impersonality, resulting in the minimization of hatred, of affection, and of enthusiasm.

He felt that the superiority over other forms of organization lay in its capacity to command and to utilize technical knowledge; or as we would say, in specialization. "The choice is only that between bureaucracy and dilettantism in the field of administration."[2]

SOME CHARACTERISTICS OF MODERN BUREAUCRACY

Although Weber sought to explain bureaucracy by means of a perhaps dubious historical law of increasing rationality, his description of bureaucratic organization seems, in effect, to be consistent with our own. Modern organization has evolved from earlier forms by incorporating advancing specialization. In an earlier period organizations could depend much more on the "line of command." The superior could tell others what to do because he could master the knowledge and techniques necessary to do so intelligently. As science and technology developed, the superior lost to experts the *ability* to command in one field after another, but he retained the *right* as part of his role.

A great structure of specialized competencies has grown up around the chain of command. Organizations have grown in size because they must be able fully to employ the new specialists and the specialized equipment associated with them if the organizations are to meet their competition. As more specialists appear and the organization continues to grow in size, it becomes necessary to group employees into units, and the units into larger units. Some of the larger of these units in government have been called

---

[1] Max Weber, *The Theory of Social and Economic Organization*. Trans. A. M. Henderson and Talcott Parsons, ed. Talcott Parsons. (New York: Oxford University Press, Inc., 1947). [First published in 1922.—Eds.]

[2] *Ibid.*, p. 336.

"bureaus," and so the kind of organization resulting from this process has been called "bureaucracy." (These units were called "bureaus" from the French word for writing table or desk.)

The impact of specialization upon modern organization accounts for many of the latter's characteristic features. Because the modern organization evolves in response to modern science and technology, it reflects the guiding spirit of science and technology. This is the spirit of *rationalism*.[3] No longer are traditional or religious standards to be the guardians of knowledge. The quest for truth is to be limited and guided only by reason and empirical verification. Within the modern bureaucratic organization this rationalism expresses itself in constant self-scrutiny. The pragmatic test grows in importance. "How does it promote the organizational goal?" is the question most often heard. Although other evaluative criteria can be observed in modern bureaucracy, the pragmatic test seems to have become institutionalized. By this we mean that people seem to feel that they ought to apply that test to all arrangements.

The growing dominance of the spirit of rationalism in modern bureaucracy simply reflects the growing influence of scientific and technical specialists upon organizational decisions. The bureaucratic organization is the arena where science and technology are applied. With a few rapidly disappearing exceptions, such as medicine, we can say that the application and development of science and technology depend upon bureaucratic organization. As a consequence of the dominance of this spirit of rationalism and the influence of specialists on decisions, modern bureaucratic organization is the most productive arrangement of human effort that man has thus far contrived. Its ability to accomplish objective organizational goals had produced the highest standard of living yet achieved by man, while allowing populations to expand enormously at the same time. Not only has the poverty of the industrial worker been eliminated . . . , the industrial laborer is becoming a technically trained specialist.

Dependence upon highly trained specialists requires *appointment by merit* rather than election or political appointment. It requires *a system of assured careers*; otherwise, the individual would not invest the time needed to acquire specialized skill. It requires that the organization have a definite and reasonably assured division of work into defined jobs or offices. The trained specialist would not usually allow himself to be used as a jack-of-all-trades. In fact, the division of work in organizations for the most part

simply follows the existing specializations in society at large.

As Weber said, charismatic forms of organization give way to bureaucracy because the former are inadequate for daily, regularized activity. Charisma functions in new situations and is not compatible with highly defined situations. Charismatic organization is dependent upon the reputed genius of individuals and is, therefore, unstable and precarious. To secure stability, continuity, and predictability of product, the activities of the organization are reduced to procedures or routines. *Routinization of organizational activity* is implicit in the process of specialization and is a characteristic of bureaucracy. Specialization requires a stable environment and a guarantee of continuity of function. Within the organization, the specialist must practice his specialty—a group of related routines. Although managerial ideology still strongly contains the charismatic image, bureaucratic organizations seek to avoid dependence upon individuals by reducing relevant information to classes, and organizational activity to routines which are activated when the appropriate class of information is perceived. It would seem, therefore, that the advance of specialization requires routinization, one of the central characteristics of bureaucratic organization.

Organizations as problem-solving mechanisms depend upon a *factoring of the general goal into subgoals* and these into sub-subgoals, and so on, until concrete routines are reached. These subgoals are allocated to organizational units and become the goals of those units. Individuals in the units are not given the impossible task, therefore, of evaluating their every action in terms of the general goal of the organization, but only in terms of the particular subgoal allocated to their unit. The definition of the situation is sufficiently simplified to bring it within the rational capacity of the human mind. If the factoring is accurate, rationality in terms of each unit will be rationality in terms of the organization as a whole. In this way, bureaucratic organizations achieve rationality far beyond the capacity of any individual.

In addition to accurate factoring, rationality in terms of the whole organization requires that individuals in the subunits accept their assigned subgoal as the end or objective of their activities. It must be the principal given value. Normally, individuals accept the assignment, since they accept the authority of the organization. Various forces, in addition, reinforce this identification with subgoals, particularly the fact that communication within the unit, and between it and the rest of the organization is heavily concerned with the subgoal. Looked at from our point of view, factoring of the organizational goal is simply differentiation of function—namely, specialization. People are to be concerned with a certain area of activities,

[3] We are using the term "rationalism" and its various derivatives according to common usage—not in its philosophically technical sense as an antiempirical theory of knowledge.

not with all activities. Thus, specialization results in strong attachment to subgoals.

From a point of view outside a particular unit, the unit's goal is seen not as a goal, but as a means to a larger goal. From this external vantage point, therefore, the members of a unit seem to be attached to means rather than ends. One of the characteristics of bureaucratic organization based on specialization, consequently, is an *apparent inversion of ends and means.* For example, people outside a budget office frequently accuse budget officers of believing the organization exists for the purpose of operating budget procedures. From the point of view of a client interested in the general organizational goal, members of all subunits appear to have inverted means into ends. Such "inversion" may be a problem of factoring, of dividing up the work; and any necessary corrections may not be in the direction of reducing subgoal identification but, rather, of reorganization.

A *formalistic impersonality* is a readily discernible characteristic of modern organization. In interpersonal relationships, total involvement probably never occurs. Each person is concerned with somewhat less than all of the actual or potential needs of the other. In specialist relationships, involvement is limited to the needs for which the specialized function is relevant. The relationship is partial, and functional; it is "secondary" rather than "primary." The specialist performs his function for many, and so he must limit his participation to the relationship to the area of his specialty. The resulting "impersonal" relationship need not be cold or painful. When both sides recognize their mutual interdependence—the client's dependence on the specialist for the fulfillment of some need, and the specialist's dependence on the client for the opportunity to work at his calling—the relationship is not necessarily without human warmth and mutual appreciation. Pleasant though impersonal relationships of mutual interdependence abound in everyday life—the motorist and the mechanic, the doctor and the patient, the householder and the postman. Impersonality is inevitably associated with bureaucratic organization, resting as it does on specialization.

An organization based on specialization must allow specialists to practice their specialties, to carry out the routines of which their specialties are composed. Specialists do not improvise for each unique event. Improvisation is charismatic, "dilettantish." Although there are unique aspects to all events, it is only to the repeated aspects that the routines of the specialty can be applied. Consequently, specialization requires that the raw data of reality be organized into classes or categories that often recur. Furthermore, enormous amounts of information needed in a specialized world can be summarized and communicated quickly by *categorization of data,* thereby greatly facilitating the solution of problems. Therefore, although an individual is to himself a total, complete person, in some ways unique, to the specialist he is a carrier of a class of data relevant to the practice of the specialty in question. He is a speeder, an income-tax evader, a disciplinary case, an applicant for a job, a coronary, etc. The reality of the specialist is created by his classes and categories. We are all specialists in some sense, so that the realities we perceive vary from person to person. In fact, language itself is a system of categories by which we organize the raw sensory data of experience. There would appear to be no basis, therefore, for criticizing bureaucratic organizations merely because they interpret reality through specialist categories and classes. What may be important, however, is to ensure through organization that differing conceptions of reality have ample opportunity to be heard and are not simply buried under an official reality.

Bureaucratic classification of persons for differential treatment is reinforced by the confusion in our culture between the norm of "evenhanded" justice, on the one hand, and on the other, the ideal conception of justice as giving to each man his due. People want equality before the law in general, but individualized treatment in particular. The grouping of individuals into classes is an attempt to come closer to ideal justice without losing equality before the law. Clientele behavior enforces classification. If one individual is treated out of class, many persons who feel similarly situated will insist on equal treatment. If they are denied, it is called "discrimination." This reaction shows that these classes do exist subjectively in the particular society. Frequently this process results in the creation of new classes. Elaboration of the system of client classification approaches the ideal of individual justice. Whether one's function is regulation or service, he disregards this social process of classification at his peril.

A final aspect of bureaucratic organizations, and one which often comes under criticism, is their *seeming slowness to act or to change.* In discussing this topic we must concede at the outset that bureaucratic organizations, in the face of emergencies, do often act with tremendous speed. A serious note is received from Russia, let us say, in the morning, and a reply with warlike implications is dispatched in the afternoon. A rush order is received, and all regular procedures are tacitly suspended, protocol is forgotten, and a busy, happy, problem-solving atmosphere pervades the organization until the order is out. . . . Crisis situations, since they are by definition ones for which routines are not available, evoke a nonroutinized approach—a charismatic rather than a bureaucratic approach.

Under more normal conditions, organizations based upon specialization and its routines cannot be expected to react immediately to each stimulus. Great amounts of information must be accumulated if knowledge is to be substituted for impulse, thus assuring greater effectiveness of action and greater chance of success. Since action involves many interdependent specialists, co-ordination time must be expanded. In order that all necessary parts of the organization act in co-ordinated fashion, clearances must be obtained, meetings held, many copies of proposals and information memoranda prepared and properly routed. In short, if the organization could act with the speed of an individual, the organization would not be needed.

With regard to *resistance to change*, it should be noted that this phenomenon is not uniquely related to bureaucratic organizations but is a characteristic of all institutions—hence the term "cultural lag." In the case of the bureaucratic organization, however, there is special need for caution with regard to change. As we have said before, specialization requires some guarantee of stability. Specialties must not soon go out of date, or people would not invest the time needed to acquire them.

Furthermore, the members of an organization become socially specialized. They become specialized in working with one another. It takes time to convert a number of abstract, related positions into a flesh-and-blood working organization. Consequently, any suggestion for change must be measured against its effect on the co-operative system as a whole. Bureaucratic organizations must plan and control changes. Although the persons urging change may feel that the resistances they encounter represent "bureaucratic" stubbornness, the desirability of any particular change, all things considered, is usually an open question.

Internally, the bureaucratic organization is a complex structure of technical interdependence superimposed upon a strict hierarchy of authority. The entire structure is characterized by a *preoccupation with the monistic ideal*. The hierarchical institution is monocratic. It is a system of superior and subordinate role-relationships in which the superior is the *only* source of legitimate influence upon the subordinate. Everyone in the organization finds himself in such a relationship. Since this was the original organizational relationship, it has dominated organizational theory and practice and still does so. This exclusive emphasis on hierarchy has produced our prevailing organizational theory and informed management practice . . .

Preoccupation with hierarchy governs the distribution of rewards by modern organizations. Ranks of deference correspond to ranks of authority, and deference is manifested by the bestowal of good things. Success within our society means, for the most part, progression up an organizational hierarchy. Modern organizations, consequently, face a growing problem of rewarding specialists. To be socially regarded as successful, specialists must give up their technical fields and ender a hierarchy. Many do, leaving us with growing shortages of many kinds of technically trained people. A few entrepreneurial specialists, such as medical doctors, have been able to avoid this dilemma, but the advance of specialization will force them all into organizations eventually—in the case of medical doctors because specialized equipment will be too costly for an individual to own, and because the health of the patient will require the co-ordinated services of many specialists.

All organizations share certain characteristics in their structures, regardless of whether their goals are political, economic, cultural, or social welfare. The identification of such underlying uniformities is the subject of James D. Thompson's selection.

The fact of structural similarity among organizations has practiced implications for the leadership of voluntary associations. Many board members, professional executives, and volunteers are recruited who have had previous experience in organizations with other goals. The fact that a person has been successful before (such as the manager of a business firm or the director of a government agency) fosters high hopes in the association. Thompson's essay reminds the association leader to identify both the con-

tinuities and the discontinuities between the particular association job and the job in the other organization where the new member has been employed. Recruitment from a similar job in a comparable organization may facilitate adjustment better than recruitment from another source. Success in a different type of job in a different kind of organization may not always predict success in association activity; mediocre performance in one does not inevitably mean mediocrity in the other.

COMMON ELEMENTS IN ADMINISTRATION*

James D. Thompson

If the administrative process is performed adequately, the areas of decision and the functions performed will be similar in all large organizations. We believe this to be true also of the very small organization, where the total administrative process is the responsibility of one individual. But our deliberations have revolved around what we label as the "multiple-purpose" organization, that is, the type which includes two or more distinctly different professional or technical processes. An example may be helpful at this point: a firm devoted solely to the manufacture of automobile batteries for one client would be a single-operation organization, whereas a firm devoted to the manufacture of several product lines, to research, and to sales would be a multiple-purpose organization. Similarly, the welfare agency concerned only with placing children in foster homes might be considered a single-purpose organization, whereas the agency which provides a sheltered workshop, a recreation program, and a casework program would be a multiple-purpose organization. The importance of this distinction will emerge later, but we want to make it clear now that we considered administration of the relatively large and relatively complex organizations in our several fields.

We see three major functions performed by the administrative process, and we believe that usually there is a close correspondence between these three functions and three general levels in the organizational hierarchy. We called one important function "organization-directing," in the sense of discovering opportunities for the organization to satisfy needs or demands of the environment, and in the sense of winning environmental support for organizational goals—not in the narrow sense of issuing orders to members of the organization. This function is concerned with what the organization as a total entity is

now, is becoming, and should become, and with making sure that the organization continues to fit into the changing scheme of things.

Normally, we think of this organization-directing function as the responsibility of a board of trustees or directors or of a commission or a legislative body, such as a city council. But we know that often the chief executive is the key member of such a group and that when the board or council does effectively discharge organization-directing responsibilities, this fact frequently reflects the chief executive's capacity to energize his board or council. We believe that for the administrative process to operate effectively the chief executive must play an important part in the organization-directing function, and that this also enables him to link the directing function to the second of our three—the "organization-managing" function.

The organization-managing function is concerned with the sustenance of the organization as a total entity, that is, with acquiring, assigning, and planning for the orderly and coherent utilization of resources, namely finances, personnel, physical facilities and materials, and authority. The organization-managing function of the administrative process does not accomplish the ultimate work of the organization, but it provides the ingredients, instructions, and climate essential to that ultimate work. It uses as one of its criteria the goals and objectives established in the organization-directing function, but it uses as another important criterion for decisions the realities of the technical and professional processes necessary to accomplish the ultimate work of the organization—operating the machinery which manufactures a product, calling on sales accounts, interviewing clients, treating patients, dispensing advice, and so forth. We do not conceive of these technical behaviors as part of the administrative process as defined above; rather we believe that the administrative process serves to give over-all direction and meaning to technical and professional processes and to acquire and regulate the use of resources required by technical and professional activity. We do believe, however, that technical and professional actions must interlink with the administrative process, and it is at this point that we

* From James D. Thompson, "Common Elements in Administration," in Ella W. Reed (editor), *Social Welfare Administration* (New York: Columbia University Press, 1961), pp. 18-29. Reprinted with the permission of the author and the National Conference on Social Welfare. Thompson's paper was first presented at the Eighty-Seventh Annual Forum of the National Conference on Social Welfare in Atlantic City, New Jersey.

find the third major function of administration, which we refer to as the "supervisory" function.

In our view, the supervisory function of administration governs the utilization of the resources provided by the organization-managing aspect of administration, and orients their utilization in the way outlined by the organization-directing function of administration. The supervisory function results in the coordination of technical or professional activities, making sure that these are done at appropriate times and places and in generally accepted fashion.

To recapitulate: we find administrative roles at three major levels of the organization. At each level, administration performs a different function, and each level overlaps with and links those above and below it.

Now, in order to identify common elements of administration, and to compare administrative roles in different organizations, we must first determine which functions of administration involve the roles in question. We cannot do this simply by comparing similarly labeled roles, for the word "foreman" may be applied to one kind of role in one industrial firm and to a rather different kind of role in another industrial firm. Similarly, we cannot assume that "foundry foreman" is equivalent in the administrative process to "casework supervisor"—or that it is not. The personnel manager may have one kind of role in this organization and a rather different one in that organization. And so on.

We must emphasize, then, that in the following remarks we will be comparing roles in terms of the kinds of responsibilities outlined above, irrespective of the variety of labels which organizations may attach to those roles.

We believe there are significant elements in the supervisory function of administration which are common to large organizations in all fields. Whatever the technical and professional processes, those at the supervisory level are dealing with people and therefore must give attention to interpersonal communications practices, to motivation, to performance appraisal. More generally stated, concern with human relations is a common element of administration at the supervisory level, regardless of the field. A second important element at the supervisory level, common to all fields, is concerned with establishing work priorities, with shifting work loads as bottlenecks develop, with making sure that the activities of various technical specialists or professionals intermesh—in short, with coordination. A third common element at the supervisory level is the linking of the technical and professional processes to the managerial function and level of administration by anticipating future resource needs, negotiating with managers, and so on.

These, we believe, are the three major components

of supervisory roles, and they are common to all types of large, complex organizations. We will have more to say about the types of persons who can move from one field to another, but the only job-produced barrier to the transfer of supervisors between fields would be found in those instances where the supervisory job has in addition a nonsupervisory technical or professional component; that is, where the supervisor, in addition to supervising, must exercise the same specialized expertise as those he supervises, or must train and develop that expertise in his staff members.

Turning now to the organization-directing function and level of administration, we believe that some of the essential elements are common to all types of large organization. Irrespective of the technological or professional bases of the organization, this function of administration identifies social, economic, and political trends which open new opportunities to the organization or pose new problems for it; it determines the elements of the environment to which the organization seeks to be related, and determines strategy for reacting to pressure groups or organized blocs in the environment. This is the broadest of the administrative functions, requiring consideration of the distant future. Regardless of the specific lines of responsibility—to stockholders, to electors, or to a voluntary public—the individuals or groups performing the organization-directing function of administration need essentially the same kinds of abilities whatever the field, and the able person in this category frequently holds responsibilities in several different kinds of organizations simultaneously.

Now we move to the organization-managing function of administration. Here again the problems and procedures appear to be essentially the same in the several fields. Regardless of the technical or professional bases of administration, there are common practices for financial planning and management, personnel development, program planning, control and review, purchasing and property control, and so on. For each of these managerial activities the basic machinery is common in all types of large organization, and the differences in technique represent only variations on a common theme.

Even more important at the organization-managing level of the organization is the essential responsibility for meshing the several managerial activities into one cohesive whole which is both consistent with the over-all direction established for the organization and supportive of the technological or professional processes required by that over-all direction. This problem of keeping the parts integrated into a whole is common, at the organization-managing level, to all types of large, complex organizations.

One of the questions which persisted through all our deliberations was the extent to which administrative ability is or can be transferable from one field to another. It is helpful to distinguish between the transfer of administrative techniques and the transfer of administrators. We are aware of instances of both, but it seems probable that the transfer of administrative techniques is more frequent and easier to accomplish.

Systems and procedures developed in one field frequently have been adopted and adapted by others, and we think it is likely that this kind of diffusion will increase. It is generally true that for each field to discover by trial and error what has already been refined in another field is uneconomical; the belief that each field is entirely unique can be a major deterrent to the economy of borrowing. The fact that adaptation may be necessary when systems and procedures are borrowed does not discourage us, for within fields refinements are constantly being developed and systems modified to fit evolving technologies and changing circumstances.

With respect to the transferability of individuals, the picture is more complicated, for several kinds of transfer are possible. At the level of organization-directing, the practice of appointing individuals from one field to responsibilities in quite a different field is widespread. It is not unusual for an individual to be a board member in several distinctly different fields, and where individuals are selected for their competence rather than for prestige or on the basis of occupational history they can bring new insights and stimulation to the organization.

We believe that the transferability of individuals at the supervisory and organization-managing levels of administration is largely governed by the evolutionary stage of the fields involved. Where the evolution of multiple purpose organizations has been recent and rapid, supervisory roles may be built by adding to professional or technical roles, so that the supervisor is viewed merely as a supertechnician or a superprofessional. When this is true, the supervisor in Department or Division A is automatically disqualified from moving to Department or Division B, which uses another variety of professional skills. But when the evolution has progressed far enough to have clearly distinguished between supervisory roles and professional roles, the multiple-purpose organization frequently finds it desirable to transfer supervisors from one department to another, and might indeed be inefficient if it refused to consider such transfers.

Similarly, in the rapidly evolving organization, organization-managing positions may be viewed as supersupervisory positions, with the responsibilities and activities of those in managerial positions reflecting the peculiarities of the technical bases of the organization. During this period of evolution the organization is likely to have difficulties, with managers giving too much attention to operational details, or too little attention to the acquisition and control of resources, or both. During this stage of evolution there are likely to be growing pains in the form of controversy over the importance of technical or professional expertness as a qualification for organization-managing roles. We believe this is a temporary issue, however, for the continued expansion of technical knowledge will result in greater size and complexity of organizations in all fields, and will make mandatory the recognition of administrative roles as distinct from expert roles.

The role of chief executive is particularly important in this respect. As organizations become multiple-purpose ones, and as they recognize the need for managerial specialists of various types, it becomes impossible for the chief executive to have expert knowledge of either the technical processes or the several aspects of management. In these complicated organizations, then, the chief executive must be able to comprehend a variety of things, for administrative purposes, and he must be able to fit them together. This is a "generalist" role, and indeed, the chief executive with expert knowledge in one of the organization's operations may be handicapped if he behaves like a generalist—at least until his specialized technical knowledge has faded into memory or been subjected to self-control.

We believe that usually the chief executive first becomes one by transferring from a more specialized managerial role. In the early stages of an organization's evolution it frequently is the case that only those who at some point have been identified directly with the basic professional work of the organization are considered qualified to step into the chief executive role. When the organization becomes a multiple-purpose one, service at any of several professional starting points may qualify an individual for consideration as the chief executive. When such organizations mature, however, it seems to us that the starting point and the route taken by the individual becomes of minor importance. Entering the organization by way of one of the managerial specialties, such as finance or personnel, may prepare him for executive responsibilities just as well as entering through one or another of the professions associated with the ultimate work of that organization. We know that this view is not fully accepted in all quarters but we believe it will become increasingly evident that the abilities of the individual, rather than arbitrary credentials, must be the basis of administration selection—and that these abilities can be acquired in various ways.

On the other hand we do not imply that an administrator judged "successful" in one organization would necessarily be successful in another. The transferability of an individual depends on several important variables, including:

1. *Adaptability.* This quality, of course, is as necessary for the administrator who remains stationary as for the one who transfers, for in both cases the individual should be flexible enough to adopt new techniques and new procedures for solving administrative problems whenever and wherever he finds them. The administrator who never changes his techniques can only appear to be successful when purposes and conditions remain unchanged, and this is unusual. The administrator who transfers from one field to another must also be able to adopt criteria for decision which are appropriate to the mission, and to reject criteria for decision which might have been appropriate for other missions but not for this one.

2. *Acceptability.* This implies acceptability not only to technical specialists and interested groups outside the organization, but also to others in the administrative process with whom his activities must be closely linked. Even when he transfers from one organization to another in the same field, the individual must win the confidence and acceptance of others involved in the administrative process, and his ability to do so may depend on such matters as the prior image he has created, his personality and personal prestige, and his persuasiveness.

3. *Commitment.* Here we have in mind the psychological readiness of the individual to identify himself with the purpose of the organization, and to relate to those outside the organization who believe in that purpose. Commitment to one single professional field rather than to an organizational mission can lead to rigidity.

4. *Awareness.* By this we refer to the administrator's ability to identify the underlying assumptions he has been able to make in his old position and to recognize that these assumptions may not be appropriate in his new position. These underlying assumptions describe the political nature of an organization, for they deal with sources of power and authority. The individual who assumes that the political nature of all organizations is identical can make serious mistakes. The military administrator who successfully transfers to an educational position modifies his behavior to accord with the differing sources and balance of power and authority, just as the business ad-

ministrator who serves in Washington learns that prior assumptions must be set aside.

The preceding analysis and our experiences which led to it have left us with the following convictions:

1. As organization-managing roles become differentiated from supervisory and organization-directing roles, the differences are not only of scope but also of quality.

2. As organizations become larger and more complex, we doubt that the best technician is necessarily the best candidate for a supervisory position, and we are even more certain that the best supervisor is not necessarily the best candidate for a managerial position.

3. We feel that rigid requirements, such as certain kinds of professional degrees, unnecessarily restrict the sources from which administrators can be drawn and are therefore unduly restricting on the fields which need increasingly effective administration. The focus should be on administrative ability rather than on career history; on readiness for the new responsibilities rather than on competence in a prior position.

4. Finally, we would like to see more serious thought given to questions of the recruitment and training of future administrators. We doubt that schools—of social work, public administration, business administration, education, hospital administration, or in any other field—have squarely faced the question of what kinds of administrative abilities and qualities will be needed in the next decade or two and asked themselves how to select and prepare individuals for those future needs.

Imagination and innovation are as desirable in administration as in any other activity, and they are likely to become increasingly necessary as our organizations and their environments become more complex. We wonder whether administrative improvements and new insights are more likely to come from executives who move from one field to another, from those who are appointed from within a major profession on which the organization relies, or from those who move from managerial specialties within the organization. This undoubtedly is related to the questions we raised of acceptability, adaptability, commitment, and awareness, and probably varies with the evolutionary stage of the field, but we believe it warrants further study.

A. CONTROL AND COORDINATION

One's initial image of an organization is usually a hierarchy of jobs and tasks, with higher-ups giving orders to and getting reports from lower-downs. Armies, business firms, and government agencies are often believed to be the organizations most closely approximating such chains of command. The selection by John M. Pfiffner and Frank P. Sherwood describes the highly bureaucratized and disciplined systems of such action-oriented or production-oriented organizations. The authors summarize the tasks of each managerial rank. Although the authors' ideas were derived from industry, they demonstrate their applicability to government. The leader of a voluntary association might find that some of the descriptions of echelons apply to his own organization directly or with modifications. The hierarchical and disciplined structure pictured by Pfiffner and Sherwood will describe some associations better than others. Within each association, their model will describe certain departments—such as the accounting division staffed by salaried employees—better than others.

LEVELS OF SPECIALIZATION AND COORDINATION*

John M. Pfiffner and Frank P. Sherwood

The heart of formal structure is the job-task-pyramid, which consists of tasks grouped into jobs (more accurately, positions), and jobs grouped into functional units, or boxes as depicted on the organization charts. These boxes are arranged into the pyramid both horizontally and vertically. The pyramid may be steep, in which case there are many echelons or horizontal levels, or it may be "flat," meaning that there are fewer horizontal levels but larger numbers of units on each echelon.

Unity of command. According to formal organization theory the lines of official authority run from boxes on a subordinate echelon to boxes on the next higher, and so on until they all converge at a single box at the top. At each level there are evidences of *unity of command*, meaning that subordinates formally report to only one boss. Ultimately all authority and responsibility rests in the top box. This is the supreme coordinating entity with official authority to impose its fiat upon all subordinate echelons. Sociological concepts of authority as advanced by Barnard and Simon throw doubt upon the validity of this extreme view of unity of command, but here we are attempting to set forth the main precepts of tradi-

* From John M. Pfiffner and Frank P. Sherwood, *Administrative Organization*, pp. 134-149. © 1960. Reprinted by permission of the authors and Prentice-Hall, Inc., Englewood Cliffs, N.J.

tional organization theory as they apply to superior-subordinate relationships. The myth of unity of command, using the term "myth" as a bit of folklore widely believed rather than in its vernacular meaning as being at least partially false, constitutes a major concept of the theory of formal organization.

Inasmuch as the term came (at least presumably) from the military, perhaps the traditional infantry regiment would be an example familiar to most male readers. At the bottom is the squad led by a sergeant; three or four squads constitute a platoon led by a sergeant or lieutenant; two or more platoons make a company led by a captain; three or four companies form a battalion led by a lieutenant colonel; and several battalions go to make up a regiment commanded by a colonel. In the composition of a traditional division two or more regiments make a brigade commanded by a brigadier general and two or more brigades comprise a division commanded by a major general. Above these is the corps, a grouping of divisions, and the army, a grouping of several corps.

CHANNELS AND CHAINS OF COMMAND

The chain of command constitutes the conduit through which commands and communications travel between superior and subordinate commanders. According to traditional organization theory, commands flow downward and information relative to achievement against prescribed goals flows upward. Communications and orders flow "through channels"; that is, they do not skip levels or echelons. On the plus side this pattern strengthens the positions of subordinate commanders by assuring them that their own subordinates will not receive orders directly from someone on a different level, a very demoralizing practice. The requirement that orders and communications go through channels also makes for coordination because everyone on the chain of command will have seen the communication and thus be "in the know."

Communication aspects. One of the principal disadvantages of the requirement that communications go through channels is that it slows down communications by requiring them to pursue a circuitous route. This is particularly aggravating in a situation where a communication to an office nearby has to go up through several echelons and back down through a branch chain. Those familiar with the military will perhaps have had experience with the system known as "endorsements" wherein a communication is added at each successive level and "endorsed" by the appropriate commander. If such a communication has to follow a long hierarchical route it may become a thick bundle of endorsements; furthermore, its travel time may have been slowed down considerably by waiting for attention at the several endorsing echelons.

As will be pointed out later in the chapter on communication, modern hierarchies, both military and civilian, provide for channels of communication that follow oblique and horizontal lines without infringing upon the integrity of the unity of command concept. Nevertheless, the folklore of formal organization theory is so strong that the organization analyst is likely to discover slavish adherence to "channels" in many cases where it is not necessary and where streams clogged with the debris of correspondence can be cleared by redirecting the flow through shorter conduits. With the "exception" principle and modern concepts of communications as a circuit rather than a pyramid, it is not necessary for a commander on each echelon to have seen and read every message, but only those which require his attention for purposes of information or decision.

Upward focus. In the theory of formal organization the attention of subordinates is toward the boss and higher echelons, in general. Everyone is busy watching the boss and he in turn is observing his boss. Orders flow downward as does the dispensation of rewards and benefits. Recent researches have indicated that this is perhaps more true of the mobile members of the organization than of those who have become "frozen," that is, who have reached their ceilings. The latter tend to seek rewards which management cannot give, namely, the social group membership dispensed only by their fellow workers.[1] Indeed, perhaps the major problem of motivation is to devise ways and means of "unfreezing" the workers, that is, in a sense, to get them to look more eagerly upward.

Nevertheless, the dominant spirit prevailing in most organizations is that of the pyramid rather than the circle. Significant decisions tend to be made on the higher echelons; the important orders emanate from there; the formulation of major policy originates there; and personnel actions affecting the personal fortunes of individuals are taken by bosses rather than peers. Hence the focus upward prevails . . .

AN OUTLINE OF TASK DIFFERENTIATION BY ECHELON

Large-scale organizations may have as many as a dozen supervisorial levels or echelons between the person performing "direct labor" in the factory or the field and the top echelon at headquarters. However, it is our hypothesis that these levels of leadership and sub-leadership can be divided into four distinct categories on the basis of similarity of task. These are (1) corporate management, (2) top production management, (3) middle management, and (4) supervisory management. Obviously what people do, the tasks they perform, differs from one of these management levels to another.

Furthermore, a person who performs well on one of these levels may not do equally well on another. This may be because of inherent personal qualities which cannot be altered or because of a failure to perceive the need to change behavior which one has followed in the old job. For example, the corporate level is a relatively new organization device. While it may have existed in organizations of the past, American corporations are just beginning to adjust themselves to the realization that the tasks of corporate management differ from those of production management. The corporate executive committee, which tends to be the power center at the corporate level, spends a great deal of time in reading reports, digesting information, deliberating, planning, and formulating over-all long-range policy. The natural place to look for corporate managers is at the production management level, but that is a place of action rather than of deliberation, with the result that the transition from production management to corporate management may be difficult.

Similarly, the supervisory management level often

[1] A. Zaleznik, C. R. Christensen, and F. J. Roethlisberger, *The Motivation, Productivity, and Satisfaction of Workers* (Boston: Harvard Business School, 1958).

requires a behavior in which, in order to get things done, the supervisor seems to compromise. He is often referred to as a "double talker." He must have one ear cocked to the sentiment of the work group while listening to the production logic of management with the other. In order to preserve a desirable equilibrium he attempts to mollify both sides, but in doing so he fails to manifest the ascendancy traits which attract the attention of higher-ups. The levels above him call for a management ideology characterized by a rational emphasis on maximizing productivity, and upward social mobility. These are values which the environment of the production levels does not foster.

THE CORPORATE LEVEL

In smaller organizations there may be no distinction between corporate management and production management. But as organizations grow beyond a certain size, stresses and strains develop because people at headquarters continue to function as though they were production managers. There is a tendency in such an organization toward line functionalism, that is, the headquarters people deal with manufacturing, supply, engineering, and marketing as though they had to assume control and direction at the operating level.

Experience of the aircraft industry. One of the best laboratories for observing the emergence of the corporate level is the aircraft industry, where in the fifteen years from 1940 to 1955 there took place an evolution which in most organizations lasts for several decades. They started out in limited quarters with a few hundred employees, and were led by flying or engineering enthusiasts who had little or no managerial background. The experience of one such company may be typical. From 1936 to 1943 it jumped from 5,000 to 90,000 employees. When the government began to ask for cost figures and more production, the existing system would yield neither. Management, experimentation, and production tended to operate together at the shop level. Then size and government pressure forced the adoption of system (bureaucratization). But top management continued to be housed on the factory premises, where it concerned itself with the minutiae of day-to-day operations.

Then came three developments which forced the recognition of the corporate level as a distinct entity in itself. The first was geographical decentralization by the establishment of plants at different locations, some hundreds or thousands of miles away, such as Lockheed in Georgia and at Sunnyvale, California, and Boeing in Seattle and Wichita. The second was diversification, such as North American's move into the field of atomic energy. The third was the need for administrative decentralization because of size and bureaucratic ponderousness. This trend was capped by the erection in 1957-58 of buildings devoted exclusively to corporate activities for two of the California aircraft companies.

Other perspectives. Management below the corporate level tends to be parochial; it is composed of people who are unifunctionally oriented, that is, they have one objective such as making a particular automobile, paint, or fabric. As organizations grow there is a tendency at first to have production executives double in brass as members of the corporate executive committee. This has two disadvantages, in addition to overworking the individual involved. In the first place, production executives tend to have an eye cocked toward the interests of their own separate bailiwicks in making decisions which should be based on broader considerations. Secondly, their habits, visions, and outlook are focused toward day-to-day productivity rather than planning and general guidance. The result is that it has been found advisable to relieve members of executive committees from operating duties, a step which took place at DuPont twenty or more years ago and in the Bank of America in the 1950's.

Drucker's study of General Motors describes central management's role as "to weld several hundred aggressive, highly individual and very independent divisional top executives into one team."[2] He goes on to state five main ways in which this is accomplished: (1) setting goals, (2) defining limits of authority, (3) constantly checking on divisional problems and progress, (4) relieving divisional management of problems not strictly a part of production and selling, and (5) furnishing staff advice and service.

The problem of the corporate level is to boss without seeming to boss; to watch productivity without taking over direct responsibility—therefore, to know what takes place without seeming nosey; and to maintain control without stifling initiative and self-reliance.

It is not only a matter of giving up power, but learning to operate in a different manner (changing behavior). The new dispensation in organization behavior aims to reverse the cultural values extant in the world throughout human existence. It seeks to modify the hierarchy wherein a great Caesar at the top directs the most minute actions of a chain of little Caesars beneath him. The hierarchy is retained but its harsher features are disguised. Each echelon of leadership leads without seeming to; each leader is encouraged to make decisions on his own responsibil-

[2] Peter Drucker, *The Concept of the Corporation* (New York: The John Day Company, 1946), p. 49.

ity. Indeed, the whole effort is directed toward developing strength and resourcefulness at the operating levels. That is why, when a production manager is promoted to the corporate level, he finds it difficult to adjust; he is not used to a role characterized by planning, deliberation, review, reading, and long-run perspective. The result is that he sometimes disturbs subordinate echelons by his tendency to reach down into production as an agent for action and troubleshooting.

Application to government. While it may be difficult to apply the corporate level concept to specific governmental institutions, it surely has relevance to the behavior of specific units. Thus, in federal administration it would seem that both the presidency and the top echelons of the great executive departments are essentially corporate from the standpoint of differentiation of tasks. One could say the same of the office of governor in the states and mayor in the larger cities. Each of these positions embraces tasks that require a behavior essentially corporate rather than productive in nature. These include: (1) coordinating a wide variety of agencies with separate and distinct technologies and objectives, (2) doing this without making operating decisions, (3) planning for the long run, (4) evaluating results without constantly "telling how" to do it, (5) developing policy which has over-all implications, and (6) providing and allocating finances.

TOP PRODUCTION MANAGEMENT

By top production management is meant the leadership jobs at what is known as the division level in industry and perhaps the bureau and regional office level in the federal government. These are at the top of a unifunctional sub-hierarchy, such as production of a particular brand of automobile or administering the national forests. At the top of the production hierarchy is found a replica of the subunits at corporate headquarters. In industry these would include manufacturing, sales, engineering, and finance.

Since present management philosophy calls for the decentralization of decision-making at all levels, production management, like corporate management, must condition itself to a hands-off type of behavior, in this case toward middle management. But top production management differs from corporate management in other respects. First, it is nearer to the scene of production. Second, while a "breathing down the necks" type of supervision may be frowned upon, production management is nevertheless directly interested in production and the chances are that it gets daily feedback reports that are closely scrutinized and

questioned. This means, third, that the prevailing psychological atmosphere is centered upon operations and what goes on in the factory or field.

MIDDLE MANAGEMENT

Middle management is a generic term that may be difficult to apply to positions in specific organizations. It includes the echelons of leadership immediately below those of top production management. The terminology used may be department head or division head, and also included are those staff, technical, and engineering personnel who are production-centered.

A psychological study of how top and middle management looked at itself demonstrated marked variations between the two.[3] Individuals in the top management group perceived themselves as active, self-reliant and willing to act on the basis of their abilities. They were ready to take risks. They possessed confidence that their decisions would lead to success, and their interpersonal behavior was characterized as candid and straightforward.

Middle managers saw themselves as careful planners who displayed well controlled behavior and whose actions were carefully thought out. They seemed to place more reliance on operating within the rules and conditions of the system than in plunging ahead on their own ideas. They wanted to avoid the appearance of being controversial personalities. They saw themselves as stable and dependable persons who tended to hew to the line.

SUPERVISORY MANAGEMENT

Supervisory management embraces what may be three or four levels, constituting those jobs whose duties typically involve immediate and continuing contact with production workers. It should be noted, however, that there may be some supervision on virtually all levels, including the top where a head clerk is in charge of clerical help in an executive suite. However, we ordinarily think of supervisory management as being in charge of direct labor in the factory or field. Foreman is the term most generally applied to the lowest level of full-time supervision. He may have an assistant foreman and may himself report to a general foreman.

The tasks of supervisory management are in many respects similar in kind to those of management on other levels, because supervisors plan, implement policy, and organize—and would seem to be acquiring increasing duties in the realm of budgeting and finance. Indeed, the prevailing climate of decentralization tends to picture the foreman's bailiwick as a

---

[3] L. W. Porter and E. E. Ghiselli, "The Self Perceptions of Top and Middle Management Personnel," *Personnel Psychology*, Volume 10 (Winter 1957), pp. 397-406.

microcosm wherein he exercises a maximum of decision-making authority, a situation which is perhaps more of an aspiration or virtuous avowal of intent than it is an actual achievement in most organizations.

But perhaps the distinguishing feature of the supervisory level is propinquity to the mass of production workers. A recent study of the foreman's tasks discovered the three broad areas of critical competencies to be in administrative matters, in supervising subordinates, and in relations with equals and superiors. The second category was broken down into the following six: (1) development of subordinates, (2) correction of undesirable behavior, (3) giving credit where due, (4) equality of treatment, (5) concern for employee's welfare, and (6) keeping subordinates informed. Of the 16 critical factors in the three broad categories, ten were based directly on *interpersonal relations*.[4]

BEHAVIOR-TASK GUIDES
FOR EACH ECHELON

Each of the four managerial levels has tasks which are essentially alike in kind but vary in degree. And much of the difference in degree lies in the extent to which decision-making is decentralized. Though the idea of levels in organization is old, present theories as to the nature and function of these levels derive clearly from the decentralization concept. This general question of relating levels to the new decentralization trend is a timely one, which is attested by the appearance of three studies almost simultaneously. Each describes the problems encountered in industrial organizations undergoing decentralization where relations between the various functional specialists and the operating people was particularly delicate.[5] In each case one of the major problems encountered was the inability or unwillingness of people who had previously been in positions of operating control to change over to specialist advisory positions . . .

As a concrete means of identifying the nature of these responsibilities at the various levels, a set of broad behavior-task guides for the four levels are suggested. They assume the existence of a philosophy of decentralization within the organization and a full complement of functional specialists.

4 Brian R. Kay, "Key Factors in Effective Foreman Behavior," *Personnel*, Volume 36 (January-February 1959), pp. 25, 27.
5 Eli Ginzberg and Ewing W. Reilley, *Effecting Change in Large Organizations* (New York: Columbia University Press, 1957); George Albert Smith, Jr., *Managing Geographically Decentralized Companies* (Boston: Harvard Business School, 1958); Paul R. Lawrence, *The Changing of Organizational Behavior Patterns* (Boston: Harvard Business School, 1958).

CORPORATE MANAGEMENT LEVEL

Spends comparatively more time in reflection and deliberation; reads staff reports.

Attends many meetings.

Meticulously avoids becoming involved in day-to-day operations at production levels.

Specialized units act in pure staff relationship to subordinate echelons.

Contacts with operating officials deal with over-all and long-run goals rather than day-to-day problems and achievements.

Makes long-range plans.

Makes policy which serves as guides rather than directions.

Sets goals and devises feedback control in such a way as to stay out of day-to-day operations.

Has public relations contacts with government officials, national pressure groups, and client (customer) organizations.

Travels a great deal; visits to branches consultative rather than punitive; inspection.

Evaluates personnel from standpoint of choosing future executives.

TOP PRODUCTION
MANAGEMENT LEVEL

Focus is on immediate production, whether manufacturing, sales or service.

Makes policy decisions within framework laid down at corporate level, but does not hesitate to plow new ground when circumstances warrant.

Gets daily feedback on productivity and takes personal and immediate interest in trouble spots.

Lets subordinates handle trouble, but makes his own interest felt.

Specialized units act in staff capacity, but have intimate and constant contact with production.

Engages in long-run planning which is synchronized with corporate level.

Evaluates personnel for promotability.

MIDDLE MANAGEMENT LEVEL

Maintains closer contact with day-to-day results.

Participates in operating decisions.

Evaluates production results rather than program.

Evaluates personnel from standpoint of immediate usefulness than future potential.

Press of events minimizes time spent in reading and reflection.

Deliberation with colleagues more likely to be spent in solving urgent and immediate problems.

Makes plans for achieving goals established by corporate level.

Implements policy decisions within the limitations set by higher echelons.

SUPERVISORY MANAGEMENT LEVEL

Plans day-to-day production within goals set from above.

Assigns personnel to specific jobs and tasks.

Watches hour-to-hour results.

Reports feedback information daily.

Takes corrective action on the spot.

Maintains personal and immediate contact with production personnel.

Evaluates personnel from standpoint of immediate needs.

Implements policy decisions within the limitations set by higher echelons.

Informal custom not prescribed or proscribed.

Pfiffner and Sherwood describe the tasks at various levels of the hierarchy in organizations. An organization is not only hierarchical; it is also pyramidal. Ideally, the top leadership group should be small, even for large organizations that have many members and many functions at the grass roots. The organization should be so constructed that the leadership is in touch with the membership in an exchange of information, in communicating decisions, and in reviewing performance. But since one leader possesses neither the time nor the energy to be in touch with every grass-roots member and office, his supervision and communication always must be performed indirectly and through functionally separate channels.

Leaders of every organization must decide the number of channels, i.e., the shapes of the organizational pyramid. In traditional management theory, this is called deciding the executive's "span of control," and the reader can find pertinent advice in many management textbooks. The reader can also learn the practices of American corporations from a questionnaire survey of 150 corporations, carried out by the American Management Association. The survey found that the number of executives reporting to the corporation president was more than the number foreseen by classical span-of-control theory (actually between seven and eight instead of the theoretical three to four). The presidents' need to keep in touch with company activity, the need to avoid the inefficiency and communication blockage resulting from too many intermediate levels, and other considerations thus involve presidents in company affairs more closely than was traditionally assumed necessary. Certain departments report to the president more directly than others—i.e., production, marketing, and personnel, more often than public relations and advertising.* Leaders of voluntary associations may find in such surveys of business experience useful background information when they must decide how to construct their own organizations. Similar surveys of a large number of voluntary associations have yet to be made.

Subordinates' compliance with leaders' directions is essential to the success of an organization. From a common-sense perspective, one may think initially that the leader's rewards and sanctions are the basis of compliance, but research about leader–follower relations in organizations shows that the reasons for compliance in each instance may be multiple, and different reasons may govern different situations. In the next selection, Herbert A. Simon says that compliance with authority may be the result of the leader's

* Ernest Dale, *Planning and Developing the Company Organization Structure* (New York: American Management Association, 1952), pp. 51-60.

proffered rewards, the leader's threatened sanctions, the subordinate's peers, and the socially-recognized competence of the leader. Rewards and sanctions have limited efficacy, and successful organizations are those that somehow tap the voluntary loyalties of their members.

Simon discusses certain dilemmas resulting from the discoveries by management experts and behavioral scientists that rewards and sanctions are used much less frequently and effectively than previously believed, and that employee loyalty must be developed and used. In organizational theory and (to a lesser extent) in organizational practice, a "human relations" school has claimed that effective compliance always necessitates the persuasion and voluntary participation of subordinates. Simon describes the disadvantages of excessive reliance on either authoritarianism or "human relations" alone. One of the merits of the selection is its expression of the qualifications many behavioral scientists now add to the once fashionable but oversimplified "human relations" approach to the management of organizations.

THE NATURE OF AUTHORITY*
Herbert A. Simon

Without disputing the right of anyone else to use words as he pleases, I should like to state what I shall mean by *authority* in the remainder of this essay.

An individual accepts authority when he sets himself a general rule that permits the communicated decision of another to guide his own choice (i.e., to serve as a premise of that choice) independently of his judgment of the correctness of acceptability of the premise. . . .[1]

If we use the term "influence" to denote any change in behavior induced in one person by one or more others, then authority is one of the forms of influence, the other (persuasion) being change induced by information and conviction. In any concrete instance, authority is unlikely to be observed in pure form, but, instead, is usually liberally admixed with persuasion.

MOTIVATIONS FOR THE ACCEPTANCE OF AUTHORITY

Having settled definitional questions, we come to the real problems with which a study of authority in organizations must deal. First, under what circumstances and to what extent do individuals accept authority as a basis for their choices and behavior? Second, what motivates individuals to accept authority? Third, what are the consequences of an authority

relation for those who exercise it and for those who accept it? Since our primary concern here is with the questions of policy and value that stem from the phenomena of authority, I shall proceed directly to the second and third questions.

What are the motivations for acceptance of authority? There are at least four that are of considerable importance:

I. REWARDS AND SANCTIONS

Authority is accepted because the person exercising it can attach pleasant or unpleasant consequences to action through the system of rewards and sanctions. (I will use the term "sanctions" to refer generically to both rewards and negative sanctions.) The most important sanctions of managers over workers in industrial organizations are (a) power to hire and fire, (b) power to promote and demote, and (c) incentive rewards.

The management of an industrial concern has these sanctions at its immediate disposal to a greater or lesser degree depending, among other things, upon alternative opportunities open to employees and upon strength of employee unions. In addition, society, through its legal system and courts, lends to members of industrial organizations other sanctions whose exercise is based on the law of contracts and property and upon special rights defined by statute (e.g., wage and hour legislation).

In the employer-employee relation the employer by no means possesses a monopoly of sanctions. We shall see, when we come to discuss the "poverty of power," that employees, particularly when they are organized in unions but even when they are not, have a number of effective sanctions at their disposal which they can use to neutralize the power of the em-

* From *Research in Industrial Human Relations*, edited by Conrad M. Arensberg, et al. Copyright © 1957 by Harper & Brothers: pages 103-115, "Authority" by Herbert A. Simon. Reprinted with the permission of the author and publisher.
[1] For a fuller discussion, see the author's *Administrative Behavior* (New York: Macmillan, 1947, p. 125); his *Public Administration* (New York: Alfred A. Knopf, 1950), pp. 180-182; and Chester I. Barnard's *The Functions of the Executive* (Cambridge: Harvard University Press, 1938), p. 163.

ployer. Hence the relation is not nearly as one-sided as a narrow view of the legal and formal implications of the employment contract would imply.

2. LEGITIMACY

The motive of legitimacy refers to the tendency of people to do what they feel they "ought" to do. The terms "right" and "wrong" are sometimes defined substantively—"Thou shalt not kill!"—but more often procedurally—"Thou shalt obey the law!" To the extent that people respond to the motive of legitimacy, the acceptance of authority can be secured by legitimizing the right to give orders and the obligation to accept them. "Legitimizing" is used here as a psychological term—the creation of a set of attitudes. The basic psychological mechanisms that create and maintain attitudes of acceptance of legitimate authority are identical with those responsible for the acquisition and internalization of other attitudes.

3. SOCIAL APPROVAL

Authority is accepted when rejection would incur disapproval from persons whom an individual regards as his "reference group"—a group in which he wants acceptance and approval. Approval and disapproval may properly be regarded as sanctions, but since the reference group is often not the group that can dispose of the other sanctions, the approval-disapproval sanction deserves separate consideration. For the same reason, acceptance of the one authority may entail rejection of the other. Important situations where this occurs will come readily to mind.

There is an important interaction between social approval and the legitimacy motive. When a particular system of authority is accepted as legitimate by members of a group, not only do they tend to accept authority in their own behavior, but they tend also to exhibit disapproval toward members of the group who do not accept it. I would conjecture that it is through this indirect mechanism that the motive of legitimacy obtains its greatest force. The approval mechanism operates as a powerful amplifier to secure compliance with the particular system of authority that the group accepts as legitimate.

4. CONFIDENCE

Authority is accepted when a decision premise comes from a source that is regarded as technically competent to provide that premise. The authority of a doctor over his patient, of an attorney over his client, are typical examples of the authority of confidence. Both inside and outside organizations much of the authority of the technical specialist derives from this source —particularly the authority that operates upwards and sidewise in the formal organizational hierarchy. The authority of confidence is generally an important

part, too, of the authority relation between superiors and subordinates although—as we have just seen—it is not limited to that relation.

Debates about the "proper" definition of the term "authority" usually center around the issue of whether acceptance of behavior premises should be called "authority" regardless of which of the four motivational mechanisms caused the acceptance, or whether the term should be limited to acceptance due to rewards and sanctions, or to the legitimacy motive. We will use here an inclusive definition that embraces all instances of the exercise and acceptance of authority, whatever the motivational base. When it becomes necessary to distinguish among the motivations, we will refer to "authority of sanctions," "authority of legitimacy," "authority of social approval," and "authority of confidence."

AUTHORITY, COERCION, AND MANIPULATION

It is not easy in our society at the present time to use "authority" as a neutral, descriptive term. It transforms itself too easily into "authoritarian," which is more epithet than description. But authority, as I have defined it, is neither good nor bad. It becomes good or bad in particular situations on the basis of our evaluation of the social consequences of its exercise. We regard authority as "coercion" when it rests primarily on sanctions and is used to advance the interests of the party who possesses it against the interests of the other. We regard influence (authority or persuasion) as "manipulation" when it rests on disparity between the parties in their skill and technique of persuasion and negotiation, and when the disparity is used to advance the interests of the stronger against those of the weaker. . . .

Authority that is viewed as legitimate is not felt as coercion or manipulation, either by the man who exercises it or by the man who accepts it. Hence, the scientist who wishes to deal with issues of manipulation that are sometimes raised in human relations research must be aware of his own attitudes of legitimacy. In particular, he must understand his own beliefs as to the scope of legitimate authority that is implied by an employment relation. If he regards the area of legitimate authority as narrow, many practices will appear to him coercive or manipulative that would not seem so with a broader criterion of legitimacy.

THE POVERTY OF POWER

When we are confronted with a discrepancy in the views of several parties to an agreement as to what they have agreed to do, it is natural to ask who has, in fact, the power to enforce his viewpoint with sanctions. Modern students of authority—Charles E. Merriam and Chester I. Barnard prominent among them —have observed that the study of enforceability should start with the person who accepts authority rather than the person who seeks to wield it.

The reason is that the behavior authority seeks to control is the behavior of the subordinate, not the behavior of the superior. The acceptance that is secured may be the "I do" of a shotgun wedding, but acceptance there must be. This is not merely a verbal quibble, for it implies that wherever the authority relation exists there must be a mechanism to maintain it, and this mechanism must be efficacious.

In the employment relation, the employer has the sanctions of firing, the lockout, incentive pay, and promotion. But the employee has the sanctions of quitting, the strike, and the slowdown—as well as more subtle means of job control. The strengths of each of these as rewards and sanctions will depend on the state of supply and demand for labor, the degree of organization of labor, the legitimacy or illegitimacy attached by the courts and the state of these several sanctions, and numerous other factors.

When the balance of sanctions is not completely one-sided, however, it is the employer who is faced with the problem of securing acceptance of authority from the employee, and not vice versa. It is this asymmetry that improverishes the power of sanctions. The employee has at his disposal a whole range of weapons of minimal performance, literal performance, and nonperformance to help him resist attempted exercises of authority that appear to him illegitimate or unwelcome, and hence to enforce his version of the employment bargain.

Under these circumstances, "human relations" may take on very different meanings for the employee and the employer, respectively. The employee wishes to emphasize that when he sells his services he does not sell a commodity. He has feelings and attitudes both about what he is asked to do on the job and how he is asked to do it. If the employer does not enlist his willing acceptance by paying attention to these aspects of the job, the employee may feel justified in demonstrating the employer's inability to compel his acceptance.

When the employer is confronted with the poverty of his power, he too may turn to "human relations." Finding little common ground with the employee as to the legitimate boundaries of his authority, and finding sanctions ineffective as means for motivating acceptance, he may want to find what other motivations there are—and discover the answer in some of the findings of human relations research.

In the problem posed by the two previous paragraphs lie some of the central difficulties of securing acceptance for research in human relations as a neutral scientific activity. I do not mean to assert that human relations research always *has* been entirely neutral, but that even if it had, it would have a hard time convincing the parties to the employment contract that it was so. Let us look at what some human relations research has had to say about the authority concept.

THE SUPERIORITY OF "DEMOCRACY"

Perhaps I should indicate what I am including in the term "human relations research." Broadly, I mean research that is directed at understanding the motivations and behaviors of humans in groups; somewhat more narrowly, I mean research on human behavior in the industrial setting.

There is, of course, no official body of "human relations" doctrine. On the other hand, there is a considerable measure of agreement among the principal investigators about several central generalizations. One such generalization is the *participation hypothesis*: to bring about change in behavior in an organization and to get effective acceptance of new practices, it is necessary to secure the active participation in the decision of those whose behavior will be affected by the change.

A second generalization is the *social approval hypothesis*: the most powerful sanction influencing an individual employee is the approval and disapproval of the other members of his work group.

An employer who experiences the poverty of power and finds the authority of legitimacy and sanctions inadequate to his managerial tasks may seek to enlist the mechanisms of participation and social approval as means of persuasion and as additional motivations for the acceptance of authority. He is likely to be successful to the extent that the several parties to the employment contract *perceive* their goals to be more or less parallel.

Let us consider first the social approval hypothesis. I have stated the hypothesis in a weaker form than one usually finds in the literature. The statement often is that increase in social cohesion of the work group will increase the productivity of the employee. Evidence from studies of productivity and morale does not bear out this stronger hypothesis with any consistency. The reason is that there will be a positive correlation between productivity and morale only to the extent that goals approved by the work group are consistent with goals of management. Both reason and empirical evidence generally support this more qualified statement.

It is also clear why the participation mechanism is useful to the employer only under the assumption of substantial parallelism of interests. The employer can tolerate genuine participation in decision-making only when he believes that reasonable men, knowing the relevant facts and thinking through the problem, will reach a decision that is generally consistent with *his* goals and interests in the situation. This requires that they must, at least in part, share those goals and interests or have parallel ones. Participation can bolster the authority of confidence and can supplement authority with persuasion, but it can do these things only to the extent that the parties perceive themselves as working toward common goals.

Pioneer research in human relations has been much criticized for the enthusiasm with which it advocated participation in decision-making and encouragement of group cohesion as solutions for the human problems of the workplace. The basis for that criticism has been sketched in the preceding paragraphs. The error arose because it was assumed implicitly that there was an underlying community of goals between employer and employees and because this assumption was never made explicit or subjected to careful empirical examination.

Because symptoms of industrial strife are so easily and commonly observed, a lack of good faith has sometimes been charged against persons who have made the implicit assumption of community of goals in interpreting their research findings, and the adjective "manipulative" has been applied to human relations techniques. I have no way of knowing whether employers have accepted and attempted to apply the findings of human relations research in good or in bad faith. But I think it is easy enough to explain how a reasonable man, even in the face of evidence of industrial strife, still could make the assumption of community of goals.

It has been an overwhelming prevalent ideology in this country that the way to get more pie is to bake a larger one, not to quarrel about the slicing of the smaller one. (I am not concerned with the truth of the statement, but with widespread belief in it.) How could an employer reconcile his acceptance of this tenet, and his belief that his employees accepted it, with their observable resistance to his authority—his "managerial prerogatives"?

1. He could suppose that he had misjudged their goals—that they were interested not merely in the pay envelope but also in satisfactions, social and otherwise, associated directly with the job.

2. He could suppose that they did not have a complete enough understanding of the advantages to them (through the increased size of the pie) of the action he was proposing.

If the employer adopted the first line of interpretation, he would likely have become, a generation ago, a highly paternalistic employer, or, today, an enthusiastic "human relator." If the employer adopted the second line of interpretation, he would seek, via the participation mechanism, to supplant the employees' "sentiments" with his own "logic." In all these cases the outcome would depend not only on what he did, but on how his employees interpreted his actions.

We see that the findings of human relations research, *if* they are combined explicitly with the assumption of community of goals, can be used to show a deep lying consistency between good and effective managerial practices, on the one hand, and the generally accepted values of our culture on the other:

1. Employer and employee have the common goal of creating a larger product that will be shared not only between them, but with the consumer and the investor as well.

2. Excessive reliance on formal authority and the authority derivable from sanctions is not an effective way of producing this larger product. Hence there is no conflict of good managerial practice with the democratic and antiauthoritarian values of our culture.

3. The pleasant workplace is the productive workplace. Hence there is no conflict of good managerial practice with the desires of employees to derive satisfactions from their jobs and from social activity connected with their work.

EFFICIENCY OR SATISFACTION

Each of the three main tenets of the doctrine sketched in the preceding section has been the subject of critical re-examination. The question of size of the pie and who shares it is beyond the scope of the present essay—it would lead us over the whole area of industrial relations, anti-trust policy, government-business relations, and what not. Our concern will be with the other two issues, which we will find it convenient to label "authority or democracy" and "efficiency or satisfaction," respectively.

The doctrine has not gone unchallenged that "democratic" administration or administration that depends heavily upon participation in decisions and that does not brandish its formal authority—is the most effective administration. Without attempting to survey the literature in detail, one might note particularly the work of Barnard, Homans, and Argyris in re-examining the functions of status differentials in organizations and in challenging the notion that a large-scale organization can or should be egalitarian.

The situation with respect to efficiency and satisfaction is somewhat more complicated. Early proponents of scientific management adopted a fairly narrow, almost physiological, point of view; emphasized short-term efficiency through specialization; and pretty well neglected the subtler motivational aspects of the problem—including the satisfactions of the worker *on the job.* Early human relations research directed attention to the worker's job satisfactions and the long-run feedback of these upon performance; it undoubtedly swung the pendulum too far in assuming that if job satisfactions were handled, efficiency would take care of itself. More recent studies—e.g., the work of Bavelas and Leavitt with small laboratory "organizations"—re-emphasize the short-term conflict between work arrangements that are physiologically efficient and those that produce satisfaction, and cast doubt on the thesis that maintenance of an appropriate level of satisfaction will automatically assure a high level of productive efficiency.

The consequences of taking the middle ground with respect to either of these issues—authority v. democracy or efficiency v. satisfaction—do not seem to me particularly disturbing. We need simply to accept the fact that designing organizations, like designing the buildings that house them, is a rather complex activity and that organization design, like architecture, is a process of continual compromise in which we are always deciding how we shall divide our limited budget between more floor space and more attractive furnishings.

As long as these compromises have to be made, we must expect that employers and employees will often disagree as to the weights to be assigned to conflicting goals. What these weights should be is a matter to be settled by bargaining, not by scientific evidence. . . .

IN CONCLUSION

Management involves a combination of persuasion and the exercise of authority. It has to operate within a context that is perceived as involving both conflicting and parallel interests. Authority that rests solely or largely on sanctions is inadequate to the tasks of management, for the sanctions do not all lie on one side of the employment relation and the employee has many means of defending himself from the manager's attempts to enforce his authority.

Managerial authority may seek its second support in the mechanism of legitimacy, but this support extends only to the limits of the employees' acceptance of legitimacy. If authority is to extend beyond these limits, it must depend on other mechanisms—upon social approval and on confidence.

Much contemporary human relations research may be interpreted as seeking to enlarge the means for motivating members of organizations toward the acceptance of organization goals and of organization authority. The research has resulted in increased emphasis upon the mechanisms of persuasion, social approval, and confidence. Employee participation in decision-making and the strengthening of work-group influence over individual employees have been proposed as two important organizational techniques to this end.

The more recent work along these lines has shown however, that authority based on social approval and confidence depends heavily upon perceived parallelism of interest between employers and employees. We have had to moderate the optimism of some of the early human relations research which took that parallelism for granted and equated conflict with ignorance or lack of skill in human relations. Our present view is more balanced—at the expense of being more complex and less easily applied. In a world in which there was always a complete conflict of interests, . . . the terms "authority," "power," "coercion," and "manipulation" would be used almost synonymously. In such a world authority would extend only as far as the club could reach that enforced it, and the only function of knowledge of human behavior would be to give the party who possessed it power to manipulate. All bargains would be necessitous.

Clearly, most of us do not view the world in quite this way. We recognize areas of competition, but we do not regard these areas as coterminous with the whole of social life, nor the competition as lawless. Hence, we distinguish between an authority relation —which seems to us an acceptable and frequently useful pattern of social behavior—and a coercive or manipulative relationship, of which we disapprove. The problem of authority is one of the central issues that is always present, whether acknowledged or not, at the bargaining table. As management representatives and union leaders gain a deeper understanding of this problem they will be prepared increasingly to search for ways of enlisting the authority of legitimacy, of social approval, and of confidence in the pursuit of goals that employer and employee can both accept.

The leaders of every organization must achieve coordination in three direc-tions—with their governing body, among the organization's executives and departments, and with their subordinates. Behavioral scientists have not yet studied governing boards and the relations between executives and boards, so we cannot present any reports of research. However, several manuals of advice have been published about how to organize boards and how execu-tives should deal with boards, and the leader of a voluntary association is urged to consult them.* They are written from the perspective of personal managerial experience rather than social science research.

In most large organizations, committee meetings are commonly used as coordination devices so that heads of different departments can exchange information and make joint decisions. Every leader of a voluntary associ-ation must spend much of his time in committee meetings. From the stand-point of the organization, the leadership must choose whether individual action or committees should be used for specific decisions, and whether the gains from committee procedures outweigh their costs. The uses, advan-tages, and disadvantages of committees were subjects in the American Management Association's survey of the managerial practice of 150 large American companies, and the results may interest leaders of voluntary as-sociations. Most companies have committees that meet regularly, particu-larly in the policy-making areas of planning, control, formulation of objec-tives, organization, and the solution of jurisdictional questions. Committees are often used in administrative areas, such as setting administrative guide-lines, appointing personnel, and evaluating proposed innovations. Success-full committee work presupposes the right staff preparation by individuals.†

If an organization uses committees, the problem is to make them effec-tive. Many an executive has wished for guidelines for running committees, so that the best informed decisions can emerge at the least cost in time and with the least strain. Many committee participants have private impres-sions about good and bad methods based on personal experience, but gen-eral principles based on research are preferable.

A committee in an organization may be viewed as a small group, suscep-tible to the same research techniques used in small group research. In the next selection, Robert F. Bales, who has studied small groups extensively, describes the structures he has discovered in committees and suggests some guidelines. Many of his conclusions are directly applicable to the conduct of committees in voluntary associations; others could be adapted to fit special circumstances. Bales discusses fairly small committees, and somewhat different techniques may be needed to conduct larger meetings.

Bales' article mentions an important contribution of his small group research to leadership theory. Every group tends to develop at least two distinct leadership roles, one for task performance and one for the mainte-nance of morale. Few individuals can occupy both roles. The stability and success of the group depend on effective collaboration between these two types of leaders.

---

* See especially Cyril Houle, *The Effective Board* (New York: The Association Press, 1960).
† A more complete summary of facts and advice appears in Ernest Dale, *Planning and Developing the Company Organization Structure* (New York: American Manage-ment Association, 1952), pp. 86-97.

THE COMMITTEE MEETING*

Robert F. Bales

Not many years ago nobody seriously supposed that the subtle aspects of face-to-face human relations could be studied experimentally in the laboratory. All sorts of skeptical objections appeared, even among social scientists, when a few of their more hopeful colleagues began to set up small groups of subjects under laboratory conditions and study social behavior by direct observation. Now a number of such laboratories are in operation, and findings of possible practical importance are beginning to appear.

One of the early installations was set up by the Laboratory of Social Relations at Harvard University in 1947. This laboratory and some of its findings will serve as an illustration of the type of research now going on in a number of centers:

On the third floor of Harvard's Emerson Hall there is a specially designed room for the purpose of observing the operation of committees and similar types of small groups. Containing chairs and a table which can be varied in size, it is well lighted and surfaced in acoustic tile. On one wall is a chalkboard and on another a large mirror. Behind the mirror is an observation room, for in reality the mirror is a one-way glass through which a team of observers on the other side may watch without disturbing the subjects. While the subject group is aware that it is being watched, the illusion is such that any self-consciousness is only brief and the "mirror" is ignored and soon forgotten.

The groups vary in size from two to seven members, depending on the particular problem under discussion. The problem for discussion may be industrial, governmental, military, or educational in character, but in any case it has to do with administration and requires a decision or recommendation of some kind.

During the discussion the observers behind the "mirror" note the action within the group: who speaks, to whom he speaks, and how he speaks. The actual subject matter is not the primary concern, except as it indicates the speaker's feelings.

An ingenious machine, built by the laboratory, makes it easy for the observer to classify each statement as it is made. Observers are trained until they are able to classify within a second or so any remark

that is made into one of 12 descriptive categories. (Originally there were 87 categories of response, but gradually the list has been reduced to 12.) In addition, the conversation is sound-recorded for later checking.

Each experimental group takes part in 4 sessions of 40 minutes each. By the end of this time, an accurate appraisal of the way in which it operates *as a group* is possible, and the relationships between members can be predicted with some confidence should it ever meet again.

KINDS OF BEHAVIOR

All the behavior that goes on in a committee (or indeed, in any verbal interchange) can be viewed as a sequence of questions, answers, and positive and negative reactions to the questions and answers. Three types of questions are distinguished: *asking for information, opinion,* and *suggestion.* Corresponding to these three types of questions are three types of answers: *giving information, opinion,* and *suggestion.* These answers are problem-solving attempts, and they call for reactions. Negative reactions include: *showing disagreement, tension,* or *antagonism.* On the positive side the corresponding reactions include: *showing agreement, tension release,* and *friendly solidarity.* These are the 12 categories of remarks used as a basis of analysis in the Harvard experiments.

SUCCESSFUL DECISIONS

It is interesting to note that, on the average, about 50% of all remarks made in meetings are answers while the remaining 50% consist of questions and reactions. Such a 50-50 balance (or something close to it) may be one characteristic of successful communication. Problem-solving attempts are needed to reach a decision, but that is not all. It may very well be that if enough time is not regularly allowed also for questioning and reaction to occur in the meeting, the members will carry away tensions that will eventually operate to vitiate an apparently successful but actually superficial decision.

PARTICIPATION OF MEMBERS

A decision is not a successful decision unless each member who is supposed to have been involved in its making is actually bound by it in such a way that his later behavior conforms to it.

By and large, members do not seem to feel strongly

* From Robert F. Bales, "In Conference," *Harvard Business Review*, Volume 32, Number 2 (March-April 1954), pp. 44-50. Reprinted with the permission of the author and the publisher. Bales' methods are described in his book *Interaction Process Analysis* (Cambridge: Addison-Wesley Press, 1950). Additional findings on the behavior of experimental committees are reported in his article "How People Interact in Conferences," *Scientific American*, Volume 192, Number 3 (March 1955).

bound by a decision unless they have participated in making it. However, participation does not necessarily mean that each member has to talk an equal amount. As a matter of fact, even approximate equality of actual talking time among members is very rare; and, when it does appear, it is usually associated with a free-for-all conflict. A moderate gradient among members in talking time is the more usual thing.

More significantly, participation means that the meeting operates under the presumption that each member has an equal right to ask questions or voice negative or positive reactions to any proposal made, if he wishes, and a right to expect that, if he makes a proposal, it will receive an appropriate reaction from some other member. Because of time exigencies, most members, most frequently, allow a voiced proposal to represent what they themselves would say, and a voiced reaction to represent what they themselves might respond.

On the other hand, it is difficult to know when a member's feelings and interests are being adequately represented and when they are not. The difference is so subtle that he himself is not always able to tell. He may go away dissatisfied without knowing quite why. Hence there is probably no adequate substitute for *some* actual verbal participation of each member. A few words on his part will serve to express and solidify his involvement, and to avoid his subsequent dissatisfaction.

OPTIMUM BALANCE

There are about twice as many positive reactions in most meetings as there are negative reactions. One might suppose that the more successful the meeting, the fewer negative reactions and the more positive reactions one would find. But the evidence does not support this view. Rather, there appears to be a kind of optimum balance. Departures too far to either side are indicators of trouble.

Disagreement. Rates of disagreement and antagonism that are too high are sure indicators of trouble. Apparently, when ill feeling rises above some critical point, a "chain reaction" or "vicious circle" tends to set in. Logic and the practical demands of the task cease to be governing factors. Such an occurrence is an impressive experience when seen from the perspective of the observer behind the one-way glass in the laboratory:

The observer is unseen by the subjects, cannot communicate with them, and so in a basic sense is "not involved." He knows that no action will be taken on the decision of the committee. He may have heard

the same case discussed hundreds of times before. Nevertheless, he is "caught in the illusion of reality" as the temperature of the group begins to rise.

Suddenly the credulity of the observer is strained beyond some critical point. The illusion that the group is dealing with some external problem breaks. It becomes perfectly transparent—to the observer—that emotions have taken over, and that what one member is saying does not refer at all to some external situation but to himself and the other members present.

"Facts" are unwittingly invented or are falsified. Other facts drop out of sight entirely. When one members insists that "people in this office should be treated like human beings," it is clear that he refers to himself and how he feels he should be treated in this group. When his opponent insists that "troublemakers should be fired," it is equally clear that he refers to the man who just spoke to him.

The decision, if any, reached by a group in this state has all the characteristics of a "bad dream," indeed.

Agreement. There can also be too many agreements and too few disagreements. This condition may be an indication either of lack of involvement in the practical demands of the task or of an atmosphere so inhibited and constrained that nobody dares risk disagreement. In the ordinary mill run of opinions and suggestions, there is always a certain percentage so unrealistic, exaggerated, or unsuitable that not to disagree means not to solve the problem.

Closely related to the rate of agreement is the rate of suggestion. Groups in a smoothly operating condition tend to show relatively high rates of suggestion, as well as of agreement. But there is a joker in this finding. This condition is an *outcome* of smooth sailing, *not* a way to attain it.

As most people would suppose, giving facts is fairly safe. The probability of arousing disagreement by reviewing the facts of the case is relatively low. But giving opinions is more risky, for in so doing a man gives his inferences and expresses his feelings and values, including his prejudices. Others are more likely to disagree, and the means of resolving disagreements are much more vague and indirect than in the case of disputed facts.

Indeed, a suggestion can cause a real bottleneck. If a man agrees to the suggestion, he must embrace all it implies, assumes, or involves. He has bound himself to future action. Most people are quite sensitive to this kind of constriction, even though they know that a decision is necessary. That is why, as the rate of giving suggestions goes up, the rate of negative reactions also tends to increase.

REDUCING THE RISK

Of course suggestions are necessary before a decision is reached. The decision point is inevitably a crisis point. But this is the risk that all decision-making groups have to take. The wise strategist should seek to reduce his risks to a calculated minimum, which is something quite different from trying to escape them entirely. But how: The laboratory observations suggest a reasonable solution. Most successful groups go through an ordered series of three phases or stages in the solution of a problem:

(1) They attempt to assemble the largest possible pool of common information about the facts of the case.

(2) They make inferences and evaluations, and try to form common opinions in a general way.

(3) Only in the final phase do they get around to more specific suggestions, after an extensive groundwork has been laid.

Not all groups do this, by any means. Some start the other end to, and some start with an outburst of opinions before they ever look at a fact. Indeed, many of the members are hardly conscious of any difference between a fact and an opinion.

It is probably not any excess of wisdom or extraordinary sensitivity that produces the typical order of stages. It is rather, we may suppose, the "brute logic of natural selection." A suggestion given at a premature stage simply dies for lack of support, or is trampled to death in the general melee. Gradually the discussion is forced back to facts, where agreement can be reached.

In an environment barren of consensus, only a fact can survive; and, where there is hostility, even facts find a slim foothold. But a rich background of common facts lays the groundwork for the development of common inferences and sentiments, and out of these common decisions can grow. No decision rests on "facts" alone, but there is no better starting point. To start the decision-making process at any other point is to multiply the risk of a vicious circle of disagreement—and at no saving of time in the long run.

DUAL LEADERSHIP

One of the most startling implications of the laboratory research so far is that the concept of "leader," if it is taken too literally, can cause the man who thinks he *is* one to disregard a most important fact—namely, that there is usually *another* leader in the group whom he can overlook only at his peril.

SEPARATE ROLES

The laboratory findings, while still tentative, indicate that the man who is judged by the group members to have the "best ideas" contributing to the decision is *not* generally the "best-liked." There are two separate roles—that of task leader and that of social leader. If a man comes into a task-leadership position because he is popular or best liked, he is ordinarily confronted with a choice: (1) If he chooses to try to keep the task leadership of the group, he tends to lose some of his popularity and to collect some dislikes. (2) If he chooses to try to keep his popularity, he tends to lose the task leadership. People differ in the way they solve this dilemma, although most tend to prefer to keep the popularity rather than the task leadership.

The difficulty becomes more acute with time. At the end of the group's first meeting there is 1 chance in 2 that the task leader will be the most liked. At the end of the second meeting the chances are reduced to 1 in 4. At the end of the third they are 1 in 6, and at the end of the fourth they are only 1 to 7.

There are apparently few men who can hold both roles; instead, the tendency is for these positions to be held by two different men. Each is in reality a leader, and each is important to the stability of the group. The task leader helps to keep the group engaged in the work, but the pressure of decision and work tends to provoke irritation and injure the unity of the group. The best-liked man helps to restore this unity and to keep the members aware of their importance as particular individuals, whose special needs and values are respected. These men complement each other, and they are both necessary for smooth operation of a committee.

It is especially important for these two men to recognize each other's roles and in effect to form a coalition. The most stable groups observed have been those in which this coalition has taken place. There are indications that such durable groups as the family and simple small communities are constructed this way, and apparently the coalition also takes place in many administrative staffs, sometimes consciously but more often accidentally.

These findings challenge some very basic concepts of leadership. Millions are spent each year by business, government, and the armed forces in developing means for recognizing leaders, and much has been written about the "characteristics" of leadership. Yet it appears that whatever superior qualities the individual may possess as a simple individual, he may be unable, just because of the way groups work, to maintain a stable leadership position without a co-leader of complementary qualities.

COMMUNICATION NETWORKS

Significantly, among the half-dozen instances where the observation room and equipment at the Harvard laboratory have been duplicated are several installations by the military:

The Air Force has built a room at Maxwell Field, Alabama, for testing and predicting leadership ability. Other divisions of the armed forces are also engaged in the same kind of experimentation, for one of the most pressing problems they face is the development of leaders and the selection of personnel who have to work in small groups—bomber and submarine crews, intelligence teams, and communications centers—particularly in situations where immediate processing of information and rapid but wise decisions are a tactical necessity.

One of the persistent problems in rapid communications networks such as those found in military defense is how to keep the actual control over critical decisions in the hands of the person or persons who will later bear the formal responsibility for the decision. Practically, the decision-making function on the tactical level tends to gravitate to the person who is at the center of the communication network, where information about the tactical situation is immediately available. But this tactical information center tends not to coincide with the top spot in the chain of command, where formal authority and responsibility are centered.

Here again is an instance where it is unrealistic to operate with a simple notion of a single "leader" in whom all essential leadership functions can be vested. Although this problem appears most clearly in larger organizations, it is essentially a large-scale version of the same tendency toward division of labor in leadership that can be seen in a committee.

COMMITTEE MEMBERSHIP

If all this is true, the emphasis should shift from seeking the ideal leader to trying to compose the ideal total group. Accordingly, at Harvard the next few years will be devoted to observing groups for the specific purpose of assessing the personnel, then attempting actually to compose new committees from them which will function in a predicted way. With the right kind of assessment of each person's action within a group, it may be possible to pick, say, two people who would appear to be complementary leaders, put them with three more "neutral" people, and thus form a committee which would theoretically function at a certain predicted level of effectiveness. This at least is a start in the direction of rational composition of total groups.

OPTIMUM SIZE

Just to take one of the elementary problems, the question of optimum size of a committee has received many interesting answers, but so far they seem to come mostly from numerology rather than from scientific research. For the particular task and time lim-

its given to subjects in the Harvard laboratory, five seems to be the preferred number. Below that size subjects begin to complain that the group is too small, and above it that the group is too large. The fact that there is a distinct "saddle point" at five suggests that the notion of an optimum size is meaningful, if the task, time, and other circumstances are well enough specified. But the optimum size must surely vary according to conditions.

There seems to be a crucial point at seven. Below seven, for the most part, each person in the group says a least something to each other person. In groups over seven the low participators tend to stop talking to each other and center their communications on the few top men. The tendencies toward centralization of communication seem to increase rather powerfully as size increases.

At the same time, there are certain difficulties inherent in groups of as low as two and three members. In a two-man group no majority short of unanimity can form. Each person can exercise a complete veto over the other. One person can exercise power quite as effectively by simply refusing to react as he can by making suggestions, and this tendency toward withdrawal of one member appears with some frequency.

In a three-man group the tendency of two to form a combination against the third seems fairly strong. If this happens, the would-be task leader may be overcautious because he knows that, if his lieutenant disagrees with him, he may be left in the minority. The lieutenant knows he has this power but that, if he exercises it, the third man may step in to take his place. The third man on the outside of the coalition is left powerless whether he agrees or disagrees, so long as the other two agree, and tends either to withdraw or set up a damaging but unsuccessful protest. It is hard for a three-man group to have a "healthy" amount of disagreement. The structure is too sensitive to disagreement, and therefore it tends to an all-or-none extreme.

RECOMMENDATIONS

It is important to realize that basic research is a long, slow process which really cannot be short-cut by concentration on the need for practical results. Some of the generalizations ventured above actually go somewhat beyond the base of firmly established facts, and all of them should be taken with a generous grain of salt in any attempted application, since circumstances alter cases. With proper precautions, however, a summary of "rules of thumb" may be helpful in pinpointing some possible applications based on the experience of observing many laboratory groups:

(1) Avoid appointing committees larger than

seven members unless necessary to obtain representation of all relevant points of view. Try to set up conditions of size, seating, and time allowed so that each member has an adequate opportunity to communicate directly with each other member.

(2) Avoid appointing committees as small as two or three members if the power problem between members is likely to be critical.

(3) Choose members who will tend to fall naturally into a moderate gradient of participation. Groups made up of all high participators will tend to suffer from competition. Groups made up of all lows may find themselves short on ideas.

(4) Avoid the assumption that a good committee is made up of one good "leader" and several "followers." Try to provide the group with both a task leader and a social leader, who will support each other. It is probably not a bad idea to include a humorist if the social leader does not have a light touch. A few strong but more silent men add judicious balance to the group.

A group of otherwise balanced composition can probably absorb one "difficult" member—one of the type, for example, who talks too much, is short on problem-solving ability, tends to arouse dislikes, and cannot be changed by ordinary social pressures. If such a member must be included, probably the best strategy is to "surround" him.

(5) In actual procedure, start with facts if possible. Even where the facts are thought to be well known to all members, a short review is seldom a waste of time. A good general procedure is probably to plan to deal with three questions on each major agenda item:

"What are the facts pertaining to the problem?"
"How do we feel about them?"
"What shall we do about the problem?"

This is probably the preferred order. Take time to lay the groundwork before getting to specific suggestions, the third stage. It may be noted, by the way, that the order recommended is the exact opposite of that which is characteristic of formal parliamentary procedure.

(6) Solicit the opinions and experiences of others, especially when disagreements begin to crop up. People often think they disagree when actually they simply are not talking about the same experiences. In such cases they do not draw each other out far enough to realize that, although they are using the same *words*, they are thinking about different *experiences*. Try to get past the words and general statements the other man uses to the experiences he is trying to represent. Members of the group may agree with his experiences.

(7) When somebody else is talking, listen, and keep indicating your reactions actively. Most people are not much good at reading your mind. Besides that, they need the recognition you can give them by your honest reaction, whether positive or negative.

(8) Keep your eyes on the group. When you are talking, talk to the group as a whole rather than to one of your cronies or to one of your special opponents. Search around constantly for reactions to what you are saying. A good deal of communication goes on at a subverbal level. Nothing tones up the general harmony of a group like a good strong undercurrent of direct eye contact.

(9) When you scent trouble coming up, break off the argument and backtrack to further work on the facts and direct experience. In some instances the best way to get started on a cooperative track again after a period of difficulty is to agree to go out and gather some facts together by direct experience.

(10) Keep your ear to the ground. No recipe or set of rules can substitute for constant, sensitive, and sympathetic attention to what is going on in the relations between members. Do not get so engrossed in getting the job done that you lose track of what is the first prerequisite of success—keeping the committee in good operating condition.

Every leader must understand and regulate a variety of organizational activities at lower levels that are not directly visible to him, and he must base his judgments on patterns of activity, rather than on individual acts. Every organization has a flow of reports and ways of consolidating individual reports into general patterns. In the next selection, Eliot D. Chapple and Leonard R. Sayles describe the various reporting methods used to control subordinate units in American business firms and in many other organiza-

tions. Leaders of voluntary associations will find some parallels in their own experiences. The authors describe the administrative problems of adapting budgetary, statistical, and other techniques to the accomplishment of the desired ends of accurate reporting and guidance in reorganization and in personnel assignment.

ORGANIZATIONAL CONTROLS*

Eliot D. Chapple and Leonard R. Sayles

The volume of paper that passes over an executive's desk in any American company would suggest that too much information is provided, not too little. Yet, a few casual questions about the value of all these forms, reports, memos, and correspondence would create the impression that there is probably no substitute for going into the shop or the field and finding out for oneself. Most managers are in fact sensitive about their lack of adequate information! "We wish we knew how things were really going down in the shop" is a typical remark.

But organizational complexity, both geographical and administrative, makes such personal observation impractical. In addition, only a kind of administrative extrasensory perception, not possessed by most people, would enable the executive to know what to look at, whom to ask, and what information to request.

Many companies preserve the fiction that top management is in close touch with what is going on at the first level. The executives sally forth from time to time to "look into a problem," but usually plenty of advance warning reaches the department through the company grapevine. Even though there are ceremonial virtues in such visits and the possibility that some exchange of information may occur on a variety of subjects, the yield is liable to be strikingly low even if an agenda is carefully planned. Besides the natural tendency of divisional or plant managers to spruce things up and sweep the problems under the rug in their front office, the framework for pinpointing difficulties is simply not present.

ACCOUNTING TECHNIQUES MAY NOT PROVIDE CONTROL

The information available to the executive, or even top management for that matter, touches only a segment of the total operation, and most of this is primarily designed to fit the special needs of the accountants. Historically, these reports develop out of and have been strongly influenced by the public func-

tion of the auditor. The balance sheet and operating statements of the company are prepared for the stockholders and for the government, and they relate only incidentally to the operating needs of management.

Unfortunately, although management should be evaluated in terms of the financial statements of the company, the statements are not built up from the realities of operation of the smallest unit, which for organizational efficiency would be a unit work flow, and then combined into larger systems until the total organization is described.

Instead, the accountants have started with the total company and then tried with growing sophistication to set up similar reporting systems for smaller units. The Chart of Accounts, through which income and expense are assigned to organizational units, reflects and is patterned on the functional classification of organization activities. As a result, endless effort is expended on distribution of expense, prorates and all the other fictions that make it possible to put the dollars somewhere to produce a statement that can finally be audited.

Skillful executives learn to maneuver within this framework because they know they are judged by what the figures show. "Balloon squeezing" then becomes a major art; one tries to make his financial statements look good by shoving expense off on less astute colleagues. Although the total picture of the company does not improve, the steady flow of reports is the index of performance for top management that determine the method of reward and punishment, no matter how unreal.

Thus, in some companies, as experienced accountants know, more executive energy is devoted to manipulating the figures than improving productive efficiency. But such behavior is a product of the incentive system management itself designs by using such auditing procedures as control measures of managerial effectiveness. The manager who plays along is responding as might be predicted with this type of situation . . .

But where the game becomes more serious for the organization is the difficulty of proceeding from a line on the operating statement to an individual's responsibility. Who is responsible when expense is up and

* Reprinted with permission of The Macmillan Company and the authors from pages 69-75 of *The Measure of Management* by Eliot D. Chapple and Leonard R. Sayles. Copyright © The Macmillan Company, 1961.

income down? Even if it is assumed that the accountants completely describe the operation of the company (which is not usually the case), only a series of shaky fictions can lead from the operating statement of the smallest unit to the summation for the total company. Who should be held responsible, and can any single individual justifiably be accountable for what the figures show?

Top management people are actually even worse off than those on lower levels because they have to depend so much on what the figures show. Making decisions on the basis of what financial reports reflect, as they must be made, assumes the figures are organizationally defined. The action taken is often completely unrelated to the problem. Consequently, management tries to supplement the decisions that they are compelled to make when the "figures" show some significant change through the use of personal visitations, hunches, or special studies.

Moreover, . . . company financial records are often produced for the convenience of accountants, not management. Accountants are responsible for the financial accuracy of their statements, so it is only natural that this should be an overriding concern. The profit-and-loss statement must be ready for the directors at their monthly meeting or for inspection by the banks or insurance companies which provide financing and it must be balanced to the last penny no matter how much time it takes. Therefore, under the present rules of the game, the operating statements on which internal operation depends are always after the fact, matters of ancient history. They are of no use to the executive as a means of control. This is ironic because the chief accounting officer is the controller, illustrating the semantic difficulties of the word "control."

Controllers are generally concerned by their uncertain relationship to top management. Having the tools of budgeting and accounting in their hands, they do not know why they do not have the full responsibility for control. For them, the term implies the detection of deviations and the authority to require the guilty party to correct the situation forthwith. Although they concede the manager has the first responsibility, at heart they usually consider themselves as watchdogs of the operations of the company, ready to bite.

THE REAL MEANING OF CONTROL

The reason for the ambivalent treatment accountants received from management is the real distinction between keeping records and the administrative behavior that makes the records actually happen. Management, often only intuitively, is aware that record keeping indicates what has happened, not what is going to happen, and a controller can play his part in management only as control is limited to anticipation and prediction. The problem, therefore, can be reduced to asking, "How can we predict from our records, whatever they are, that a deviation is *about to take place* in the near or distant future so we as managers can take preventive steps in advance?" Because the whole orientation of the controller, who is trained as an accountant, is toward the production of accurate but after-the-fact reports, it is little wonder he often fails to understand that what he calls "control" does not mean the same thing to management. The field of management accounting is working in this direction, but, as mentioned earlier, it is not yet adequately synthesized with the organizational realities.

What is required to develop a system of controls for the organization? To find out, it is necessary to go back to the work flows of the company that are the ultimate sources of record keeping and ask, "Do managers now get information on every point of disturbance so they can anticipate disturbances before they happen?" In most companies, executives do not, but it may be worth considering the part the unit work-flow supervisor plays in managing disturbance and with what the work-flow system manager and his staff of specialists are necessarily concerned.

In the old-fashioned days, the foreman operated entirely by "feel." Constantly disdaining records of any sort, his ear told him a machine was beginning to slip in its performance and his eyes detected when the material was slightly off in specifications. From close moment-to-moment contact, he could tell if an operator was upset, and, by constant and continuous effort, he was able to anticipate every kind of disturbance to the smooth flow of work in his shop and take corrective actions.

Now, the foreman has become an executive or, some would say, a clerical employee, who is more liable to be found in his office than on the line. Like his superiors, he is kept busy preparing and studying reports, many of which are only peripheral in his operation. To supervise his department, he needs exactly the same kind of data coming to him that his predecessor obtained from direct contact. The same information affects stability of operation (and costs). The span of his control, using management terminology, depends *not* on the number of people to be supervised but on the frequency and duration of disturbances within his work-flow unit and the length of time required for him to correct them. Thus, two considerations need to be made in planning his job: the ease with which disturbances can be detected, and the freedom he has to do something about them.

The nature of the work-flow system he has to work with, however, imposes real limitations on what he can do unaided. If his equipment has a high frequency of mechanical problems or his processing difficulties stem from another unit work flow in the system, intervention by the work-flow system manager, that is, the second-level supervisor, and his specialists is necessary. Perhaps a study of the machines that are causing trouble by the mechanical specialist (staff) will lead to action to lower significantly the frequency of machine problems as a source of disturbance, and concentrated attention by the manager on coordination between two unit work-flow groups will reduce delays that introduce an erratic element into his operating system.

However, both the first-line supervisor or foreman and the work-flow system manager and his specialists need continuous data on the various technical and human problems of the constituent systems. This involves a reporting system to identify the specific sources of deviation from smooth performance. If the span of supervision is to be increased to a total unit work flow, work flows cannot be split into small segments in order to make it possible for an experienced foreman to anticipate trouble before it happens. A further difficulty with that approach is that too few foremen have such operating perception; because it is largely intuitive, there is little possibility for the specialists either to recognize a problem or to diagnose it. Under the old system of organization, the foreman usually regarded the specialists as interlopers and there was no conceptual and objective framework of analysis for them to use to talk effectively to each other.

Staff projects should be a product of the control system, not of someone's ambitions. Most of the specialists—engineering, personnel, methods, etc.—are present to make improvements in the functioning of the organization. Unfortunately, unless the control system identifies the sources of difficulty, staff activities are likely to be independent of the work flow. Someone who has an idea "sells it" to a manager, and a major staff activity is underway. Unless there are adequate controls to assess the degree of improvement resulting from such programs, it is likely that they will fail to accomplish their assumed objective. The criterion should be the contribution of a particular staff activity in reducing the frequency or the severity of a particular type of disturbance, whether its source is disturbed employees, equipment, or systems.

USE OF THE STATISTICAL QUALITY CONTROL CONCEPT

Modern statistics has provided a means by which controls, in the sense used here, can be provided with great power and effectiveness. Best known in the area of quality control, the principles can be stated rather simply. Something is in control when the limits within which past variation will repeat itself in the future can be predicted. Although nothing will be exactly the same each time it is measured or counted, as long as the variation falls within statistically defined limits, predictions can be made for the future. If, after a condition of control is shown, the measurements suddenly or gradually move outside the established limits, it is assumed that some unknown or assignable factor has intervened.

To use one illustration of quality control, inspectors take routine measurements of samples of parts that are being manufactured. If the measurements begin to fall outside the limits set up by past performance, it signals trouble. Perhaps the machine is going out of adjustment, the material has changed its metallurgical composition, or the operator is not following instructions. Therefore, the signal set up by consecutive sampling tells the supervisor that action is needed, and he must investigate to find the cause for the significant deviation in the values.

IDENTIFYING SOURCE OF TROUBLE

In more advanced systems of control, the probable causes of deviation are also controlled. Routine measures of revolutions per minute, machine settings, etc., are made to prevent the machine from causing trouble; routine chemical analyses of the raw material are performed; and the operator's performance of instructions is checked. As a result, the supervisor's time is saved because the amount of trouble shooting is reduced to a minimum and the guesswork technique to locate the source of poor quality is eliminated.

These various types of statistical control systems are important because they anticipate the source of difficulty or disturbance long before it becomes evident by methods of observation. Thus, quality defects that are not apparent in the inspection of individual parts do show up through sampling by the statistical trends toward greater variability, although for some time thereafter there is no increase in the actual rejects by usual inspection techniques. The application of this theory to situations where stability or repetition can be determined makes possible the prediction of disturbance before it happens. This provides the supervisor with the opportunity to correct it before the operation of his work-flow system is seriously affected.

Using the yardsticks of interaction, measurement, based on the time and frequency of occurrence, a statistical control system for organization, exactly comparable to the controls of quality or productivity, is available. The only difference is that the mathematical properties of the frequency of intervals of action and inaction follow a different law than the normal law introduced in elementary statistics. From the point of view of understanding control, this is irrelevant and of concern only to the mathematicians who work out the methods of sampling, the methods of calculating limits, and the amount of change that signals trouble.

As a consequence, two interdependent systems can be used: the measures of quality and quantity and their dependent variables, such as machine performance, etc., and the measurement of action and interaction. A shift in interaction can cause a significant deviation in quality or output; and a disturbance in the even flow of work changes interaction. Consecutive samples from both of these areas provide the supervisors with the data needed for control. If controls are set up to obtain samples from all potential assignable causes shown by experience to be sources of trouble, they automatically prescribe for the supervisor the pattern of remedial actions to take and where to take it. Thus human relations variables are subject to the same type of control as production variables . . .

[Chapple and Sayles, *The Measure of Management*, provides more details of proposed techniques for statistical control reports about social interaction in work flows.—Eds.]

B. GROUP RELATIONS

The informal relations within an organization have an enormous impact: they develop or lower morale, stimulate or hinder productivity, create alliances or information networks contrary to the organizational chart, etc. Much of the research conducted by behavioral scientists in large organizations has been oriented toward specifying the precise ways in which the informal relations of the work group actually influence the organization. In his selection, Leonard R. Sayles reviews much of this research and summarizes its importance for organizational leaders.

THE BEHAVIOR OF WORK GROUPS*

Leonard R. Sayles

The individual's most immediate and meaningful experiences of work are obtained in the context of the work group and his work associates. The largest organization is experienced by indirection, but membership in the small group contributes directly to the shaping of attitudes and behavior toward the entire world of work. For this reason of potency, therefore, the contribution of the small group to the total organization has been a subject of substantial research by those interested in human relations in industry.

CONCEPTIONS OF THE WORK GROUP

As Whyte observes, the individual is *not* a member of a single group within a larger structure.[1] Rather, he typically interacts in a variety of settings within the organization. It is the task of the researcher to identify those interaction patterns which are focused and concentrated so that it is reasonable to speak of a "group."

If we follow all the members of the organization through their hours on the job, or find some "high" vantage point and observe the total of all interactions, we are likely to be impressed with this proliferation of memberships. Most apparent is membership, except for that unique individual, the president, in some *command group;* that is, the employee shares a common supervisor with a number of colleagues. Distinguishable from this group, but closely related, is a *functional* or *task group*—those employees who must collaborate in some fashion if the work task defined by the organization is to be accomplished. In fact, both of these groups are rather well defined by the larger organization, and the group typically retains those boundaries.

However, there are two other kinds of clusterings that tend to overlap and penetrate the organization in unexpected ways. They are not defined by the formal organization and are often included under the general term, informal organization. One has received much attention from researchers: the *friendship clique.* The other is less well studied, but equally important. That is the *interest group.* This is comprised of those employees who share a common economic interest and seek to gain some objective relating to the larger organization.

Memberships in these groups are not exclusive;

* From *Research in Industrial Human Relations,* edited by Conrad M. Arensberg, et al. Copyright © 1957 by Harper & Brothers: pages 131-145, "Work Group Behavior and the Larger Organization," by Leonard R. Sayles. Reprinted with the permission of the author and publisher.
1 William F. Whyte, "Small Groups in Large Organizations," in John Rohrer and Muzafer Sherif (Editors), *Social Psychology at the Crossroads* (New York: Harper & Brothers, 1951), pp. 303-304.

often they will overlap considerably. However, the motivations of the members, and, more important, their behavior, are distinctive; and we have no reason to believe that the boundaries will be perfectly coincident.

THE COMMAND GROUP

Perhaps the most obvious kind of small group in the large organization is composed of the supervisor and his immediate subordinates. As Jacques observes, the entire organization is composed of interconnected *command groups*, the subordinates in one group being the superiors in their own command group, with the exception of the first level.[2] While we might expect that research would have emphasized this unit of the organization, if we exclude the manifold studies of leadership styles dealt with elsewhere in this volume, there are relatively few systematic explorations of the relationship between the leader and his subordinates as a group, as individuals, and among the subordinates themselves. Jacques' volume is a notable exception. His examination of the command group has a strong psychiatric flavor. He stresses the leader's ambivalence: his *authority* over his subordinates and *dependence* upon them, his sense of isolation, the problem of integrating pair relationships (leader and individual subordinates) with cohesiveness among subordinates, and the mixed feelings of the subordinates as a group who find the leader both expendable and indispensable (one to be protected or exposed?).

THE FRIENDSHIP CLIQUE

This has been conceived as the elementary building block of human organization. As Mayo writes, "Man's desire to be continuously associated with his fellows is a strong, if not the strongest human characteristic."[3]

At the workplace we find a multitude of friendship groups representing the diverse interests of the workers placed there by the organization. The boundaries of these clusterings appear to reflect the employees' off-the-job interests and associations or previous work experience. Age, ethnic background, outside activities, sex, marital status, and so on, comprise the mortar that binds the clique together.

The friendship group has emerged as the agency which welds the individual to the organization. Loyalty, even attachment, to the total organization with its impersonality, extended hierarchy, and social distance becomes ambiguous. However, attachment to the immediate and easily perceived face-to-face group

is the predominant reality of organization experience. For the individual it provides a source of personal security in an impersonal environment.

Where cliques are largely nonexistent, as in the rapidly expanding aircraft plants of California, turnover can be enormous. The presumption is that stable social groups take time to crystallize; during the period of formation many potential members will leave voluntarily because they do not find an established unit with which they can affiliate. This in turn inhibits the formation of permanent groups; the process is self-defeating.

Thus Lombard and Mayo conclude that the naive administrator who seeks to break up these cliques because of the inefficiency and wasted motion of the purely social activities involved is actually doing a disservice to the organization.[4] In fact, they find that it takes skillful leadership to encourage their formation, at least in organizations undergoing rapid expansion. A recent well-received text[5] in the field of public administration comes out strongly on the side of encouraging on-the-job social life, concluding that production increased when social conversation was allowed. However, a study employing methods of precise interaction observation is unique in casting some doubts as to the positive correlation between social interaction and productivity.[6]

More serious criticism of the universal efficacy of friendship cliques, however, involves considerations of personality and work structure differences. A study of "rate busters" disclosed a significant majority who were indifferent to, if not hostile to, the social groupings they found on the job.[7]

A recent examination of British longshoremen finds that approximately half of the longshoremen on the docks studied have consciously avoided social entanglements of work group membership. Given an opportunity to join semi-permanent gangs, they prefer random work assignments that leave them free to come and go at will, with no group responsibility.[8]

Formation of social groups also appears to be a function of the structure of the work situation itself. Argyris, in his Bank study, finds that incidence of in-

---

2   Elliot Jacques, *The Changing Culture of a Factory* (New York: Dryden Press, 1952), pp. 273-297.
3   Elton Mayo, *Social Problems of an Industrial Civilizations* (Boston: Graduate School of Business Administration, Harvard University, 1945), p. 111.
4   Elton Mayo and George F. Lombard, *Teamwork and Labor Turnover in the Aircraft Industry of Southern California* (Boston: Graduate School of Business Administration, Harvard University, 1940).
5   Herbert Simon, Donald Smithburg, and Victor Thompson, *Public Administration* (New York: Alfred A. Knopf, 1950), pp. 113-114.
6   Alfred A. Horsfall and Conrad Arensberg, "Teamwork and Productivity in a Shoe Factory," *Human Organization*, Volume VIII (Winter 1949), pp. 21 ff.
7   These men tended to have a rural background emphasizing individualism. Orvis Collins and Donald Roy, "Restriction of Output and Social Cleavage in Industry," *Applied Anthropology*, Volume V (Summer 1946), pp. 1-14.
8   University of Liverpool, *The Dock Worker* (Liverpool: University Press of Liverpool, 1954), pp. 61 ff.

formal social groupings among tellers is less than for bank employees who have less interaction with customers.[9] . . .

From this theoretical approach, we would expect that the whole range of group activities, not just social life, would be influenced by the interaction pattern fostered by the job. The previously cited study by the University of Liverpool researchers, for example, notes that dockworkers who were members of semipermanent crews were rarely found among the informal leaders of the longshoremen or among the active participants in the union.[10] Moving in the other direction, Lipset concludes that because some jobs handicap workers in maintaining adequate off-the-job relations with other friends (e.g., unusual working hours as among printers, actors, and policemen), they tend to form more closely knit "fellow worker" groups, as evidenced by their record of high participation in local union activities . . .[11]

THE TASK GROUP

Perhaps one of the most important aspects of small group behavior in large organizations is their relation to the work process itself. The formally designated task builds a group structure, just as do individual social needs and the organizational authority structure.

More specifically, the work process stimulates group controls of (a) work method, (b) output standards or productivity, and (c) relative compensation and prestige relationships.

(a) *Impact on Work Method.* The experience of working in close proximity on a day-to-day basis induces methods that may depart from the organization's original conception of the job, or at least "fills in" the specific details of the operation not specified in the formal work plan. Thus, employees may exchange repetitive jobs, although such trading is illegal; one worker may do two jobs while a colleague rests; or, as Whyte found, they may change the sequence of the operations to reduce tensions and provide short cuts.[12] Roy observed similar "adjustments" in relations among tool room clerks, job setters, and machinists where the objective was maximizing piece rate earnings.[13]

Some of these informal, or unplanned for, work methods may decrease worker output. For example, workers' machinations in Roy's machine shop tended to overstate make-ready time during job changes. However, other worker innovations, such as those described by Whyte, undoubtedly increase the total product. Gross found that radar teams, through communication circuits set up during off-the-job social periods, were compensating for deficiencies in the information provided by the formal organization.[14]

Similarly researchers have analyzed the initiative exhibited by a group of department store salesmen in evolving a new work pattern that solved a serious internal morale problem created by a new incentive system.[15]

However, the work structure can be designed so that elaborations of the informal group necessarily work in opposition to the major objectives of the organization. Recent studies of changes in the method of mining coal, conducted by the Tavistock Institute in Great Britain, illustrate such organization. The change from jobs completed by small groups of miners in one shift to successive operations carried out by three shifts resulted in reduction of interaction and communication and a consequent decrease in the miners' recognition of their total responsibility for the operation.[16]

Thus the Tavistock studies suggest that the goal of the engineer in designing the technological organization is to provide the work group with a relatively autonomous task so that responsible *internal* leadership can develop. This kind of organizational structure is, in fact, the very essence of decentralization:

> A primary work organization of this type has the advantage of placing responsibility for the complete . . . task squarely on the shoulders of a single, small, face-to-face group which experiences the entire cycle of operations within the compass of its membership. For each participant the task has total significance and dynamic closure.[17]

The development of mutually convenient methods of conducting the work process can extend to the "job" of collective bargaining. We have ample evidence that union-management relationships at the work group level often depart radically from estab-

9   Chris Argyris, *Organization of a Bank* (New Haven: Labor and Management Center, Yale University, 1954), p. 129.
10   University of Liverpool, *op. cit.*, p. 72.
11   Seymour M. Lipset, "The Political Process in Trade Unions: A Theoretical Statement," in Morroe Berger *et al.* (editors), *Freedom and Control in Modern Society* (New York: D. Van Nostrand Company, 1954), pp. 101-102.
12   William F. Whyte, "The Social Structure of the Restaurant," *The American Journal of Sociology*, Volume LIV (January 1949), pp. 306-307.
13   Donald Roy, "Quota Restriction and Goldbricking in a

Machine Shop," *The American Journal of Sociology*, Volume LVII (March 1952), pp. 427-442.
14   Edward Gross, "Some Functional Consequences of Primary Controls in Formal Work Organizations," *American Sociological Review*, Volume XVIII (August 1953), pp. 370-371.
15   Nicholas Babchuk and William Goode, "Work Incentives in a Self-Determined Group," *American Sociological Review*, Volume XVI (October 1951), p. 686.
16   E. Trist and K. Bamforth, "Some Social and Psychological Consequences of the Long Wall Method of Coal-Getting," *Human Relations*, Volume IV, Number 1 (1951).
17   Trist and Bamforth, *op. cit.*, p. 6.

lished practices and attitudes prevailing at higher levels, and may in fact contradict these other, more "formal" relationships.[18]

Aside from evolving methods which seem most convenient to work group members, the pattern of doing the job is fitted to the status system of the group. Those members with most prestige, if at all possible, receive the best jobs. Where possible, working location and equipment are similarly "assigned." And where these are not under group control, helping and trading can be adjusted to the status system. The exchange-of-favors system readily responds to the prestige hierarchy. Of course, the evaluation placed on jobs is itself a product of group interaction.

The methods evolved within the group for task completion become firmly established. Where outside forces (e.g., technological change) threaten to induce changes, the ranks close and resistance is applied. In part, of course, this may be the natural reaction of the culprit fearing punishment for rules infractions. A more reasonable explanation of the informal group's resistance to change, however, is the intimate relationship between the task group as an entity and the work methods they have evolved. A threat to one is a real threat to the other.

(b) *Impact on Output Standards.* Probably more attention has been given to this aspect of task group behavior than to any other. Starting with the work of Mathewson, and extending through the Western Electric studies, a long and distinguished line of studies indicate that work groups often formulate quite specific output standards and obtain close conformity from their members in *maintaining* these standards. Productivity itself is increasingly conceived as a group phenomenon.

Several reasons have been advanced as to why output control occupies a place of such importance in the life of the group. Work standards are one of the most important aspects of the job, which can in some fashion be influenced by worker action. The energy expenditure required by the job is largely determined by the number of units required, rather than by the nature of the job itself. Presumably without group control management would be able to utilize individual differences, and competition for promotion and greater earnings, to obtain higher and higher standards. This would penalize particularly the slower worker and the older employee. It might, however, penalize all workers by cutting piece rates, where such exist, and/or reducing the number of employees required by the operation. "Run away" output might have internal ramifications. We have observed situa-

tions where group controls were weak, and younger, low-prestige employees exceeded the production and earnings records of their "betters." The results were calamitous for the status hierarchy of the department and ultimately for the effectiveness of the formal organization.

Output control is a basic objective of group action as well as an essential element in maintaining group stability. Not only the relationship of the members to one another, but the durability of the worker relationship to his job depends on the efficacy of this process. Again we need to note that the resultant is not always unfavorable to management. We have many instances on record where the group has sanctioned increasingly high productivity,[19] rejected fellow workers who could not maintain high output, and resisted threats to existing high quality standards . . .

Some of the earliest research on productivity was based on the assumption that internal harmony in the work group would produce higher performance records. Increasingly researchers have become disillusioned with the relationship between social satisfaction and worker effort. Perhaps one of the most telling blows to the impetus to devote substantial energies to building work groups that are "sociometrically sound" is the provocative study by Goode and Fowler in a low morale plant. They found "the informal relationships which developed were such as to maintain pressures toward high production in the face of considerable *animosity* toward the owners and *among the workers themselves.*"[20] While their findings are severely limited by the somewhat unique environment they chose, it has become recognized that the relationship between friendship and output is a complex one.

More recently, Seashore finds in a study in a large "heavy equipment manufacturing company" that highly "cohesive" work groups are more likely to have output records that diverge in *either direction* from plant averages.[21] By implication, then, tightly knit work groups are almost as likely to have notably *poor* production records as outstandingly *good* ones.

The present author is inclined to believe that these inconsistencies in research results are due to an overemphasis on output as a part of informal group equilibrium. Control over output is also a major weapon in the arsenal of the group engaging in conflict with management, other work groups, and even the local union. We need to know more about the *total situa-*

18 Cf. Melville Dalton, "Unofficial Union–Management Relations," *American Sociological Review*, Volume XV (October 1950), pp. 611-619.

19 Cf. George Strauss, "Group Dynamics and Intergroup Relations," in William F. Whyte and others, *Money and Motivation*, (New York: Harper & Brothers, 1955), pp. 90-96.
20 William Goode and Irving Fowler, "Incentive Factors in a Low Morale Plant," *American Sociological Review*, Volume XIV (October 1949), p. 624.
21 Stanley Seashore, *Group Cohesiveness in the Industrial Work Group* (Ann Arbor: Institute for Social Research, University of Michigan, 1954), p. 98.

tion facing a given work group, including these external factors, before predicting its work performance.

The evolution of the method of *group decision* for gaining acceptance for changes in production methods and output standards is recognition of the potency of group standards. The theory presumes that leadership methods that involve the entire work group in the change process have two major advantages:

1. They can eliminate the major barrier of existing group standards which militate against any change, per se.

2. More positively, they commit the individual to new efforts in the context of his group membership. In a sense, the individual "promises" his fellows to accomplish some change in his behavior. Valuing the opinions of his associates, he feels bound to maintain his agreement.

Ideally the "decision" itself becomes the new standard or norm of conduct for the task group. Similarly efforts to develop plantwide incentive systems are premised on the assumption that output and effort are dependent on the relation of the work group to the total social system of the plant.[22]

(c) *Impact on Relative Compensation and Prestige Relationships.* The fact that jobs take on a significant social meaning can be seen in the importance attached to wage differentials within the group itself. For example, we have many instances on record when management assigned an equal value to each job and the group found significant distinguishing characteristics. Jobs ranked by employees as *more important or desirable* are expected to have higher earnings than jobs ranked below. The established hierarchy is reinforced over time by the gradual perfection of the correlation between esteem accorded particular workers and prestige accorded to their jobs. The "more important" workers have moved to the "more important" jobs. (The importance attached to the job is not only a function of the earning capacity but also the quality of the surroundings, equipment, the tempo of the work required, etc.) Problems occur only when changes are introduced which violate the established hierarchy.

A persistent problem has been that jobs which the group evaluates as relatively undesirable may need to be compensated at a higher rate than the "desirable" jobs, in order to attract adequate personnel. However, this differential may be contrary to the status system of the work group. Similarly, jobs evaluated (by the group) as desirable may lack characteristics which would bring them a high rating under the organization's formal ranking plan. These contradictions between the group and the organization's ranking system become more important during periods of relative labor shortage, when new recruits are difficult to obtain and when the group undergoes aging.

While these several concepts of the "informal group" are not identical, and in some cases not even complementary in their basic dimensions, they do have one common feature. All stress equilibrium, the development of a system of interpersonal relations which stabilizes the work situation (among subordinates and between superior and subordinates), an interconnected series of friendship linkages, work flow relationships, output levels, and status-income relations. The objectives are the maintenance of individual and group stability by insuring a predictability of day-to-day events and effecting a *modus vivendi* as between individual on-the-job needs and the requirements of the formal organization.

As such, the *informal group* in any and all of its meanings is serving well-recognized and accepted human needs. Its existence and continued preservation are hardly matters for surprise. The building up of routines, of established methods of accomplishing tasks, of predictable social relationships, of group roles—these are all elements of structuring which social scientists have found typical of the human group. In fact, the elements define the group.

Particularly through the setting and maintenance of group standards, informal groups have protected their memberships from possible indiscretions that might reflect adversely on them all; also they have provided support for the individual, by acting as a buffer to outside organizations and by sustaining him through the provision of *known and acceptable* routines of behaving within the face-to-face work group.

Thus the informal group, as perceived in such studies, *reacts to* the initiations of other organizations, particularly management. Being defined in equilibrium terms, the reaction is always an attempt to *regain* the previous undisturbed state—to protect work methods, social relationships, and output levels incorporated in the norms of the group.

CONCERTED INTEREST AS THE FOCUS

Workers also band together into *interest groups.* These are formed not only to protect their members but also to exploit *opportunities* to improve their relative position. Improvements can take the form of "looser standards," a preferred seniority position, more overtime, more sympathetic supervision, correction of "inequities," better equipment, and countless other less tangible goals that make the job a better one and that often serve to substitute for the more traditional kinds of promotions and mobility.

Distribution of these benefits may be much influenced by pressures of united and determined infor-

22 Cf. William F. Whyte and others, *Money and Motivation, op. cit.,* p. 225.

mal groups. What management feels is "equitable," just as what the union determines is in the "members' interest," is determined to a large extent by attitudes expressed by those individuals who can support their demands by group reinforcements. Those work groups which for one reason or another are unable to exercise similar power in the market place of the plant are penalized.

This is not the traditional concept of the informal group seeking conformity with established norms of conduct. These are much more "free enterprise" units, interacting in a struggle for maximization of utility. All are not equally aggressive in the struggle for self-improvement or equally well-equipped with the wherewithal to do battle via the grievance procedure and the more direct pressure tactics on union and management. Some lack the spirit of combat, others the means, while only a restricted few are endowed with the characteristics associated with sustained "activity" and progress toward the goals they seek.

Much of what we say implies a degree of dual or even treble *disloyalty*. Other groups, management, the union, and fellow workers, are perceived as either barriers or sources of assistance. From the point of view of the interest group, it is not high identification or loyalty that counts, but rather the right tactics in using or ignoring these other aggregations.

Thus, management is neither "good" nor "bad," liked or disliked as such. In fact, this approach suggests that it may not always be fruitful to think in pro-management and pro-union terms. It may well be that a group which is satisfied with *itself*, with its ability to protect and improve its own interests, is more favorable to *both* union and management.[23]

The results for the larger plant may not be a system tending toward equilibrium at all. We might expect that certain combinations of pressure groups actually involve the organization in increasing instability—a trend toward disequilibrium. We have observed plants where the interaction of these groups involves increasingly greater discontent, turmoil, and nonadaptive behavior. That is, their behavior tends to reinforce the very problems it was designed to solve.

Similarly, the internal structure of these groups is much more responsive to changes in its external environment than is often implied in the concept of the informal work group as a relatively durable, impervious entity. Literally overnight, technical changes introduced by management can convert a cohesive task force into a disunited, apathetic "rabble," squabbling over internal differences. Similarly, we have observed a group of weakly-united employees become a force of some magnitude in the social system of the plant within a brief period, with no changes in personnel.

The existence of these *interest group* types suggests that greater attention should be given to matching supervisory "types" with group "types." We have tended to think of effective supervision as being the product of a relationship between a good leader and his group, on the assumption that the group of subordinates was a constant. In fact, variations in the effectiveness of supervision may be as much due to inherent differences in the group itself as to the leadership practices exhibited by the supervisor . . .

CONCLUSION

Clustering of workers-on-the-job all have these characteristics: They stem from the uniqueness of individual personality, which refuses to combine into larger "wholes" without changing those entities. The sum of a group of individuals is something more than the total of the constituents; it is a new organization, because most of the members (there are significant exceptions as we have noted) obtain satisfaction in gaining acceptance as a part of the group, and the group itself wields an influence over its members. Put in another way, there are pressures toward conformity within the group. These pressures result in the establishment of accepted ways of living together. The way of life of the group includes a complex system of customs and rules, vested interests, and interaction patterns which govern the relationship of members of the group to one another and to the larger environment of which it is a part.

This observance of group-sanctioned behavior and attitudes "fills out" the rationally conceived organization. What is on paper an organization becomes a "living, breathing" social organism, with all the intricacies, emotions, and contradictions we associate with human relations. While no organization would long persist which did not provide its members with this opportunity for spontaneous "human relations," a major problem of the larger organization becomes one of successfully incorporating the small group.

23 These areas are further elaborated in the author's study, *Technology and Work Group Behavior* (Ann Arbor: Bureau of Industrial Relations, University of Michigan, 1956).

A. FORMAL AND INFORMAL COMMUNICATION

Organizations may be viewed as communication structures in which information is brought to bear upon the making of decisions. Empirical research using this viewpoint is concerned with the content and efficiency of message flow among the various levels of an organization, and between the organization and its environment. In their selection, John M. Pfiffner and Frank P. Sherwood summarize a communication model of this kind and report some evidence about the various decisions made and the internal administrative problems that result from various types of organizational structures. The communication model may seem novel to a leader of a voluntary association, but his organization can be pictured as a communication structure like any other organization, and he can use communication efficiency as a criterion for evaluating the effectiveness of his organization.

This selection is a good example of how behavioral scientists develop theoretical models as guides to empirical research or as standards for evaluating the efficiency of actual organizations. If one is interested in studying productivity or work relationships rather than communication, he could devise a theoretical model of work functions and work flows; an actual voluntary association thus might be compared with such a theoretical model, in a study either of its efficiency or of its work flow.

FORMAL ORGANIZATION AS A COMMUNICATION STRUCTURE*

John M. Pfiffner and Frank P. Sherwood

THE THEORETICAL MODEL

If the viewpoint is taken that information constitutes the lifeblood of the functioning organization, the channels and apparatus for the transmission of such information become the organization structure. Wiener's thesis is that man can control his environment only through information, which is transmitted through units called *messages*. Thus the message becomes in a sense the basic component of organization analysis, although Wiener does not say this in so many words. He compares what goes on in organizations with both the model of the automatic machine and nervous system of animals.

Much of modern communication theory is traceable to the relatively new discipline of communication engineering, which is in turn a product of the electronic age and its expansion during and after World War II. That is why much of the terminology is expressed in engineering terms. Thus "entropy" comes from the second law of thermodynamics.[1] "Feedback" is essentially an engineering concept, and such phraseology as "network," "loop," and "circuit" flows from electronic and machine applications. Indeed, modern large scale organization is being seriously affected, if not modified, by communication engineering.

Entropy. The concept of *entropy* in physics has surprising relevance to any discussion of the communications structure. It is a term which suggests the degree of ignorance, chaos, and randomness in a system. It is closely interlinked with notions of organization and information. Entropy can be resisted only by organization; and organization depends primarily on information. It is interesting that scientists were only able to develop highly complex heat machines when they turned their attention to questions of entropy and communication.

For our purposes it is important to realize that

* From John M. Pfiffner and Frank P. Sherwood, *Administrative Organization*, pp. 296-308. © 1960. Reprinted by permission of the authors and Prentice-Hall, Inc., Englewood Cliffs, N. J.

[1] Norbert Wiener, *The Human Use of Human Beings* (Garden City: Doubleday Anchor Books, Second edition, 1954), pp. 28-29. [The Pfiffner–Sherwood presentation relies heavily upon the cybernetic model developed by Wiener.—Eds.]

there is a strong tendency toward disequilibrium both in the physical and social world. The physicists' problem of developing informational devices that would provide proper systems of control for their heat machines is a case in point. The same kinds of problems obviously exist in human organizations. Indeed such factors may very well be critical in limiting size and specialization in our modern organizations. In the physical world, entropy is measurable. It represents the amount of "slippage" in performance that results from communications shortcomings. Thus the "information concept has made entropy, as a measure of ignorance, precise in an extended domain. . . ." [2]

In any given situation there are of course limits to the amount of entropy that can be tolerated; and the system of organization must be sufficient to secure the performance of a specified function. There is, too, a certain amount of "noise" entropy in each situation. it arises from errors and distortions in the communications system. This type of entropy is particularly a problem in human organizations.

As an example well known to those familiar with production organizations is the practice of filtering information as it travels through various hierarchical stages. People on the lower echelons deliberately distort messages going up in order (1) to give the boss the information that will please him, and (2) to present their own performances in the best light. In the same manner, messages going down the hierarchy are often deliberately altered for various reasons. Sometimes staff people on subordinate levels "edit" the message in order to assert authority or to put it in line with their own interpretations of policy. In other cases the messages are altered by intermediate echelons because the leaders there know that such alterations will make them more acceptable to those below.

But perhaps the principal cause of "noise" entropy in large-scale organization is the sheer size and weight of hierarchy, coupled with the disposition of people to resist regimentation. In the one case the vast impersonal nature of hierarchy builds inertia. In the other instance people tend to hear what they want to hear and ignore that which they do not want to hear. They even go so far as to devise defensive "noise."

Homeostasis. Just as entropy represents a tendency toward ignorance and chaos, there are forces in nature which cause us to resist these things. Such a behavior incentive, to be found in both the plant and animal world, is sometimes called *hemeostasis*.[3] It

impels a striving toward equilibrium and stability while embodying that type of change which is necessary to maintain health. Homeostasis is thus dynamic and variable in nature while striving for orderliness and system.

In the world of human organization it is encouraging to know that there is strong motivation toward such self-regulation and stability. It suggests that people will respond to planning and coordination. Furthermore the idea of homeostasis helps to provide some perspective on the reasons why humans have, in a naturalistic way, moved in the direction of very complicated interpersonal organizations.

Feedback. This recognition of the need to resist entropy spawned a new discipline in the post-World War II years. It is known as *cybernetics*, a word borrowed from the Greek and meaning *governor*. Cybernetics is the study of control and communication. Its purpose, as Wiener reported, is to develop a language and techniques that will not only attack the general problem of control and communication but will also find ". . . the proper repertory of ideas and techniques to classify their particular manifestations . . ." [4] The central idea in cybernetics is feedback. In its simplest form, feedback is the kind of communication an actor receives from a live audience. If the crowd is enthusiastic, the performer reacts with similar enthusiasm. There is in a way a closed circuit between performer and audience with continuing interchange of information. That circuit is not possible on TV. As a consequence many performers find it a frightening medium. There is no feedback, no communication, no control.

Essential to feedback is the notion that the flow of information is actually having a reciprocating effect on behavior. That is why the term *loop* is frequently associated with feedback. This circular pattern involves the flow of information to the point of action, a flow back to the point of decision with information on the action, and then a return to the point of action with new information and perhaps instructions. A primary element in this process is the sensory organ, the instrument through which information is obtained. Until recently only the animal organism, particularly the human brain and nervous system, was sufficiently developed to possess this capacity. For us humans the message comes through pretty rapidly when we put our finger on a hot stove.

The automatic machine. But we have now reached the point where we can equip our automatic machines with sensory organs; and thus the same general prin-

[2] Jerome Rothstein, *Communication, Organization, and Science* (Indian Hills, Colorado: The Falcon's Wing Press, 1958), p. 34.
[3] For discussions of homeostasis as applied to social theory see Roy R. Grinker (editor), *Toward a Unified Theory of Human Behavior* (New York: Basic Books, 1956), pp. 147, 264.
[4] Wiener, *The Human Use of Human Beings*, p. 17.

ciples of feedback can be applied mechanically. In fact, it has been said that our new highly complicated machines are an imitation of life. While it is not necessary here to discuss such interesting clichés as machines' inability to "think" for themselves—their reliance on the brain of man for succor—the fact remains that they do have the ability to combat entropy. Their sense organs detect errors and thus facilitate "negative feedback," by which is meant messages warning of danger or the need to take a different course. The sense organs in the earlier machines were vacuum tubes such as those in radios or television sets, but now the smaller transistors are coming into use.

The machines also have "memory" in the sense that they can store up information for future use. This memory may be of a rather simple nature as when in preparing a payroll a series of holes on a punch card recall the alphabetical spelling out of a payee's name on a check and cause the machine to print it, as well as the amount due. But they can also store much more complex information such as directions for a lathe to mold a particular piece of metal into the desired shape. Visitors to the Brussels Fair of 1958 will remember that one of the American exhibits was a computer which could be manipulated to deliver answers to a variety of questions, even the recounting of events in history. Some of these machines have gone beyond the punch card stage and now use either punched or magnetic tape.

THE ORGANIZATION ANALOGY

Having granted that automatic machines resemble biological organisms and that communication is an important factor in the physiology of organization, the skeptical observer might still question the analogy between animals, machines, and production organizations. The crux of the problem would seem to be the importance one places upon the feedback apparatus as an element in organization. And it may very well loom larger in some enterprises than in others, but one is hard put to think of anywhere it is not essential. Organizations, in common with human beings and machines, seem to have such attributes as ability to learn, memory, will, and consciousness. All of these are related to messages and the communication process.

Organization. One of the chief processes by means of which machines and organizations learn is through feedback, combined with memory. The original "teaching" perhaps comes from goal-centered messages which issue from the decision centers to the performers who have sensory organs which react to such messages. In the animal organism these are nerve centers, in the machine they are vacuum tubes

or transistors, and in the organization, communication centers. Learning through feedback is a dynamic and continuous process wherein there is mutual and reciprocating accommodation.

The sensory organ communicates error. In the machine it may take the form of a message signalling danger that tolerance is being exceeded. In the human organism the nerve cells in the housewife's finger tell the brain that the iron is hot. In the organization the signal of error will refer to production goals. These compensating messages may go on *ad infinitum* and in their totality they constitute the outward manifestation of the learning process because each message modifies the other and governs ensuing behavior.

Organizational memory. Memory in the automatic machine is manifested by either the form, die, or cams which guide the cutting or shaping of parts, or the data on the punched cards or tape. These memory data are "stored" so that they can be called up in case of need. The same is true of the organization where the memory is contained in all of the enduring records such as accounting ledgers, correspondence files, statistical tabulations, or production reports. The organization manual and job descriptions, as well as standard practice writings constitute parts of the organization's memory. Thus communication centers are located near to memory storage points, convenient to the sources of information. Messages are effective in resisting entropy and promoting homeostasis to the extent that they reflect reality. Hence facts must be stored so that they will be available when needed.

Organization consciousness. Several years ago when electronic data-processing was beginning to force itself on the attention of management a worried questioner asked a speaker at a management conference how a decision-maker was to defend himself against being swamped by the torrent of data which the machines were about to gush forth. The answer is, of course, that the machines furnish that defense through the concept of consciousness, another analogy with the animal organism. It also has its counterpart in traditional management ideology, just as feedback was foreshadowed by Fayol and others. Consciousness is little if any different from the "exception principle" so familiar to the orthodox management ideology. The manager who is a delegator and who practices the "clean desk" maxim gives his attention only to the exceptional situations which are called to his attention by various types of reports signalling danger points.

The same is true of a mechanized data-processing network; the great mass of material goes through and is stored in the memory cells without being noticed.

Certain tolerances are established and when the sensory organs detect that those tolerances are being approached, signals are sent out. They call the dangerous situation to the attention of the decision-makers, who formulate and transmit corrective messages. When the emergency is past, the great mass of data continues to go into memory storage without notice until another emergency is signalled.

The problem of consciousness is related to the existence of policy because decision and action tend to become routine where policy is established and well known. Communications flow, decisions are made, and actions are taken automatically without requiring conscious attention. Thus policy is a product of role expectations. People in an organization will behave in accordance with a pattern expected by others; and this pattern becomes policy when it is stabilized in types of situations which recur frequently or repetitively.[5] The messages and signals become routine except when decision or action out of the ordinary occurs, in which case danger signals arouse consciousness on the part of those whose role it is to attend to the problem at hand.

Organization will. An organization is said to have a "will," composed of "the set of internally labeled decisions and anticipated results, proposed by the application of the system's past and by blocking of incomparable impulses or data from the system's present or future."[6] Examples of "will" in familiar settings are: (1) the United States Forest Service's long-standing preference for selective cutting of timber as against clean-cutting; (2) the pacifism of the Quakers; and (3) a department store's refusal to open its display windows on Sunday. The latter is a perfect example of organization memory sending a message from the past which reflected the religious scruples of the long dead founder.

INFORMATION CHANNELS AND HIERARCHY

It is quite apparent that information is a principal basis for decision. The information needed in making a decision is likely to exist in many places with the result that facilities must be provided for transmitting that information to the decision centers. The conduits for such transmission may or may not follow hierarchical channels. One writer distinguishes between structure and dynamics, stating that dynamically, "administration appears as a patterned whirl and flow of communications. . . ."[7]

It is at this point, of course, that some of the new concepts come most directly into conflict, with one of the dominant aspects of traditional organization theory, the requirement that communications shall flow through command channels. Today we find that such a precept is no longer as sacred as it once was. No less an administrator than Ralph J. Cordiner has insisted that communications should never bog down in channels. A person in one division is expected to seek information from another division by calling "straight across the company" on the telephone.[8]

STRUCTURING COMMUNICATION FLOW

Reasons for observing channels. In general, however, it is desirable to spell out who shall communicate with whom and what matters are to be limited in circulation. There are at least three reasons for this. In the *first* place, it may be desirable to render obeisance to hierarchy in certain instances where a tense atmosphere has not yet subsided into that desired equilibrium which tolerates communication outside of channels. In other words there may be fewer ruffled feathers if the orthodoxy of "through channels" is observed. *Secondly,* organization objectives will often be better served if certain messages are kept secret—future intention to purchase land or establish a new branch, or development of new products for a competitive market. A *third* factor is discussed at greater length below: the proposition that the structuring of communications leads to more effective results than when they are unstructured.

Need for conscious structuring. If "many alternative channels are available for few messages, the functioning of the network may be hampered by indecision; if many messages have to compete for few channels, it may be hampered by 'jamming'."[9] The result is that the communication system needs to be based on some relatively stable operating rules; the channels should be specified, and the priorities and preferences for various types of messages indicated. From the standpoint of traditional management ideology, one of the most sensitive points involves conflict between the functional network and line of command. It may be desirable to minimize such tensions by spelling out what kinds of messages functional specialists may transmit without pre-consultation with the line of command, and *vice versa* messages from subordinates in the line of command to functional specialists on a superior echelon.

[5] John T. Dorsey, Jr., "A Communication Model for Administration," *Administrative Science Quarterly*, Volume 2 (December 1957), pp. 307-310.
[6] Karl W. Deutsch, "Mechanism, Teleology, and Mind," *Philosophy and Phenomenological Research*, Volume 12 (December 1951), p. 209.

[7] Dorsey, *op. cit.*, pp. 307, 310.
[8] Ralph J. Cordiner, *New Frontiers for Professional Managers* (New York: McGraw-Hill Book Company, 1956), pp. 65-66.
[9] Deutsch, *op. cit.*, p. 202.

There are undoubtedly types of organizations in which channels tend to become secondary. For instance, this was found to be the case in a unit devoted wholly to scientific research.[10] Easy access and informal interchange outside of channels became the rule. One's standing in the group was enhanced by a reputation for maintaining an open door.

RESEARCH FINDINGS

All of this talk about networks, grids, and loops should not cause one to jump to the conclusion that the hierarchical concept is to be banished from organization theory. *Far from it!* Experiments conducted by Bavelas indicated that the communicator's centrality of location facilitates his recognition as a leader by the group. Furthermore, in groups where the locations of the members favor centrality of leadership, communication is more effective. In other words hierarchy facilitated communications, as against laissez-faire evolution of group relationships. However, morale was greater under laissez-faire than under hierarchy.[11] A replication of Bavelas's experiment by Guetzkow and Simon showed that communication was more effective in groups that had centrally structured leadership. They remark, however, that "current management literature on the topic of communication leaves one with the expectation that certainly a reduction in communication restrictions should lead to a more adequately functioning organization." [12] They go on to say that their findings do not warrant any such conclusions, and warn "the practical communications expert working in industry or government" to be wary of the advice of those who advocate less structure in communications.

INFORMATION AND DECISION-MAKING

There are those who see the communication and decision-making processes as, if not identical, at least so interdependent that they become inseparable in practice. Dorsey says that a decision occurs on "the receipt of some kind of communication, it consists of a complicated process of combining communications from various sources and it results in the transmission of further communication." [13] Decision centers

must of necessity either coincide with or be in conjunction with communication centers.[14]. . .

A more correct characterization of the decision-communication process would be to refer to "decision chains," or a system of "sequential decisions." While information may sometimes follow a circular path the chain of decision centers takes on hierarchical conformation. The circular element is nevertheless present in the necessity for reciprocation, which is the very essence of feedback in modern communications systems. Thus there was the case of the captain of an infantry company who, after the Remagen bridge break-through, received a written order from his battalion commander to undertake a frontal assault on a hill position. The company commander conducted a reconnaissance which indicated that a frontal assault would court disaster whereas a flank attack had chances of success. He communicated this information to the battalion commander who somewhat reluctantly modified the order. The hill was taken by roundabout means with minimal cost. The reporter of the case, a veteran infantry officer, claimed that military concepts of hierarchical relationships would have inhibited this type of reciprocal communication in former days. The more likely procedure would have been to start the attack as per orders and change plans to meet the situations encountered.

Sometimes a breakdown in communication requires an on-the-spot decision to be made by the most likely person in the scalar chain. The foreman of a subcontractor requisitioned construction materials according to the plans in his possession, but someone at the yard pointed out that the job did not call for that type of material. This was communicated to the superintendent who immediately consulted the estimator. His notes showed that the material in present plans was not that used in figuring the estimates. Somewhere between the original and final plans a more costly item was included. The subcontractor's superintendent decided to authorize construction according to revised plans, even though it might entail loss, rather than hold up construction. Did this constitute circular decision-making?

Another decision actually took on aspects which were definitely circular in structure because the organization was more circular than hierarchical. This was a weak mayor-council city with a chief administrative officer reporting to both the mayor and the council. The question was whether to buy a machine that would save $6,000 a year in clerical expense. The department had the money and requisitioned the item, but an analyst under the administrative officer vetoed it under a mayor's directive to suspend capital expenditures. The city council was approached and it

10 Robert S. Weiss, *Processes of Organization* (Ann Arbor, Mich.: Survey Research Center, 1956), p. 9.
11 Alex Bavelas, "Communication Patterns in Task-oriented Groups," in Dorwin Cartwright and Alvin Zander, *Group Dynamics Research and Theory* (Evanston, Ill.: Row, Peterson, 1953), p. 505. (Reprinted from the *Journal of the Acoustical Society of America*, Volume 22, 1950, pp. 725-730.)
12 Harold Guetzkow and Herbert A. Simon, "The Impact of Communication Nets upon Organization and Performance in Task-oriented Groups," *Management Science*, Volume 1 (July 1955), pp. 233, 250.
13 Dorsey, *op. cit.*, p. 309.
14 Herbert A. Simon, *Administrative Behavior* (New York: The Macmillan Company, 1957), pp. 155-156.

asked the administrative officer to reconsider but he backed up his aide. Council members appealed informally to the mayor's office, where it was suggested that the work could be processed by machines existing in the elective controller's office. This proved feasible and that was the solution.

SUMMARY

There can be little doubt that communication is central to the life of organizations. Some even say it is a the base of organization structure. Indeed the traditional theory of organization places great emphasis on "going through channels" as the basic means of preserving unity of command within the pyramid.

In more recent years communications theory has become the central concept in developments in electronics and automation. It is postulated that man can only control his environment through information. Yet there are continuous forces at work which tend to distort communication and to promote disorganization. These forces are sometimes called *entropy,* from the concept so called in mathematical physics. They are counterbalanced by a seemingly natural tendency toward stability and equilibrium, which in itself is dynamic. This is sometimes known as *homeostasis.*

In the drive to resist entropy and induce homeostasis, the effectiveness of the communication process is central. If an appropriate feedback loop has been created which provides a reciprocal and compensating pattern of messages, the organization should function in a stable fashion. Both the animal organism and the automatic machines provide the model for this system of control through communication.

The effect of these new theoretical constructs has been to place great emphasis on opening any communications blocks within the organization. And unfortunately the traditional pattern of "going through channels" has in many circumstances been cumbersome, occasionally contributed to distortion, and been time-consuming. In a sense it is the concept of hierarchy which has been on trial; for the burden of much of the recent theory is to permit no tampering with the communication channels for the sake of the command channels. In other words, if the hierarchy cannot accommodate itself to the new significance of communications, it is the traditional notion of hierarchy which must be amended. Ralph Cordiner, for example, has insisted that communication should never bog down in channels. The communications must get through, even if the niceties of hierarchy must be forsaken.

In actual practice, some communications have gone through channels and some have not. This has led to a rather popular notion that fewer hierarchical restrictions on communication—that is, less structuring—would improve organization performance. Research evidence, however, does not necessarily support this view. Bavelas found, for example, that the hierarchical principle provides for a more *efficient* system of communication, though it may be harder on the morale of the participants. Guetzkow and Simon also found that communication was more effective in groups which had centrally structured leadership. Thus it would seem that the consequence of developments in communication theory has been to place greater emphasis on communications as an organizational factor and as a means of creating structure. It does not necessarily mean that traditional notions of hierarchy should be completely sacked.

The relationship between the communications system and decision-making is extremely important. If decision-making and communication processes are not identical, they are so interdependent they become inseparable in practice. As a result all studies of communication inevitably involve decision-making.

When studying communication in organizations, a central problem is to identify the types of networks that produce various consequences for the knowledge and performance of participants. One research technique involves the use of experimental groups, such as those created by Robert F. Bales during his simulation of committee meetings, summarized in Chapter 9 of this volume. Alex Bavelas has attempted to identify communication patterns by such laboratory techniques. In the next selection, Bavelas and Barrett describe his methods and some findings.

EXPERIMENTS IN ORGANIZATIONAL COMMUNICATION*

Alex Bavelas and Dermot Barrett

An organizational system of communication is usually created by the setting up of formal systems of responsibility and by explicit delegations of duties. These categories include statements, often implicitly, of the nature, content, and direction of the communication which is considered necessary for the performance of the group. Students of organization, however, have pointed out repeatedly that groups tend to depart from such formal statements and to create other channels of communication and dependence. In other words, informal organizational systems emerge. One may take the view that these changes are adaptations by the individuals involved in the direction of easier and more effective ways of working, or, perhaps, not working. It is no secret that informal groups are not always viewed by managers as favorable to the goals of the larger body. Also, it is by no means obvious that those informal groupings which evolve out of social and personality factors are likely to be more efficient (with respect to organizational tasks) than those set up formally by the managers. Altogether, if one considers how intimate the relations are between communication channels and control, it is not surprising that the managers of organizations would prefer explicit and orderly communication lines.

IS THERE "ONE BEST WAY"?

Unfortunately, there seems to be no organized body of knowledge out of which one can derive, for a given organization, an optimal communications system. Administrative thinking on this point commonly rests upon the assumption that the optimum system *can* be derived from a statement of the task to be performed. It is not difficult to show, however, that from a given set of specifications one may derive not a single communication pattern but a whole set of them, all logically adequate for the successful performance of the task in question. Which pattern from this set should be chosen? The choice, in practice, is usually made either in terms of a group of assumptions (often quite untenable) about human nature, or in terms of a personal bias on the part of the chooser. The seriousness of this situation is illustrated by the following example.

Let us assume that we have a group of five individuals who, in order to solve a problem, must share as quickly as possible the information each person possesses. Let us also assume that there are reasons which prevent them from meeting around a table, and that they must share this information by writing notes. To avoid the confusion and waste of time of each person writing a message to each of the others, a supervisor decides to set up channels in which the notes must go. He strikes upon the pattern shown in Fig. 1.

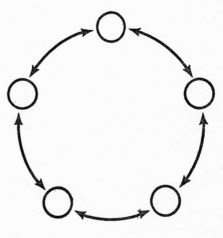

FIGURE 1

In this arrangement each individual can send to and receive messages from two others, one on his "left" and one on his "right." Experiments actually performed with this kind of situation show that the number of mistakes made by individuals working in such a "circle" pattern can be reduced by fully 60 per cent by the simple measure of *removing one link*, thus making the pattern a "chain" as shown in Fig. 2. The relevance of such a result to organization communication is obvious, simple though the example is. The sad truth, however, is that this phenomenon is not clearly derivable either from traditional "individ-

* From Alex Bavelas and Dermot Barrett, "An Experimental Approach to Organizational Communication," *Personnel*, Volume 27, Number 5 (March 1951), pp. 366-371. Reprinted with the permission of the authors and the publisher, the American Management Association, Inc.

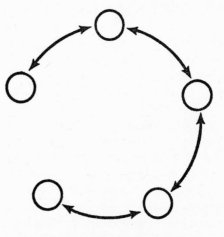

FIGURE 2

ual psychology" or from commonly held theories of group communication . . .

PATTERNS OF COMMUNICATION

About two years ago a series of studies was begun whose purpose was to isolate and study certain general properties of information handling systems. The first phase of this research program[1] is directed at a basic property of all communication systems, that of connection or "who can talk to whom."

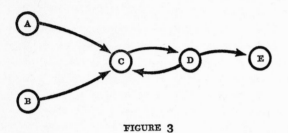

FIGURE 3

The property of connection can be conveniently expressed by diagrams. The meaning of the picture in Fig. 3 is obvious. Individuals A and B can send messages to C but they receive messages from no one; C and D can exchange messages; E can receive messages from D, but he can send messages to no one. The pattern shown in Fig. 3, however, is only one of the many that are possible. A group of others is shown in Fig. 4. An examination of these patterns will show that they fall into two classes, separated by

[1] These studies are supported jointly by the Rand Corporation and the Research Laboratory of Electronics at M.I.T.

FIGURE 4

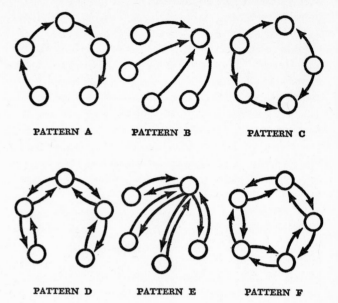

PATTERN A   PATTERN B   PATTERN C

PATTERN D   PATTERN E   PATTERN F

a very important difference. Any pair of individuals in each of the patterns, d, e, and f can exchange messages either directly or indirectly over some route. No pair of individuals in each of the patterns a, b, and c can exchange messages. Patterns like, a, b, and c obviously make any coordination of thought or action virtually impossible; we will be concerned from this point on only with patterns like d, e and f.

Since the individuals in any connected pattern like d, e, and f can share ideas completely, should we expect that the effectiveness of individuals in performing group tasks or solving group problems would be

FIGURE 5

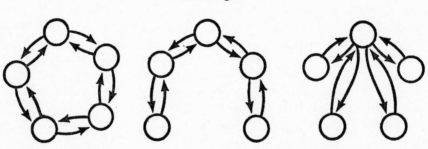

Speed	slow	fast	fast
Accuracy	poor	good	good
Organization	no stable form of organization	slowly emerging but stable organization	almost immediate and stable organization
Emergence of leader	none	marked	very pronounced
Morale	very good	poor	very poor

the same in patterns d, e and f except for differences in ability, knowledge, and personality? Should we expect differences in quality and speed of performance? Is it likely that the individuals working in one pattern would show significantly better morale than the individuals working in a different pattern? Sidney Smith and Harold J. Leavitt conducted a series of experiments[2] which yielded very definite answers to these questions. An experimental design was used which made it possible to equate the difficulty of the task which the groups performed, and which permitted the cancelling of individual differences by randomizing the assignment of subjects to patterns. Also, the experiment was repeated with different groups enough times to establish the consistency of the results. A brief summary of the findings is given in Fig. 5. The use of qualitative terms in Fig. 5 in place of the quantitative measurements which were actually made blurs the comparison somewhat, but it gives a fair picture of the way these patterns performed. Since the original experiments were done by Smith and Leavitt, this experiment has been repeated with no change in the findings.

The question very properly arises here as to whether these findings can be "explained" in the sense of being related to the connection properties of the patterns themselves. The answer to this question is a qualified yes. Without developing the mathematical analysis, which can be found in Leavitt's paper, the following statements can be made:

For any connected pattern, an *index of dispersion* can be calculated. Relative to this index, there can be calculated *for each position in each pattern* an *index of centrality*, and an *index of peripherality*. The data suggest strongly that the rapidity with which organization emerges and the stability it displays are related to the gradient of the indices of centrality in the pattern. In Fig. 6 these indices are given for each position. It should be added at this point that in the patterns in which leadership emerged, the leader was invariably that person who occupied the position of highest centrality.

The index of peripherality appears to be related strongly to morale. In Fig. 7 the indices of peripherality are given by position. Those individuals who occupied positions of low or zero peripherality showed in their actions as well as in self-ratings (made at the end of the experiments) that they were satisfied, in high spirits, and generally pleased with the work they had done. Those individuals who occupied positions of high peripherality invariably displayed either apathetic or destructive and uncooperative behavior dur-

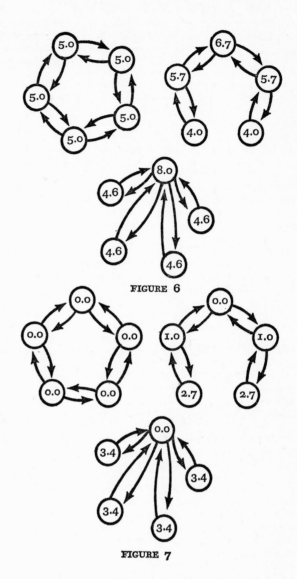

FIGURE 6

FIGURE 7

ing the group effort, and rated themselves as dissatisfied and critical of the group's operation.

A word of caution should be given concerning the slow, inaccurate, but happy "circle" pattern. Subsequent experiments by Sidney Smith indicate that this pattern possesses unusual abilities for adaptation to sudden and confusing changes of task—a quality lacking in the other two patterns.

A PROMISING FIELD FOR RESEARCH

Clearly, these experiments are only the beginning of a long story. The findings, although they promise much, settle nothing; but they do suggest that an experimental approach to certain aspects of organizational communication is possible and that, in all probability, it would be practically rewarding. As the characteristics of communication nets and their effects upon human performance *as they occur in the laboratory* become better understood, the need will grow for systematic studies of actual operating organizations. The

[2] Harold J. Leavitt reports these experiments in detail in the January, 1951, issue of the *Journal of Abnormal and Social Psychology*.

job of mapping an existing net of communications even in a relatively small company is a complicated and difficult one, but it is not impossible. Some work is beginning on the development of field methods of observation. The importance of bridging the gap between the simple, directly controlled experiment and the very complex, indirectly controlled social situation cannot be overestimated.

As Bavelas and Barrett say, generalizations about communications should be based on observations of actual organizations as well as on laboratory experiments. At the same time as Bavelas' experiments with small laboratory groups have been taking place, other researchers have been using participant–observation and interviews to study the communication of real-life information in actual organizations. In Keith Davis' "Communication and the Grapevine," the author tells how he identified the structure of an informal communication network in an organization; he describes the significance of this structure for the larger structure and decisions of the organization; and he suggests some lessons for management. In previous selections, the distinction between the formal and informal structures of an organization has been made; Davis' selection demonstrates some of the techniques that may identify the unpublicized and often unrecognized informal structure. The leader of a voluntary association must be alert to the consequences of the informal communications networks that exist among both the employees and the volunteers of his organization.

COMMUNICATION AND THE GRAPEVINE*

Keith Davis

A particularly neglected aspect of management communication concerns that informal channel, the grapevine. There is no dodging the fact that, as a carrier of news and gossip among executives and supervisors, the grapevine often affects the affairs of management. The proof of this is the strong feelings that different executives have about it. Some regard the grapevine as an evil—a thorn in the side which regularly spreads rumor, destroys morale and reputations, leads to irresponsible actions, and challenges authority. Some regard it as a good thing because it acts as a safety valve and carries news fast. Others regard it as a very mixed blessing.

Whether the grapevine is considered an asset or a liability, it is important for executives to try to understand it. For one thing is sure; although no executive can absolutely control the grapevine, he can *influence* it. And since it is here to stay, he should learn to live with it.

PERSPECTIVE

Of course, the grapevine is only part of the picture of communication in management. There is also formal communication—via conferences, reports, memoranda, and so on; this provides the basic core of information, and many administrators rely on it almost exclusively because they think it makes their job simpler to have everything reduced to explicit terms —as if that were possible! Another important part of the picture is the expression of attitudes, as contrasted with the transmission of information (which is what we will be dealing with in this article). Needless to say, all these factors influence the way the grapevine works in a given company, just as the grapevine in turn influences them.

In this article I want to examine (a) the significance, character, and operation of management communication patterns, with particular emphasis on the grapevine; and (b) the influence that various fac-

* From Keith Davis, "Management Communication and the Grapevine," *Harvard Business Review*, Volume 31, Number 5 (September-October 1953), pp. 43-49. Reprinted with the permission of the author and the publisher.

tors, such as organization and the chain of procedure, have upon such patterns. From this analysis, then it will be possible to point up (c) the practical implications for management.

As for the research basis of the analysis, the major points are these:

1. Company studied. The company upon which the research is based is a real one. I shall refer to it as the "Jason Company." A manufacturer of leather goods, it has 67 people in the management group (that is, all people who supervise the work of others, from top executives to foremen) and about 600 employees. It is located in a rural town of 10,000 persons, and its products are distributed nationally.

In my opinion, the pattern of management communication at the Jason Company is typical of that in many businesses; there were no special conditions likely to make the executives and supervisors act differently from their counterparts in other companies. But let me emphasize that this is a matter of judgment, and hence broader generalizations cannot be made until further research is undertaken. . . .

2. Methodology. The methods used to study management communication in the Jason Company are new ones. Briefly, the basic approach was to learn from each communication recipient how he first received a given piece of information and then to trace it back to its source. Suppose D and E said they received it from G; G said he received it from B; and B from A. All the chains or sequences were plotted in this way—A to B to G to D and E—and when the data from all recipients were assembled, the pattern of the flow of communication emerged. The findings could be verified and developed further with the help of other data secured from the communication recipients.

This research approach, which I have called "ecco analysis," is discussed in detail elsewhere.[1]

SIGNIFICANT CHARACTERISTICS

In the Jason Company many of the usual grapevine characteristics were found along with others less well known. For purposes of this discussion, the four most significant characteristics are these:

1. Speed of transmission. Traditionally the grapevine is fast, and this showed up in the Jason Company.

For example, a certain manager had an addition to his family at the local hospital at 11 o'clock at night,

[1] Keith Davis, "A Method of Studying Communication Patterns in Organizations," *Personnel Psychology* (Fall, 1953).

and by 2:00 P.M. the next day 46% of the whole management group knew about the event. The news was transmitted only by grapevine and mostly by face-to-face conversation, with an occasional inter-office telephone call. Most communications occurred immediately before work began, during "coffee hours," and during lunch hour. The five staff executives who knew of the event learned of it during "coffee hour," indicating that the morning rest period performed an important social function for the staff as well as providing relaxation.

2. Degree of selectivity. It is often said that the grapevine acts without conscious direction or thought —that it will carry anything, any time, anywhere. This viewpoint has been epitomized in the statement that "the grapevine is without conscience or consciousness." But flagrant grapevine irresponsibility was not evident in the Jason Company. In fact, the grapevine here showed that it could be highly selective and discriminating.

For example, the local representative of the company which carried the employee group insurance contract planned a picnic for company executives. The Jason Company president decided to invite 36 executives, mostly from higher executive levels. The grapevine immediately went to work spreading this information, but it was carried to *only two of the 31 executives not invited*. The grapevine communicators thought the news was confidential, so they had told only those who they thought would be invited (they had to guess, since they did not have access to the invitation list). The two uninvited executives who knew the information were foremen who were told by their invited superintendent; he had a very close working relationship with them and generally kept them well informed.

Many illustrations like the above could be gathered to show that the grapevine can be discriminating. Whether it may be *counted on* in that respect, however, is another question. The answer would of course differ with each case and would depend on many variables, including other factors in the communication picture having to do with attitudes, executive relationships, and so forth.

3. Locale of operation. The grapevine of company news operates mostly at the place of work.

Jason managers were frequently in contact with each other after work because the town is small; yet grapevine communications about company activities predominantly took place at the plant, rather than away from it. It was at the plant that executives and supervisors learned, for instance, that the president was taking a two weeks' business trip, that the style designer had gone to Florida to study fashion trends, and that an executive had resigned to begin a local insurance business.

The significance of at-the-company grapevines is this: since management has some control over the work environment, it has an opportunity to influence the grapevine. By exerting such influence the manager can more closely integrate grapevine interests with those of the formal communication system, and he can use it for effectively spreading more significant items of information than those commonly carried.

4. Relation to formal communication. Formal and informal communication systems tend to be jointly active, or jointly inactive. Where formal communication was inactive at the Jason Company, the grapevine did not rush in to fill the void (as has often been suggested);[2] instead, there simply was lack of communication. Similarly, where there was effective formal communication, there was an active grapevine.

Informal and formal communication may supplement each other. Often formal communication is simply used to confirm or to expand what has already been communicated by grapevine. Thus in the case of the picnic, as just described, management issued formal invitations even to those who already knew they were invited. This necessary process of confirmation results partly because of the speed of the grapevine, which formal systems fail to match, partly because of its unofficial function, and partly because of its transient nature. Formal communication needs to come along to stamp "Official" on the news and to put it "on the record," which the grapevine cannot suitably do.

SPREADING INFORMATION

Now let us turn to the actual operation of the grapevine. How is information passed along? What is the relationship among the various people who are involved?

Human communication requires at least two persons, but each person acts independently. Person A may talk or write, but he has not *communicated* until person B receives. The individual is, therefore, a basic communication unit. That is, he is one "link" in the communication "chain" for any bit of information.

The formal communication chain is largely determined by the chain of command or by formal procedures, but the grapevine chain is more flexible. There are four different ways of visualizing it, as Figure 1 indicates:

1. The single-strand chain. A tells B, who tells C, who tells D, and so on; this makes for a tenuous chain to a distant receiver. Such a chain is usually in mind when one speaks of how the grapevine distorts and filters information until the original item is not recognizable.

2. The gossip chain. A seeks and tells everyone else.

3. The probability chain. A communicates randomly, say, to F and D, in accordance with the laws of probability; then F and D tell others in the same manner.

4. The cluster chain. A tells three selected others; perhaps one of them tells two others, and then one of these two tells one other. This was virtually the only kind of chain found in the Jason Company, and may well be the normal one in industry generally.

FIGURE I. *Types of communication chains*

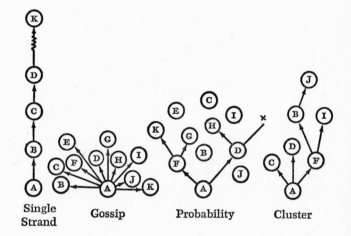

Single Strand   Gossip   Probability   Cluster

ACTIVE MINORITY

The predominance of the cluster chain at the Jason Company means that only a few of the persons who knew a unit of information even transmitted it—what Jacobson and Seashore call the "liaison" individuals.[3] All others who received the information did not transmit it; they acted merely as passive receivers.

For example, when a quality-control problem occurred, 68% of the executives received the information, but only 20% transmitted it. Again, when an executive planned to resign to enter the insurance business, 81% of the executives knew about it, but only 11% passed the news on to others. Those liaison

2 For example, see National Industrial Conference Board, *Communicating with Employees,* Studies in Personnel Policy, No. 129 (New York, 1952), p. 34.

3 Eugene Jacobson and Stanley E. Seashore, "Communication Practices in Complex Organization," *The Journal of Social Issues,* Volume 7, Number 3 (1951), p. 37.

individuals who told the news to more than one other person amounted to less than 10% of the 67 executives in each case.

These active groups varied in membership. There was no evidence that any one group consistently acted as liaison persons; instead, different types of information passed through different liaison persons. However, as will be shown later, some individuals were invariably communication "isolates"; they received and transmitted information poorly or not at all.

The above findings indicate that if management wants more communication, it should increase the number and/or effectiveness of its liaison individuals. This appears to be a large order, but it is entirely possible. Liaison individuals tend to act in a predictable way. If an individual's unit of information concerns a job function in which he is interested, he is likely to tell others. If his information is about a person with whom he is associated socially, he also is likely to tell others. Furthermore, the sooner he knows of an event after it happened, the more likely he is to tell others. If he gets the information late, he does not want to advertise his late receipt of it by telling it to others.

In other words, three well-known communication principles which are so often mentioned in relation to attitudes also have a major influence on the spread of information by liaison individuals:

(1) Tell people about what will affect them (job interest).

(2) Tell people what they want to know, rather than simply what you want them to know (job and social interest).

(3) Tell people soon (timing).

ORGANIZATIONAL EFFECTS

The way an organization is divided horizontally into organizational levels and vertically into functions such as production and sales, obviously has effects on management communication, for it cuts each company's over-all administrative function into small work assignments, or jobs, and sets each management person in certain relationships to others in his company.

HORIZONTAL LEVELS

Organizational levels are perhaps the more dramatic in effect because they usually carry authority, pay increases, and status. From the communication point of view, they are especially important because of their number. In a typical firm there are usually several management levels, but only one or two worker levels; furthermore, as the firm grows, the management levels increase in number, while the worker levels remain stationary.

Communication problems are aggravated by these additional levels because the chain of communication is lengthened and complicated. Indeed, just because of this, some companies have been led to try to reduce the number of intermediate management levels. Our concern here is with the patterns of communication among individuals at the different levels.

At the Jason Company, executives at *higher* levels communicated more often and with more people than did executives at *lower* levels. In other words, the predominant communication flow was downward or horizontal. When an event happened at the bottom level, usually the news did reach a high level; but a single line of communication sufficed to carry it there, and from that point it went downward and outward in the same volume and manner (cluster chain) as if it had originated at the top.

Accordingly, the higher an executive was in the organizational hierarchy (with the exception of nonresident executives), the greater was his knowledge of company events. This was true of events which happened both above his level and below his level. Thus, if the president was out of town, a greater proportion at the fourth level knew of it than at the sixth level. Or—and this is less to be expected if a foreman at the sixth level had an accident, a larger proportion of executives at the third level knew of it than at the fourth level, or even than at the sixth level where the accident happened. The more noteworthy the event, of course, the more likely it was to be known at upper levels—but, in a company of this size, it had to be quite trivial indeed before it failed to reach the ears of top executives.

The converse follows that in terms of communications transmitted and received the sixth and lowest level of supervision, the foreman level, was largely isolated from all other management. The average foreman was very hesitant to communicate with other members of management; and on the rare occasions when he did, he usually chose someone at his own level and preferably in his own department. Members of this group tended to be the last links in management communication, regardless of whether the chains were formal or informal.

A further significant fact concerns the eight departmental superintendents at the fourth level. Six of them supervised foremen directly; two others, with larger departments, each had a single line assistant between him and his foremen. The two who had line assistants were much more active in the communication chains than were the six others; indeed, all but one of the six appeared to have little to do with their foremen except in a formal way.

Perhaps the clue is that, with increased organizational levels, those at the higher (and hence further removed) levels both recognize a greater need for communication and have more time to practice it!

FUNCTIONAL GROUPS

Functionalization, the second important way in which an organization is "cut up," also has a significant impact on communication in management. The functions which are delegated to a manager help to determine the people he contacts, his relationships with them, his status, and as a result, the degree to which he receives and transmits information. More specifically, his role in communication is affected (a) by his position in the chain of command and (b) by his position in the chain of procedure, which involves the sequence of work performance and cuts across chains of command, as when a report goes from the superintendent in one chain of command to the chief engineer in another chain of command and to the controller in still another.

In the Jason Company the effects of functionalization showed up in three major ways:

1. Staff men "in the know." More staff executives than line men usually knew about any company event. This was true at each level of management as well as for the management group as a whole. For example, when the president of the company made a trip to seek increased governmental allotments of hides to keep the line tannery operating at capacity, only 4% of the line executives knew the purpose of the trip, but 25% of the staff men did. In another case, when a popular line superintendent was awarded a hat as a prize in a training program for line superintendents, within six days a larger proportion of the staff executives than of the line executives knew about this event.

The explanation is not just that, with one staff executive to every three line executives, there were more line executives to be informed. More important is the fact that the *chain of procedure* usually involved more staff executives than line executives. Thus, when the superintendent was awarded his hat, a line executive had approved the award, but a staff personnel executive had processed it and a staff accounting executive had arranged for the special check.

Also the staff was more *mobile* than the line. Staff executives in such areas as personnel and control found that their duties both required and allowed them to get out of their offices, made it easy for them to walk through other departments without someone wondering whether they were "not working," to get away for coffee, and so on—all of which meant they heard more news from the other executives they talked with. (In a larger company staff members might be more fixed to their chairs, but the situation in the Jason Company doubtless applies to a great many other businesses.)

Because of its mobility and its role in the chain of procedure, the staff not only received but also transmitted communications more actively than did the line. Most of these communications were oral; at least in this respect, the staff was not the "paper mill" it is often said to be. It seems obvious that management would do well to make conscious use of staff men as communicators.

2. Cross-communication. A second significant effect of functionalization in the Jason Company was that the predominant flow of information for events of general interest was between the four large areas of production, sales, finance and office, and industrial relations, rather than within them. That is, if a production executive had a bit of news of general interest, he was more likely to tell a sales, finance, or personnel executive than another production executive.

Social relationships played a part in this, with executives in the various groups being lodge brothers, members of the same church, neighbors, parents of children in the same schools, and so on. In these relationships the desire to make an impression was a strong motivation for cross-communication, since imparting information to executives outside his own area served to make a man feel that the others would consider him "in the know." Procedural relationships, discussed earlier, also encouraged the executives to communicate across functional lines.

Since communications tended not to stay within an area, such as production, they tended even less to follow chains of command from boss to sub-boss to sub-sub-boss. Indeed, the chain of command was seldom used in this company except for very formal communications. Thus Figure 2 reproduces a communication chain concerning a quality control problem in production, first brought to the attention of a group sales manager in a letter from a customer. Although it was the type of problem that could have been communicated along the chain of command, the exhibit shows that, of 14 communications, only 3 were within the chain of command and only 6 remained within one functional area—sales—where the information was first received.

The fact that the chain of command may affect management communication patterns less than procedural and social influences—which has shown up in other companies too[4]—means that management needs to devote considerably more attention to the problems and opportunities of cross-communication.

[4] See Carroll L. Shartle, "Leadership and Executive Performance," *Personnel* (March, 1949), pp. 377-378.

FIGURE 2. *Communication chain for a quality control problem*

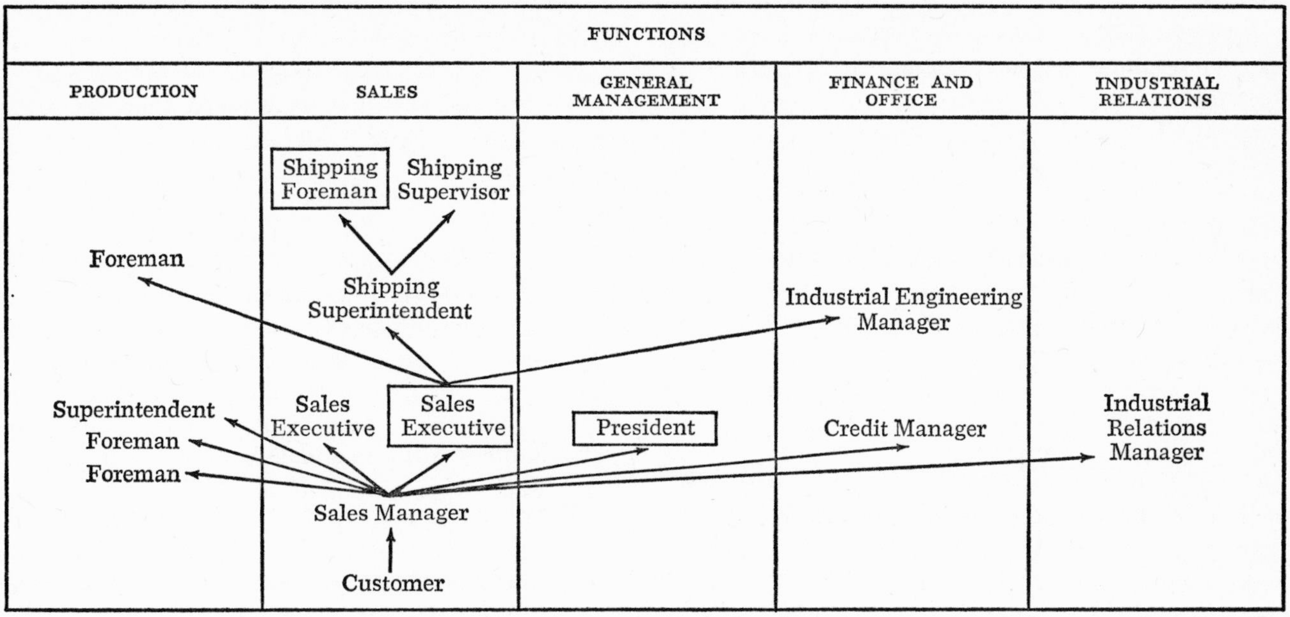

FUNCTIONS				
PRODUCTION	SALES	GENERAL MANAGEMENT	FINANCE AND OFFICE	INDUSTRIAL RELATIONS

NOTE: *Executives in boxes received chain-of-command communications.*

3. *Group isolation.* The research in the Jason Company revealed that some functional groups were consistently isolated from communication chains. Also, there were other groups which received information but did not transmit it, and thus contributed to the same problem—the uneven spread of information through the company. Here are three examples at the foreman level illustrating different degrees of failure to participate in the communication process and different reasons for this failure:

(a) The foremen in one group were generally left out of communication chains. These men were of a different nationality from that of the rest of the employees, performed dirty work, and worked in a separate building. Also, their work fitted into the manufacturing process in such a way that it was seldom necessary for other executives to visit their work location.

(b) Another group often was in a communication chain but on the tail end of it. They were in a separate building some distance from the main manufacturing area, their function was not in the main manufacturing procedure, and they usually received information late. They had little chance or incentive to communicate to other executives.

(c) A third group both received and transmitted information, but transmitted only within a narrow radius. Although they were in the midst of the main work area, they failed to communicate with other functional groups because their jobs required constant attention and they felt socially isolated.

In sum, the reasons for group isolation at the Jason Company were: geographical separation; work association (being outside the main procedures or at the end of them); social isolation; and organizational level (the lower the level of a group, the greater its tendency to be isolated).

Obviously, it is not often feasible for management to undertake to remove such causes of group isolation as geographical or social separation. On the other hand, it may well be possible to compensate for them. For example, perhaps the volume of formal communication to men who happen to be in a separate building can be increased, or arrangements can be made for a coffee break that will bring men who are isolated because of the nature of their work or their nationality into greater contact with other supervisors. In each situation management should be able to work out measures that would be appropriate to the individual circumstances.

CONCLUSION

The findings at the Jason Company have yet to be generalized by research in other industries, but they provide these starting points for action:

(1) If management wants more communication among executives and supervisors, one way is to increase the number and effectiveness of the liaison individuals.

(2) It should count on staff executives to be more active than lines executives in spreading information.

(3) It should devote more attention to cross-

communication—that is, communication between men in different departments. It is erroneous to consider the chain of command as *the* communication system because it is only one of many influences. Indeed, procedural and social factors are even more important.

(4) It should take steps to compensate for the fact that some groups are "isolated" from communication chains.

(5) It should encourage further research about management grapevines in order to provide managers with a deeper understanding of them and to find new ways of integrating grapevine activities with the objectives of the firm.

(6) "Ecco analysis," the recently developed research approach used at the Jason Company, should be useful for future studies.

If management wants to do a first-class communication job, at this stage it needs fewer medicines and more diagnoses. Communication analysis has now passed beyond "pure research" to a point where it is immediately useful to top management in the individual firm. The patterns of communication that show up should serve to indicate both the areas where communication is most deficient and the channels through which information can be made to flow most effectively.

In particular, no administrator in his right mind would try to abolish the management grapevine. It is as permanent as humanity is. Nevertheless, many administrators have abolished the grapevine from *their own minds.* They think and act without giving adequate weight to it or, worse, try to ignore it. This is a mistake. The grapevine is a factor to be reckoned with in the affairs of management. The administrator should analyze it and should consciously try to influence it.

Social distance can be as much of a barrier to communication as physical distance; when organizations contain individuals of sharply different statuses, communication can be impaired. For example, sociologists and social psychologists in the Research Branch of the Army during World War II, in studies of officers and enlisted men, found that the two groups had widely divergent views about the army and about each other. Each group misperceived the opinions held by the other, as judged by responses to such questions (to enlisted men) as "Most officers believe that. . . ." The researchers concluded that status barriers prevented each group from communicating freely with the other.*

Since numerous barriers to communication are lodged both in individuals and in the social structure, special effort must be made to ensure that communication be efficient enough to enable the organization to achieve its goals. In their selection, George Strauss and Leonard R. Sayles offer advice based on sociological and psychological research.

OVERCOMING BARRIERS TO COMMUNICATION†

George Strauss and Leonard R. Sayles

We now know many techniques for improving communications, though—it should be emphasized—none is a cure-all. Perfect understanding between people is impossible. . . . At first glance, these techniques may appear mechanical substitutes for mutual trust and understanding. However, a wide variety of research confirms the efficacy of considering communications as a type of engineering problem—the problem of transmitting information from one point to another.

UTILIZE FEEDBACK

Perhaps the single most important method of improving communications is *feedback.* This term, adopted

* Samuel Stouffer et al., *The American Soldier* (Princeton: Princeton University Press, 1949).
† From George Strauss and Leonard R. Sayles, *Personnel: The Human Problems of Management*, pp. 203-213. © 1960. Reprinted by permission of the authors and the publisher, Prentice-Hall, Inc., Englewood Cliffs, N.J.

from engineering refers to the ability of certain complex machines (technically: systems) to check on their own performance and to correct it if necessary.

We all use this principle of feedback in our human communications—perhaps without realizing it. Even in casual conversations we are constantly on the alert for cues to whether we are being understood (e.g., attentive nods from the other person). Similarly, a good teacher is always interested in audience reaction among his students. If they seem confused or drowsy, he knows his lecture isn't getting across. The good supervisor is equally conscious of the need to determine his subordinates' reactions to what he is trying to communicate.

An interesting study conducted by Dr. Alex Bavelas illustrates the importance of feedback.[1] Two students were placed in different rooms and one was asked to communicate to the other the position of an interconnected series of dominoes placed on a grid. Both had identical grids in front of them. The sender was permitted to explain to the receiver, in any way he saw fit, the relative positions of the dominoes. It was impossible to complete the task successfully when the receiver was forbidden to respond—that is, when communications were entirely one-way. No matter how painstakingly the sender explained the pattern, the receiver never understood all of it. Apparently some opportunity to ask for further information, at least to answer "yes" or "no" to the questions of the sender (e.g., Did you understand what I said?), is essential if complex information is to be communicated. Without feedback, false perceptions creep in, and even a small error that goes uncorrected may become magnified into a major distortion.

Bavelas' experiment also revealed that communications gain in speed and efficiency as more and more feedback is permitted. Limiting the receiver to "yes" or "no" responses is less effective than allowing him to expand his comments to whatever he deems appropriate.

MAXIMIZE FEEDBACK BY USING MANY
CHANNELS OF COMMUNICATION

How do we know if the person to whom we are communicating understands, agrees, or sympathizes with us, or is indifferent, hostile, or confused? There are several techniques for maximizing feedback.

Observation. In a face-to-face situation, we can observe the other person and judge his responses by his total behavioral set. We can watch for non-verbal cues—the expressions of puzzlement, anger, or comprehension that flicker across the face of the listener, or the subtle body motions that reveal impatience, animosity, or agreement. These cues give eloquent expression to attitudes that the receiver may be reluctant or unable to express in words.

Indeed, by their posture and facial expression, the set of their lips, the movement of an eyebrow, people often tell us more than they do in hours of talk or scores of written memoranda. A subordinate is seldom eager to challenge the orders of his superior. But in the course of informal, face-to-face discussion, an alert supervisor can detect the subordinate's lack of enthusiasm by his tone of voice and his general physical behavior.

Few of us appreciate just how much valuable information these nonverbal cues transmit. As one social scientist has observed, "When communication is at peak efficiency, in the most intimately shared situations, words are often superfluous. Good examples of this are the hospital operating room, the jazz band, and some small interdependent work teams in industry."[2] The close coordination necessary for these groups to achieve their goal is attained exclusively through occasional nods and glances.

Listening with a "third ear." We must listen carefully if we are to discover what a person is trying to say. Though few of us can qualify as psychiatrists, we can learn to listen with a "third ear" by asking ourselves such questions as "What did Joe really mean when he told me he was 'fed up'? Was it his assignment? His family? His chances for promotion? Me, as his boss? Why did he remain silent when I asked him for details?"

There is a hidden content in many communications that can only be inferred by the listener. (This non-logical element is frequently referred to as the *latent* content as distinct from the *manifest* content.) While the listener should keep his imagination in check, he should try to go beyond the logical verbal meaning where there is some evidence that emotional feeling is involved. Most communications are in fact a combination of fact and feeling.

A good example of this hidden content is provided by the word "communications" itself. An office manager complains to the personnel director that all his human-relations problems stem from "poor communications." If the personnel director wants to be of assistance, he will try to get behind the manager's use of the word "communications." The manager might mean that there are divisive cliques that tend to distort his orders or that he, the boss, never hears the "real truth" about what is going on in the office. He might be using the word communications to mean that cooperative teamwork is lacking, or to mean many other things. The point is that the words used by a speaker may not be very informative until we

---

[1] As described to his students at M.I.T.

[2] From a lecture by Dr. Robert N. Wilson, Executive Development Program, Cornell University, 1952.

have an opportunity to question him on what he really means in terms of actual observable behavior. The listener must try to get back to the referents of the speaker and to avoid the easy assumption that both people are attaching the same meaning to abstract words.

Checking on reception. The speaker himself may have to initiate queries to insure that the message he is transmitting is actually being received. For instance, he might ask the receiver to repeat complex verbal orders. Or he might simply ask, "Do you understand? Is this clear?" (This is one of the functions of the classroom recitation.)

Feedback is particularly hard to obtain in a large organization. When top management wants to discover whether its directives are being understood, face-to-face exchanges are often impossible. Morale surveys and suggestion systems sometimes help to bridge the gap between top management and subordinates, but . . . the best way to promote feedback is through changes in organizational structure and overall supervisory attitudes.

USE FACE-TO-FACE COMMUNICATIONS

Face-to-face communications are superior, under most circumstances, to written orders, printed announcements, or newspaper articles. Only when the sender is able to experience direct feedback from the receiver can he really know what the receiver is hearing and what he is failing to hear. How else can the sender become aware of the hidden meanings—the symbolic significance the receiver is ascribing to his words? How else can he bring out into the open contradictory information already in the receiver's mind that may cause him to reject or ignore the communication?

Another reason for the greater effectiveness of voice communications is that most of us communicate more easily, completely, and more frequently by voice.

Probably the greatest advantage of voice communications is that they provide immediate feedback. Merely by looking at the audience, the skillful speaker can judge how it is reacting to what he is saying. If necessary he can modify his approach or vary the intensity of his voice. (The human voice can provide a wider variety of emphasis and pace than any printed page, regardless of the number of type fonts used.)

Even better feedback is possible if the recipients of the message are allowed to comment or ask questions. This gives the supervisor an opportunity to explain his meaning or to consider unexpected problems. (Printed material can provide explanations, but few writers can anticipate all the questions that might be asked.)

Furthermore, we usually ascribe more credibility to what we hear someone say than to words attributed to him in print. Employees conditioned to the "slick" releases of public relations offices tend to discount many of the printed announcements they read. Actually hearing the boss say that the company is in serious trouble, however, may carry a great deal more weight than would a statement in the house organ, particularly if employees have an opportunity to ask the boss direct questions . . .

Does all this mean that written messages have no place in the organization? Not at all. In fact, they are often indispensable. Lengthy, detailed instructions must be put in writing so that the person to whom they are addressed can have a chance to study them at leisure. The spoken word exists only for an instant, and then vanishes. The written message provides a permanent record to which the receiver can refer to make sure he understands what has been said, and to which the sender can refer as evidence that he has in fact said it. Frequently, too, the relative formality of written communications gives the message greater weight than it would have if it were delivered orally.

For very important messages, both the spoken and written word may be used in combination. For instance, if a new procedure is to be introduced, the supervisor might call a meeting of his subordinates to give them a rough outline of the change. At this point he could (1) explain why the change is necessary, (2) answer their questions, and (3) perhaps make adjustments to meet objections. Once general agreement has been reached, the new procedure can be reduced to writing for future reference.

BE SENSITIVE TO THE WORLD OF THE RECEIVER

It is extremely difficult to get through to a listener when what we are trying to communicate contradicts his expectations and predilections. If our typist has been in the habit of preparing only a single carbon, we must stress our request for two carbons. If being sent to the front office is regarded by employees as a sign of impending discipline, we must take pains to communicate that this is *not* the reason, if in fact it is not.

In short we must be sensitive to the private world of the receiver and try to predict the impact of what we say and do on his feelings and attitudes. The greater the gap between our background and experience and that of the receiver, the greater the effort we must make to find some common ground of understanding. If the supervisor really wants to communicate with the sweeper, for example, he must find a way of (a) fitting his remarks to the sweeper's attitudes and beliefs, (b) making some appeal to the needs of the sweeper, and (c) constantly testing (via feedback) whether his message is being received.

This same problem arises when management attempts to communicate to employees through company newspapers (house organs) or reports. Management often relies on such publications to tell employees about personnel changes, the company's economic condition, cost problems, cost-reduction programs, future prospects for company business, how company products and services are being used, and the "why" and "how" of doing things throughout the organization. For obvious reasons management thinks these are matters of importance and wants all employees to understand as much as possible about them. Unfortunately, however, management is often insensitive to the world of the employees and tries to project its own interests onto them. The employees down the line may be bored by information on the sources of company funds or the painstaking engineering that lies behind the company's products, though these are subjects of great importance to management.

Management often spends a great deal of time and money to present information of this sort in a way that will capture the interest of the employees when they read the house organ. But what happens is that the carefully worded story simply passes over the heads of the majority of employees whose interest in the subject is limited or downright nonexistent.

Many companies try to get around this problem by including information that *is* relevant to rank-and-file employees—information on their own world of activities and interests. They feature news of company-sponsored athletic events, social notes, announcements of weddings, births, retirements, and so forth. Departmental correspondents are appointed to broaden the coverage. The objective is to improve morale and enhance employee identification with the company.

The Detroit Edison Company has adopted an interesting approach. Its house organ features a "rumor clinic" in which top management deals candidly with questions raised by employees on such subjects as: alleged pay and vacation inequities, why some employees receive company-bought clothing and others do not, the quality and price of cafeteria food, and the reasons for layoffs or overtime. In answering questions submitted by workers, management has an opportunity to communicate information about the company's economic condition, engineering and sales problems, and so on—and in terms of direct interest to employees.

BE AWARE OF SYMBOLIC MEANING

As we have seen, symbols play a vital role in the "private world" of the listener. Here is a case in which effective communication was blocked until symbolic meanings were taken into account:

To help in the preparation of market analyses the District Sales Manager asked the salesmen to compute correlation coefficients from their records. These coefficients could be calculated quite simply and painlessly by use of a simple formula. But the salesmen refused to do what they were asked. One excuse followed another: the computations were too complicated, it was clerk's work and not part of their job description, the coefficients were really useless, and so on. There seemed to be no way to convince the men to perform this simple task, and their persistent refusal seemed out of all proportion to the issue at hand.

Why was this modest request greeted with such stubborn resistance? The very degree of the salesmen's reaction was the key to the problem. Investigation revealed that coefficient correlations had been tried three years earlier, when the department was headed by an inept supervisor who had earned the universal dislike of his subordinates. Among other things, he had tried to revamp all the departmental procedures and in the process had introduced this statistical technique. Ever since, the salesmen had associated the term "coefficient correlation" with autocratic supervision. To them it had become a symbol of oppressive management. Once the company had plumbed this seemingly irrational attitude, it was a simple matter to develop a different terminology for the operation, to conduct training in how the computations should be carried out, and to gain ready acceptance for the whole activity.

The moral of this story is clear; if there is extraordinary, unexpected resistance to a proposal, try to find out whether some symbolic meaning is associated with it.

TIME YOUR MESSAGES CAREFULLY

We have already noted that our current beliefs often distort the meaning we ascribe to what we hear or see. There is an analogy here to the concept of "noise" as used by the communications engineer. The supervisor must recognize that when he is trying to tell his subordinate something, other things are being heard simultaneously that may distort his message.

One way of limiting the amount of noise or distortion is to communicate your message before those other beliefs or attitudes come into play. Then the communication will meet less resistance and your chances of getting it accepted will be greatly increased.

Management announced that Foreman Green would retire in a few months and would be replaced by a man named Williams from another department. One of the men felt that Williams had done him an injustice years ago, and spread the word among his fellow employees that Williams was a tyrant who played favorites.

Long before Williams set foot in the new department, a petition was sent to top management requesting that a different foreman be assigned. And once Williams showed up, everything he said and did was fitted into the picture the employees had already established. Every job assignment he made was scrutinized for favoritism. Even harmless statements were often interpreted as threats.

A situation like this is an ideal breeding-ground for misunderstanding and unrest. Yet management could have minimized the problem by taking positive action before the picture of the new supervisor got established, perhaps by having the employees meet him as soon as the announcement was made.

REINFORCE WORDS WITH ACTIONS

Words by themselves are suspect. Employees are more likely to accept new propositions when they observe an actual change in behavior or participate themselves in the process of change. For example, supervisors in one company were told that they would have the final say in granting individual pay increases. This was a radical departure from past practice. Most of the supervisors were skeptical about whether management really meant what it said. But this feeling disappeared when they began filling out recommendation forms themselves and sending them to the Personnel Department (a minor clerical job that in the past had been done in the superintendent's office). The consistent reinforcement of verbal announcements by action increases the likelihood that the communication will be accepted.

Management must be careful not to allow super-salesmanship techniques to dominate its thinking in communicating to employees. Because employees are able to judge for themselves the quality of the relationship they enjoy with a company, sustained repetition of slick slogans will not be effective. One cannot advertise one type of personnel program and deliver another. In the same vein, low-pressure statements are probably more effective than high-pressure pronouncements. Instead of telling workers how generous their pension benefits are, it may be more effective to give them the facts (comparative data on pension plans for the industry or community) and let them draw their own conclusion. It is difficult if not impossible to communicate "values"; facts can be transmitted with some success, but even facts are subject to distortion.

Once management has acquired a reputation for accuracy and reliability in its communications, it can do a more effective job of communicating information on new problems. The British learned this lesson during the war.

> Early in World War II, when the radio stations of most countries were widely suspected of distorting the war news, the British Broadcasting System adopted a policy of frankly reporting Allied setbacks. This gave the British a morale and tactical advantage over their enemies when the tide turned in favor of the Allies, for Europeans of all nationalities were ready to believe the news of the German rout— simply because it came from a source that had proved itself trustworthy.

USE DIRECT, SIMPLE LANGUAGE

Written communications should be as intelligible and readable as possible. Rudolf Flesch, one of the foremost proponents of simple, clear, direct writing and speaking, urges that multisyllable and erudite words be avoided, that lengthy sentences be broken down into more manageable units, and that metaphors, irony, and other indirect devices be shunned.[3] He has developed various scales by which the readability of material may be related to the education and comprehension level of different groups of readers.[4] Flesch and others who have specialized in research of this sort also advocate the use of words and phrases that personalize the material and make it more concrete and immediately intelligible.

Every manager must insure that his announcements, public statements, and directives are couched in simple, direct language. Government agencies have been the favorite butt of jokes about "gobbledegook," but many private organizations also are guilty of torturing simple statements into complicated puzzles, and of using specialized and complex jargon. Low readability is undoubtedly a factor in the breakdown of communications. (And since most people talk more simply than they write, it is another reason for using face-to-face communications whenever possible.) High readability, however, is not an answer in itself to the fundamental barriers to communication that we have discussed.

INTRODUCE PROPER AMOUNT OF REDUNDANCY

Communications engineers have developed techniques for measuring the amount of "redundancy" in a message—roughly the amount of repetition it contains. The supervisor who wants to give a direct order or transmit technical information should make sure that his message includes substantial redundancy. Then, if any word or phrase is misunderstood, there are other elements in the communication that will carry his point.

> To give a very simple example: a firm manufacturing several thousand varieties of chemical compounds used a numerical coding system to refer to each of the products. Increasingly, management found that mistakes were creeping into the ordering system. When a supervisor requested a shipment of compound #28394, a clerical error would occasionally result in a wasted shipment of #23894. Each digit was crucial, and the slightest mistake was costly. Eventually the firm adopted individual

[3] Rudolf Flesch, *The Art of Plain Talk* (New York: Harper, 1946), and *The Art of Readable Writing* (New York: Harper, 1949).
[4] For instance, the Flesch index for this section is 5.45 or difficult. According to Flesch, it should have a potential audience of 24 per cent of all readers. *The Art of Plain Talk*, p. 205.

names for each compound and these words had a great deal of built-in redundancy, as do nearly all words. If a clerk ordered "calitin" instead of "calithin," the shipping department knew what he meant.

If each word is crucially important, it pays to say the same thing in several ways. In giving complicated directions, for example, it is wise to repeat them several times, perhaps in different ways, to guarantee successful transmission.

At times, however, the manager may want to avoid redundancy, and concentrate instead on introducing novelty or originality into his communications. We tend to ignore many of the messages we receive simply because they sound so familiar. Most of us are guilty of repeating our favorite clichés to the point where people no longer listen to what we say because it is all so predictable. ("I know what the boss is going to say the minute he starts on that line about us all being one big happy team.")

There is some need for surprise, in modest doses to be sure, if we are to gain the attention of those with whom we wish to communicate. This is particularly true when our message contains something that contradicts expectations. For instance, to repeat our previous example, if our typist has been in the habit of preparing only one carbon, we must stress our request for two carbons.

Thus the supervisor needs to balance carefully the redundancy and surprise elements of his communication.

OVERCOMING BARRIERS: CONCLUSION

The swiftest, most effective communication takes place among people with common points of view. The supervisor who enjoys a good relationship with his subordinates has much less difficulty in explaining why air-conditioning equipment cannot be installed for another year than does the supervisor who is not trusted by his men. When people feel secure, they can talk to one another easily. Where discontent is rife, so is misunderstanding, misinterpretation, rumor, and distortion. In this sense, communication is a dependent variable. Where human relations is good, it is easy; where they are poor, it is almost impossible. Therefore the communications area is *not* the place to start improving supervisor-subordinate relationships.

Nearly every aspect of personnel work and of supervisor-subordinate relations involves communications. Even the structure of the organization—affecting as it does status relations and the number of levels between top management and the worker at the bottom—has a most significant effect on the ability of people to communicate easily and quickly.

Personnel programs . . . also have a profound effect on communications. When a selection policy is geared to admit people with similar backgrounds and interests, some of the problems we have discussed are minimized. Similarly, carefully planned training and orientation programs help establish a common point of view and thus tend to reduce the misunderstandings that arise out of differing frames of reference.

Nevertheless, the problem of communicating accurately and effectively in each contact makes the supervisor's job more difficult. He must guard against the natural inclination in our highly verbal society to assume that simply *telling somebody* is enough to insure successful communication. Fortunately, as we have seen, the supervisor can resort to a number of techniques to facilitate the transmission of understanding between people in their day-to-day activities.

B. THE MAKING OF DECISIONS

The practical purpose of research into communication and decision making is to provide guidance for organizational planning. That organizational structure is best which conveys the right kinds of information to decision centers. The following summary of the influential writings of Herbert A. Simon describes how organizations may be conceived as communications network and decision-making systems; how decision centers and communication channels are identified in research; and how reorganization plans are developed. A voluntary association might be analyzed and modified in the same way.

DECISION THEORY AND ITS APPLICATIONS*

John M. Pfiffner and Frank P. Sherwood

The significance of the decision as a primary orienting point in organization theory has long been central to the approach and philosophy of Herbert Simon. Like Bakke at Yale, Simon for more than two decades has been pondering these questions and evolving his own formulations. His first important work in this field was undertaken in association with Clarence Ridley, then Executive Director of the International City Managers' Association. These two refined and expanded an earlier effort by Ridley to provide a basis for decision-making in the municipality. Published in 1937, the monograph was entitled *Measuring Municipal Activities*.[1] It was in 1945, however, that Simon's pioneering and perhaps most significant work, *Administrative Behavior*, was published. With the decision as his basic frame of reference, he took to task most of the earlier propositions on organization, labeling them ambiguous and useless. Since *Administrative Behavior*, Simon has concentrated with his colleagues on the sharpening of his basic theory. This has involved considerable research at Carnegie Institute of Technology and has resulted in such publications as *Centralization versus Decentralization* (1954), *Models of Man* (1957), and *Organizations* (1958).

SIMON'S BASIC IDEAS

While it is perhaps possible to construe the decision concept in rather narrow, mechanistic terms, this has not at all been the Simon approach. . . . Simon has seen the organization problem in its total social and psychological context. His basic assumption has been that the features of organization structure and function derive from the characteristics of human problem-solving processes and rational human choice.[2] Thus the members of an organization are not to be viewed as mere mechanical instrumentalities. They must be regarded as individuals who have wants, motives, and drives, and are limited in their knowledge and in their capacities to learn and to solve problems.

The organization is, in these terms, an extension of individuals making choices and behaving on the basis of their understanding of their environment and their needs.

THE ORGANIZATION

Human organizations are regarded by Simon as systems of interdependent activity, encompassing at least several primary groups. There are three *levels* of multi-person units: (1) the *smallest* is the primary group; (2) the *largest* is the institution, such as the state, economic system, etc.; and (3) systems *in between* are organizations. In such a definition there is a great deal of ambiguity, as Simon has pointed out. Organizations may exist *within* organizations—"a whole agency, a bureau, or even a section of a large department may be regarded as *an* organization."[3]

In later writings Simon has placed increased emphasis on the human organism. Adaptive behavior, largely in terms of "one thing at a time," is basic to the existence of organization structure. Such structure exists only as patterns of behavior which are relatively stable and change slowly. People do not want to tackle too many problems at once. By necessity they must settle on some habits of conduct. These, then, constitute organization *structure;* and it is in the development of these patterns, which obviously involve decision-making, that attention can be concentrated profitably.

THE DECISION

In the very first paragraph of *Administrative Behavior*, Simon has indicated how significant the decision is to his system of thinking. He has written that traditional discussions of administration emphasize the action process, getting things done; and so-called principles are laid down to aid in achieving such action. In all such discussion scant attention has been paid to the choice which prefaces all action, to decide what is to be done rather than how to do it.[4]

The first step in building an adequate theory of organization (and hence a model) is the development of an appropriate unit of analysis. That is why Simon has placed so much emphasis on the decision. He has concluded that the analysis of the *role* played by individuals in an organization is not precise enough; similarly a study of acts or actions remains too general.

---

* From John M. Pfiffner and Frank P. Sherwood, *Administrative Organization*, pp. 385-401. © 1960. Reprinted by permission of the authors and Prentice-Hall, Inc., Englewood Cliffs, N.J.

[1] Clarence Ridley and Herbert Simon, *Measuring Municipal Activities* (Chicago: International City Managers' Association, 1937). Many writers have since joined Simon in placing emphasis on the decision. Harold J. Leavitt has recently suggested that this will be the predominant orientation of organization theory in the future: *Managerial Psychology* (Chicago: University of Chicago Press, 1958), p. 301.

[2] James G. March and Herbert A. Simon, *Organizations* (New York: John Wiley and Sons, 1959), p. 169.

[3] Herbert A. Simon, "Comments on the Theory of Organization," *American Political Science Review*, Volume 46 (December 1952), p. 1130.

[4] Herbert A. Simon, *Administrative Behavior* (New York: The Macmillan Company, Second edition, 1957), p. 1.

He regards the decision *premise* as a much smaller unit of analysis and therefore more appropriate. Many premises are involved in any specific decision or action and are incorporated in the definition of a single role. "The central notion," he has written, "is that a decision can be regarded as a conclusion drawn (though not in any strict logical sense) from premises; and that influence is exercised by transmitting decisions, which are then taken as premises for subsequent decision." [5]

In this view there is not an expectation that decision-making is necessarily rational. As a matter of fact Simon has appeared to become less sure over the years that even the rationality he assumed in *Administrative Behavior* was appropriate.[6]

The really critical factors in the decision process, then, are (1) the availability of information and (2) the computational capacities available to deal with the information. Man should not be regarded as even "intendedly" rational, as the models of economic man and administrative man suggest. We should substitute the concept of a "choosing" organism of "limited knowledge and ability." [7]

The point of reference that Simon uses to analyze organization behavior is, then, a human organism capable of choosing, problem-solving, and decision-making. But it does not possess infinite powers, it is limited to doing a few things at a time and can deal with only a small part of the information stored in its memory or existing in its environment.[8]

GENERAL COMMENTS

How can such an emphasis on decision be applied to a more general model of organization? Note that decision premises arise largely out of information and the ability of the individual to handle that information. Thus the key to this approach to organization is identification (1) of the decision centers, and (2) of the channels by which communications are carried. Put in the words of March and Simon,

    1. Communication traverses definite channels, either by formal plan or by the gradual development of informal programs.

    2. Information and stimuli move from sources to points of decision; instructions move from points of decision to points of action; information of results moves from points of decision and control.

    3. Rational organization design would call for the arrangement of these channels so as to minimize the communication burden.[9]

The manner in which this type of analysis can provide a foundation for the structuring of organization may be seen in the following hypotheses suggested by March and Simon:

As one moves toward the top of a hierarchy, the possibilities of rationality decline. He must deal with phenomena in grosser and move aggregative form.

The division of work according to purpose (or subgoals) tends to foster insularity by building in a subgoal bias. Other subgoals and other aspects of the goals of the larger organization tend to be ignored in the decisions of the subunit, even though conflicts may exist.

Division of work on the basis of process (subprograms rather than subgoals) will be carried furthest in stable environments. It is likely, too, that organizations, in order to permit a greater degree of process specialization, will devise means for increasing stability and predictability of the environment.

Specialization is most apt to be found when the organization has stability and is not continually adapting to a rapidly changing environment.

The degree of local autonomy may reflect the precision of coordination. When communication is poorly developed and control from the center made difficult, there is very apt to be a considerable degree of local discretion for the reason that little else is possible.

The influence structure in an organization is set in large part by its communication system. More precisely, it is suggested that the "locus of uncertainty absorption" is extremely significant. Thus persons closest to the reality communicate their "facts," which cannot be checked, as a conscious or unconscious means of acquiring and exercising power.

The greater the communication efficiency of a channel, the greater its usage. Further, channel usage tends to be self-reinforcing. Once the channels have been well established, their pattern will have an important influence on decision-making processes and particularly upon nonprogrammed activity.

It is apparent from these hypotheses that there has been identified in the decision premise a basic unit of analysis which appears applicable to the major questions of organization model-building. We may now turn to an instance where this approach was actually used in the creation of an organization structure.

---

[5] Simon, "Comments on the Theory of Organization," p. 1132.

[6] "I now feel that . . . I yielded too much ground to the omniscient rationality of economic man." Simon, *Administrative Behavior*, p. xxxv.

[7] Herbert A. Simon, "A Behavioral Model of Rational Choice," *Models of Man* (New York: John Wiley and Sons, Inc., 1957), p. 241.

[8] March and Simon, *Organizations*, p. 11.

[9] Quoted from March and Simon, *Organizations*, pp. 166-167; numbering added.

A PRAGMATIC USE OF THE DECISION MODEL

In any large organization the accounting department is a unit having a rather peculiar relationship to the whole. Its function cuts both horizontally and vertically, reaching down to the lowest echelon and yet affecting the most senior of men in the organization. The proper role of this unit in the total structure therefore provides a most interesting test of the decision approach.

Under the sponsorship of the Controllership Foundation, a team led by Simon studied seven large companies with geographically dispersed operations. They did not necessarily represent a cross-section of American business, but they had all approached the problem of organizing the controllership function in different ways. The question which the Carnegie Tech group sought to answer by creating an appropriate model was:

How should a company's accounting department be organized in order that the data it assembles will be of greatest usefulness to the operating executives of the *business* in making decisions and solving problems? [10]

In contrast to the more traditional approach of analyzing authority relationships, the Carnegie Tech group took these steps:

(1) Studies were made of the most important types of decisions taken in the organization; how accounting data might be useful in making these decisions; and at what point in the decision process accounting information could be most usefully injected.

> . . . By observation of the actual decision-making process, specific types of data needs were identified at particular organizational levels—the vice presidential level, the level of the factory manager, and the level of the factory head, for example—each involving quite distinct problems of communication for the accounting department.[11]

(2) Recommendations were made in terms of the accounting department's responsibility for providing information and exerting influence on these operating decisions.

> . . . Recommendations for organizational change were to be implemented by bringing about changes in the communication patterns—in the patterns of who-talks-to-whom-how-often-about-what, rather than by formal changes in the organization charts.[12]

[10] The report of this study is found in Herbert A. Simon, Harold Guetzkow, George Kozmetsky, and Gordon Tyndall, *Centralization vs. Decentralization in Organizing the Controller's Department* (New York: Controllership Foundation, Inc., 1954). [We are indebted to the publisher, the Financial Executives' Research Foundation (formerly the Controllers' Institute Foundation), for permission to quote from this report.–Eds.]
[11] Simon, *Administrative Behavior*, p. xx.
[12] *Ibid.*

TYPES OF INFORMATION REQUIRED BY MANAGEMENT

Thus the departure for this study—as might be expected—was the decision which found its premise in greater or lesser degree in accounting information. Several key points in the decision-making hierarchy were identified:

1. The Chief Executive
2. The Company Vice-Presidents for Sales and for Production
3. Division Executives
4. Factory Managers and Regional Sales Managers

The identification of these decision centers led to the further question: what *types* of accounting information are required at these points? Predictably, it was found that the executives at these various levels did *not* require the same types of information. Furthermore, it was discovered that the extent to which the information was used depended in considerable part on the closeness of the relationship between the accounting people as information sources and the operating people as consumers. What might be a good organization pattern for the use of certain types of accounting data, then, might be quite inappropriate for other types. *Three* categories of information, each serving a different purpose at a different point in the decision hierarchy, were identified:

(1) *Communication to provide information on the results of activities: Score-Card.* Here the fundamental question is, "How well am I (or is he) doing?" Such a question becomes very important to the factory supervisor who has the basic responsibility for getting the work out.

(2) *Communication to evoke programs: Attention-Directing.* Here the fundamental question is, "What problems shall I look into?" Data which serve as a score card for a lower level supervisor may very conceivably operate in an attention-directing role for a higher level official. The latter must look for the trouble spots, and be concerned about variations from the norm.

(3) *Communication to provide data for application of strategies.* Here the fundamental question is, "Which course of action is better?"

This analysis of information categories presents important insights into the organizing process as it affects the accounting function. It makes quite clear that the communications channels which operate *horizontally* must be given as much weight as those which operate vertically. Thus, in terms of "score card" analysis, the important relationship is between the cost analyst and the department head (see Chart 1) and is occasioned by the importance of standards at this level. Operating supervisors need to have confidence that standards established are realistic and that environmental factors are considered in their establishment. The same general situation applies with "attention-directing" information, with the basic horizontal contact between the factory manager and the factory accountant (Chart 1). As a consequence, the Carnegie Tech group concluded, ". . . for effective attention-directing service, it is essential for the controller's department to develop direct and active channels of communication with the operating executives at those points in the organization where operations are being measured." [13]

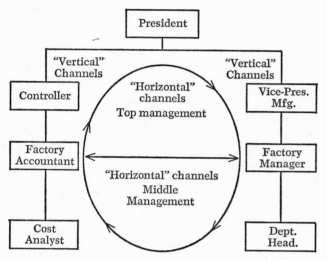

CHART 1. *"Horizontal" and "vertical" channels of communication (source: Simon et al., Centralization vs. Decentralization in Organizing the Controller's Department, p. 48).*

While the same horizontal pattern obtained in the case of problem-solving questions, i.e., factory manager to factory accountant and chief executive to company controller, a fundamental difference lies in the fact that not only are regular reports provided but also special studies are made. As a consequence there seems less need to create the same kind of close-working relationship necessary in the score-card and attention-directing areas.

To summarize, the most essential point to note is that there is no such gross product as accounting information. For purposes of organizational analysis, we must think of a number of categories of data; further, the channels through which such information should appropriately flow depend on its nature and usefulness to the various members of the organization. Put another way, there is no single "right" channel of accounting communication; and hence, a good way of organizing the accounting function involves using different channels for different purposes.

[13] Simon et al., *Centralization vs. Decentralization in Organizing the Controller's Department*, p. 3.

THE FUNCTIONS OF THE CONTROLLER

As a consequence of this analysis of communications, the Carnegie Tech group concluded that there are three major areas of the accounting function, each of which can be separated from the other. These are:

1. *Record-keeping*, which involves bookkeeping and preparation and distribution of periodic accounting reports. In making judgments as to where this mechanical aspect of the accounting function might most appropriately be located, such factors as cost, access to information, promptness in reporting, uniformity of reports, and control from an auditing viewpoint are all considered significant. It is to be noted that no special problems of communication are in-

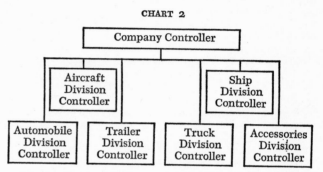

PART A: *Company-wide accounting organized on "divisional" basis.*

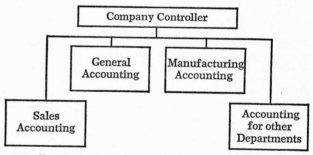

PART B: *Company-wide accounting organized on "functional" basis—paralleling as close as possible operating departments.*

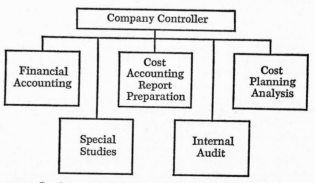

PART C: *Company-wide accounting organized on "functional" basis—using communications analysis.*

volved in the record-keeping function; hence it can be approached in rather conventional organization terms.

2. *Current analysis,* which involves assistance to the operating departments in providing meaningful score-card and attention-directing information. Here proximity to the operating units is the most important locational consideration. Not only must there be promptness of presentation but also confidence in the reliability and integrity of the data. Easy horizontal communication is therefore essential.

3. *Special studies for problem-solving purposes,* which involves participation in the use of accounting information to satisfy unique management requirements and to suggest strategies. Again the factor of horizontal communication is a most significant element. These special studies cut across departments and have to be attacked at the company-wide, or at least factory-wide, level.

Juxtaposing communications and functions, a rough model for accounting organization now begins to emerge. It can be based on the following assumptions:

(1) Communications and decision premises are largely irrelevant to organization arrangements for the *record-keeping* function.

(2) Closeness to operating units is a basic requirement in organizing for the *current analysis* function; thus decentralization would normally be indicated.

(3) An opportunity to interrelate with other major segments of the organization on a company-wide or factory-wide basis is primary in organizing for the *problem-solving, special study* function; thus centralization would normally be indicated.

THE COMPANY-WIDE CONTROLLER'S ORGANIZATION

In these few pages, it is obviously impossible to describe in detail all the steps through which the Carnegie Tech group went in arriving at certain conclusions about the most appropriate organization of a controller's department. Therefore we will look only at two structural models which have arisen from this analysis, one at the company-wide level and the other at the factory level.

At the company level two main alternatives for organizing the controllership functions are (a) "divisional" and (b) "functional." Under a *divisional* plan, the principal subordinates of the company controller are divisional controllers, each responsible for a complete system of sales, manufacturing, and general accounting for some one division of the operations (Chart 2, Part A). Obviously, if such divisions or bureaus do not exist or if the accounting function has not been decentralized to that level, such an approach would not be possible.

The *functional* basis of organization presents two alternatives:

(a) A classification of functions that parallels, as far as possible, the operating departments (see Chart 2, Part B).

(b) A classification of functions which would be based on the Carnegie Tech group's communication analysis, separating record-keeping, attention-directing services and problem-solving services (see Chart 2, Part C)

The organization model which came out of a weighing of these alternatives was "not particularly revolutionary," but it does reveal quite clearly the effects of the analysis of communications (see Chart

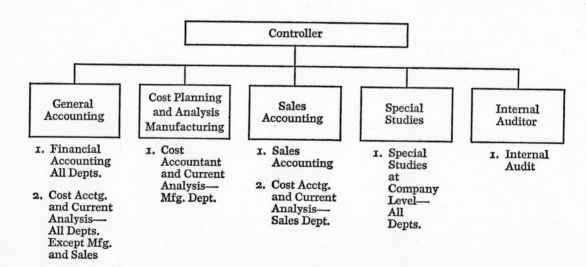

CHART 3. *Company-wide accounting organization proposed by Carnegie Tech Group (source: Simon et al.,* Centralization vs. Decentralization in Organizing the Controller's Department, *p. 71)*

3). It is really an amalgamation of both functional approaches, in which perhaps the most noteworthy element is the special studies unit. The creation of this latter section at the top-management level is clearly a consequence of the communications analysis. It may be noted, too, that the Carnegie Tech group's approach tells us as much about what *not* to fight for in an organization as what we should. In this instance top-level organization for current analysis is not of great importance because the crucial horizontal communication must occur at lower echelons with operating people. Thus the development of the organization partially along manufacturing and sales function lines does not represent any significant compromise.

RELATIONSHIPS BETWEEN FACTORY AND COMPANY HEADQUARTERS

Although the significance of communications to organization is not a new finding, practitioners have typically been unwilling to face up to its implications because of its incompatibility with one of the most time-tested of hierarchical credos, unity of command. In the relationship of the factory accounting program to the company level, however, the unity of command precept has been able to contribute little in a real sense to some difficult questions. Traditionally, there have been two authority patterns suggested for the relationship of the factory accountant to the factory manager and to the home office—both designed to avoid conflict and presumably preserve unity of command. In Chart 4 (Part A) we see the first alternative, which is to place the factory manager so that he has all units under his direct control. The Company Controller has no formal power over the person on whom he must depend at the lower level, the factory accountant. From the Controller's perspective, then, the situation is complicated by a series of relationships which in most cases can only be made to work by informal arrangements.

The second alternative, shown on Chart 4 (Part B) suggests a different orientation. Here unity of command is preserved in the relationship between the Company Controller and the Factory Accountant. It is the factory manager who suffers under this arrangement, since he has now lost control over one of his important staff people.

The problem involved here is a major one in many organizations. Since the communications pattern of Chart 1 must exist under any circumstances, the various structural approaches serve only to hamper or inhibit communications. They do not stop it. Despite this, managers as a whole have found it emotionally impossible to abandon the familiar "unity of command" principle. In most cases they prefer to live with a formal chart which they know does not repre-

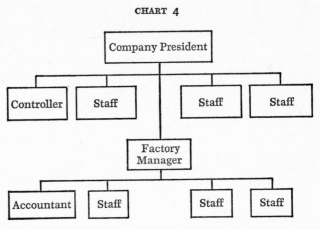

CHART 4

PART A: *A "unitary" field organization.*

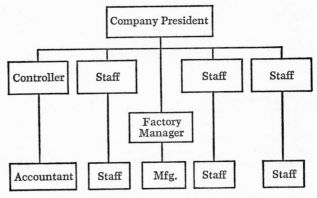

PART B: *A "functional" field organization.*
(Note that in both these alternative field organizations, the principle of "unity of command" is observed. The "functional" pattern, however, has no integrating mechanism at the field level.)

sent a true picture of authority relationships.

The Simon group's conclusions on this point are therefore of consequence. The recommendation: *Forget the unity of command idea. If it is discovered that the administrative situation requires communication to flow both vertically and horizontally, formalize this pattern in the structure.* Specifically, in the case of the factory accountant, there is much to be said for recognizing organizationally his twofold responsibility to the factory manager and to the company controller. It was found, furthermore, that some companies have created such a formal arrangement without disastrous results. On this point the Simon group has written:

> The survey team's thinking . . . has been set forth at length because there has been much disagreement among writers on administration and among practicing managers on the essentiality of unity of command. Until further studies can be made on this point, the evidence cited here indicates that a division of formal authority over the factory accountant is entirely workable, provided that the controllers' department has acceptance and support

of company manufacturing executives. A man can serve two masters provided that the two masters are not working at cross purposes.[14]

Thus the Carnegie Tech group suggests the feasibility of an organizational arrangement which is in striking contrast to traditional theory, as shown in Chart 5. Its close relationship to the communications pattern of Chart 1 is also of significance.

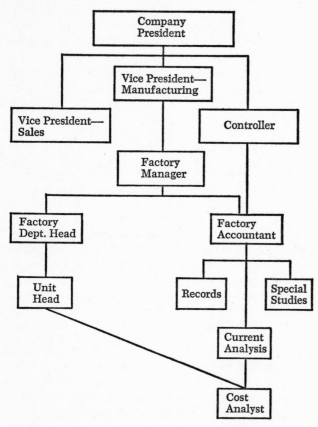

CHART 5. *A simplified view of proposals for organizing accounting function at company-wide and factory levels (note absence of unity of command).*

ORGANIZATION WITHIN THE FACTORY

As a final example of the way in which the Carnegie Tech group made its analysis (1) by looking at the

[14] *Ibid.,* p. 83.

points at which decisions were made and (2) by noting the manner in which decision premises were developed out of information, the model suggested for the internal structure of accounting in a large factory is instructive.

Here again we find the three major functions of accounting, each of which is considered separable: current analysis, record-keeping, and special studies. As might be expected, too, from a review of the points of decision and communications pattern in Chart 5, the need for horizontal communications is recognized. Hence current analysis functions are decentralized so that Department heads and cost analysts will have close contact; special studies are centralized at the factory level to afford close cooperation with other staff departments; and record-keeping is centralized for cost and other reasons.

SUMMARY

The decision model is based on the idea that human beings, with all their failings, are continually being cast into problem-solving situations where choices are made. Thus we need to know who makes decisions and the base of information from which decision premises are drawn.

In the study of controllership in several large factories, we find that this method of analysis was followed. The points of decision were identified, as were the kind of decisions to be made. Since information served as the initial stimulus for the decision, as the means of guiding action, and as the vehicle for reporting action results preparatory to taking new decisions, it was obvious also that the analysis of communications content and flow was a necessary step.

On the basis of these data, the Simon group came to certain conclusions about the nature of the accounting function in a large company. In many respects these findings were not particularly dramatic or striking, but they do suggest some rather sharp departures from classic organization. Further, it would appear that the decision, with its companion study of information flows, has proved itself to be a practicable means of organization analysis.

Private organizations are increasing their use of information provided by the behavioral sciences in making decisions concerning both policy and current operations. Proper relationships between researchers and client or-

ganizations are evolving through trial and error.* The client's problem must be specified clearly, and the research must be designed to secure pertinent information. In the following article, David L. Sills describes how a voluntary association decided that it needed information; how a research organization secured the information; and how the information was used in subsequent policy decisions.

RESEARCH AS AN INSTRUMENT FOR DECISION MAKING†

David L. Sills

Social agencies turn to research agencies for assistance for a wide variety of reasons, and one of the functions that this article hopefully will serve is that of stimulating others involved in such collaboration to provide a sufficient number of examples to make possible some preliminary codification of this process. My purpose is to describe one fairly successful, and thus fairly unusual, direct application of research, rather than to describe the process itself. But a few general remarks are necessary before the specific case at hand is described.

Social agencies and other organizations generally commission research when they are in a crisis situation. A campaign designed to inform the public is not having satisfactory results; a voluntary association is meeting resistance from its local affiliates; a new program is not understood on all echelons. Typically, requests for research are phrased in some variant of the question: "Why doesn't our public appreciate us and understand us better?" Equally typically, this question is often rephrased in the process of the research to read: "What is there about our organization and our program which people like or dislike, understand or misunderstand?" But the important fact remains that it was a crisis situation that precipitated the research in the first place.

Sometimes, however, research is commissioned not *because* of a crisis situation but in *anticipation* of one. When this happy circumstance occurs, the research report can be utilized, along with other resources, at the time the crisis is met. Very few instances of such foresight are recorded in the literature; for this reason, the case study examined here seems of more than routine interest.

The story begins in the Autumn of 1952, when it became apparent from results emerging from the laboratory of Dr. Jonas E. Salk (at the University of Pittsburgh) that a successful vaccine against para-

lytic polio might be found. The National Foundation for Infantile Paralysis, which had sponsored Salk's research, decided—in consultation with its medical and scientific advisers—that as soon as the *safety* of the vaccine had been determined, its *efficacy* would have to be ascertained on the basis of a large-scale field trial. The Spring of 1954 was selected as the earliest possible time during which to carry out this mass test. A test of this size was unprecedented in the history of medical immunization.

While the field trial was being planned in 1953, another important decision was made by the President of the Foundation: to plan, in a deliberate and rational way, even at this early date, for the consequences of a successful outcome of the field trials. The Foundation had become a large organization in the years since its establishment in 1938. It had over 3,000 local chapters—roughly one for every county in the United States; it had an estimated 80,000 volunteers on a year-round basis, and during the January March of Dimes it was able to mobilize approximately 3 million temporary volunteers; in the 1953 fundraising campaign alone over 51 million dollars was contributed by the American public; and in that year nearly 30 million dollars was spent by the Foundation to pay medical and hospital bills.[1] It was by far the largest and most successful health association in the country. A successful vaccine, and the subsequent elimination of infantile paralysis as a major threat to the health of the American public, would clearly have enormous consequences for the Foundation. How might these consequences be anticipated?

One answer to this question was social research, and two research organizations—the American Institute of Public Opinion (the Gallup Poll) and the Bureau of Applied Social Research at Columbia University—were handed an identical list of questions. They concerned such matters as how people learn about the Foundation; what motivations keep volunteers active in Foundation affairs; what motivates people to contribute to the March of Dimes; and how much continuing support the Foundation could expect if it undertook a "next program" closely related to polio (e.g.,

---

* For experiences and advice about relationships between the two groups, see Robert Tannenbaum et al., *Leadership and Organization* (New York: McGraw-Hill Book Company, 1961), ch. 23; Leon Festinger and Daniel Katz (editors), *Research Methods in the Behavioral Sciences* (New York: The Dryden Press, 1953), ch. 13.

† A previously unpublished paper. Publication A-435 of the Bureau of Applied Social Research, Columbia.

[1] See National Foundation for Infantile Paralysis, *1953 Annual Report*, p. 42.

physical rehabilitation), completely removed from polio (e.g., geriatrics), or something in-between.

This was an unusually detailed set of questions for research. However, it seems to share the characteristic of many research requests mentioned earlier—and to be referred to again—of being largely concerned with what others think of the organization and its program, rather than with what kind of an organization and what type of a program it is.

Given this assignment, the rather obvious decision was made to conduct surveys among both the general public and the volunteer members of the Foundation. The two research organizations collaborated in developing similar instruments, but they studied independently selected samples of the two populations. And they submitted independent reports to the Foundation—reports that by and large reached similar conclusions.

What kinds of reports were submitted? As far as the Bureau is concerned there were three quite different types of reports. The first type is best described as *descriptive*. It described the public image of polio and the twin themes of fear and hope that characterized the public view of polio in early 1954; it pointed out how little the public knew about the local chapters of the Foundation; it provided a description of the volunteer membership; it summarized the various images of their organization held by volunteers; it contrasted public and volunteer opinions of the Foundation's two major programs—patient care and research; it indicated the extent and type of public support given to the March of Dimes and other fund-raising campaigns conducted by voluntary health and welfare associations; and it described the satisfactions and frustrations which volunteers derive from their role as fund-raisers.

The second type was *analytical* in nature, and represented a radical departure from the emphasis upon what *others* thought that characterized the original research request. It focussed upon three components of the Foundation itself—organizational, programmatic, and symbolic—and described for each component the essential elements and their relationship to the problem of future program planning. The organizational components, for example, were described as including both structural features (the chapter system, the volunteer system) and operational features (community-level decisions, an emphasis upon economy, direct personal relationships between headquarters staff and local volunteers) that had helped shape its past and would be decisive in shaping its future.

A number of important features of the program were discussed. It was pointed out that the polio program was to a very large extent conditioned by the intrinsic characteristics of polio itself—its comparatively low incidence, its greater prevalence among up-

per income groups, its epidemic nature, its tendency to attack children, and its public image as a disease on the verge of being conquered—as well as by the strategies used to combat polio (patient care for persons afflicted and research into the causes and treatment of the disease itself). Similarly, the policies and strategies of the fund-raising program were discussed; the limitation of fund-raising to one month in the year, the ban on accepting funds collected through federated appeals, the emphasis upon the small gift given by millions of people, and the importance of one feature of the campaign—the Mothers' March on Polio.

Finally, this analytical report described the implications of the symbolic components of the Foundation: the fact that in the public mind the March of Dimes *was* the Foundation; the symbol of the crippled child; and the widespread knowledge of President Roosevelt's early association with the Foundation.

This analytical report, submitted in August 1954, reached three broad conclusions, as follows:

> The first, and most inclusive of these, is that the National Foundation has acquired a large number of organizational characteristics over the years which define the kind of organization it has become. These components of the present organization are not only assets, which serve as potential sources of future strength, but commitments which delimit the range of available alternatives for future action.
>
> Second, public support of the March of Dimes is based not so much upon polio-related attitudes as upon the fact that the overall purpose to which the funds are put is accepted by almost everyone as worthwhile. Moreover, the March of Dimes, as a symbol, is well-known and widely-accepted, and the mechanical means through which people can support the campaign are made easily available.
>
> Third, volunteer support, like that of the general public, is only indirectly based upon polio-related attitudes. Volunteers accept the bait which is offered them—the polio program—but they get hooked by the organization and what it stands for.[2]

After these two reports were submitted, a new phase of the research-into-policy process was initiated. Foundation officials were generally pleased with the results reported to them, since they indicated that public and volunteer support was at a high level. But this support was of course directed toward the *current* organization, at a time when polio incidence was near its all-time high and the Salk vaccine had not been systematically tested for its efficacy. But what of future support of a program designed to combat a health problem other than polio? How could the research be used as *prediction* rather than as analysis?

[2] Bureau of Applied Social Research, Columbia University, unpublished report. An extensive re-analysis of these materials is reported in David L. Sills, *The Volunteers: Means and Ends in a National Organization* (Glencoe, Ill.: The Free Press, 1957).

This question generated the next phase of the utilization process.

Since it was taken as axiomatic that most people are incapable of predicting their own attitudes and behavior under hypothetical future conditions, the research instruments did not include such questions as "Would you contribute to the March of Dimes if the funds were to be used to combat some other disease?" or "Will you remain an active volunteer after polio is conquered?" It was thus necessary to approach the problem of future participation in an indirect way. In consultation with Foundation officials, the decision was made to derive from the research findings the essential characteristics of the organization and its program which would remain no matter what disease or disorder it sought to combat.

Twenty-nine criteria were derived from the research; space does not permit a review of all of them. The first group of seven criteria pertained to the disorder to be attacked by the new program—for example, it should be a disorder that is a potential threat to people in all regions of the country and in all strata of society, so that it lends itself to the strategy of the small gift and the broad base of contributors. The second group of twelve criteria related to the program for attacking this disorder—for example, it should be one not already encompassed in the work of a major, well-established national voluntary association and one that lends itself to lay leadership and control, nationally and locally. The final group of ten criteria concerned the organization which would administer the program—for example, it should be one that provides for strong national control of the program and one that would make possible maintaining and strengthening the middle-class composition of the volunteer membership.

The next step in the process was to differentiate among the criteria on the basis of their importance: 10 were designated as desirable, seven as essential, and 12 as being so essential as to be granted top priority. At this point the participation of the researchers in the research-into-policy process ended, and what follows is an account—based upon interviews with officials—of how these criteria were used in the three-year process of determining a new program for the Foundation.

In setting out to develop a program that would both make maximum use of the organization and the skill developed in combating polio *and* meet a major health need in American society, Foundation officials had no precedents upon which they could rely. Never in history had a major voluntary, publicly-supported health agency consciously and with advance planning considered making a complete shift in program in order to broaden its scope and flexibility. In the words of a Foundation official:

We studied all major causes of crippling and death. When it came to outlining possible programs, we finally decided that what we had to do was take a particular program and imagine that the National Foundation would start on it at nine o'clock the next morning. We would lay out the program in detail, drawing up a plan that our people could follow and that would utilize the strengths we had. We built into such programs elements that our criteria suggested would be essential to success.

In considering various programs, the Foundation did not rely solely upon its own staff or its own medical advisory committee. Instead, scientists and doctors familiar with many health problems were consulted, and as soon as a possible program was blocked out in rough form an all-day consultation and discussion session was arranged. At each of these sessions it proved necessary to describe the criteria, and the methods by which they had been established, before describing the program which matched them, since the consultants were unable to evaluate the program without knowing the reasons underlying its selection. As these consultation sessions progressed, it became apparent that even when the experts disagreed on the proposed program they were impressed with the methodology which had been employed in developing it. After months of consultation and staff work a program deemed important and feasible—and which met the essential criteria established as a consequence of the research—was finally approved.

The Foundation's new program was announced to the public on July 22, 1958, and the National Foundation for Infantile Paralysis—renamed the National Foundation—entered a new phase of its history. Briefly, the organization continued to combat polio and support virus research and investigations of disorders of the central nervous system. But to this program was added research, and eventually patient care, in arthritis and congenital malformations. The new patient care program was broadened as funds become available; initially, financial assistance was limited to patients 18 years old and under who suffered from arthritis or congenital abnormalities of the central nervous system.[3]

The Foundation will thus carry on its program of supporting both patient care and research, with a continued emphasis upon disorders that cripple children and adolescents.

Organizational sociologists, among others, will watch its future with interest, since there are rela-

[3] For descriptions and comments upon this new program see Howard A. Rusk, "Broadened Horizons," *New York Times*, July 27, 1958, p. 50, and William L. Laurence, "Polio Foundation Announces Plans to Fight Wide Range of Disabling Diseases," *New York Times*, July 27, 1958, p. E-9. For an official description of the new program see the Special Edition of *National Foundation News*, Volume 17, Number 8 (July 22, 1958). The program in arthritis research and patient care was subsequently turned over to the Arthritis Foundation.

tively few instances of large organizations that have self-consciously changed their goals—and even fewer in which social research has been used as an instrument for selecting new goals.

The objectives of the Foundation's new program cannot be said to have been derived from social research—the scientific method can never obviate the need for subjective judgments and calculated risks—but the criteria established by the research performed the important task of defining and delimiting the area in which judgment and risk could safely be permitted to operate.

This research not only served the manifest purpose of providing criteria for the selection of a new program, but it also served important latent or unintended functions. Only time will reveal the full extent of these, but a few functions which Foundation officials have identified are worthy of mention.

First, the research served to educate the staff into the value of social research as an organizational procedure. When this research program was first being planned it was regarded by the staff as a threat to its competence. The atmosphere has now changed completely, and during staff meetings research is frequently mentioned as a possible method of illuminating an operational problem. The far-reaching implications of this for the organization are obvious.

Second, the research changed the orientation of the professional staff toward the volunteer members. This has come about in two ways. First, one of the major findings of the research was that approximately half of the volunteers interviewed did not perceive the structure of the organization as it officially existed—as a national organization having local chapters as component units—but as a federation of loosely-affiliated chapters serviced by a national headquarters. By being in a position to see themselves more as others see them, national headquarters staff members are better prepared to understand and assist the volunteers who actually carry out the local program of the Foundation. Second, the abundant evidence from the research that volunteers are drawn chiefly from the middle class, "Main Street" stratum of the community has both directed the staff's attention to the importance of Foundation activity as a medium for social mobility and forced consideration of

ways in which working class people could be more widely drawn into Foundation activities.

Third, the research served to resolve a number of questions confronting the staff. The research finding that the direct relationship between local chapters and national headquarters is a source of satisfaction to volunteers put to rest a proposal to establish state organizations which would mediate between local chapters and the central office; the conclusion that President Roosevelt's early association with the Foundation is more of an asset than a handicap put an end to discussions as to how an organization founded in the partisan atmosphere of the 1930's could serve an entire nation in a nonpartisan spirit; and the uniformly high rate of volunteer turnover revealed by the research served to define the turnover rate as normal rather than as pathological.

Fourth, the research raised the status of the professional staff in the eyes of the medical advisory committee. The doctors and scientists affiliated with the Foundation were reportedly impressed by the staff's use of the scientific method in charting the organization's future, and a new basis for understanding and collaboration between them has been established.

Finally, the research increased the stature of the Foundation among the personnel of other voluntary health associations. News of this research program spread among professionals in the social welfare field, and the Foundation was frequently consulted on problems of organizational structure or volunteer utilization.

This concludes a brief review of how one organization has used research as an instrument for the formation of policy. The emphasis has naturally been upon the positive accomplishments rather than upon the lost opportunities, and perhaps too favorable a picture has been portrayed. As is the case with most human activity, the participants would probably have done things quite differently if they had the opportunity to relive the experience; as one who participated in this process as a researcher, I can with the wisdom of hindsight think of much that could have been improved. The case study has been described in the spirit of Dr. Samuel Johnson's observation that the significance of a dancing dog is not that he dances badly, but that he dances at all.

A. FORMAL AND INFORMAL GOALS

Every organization has certain official aims that can be readily discovered in its charter and publications. In addition, every organization has certain "operative" or unofficial aims that are pursued in actual practice, with or without their full recognition by the leaders. When behavioral scientists study organizations, they try to identify both kinds of goals, as well as the social functions the organization performs in the larger social setting.

Since sociologists are interested in the relationships between a social structure and the dynamic life of the social group, those who study formal organizations try to identify relations between the structures and goals of organizations. One can examine the connection from either starting point, i.e., how goals affect structure and how structure affects the nature and attainment of goals. The first selection, by Donald R. Cressey, describes the effects of organizational aims, both stated and unstated, upon the structure of prisons. Prisons with custodial and therapeutic official aims have somewhat different internal structures, particularly in the management of prisoners. On the other hand, they share certain organizational characteristics that serve common goals. Besides their divergent official aims, Cressey found that prisons share an important unstated goal, namely protection of the individual inmate from fellow inmates, prison staff, and the public. The differences between their official aims caused differences in how they pursued their common unofficial aim; but having a common unstated goal did produce some institutional similarities.

Among voluntary associations, a comparable study could be made of the effects of goals on social structure: for each association, both official and operative goals exist; structured differences as well as similarities would be found among various associations because of differences and similarities in their several goals.

UNSTATED GOALS AND ORGANIZATIONAL STRUCTURE*

Donald R. Cressey

It is customary for both sociologists and correctional workers to adopt the viewpoint of society, rather than of the prisoner, when discussing the goals of prisons and other correctional institutions. In general, prisons, like mental hospitals, are seen as performing an integrative function for society. Usually, they are said to do this by incapacitating criminals, thus directly protecting society from them; by punishing them, thus protecting society both by reinforcing the system's anti-criminal values and by deterring potential criminals; and by reforming them, thus protecting society by restoring social integration. In short, a society assigns *incapacitation, retribution, deterrence* and *reformation* goals to prisons.

The goals of prisons also can be considered from the viewpoint of the criminal. In the past fifty years America has witnessed increasing concern for the welfare of prisoners. Probably on the theoretical ground that confinement behind bars is sufficient for incapacitation, punitive and reformation purposes, efforts have been made to improve sanitary conditions and facilities, medical and health programs and food. Also, numerous "amenities," as Reckless calls them[1] have been introduced: smoking privileges, radio, movies, sports and hobbycraft are among these. Moreover, the conception of the criminal has been slowly changing. Under the leadership of "professional" personnel such as social workers and psychiatrists, the conception of the criminal as a bad man or

* From Donald R. Cressey, "Achievement of an Unstated Organizational Goal: An Observation on Prisons," *Pacific Sociological Review*, Volume I, Number 2 (Fall 1958), pp. 43-49. Reprinted with the permission of the author and publisher.

[1] Walter C. Reckless, *The Crime Problem* (New York: Appleton-Century-Crofts, Second edition, 1955), pp. 572-573.

outlaw is giving way to a conception of him as a needy or sick person who deserves help. Both these changes are expressions of concern for the welfare of inmates and have led to the assignment of a new goal to prisons—protection of inmates from society. Although criminology textbooks and institutional policy-statements are silent regarding this relatively new goal, contemporary prisons are expected both to protect society from inmates and to protect inmates from society.

In the course of a year spent observing the structure and functioning of two prisons, we are able to document such an extension of the protective goal, just as it has been documented in reference to mental hospitals and in the area of probation and parole.[2] This was done by extensive interviews with samples of all categories of employees and a sample of inmates and by firsthand observations of the institutions in action. Although neither institution had an explicit policy regarding protection of inmates, the staffs showed considerable concern for protecting them. This protection took two principal forms.

First, there was concern for protecting inmates from the ostracism, ridicule, exploitation and even physical attack which they might have experienced had they been left in the free community. Criminals whose cases were well publicized and whose crimes were horrendous were viewed as in most need of such protection but some interviewees in both prisons said that all prisoners should be protected (a) from exploitation by gangsters, high pressure salesmen, over-zealous attorneys and other individuals; (b) from ministrations of amateur "reformers" or "researchers"; and (c) from observation and ridicule by the morbidly curious. One guard pointed out, for example, that in some states criminal statutes prohibit the "exhibition" of criminals.

Second, over half the interviews in each prison indicated, and personal observation verified, that in both institutions concerted effort was made to protect inmates from each other and from staff members. This included protection from dishonesty, ridicule and physical harm.

Generally speaking, both institutions efficiently provided the two kinds of protection. For example, individual inmates were protected in many ways from individuals who wanted to "study" them, "reform" them or use them in some way. Similarly, inmates were efficiently protected from dishonesty and physical violence on the part of staff members and other inmates. Both prisons had rules stating that no em-

ployee is to touch an inmate except to search him or to subdue him if he attacks another inmate or an employee. Despite popular beliefs that prison guards and officials are likely to be "brutal" or "sadistic," no behavior of this kind occurred during the year of observation. Also, inmates were carefully policed to insure that they did not steal from each other or fight with each other. Crime rates were low in both institutions.

Such similarities between the two prisons indicate that both are organized, at least unofficially, for the protection of inmates. Even though unstated, this goal is achieved with considerable efficiency. However, some differences were observed between the two institutions in the kind and amount of protection offered. As we shall show below, inmates in one prison were more effectively protected from observation by curious outside groups, while inmates in the other were more effectively protected from ridicule by staff members. These differences are of greater sociological significance than are the similarities, for their presence illustrates three things of concern to students of social organization: (1) the effect of official policies on accomplishment of unstated organizational goals, (2) the effect on organizational behavior of relationships which must be maintained with authority outside the system, and (3) the effects on both official and unstated goals of officially substituting informal control mechanisms for formal ones.

VARIATIONS IN OFFICIAL POLICY

The two prisons are located in the same state but their institutional "climates" were quite different. One was characterized by a "relaxed discipline" for inmates and staff alike. The administrators were "professional" persons and viewed inmates as men in need of "treatment" rather than, or in addition to, punishment and close supervision. Generally speaking, guards and other employees were expected to *understand* inmates, to help them with their problems, to avoid being "rigid" or "punitive" and to refer inmates with serious problems to professional personnel for therapy. Thus in this prison, which is for youthful offenders, official emphasis was on the fourth goal which society assigns to prisons: the reformation of criminals. Although the institution's walls, guntowers, bars, locks and lines of marching inmates revealed official concern for protecting society, the stated policy was to "coordinate all the institution's facilities in a program of individualized treatment."

The other prison housed older but not necessarily more dangerous offenders and its routine was not as "relaxed." Inmates were officially viewed as dangerous and conniving and, accordingly, were expected to obey explicit rules which were stated in advance. The

2 Alfred H. Stanton and Morris S. Schwartz, *The Mental Hospital*, (New York: Basic Books, 1954), pp. 48-55, 233-234; Lloyd E. Ohlin, Herman Pivin, and Donnell M. Pappenfort, "Major Dilemmas of the Social Worker in Probation and Parole," *National Probation and Parole Association Journal*, Volume 2 (July, 1956), pp. 211-225.

principal duty of guards and other employees was to maintain "discipline" among inmates by enforcing rules. While administrators expressed and implemented concern for rehabilitation and treatment, the institutional routine attempted to insure that a maximum number of inmates were under close surveillance at all times. Official emphasis was on the first goal which society assigns to prisons: the *incapacitation* of criminals. The official policy of this prison was stated as follows: "First of all, our purpose is protection of society; that is first and foremost."

Although the policy-statement of the first prison specifies a single goal, treatment or rehabilitation, and that of the second prison indicates the possibility of multiple goals, it must be emphasized that both statements are expressions of the *priority* to be given to the rehabilitation goal and to the incapacitation goal. Both institutions had both a rehabilitation and a custodial goal. In the first there was greater official emphasis upon meeting inmates' needs by "individualized treatment" in an effort to reform them. In the second there was more emphasis upon protecting society from inmates. Because the difference is one of emphasis, we have called the first institution a "treatment-*oriented*" prison and the second a "custodially-*oriented*" prison.

However, the differences in official policy had important implications for achieving the unstated goal of protecting inmates. Despite the fact that the treatment-oriented institution had to protect society, the commitment to individualized treatment required that inmate deviations within the prison, like criminal acts themselves, be interpreted as a consequence of *inability* to conform rather than as *intentional* and *deliberate* violation. This view is highly significant for in our culture when nonconformity is perceived as unintentional the response to it is one of "treatment" or "education," indicating immediate concern for the individual deviant rather than for the society or group disrupted by the deviation. This same response is found in criminal law theory which exempts from official punishment insane persons and very young children who are viewed as not intending the consequences of their acts, even if they are harmful. The official concern for "treatment" in the treatment-oriented prison, then, necessarily placed emphasis upon inmate welfare and, more generally, upon protection of inmates from conditions which might interfere with the "treatment." The trend toward the "professional" view that criminals are sick rather than bad has had as one of its consequences the kind of policy characterizing the treatment-oriented prison and the attendant concern for inmates rather than, or in addition to, concern for society.

On the other hand, in our culture when deviation is perceived as *intentional* or *deliberate* the reaction is punishment and/or close surveillance. In the administration of the criminal law, for example, we traditionally have assumed that most deviation is deliberate and, accordingly, a proper subject of punishment or control by force. Our conceptions of justice and civil liberties, in fact, have been constructed on the assumption that both the pain and the close surveillance which ordinarily characterize imprisonment are to be inflicted only on men who *deliberately* violate the law—on men who are "guilty." Since criminals are "guilty," society is more deserving of protection than are prisoners. It is this principle which is emphasized in the custodially-oriented prison. Although some inmates are to be "treated" and all are to be handled "humanely," the goal of protecting society from the majority of inmates is the one emphasized in the official policy-statement.

The observed difference in official policies was found to be reflected in the degree to which inmates in the two prisons were protected from ridicule and humiliation by outsiders. In the state in question, as in others, a large number of citizens want to tour penal institutions in order to "educate" themselves or, perhaps more realistically, to "amuse" themselves. During the year of observation, inmates at the treatment-oriented prison were more carefully protected from such curious tourists than were those at the custodially-oriented prison.

A decade ago almost any individual presenting himself at the gate could "go through" either institution for a small admission fee and tours were conducted almost every hour during the working day. During this period, tours for organized groups also were conducted. The tours for individuals "just passing through town" are no longer permitted in either institution but organized associations of adults can still arrange in advance for conducted tours.

Such tours are much more frequent at the custodially-oriented prison than they are at the treatment-oriented prison. During one month in a recent year over one hundred man-hours were devoted to guiding about one thousand visitors through the custodially-oriented institution. Inmates complained about being put on exhibition, guards complained about the threat to security and the administration found it necessary to maintain in the central lobby a large sign reading "Visitors must not speak to or point out prisoners." In the treatment-oriented prison, on the other hand, groups other than college classes or members of professional organizations somehow related to penology rarely were taken on tours. While nonacademic and nonprofessional groups were not prohibited from touring this prison, they were somehow discouraged from applying for tours.

The official policy-statements, thus, had important consequences for accomplishing the unstated goal.

The official emphasis upon treatment and the concomitant view that deviation is unintentional meant that inmate welfare, including protection from curious tourists, had to be given high priority, while the official emphasis on protecting society from inmates made this unnecessary. . . .

VARIATIONS IN STRUCTURE

Because the custodially-oriented prison's official policy and relationships with external authority stressed the importance of protecting society, a maximum number of treatment, educational and industrial activities were made subservient to custodial routines. Consistently, guards were expected to follow rules which had been designed to maximize safe custody of inmates. For example, they were not expected to use "discretion" in deciding whether or not behavior was an infraction of rules.

Thus, the system of control was formal. Employees were trained to view inmates as dangerous and conniving men from whom society must be protected even at risk of life. They were to maintain social distance between themselves and inmates at all times and, like inmates, were to follow rules which had been specified in advance. These rules were, generally speaking, instructions for "enforcing" rules for inmates. As indicated earlier, the general duty of guards was to "maintain discipline" among men who were, by definition, inferior to them and in need of control. "Enforcing rules" and "maintaining discipline" meant that guards were to report deviations to the central court in a routine way; captains and lieutenants gave demerits to guards who were caught deviating from this formal procedure. In a sense the prison was organized to emphasize inmate inferiority to guards and guard inferiority to officers and administrators. Although some guards occasionally withdrew from this formal system and entered into cooperative alliances with inmates, such behavior did not seem to be as extensive as it was in [studies by other criminologists].

Stated in another way, emphasis upon protecting society from inmates led to implementation of a system for controlling men who were feared. Just as a community hires policemen because it fears unapprehended criminals, it maintains prisons in part because it continues to fear these men after they have been apprehended and convicted. Within a prison which emphasizes protecting this outside community, the organizational response is a formal system designed to minimize inmate autonomy and to minimize opportunities for inmate rebellion. To this end, guards and others were trained to be alert to conditions which might stimulate inmate retaliation of either an individual or collective nature. One such

condition, administrators believed, was informal relations with inmates. Again, control systems were to be formal and emotionally neutral. For example, even if ridiculing inmates works as a short-term control measure, in the long run ridiculing men who are in a system which defines them as bad and dangerous can only be an irritant leading to individual or collective violence, both of which threaten institutional security. Further, if controls are formal any inmate hostility might be directed toward "the system," but informal control by ridicule might direct hostility toward the ridiculer and thus be personally dangerous.

At the treatment-oriented institution, on the other hand, employees were expected to view inmates as essentially maladjusted or "sick," as not entirely responsible for their actions and as in need of individualized "treatment" rather than, or in addition to, "discipline." This individualized treatment policy has definite organizational implications. Most significantly, it calls for a "relaxed discipline" in which nonprofessional employees assist professional treatment personnel with the task of treatment. There were two principal conceptions of what guards, as members of a treatment organization, should do. First, they were to act as referral agents for the professionally-trained staff. They were to discuss inmates' problems with them and, in a broad sense, to diagnose surface problems of adjustment. On the basis of these diagnoses, inmates were to be referred to the proper professional personnel for clinical handling. Second, guards were to participate more directly in treatment. Under the direction of the professional staff they were to handle inmates' minor emotional problems themselves, to counsel and encourage inmates to "talk out" their problems and to inspire them by personal example.

In either case, guards were expected to be receptive, passive and relaxed. They were to think for themselves, use discretion in deciding whether an action is a rule violation and be "professional." Relationships with inmates were to be personal and friendly rather than formal. In their roles as treatment agents, guards were expected informally to give rewards to inmates showing signs of improvement.

At the same time, however, guards had to function as guards. While they were relaxing in their relationships with inmates so as to contribute to rehabilitation, they were to maintain order and insure that inmates performed the work tasks which had to be performed if the institution were to continue operating. Although institutional policy and reference groups stressed inmate welfare, guards were expected to help protect society. Because of this obligation to *guard*, to maintain peaceful routines and to utilize inmate workcrews efficiently, guards could not behave like archetypical treatment agents. They could relax and enter into informal relations with inmates but they could not give unqualified support to meeting individual inmate needs for a relaxed "therapeutic climate." To do this would jeopardize their effectiveness as protectors of society. At the same time, to give unqualified support to a formal system of custodial control at the expense of therapeutic climate would jeopardize their effectiveness as treatment agents.

The dual role of the inmate—as patient in need of treatment and as a prisoner in need of control—thus brought into being a treatment-*oriented* organization in which it was extremely difficult for the guard to behave ideally in respect to the institution's official goal. The presence of the subsidiary goal, repression of inmates, meant that the discretion granted employees so that the organization would be therapeutic was not always used for therapeutic purposes. Rather, official decentralization of decision-making, introduced so that individualized treatment could be effected, had as one of its consequences the decentralization of *punishment*. In this institution, guards and other employees could not routinely refer inmates to a central court for disciplinary action because this would be evidence of "rigidity" and poor treatment practices. Faced, then, with the perceived need for stimulating conformity in a situation in which use of formal control mechanisms was denied them, guards used unofficial rewards and punishments to get the conformity they needed. Inmates occasionally were given duty which was dirty or unpleasant, deprived of recreational privileges or demoted from higher status jobs without ever going to a professional treatment specialist or to a disciplinary court. Probably there were few guards who did not informally use punishments in order to protect the institution and society, even if they subscribed to the notion that inmates should be understood rather than punished.

These variations in the structures of the two prisons were reflected in differences in the degree to which the unstated goal—protection of inmates—was achieved. In contradiction to the direction of the difference in protecting inmates from curious outsiders, protection from ridicule, humiliation and even physical contact by staff members was more complete at the custodially-oriented prison than at the treatment-oriented institution.

While some employees in both prisons probably ridiculed and attempted to humiliate some inmates, this practice was very rare at the custodially-oriented prison but occurred occasionally at the treatment-oriented institution. At the former but not the latter all guards were frequently and carefully warned by the chief custodian against "needling" inmates. Further, at the custodially-oriented prison guards were discouraged from holding any but very short conversations with inmates. Although they were permitted to talk briefly to inmates who came to them with questions about their work or who came to them for advice on some problem, they were not to engage in friendly or relaxed chats or to "joke" with inmates. One stated rationale for this rule was that friendly conversations and "joking" would lead to ridiculing inmates and this, in turn, might be misunderstood and lead to security problems. The investigator never heard an employee of the custodially-oriented prison call an inmate names or otherwise deliberately ridicule him about his presumed low status in either the outside community or the prison.

At the treatment-oriented prison, on the other hand, guards were encouraged to engage in conversations with inmates, and the investigator occasionally heard inmates called "no good punks," "bums" and other names to their faces. One important employee always referred to inmates he didn't like as "rum dumbs," even when they were present. Ordinarily, however, such ridicule as occurred was in the form of "joking" with the youthful inmates about their presumed inability to hold a job or earn a living outside the institution . . .

It may be concluded that the lower degree of protection of inmates from ridicule by employees in the treatment-oriented institution was a function of the kind of controls guards were expected to exert. In the custodially-oriented prison it was the duty of guards to maximize use of a formal system of control in order to protect society and this formal system operated in such a way that the unstated goal was efficiently achieved. In the treatment-oriented prison decision-making was decentralized so guards could contribute to inmate rehabilitation, but the consequent informal control mechanisms were sometimes used for the nontherapeutic purpose of protecting the institution and society. The informal control mechanisms included unofficially administered rewards and punishments. Among these were ridicule and humiliation and, generally, the granting or withholding of friendship, affection and esteem as reward or punishment. . . .

SUMMARY

Historical trends and the concern of staff members in the two institutions studied for protecting inmates from the public, from each other and from the staff indicate that an unstated goal of prisons is the protection of inmates. This unstated goal was efficiently achieved in both insitutions but two principal differences were present. Inmates of the treatment-oriented prison were more carefully protected from the stares of organized groups of tourists than were inmates of the other prison, and inmates of the custodially-oriented prison were more carefully protected from ridicule by employees than was the case in the treatment-oriented prison. Analysis of these differences suggests: (1) that an organization's official, formal, policy has important effects even on achievement of unstated, informal, goals, (2) that an organization's arrangements with the larger social system maintaining it both determine and affect the accomplishment of unstated as well as official goals, and (3) that official substitution of informal for formal control mechanisms in an organization does not necessarily produce increased efficiency in accomplishing informal, unstated, goals.

Not only can goals affect structures, but structures can affect goals. In the next selection, Charles P. Perrow describes a sequence often noticed in studies of organizations: official goals are proclaimed and an administrative apparatus is created to pursue them; the organizational structure begins to generate its own unofficial goals, either because of the philosophy of its personnel, the logical implications of its procedures, or some other reasons. Perrow describes how voluntary hospitals, despite their common official aims, may pursue diverse unofficial goals as a result of their different organizational structures. He suggests that structures may also generate unofficial goals in other voluntary associations.

THE GENESIS OF UNOFFICIAL GOALS*
Charles P. Perrow

Two major categories of goals will be discussed here, official and "operative" goals. Official goals are the general purposes of the organization as put forth in the charter, annual reports, public statements by key executives and other authoritative pronouncements. For example, the goal of an employment agency may be to place job seekers in contact with firms seeking workers. The official goal of a hospital may be to promote the health of the community through curing the ill, and sometimes through preventing illness, teaching, and conducting research. Similar organizations may emphasize different publicly acceptable goals. A business corporation, for example, may state that its goal is to make a profit or adequate return on investment, or provide a customer service, or produce goods.

This level of analysis is inadequate in itself for a full understanding of organizational behavior. Official goals are purposely vague and general and do not indicate two major factors which influence organizational behavior: the host of decisions that must be made among alternative ways of achieving official goals and the priority of multiple goals, and the many unofficial goals pursued by groups within the organization. The concept of "operative goals" will be used

* From Charles P. Perrow, "The Analysis of Goals in Complex Organizations," *American Sociological Review*, Volume 26, Number 6 (December 1961), pp. 854-866. Reprinted with the permission of the author and the publisher, the American Sociological Association.

to cover these aspects. Operative goals designate the ends sought through the actual operating policies of the organization; they tell us what the organization actually is trying to do, regardless of what the official goals say are the aims.

Where operative goals provide the specific content of official goals they reflect choices among competing values. They may be justified on the basis of an official goal, even though they may subvert another official goal. In one sense they are means to official goals, but since the latter are vague or of high abstraction, the "means" become ends in themselves when the organization is the object of analysis. For example, where profit-making is the announced goal, operative goals will specify whether quality or quantity is to be emphasized, whether profits are to be short run and risky or long run and stable, and will indicate the relative priority of diverse and somewhat conflicting ends of customer service, employee morale, competitive pricing, diversification, or liquidity. Decisions on all these factors influence the nature of the organization, and distinguish it from another with an identical official goal. An employment agency must decide whom to serve, what characteristics they favor among clients, and whether a high turnover of clients or a long run relationship is desired. In the voluntary general hospital, where the official goals are patient care, teaching, and research, the relative priority of these must be decided, as well as which group in the community is to be given priority in service, and are these services to emphasize, say, technical excellence or warmth and "hand-holding."

Unofficial operative goals, on the other hand, are tied more directly to group interests and while they may support, be irrelevant to, or subvert official goals, they bear no necessary connection with them. An interest in a major supplier may dictate the policies of a corporation executive. The prestige that attaches to utilizing elaborate high speed computers may dictate the reorganization of inventory and accounting departments. Racial prejudice may influence the selection procedures of an employment agency. The personal ambition of a hospital administrator may lead to community alliances and activities which bind the organization without enhancing its goal achievement. On the other hand, while the use of interns and residents as "cheap labor" may subvert the official goal of medical education, it may substantially further the official goal of providing a high quality of patient care.

The discernment of operative goals is, of course, difficult and subject to error. The researcher may have to determine from analysis of a series of apparently minor decisions regarding the lack of competitive bidding and quality control that an unofficial goal of a group of key executives is to maximize their individual investments in a major supplier. This unofficial goal may affect profits, quality, market position, and morale of key skill group. The executive of a correctional institution may argue that the goal of the organization is treatment, and only the lack of resources creates an apparent emphasis upon custody or deprivation. The researcher may find, however, that decisions in many areas establish the priority of custody or punishment as a goal. For example, few efforts may be made to obtain more treatment personnel; those hired are misused and mistrusted; and clients are viewed as responding only to deprivations. The president of a junior college may deny the function of the institution is to deal with the latent terminal student, but careful analysis such as Clark has made of operating policies, personnel practices, recruitment procedures, organizational alliances and personal characteristics of elites will demonstrate this to be the operative goal.[1]

THE TASK—AUTHORITY—GOAL SEQUENCE

While operative goals will only be established through intensive analysis of decisions, personnel practices, alliance and elite characteristics in each organization,

[1] Burton Clark, *The Open Door College* (New York: McGraw-Hill Book Company, 1960).

it is possible to indicate the range within which they will vary and the occasion for general shifts in goals. We will argue that if we know something about the major tasks of an organization and the characteristics of its controlling elite, we can predict its goals in general terms. The theory presented and illustrated in the rest of this paper is a first approximation and very general, but it may guide and stimulate research on this problem.

Every organization must accomplish four tasks: (1) secure inputs in the form of capital sufficient to establish itself, operate, and expand as the need arises; (2) secure acceptance in the form of basic legitimization of activity; (3) marshal the necessary skills; and (4) coordinate the activities of its members, and the relations of the organization with other organizations and with clients or consumers. All four are not likely to be equally important at any point in time. Each of these task areas provides a presumptive basis for control or domination by the group equipped to meet the problems involved. . . . The operative goals will be shaped by the dominant group, reflecting the imperatives of the particular task area that is most critical, their own background characteristics (distinctive perspectives based upon their training, career lines, and areas of competence) and the unofficial uses to which they put the organization for their own ends.

The relative emphasis upon one or another of the four tasks will vary with the nature of the work the organization does and the technology appropriate to it, and with the stage of development within the organization. An organization engaged in manufacturing in an industry where skills are routinized and the market position secure, may emphasize coordination, giving control to the experienced administrator. An extractive industry, with a low skill level in its basic tasks and a simple product, will probably emphasize the importance of capital tied up in land, specialized and expensive machinery, and transportation facilities. The chairman of the board of directors or a group within the board will probably dominate such an organization. An organization engaged in research and development, or the production of goods or services which cannot be carried out in a routinized fashion, will probably be most concerned with skills. Thus engineers or other relevant professionals will dominate. It is also possible that all three groups—trustees, representatives of critical skills, and administrators—may share power equally. This "multiple leadership" will be discussed in detail later. Of course, trustees are likely to dominate in the early history of any organization, particularly those requiring elaborate capital and facilities, or unusual legitimization. But once these requisites are secured, the nature of the tasks will determine whether trustees or others dominate. The transfer of authority, especially from trustees to another group, may be protracted, constituting a lag in adaptation.

Where major task areas do not change over time, the utility of the scheme presented here is limited to suggesting possible relations between task areas, authority structure, and operative goals. The more interesting problems, which we deal with in our illustrations below, involve organizations which experience changes in major task areas over time. If the technology or type of work changes, or if new requirements for capital or legitimization arise, control will shift from one group to another. One sequence is believed to be typical.

VOLUNTARY GENERAL HOSPITALS

We will discuss four types of hospitals, those dominated by trustees, by the medical staff (an organized group of those doctors who bring in private patients plus the few doctors who receive salaries or commissions from the hospital), by the administration, and by some form of multiple leadership. There has been a general development among hospitals from trustee domination, based on capital and legitimization, to domination by the medical staff, based upon the increasing importance of their technical skills, and, at present, a tendency towards administrative dominance based on internal and external coordination. (The administrator may or may not be a doctor himself.) Not all hospitals go through these stages, or go through them in this sequence. Each type of authority structure shapes, or sets limits to, the type of operative goals that are likely to prevail, though there will be much variation within each type.[2]

TRUSTEE DOMINATION

Voluntary general hospitals depend upon community funds for an important part of their capital and operating budget. Lacking precise indicators of efficiency or goal achievement, yet using donated funds, they must involve community representatives—trustees—in their authority structure. Trustees legitimate the non-profit status of the organization, assure that funds are not misused, and see that community needs

are being met. Officially, they are the ultimate authority in voluntary hospitals. They do not necessarily exercise the legal powers they have, but where they do, there is no question that they are in control.

The functional basis for this control is primarily financial. They have access to those who make donations, are expected to contribute heavily themselves, and control the machinery and sanctions for fund raising drives. Financial control allows them to withhold resources from recalcitrant groups in the organization, medical or non-medical.

Where these extensive powers are exercised, operative goals are likely to reflect the role of trustees as community representatives and contributors to community health. Because of their responsibility to the sponsoring community, trustees may favor conservative financial policies, opposing large financial outlays for equipment, research, and education so necessary for high medical standards. High standards also require more delegation of authority to the medical staff than trustee domination can easily allow. As representatives drawn from distinctive social groups in the community, they may be oriented towards service for a religious, ethnic, economic, or age group in the community. Such an orientation may conflict with selection procedures favored by the medical staff or administration. Trustees may also promote policies which demonstrate a contribution to community welfare on the part of an elite group, perhaps seeking to maintain a position of prominence and power within the community. The hospital may be used as a vehicle for furthering a social philosophy of philanthropy and good works; social class values regarding personal worth, economic independence and responsibility; the assimilation of a minority group; or even to further resistance to government control and socialized medicine.

Such orientations will shape operative goals in many respects, affecting standards and techniques of care, priority of services, access to care, relations with other organizations, and directions and rate of development. The administrator in such a hospital—usually called a "superintendent" under the circumstances—will have little power, prestige or responsibility. For example, trustees have been known to question the brand of grape juice the dietician orders, or insist that they approve the color of paint the administrator selects for a room.[3] Physicians may disapprove of patient selection criteria, chafe under financial restrictions which limit the resources they have to work with, and resent active control over appointments and promotions in the medical staff.

[2] The following discussion is based upon the author's study of one hospital which, in fact, passed through these stages; upon examination of published and unpublished studies of hospitals; and upon numerous conversations with administrators, doctors, and trustees in the United States. Sophisticated practitioners in the hospital field recognize and describe these types in their own fashion. See Charles Perrow, *Authority, Goals and Prestige in a General Hospital* (Berkeley: unpublished dissertation for the Ph.D. at the University of California, 1960), for fuller documentation and discussion.

[3] Edith Lentz, "Changing Concepts of Hospital Administration," *Industrial and Labor Relations Research*, Volume 3 (Summer, 1957), p. 2. Perrow, *op. cit.*, p. 86.

MEDICAL DOMINATION

Trustee domination was probably most common in the late nineteenth and early twentieth century. Medical technology made extraordinary advances in the twentieth century, and doctors possessed the skills capable of utilizing the advances. They demanded new resources and were potentially in a position to control their allocation and use. Increasingly, major decisions had to be based upon a technical competence trustees did not possess. Trustees had a continuing basis for control because of the costs of new equipment and personnel, but in many hospitals the skill factor became decisive. Some trustees felt that the technology required increased control by doctors; others lost a struggle for power to an outstanding doctor in order to increase the reputation of the hospital. Under such conditions trustees are likely to find that their legal power becomes nominal and they can only intervene in crisis situations; even financial requirements come to be set by conditions outside their control. They continue to provide the mantle of community representation and non-profit status, and become "staff" members whose major task is to secure funds.

It is sometimes hard to see why all hospitals are not controlled by the medical staff, in view of the increasing complexity and specialization of the doctor's skills, their common professional background, the power of organized medicine, and the prestige accorded the doctor in society. Furthermore, they are organized for dominance, despite their nominal status as "guests" in the house. The medical staff constitutes a "shadow" organization in hospitals, providing a ready potential for control. It is organized on bureaucratic principles with admission requirements, rewards and sanctions, and a committee structure which often duplicates the key committees of the board of directors and administrative staff. Nor are doctors in an advisory position as are "staff" groups in other organizations. Doctors perform both staff and line functions, and their presumptive right to control rests on both. Doctors also have a basic economic interest in the hospital, since it is essential to most private medical practice and career advancement. They seek extensive facilities, low hospital charges, a high quality of coordinated services, and elaborate time and energy-conserving conveniences.

Thus there is sufficient means for control by doctors, elaborated far beyond the mere provision of essential skills, and sufficient interest in control. Where doctors fully exercise their potential power the administrator functions as a superintendent or, as his co-professionals are wont to put it, as a "housekeeper." The importance of administrative skills is likely to be minimized, the administrative viewpoint on operative goals neglected, and the quality of personnel may suffer. A former nurse often serves as superintendent in this type of hospital. Policy matters are defined as medical in nature by the doctors, and neither trustees nor administrators, by definition, are qualified to have an equal voice in policy formation.

The operative goals of such a hospital are likely to be defined in strictly medical terms and the organization may achieve high technical standards of care, promote exemplary research, and provide sound training. However, there is a danger that resources will be used primarily for private (paying) patients with little attention to other community needs such as caring for the medically indigent (unless they happen to be good teaching cases), developing preventive medicine, or pioneering new organizational forms of care. Furthermore, high technical standards increasingly require efficient coordination of services and doctors may be unwilling to delegate authority to qualified administrators.

Various unofficial goals may be achieved at the expense of medical ones, or, in some cases, in conjunction with them. There are many cases of personal aggrandizement on the part of departmental chiefs and the chief of staff. The informal referral and consultation system in conjunction with promotions, bed quotas, and "privileges" to operate or treat certain types of cases, affords many occasions for the misuse of power. Interns and residents are particularly vulnerable to exploitation at the expense of teaching goals. Furthermore, as a professional, the doctor has undergone intensive socialization in his training and is called upon to exercise extraordinary judgment and skill with drastic consequences for good or ill. Thus he demands unusual deference and obedience and is invested with "charismatic" authority. He may extend this authority to the entrepreneurial aspects of his role, with the result that his "service" orientation, so taken for granted in much of the literature, sometimes means service [of the hospital] to the doctor at the expense of personnel, other patients, or even his own patient.[4]

ADMINISTRATIVE DOMINANCE

Administrative dominance is based first on the need for coordinating the increasingly complex, non-routinizable functions hospitals have undertaken. There is an increasing number of personnel that the doctor can no longer direct. The mounting concern of trustees, doctors themselves, patients and prepayment groups with more efficient and economical operation also gives the administrator more power. A second, related basis for control stems from the fact

4 Wessen notes that the doctor "sees ministering to the needs of doctors as a major function of the hospitals." Albert F. Wessen, *The Social Structure of a Modern Hospital* (New Haven: unpublished dissertation for the Ph.D. at Yale University, 1951), p. 328.

that health services in general have become increasingly interdependent and specialized. The hospital must cooperate more with other hospitals and community agencies. It must also take on more services itself, and in doing so its contacts with other agencies and professional groups outside the hospital multiply. The administrator is equipped to handle these matters because of his specialized training, often received in a professional school of hospital administration, accumulated experience and available time. These services impinge upon the doctor at many points, providing a further basis for administrative control over doctors, and they lead to commitments in which trustees find they have to acquiesce.

The administrator is also in a position to control matters which affect the doctor's demands for status, deference, and time-saving conveniences. By maintaining close supervision over employees or promoting their own independent basis for competence, and by supporting them in conflicts with doctors, the administrator can, to some degree, overcome the high functional authority that doctors command. In addition, by carefully controlling communication between trustees and key medical staff officials, he can prevent an alliance of these two groups against him.

If administrative dominance is based primarily on the complexity of basic hospital activities, rather than the organization's medical-social role in the community, the operative orientation may be toward financial solvency, careful budget controls, efficiency, and minimal development of services. For example, preventive medicine, research, and training may be minimized; a cautious approach may prevail towards new forms of care such as intensive therapy units or home care programs. Such orientations could be especially true of hospitals dominated by administrators whose background and training were as bookkeepers, comptrollers, business managers, purchasing agents, and the like. This is probably the most common form of administrative dominance.

However, increasing professionalization of hospital administrators has, on the one hand, equipped them to handle narrower administrative matters easily, and, on the other hand, alerted them to the broader medical-social role of hospitals involving organizational and financial innovations in the forms of care. Even medical standards can come under administrative control. For example, the informal system among doctors of sponsorship, referral, and consultation serves to protect informal work norms, shield members from criticism and exclude non-cooperative members. The administrator is in a position to insist that medical policing be performed by a salaried doctor who stands outside the informal system.

There is, of course, a possibility of less "progressive" consequences. Interference with medical practices in the name of either high standards or treating the "whole" person may be misguided or have latent consequences which impair therapy. Publicity-seeking innovations may be at the expense of more humdrum but crucial services such as the out-patient department, or may alienate doctors or other personnel, or may deflect administrative efforts from essential but unglamorous administrative tasks.[5] Using the organization for career advancement, they may seek to expand and publicize their hospital regardless of community needs and ability to pay. Like trustees they may favor a distinctive and medically irrelevant community relations policy, perhaps with a view towards moving upward in the community power structure. Regardless of these dangers, the number of administration dominated hospitals oriented towards broad medical–social goals will probably grow.

MULTIPLE LEADERSHIP

So far we have been considering situations where one group clearly dominates. It is possible, however, for power to be shared by two or three groups to the extent that no one is able to control all or most of the actions of the others. This we call multiple leadership: a division of labor regarding the determination of goals and the power to achieve them. This is not the same as fractionated power where several groups have small amounts of power in an unstable situation. With multiple leadership, there are two or three stable, known centers of power. Nor is it the same as decentralized power, where specialized units of the organization have considerable autonomy. In the latter case, units are free to operate as they choose only up to a point, when it becomes quite clear that there is a centralized authority. In multiple leadership there is no single ultimate power.

Multiple leadership is most likely to appear in organizations where there are multiple goals which lack precise criteria of achievement and admit of considerable tolerance with regard to achievement. Multiple goals focus interests, and achievement tolerance provides the necessary leeway for accommodation of interests and vitiation of responsibility. Many service organizations fit these criteria, but so might large, public relations-conscious business or industrial organizations where a variety of goals can be elevated to such importance that power must be shared by the representatives of each.

In one hospital where this was studied[6] it was found that multiple leadership insured that crucial group interests could be met and protected, and encouraged a high level of creative (though selective)

5 Charles Perrow, "Organizational Prestige: Some Functions and Dysfunctions," *American Journal of Sociology*, Volume 66 (January, 1961), pp. 335-341.
6 Perrow, *Authority, Goals and Prestige . . . , op. cit.*, Chs. 4, 10.

involvement by trustees, doctors, and the administration. However, the problems of goal setting, assessment of achievement and assignment of responsibility seemed abnormally high. While the three groups pursued separate and unconflicting operative goals in some cases, and were in agreement on still other goals, in areas where interests conflicted the goal conflicts were submerged in the interests of harmony. In the absense of a single authority, repetitive conflicts threatened to erode morale and waste energies. A showdown and clear solution of a conflict, furthermore, might signal defeat for one party, forcing them to abandon their interests. Thus a premium was placed on the ability of some elites to smooth over conflicts and exercise interpersonal skills. Intentions were sometimes masked and ends achieved through covert manipulation. Assessment of achievement in some areas was prevented either by the submergence of conflict or the preoccupation with segmental interests. Opportunism was encouraged: events in the environment or within the hospital were exploited without attention to the interests of the other groups or the long range development of the hospital. This left the organization open to vagrant pressures and to the operation of unintended consequences. Indeed, with conflict submerged and groups pursuing independent goals, long range planning was difficult.

This summary statement exaggerates the impact of multiple leadership in this hospital and neglects the areas of convergence on goals. Actually, the hospital prospered and led its region in progressive innovations and responsible medical-social policies despite some subversion of the official goals of patient care, teaching, research, and preventive medicine. The organization could tolerate considerable ambiguity of goals and achievements as long as standards remained high in most areas, occupancy was sufficient to operate with a minimum deficit, and a favorable public image was maintained. It remains to be seen if the costs and consequences are similar for other organizations where multiple leadership exists.

APPLICATION TO OTHER ORGANIZATIONS

VOLUNTARY SERVICE ORGANIZATIONS

Other voluntary service organizations, such as private universities, social service agencies, privately sponsored correctional institutions for juveniles, and fund raising agencies resemble hospitals in many respects. They have trustees representing the community, may have professionals playing prominent roles, and with increasing size and complexity of operation, require skilled coordination of activities. Initially at least, trustees are likely to provide a character defining

function which emphasizes community goals and goals filtered through their own social position. Examples are religious schools, or those emphasizing one field of knowledge or training; agencies caring for specialized groups such as ethnic or religious minorities, unwed mothers, and dependent and neglected children; and groups raising money for special causes. Funds of skill and knowledge accumulate around these activities, and the activities increasingly grow in complexity, requiring still more skill on the part of those performing the tasks. As the professional staff expands and professional identification grows, they may challenge the narrower orientations of trustees on the basis of their own special competence and professional ideology and seek to broaden the scope of services and the clientele. They may be supported in this by changing values in the community. Coordination of activities usually rests with professionals promoted from the staff during this second character defining phase, and these administrators retain, for a while at least, their professional identity. Trustees gradually lose the competence to interfere.

However, professionals have interests of their own which shape the organization. They may develop an identity and ethic which cuts them off from the needs of the community and favors specialized, narrow and —to critics—self-serving goals. Current criticisms of the emphasis upon research and over-specialization in graduate training at the expense of the basic task of educating undergraduates is a case in point in the universities.[7] There is also criticism of the tendency of professionals in correctional institutions to focus upon case work techniques applicable to middle-class "neurotic" delinquents at the expense of techniques for resocializing the so-called "socialized" delinquent from culturally deprived areas.[8] The latter account for most of the delinquents, but professional identity and techniques favor methods applicable to the former. Something similar may be found in social agencies. Social workers, especially the "elite" doing therapy in psychiatric and child guidance clinics and private family agencies, may become preoccupied with securing recognition, equitable financial remuneration, and status that would approach that of psychiatrists. Their attitudes may become more conservative; the social order more readily accepted and the deviant

7 Earl J. McGrath, *The Graduate School and the Doctrine of Liberal Education* (New York: Bureau of Publications, Teachers College, Columbia University, 1960).
8 Robert Vinter and Morris Janowitz, "Effective Institutions for Juvenile Delinquents: A Research Statement," *Social Service Review*, Volume 33 (June, 1957), pp. 118-122; Donald Cressey, "Changing Criminals: The Application of the Theory of Differential Association," *American Journal of Sociology*, Volume 56 (September, 1955), p. 116; Lloyd Ohlin and W. C. Lawrence, "Social Interaction Among Clients as a Treatment Problem," *Social Work*, Volume 4 (April, 1959), pp. 3-14.

adapted to it; "worthy" clients and "interesting cases" receive priority.

It is possible that with increasing complexity and growth in many of these voluntary service organizations, administrators will lose their professional identity or be recruited from outside the organization on the basis of organizational skills. In either case they will be in a position to alter the direction fostered by selective professional interests. Of course, the problem of coordinating both internal and external activities need not generate leadership seeking broadly social rather than narrowly professional goals, any more than it necessarily does in the hospital. Administrative dominance may stunt professional services and neglect social policy in the interest of economy, efficiency, or conservative policies.

NON-VOLUNTARY SERVICE ORGANIZATIONS

A different picture is presented by non-voluntary service organizations—those sponsored by governmental agencies such as county or military hospitals, city or county welfare agencies, juvenile and adult correctional agencies. Authority for goal setting, regulation, and provision of capital and operating expenses does not rest with voluntary trustees, but with governmental officials appointed to commissions. In contrast to volunteers on the board of a private service organization, commissioners are not likely to be highly identified with the organization, nor do they derive much social status from it. The organizations themselves often are tolerated only as holding operations or as "necessary evils." Commission dominance is sporadic and brief, associated with public clamor or political expediency. On the other hand, the large size of these organizations and the complex procedures for reporting to the parent body gives considerable importance to the administrative function from the outset, which is enhanced by the tenuous relationship with the commissioners. Consistent with this and reinforcing it is the low level of professionalization found in many of these agencies. The key skills are often non-professional custodial skills or their equivalent in the case of public welfare agencies (and schools). Administrators are often at the mercy of the custodial staff if, indeed, they have not themselves risen to their administrative position because of their ability to maintain order and custody.

Nevertheless, professional influence is mounting in these organizations, and professional groups outside of them have exercised considerable influence.[9] Pro-

fessionals may assume control of the organization, or administrators may be brought in whose commitment is to the positive purposes of the organization, such as rehabilitation of the clients, rather than the negative custodial functions. This appears to have happened in the case of a few federal penal institutions, a few state juvenile correctional institutions, and several Veterans Administration mental hospitals. Even where this happens, one must be alert to the influence of unofficial goals. The organizations are particularly vulnerable to exploitation by the political career interests of administrators or to irresponsible fads or cure-alls of marginal professionals. In summary, the sequence of tasks, power structure, and goals may be different in non-voluntary service organizations. The importance of administrative skills with system maintenance as the overriding operative goal does not encourage a shift in power structure; but where new technologies are introduced we are alerted to such shifts along with changes in goals.

PROFIT-MAKING ORGANIZATIONS

Our analysis may appear less applicable to profit-making organizations for two reasons. First, it could be argued, they are not characterized by multiple goals, but relate all operations to profit-making. Second, skill groups are not likely to dominate these organizations; owners control the smaller firms, and professional executives the larger ones. Thus power structure and possibly goals may merely be a function of size. We will discuss each of these points in turn.

If profit-making is an overriding goal of an organization, many operative decisions must still be made which will shape its character. Even where technology remains constant, organizations will vary with regard to personnel practices, customer services, growth, liquidity, an emphasis upon quality or quantity, or long or short run gains. An adequate understanding of the organization will require attention to alternatives in these and other areas.

Furthermore, it has often been asserted that the importance of profits, *per se*, has declined with the increased power of professional management, especially in large organizations. The argument runs that since management does not have a personal stake in profits, they consider them less important than stability, growth, solvency, and liquidity. . . .[10]

---

9 Thompson and McEwen note that the "importance of new objectives may be more readily seen by specialized segments (professionals) than by the general society" and argue that public clamor for change has not been the initiating force. James D. Thompson and William J. McEwen, "Organizational Goals and Environment," *Amer-*

ican Sociological Review, Volume 23 (February 1958), p. 29.

10 Robert A. Gordon was perhaps the first to deal at length with this proposition, and many have subsequently argued along the same lines. See Robert A. Gordon, *Business Leadership in the Large Corporation* (Washington, D. C.: Brookings Institution, 1945), pp. 308-312, 327-329, 336, 340. For similar assertions see C. E. Griffin, *Enterprise in a Free Society* (Chicago: Irwin, 1949), pp. 96-104; H. Maurer, *Great Enterprise,* (New York: Macmillan Co., 1955), p. 77-78; and F. X. Sutton, *et al., The Ameri-*

R. A. Gordon and others have asserted that in large corporations it is the executive group, rather than stockholders or the board of trustees, that generally dominates.[11] A study of the role of trustees, frankly in favor of their exercising leadership and control, actually shows through its many case studies that trustees exercise leadership mainly in times of crisis.[12] The generalization of Gordon, almost a commonplace today, appears to be sound: he asserts that the common pattern of evolution is for active leadership by owners in the early years of the firm, then it is passed on to new generations of the families concerned, and gradually responsibility for decision-making passes to professional executives who frequently have been trained by the original leaders. Goals likewise shift from rapid development and a concern with profits to more conservative policies emphasizing coordination, stability and security of employment.[13]

But does this mean that for large, old, and stable firms that operative goals are substantially similar, reflecting professional administration? Does it also mean that for profit-making organizations in general there are only two alternative sources of domination, trustees (including owners) and professional administrators? Our theoretical scheme suggests that neither may be true, but the evidence is scanty. Certainly within the organizations dominated by professional managers there is ample opportunity for a variety of operational goals less general than, say, stability and security of employment. Even these are likely to vary and to shape the nature of the firm. (We exclude, of course, the failure to achieve these broad goals because of poor management or environmental factors over which the organization has no control; we are dealing with operating policies which may not be achieved.) Gordon notes that the "historical background" of a company (he does not elaborate this phrase) and especially the training received by its leading executives may be a powerful factor in shaping management decisions. "It is the 'Rockefeller tra-

dition' rather than the present Rockefeller holdings which actively conditions the management decisions in the Standard Oil Companies. This tradition is largely responsible for present methods of management organization and internal control, use of the committee system and the domination of boards of directors by [company executives]." [14] Historical factors will certainly shape decisions, but the nature of technology in the oil industry and the trustees' awareness of the prime importance of coordination may have been decisive in that historical experience.

Domination by skill groups is possible in two ways. On the one hand, a department—for example, sales, engineering, research and development, or finance—may, because of the technology and stage of growth, effectively exercise a veto on the executive's decisions and substantially shape decisions in other departments. Second, lines of promotion may be such that top executives are drawn from one powerful department, and retain their identification with the parochial goals of that department. Gordon asserts that chief executives with a legal background are conservative in making price changes and find 'order in the industry' more appealing than aggressive price competition.[15] It is possible that engineers, sales executives, and financial executives all have distinctive views on what the operating policies should be.

Thus, goals may vary widely in profit-making organizations, and power may rest not only with trustees or professional administrators, but with skill groups or administrators influenced by their skill background. Of course, one task area may so dominate a firm that there will be no shifts in power, and operative goals will remain fairly stable within the limits of the changing values of society. But where basic tasks shift, either because of growth or changing technology, the scheme presented here at least alerts us to potential goal changes and their consequences. An ideal-typical sequence would be as follows: trustee domination in initial stages of financing, setting direction for development and recruitment of technical or professional skills; then dominance by the skill group during product or service development and research, only to have subsequent control pass to coordination of fairly routinized activities. As the market and technology change, this cycle could be repeated. During the course of this sequence, operative goals may shift from quantity production and short-run profits as emphasized by trustees, to the engineer's preoccupation with quality at the expense of quantity or styling, with this succeeded by a priority upon styling and unessential innovations demanded by the sales force, and finally with an emphasis upon the long-run market position, conserva-

can Business Creed (Cambridge: Harvard University Press, 1956), pp. 57-58. For a contrary view see G. Katona, *Psychological Analysis of Economic Behavior* (New York: McGraw-Hill, 1951), p. 197.

[11] Gordon, *op. cit.*, pp. 114, 131-132, 145-146, 180, 347.

[12] M. T. Copeland and A. Towl, *The Board of Directors and Business Management* (Boston: Harvard University, 1947). For a similar conclusion and excellent discussion of these matters see R. H. Dahl, "Business and Politics," *American Political Science Review*, Volume 53 (March, 1959), p. 6. The argument for increasing managerial control was, of course, also put forth by Burnham in 1941, but he was only faintly interested in the effects upon organizations, his thesis being that managers would supplant capitalists in the national and world power elite. See *The Managerial Revolution* (New York: John Day, 1941).

[13] Gordon, *op. cit.*, pp. 180, 327, 339. See his illustrations from General Motors and U. S. Rubber Company in Chapter 7 of his book.

[14] *Ibid.*, p. 188.

[15] *Ibid.*, p. 264.

tive attitude towards innovation, and considerable investment in employee-centered policies and programs by management. It is important to note that the formal authority structure may not vary during this sequence, but recruitment into managerial positions and the actual power of management, trustees or skill groups would shift with each new problem focus. Multiple leadership is also possible, as noted in an earlier section.

There are many critical variables influencing the selection of key problem areas and thus the characteristics of the controlling elite and operative goals. They will be applicable to the analysis of any complex organization, whether business, governmental, or voluntary. Among those that should be considered are capital needs and legitimization, the amount of routinization possible, adaptability of technology to mar-

ket shifts and consumer behavior, possible or required professionalization, and the nature of the work force. Our analysis of profit-making organizations suggests that we should be alert to the possibility of a natural history of changes in task areas, authority, and goals which parallels that of hospitals and other voluntary service organizations. Non-voluntary service organizations may systematically deviate from this sequence because of the source of capital (government) which influences the commitments of appointive trustees (commissioners), and the character of the administrative tasks. The scheme presented here, when used in conjunction with the concept of operative goals, may provide a tool for analyzing the dynamics of goal setting and goal changing in all complex organizations.

B. THE DISPLACEMENT OF GOALS

The emergence in an organization of what Perrow calls operative goals may lead to a neglect of the official goals; if it does, the process is often termed the displacement of goals. Many students of organizations have cited instances of this familiar process.* One of the classic studies is Philip Selznick's analysis of the Tennessee Valley Authority. Selznick reports that the central administration delegated responsibility for many programs to local organizations, and that this delegation led to unanticipated consequences.

One of the motivating theories of the TVA was that it must and could earn acceptance from its constituency by giving the population of the Tennessee Valley an opportunity to participate in the execution of the agricultural and other programs. In practice, the programs were delegated to local farm organizations by a virtual merger of local TVA offices and local groups. The programs were accepted by local populations but diverged from the original intentions of the TVA's founders and pitted the TVA against certain other New Deal agencies that were more responsive to Administration policy. For example, the TVA was supposed to be a conservationist-minded agency, but it gradually de-emphasized conservation in response to grass-roots farm interests.†

Delegation upward may also lead to an unintended deflection from the organization's official goals. The Baptist Church emphasizes personal freedom and congregational self-government; it has no doctrinal basis for any kind of authoritative national hierarchy. All church functions and decisions are supposed to be local. But the need to conduct foreign missionary work led to the creation of the American Baptist Convention, a central body that was supposed to be the limited tool of the local congregations. Once established, the Convention acquired budgets, ambitious personnel, and an accumulation of tasks. Formal procedures began to govern relations between the Convention and the local congregation. Convention executives began to act as national leaders and spokesmen of the church, the Convention began to originate its own policies and activities, and Convention executives began to exercise controls over local congregations—all

* For a summary of the research literature on the displacement of goals, see David L. Sills, *The Volunteers: Means and Ends in a National Organization* (Glencoe: The Free Press, 1957), pp. 62-69.
† Philip Selznick, *T.V.A. and the Grass Roots* (Berkeley: University of California Press, 1949).

contrary to official religious doctrine and all unanticipated when the Convention was originally established.* The dilemma of combining national coordination with local autonomy is familiar to many leaders of voluntary associations: some can recall cases like the TVA experience, when national policy could not be executed except by local units, but the local agencies deviated from national policy; other leaders can recall cases like the Baptist Convention, when local units required a national office to organize a nation-wide effort, but the national office then pursued its own aims.

Social scientists have studied other processes causing goal displacement. Peter Blau's research in government agencies shows how the administrative chain of command between leader and employee led the organization to function in undesired ways. The danger of disapproval by superiors sometimes led to over-literal application of rules, over-cautious procedures, and resistance to innovations—all of which reduced work output. During periods when supervisors were checking implementation of new regulations in a law enforcement agency, investigators made extra efforts to find violations among the public, since such cases would bring the employee to the presumably favorable attention of the supervisor. Evaluation of investigators by statistical indices (such as number of violations found) induced them to classify minor mistakes by business men as violations and sometimes led them to avoid investigating the types of business firms that yielded few violations.†

In Chapter 13 of this book, we describe factional divisions within organizations. If policy-makers and administrators belong to opposing factions, the administrators may use bureaucratic routine to implement their own rather than the official policy-makers' goals. For example, Seymour M. Lipset's study of the new socialist government of Saskatchewan showed how social change carried innovating leaders into the government agencies of the province, while the bureaucracy remained filled with persons who had traditional conceptions of government and who preferred to continue familiar administrative routines. The social reforms sought by the elected leaders were reduced and sometimes nullified because of the bureaucrats' power to advise the leaders, to control the kinds of information available to them, and to interpret and actually alter the orders given by them.‡

The next selection, by Philip Selznick, sets the entire problem of goal displacement within a theory of bureaucracy. As he makes clear, Selznick uses the words "bureaucracy" and "bureaucratization" in special ways, to refer to specific processes within organizations, including the displacement of goals. Other selections in this volume, such as Victor A. Thompson's summary in Chapter 8 of Max Weber's writings on bureaucracy, use the term "bureaucracy" in a more general sense to refer to a specific type of formal administrative structure.

* Paul M. Harrison, *Authority and Power in the Free Church Tradition* (Princeton: Princeton University Press, 1959).
† Peter M. Blau, *The Dynamics of Bureaucracy* (Chicago: University of Chicago Press, 2nd ed. rev. 1963). Another study of goal displacement resulting from an over-preoccupation with administrative routines is Arthur K. Davis, "Bureaucratic Patterns in the Navy Officer Corps," *Social Forces*, Volume XXVII (1948), pp. 143-153.
‡ Seymour M. Lipset, *Agrarian Socialism* (Berkeley: University of California Press, 1950), pp. 255-275.

INHERENT TENDENCIES OF BUREAUCRACIES*
Philip Selznick

PROFESSED AND OPERATIONAL GOALS

Running an organization. . . . generates problems that have no necessary (and often an opposed) relation to the professed or "original" goals of the organization. The day-to-day behavior of the group becomes centered around specific problems and proximate goals that have primarily an internal relevance. Since these activities come to consume an increasing proportion of the time and thoughts of the participants, they are—from the point of view of actual behavior—*substituted* for the professed goals.

The day-to-day activity of men is ordered by specific problems of a direct relevance to the materials with which they have to deal. "Ultimate" issues and highly abstract ideas which do not specify any concrete behavior have therefore little direct influence on the bulk of human activities. (The general ideas, of course, may influence action by setting its context and, often, defining its limits.) This is true not because men are evil or unintelligent, but because the "ultimate" formulations are not *helpful* in the constant effort to achieve that series of equilibria which represent behavioral solutions to the specific problems posed by day-to-day living. Besides those professed goals which do not specify any concrete behavior, analogous to nonprocedural formulations in science, there are other professed goals which require actions that conflict with what must be done in the daily business of running an organization. In that conflict the professed goals will tend to go down in defeat, usually through the process of being extensively ignored. This phenomenon may be introduced as a hypothesis in the general theory of organization:

> The actual procedures of every organization tend to be molded by action toward these goals which provide operationally relevant solutions for the daily problems of the organization as such.

This hypothesis does not deny that operational goals may be, and very often are, specified in the formulation of the professed goals of the organization. But in any case it is the operational goals which must be looked to for an understanding of the conduct of the organization.

What is meant by the "daily problems?" Consider a boys' reformatory. The institution is organized on the basis of progressive ideals as specified in the social work literature. But the processes of constructing and operating the organization create problems and de-

* From Philip Selznick, "An Approach to a Theory of Bureaucracy," *American Sociological Review*, Volume 8, Number 1 (February 1943), pp. 48-54. Reprinted with the permission of the author and the publisher, the American Sociological Association.

mands, effective daily, to which the general ideals give no adequate answer. Since, however, the existence of the organization depends upon such answers, and since the way of life of everyone concerned depends on the continued existence of the organization, a set of procedural rules is worked out which is *helpful* in solving these problems. These rules are, in practice, substituted for the professed ideals. "The social work ideals are fine, but how can we do otherwise than use techniques of discipline, regimentation, spying, etc." This is the cry of those who must meet daily crises in the institutions of segregative care. "Holiday speech," "lipservice," "we've got to be practical" are expressions which confirm from ordinary experience, repeated over and over again, the validity of this hypothesis . . .

THE TERM BUREAUCRACY

"Bureaucratic behavior" will designate that behavior of *agents in social action* which:

(1) tends to create the organization-paradox, that is, the modification of the professed aims of the organization—aims toward which the agent is formally supposed to strive; this process obtains

(2) through such behavior patterns in the informal organization as are centered primarily around the ties of influence among the functionaries, and as tend to concentrate the locus of power in the hands of the officials; and

(3) through such patterns as develop through the displacement of the functionaries' motives on the habit level, e.g., routinization.

This does not mean that every situation in which the organization paradox is found is a bureaucratic one. Bureaucracy is concerned with the behavior of officials, while the action of, say, worker groups, may also lead to deflection of an organization. It is clear from this definition that the emphasis is on the *informal* structure as the mechanism or manifestation of bureaucratic patterns; it does not follow, of course, that those patterns are uninfluenced by the character of the formal organization . . .

BUREAUCRATIZATION: A GENERAL FORMULATION

A brief analytical formula stating the general character of the process of bureaucratization may here be introduced:

(1) Co-operative effort, under the conditions of increasing number and complexity of functions, requires the *delegation of functions*. Thus action which

seeks more than limited, individual results becomes *action through agents*. It is the activity of officials acting as agents with which the discussion of bureaucracy is concerned.

(2) The use of intermediaries creates a tendency toward a *bifurcation of interest* between the initiator of the action and the agent employed. This is due to the creation of two sets of problems: for the initiator, the achievement of the goal which spurred him to action, and for the intermediary, problems which are concerned chiefly with his social position as agent. The character of the agent's new values are such as to generate actions whose objective consequences undermine the professed aims of the organization. This conflict need not be between the employer as a person or a group and the agent, for the latter may be able to manipulate the ideas of the former, but between the actual course of the organization and those aims formally asserted, whether the employer recognizes the conflict or not.

(3) This bifurcation of interest makes dominant, for initiator and agent alike, the issue of *control*. What is at stake for each is the control of the conditions (the organizational mechanism) which each group will want to manipulate (not necessarily consciously) toward solving its special problems. In this struggle for control, an *informal structure* is created, based largely on relationships involving personal influences rather than formal rules.

(4) Because of the concentration of skill and the control of the organizational mechanism in the hands of the intermediaries, it becomes possible for the problems of the officials as such to become those which operate *for the organization*. The action of the officials tends to have an increasingly *internal relevance*, which may result in the deflection of the organization from its original path, which, however, usually remains as the formally professed aim of the organization.

THE BUREAUCRATIC LEADER VS. THE RANK AND FILE WHICH EMPLOYS HIM

Utilizing the scheme outlined above, let us examine a concrete type of bureaucratic situation, that which opposes a bureaucratic leader to the rank and file for which he is formally an agent. This situation tends to arise whenever a group of people organize for the attainment of shared objectives, with the additional aim of conducting their organization along democratic lines. Common examples are political parties, trade unions, a national political democracy.

(1) The need for the delegation of functions to a leader arises from the pressure of the wide range of problems, with which every individual must deal in his social existence, against strictly limited time and ability as well as against the social pressures which limit the exercise of certain functions to only some personality types and to members of only some classes. Even in a small group, individual differences in terms of aptitude for the various functions of organized effort (speaker, writer, record-keeper, etc.) play an important role in creating a leader–ranks relationship.

(2) Another bifurcation of problems arises from the fact that the problems and interests which impel men to organization are of a quite different kind from those which occur in running the organization. Whenever the ranks are needed to carry out the work of the organization, this gap becomes of real importance. Spurts in organizational effort on the part of the members occur when a direct connection can be seen between this organizational work and the reason for allegiance to the organization. Thus a political party can get "activity" when it carries on direct political propaganda—but the day-to-day task of keeping the party together, shaping its character, and strengthening its roots in various centers of power are tasks too far divorced from the original problems to stir most people from their ordinary way of living. In a political democracy, too, only heated contests over broad issues can really "bring out the vote," while the day-to-day changes which in the long run are decisive remain uninfluenced by the mass.

(3) There is a hierarchy of values attached to *kinds of work*. Thus even equality between a worker in a unionized plant and the union organizer, in terms of money, does not alter the situation. It is the kind of work involved which is valued above the work of the ordinary members. Not only is there the fact of being well-known (the prestige of bare celebrity), but the facts of having certain powers, however small, of being associated with the incumbent leadership and of being acquainted with the "mysteries" of organization are important. There are always men who *want* to be officials.

(4) Positive valuation of the office as such raises new problems for the bureaucrat. His interest in the ultimate purpose of the organization, or in the "common good," becomes subordinate to his preoccupation with the problems involved in the *maintenance* of his post. This is not the same thing as the attempt to hold on to an official sinecure; for in this case, the post is primarily a source of social prestige and power. In many cases, the leaders could obtain better positions financially in another field. The leader of a women's club who, *because she has a following,* is treated with respect by political or other socially important forces, has more than a merely well-paid position. A. J. Muste, in his discussion of factional fights in trades unions, deals with the problem of why a

leadership seeks to maintain its status.[1] He points to reasons such as those already mentioned: the positions are pleasant, the return to the shop is humiliating, the official tends to become less efficient in his old trade. In addition there are motives connected with what they honestly consider to be the good of the union. They feel that they are better (more competent, have a better policy) than the opposition and that they have given more to the union and deserve to be left in power. This is often quite sincere and even *objectively a correct appraisal*. For our purposes that changes nothing: whether honest or corrupt, the tendency is for leaders to use the same general procedures for the maintenance of their power. This ought not to be surprising: if the question of organizational dominance as such becomes directive in action, and the available means are limited, it is to be expected that the characters of their procedures would converge toward a common type, regardless of their ultimate reasons for desiring dominance.

(5) The delegation of functions introduces a relation of *dependence*. This is enforced by and perhaps directly dependent upon the *professionalization* of the work of the officialdom. To the extent that the necessary knowledge and skill are increased, the possibilities for replacement of the leadership are diminished. The existence of the organization itself becomes dependent on the continued functioning of the incumbent leadership. And so long as this is true, and the ranks still require the organization (or think they require it), their dependence upon the leaders becomes firmly established. This has nothing to do with the existence of formal (e.g. constitutional) procedures for replacing leaders; these may continue to exist, but they are relatively harmless to the intrenched leaders (because functionless) so long as the ranks fear the consequences of using them.

(6) In order to be secure in his position, the leader–bureaucrat must strive to make himself as independent as possible from the ranks. He must seek a power-base which is not controlled by them. He may attempt to derive his strength from an electorate more general than the party or union membership. Thus he will be able to follow independent policies by claiming that he has a responsibility to a broader base than the party ranks; and the ranks cannot do without his influence on outside groups. In a nation, an independent politician tends to cultivate those forces, such as a ruling economic group, which control the instruments which shape mass opinion as well as the electoral machinery, but which are not themselves controlled by the mass. It is a well-established political principle that a politician reacts most sensitively

to those forces to which he owes the maintenance of his position; to the extent that forces can be developed apart from the electorate, he can—and often must, because he becomes dependent on the new force—assert his independence from his formal constituency.

(7) The leader–bureaucrat must seek a personal base *within* the group itself; some mechanism directly dependent on, devoted to, or in alliance with him which can be used to maintain his organizational fences. A class base in a nation, a political faction in a trade union, paid gangsters, an elite guard, a secret police force, proteges and confidants—these are the weapons which he must use in order to be independent of the shifting sands of public favor.

(8) Because of this series of problems which the bureaucrat must face, his action in the name of the group, that is, that activity carried on to further its professed purposes, comes to have more and more a chiefly *internal relevance*. Actions are taken, policies adopted, with an eye more to the effect of the action or policy on the power-relations *inside* the organization than to the achievement of its professed goals. An organization drive in a trade union, party activity, legislative action, even the "activities program" of a club—all come to be oriented toward the problem of self-maintenance before possible onslaughts from the membership. Factors of "morale"—the condition wherein the ranks support the incumbent leadership—become dominant. *Bureaucratization is in a sense the process of transforming this set of procedures from a minor aspect of organization into a leading consideration in the behavior of the leadership.*

(9) Struggles within a group tend to become exclusively struggles *between leaders*. The masses (rank and file) play the role of manipulable weapons in the conflict between the controlling groups. The struggle for control between the initiators and the agent-officials is a very complex problem. The rank and file as a group (and in an important sense the leader, too, because he has to build an apparatus which creates new problems for him) cannot exercise *direct* control. Even a struggle against an incumbent leadership must be carried on through intermediaries. When a faction is formed, it being an organization too, the relations which operated for the organization as a whole come to be effective within the faction. The faction leaders assert their dominance over their groups and come to grips with one another as leaders whose strength is measured by the forces they can deploy. There are, however, three ways in which the influence of the rank and file is felt in a democratic organization: (a) the threat of spontaneous rank and file action and of a consequent internal revolt makes the construction of bureaucratic power-relationships

[1] "Factional Fights in Trade Unions," in J. B. S. Hardman (editor), *American Labor Dynamics* (New York: Harcourt, Brace and Company, 1928).

necessary as a preventive measure; (b) opposing faction leaders tend to champion the professed aim of the organization against the leaders who abandoned it, thus expressing, if temporarily, the desires of the rank and file; and (c) pressure groups, often spontaneous, which do not seek the seizure of the organizational reins, may influence the course of the leadership in directions desired by the mass. This last, however, has usually a limited measure of success precisely because no direct threat to the power of the leadership is offered. It is significant that tolerance of these groups is a function of the extent to which they are interested in "new leadership." . . .

The above discussion emphasizes certain characteristic tendencies in the organizational process.

These tendencies are, however, analytical: they represent abstractions from concrete organizational patterns. To state these tendencies is merely to *set* a problem, for although they ascribe to organizations in general an *initial presumption of bureaucratic consequence*, it always remains to be determined to what degree the bureaucratic tendencies have become dominant. It may be said, indeed, that this is the way organizations will develop if they are permitted to follow the line of least resistance. That is what does happen, often enough. But in the real world of living organizations there is always the possibility of counter-pressure, of devising techniques for blocking the bureaucratic drift.

C. THE SUCCESSION OF GOALS

The process of goal displacement—as Selznick makes clear—generally leads to unanticipated consequences that are pathological for an organization. The tendencies in organizations that lead to pathological goal displacement may, however, lead to the special type of goal displacement that Peter Blau first identified as the succession of goals. That is, an organization may develop new goals to replace goals that have been achieved or rendered irrelevant by changes in the environment.

In the following selection, David L. Sills cites a number of instances of organizations that have developed new goals to replace old ones, and analyzes in greater detail the history of goal succession in four voluntary associations.

GOAL SUCCESSION IN FOUR VOLUNTARY ASSOCIATIONS*
David L. Sills

In order to achieve a perspective through which to approach the topic of the future of the Foundation it is helpful to recall the major conclusions reached by Philip Selznick in his analysis of the relationship between doctrine and action in the Tennessee Valley Authority. Organizations, Selznick notes, develop obligations over a period of time to act in a certain way, obligations which Selznick terms "commitments." He summarizes the importance of these commitments as follows:

> The systematized commitments of an organization define its character. Day-to-day decision, relevant to the actual problems met in the translation of policy into action, create precedents, alliances, effective symbols, and personal loyalties which transform the organization from a profane, manipulable instrument into something having a sacred status and thus resistant to treatment simply as a means of some external goal. This is why organizations are often cast aside when new goals are sought. . . .

> So long as goals are given, and the impulse to act persists, there will be a series of enforced lines of action demanded by the nature of the tools at hand. These commitments may lead to unanticipated consequences resulting in a deflection of original goals.[1]

Although Selznick's research was restricted to one organization, he clearly intended his conclusions to apply to other organizations as well. For this reason, it is appropriate to examine the extent to which this formulation of the consequences of organizational commitments may be said to characterize the situation which may soon confront the Foundation.

The passage cited is composed of two parts. First, it states that "day-to-day decisions" (i.e., those made in order to solve immediate and pressing problems) lead to "commitments" which in turn define the "character" of an organization. Second, it states that this process may have two consequences: an organization may be "deflected from its original goals" and it may be "cast aside when new goals are sought."

[1] Philip Selznick, *TVA and the Grass Roots* (Berkeley and Los Angeles: University of California Press, 1949), pp. 258-59.

Although the major focus of this study has been the current membership and activities of the Foundation, rather than the details of its history, sufficient attention has been given to the circumstances surrounding the original emergence of various features of the organization to document the first of these two statements—that decisions made for the purpose of solving immediate problems often determine the ultimate character of an organization. It has been noted, for example, that the Foundation's almost total dependence upon a fund-raising strategy based upon obtaining small gifts from large numbers of people emerged from two decisions made in the Depression year 1933: to solicit gifts from the people of Georgia in order to finance the construction of a new building at Georgia Warm Springs, and to raise funds nationally by sponsoring President's Birthday Balls; that the characteristically middle-class composition of the Foundation's Volunteer membership may be traced in large part to the decision to ask postmasters, Democrats, and persons of civic prominence generally to organize these Birthday Balls; and that the patient care program is a direct outgrowth of the decision to permit local Committees for the Celebration of the President's Birthday to retain for use in their own communities a portion of the funds raised in 1935. This brief listing of examples suggests the general applicability to the Foundation of this aspect of Selznick's thesis: the Foundation's "character" today is clearly in many respects the result of decisions made with other ends in view.

The second part of Selznick's statement concerns the consequences which may result from the emergence of organizational commitments—goal displacement and the destruction of the organization itself. Sufficient evidence from other studies has been cited throughout this volume to suggest the near-universality of the phenomenon of goal displacement within organizations, and a number of reasons underlying the Foundation's capacity to maintain itself as a goal-oriented organization have been cited. But what of the Foundation's capacity to maintain itself as an organization after its initial goals have been realized, and "new goals are sought"? Will its organizational structure be "cast aside"? It is to be a consideration of these questions that the discussion now turns.

It should be noted first of all that Selznick is not alone in asserting the close relationship between organizational goals and organizational survival. Arnold Rose, for example, has stated that the purposes of voluntary associations are limited and "almost never will an association act for a purpose different from the original one which brought the members together." [2] And the Kluckhohns have observed that

"American associations are also a way that an anti-feudalistic society chooses to 'get things done.' We form thousands of organizations to accomplish a specific purpose and then dissolve them." [3]

It is not difficult to find illustrations in American history which document the truth of these assertions. For example, two important voluntary associations in our early history, the Sons of Liberty and the Committees of Correspondence, were dissolved when the anti-British purposes for which they were established culminated in the American Revolution and the establishment of the Continental Congress. Sometimes organizations decline long before their goals are achieved, as, for example, the American Anti-Slavery Society, which split through internal dissension and controversy over policy matters some twenty years before the Emancipation Proclamation. And sometimes they are dissolved when their functions are taken over by governmental bodies, as happened to the Public School Society of New York City when the public school system was established.

THE SUCCESSION OF GOALS

Dissolution, however, is not the only course of action open to an organization when its purposes are either achieved or become irrelevant because of changes in the social environment; in fact, it is equally easy to find examples of organizations which have remained intact for the purpose of working toward new or sharply modified objectives. Peter Blau has called this process the "succession of goals," which he states is "the reverse of the displacement of goals." [4] He describes the process in these terms:

> The attainment of organizational objectives generates a strain toward finding new objectives. To provide incentives for its members and to justify its existence, an organization has to adopt new goals as its old ones are realized. Unions illustrate this transformation of ends into means. After a union establishes the right of collective bargaining, this original objective becomes a means for the accomplishment of new objectives, such as pensions and seniority rights for workers. [5]

Unions are of course not the only illustration of the tendency of organizations to seek new objectives, nor do organizations necessarily wait until the achieve-

---

2 Arnold M. Rose, *Theory and Method in the Social Sci-ences* (Minneapolis: University of Minnesota Press, 1954), p. 58.

3 Clyde Kluckhohn and Florence R. Kluckhohn, "American Culture: Generalized Orientations and Class Patterns," in Lyman Bryson, Louis Finkelstein, and R. M. MacIver (eds.), *Conflicts of Power in Modern Culture* (New York: Harper and Brothers, 1947), p. 116.

4 Peter M. Blau, *The Dynamics of Bureaucracy* (Chicago: University of Chicago Press, 1955), p. 195. See also Peter M. Blau, *Bureaucracy in Modern Society* (New York: Random House, 1956), pp. 95-96.

5 Blau, *The Dynamics of Bureaucracy*, p. 195.

ment of their original objectives before they establish new ones. The American Legion, to cite one example, was originally established in order to preserve the spirit which characterized the American Expeditionary Force in World War I, but it very soon included in its objectives the protection of the rights of veterans and, particularly among local Posts, the instigation of community service projects. Dartmouth College, to cite another example, was originally founded primarily in order to educate and Christianize the Indians of New England, but it experienced no great difficulty in transforming itself into a general liberal arts college.

Voluntary health and welfare agencies exhibit similar tendencies. The Birth Control Federation, for example, in 1942 adopted the more comprehensive name of the Planned Parenthood Federation of America, and has since that time expanded its objectives to include treatment for infertility, education for marriage, and marriage counseling.[6] The American Social Hygiene Association, which has traditionally concerned itself with combating both prostitution and venereal diseases, has in recent years adjusted to the decline in organized prostitution and the drastic lowering of the incidence of venereal diseases, and has established such new objectives as supporting family life education and preparing high school boys for the social and psychological strains which they will undergo during military service.[7] In fact, thousands of organizations of all kinds have adapted in one way or another to external conditions affecting the relevance of their objectives, but there have been very few systematic analyses of such organizations from this point of view. It is therefore instructive to examine briefly the process of organizational adaptation as it has taken place in four organizations for which relatively complete information is available. Two of these organizations, the Woman's Christian Temperance Union and the Townsend Organization, have failed to adjust themselves to a changed environment, and exist today as fossil remains of their previous life. The other two, the Young Men's Christian Association and the American National Red Cross, have made highly successful adaptations.

THE YOUNG MEN'S CHRISTIAN ASSOCIATION

Although there have been a number of organizational histories of the Y.M.C.A., Owen Pence's volume, *The Y.M.C.A. and Social Need*, is most useful for an examination of the Y.M.C.A. as an illustration of the process of organizational adaptation.[8] The book is sub-titled, "A Study of Institutional Adaptation"; more specifically, it is an examination of how the goals of the Y.M.C.A. have changed in response to various changes in the social environment, particularly the secularization of American society which has taken place in the past century.

Today the Y.M.C.A. places a great deal of emphasis upon the opportunities for recreation and physical exercise which it offers, but the first Association in London stated that its objective was "to improve the spiritual condition of young men engaged in the drapery and other trades"; the first Association in America, in Boston, expanded its objective to include "the improvement of the spiritual and mental condition of young men"; and the first New York Association included in its objectives the following:

> The object of this Association shall be the improvement of the spiritual, mental, and social condition of young men . . . to bring them under moral and religious influences, by aiding them in the selection of suitable boarding places and employment. . . .[9]

With the passing years, as Pence shows, the Y.M.C.A. has devoted increasing attention to its physical and social goals, and less attention to its original religious and spiritual aims. This transition is summarized in these terms:

> In contrast with the conception of earlier years, when the principal concern of the Association was with the securing of individual commitments to the Christian life, the realization has steadily grown in recent years that religious living and interests are so gravely conditioned by the total social experience that the two cannot be dealt with separately.[10]

And again, in more direct language:

> In time, the Association began to take their objectives for granted. In their place activity (that is, whatever met and satisfied expressed interests of members), became the real objective.[11]

The Y.M.C.A., therefore, is an example of an organization whose goals have changed not because they were achieved, but rather because of fundamental changes in the social environment in which its activities were carried out. The "spiritual improvement" of young men has come to be regarded as less relevant than it was in the 19th century, and other activities have achieved greater relevance. As a result, the organization's membership has been broadened to include boys, women and non-Protestants; profession-

[6] Planned Parenthood Federation of America, *Birth Control U.S.A.: Highlights of the Program*, p. 8; *The Most Important Thing*, p. 3.

[7] American Social Hygiene Association, *Social Hygiene News*, April, 1955.

[8] Owen E. Pence, *The Y.M.C.A. and Social Need* (New York: Association Press, 1939).

[9] *Ibid.*, p. 12.

[10] *Ibid.*, p. 315.

[11] *Ibid.*, p. 236.

ally-trained group leaders have often replaced the original laymen who served as volunteer workers; and an increased emphasis has been placed upon the construction of adequate buildings in which to carry out its broadened program.

Today the Y.M.C.A. is a highly successful organization, and it would be presumptuous to suggest that its success bears no relationship to the Christian ideals held by so many of its leaders. In fact, if its original objective had been to provide recreational facilities to "young men engaged in the drapery and other trades," it is highly probable that it would exist today only as some sort of athletic club in London. But the evidence is also quite clear that its success is in large part attributable to the fact that it has had the flexibility, in keeping with its Christian ideals, to redefine its objectives in accordance with the needs of the society which it serves.

THE WOMAN'S CHRISTIAN TEMPERANCE UNION

The central problem which led Joseph Gusfield to study the W.C.T.U. is the fact that changes in American drinking habits and the increased acceptance of drinking as a part of general social life "have presented the W.C.T.U. with an environment more hostile to the doctrine of total abstinence than was true in the years of the organization's formation and development." [12] In the face of this situation, Gusfield sought both to determine "whether the change in environment has led to changes in the goals and doctrine of the movement" and to explain "changes, or lack of change, in the organization." [13]

In many respects, the Y.M.C.A. and the W.C.T.U. have had similar histories. Both organizations were established at a time when a powerful middle class believed that its mission was to improve the social conditions under which the lower class lived. The Y.M.C.A. sought to improve these conditions by Christianizing and educating young men; the W.C.T.U. believed that working class people could enjoy the benefits of middle class life if they stopped drinking— "drink is the curse of the working classes" was a popular slogan of the 19th century temperance movement.[14] And both organizations have survived in spite of a sharp decline in the popularity of these theories of humanitarian reform. But they differ greatly in the manner in which they have survived.

As previously indicated, the Y.M.C.A.'s history has

been characterized by successive adjustments to its social environment. The W.C.T.U., on the other hand, has not adjusted:

> Today the W.C.T.U. is an organization in retreat. Contrary to the expectations of theories of institutionalization, the movement has not acted to preserve organizational values at the expense of past doctrine.[15]

How has this been possible? As Gusfield shows, the W.C.T.U. has not abandoned its goal of establishing temperance norms, but has instead shifted its attention to a new audience. Originally the organization was composed largely of middle- and upper middle-class women who sought both to dissuade working class people from drinking and to improve their general welfare in other ways; today it is less upper middle-class and more lower middle- and working-class in composition, and its chief target is the drinking habits of middle-class groups. In short, the W.C.T.U. has elected *not* to change its goals to meet changed conditions, although Gusfield suggests two courses of action it might have taken:

> One possible position would be a reversal of past doctrine and the embracing of a doctrine of moderate drinking. This would be the acceptance of the new standard of the middle classes. Another possibility might be a de-emphasis of temperance aims and a substitution of other aims, such as those of a social welfare nature or an attack on "popular" enemies, such as drug addiction or juvenile delinquency.[16]

Instead, the organization has changed the composition of its membership, limited its goals to the discouragement of middle-class drinking, and shifted its strategy from active campaigning against intemperance to indulging in what Gusfield terms "moral indignation." [17]

THE TOWNSEND ORGANIZATION

The Y.M.C.A. is an example of an organization which has succeeded through successive adaptations to its social environment; the W.C.T.U. is an organization which is in a state of decline because of its failure to adjust to changes in its environment; and the Townsend Organization, as Sheldon Messinger has demonstrated, is one which has nearly vanished because its major goal, alleviating or preventing economic dislocation, has at least temporarily been achieved—not, however, through the efforts of the organization.[18]

12 Joseph R. Gusfield, "Social Structure and Moral Reform: A Study of the Woman's Christian Temperance Union," *American Journal of Sociology*, 61 (1955), pp. 221-32. The discussion in the text is based entirely upon this study.
13 *Ibid.*, p. 222.
14 *Ibid.*, p. 225.

15 *Ibid.*, p. 232.
16 *Ibid.*, p. 228.
17 *Ibid.*
18 Sheldon L. Messinger, "Organizational Transformation: A Case Study of a Declining Social Movement," *American Sociological Review*, 20 (1955), pp. 3-10. The discussion which follows is based largely upon this study. See Arnold W. Green, *Sociology* (New York: McGraw-

Dr. Francis E. Townsend first proposed his plan to end the Depression by retiring all United States citizens at the age of sixty on a monthly pension of $200 in September, 1933; by 1936 the Townsend Organization had 2,250,000 members. In 1935, however, the Social Security Act was passed, and by 1951 the organization had only 56,656 members, a loss of more than 97 per cent.[19] In the intervening years, the expansion of social security legislation, of pension plans by private employers, and of the national economy itself largely eliminated public interest in a program designed to end the Depression of the 1930's. In the face of these changes in the relevance of its original goals, how has the Townsend Organization survived at all?

Messinger outlines three organizational transformations which have taken place. First, there has been a tendency to support other measures affecting the aged, a tendency which the leaders themselves have checked since they realized it could lead only to a break-up of the organization. Second, there has been a tendency to obtain financial support by selling consumer goods of one kind or another, e.g., vitamin pills. Finally, there has been a tendency to convert membership meetings into social gatherings, and to hold other social events as well. On the basis of these tendencies, as well as of other aspects of the transformation of the Townsend Organization, Messinger draws this conclusion:

> The organized arms of declining social movements will tend to adapt to these changed conditions in characteristic ways. We can broadly describe this adaptation by asserting that the dominating orientation of leaders and members shifts *from the implementation of the values the organization is taken to represent* (by leaders, members, and public alike), *to maintaining the organizational structure as such,* even at the loss of the organization's central mission.[20]

The Townsend Organization, in short, has adjusted to changes in its environment in ways quite different from those followed by the W.C.T.U. Instead of modifying its membership and its goals, it has virtually abandoned its original goals and has concentrated its attention, not very successfully, upon maintaining its organizational structure.

THE AMERICAN NATIONAL RED CROSS[21]

Like the Y.M.C.A., the Red Cross is a highly successful organization, and for much the same reasons: it has made successive adjustments to changes in its social environment. Its initial objective, as set forth in its first constitution, was "to hold itself in readiness in the event of war or any calamity great enough to be considered national, to inaugurate such practical measures in mitigation of the suffering and for the protection and relief of sick and wounded as may be consistent with the objects of the Association. . . ."[22] The organization was small in its early years, and floods and other disasters, the Spanish–American War, and most importantly, World War I, provided sufficient challenges to its resources to make any expansion of its objectives unnecessary. The end of World War I, however, found a greatly expanded Red Cross without an objective of sufficient scope to maintain the organization. There was a decline in membership interest, and the leaders feared the organization would suffer. Foster Dulles has summarized this crisis in the Red Cross's history in these terms:

> The officers of the Red Cross, discouraged but not dismayed, were determined to find a way out in spite of chapter apathy. There was a natural desire on their part to see the American Red Cross maintain its position and still further broaden its field of usefulness, not only for the sake of whatever contributions could be made toward improving the conditions of American life, *but for the sake of the organization itself.*[23]

This crisis was surmounted by adopting a new program—"the preservation and improvement of the public health"[24]—and the Red Cross had no need to question the adequacy of its objectives until the Depression of the 1930's, when there was disagreement among the leaders concerning the role the organization should play in dispensing unemployment relief.[25] But the most severe test to date of the adequacy of the Red Cross's objectives came at the end of World War II, when again a greatly expanded organization found that its capacity to act outpaced its goals. Furthermore, there now existed a new threat to the organization—the increased intervention of the Government in welfare and relief activities as a result of the responsibilities it had assumed during the Depression and War years. "Clouds are appearing on the disaster relief horizon," wrote one Red Cross disaster worker in 1946. "Government today is rendering a number of services to disaster sufferers that were rendered by Red Cross disaster relief 10, 15, or 20 years ago."[26] This new crisis was summarized by Basil O'Connor, who was then National Chairman of the American Red Cross, at the 1949 annual convention, in a

Hill Book Co., 1956), pp. 547-55, for further details of the Townsend Movement.
[19] Messinger, *op. cit.,* p. 4.
[20] *Ibid.,* p. 10.
[21] The discussion of the Red Cross in the text is based

entirely upon Foster R. Dulles, *The American Red Cross: A History* (New York: Harper and Brothers, 1950).
[22] Cited in Dulles, *op. cit.,* p. 16.
[23] *Ibid.,* p. 218. Italics supplied.
[24] *Ibid.,* p. 219.
[25] *Ibid.,* pp. 276-94.
[26] Cited in *ibid.,* p. 521.

speech entitled "Can the Red Cross Survive?" Dulles summarizes this speech as follows:

> The convention delegates were told that it was not only necessary to re-evaluate the mission of the American Red Cross, but to ask themselves the fundamental question of whether an organization founded in the remote past of the nineteenth century still had any place at all in the vastly altered world of the mid-twentieth century. O'Connor's own answer was strongly affirmative.[27]

It was of course not sufficient to give an affirmative answer to this question; it was necessary as well to establish new objectives and new activities. These were found in "the adoption of a national blood donor program as the core of its peacetime activities apart from disaster relief." [28] In this way the most recent crisis has been met, and the Red Cross has both maintained an active program and obtained adequate volunteer and public support in the postwar years. The decision to embark upon this program was made with full realization of its implications for the organization's survival:

> Apart from meeting a very real need, the national blood program also appeared the best possible thing for the Red Cross to undertake on its own account. Just as health activities had been promoted after the First World War to give the chapters something to do as well as to advance public health, so the new project was expected to provide an outlet for volunteer activity in the new period of peace which would bring together, in one unified undertaking, the varied interests of the volunteer services.[29]

This brief review of the history of four organizations has of necessity mentioned only a few of the major conclusions reached by the authors cited. Nevertheless, it has called attention to the fact that organizations are by no means necessarily "cast aside when new goals are sought" and indicated some of the ways in which organizations have adjusted to changes in their environment and the relevancy of their goals. Furthermore, the histories of these four organizations suggest that the fate of an organization after its goals have been either achieved or rendered irrelevant cannot be determined on *a priori* grounds, but is rather a resultant of a given set of forces. "What," Blau asks, "determines whether displacement of goals or succession of goals predominates in an organization?" [30] Although he admits that this crucial question can be answered only in part, Blau does suggest two determining factors: "structural constraints in the organization" and acceptance on the part of the community. "When the community permits an organization . . . to become established and attain at least some of its first objectives in a relatively short period, it will probably find new fields to conquer in the course of its development." [31]

[27] *Ibid.*, p. 527.
[28] *Ibid.*
[29] *Ibid.*, p. 528.
[30] Blau, *Bureaucracy in Modern Society*, p. 95.
[31] *Ibid.*, pp. 95-96.

A. PERSONNEL

In order to achieve its goals, an organization must continually secure both people and funds from its environment. The voluntary association has the double problem of recruiting unpaid volunteers as well as salaried employees. Leaders of voluntary associations must learn the personal and social characteristics of their volunteers and the reasons why they volunteer, in order to know where to recruit volunteers and how to keep them.

Chapter 3 of this book includes two selections that indicate which sectors of American society provide many and which provide few members. Such participation data are now plentiful, but few studies have yet been made of the characteristics of an individual association's voluntary workers and the motivational process that brought them to the association. In their selection, Seth Arsenian and Arthur Blumberg report the results of a small survey of Y.M.C.A. volunteers. They found that active participation in an association is part of a general mode of life in which the individual participates in other primary social groups (such as active family and visiting patterns) and often in a few other voluntary associations. Personal influence is important in recruiting a volunteer; often he is asked to join by a friend with whom he has worked in some other group or voluntary association.

Such research could be conducted in any association—and would give guidelines to leaders. If the findings about the social determinants of recruitment are repeated, they would show the importance of an organized campaign to secure new volunteers through the influence of the current volunteers and friends of the association. Perhaps no association can rely completely on self-recruited volunteers. On the other hand, some findings—such as the high social class background of Y.M.C.A. board members—might cause some leaders to wonder whether or not their present recruitment patterns are adequate.

VOLUNTEERS IN THE Y.M.C.A.*

Seth Arsenian and Arthur Blumberg

The Young Men's Christian Association is a volunteer organization, both in membership as well as in leadership. The "Y" carries on its work for over two million members almost entirely by volunteer leaders. There is one volunteer worker for each five members, while the number of its employed officers is only about one for five hundred members. The problems of understanding, recruiting, selecting, training, supervising, and meeting the legitimate needs of the volunteer workers is of tremendous importance in the Y.M.C.A. A staff committee of the Baltimore Y.M.C.A. in a recent article . . . states: "Therefore, it behooves every Y.M.C.A. Secretary to give his whole-hearted effort to discovering, enlisting, and developing laymen . . . because maintenance and development of the lay character of the Movement is a fundamental method of accomplishing our purpose and of maintaining our direction and rootage." [1] This same article describes types of services involving laymen and gives a list of suggestions for locating, enlisting, and developing laymen in Y.M.C.A. But what do we know, in a systematic way, of our laymen or volunteers—who they are, why and how they came into the "Y", or how well the "Y" meets their expectations and needs, of how effectively it utilizes the abilities and energies of the volunteers. Undoubtedly a certain set of assumptions and attitudes guides the work of individual secretaries in recruiting or utiliz-

* From Seth Arsenian and Arthur Blumberg, "Volunteers in the Y.M.C.A.," *Association Forum,* Volume 40, Number 6 (November-December 1959), pp. 4-9. Reprinted with the permission of the authors and the publisher, The Young Men's Christian Association.

[1] "The Secretary Works With and Through Laymen," *Association Forum,* July-August 1958.

ing their volunteer help, but are there any systematic studies examining these assumptions and attitudes and testing their validity or their relative fruitfulness against some empirical facts and findings? We have not found such studies in the Y.M.C.A. In fact there are very few scientific studies on volunteerism outside the Y.M.C.A. And yet the topic is of primary importance not only for the "Y" but for all other community organizations whose very existence and services depend on the participation and leadership of volunteers.

In this article we are presenting a brief report, shorn of its technical niceties, of some of the findings of a pilot study which grew out of certain discussions on volunteer leadership in the Research Council of the National Board of the Y.M.C.A. in 1956. The findings to be reported are based on a study sample of . . . Y.M.C.A. volunteer workers—about one-half board members, and the other half group leaders—in Massachusetts and Rhode Island [2] . . .

We of course make no claim for the adequacy of our sample. Our results may not be representative of the volunteer situation in the entire Y.M.C.A. Our generalizations must be limited to our sample of participant volunteers. Since this was a pilot study we were much less concerned with definitive findings than with pointing out issues, suggesting methods, recommending research investigations, and making a strong plea for systematic studies of this important problem in the Y.M.C.A.

CERTAIN CHARACTERISTICS OF "Y" VOLUNTEERS

Certain of the characteristics of the volunteers in our sample were as follows:

AGE

The board members ranged in age from 30 to 78 with a median of 48, and the group leaders from 14 to 54 with a median age of 34. Approximately 50% of the total group was in the age range of 30 to 47. It is apparent that the characteristic age range for volunteers is middle age and that the board members as a group are definitely older than the group leaders.

SEX

The volunteers belong predominantly to the male sex. It is noteworthy, however, that 18% of the board members, and 23% of these group leaders are female. This development is probably new in the Association, but it will be worth observing its increase and its influence in the Y.M.C.A. program.

[2] The number of people who completed and returned the questionnaire was 93 . . . of this number, 49 were group leaders and 44 were board members.

MARITAL STATUS AND CHILDREN PER FAMILY

Ninety-one percent of the board members and 61% of the group leaders are married persons. The median number of children in the board-member families was 3, that in the group-leader families was 1.5. The difference is probably accounted for by the younger age range of the group leaders.

RELIGIOUS AFFILIATION

Eighty-one percent of the volunteers are Protestant, 17% Catholic, and 2% Jewish. It should be noted, however, that while 23% of the group leaders are Catholic, only 9% of the board members are of that faith. It is possible that this reflects more of a willingness of the Catholics to become involved on the activity level than on the management and policy-making level. On the other hand, it may reflect the selection policies of the general secretary in regard to his board. A third possibility, not involved in this particular study, would be concerned with the character of the constituency of a particular association.

FORMAL EDUCATION

Sixty-five percent of the board members and 37% of the group leaders have been to college or graduate school. Further analysis of our figures raises some interesting questions. It is quite evident that a greater number of board members have college and graduate education than have group leaders, a majority of whom went no further than high school. This would seem to have some relationship, though not necessarily a causal one, to the matter of selection and recruitment of board members. Whether by chance or design, selection of board members is related to the amount of education one has. If this is the case (we bear in mind the age differential and student status of a number of group leaders) it would seem that group leaders have less than an equal chance of rising to board membership. Whether or not this is desirable is another question, but in light of the possibility of greater potential involvement in the Y.M.C.A. by group leaders, this would appear to be a problem for further study and consideration.

OCCUPATION

Seventy-four percent of the board members and thirty-seven percent of the group leaders occupied executive, supervisory or professional positions. In general, the board members seem to hold a higher level of elevation on the community status ladder. The question which arises, and which can not be answered by our data, is whether or not the group leaders as they grow older will occupy these same occupational positions. Or, are we dealing here with essentially two discontinuous groups, whereby as in the formal education picture, the group leaders are not likely to become board members.

COMMUNITY ACTIVITIES

Both board members and group leaders are involved in other community activities. The average number of memberships for board members is 5.2 and for group leaders is 3.3. Actually, board members are involved in 63% more organizations on a membership level and 56% more on a leadership level than are the group leaders.

It is interesting to note that the March of Dimes volunteers also participate in a number of other community organizations; "Seven out of every ten belong to at least three other organizations than the Foundation." [3] One wonders if there is a general trait of volunteerism. In other words, certain people in a community do not volunteer, others do, and when they do they belong to more than one voluntary organization or activity.

RESIDENCE IN THE COMMUNITY

The median length of residence for the board members was 22 years, that for group leaders was 16 years. Further examination of our figures indicates that no board member had less than six years of continuous residence while 17% of the group leaders had been living in the community for five years or less. It is apparent that in both cases reasonably long residence in the community seems to be the prevailing condition, and especially so, for board members. This picture is in harmony with the findings of Sills for the Foundation Volunteers.[4]

PREVIOUS Y.M.C.A EXPERIENCE

One-half the board members and two-thirds of the group leaders had previous Y.M.C.A. experience. It would seem that previous experience with the "Y" is more of an attendant condition for group leaders than for board members whose position and prestige in the community were of greater importance. Also, there is some indication in our data that those whose previous experience was rated "very satisfactory" played more frequently a leadership function in the "Y."

CHURCH MEMBERSHIP ACTIVITY

Ninety-eight percent of the board members and eighty-two percent of the group leaders were members of churches. As a group, the board members considered themselves more active in church affairs than did the group leaders.

PARENTAL FAMILY ACTIVITY IN COMMUNITY AND/OR CHURCH AFFAIRS

Sixty-eight percent of the board members' and fifty-one percent of the group leaders' parental families were reported active in community and church activities. It seems then that there is some relationship between parental and filial participation in voluntary activities. In other words, volunteers in Y.M.C.A. are more likely to come from families where there has been a tradition of voluntary activity in Y.M.C.A. or other community affairs.

In general, one may characterize the volunteer in Y.M.C.A. as having the following characteristics: he is a middle aged person, somewhat older if he is a board member; he is male, although a few females enter and participate more frequently at the activity level; he is more likely to be a married person and to have children; he is more likely to be a Protestant, although Catholics and Jews, depending upon the character of the community also participate; his formal education is above the average of the general American population, and he is more than likely a college graduate if he is a board member; he comes from the middle class and higher echelons of occupations, the latter more true if he is a board member; he is generally active in and a relatively long resident of his community, especially true of board members; he is an active church member; he comes from a family that has traditionally been and is currently active in church and other community activities; he, and more likely his parents, have had some satisfying experience with Y.M.C.A. where they have played some leadership role. There are of course always some variations, but these are some of the apparent characteristics of the volunteer in Y.M.C.A.

WHY VOLUNTEERS VOLUNTEER

The problem of motivation in volunteering is a complex and difficult one. The results of the very few studies we have on this topic are controversial. Some investigators have suggested that the volunteer is a maladjusted person: he is running away from himself, or is in dire need of security, belongingness, or importance and rushes to join any social movement that promises these things like the Kingdom of Father Divine, the Townsend Plan, or the Nazi Party.[5] Other investigators have pointed out that the volunteer is a relatively well-adjusted person and has leadership qualities, that he is moved by humanitarian fervor, and missionary zeal to help others, to serve his soci-

3 David L. Sills, *The Volunteers* (Glencoe: The Free Press, 1957), p. 30.
4 *Ibid.*, p. 30.

5 John T. Bair and Thomas J. Gallagher, "Volunteering for Extra-Hazardous Duty," *Research Reviews O.V.R.*, November 1958; Hadley Cantril, *The Psychology of Social Movements* (New York: John Wiley and Sons, 1941).

ety, and that essentially he is a person seeking healthy self-fulfillment.[6] It is likely that these conclusions point to the two ends of a motivational dimension, and that the total dynamics of the volunteer may involve both healthy and pathological motivations, and that his influence on persons he "serves" may be both good and bad, depending in good measure upon the character of his motivations. What we know about motivation is that a good part of it is unconscious and the individual may not know what is moving him in certain directions he "wants" to go. Our own study did not delve into the unconscious motivations of the "Y" volunteers. It did, however, attempt to look into some motivational factors and the satisfactions that the volunteers said they derived from their volunteer work in Y.M.C.A.

To begin with, the volunteers participating in our study were asked to fill out a well known inventory on relative dominance of values.[7] The analysis of results shows that the "Y" volunteer group, both board members and group leaders, fall within the average range of the general population but that in respect to the relative dominance of six values assessed, they stand in the order of: religious, social, theoretical, economic, political, and aesthetic. This order of values is the same in both board member and group leader groups, although in the latter group there is greater variability and somewhat lower average score in religious values. This difference in the two groups may be accounted for, in part or entirely, by the relative youth of the group leaders. We do not have any precise information as to the reasons for this difference, nor whether or not this kind of difference may be expected in all comparisons of the religious values of board members and group leaders. Additional research will tell.

In addition to values, interests also play a directive role in an individual's behavior. We, therefore, used another well-known inventory, namely, the Kuder Preference Record—Vocational, Form C.[8] Without giving all the details of the analysis of the results of this inventory it will suffice to say that the interest pattern of board members and group leaders was very similar, and that on the average the preferred occupational interests of "Y" volunteers fall in social service, musical, artistic, literary, and persuasive fields rather than in mechanical, scientific, computational, clerical and outdoor occupational fields. It is to be noted that even if some of these people are employed in mechan-

ical or clerical occupations yet their interest patterns fall in the social service field. This may be accounted for either by the fact that some of these people are dissatisfied with their actual jobs and are seeking by volunteer work to satisfy their human relations interests, or that while employed in mechanical or clerical occupations they may hold positions that have more human relations than mechanical aspects or responsibilities.

With reference to the results of both the values and interest inventories, which have been reported but briefly, one must bear in mind that there are great individual differences and that we have here talked only about averages, which sometimes are quite different from the actual, individual case you and we might know.

In addition to the use of standardized inventories we asked directly of the volunteers the reasons for their present Y.M.C.A. involvement. . . . The factor most frequently mentioned is that the volunteer was *asked* by some one for his participation. Certainly some favorable motivation to participate must be present, but that alone is not sufficient in most instances. People will not run to the Y.M.C.A. to volunteer their services, they want to be asked (one might presume that in instances of strong, perhaps pathological, motivation the volunteer will push his volunteerism on others even when not asked or encouraged). Secondly, an agreement with or commitment to Y.M.C.A. principles is hardly mentioned. It may be that this is involved in whatever other motivation is stated by the volunteer. It may be that other inducements to enter volunteer work are more influential than the commitment. It would be interesting to follow up the careers of volunteers who join the "Y" seeing there a mission and commitment and others who state other considerations.

Another pertinent item may be mentioned. There seems to be an increasing tendency on the part of some business or industrial organizations to encourage the participation of their employees in church and community affairs. In some cases the motives are probably idealistic, in other cases "it is good public relations." A very substantial majority of both board members and group leaders stated that the companies or organizations in which they were employed encouraged participation in community activities by means such as: giving the employees necessary time off, paying membership and other participation fees, making use of the house organ to publicize activities, the higher executives setting example, in some instances requesting and generally looking favorably on those employees who did volunteer work. Here again it will be worth investigating further the extent of company encouragement or possibly coercion for "volunteer" participation of their employees, the in-

[6] Eduard C. Lindeman, "Motivations of Volunteers in Community Service," *Community Chests and Councils in America*, 1948, mimeographed; Sills, *op. cit.*; Bair, *op. cit.*
[7] G. W. Allport, P. E. Vernon, and G. Lindzey, *Study of Values* (Boston: Houghton Mifflin Company, Revised Edition, 1951).
[8] Published by Science Research Associates, Chicago, Illinois.

fluence of this on the "volunteer," or the quality of his participation in the Y.M.C.A.

The final question of our questionnaire also dealt with motivation. We asked the volunteers to state in their own words the satisfactions which they derived from Y.M.C.A. work as a volunteer. . . .

TABLE I

Satisfactions derived from Y.M.C.A. work

	Number of times mentioned by:	
	Board members	Group leaders
Service to others	17	22
Fellowship	11	1
Sense of civic duty upheld	11	0
Being part of a developing institution	5	1
Holding high regard for the purposes of Y.M.C.A.	4	0
* Am able to see individuals and groups develop	4	18
Enjoy interracial and religious cooperation	2	1
Pride in accomplishment	0	8
Learning to work with others	0	6
† Feeling of helping others as I was	0	6
Watching children enjoy themselves	0	5
Recognition	0	4
Enjoy what I do	0	3
Meet new people	0	3
Establishing a close relationship with a group	0	3
Enjoy working with the professional staff	1	2
Gives me greater understanding of people	0	2
Personal development	3	2
Participation in wholesome Christian activities involving youth	2	0
Religious reasons	2	0

* For group leaders this category should read "Am able to work with and see. . . ."
† A differentiation is made between this item and the first on the list because of what seems to be a verbalized antecedent for satisfactions perceived.

These results provide a number of interesting observations. It is understood that some of these are verbalizations, that is, they represent what the volunteers feel they *should* say. It is important to note what they do say or omit to say. First of all, there seems to be some difference between the patterns of satisfaction of board members and group leaders. For the board members the most frequent satisfactions perceived are "service," "fellowship," and "civic duty." It is likely that these people, older in age, better and longer settled in the community and their respective occupations, and assumedly economically much better off than the group leaders, who are still on the initial rungs of the occupational and economic ladder, feel a sense of obligation and freely devote their efforts to the welfare of others. It may also be that there are other satisfactions, unstated or unanalyzed, such as prestige, importance, example to others, "noblesse oblige," which are operative. Only additional research can tell us of the true set of motivations involved. Among the group leaders, in addition to the stated "service" motive, the other satisfactions center around learning, doing, watching people grow. The stated motivations in this group show greater variability, are more concrete and perhaps more realistic.

It is interesting that in neither group is the voluntary participation predicated on "holding high regard for the purposes of Y.M.C.A.", "wholesome Christian activities involving youth," "religious reasons," etc. Are such motivations no longer socially or personally admissible? Would these people just as readily volunteer in some other agency? Is there some uniqueness to the purposes of Y.M.C.A.? Are the Y.M.C.A. purposes made manifest to the volunteers? Does this matter? Here is a host of questions which arise and must wait for the results of additional studies.

Several decades ago, when personnel screening was introduced into business and government, the problem was considered quite simple: criteria of desirable personalities would be adopted; testing techniques would be developed; job applicants with the desired personalities would be hired and the others rejected. This scheme has for the most part failed because, among other reasons, the problem has been incorrectly defined. The candidate is not being considered for employment in general but for a particular job, and each job has certain requirements. Someone with apparently attractive personality traits may or may not be suitable for the particular job requirements in question. A second defect with the traditional approach is *that no organization gets a sufficient supply of ideal applicants: an organization must hire imperfect people.**

Personnel psychologists have recently developed a different approach. Ideally, a job description is developed for each opening, potential employees' personalities are assessed for suitability, and persons are assigned to those jobs where they can perform best. If certain jobs seem to have excessively demanding job descriptions, they may be reorganized to fit the available personnel. For example, if a job description expects the incumbent to perform certain specialized tasks and also to supervise several assistants, and if no one is available to perform both the technical and supervisory functions, the work may be divided and redistributed in accordance with the capacities of the candidates. The personnel psychologist has become an analyst of organizational structure as well as of individual personalities.†

Several psychologists have become interested in the mutual adaptation of organizations and individual personalities from the standpoint of mental health. Specialized jobs, repetitive tasks, unexplained orders, individual powerlessness, and many other characteristics of some organizations bore and frustrate employees. If many people in a society are bored and frustrated, warn these psychologists, considerable unrest and deviant behavior will result. Besides the cost for the larger society, the organization itself will not achieve its greatest stability and productivity. These authors recommend the reorganization of work and social relationships within organizations in order to give the individual a greater sense of variety, meaning, and power in his job.‡

To enable them to put their advice into practice, an increasing number of organizations has retained psychologists as members of management or as consultants. Some provide advice about how to organize work and select personnel. Others conduct management workshops designed to instruct executives and foremen in the sensitive understanding and supervision of personnel.

B. FUND RAISING

Since the leader of a voluntary association often must depend heavily on volunteers for fund-raising, he must understand the motives and satisfactions of fund-raisers. Some of these motives can be used to gain more volunteers and raise more funds; others may limit what an association can accomplish.§ In the next selection, David L. Sills reports the motives and activities of voluntary fund-raisers in the National Foundation. Similar questionnaire surveys could be carried out among voluntary fund-raisers in other associations, although the differences in their organizational goals

---

* An important turning point in personnel psychology was World War II, when some of America's leading psychologists were asked to develop the best possible selection techniques for the Office of Strategic Services and for the United States Army Air Force. The experiences of this period pointed up the defects in traditional psychological screening, among them the failure to fit screening techniques to specific job descriptions. The O.S.S. Assessment Staff's work is described in their book, *Assessment of Men* (New York: Rinehart & Company, 1948). Parenthetically, World War II was also an important period of public recognition and research experience for the sociologists and social psychologists. Many of them worked for the Research Branch that studied the social organization of the U. S. Army. See Samuel Stouffer *et al.*, *Studies in Social Psychology in World War II* (Princeton: Princeton University Press, 1949-1950, Four Volumes).
† The interaction among the development of job descriptions, the selection of personnel, the classification of personnel, and the adaptation of organizational structure is described in Edwin E. Ghiselli and Clarence W. Brown, *Personnel and Industrial Psychology* (New York: McGraw-Hill Book Company, 1955), Chs. 1-5.
‡ Examples of these arguments are Chris Argyris, *Integrating the Individual and the Organization* (New York: John Wiley and Sons, 1964); and Louis E. Davis, "Job Design and Productivity," *Personnel*, Volume 33, Number 5 (March 1957), pp. 418-430.
§ In addition, the leader must understand donors' motives and must know which sectors of the population are more likely to donate than others. Questionnaire surveys of the public's donations are reported in David L. Sills, *The Volunteers*, Ch. VI; F. Emerson Andrews, *Attitudes Toward Giving* (New York: Russell Sage Foundation, 1953); Belle Wiggins, *Dynamics of Public Support of Voluntary Health and Welfare Associations* (New York: Bureau of Applied Social Research, Columbia University, 1960), Ch. 4.

and methods doubtless would result in differences in the motives and commitments of their volunteers. In examining the Sills data, the leader should note the distinction between the motives of the organization (i.e., to raise money) and the personal satisfactions gained by the individual volunteer from participation. The individual's gains often seem quite different from the mere accumulation of funds. The successful leader of an association must know how to conduct a fund drive that will satisfy the nonmonetary personal goals of the solicitors.*

THE MARCH OF DIMES†

David L. Sills

[The National Foundation is organized into a series of local chapters and local March of Dimes organizations. The chapter is the administrative unit that carries out Foundation programs, such as providing services to patients. The March of Dimes organizations raise funds. Both use volunteers]. . . . Local Chapters are relatively small, year-round organizations whose members for the most part also play an active but generally not a top leadership role in the March of Dimes campaign. March of Dimes organizations, on the other hand, are quite large, even in small counties, and are ephemeral. The leaders start holding informal meetings in the Fall, but the vast majority of March of Dimes Volunteers is not recruited until December or in some cases early January. At the end of January, or early in February, the organization is disbanded.

As a result of these structural differences, participation as a Volunteer involves a quite different type of commitment in each organization. Consider first the amount of time which Volunteers spend in Foundation activities. Some Chapter Volunteers, as already indicated, spend many hours a week handling the affairs of their Chapter; others devote only a few hours each month to one or another committee meeting. But meetings and correspondence and conferences with the families of patients—to say nothing of the enormous work load which accompanies a polio epidemic—add up over the course of a year to a considerable time commitment on the part of many Chapter Volunteers. Most March of Dimes Volunteers, on the other hand, devote relatively little time to the organization. . . .

The March of Dimes campaign is designed to obtain small gifts from large numbers of people, and this objective requires a large number of Volunteer fund-raisers if it is to be achieved. March of Dimes activities are for the most part both of brief duration and highly specialized. These conditions lead naturally to the question of why so many people are willing to take part in an activity which on the surface seems to offer so few rewards. . . .

Participation as a Volunteer fund-raiser offers satisfactions of a quite different character than those derived from participation in the patient care program. While Chapter Volunteers are rewarded by the satisfactions which come from considering themselves benefactors, or the purveyors of information of vital importance to the welfare of the community, or the intermediaries between polio patients and the medical profession, participants in the March of Dimes are more likely to derive intrinsic enjoyment from the activities themselves, rather than from contemplating their broader significance. The key word which summarizes the satisfactions provided by the patient care program is "service"; the parallel term to describe the rewards of fund-raising is "performance."

The March of Dimes campaign provides opportunities for three types of performance. First, Volunteers obtain a sense of accomplishment from achieving the short-term, pragmatic goal of the campaign—raising money. Second, they obtain satisfactions from putting into practice organizing skills which they have learned either through their businesses or professions or through taking part in other fund-raising activities. Third, they obtain satisfactions from creativity, since the March of Dimes campaign places a premium upon initiative and imagination as tools for attracting public attention and support. Accordingly, the satisfactions derived from fund-raising are best described by considering each of these three types in turn.

THE SATISFACTIONS OF ACCOMPLISHMENT

. . . A major distinguishing feature of the March of Dimes campaign is that it has a finite goal—raising as much money as possible during the month of Jan-

---

* For a thorough study of the organization and management of fund-raising, see John R. Seeley *et al., Community Chest* (Toronto: University of Toronto Press, 1957), especially Chs. 10 and 11. The authors compare the administrative practices and success of the Community Chest and the Red Cross.
† Reprinted with permission of The Free Press and the author from pages 151-158 of *The Volunteers: Means and Ends in a National Organization* by David L. Sills. Copyright 1957 by The Free Press, a corporation.

uary. It is important to note, however, that National Headquarters does not actually set quotas which local organizations are expected to meet, although it does announce to Volunteers how much money is needed to meet anticipated expenses. Since in recent years the costs of both research and patient care have been increasing, there is a tendency for March of Dimes Volunteers to compute on their own initiative how much more than last year's total must be raised in the county if the sum is to contribute its proportionate share to the increased national budget. As a result, Volunteers talk about a "quota" as if one had actually been given them. The Campaign Director in Eastern City, for example, declared that his "greatest satisfaction was exceeding the quota last year." Referring to the current campaign, he remarked that it was impossible to tell about its outcome at that point, but that "if we were assigned last year's quota we could have made that. Still hope to meet [this year's quota]."

The fact that March of Dimes Volunteers assign quotas to themselves is symptomatic not only of their need to define the task ahead but also of their need to interject a note of challenge into an activity which might well become routine. The March of Dimes has such widespread public acceptance that most local organizations can raise a good share of their proceeds with minimum effort: it is the final 10 or 20 per cent which presents a challenge to the enterprising Campaign Director. There is evidence also that for some March of Dimes leaders the element of competition which they themselves inject into the campaign gives added spice to their activities. Witness, for example, the statement of a March of Dimes Chairman in Glass City, who declared that what was important to him was "to see each year's drive larger than the past."

Volunteers who serve as Chairmen for several consecutive years have themselves as competitors. "I've been Chairman three years," recalled the Campaign Director in Power City, "and each and every year we've had higher contributions." And new Chairmen are in competition with their predecessors. A Chairman in Suburb County, for example, reported his greatest satisfaction came from "sweating to outdo the people who did it before," and a Chairman in College Town boasted he had netted in his first year as a Volunteer "three thousand dollars more than the person who preceded me. The next year, I got three thousand more."

THE SATISFACTIONS OF ORGANIZING

Although National Headquarters distributes a *March of Dimes Guide* to each local organization, and even distributes training films which describe how to organize a campaign, the actual organization of the campaign is in the hands of the local Chairmen. Be-

cause the campaign has so many facets, it is often possible to recruit Chairmen for special activities who know from their professional or business experience a great many of the details involved in organization. Newspaper and radio editors become Publicity Chairmen; high school principals become Chairmen of Schools and Colleges; managers of beverage distribution companies become Chairmen of Coin Collectors; proprietors of movie houses become Theater Chairmen; local sports figures become Chairmen of the Sports Committee, etc. This detailed organization not only provides many individuals with the satisfaction of being "in charge"; it also makes the task less formidable, since it is "all part of a day's work."

It is not however the utilization of their professionally-learned skills which gives volunteers the greatest sense of satisfaction, but rather the fact that the campaign affords opportunities for the display of amateur organizing skills. The joys of generalship are most apparent in statements which make reference to the "fun" of organizing. "I think the part I enjoyed most in the drive," recalled a Chairman in Corn City, "was organizing fund-raising activities, contacting the people, getting them to help me and helping them get rolling." Witness also the prideful account provided by the Fabric Town Campaign Director:

> I have thirty-two people under me, all of them local Chairmen. When I call up Mr. X, he sets up an even larger organization than I have for the whole county. It's like a pyramid, with other small pyramids. Eventually you get everybody in on it. You've got to know how to organize.

For other Volunteers the task of organizing the campaign offers a different type of reward: a sense of participation in a "team," of finding a ready response from people who are approached to donate time and effort. "Just the way this campaign alone is run is terrific," the Market Town Campaign Director commented enthusiastically. "When a new idea comes up you just throw it to someone else and they run with it." For the Campaign Director in Pulpwood City, a signal satisfaction was "the fun of getting people together who are willing to work. You get a sense of accomplishment." And the College Town Campaign Director noted that the most rewarding aspect of his activities had been "finding the warmth and response in the people you're working with. They're truly inspired. It brings out the best in them. That's outside of the satisfaction you get from raising the money you hoped for."

THE SATISFACTIONS OF CREATIVITY

The March of Dimes is accepted by Volunteers as a challenge not only to their energy and their organizing skills, but to their imagination as well. The interview transcripts are replete with accounts of feats of local improvisation which give the campaign almost a Mardi Gras character. To cite one example, here is a story told with gleeful pride by a March of Dimes Chairman in Suburb County:

> I'll never forget one thing we did. We pulled into the Market Basket [supermarket] Friday night. We said [over a loudspeaker]—the parking lot was full of cars you see—"There's a *killer* loose in this vicinity!" People jumped out of cars—that got a lot of attention you see. Then we informed them that it was infantile paralysis that was loose. Next day downtown everybody was talking about it, and they gave "like mad." I think the drive would be a real success if kept hot and strong the whole month.

There are other similar examples of Volunteer efforts to keep the March of Dimes "hot and strong" all month. Typical of these activities are the wheelbarrow collections in another town in Suburb County, in which passers-by were "cornered" by determined Volunteers until they contributed; the Robin Hood campaign in Oldtown, where the Sheriff "held up" passing motorists for donations; the public auction in Market Town, at which the clothes of the fattest man in town, a well-known bank official, were sold to the highest bidder; and the emergency Mother's March held in a small town near Lumber City, in which the volunteer firemen donned their wives' dresses and canvassed the entire town in the fire truck. By and large these ebullient schemes were thought up by Volunteers themselves, although sometimes the idea first came to their attention in the campaign guide, which publishes each year stories of particularly successful special events. Through the medium of this guide, one man's "bright idea" becomes a standard feature of the next year's nationwide campaign.

The immediate significance of this type of behavior, and of the obvious satisfactions which it brings to participants, is that the campaign is, to quote one Volunteer, "full of pep and vinegar"—an energetic, original project of amateurs, not a packaged program promoted by professional fund-raisers. Of more fundamental importance, however, is the fact that fundraising can assume, in some of its phases, some of the characteristics of legitimized play. In the eyes of Volunteers there is apparently no loss of dignity involved in the "high jinks" which serve as a release for the type of spontaneous creativity usually associated with the conventions of fraternal associations, or with college class reunions. In this case, however, decorum can be set aside by the participants with impunity, since the ultimate purpose which is served by the "stunts" they create and the "gimmicks" they invent is fundamentally serious and respected by the community at large.

[Subsequent pages in this chapter of Sills' book describe the techniques used by volunteers when soliciting money from the public.—Eds.]

13 INTERNAL DIVISIONS

A. DIFFERENCES IN STATUS

Every social structure is composed of a series of positions (or "statuses") with different tasks, different outlooks, and different personnel. In Part Two of this book we described how the variety of statuses in the larger society supplies different numbers and types of recruits for voluntary associations.

The diverse outlooks and interests among social statuses are evident within organizations, since every organization contains different statuses within its structure (i.e., manager, clerk, janitor, etc.) and since every organization recruits people from different social statuses (e.g., some recruit both Protestants and Roman Catholics, some both rich and poor, some both men and women). Under some conditions, the diversity of viewpoint may produce conflict among statuses within an organization. For a long time, behavioral scientists have studied intergroup disagreements within political and industrial organizations, but recently they have begun such studies in hospitals, schools, scientific laboratories, and other organizations.

An obvious starting point for research into intergroup relations is the fact that an organization consists of people with different ranks and tasks. As a result of differences in their organizational power, tasks, and prior training, the occupants of these statuses may differ in their attitudes toward the organization's goals and in their opinions about the proper structure of the organization. In the next selection, Amitai Etzioni compares differences between managers and experts in their organizational roles, personalities, background, and attitudes toward the organization. As Etzioni's comments demonstrate, differences between managers and experts exist in all organizations, and the character and outcomes of these differences depend on the type of organization. In a business firm, decision-making authority is located in the top manager, power is delegated throughout a hierarchy of administrators, the experts are advisers and helpers to the managers, and the characteristics and outlooks of administrators and experts coincide with the system. But the goals and authority structure of professional organizations are much different and, as a result, the relative power, characteristics, roles, and outlook of administrators and experts are unlike those of their counterparts in business firms.

Similar research would show that the occupants of different positions in a voluntary association vary in roles, personality, background, and outlook toward the organization. The leader must understand such differences in order to avoid communication barriers, interpersonal strains, resistance to directives, and undue membership turnover. Research into voluntary associations as social organizations would be needed to identify how closely they resemble business firms and how closely in other respects they resemble professional organizations.

Etzioni also discusses the nature of the role conflicts that occur when a person's position exposes him to conflicting demands from various groups. He illustrates role conflicts by describing leadership dilemmas in universities, research centers, and other professional organizations; any leader of a voluntary association has encountered similar situations when he was expected to please people with conflicting expectations.

MANAGERS AND EXPERTS*

Amitai Etzioni

There are two approaches to the relationship between staff and line.† According to one approach the staff has no direct authority whatsoever. It advises the executive (line authority) on what action to take. According to the second approach the staff, while advising the line on various issues, also takes responsibility for limited areas of activity.[1] In spite of important differences between the two approaches both agree that staff authority is subordinate to line authority, and they tend to identify line with managers or administrators and staff with experts and specialists. While it is obvious that there are some staff functions which are not carried out by experts and that there are some experts among the line personnel, it is suggested that there is a high correlation between line and managers and between staff and experts.

What is the relation between these two groups and the organizational goals? Managers are generally considered as those who have the major (line) authority because they direct the major goal activity. Experts deal only with means, with secondary activities. Therefore it is functional for them to have no, or only limited (staff), authority.

Manager and expert are the two major terms used in this paper. Therefore a few lines will be devoted here to some conceptual clarification. Managers and experts may be differentiated from four points of view: (a) role structure, (b) personality, (c) background, mainly in terms of educational and occupational experience, and (d) normative orientations.

The *role* of the expert is to create and institutionalize knowledge. The role of the manager is to integrate (create or maintain) organizational systems or subsystems from the point of view of the institutional goals and needs.[2] The expert typically deals with symbols and materials (although there are many who

disagree with this point of view).[3] The manager deals with people. The two role types require different *personality* types. The expert who has intensive knowledge in a limited area, tends to have a restricted perspective. The manager has extensive, though limited, knowledge of many areas, and the resulting broad perspective is essential for his role. Experts are committed to abstract ideas and therefore tend to be unrealistic, whereas managers are more practical. Managers are skilled in human relations; experts are temperamental.[4]

Managers and experts differ in *background*. Experts usually have higher educations than managers and tend to enter their first job at a later age and at higher initial salaries. They often start at relatively high positions in the hierarchy but are limited in the range of their mobility. Managers enter their first job at a younger age, with less education, and at lower positions, but they move upward faster than the experts and some of them eventually get higher than any expert.[5] Whereas many experts remain more or less restricted to the same organizational functions, the typical manager is assigned to a large variety of tasks in what is called the process of broadening.

Managers' *orientations* differ considerably from those of experts. Managers are more committed or loyal to their specific organization than are experts.[6] Experts are often primarily oriented toward their professional reference and membership groups. While managers are often committed to the organization's particular goals, experts are committed to the scientific and professional ethos regardless of the particular needs and goals of their institution.[7]

Obviously though there is a high correlation among these four variables, they are not inevitably associated. Two major mechanisms explain how the corre-

---

* Reprinted from Amitai Etzioni, "Authority Structure and Organizational Effectiveness," *Administrative Science Quarterly*, Volume 4, Number 1 (June 1959), pp. 45-54. Reprinted with the permission of the author and the publisher.

† [In traditional literature about administration, "line" refers to those persons who occupy positions in the administrative chain of command. "Staff" personnel act as advisers and assistants to "line" officials but have little or no administrative authority of their own. As Etzioni says, writers disagree whether "staff" persons have little or no administrative authority as a consequence of their organizational positions.—Eds.]

1 On the two approaches, see Herbert A. Simon *et al.*, *Public Administration* (New York: Alfred A. Knopf, 1956), pp. 280-295; and Alvin W. Gouldner, *Patterns of Industrial Bureaucracy* (Glencoe: The Free Press, 1954), pp. 224-228.

2 The roles of managers will be discussed here only with regard to the internal functions of the organizations. Their roles with regards to environment will be disregarded because of space limitations.

3 Experts can be arranged in a continuum from the less to the more skilled in human relations. Chemists, for instance, are on the average less skilled from this point of view than labor relations experts. See L. E. Danielson, "Management's Relations with Engineers and Scientists," *Proceedings of Industrial Relations Research Association*, Tenth Annual Meeting, 1957, pp. 314-321.

4 See Robert Dubin, *Human Relations in Administration* (New York: Prentice-Hall, 1951), pp. 113-138.

5 For a comparison, see Melville Dalton, "Conflicts between Staff and Line Managerial Officers," *American Sociological Review*, Volume 15, Number 3 (June 1950), pp. 342-351; and C. A. Myers and J. G. Turnbull, "Line and Staff in Industrial Relations," *Harvard Business Review*, Volume 34 (July-August 1956), pp. 113-124.

6 For a case study which brings out this point, see Alfred H. Stanton and Morris S. Schwartz, *The Mental Hospital* (New York: Basic Books, 1954).

7 Alvin W. Gouldner, "Cosmopolitans and Locals: Toward an Analysis of Latent Social Roles," *Administrative Science Quarterly*, Volume 2, Numbers 3 and 4 (December 1957 and March 1958).

lation is maintained. First of all there is *selective recruitment*. People with managerial personalities and background are recruited to managerial roles, and those with the personalities and education of experts tend to enter staff positions. The second mechanism is *role adaptation*. People who enter roles which are initially incompatible with their personalities often adjust to their new roles. In such adjustment the process of broadening produces managers from initial specialists; a parallel process produces semi-experts from managers who entered managerial roles in professional organizations. These processes explain in part also why there is no perfect correlation among the four variables discussed above. For example, people with the background of experts may fulfill managerial roles.

INSTITUTIONAL HEADS

It is one of the basic characteristics of bureaucratic organizational structures to have one and only one center of authority. This is often vested in the role of the head of the organization. He is seen as the top of the chain of command, as the ultimate authority in the internal structure and as ultimately responsible for the organizational activity relative to external structures such as the community and the government. Institutional heads are often symbols of identification for members and employees of the organization. Customers and other outsiders, such as the personnel of other organizations, tend to identify an organization with the organizational head. Institutional heads are in a strategic position to influence the implementation of proclaimed organizational goals.

All organizations need to integrate their various activities into one operating whole. This function is partially fulfilled by the organizational head. Since integrating is a managerial role, it follows that managers and not experts will head organizations. We shall return to this point.

ORGANIZATIONS ARE MONOCRATIC

As noted above, bureaucratic organizations have one center of authority. This is one of the important characteristics which differentiate bureaucracies from feudal regimes. This does not mean that all activities are directed from one center. Authority is often delegated. Organizations can be compared with respect to the degree to which authority is centralized. But even in decentralized organizations there is one center of authority where final decisions are made and conflicts among lower authorities can be resolved. The monocratic structure is one of the more important reasons why bureaucracies are considered as the most effective form of organization. Such a structure enables the top central authority, which is often strongly committed to the organizational goals, to retain control of much of the organizational activity.

On the basis of existing theory, then, one would hold three expectations: (a) Managers have the major (line) authority whereas experts deal with secondary activities, and therefore have only limited (staff) authority. (b) Institutional heads have to be manager oriented because their role is a role of system integration. If an expert-oriented person were to hold this role, the system would be alienated from its goals and might even eventually disintegrate because some functions would be overemphasized while others would be neglected. (c) Organizational goals can be maintained more effectively in organizations with one center of authority.

The rest of this paper will be devoted to an attempt to show that these generalizations apply to some organizations but not to others.

THE PRIVATE BUSINESS: AN AFFIRMATION

The organizational goal of private business is to make profits. The major means are production and exchange. While experts deal with various aspects of the production and exchange process, that is, with means such as engineering, labor relations, quality control, and marketing, the manager is the one who co-ordinates the various activities in such a way that the major organizational goal will be maximized. Profit making is his responsibility. That seems to be one of the reasons why modern corporations prefer to have people with administrative experience as top executives rather than former specialists such as engineers. In a study of the chief executives of American industry in 1950 administration was found to be the principal occupation of 43.1 percent; finance the field of only 12.4 percent; 11.8 percent were defined as entrepreneurs; and only 12.6 percent had been engineers.[8] People with scientific background such as research workers are even less likely to become heads of private business. Only about 4 percent of the presidents of American corporations had such a background. Corporations have different types of heads at different periods in their life cycle. But the heads are usually not experts at any period.

In general the goals of private business are consistent with managerial orientations. The economic goals of the organization and the bureaucratic orientations of the managerial role have in common the orientation toward rational use of means and development of rational procedures to maximize goals which are considered as given. The social and cultural conditions

[8] Mabel Newcomer, *The Big Business Executive* (New York: Columbia University Press, 1955).

that support modern economic activities also support modern administration.

When people with strong expert orientations take over the managerial role of the institutional head, a conflict between the organizational goals and the expert orientation can be predicted. The case described in *Executive Suite*, where the design engineer with strong craftsman commitments takes over the presidency of a private corporation, should be considered atypical.[9] Usually commitment to professional values runs counter to the economic values of the organization.

Homans reports an interesting case in which the influence of the experts was greater than it is in most corporations.[10] He discusses an electrical equipment company, which was owned, managed, and staffed by engineers. Management, which was in the hand of manager-oriented engineers, suffered from pressure toward professional values from the design engineers. The design engineers in the eyes of management were "prima donnas" and "temperamental," terms often used by management to describe experts. Furthermore, they were indifferent "to the general welfare of the company," that is, to profit making, as "shown by their lack of concern with finance, sales, and the practical needs of the consumer and by their habit of spending months on an aspect of design that had only theoretical importance." This caused considerable tension between the managerial and expert-oriented groups, tension to which this company was especially sensitive because of its high dependence on expert work and the special structure of ownership. A power struggle resulted, ending with a clearer subordination of the design engineers (staff) to the managerial engineers (line). This was mandatory "if the company was to survive and increase its sales," as Homans puts it. The treasurer (a nonexpert in this context) became the most influential member of the new management. In short, in a corporation where the experts had a strong power position, the existence of the organization was threatened, considerable internal tension was generated, and finally the organizational structure was changed toward a more usual structure with a clearer subordination of the experts. In other words, the organizational authority structure was made more compatible with the goals of the organization. Manager orientations and the institutional goals of private business seem to match. When an expert orientation dominates, this is dysfunctional to the organizational purposes.

To sum up, the study of private business as an or-

ganization can be seen as an affirmation of the three generalizations of organizational theory presented above. Managers direct the major goal activities and have the major authority; experts deal with means and are in minor and subordinated authority positions. The organizational heads are manager oriented, and there is only one internal center of authority. All business organizations studied, including such decentralized organizations as General Motors and Bata seem to have one center of authority . . .

PROFESSIONAL ORGANIZATIONS: A NEGATIVE CASE

Professional organizations are organizations whose major goal is to institutionalize knowledge and to sustain its creation. Knowledge is created in research organizations (such as the Rand Corporation), spread in schools, created and spread in universities, and applied in hospitals. Knowledge is also created and institutionalized in organizations other than professional ones, but only in professional organizations are these functions the predominant goals.

STAFF AND LINE IN PROFESSIONAL ORGANIZATIONS

We would like to suggest that in professional organizations the staff-expert line-manager correlation, insofar as such a correlation exists at all, is reversed. Although manager orientations are suitable for the major goal activities in private business, the major goal activity of professional organizations is, in its nature, expertness. Managers in professional organizations are in charge of secondary activities; they administer *means* to the major activity carried out by experts. In other words, if there is a staff-line relationship at all, experts constitute the line (major authority) structure and managers the staff. Managers give advice about the economic and administrative implications of various activities planned by the professionals. The final internal decision is, functionally speaking, in the hands of the various professionals and their decision-making bodies. The professor decides what research he is going to undertake and to a large degree what he is going to teach; the physician determines what treatment should be given to the patient.

Administrators may raise objections to planned activities. They may point out that a certain drug is too expensive or that a certain teaching policy will decrease the number of students in a way that endangers the financing of a university. But functionally the professional is the one to decide whether to accept these limitations on his discretion and whether the administrator is right in bringing up his limited point of view. It is of interest to note that some of the com-

---

9 See Eric Larrabee and David Riesman, "The Role of Business in 'Executive Suite,'" in Bernard Rosenberg and D. M. White (editors), *Mass Culture* (Glencoe: The Free Press, 1957), pp. 325-340.
10 George C. Homans, *The Human Group* (New York: Harcourt, Brace and Company, 1950), pp. 369-414.

plaints usually launched against experts in private business are launched against administrators in professional organizations: they are said to lose sight of the major function of the organization in pursuit of their specific limited responsibilities. Experts in private business are sometimes criticized as being too committed to science, craftsmanship, and abstract ideas; administrators in professional organizations are deplored because they are too committed to their specialties—efficiency and economy.

Many of the sociological characteristics of experts and managers in private business cannot be found in professional organizations. Experts enter professional organizations younger and at lower positions (namely, as students, research assistants, or interns) than managers do. Although the range of mobility of managers is usually relatively limited, a professional is more likely to reach the top position of the institutional head.

In private business, [too much] influence by experts threatens the realization of organizational goals, sometimes even the organization's existence. In professional organizations, [too much] influence by the administration is considered as ritualization of means, undermining the goals for which the organization has been established, and endangering the conditions under which knowledge can be created and institutionalized (as for instance, academic freedom).

INSTITUTIONAL HEADS—A ROLE CONFLICT

The role of the institutional head in professional organizations constitutes a dilemma. It is a typical case of institutionalized role conflict.* On the one hand the role should be in the hands of an expert in order to ensure that the orientation of the head will match organizational goals. An expert at the head of the authority structure will mean that expert activity is recognized as the major goal activity and that the needs of professionals will be more likely to receive understanding attention. On the other hand organizations have functional requisites that are unrelated to their specific goal activity. Organizations have to obtain funds to finance their activities, recruit personnel to staff the various functions, and allocate the funds and personnel which have been recruited. Organiza-

tional heads must know how to keep the system integrated by giving the right amount of attention and funds to the various organizational needs, including secondary needs.† An expert may endanger the integration of the professional organization by overemphasizing the major goal activity, neglecting secondary functions, and lacking skill in human relations. Thus the role of head of professional organizations requires two incompatible sets of orientations, personal characteristics, and aptitudes. If the role is performed by either a lay administrator or a typical expert, considerable organizational strain can be expected.

So far the organizational needs have been discussed. The severity of the dilemma is increased because of the motivational structure of typical experts. Most successful experts are not motivated to become administrators. Some would refuse any administrative role, including that of university president or hospital chief, because of their commitment to professional values and professional groups and because they feel that they would not be capable of performing the administrative role successfully. Even those professionals who would not reject the distinguished and powerful role of organizational head avoid the administrative roles that are training grounds and channels of mobility to these top positions. Thus many academicians refuse to become deans and try to avoid if possible the role of department chairman. Those who are willing to accept administrative roles are often less committed to professional values than their colleagues.[11] The same can be said about administrative appointments in hospitals. Thus, for instance, in the mental hospital studied by Stanton and Schwartz the role of administrative psychiatrist is fulfilled at the beginning of the training period. It is considered an undesirable chore that must be endured before turning to the real job. Psychiatrists who complete their training tend to withdraw to private practice. From other studies, especially those of state mental hospitals, it appears that those who stay are often less competent and less committed to professional values than those who leave.[12]

[In the rest of his article, Etzioni describes various devices for the avoidance of conflict between manager and expert in professional organizations. One is the development of "semi-experts," persons with professional training who perform managerial jobs. The semi-expert can synthesize managerial and professional attitudes and aims when making decisions;

* ["Role conflict" refers to contradictory demands placed on the occupant of a status by the different groups of people with whom he must deal. Role conflict is "institutionalized" when the social structure in which the job is set exposes the occupant unavoidably to contradictory groups. For research about role conflicts, see in particular two studies of the dilemmas experienced by school superintendents: Neal Gross *et al.*, *Explorations in Role Analysis* (New York: John Wiley and Sons, 1958); and Melvin Seeman, "Role Conflict and Ambivalent Leadership," *American Sociological Review*, Volume 18, Number 2 (April 1953), pp. 373-380.—Eds.]

† ["Secondary needs" refer to the needs for money, equipment, personnel, etc. just to keep the organization in existence. Every organization has "secondary needs" regardless of its manifest goals. "Primary needs" refer to the needs for the means enabling the organization to attain its manifest goals.—Eds.]

11 Gouldner, "Cosmopolitans and Locals," *op. cit.*

12 Ivan Belknap, *Human Problems of a State Mental Hospital* (New York: McGraw-Hill Book Company, 1956).

he can conciliate the specialized managers and the specialized experts within the organization.

[Another adjustment technique is construction of professional organizations without monocratic bureaucratic hierarchies. The managers run bureaucratically organized administrative sectors, but the professional personnel have considerable autonomy.

Managers and experts have only limited authority over another professional. Some voluntary associations are organized on similar principles.

[Etzioni also describes conflicts between lay managers and professionals in hospitals, schools, and other professional organizations that have not adopted adjustment mechanisms.—Eds.]

As in every other organization, a voluntary association contains various statuses whose occupants have different conceptions of the goals, methods, and spirit of the association. For example, in the following excerpt—from a study of the Community Chest of Indianapolis—John Seeley and his associates report certain value conflicts within the organization. Sometimes the disagreements found lay volunteers and the professional staff on opposite sides, sometimes the viewpoints cut across these statuses rather than dividing them. Where opposing viewpoints cut across different statuses, the organization faces much less danger of internal disruption than if the viewpoints separate the statuses.

LAYMEN AND PROFESSIONALS*
John R. Seeley, Buford H. Junker, and R. Wallace Jones, Jr.

BUSINESS SUCCESS VERSUS COMMUNITY ORGANIZATION

In a recent campaign a very prominent layman shocked some part, at least, of the Chest's staff by referring to the Chest as essentially a "collecting agency" (for the social agencies). What was shocking to the staff people was not so much the possibility of a public-relations error in referring to the Chest's function so baldly and unemotionally. Rather they received a genuine moral shock—a sudden feeling of social distance and alienation between those who regard the Chest primarily as a semi-sacred movement in the realm of "community organization" (for which money is, incidentally, needed) and those who regard money-raising as the commonsense and natural heart of the enterprise (for which some community organization is, incidentally, necessary). Persons may be found, probably, in every intermediate position from those who consider the money-raising function nearly all-important to those who consider the community organization nearly all-important. For some, the

Chest represents almost a venture in brotherhood in which money-raising occurs; for others, it is almost an adventure in otherhood, in which the emotional focus is on the money-extracting process.

These alternate views as to the paramount or primary interest to be served do not represent merely matters of interpretation of what is going on, or more or less devotion to or interest in different elements of a total program. They may not represent purely opposed alternatives, such as, say, the alternative between driving north or driving south; but they do represent substantial opposition, such as, say, driving northeast or driving southeast—one gets east in either case, but not at the same point or near it.

The conflict has a bearing on practical matters. Should the primary criterion of the Chest's success, for instance, be a campaign measure such as "participation," or "gift per donor," or "per capita gift," or should it be a non-campaign measure such as would be reflected in an estimate of the proportion of people that "knew about" the Chest or "were in favor of" the Chest, whether or not they could or did contribute. No one perhaps took seriously any attempt to set one of these as having exclusive priority or value; this was particularly true of those who thought some non-financial measure "really" most important—i.e., no one could be found to say that the education of the

* From John R. Seeley, Buford H. Junker, and R. Wallace Jones, Jr., with the assistance of N. C. Jenkins, M. T. Haugh, and I. Miller, *Community Chest: A Case Study in Philanthropy* (Toronto: University of Toronto Press, 1957), pp. 109-120. Reprinted with the permission of the senior authors and the publisher.

community or its organization sentimentally was justifiable if it yielded no money or a net loss. But those who thought that participation was more important as an immediate issue than per capita really felt divided from the others, and were inclined to promote or pursue other policies in practice.

Among those who thought first priority ought to be given to increasing participation were people convinced either that existing givers were giving "enough" (an ethical judgment) or "about as much as they're going to give, anyway" (a judgment of fact or of practicality). On this view, since either no increase should be demanded of the givers or no such demand would be effective, the only possible source of increase is the non-giver, the successful persuasion of whom would then increase participation.

Others among the participation-emphasizers, however, had different practical and ethical reasons to adduce for their preferences. One of the practical arguments, quite credible on its face, ran to the effect that in any giving unit (such as the employees in a factory department) the acts of giving are more interdependent when it comes to the question of *whether* to give at all (which is frequently known to everyone in the unit) than they are when it comes to the alternative question as to *how much* to give (which is frequently not known to most of them). On this view, it is "easier" to use social interaction to increase participation than it is to use interaction to increase percapita. And what is easiest ought to be done first. Another practical argument rests on an "intuitive" conviction that the ease of getting another giver out of any particular group is in some way related to the number one already has got—so that great attention to participation is justified from the viewpoint of economizing persuasive resources.

In any case, the gulf between the percapita-minded and the participation-minded is less often founded on such practical arguments, and much more frequently on an important difference in general orientation, value-system, or ethical set. For those oriented to participation, the question of the relative ease or difficulty of securing increased participation as against increased percapita is largely irrelevant, since their question is not "What is easy" but "What is *right*?" or "What is *good*?"

The participation-minded and the percapita-minded are found among both the laymen and the professionals, although their reasons for occupying these positions are somewhat different.

The percapita-minded professionals tend to pay attention to the "under-giving" of those who do give; they feel (comparing their city with other cities, or comparing different classes of givers, or contrasting actuality with wish): (1) that the givers give too little, (2) that this is "wrong" and should be "righted,"

and (3) that the fact that these givers give at all shows recognition of an obligation, which it would take relatively little effort to get discharged on a more appropriate scale. The percapita-minded laymen, on the other hand, tend towards the same conclusion on one of two very different urgings: (1) a sense of *noblesse oblige* (or, more exactly, *argent oblige*)—a feeling that they and their peers are not giving enough in proportion to their "potential," or (2) a feeling of "injustice" or unfairness in that, while *they* give enough, the givers among their peers do not, and that this is urgent for correction.

The lay and professional participation-minded differ similarly. This layman feels that low participation is "bad" either because it is "poor public relations" or because, without the check of "saleability," he considers that he has, himself, little or no basis for judging value. It is "poor public relations" because it is "risky to get too far out ahead of the crowd." The second reason means that, probably, "if the crowd won't buy it, it shouldn't be sold," i.e., the unpopular isn't worthy of support. The high premium put on participation is in the first case a measure of safety; in the second, a check by the market, as it were, on selling enthusiasm.

The professional, on the other hand, is less likely to feel that his enthusiasm needs check, or that the value of his product needs proof or supporting evidence. He is likely to take his stand on a feeling, a mystique almost,[1] that flows from his high valuation of, and his interpretation of what is involved in, "democracy." The general feeling that, in all matters that concern them, as many people as possible should be "involved"—ideally "all the people"—runs like a thread thick and strong through much of the social-work fabric, and participation in money-giving on a wide scale is just one particular expression of the desire to "get everybody in" so it will be "democratic," i.e., from this viewpoint, right.

DEMOCRATIC VERSUS ARISTOCRATIC ORIENTATION

The discussion of the "business success" versus "community organization" (and percapita versus partici-

---

[1] There is something also in the occupation of the Chest or agency executive that urges him strongly in the same direction: this is his power-situation vis-à-vis his governing board, invariably more representative ideologically of élite large donors (or potential donors) than of mass small donors (or potential donors). If his organization has mass-participation, he may feel that he can speak for the unrepresented interest, and, therefore, in an important sense, act as a counterpart to his Board and (since he then has many masters) as a relatively free agent. He may prefer this position either because he "likes to" be relatively free, or because he thinks it "wrong" that he should be so wholly and indefensibly responsible to a segment of the community.

pation) orientation has brought us to the edge of another distinction or division of view as to aims and purposes: what might be called an "aristocratic" view of the organization as against what might be called a "democratic" view.

The "aristocratic" view takes it for granted that the Chest is inevitably, or "ought" to be, an organization of the "best" people for the sake of "those not so favored." If this is the case, or if it ought to be, then the Chest's principal advantage is (or would be) just precisely that it is able to indulge the aristocratic virtues —nobility, generosity, a certain ability to deal largely and openhandedly and to make quick decisions on large events without being unduly sensitive to public relations and general opinion.

The "democratic" view maintains that, on the contrary, an organization like the Chest ought to be essentially an organization of "all the people" or, at the very least, an organization that "represents" all the people.

Again, the differences in view have considerable practical consequences; some effort will be made by the democratic-minded to secure the involvement of "more people" or the "representation" of "more groups," or at least the semblance of the latter. The "aristocratic-minded" may, and some do, feel that the representation of fewer interests would lead to a firmer and more certain policy and one that would involve the relevant few (relevant in terms of power in the community and ability to give or cause giving) more deeply and enthusiastically. They may well feel that too many people are already engaged in decision-making for resultant decisions to be really bold and commanding of effective support.

Some compromise clearly characterizes the Indianapolis Chest as it probably does most Chests. The typical compromise is to extend the nominal governorship of the institution, while effectively concentrating power in "committees" on which the élite or community power-group is disproportionately represented.

The greatest loss in connection with this unresolved, and largely unconfronted, issue comes, however, not so much, we suspect, from actual struggles to concentrate or disperse power in line with the respective views as it does from a vague uneasiness or distress or feeling of "bad conscience," stemming from the discrepancy between what many feel to be "proper" or ideal and what is actually the case or what may be the only possibility. There is little or no open—as against "off the record"—discussion of what is involved, and particularly little facing of the possibility that for an organization like the Chest an élite or power-group control might be not only inevitable but appropriate. For some others, distress arises less because of the discrepancy in this respect between what the Chest is and what it ought to be, and much more

because of a felt discrepancy between what it is and what it makes itself out to be. What it makes itself out to be is very various, depending at least on the particular audience addressed and the purpose of the "message." But with sometimes one emphasis, sometimes the other, and, most often, both, it makes itself out either as an organization of the very best people, the leaders of the leaders, or as a "representative" group "no different from you or me," almost in the sense of a random sample of the community population. That the latter version has always or nearly always to be emphasized indicates the feeling either that it ought to be the true one, or that it must be made to appear so.

The preceding discussion brings us face to face with another perennial issue: appearance versus substance.

APPEARANCE VERSUS SUBSTANCE

A famous recommendation to effective government may be found in Machiavelli's *Discourses*: the Prince, to be "successful," should seem to be honest. A more long-standing recommendation, also embedded in Judeo-Christian culture, is found in the unconditional "Thou shalt not lie."

The choice between (relative) honesty as a goal and the mere appearance of it is not, of course, peculiar to any one human organization. For some, it hardly appears as a problem at all. A vendor in the more high, wide, and handsome days of selling, when even the legal maxim bade the buyer beware, could scarcely feel himself enjoined to any more honesty than made for effective selling (in the short run), which was often not a very great deal. In more recent days, while honesty is said to be the best policy, some allowance is commonly made in practice for something less than "full, frank and free disclosure." The amount of what may be called "permissible dishonesty" will vary from enterprise to enterprise and business to business, though all will permit themselves some leeway.

In many, if not most, human enterprises that fall clearly within *either* the secular field or the sacred field, the weight to be given to honesty as against its semblance is determined with relative ease by the definition of the field within which each falls. When, moreover, many years of operation have permitted what was once contrived and conscious to become habitual and largely unconscious, tradition acts as a buffer to unease; indeed, for most people, the standard of honesty is probably the standard of what is customary.

But, when, on the contrary, a movement is both sufficiently new, so that no tradition has had opportunity to crystallize, and also, for some, on the border between sacred and secular, for others an admixture of both, for still others a secular expression of sacred motives and for yet others a secular substitute for sacred function, it is likely that there will be marked differences of opinion as to what constitutes proper behavior, and marked conflict will probably prevail within and between people as a consequence. Such conflict might be expected to be peculiarly acute in an organization that aims to be at one and the same time the epitome of business—money-getting—and a major focus for the American secular religion of "service."

Unfortunately for simplicity, we cannot attribute the differential concern with honesty (as against enough appearance of it to "get by") to one party or the other, either layman or professional. One cannot, even for the same person, count upon consistent differential concern, one way or the other, as he shifts about from role to role. A layman sitting temporarily on a budget committee, or critically examining an internal financial statement, will have standards of accuracy very different from those he will have as a campaign chairman. Similarly, the same professional, acting now as general manager now as campaign director, will also have different standards on different occasions, and will feel some strain and consequently exhibit some cynicism.

Each will, generally, also allow himself much greater leeway with the facts when he is addressing a large audience than when he is addressing a small one. The addresses may otherwise be the same, but large numbers reduce intimacy and therewith, simultaneously, the felt mandate to honesty and the possibility of cross-examination, i.e., the internal and external checks on wish and imagination . . .

LONG-RUN AND SHORT-RUN
EMPHASIS

But this brings us to another type of division within and between people as we have encountered them. And this difference also characterizes laymen and professionals.

The difference is essentially between those with predominantly short-run preoccupations and those with predominantly long-run ones. If a simile can be permitted that treats the population of potential givers as a "field," the difference lies between those who would "farm the land" and those who would "mine the land," between the "cultivators" and the "exploiters," the "conservators" and the "harvesters." One group tends to think in terms of maximum yield now; the other, in terms of greatest total yield over an indefinitely long life, perhaps extending beyond the present generation.

It is a well-known fact that most of the "leading citizens" associated with a movement such as the Chest will ordinarily regard themselves as more permanent members of the community, while many if not most professionals will recognize that, willing or not, they are relatively transient through it. It is widely believed, upon this ground, that the laymen will incline to the long-run view and the professionals to the short. Again, unfortunately for simplicity, this appears simply not to be the case.

In the first place, the laymen, even the town's "leading citizens," are no longer, in these days of large national firms, so predominantly people whose past is that of their present community or whose future—if they are "successful"—is bound up with the future of any one city. They were born elsewhere, and they expect and frequently hope to be yet elsewhere soon. They are therefore, even though otherwise conservative, under some necessity to follow the mandate "That thou doest, do quickly."

For many other leading laymen, moreover, time presses in the sense that their "period of service" in such organizations as the Chest has to fit into increasingly stringent career requirements. If the "service" is to be useful to the career it must not come too early in it or too late, and this means that whatever is to be done must be done fast; it also means that what is done fast should be "successful," for little credit, relatively, accrues to the businessman in the business world from service in a "failing" organization. For both of these reasons there is considerable pressure on laymen to produce notable results immediately. One would have to add to these complications a third: that under some circumstances leaders who are in one or many senses marginal to the "top top leadership" will be called into positions of most active direction precisely *because* their marginality will permit or encourage them to take steps that are, to say the least, not traditional and therefore, while potentially "successful," not open to the "top top leadership." Such steps are almost inevitably in the direction of improvising relatively startling schemes for relatively short-run ends, with reduced regard for long-run consequences.

On the other side, for the professional, is the erroneous guess that his transience would invariably give him a short-run view. Three factors in his situation, and perhaps a fourth, incline him, however, in the opposite direction: (1) his professional past and (2) his professional future, (3) his immediate social relations, and (4) his (somewhat remoter) relations to other fundraisers. His past experience and his expectation of a permanent career in fundraising somewhere, give his knowledge some extension by way of information as to what has succeeded and failed elsewhere, and put him under some pressure to develop a personal ethic and a relatively long-run policy for himself. His relative social distance from business-men and his relative social closeness to social workers incline him perhaps to take a "professional" view of what is involved, and therefore to view it in a longer time-perspective. His association with other fund-raisers works probably ambiguously, since the ethics of stewardship seem no more dominantly represented in their gatherings than the ethics of exploit[2] . . .

VOLUNTEER AND CONSCRIPT: SUASION AND PRESSURE

One might suppose that the ideal situation for a fund-raising outfit would be one in which enough people would spontaneously (preferably for the "right" reasons) send in enough money, often enough and with enough promptness, to make any large effort unnecessary and, therefore, any large organization superfluous.

Since people do not in general so act, it appears that they must be "sold," and in order to sell them, a vast organization of salesmen—"volunteers"—must be recruited, trained, motivated, controlled, and maintained. Ideally, again—even if spontaneous money-giving on a wide scale cannot be had—it would be desirable that the army of "volunteer" sales-men or persuaders should be genuinely a volunteer army. It seems obvious that, in practice, this cannot be had either, and there must therefore be a prior process to "persuade" the army of workers who are to "persuade" the much larger population of "givers." "Voluntary gifts" which are not wholly voluntary must thus be collected by "volunteer solicitors" who are not wholly volunteers.

Every voluntary organization, no doubt, would wish to appear to be as voluntary as possible, while desire for "efficiency" tempts it constantly to mobilize all the sanctions—rewards or penalties—it can muster to ensure that "free" choice shall have a foregone outcome. But for every organization this poses at least three problems: where shall the actuality be located (how much "pressure" is actually to be used—or is it "proper" to use); where shall the public image be located ("What is our pitch here?"); and how is the discrepancy between the two to be accounted for and thus rendered harmless or even palatable? For an organization like the Chest (or probably for any fund-raising organization) these problems are peculiarly acute since the need to *seem* ethical—for the sake of efficiency—referred to earlier is conjoined with the need (for many) to *be* ethical—which stems from the Chest's origins and from the meaning the whole oper-

ation has for many laymen and professionals involved in it.

The tendency, in practice, is to locate the public representation close to the "voluntary" pole, so that, with rare exceptions, the public image fostered or the private image cherished is very largely one of free men willingly banded together to achieve an object that most or all actively desire. The main difficulties and conflicts, therefore, occur chiefly around where to locate the actual level of coercion; and, to a less degree, how to deal with the gap between appearance and reality. Both difficulties have to do with pressuring the pressurers ("recruitment"), and the pressurers' pressuring the givers ("soliciting").

There are really two problems in connection with "pressure" that are often sharply felt but only dimly distinguished; these have to do, severally, with the amount of pressure applied and with its nature or character. Pressure may be much or little, high or low as to amount; it may also, in its nature, be relevant to the issue at hand or largely irrelevant. Relevant pressure means pressure that really addresses itself to the issues at hand; irrelevant pressure makes use of rewards or sanctions that have little or nothing to do with any natural consequence of the choice, for example, a threat to cease trading with a given individual unless a gift is forthcoming. The accompanying schema may make the various kinds of pressure clear. Among both laymen and professionals can be found those who are willing or eager to use each of these types of pressure, some of them or all of them, according to need or circumstance. A few laymen think that none should be used, and many people "wish" none need be.

TABLE I

Types of pressure

Kind of pressure	Degree of pressure	
	Relatively low	Relatively high
Largely relevant	Type I $\longrightarrow$	Type III
Largely irrelevant	Type II $\longrightarrow$	Type IV

Note: The arrows indicate the directions in which one kind of pressure tends to pass into another.

Suggestions as to how best to secure results range through all these types of pressure: from gently (by printed matter and mail) "telling people about the need" (Type I) to trying to involve them in games and stunts and mild competition which "people don't like to miss" (Type II) to earnest, forceful, face-to-face and heart-to-heart talk about the facts and the

2   Indeed, on the limited evidence we have, we should be driven to guess that the ethics of exploit are at present becoming dominant over those of stewardship. The future lies most probably with the smart young operators—at least, for the next decade, at a guess.

moral issues involved (Type III) to the idea of publishing a "blacklist" of non-donors or "inadequate" donors, which, hopefully, would "bring a man around" under pressure of threat to his business or livelihood. The major conflict is, however, between those who would wish to see only Type I pressure employed ("just give people the opportunity to give") and those who favor fairly widespread use of Type IV ("There are always some —'s that are hard to get in").

The division of opinion as to what is legitimate and proper, here, is of course highly correlated with the division between those who think dominantly in financial terms and those who think dominantly in human terms. But the coincidence is not exact, for among those who do think predominantly in terms of human values, many are so deeply impressed with the need of the ultimate beneficiaries (whom they see largely as the poor or disadvantaged) that the end of serving them adequately justifies the use of almost any means; and among some who do think primarily in financial terms there is a realization that, except in the very short run, some bounds on pressure may actually yield more money.

For obvious reasons, there is also some correlation between those who divide on the issue of pressure and those who divide on short-run versus long-run perspective. But again the coincidence is not perfect since more considerations than these enter into a decision as to what kinds of pressure to apply. . . .

CHARITY AND SERVICE

One more continuous latent conflict (probably less important than the foregoing) lies between those who think the Chest is or ought to be primarily a "charity" organization and those who think of it primarily as a "community service" organization.

For some, mostly laymen, the whole meaning of the enterprise is that it represents or makes possible the discharge of the impulse or deep desire to help the less fortunate. On humane or religious grounds or both, it is deemed desirable or necessary to give aid, in suitable form and under suitable safeguards, to the disadvantaged; the Chest is intended as the major vehicle for the performance of this privilege or duty.

For others, this is almost the exact antithesis of what they would wish to think of the Chest as being,

or what they would wish it to become, in so far as they can at all affect policy. The discharge of the obligation to "clothe the naked, feed the hungry, visit the sick, and comfort the fatherless" they would regard as being sufficiently met by government at various levels: "For that, we pay taxes." The object of a *Community Chest* should be, they feel, the provision of a better life for all, but most particularly the provision of "services," not for the unfortunate, but for those most worthy or promising, the solid, substantial "backbone of the community" or "promise of America's future."

Few see this as an all-or-none choice between sharply defined alternatives, but many would wish to reduce in fact or play down in publicity the one element or the other in what the Chest "supports." Indeed there are four related sets of preferences, presented in the accompanying diagram, upon which individuals will express preferences, sometimes very strong ones. Those who are attracted to one end of

TABLE 2

any one scale are usually similarly attracted to the same end of the other scales: indeed, one could work out combinations showing polar opposite preferences such as: a character-building agency giving service to young and not-needy boys *versus* a charity agency relieving the needs of old women.

For those who have strong preferences, the Chest is in the perhaps unfortunate position that it and a great many of "its" agencies do not represent in anything like pure form either one type of program or the other. Many agencies incorporated in the Chest's appeal have both a "charitable" function and a "service" one; some agencies incline more heavily one way or the other (e.g., the . . . Mission as against, say, the Boy Scouts), but few, if any, represent pure cases, and the Chest cannot successfully represent itself as fulfilling either the one or the other function . . .

Etzioni's selection describes differences in roles and outlooks that inhere in different organizational statuses. Some differences among employees originate from sources extrinsic to the organization: the community is divided, and traditionally certain social statuses in the community supply personnel for certain jobs while employees are recruited for other jobs from other social statuses. In his selection, Orvis Collins describes how the inherited nationality statuses in a community traditionally become associated with various jobs in an organization which, by rational criteria, could select employees from any source. In Collins' factory—and often in other organizations—recruitment and promotion contrary to the traditional patterns would arouse criticism and resistance that the leader must foresee and mute. Members of organizations will consider an associate or a superior legitimate only if the latter possesses all of the personal characteristics that are consistent with the organization's customary image of that particular job. In Collins' factory, harmony was preserved only when recruitment and promotion were conducted according to community customs—even if they might seem irrelevant to industrial efficiency.

ETHNIC ORIGINS*
Orvis Collins

It is one of the shibboleths of modern management that advancement from job to job must be based on efficiency. By "efficiency" is meant the capacity to do work. Management argues that, if an institution is to continue to function, the majority of its members (in this case job-holders) must have at least a minimum capacity for performing their individual functions. Within the factory such attributes as physical strength, education, and age are all at one time or another implied by the term "capacity to do work." To a production engineer a division of labor is necessary, since, for one reason, a 200-pound male can perform certain work more efficiently than a 110-pound female; a man of thirty is able to perform certain physical tasks too great for the strength of the average man of sixty-five; and a graduate of an engineering school can perform work involving mathematics quite beyond a person who left school in the eighth grade.

Once, however, several candidates are admitted to possess the technical efficiency required for performance of the work, other qualifications become important. And at Somerset, a New England factory, the most important of these is the ethnic identification of the individuals involved. In this factory individuals must be ethnically qualified to hold certain jobs, a circumstance which has resulted in the development of a pattern of ethnic job expectations, sponsorship, and rejection. This paper is an analysis of the system in operation, with a description of the maneuvers which accompanied attempted promotions on the part of

* From Orvis Collins, "Ethnic Behavior in Industry," *The American Journal of Sociology*, Volume LI, Number 4 (January 1946), pp. 293-298. © 1946, The University of Chicago Press. Reprinted by permission of the author and the publisher.

one group and those which accompanied successful or unsuccessful attempts to reject these promotions.

I gathered the information which will be used to demonstrate the presence and functioning of this system during two years while employed as a workman at Somerset, a management-owned industry employing a labor force which varied between 1,800 and 2,000. Officially I was first a moveman and later a cutting-machine operator. While these were my formal duties, I was also editor of the union local's news-bulletin, secretary of the Labor–Management Committee, and a member of the contract-negotiating committee. Thus it was possible for me to observe the interrelationships of the plant system at crucial points at which labor interacted with management . . .

I soon became aware of an ethnic structure within the factory; among my fellow-workers expression of this fact was often made. A Negro friend remarked, "You got to be a Mason or a Catholic to get anywhere around here." When I asked about one of the Irish foremen, a fellow-worker said, "With a name like Collins you'll fit with him all right." Later it became apparent that there existed at Somerset a clearly definable system of ethnic sponsorship in matters of promotion. The proposition here will be that, whatever other considerations may have been involved in the promotion of employees, one of the key issues was always the ethnic identification of employees, one of the key issues was always the ethnic identification of the individual proposed for promotion. Nationality or race was almost never explicitly declared to be a consideration in these situations but was always present.

Chart I is a representation of the ethnic-job hierarchy at Somerset. The letters Y, I and O have been used to indicate three categories: Yankees, Irish, and Others . . .

It should be pointed out that in such an urban-ethnic area family names are important as one of the most obvious ethnic symbols, but they are not always

CHART I

Job–Ethnic hierarchy

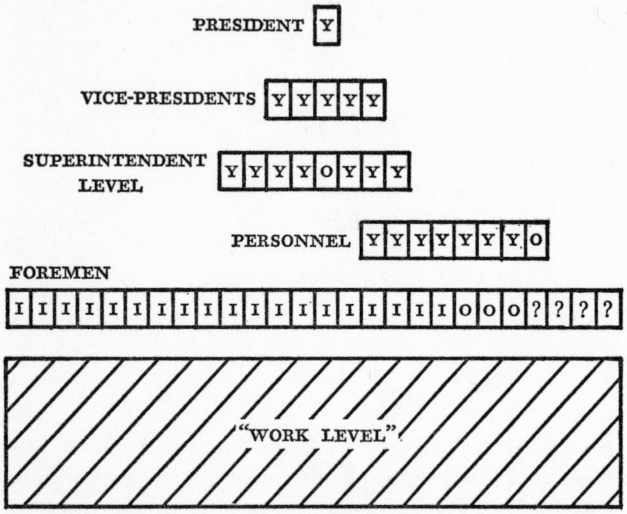

PRESIDENT [Y]

VICE-PRESIDENTS [Y][Y][Y][Y]

SUPERINTENDENT LEVEL [Y][Y][Y][Y][O][Y][Y]

PERSONNEL [Y][Y][Y][Y][Y][Y][Y][O]

FOREMEN

[I][I][I][I][I][I][I][I][I][I][I][I][I][I][I][I][I][I][I][I][I][O][O][O][?][?][?][?]

"WORK LEVEL"

Y = Yankee; I = Irish; O = Other than Yankee or Irish; ? = Not identified. The non-Yankee at the superintendent level is a testing engineer. The non-Yankee member of the personnel group is a young Italian who does safety cartoons and acts as general errand boy.

reliable as such. A newcomer to any group is immediately placed by his name. Later other factors may qualify or even nullify this early judgment. For this reason anyone who has lived in a New England urban area learns a new respect for the adage, "What's in a name?" Shea, for instance, may be the "handle" of a "lace-curtain" (or, for that matter, a "shanty") Irishman, but it was borne also by an eminent officer of the American Revolutionary Army. During my stay at Somerset there were three members of lower top management whose names seemed to indicate that they had other than good English blood in their veins. No matter, however, what may have been the indiscretions of their ancestors, Holzer, O'Brian, and Orlando had adopted all the Yankee symbols, including a typical Yankee abhorrence for what many Yankess consider a typical Irish invention—the union shop with its forced extortion of dues from factory employees. For this reason they have been placed on the chart as Yankee, rather than as Old German, Old Irish, and Old Italian.

Furthermore, wherever an ethnic status system develops, there is likely to develop a pattern of name-changing. During my stay at Somerset I think I heard this story, or variations of it, at least half-a-dozen times:

You know the ditty,

"Here's to Boston, the land of the bean and the cod
Where the Cabots speak only to Lowells
And the Lowells speak only to God."

Well, Judge So-and-so after a hard day at the bench during which he had taken care of numerous pleas by various foreign gentlemen came home and said to his wife:

"Here's to Boston, the land of the bean and the cod
Where the Cabots have no one to speak to,
The Lowells speak Polish, by God."

For "Polish" is substituted "Yiddish," "Guinea" (Italian), "Russian," "Slovak," or the language of whatever ethnic group the storyteller may be using as his target. Such a story illustrates the feeling entertained by individuals of English-speaking stock about the "borrowing" of one of their most prized symbols by individuals socially subordinate but upwardly mobile.

But the same Yankees who defend this name symbol through ridicule at one time forced English names on newcomers to New England. Industrial organizations, and Somerset was very much among them, went in heavily during one period for what was called "hiring off the dock." Through the merits of this system the newly arrived European found himself possessed of (or by, if you choose) an already prepared lodging, a job, and a new name pronounceable by English tongues. The employers in turn obtained a new workman whose peasant soul had not been besmirched by the Irish heresies of wages, hours, and working conditions. Tony Taylor, Joe Brown, and Chris Cook were typical recipients of such New England generosity.

For these reasons I have placed a question mark after some of the foreman positions. There were twenty-six foreman, and I do not feel that I knew enough about some of them to judge their ethnic identification.

Chart I indicates not only that certain jobs were held by the ethnically acceptable but that large areas of the plant hierarchy are almost completely occupied by members of one ethnic group. Jobs of managerial type are held by individuals of native or Yankee stock, and jobs of supervisory nature are held almost exclusively by Irish. "He is a foreman, although not Irish," is a succinct and commonly made statement of a Somerset pattern of expectation: the exception calls forth comment. One can see also that a member of top management, a superintendent, for example, can be expected to be a Yankee and that the personnel department is Yankee-monopolized.

If, then, the Irish-and Yankee-held positions as shown by the chart are separated by encircling, two sharply defined areas are set up. These areas quite clearly coincide with the management and with the supervisory areas of the factory structure. In the remaining portion of the chart are the individuals at the working level. As they are represented, they appear to be an undifferentiated mass. If, however, it were our purpose here to examine them more closely, we should find that there also are certain structures of job occupancy among the worker group.

Because this ethnic pattern of job occupancy has existed so long at Somerset (the company was established about 1890), an ethnic pattern of expectation has developed. What happens to the social organization and to the individuals when these expectations are upset? It should, I suppose, be pointed out that, when I speak of "job expectation," I have in mind not what the individual expects for himself (which is the usual meaning conveyed by the word) but the fact that a significant number of the people participating share the expectation that a person of certain identification will be promoted to fill a vacancy or a newly created job. In other words, this is a social, as distinct from an individual, expectation.

Since most of the foremen at Somerset are Irish, both Irish and non-Irish have come to expect newly appointed members of supervision to be Irish. This does not mean that all individuals in this position must be Irish, but it does mean that, when management appoints a non-Irish person to a supervisory job, it should be very sure that it has an especially good reason for making the appointment.

Since members of both management and labor have learned to recognize this system of ethnic job expectations and know fairly well how to adapt themselves to it, promotions are made year after year without, in the majority of cases, conflicts developing. But, when the pattern is violated, there is usually trouble.

Management, of course, has the formal prerogative of selecting whichever individuals it feels are capable of filling openings, and this is explicitly recognized by the union. Any action, therefore, which develops in opposition to a promotion is highly informal, as the following illustrates.

In the spring of 1942 the subforeman in charge of one of the special-treating work groups decided to go into the armed services. Sullivan had been "Old Country" Irish and was exceedingly popular with his men. When he left, the management announced that a Yankee by the name of Peters was to replace him. Peters had been in the department a considerable length of time and seems to have been well liked by the other men. But, when I came to work on the second shift, I heard that there had been a threat of a walkout in the special-treating department. I do not recall the exact conversation, but most of the discussion was centered around Donovan, another employee of the depart-

ment, who the men seemed to think should have been given the job.

A walkout materialized and lasted for one shift. From examination of the grievance records and through talking, a year later, with some of the principals involved, I was able to piece together this story:

When the president of the local heard that a walkout was threatened in the special-treating department, he and the business agent made a tour of the plant and, according to the story they told, informed all employees that the walkout was "wildcat" and not supported by the local. According to the president of the company, however, the labor leaders did not actively discourage the walkout—but informed the workmen that the local was "neutral."

A formal grievance was lodged with management charging that Donovan had been discriminated against. Obviously the local did not have a legal leg to stand on, since the right of promotion is vested in management. I do not know that either side took the grievance statement seriously. The filing of the grievance merely served as an excuse for the men to return to work while the local handled matters through regular channels. But social pressure within a tightly integrated work group is terrific. Several days later Peters, the Yankee, failed to come to work, the report was circulated that he was ill, and management selected a man named Murphy to take over for him. Peters did not return to work, and Murphy was later made subforeman.

I was fortunate in having a chance later to talk over what happened with one of the members of the special-treating department. He explained it this way: "Management went over Conner's [the foreman's] head by making one of his subforemen for him. It wasn't right, and Holzer [the plant manager] knew it; but he did it anyway, and Conner couldn't make a peep. No [in answer to a question], we weren't backing Conner specially; we just did what was right."

The group rationalization seems to have been: It has always been the duty of the foreman to help choose his subforemen, but management appointed a subforeman, a Yankee, without consulting the foreman under whom he was to work. If Conner had not been cheated of this privilege, he would have insisted upon an Irish assistant. Donovan is Irish and the leader of the gang; therefore, it is up to us to see that Donovan gets the job by inducing the Yankee, Peters, to leave. But if Murphy gets the job that's all right because he is Irish, too. That is the sort of situation which arose when management failed to promote in accordance with the expectations of the individuals involved. In this instance the labor group clearly demonstrated its ability to reject a promotion which did not fit into the ethnic pattern.

Incidentally, Murphy and Donovan "fitted" and were friendly after this episode. They were seen together constantly at the bowling alleys. One inference might be that Murphy had aided rather than injured Donovan by accepting the job. Another Yankee chosen to replace Peters would probably have had a rather rough time of it.

It is significant, however, that no opposition is given to Yankees promoted to fill jobs within the area of the hierarchy dominated by Yankees. At Somerset staff jobs of a certain type are distinguished by the term "administrative." Personnel jobs are always spoken of as "administrative," and jobs of this sort are pretty well monopolized by Yankees. Accordingly, when wartime expansion made necessary a series of new administrative posts, the management without exception selected Yankees to fill them. Fawn, for instance, who had worked several years in the rubber-treating department as a clerk, was chosen safety engineer. Stillwell, who had been a clerk in the container department, was placed in charge of a foreman-training program. And, most significant, the man appointed director of the newly organized personnel department was an engineer by the name of Ball. Each of these men had two things in common. They were not from the labor group and they were Yankees. For these reasons promotion through the supervisory structure had been pretty definitely closed for them. What, however, was the non-Yankee attitude toward them as recipients of the new jobs? They accepted the three men because they were well liked by the foremen and by the union leaders, the two most important non-Yankee groups.

Sometimes, when a new job is created, the people involved are not sure whether it is a supervisory or an administrative position. This does not often happen, but I was able to observe one such incident.

During wartime expansion Somerset had overlooked the need for improved toilet and janitorial facilities. In one of the earlier labor-management meetings a discussion of these conditions was introduced, and after several weeks of debate, of "kicking the thing around," it was agreed that a new department should be organized under the auspices of the safety and health subcommittee of the Labor–Management Committee. This new department was to be known as the "Central Janitor Service," and the janitors from each department were to be reassigned to it. Management agreed that if the safety and health subcommittee (one of whose members was the vice-president in charge of production) was to assume responsibility for plant cleanliness, management would not interfere with its running of the janitor service without the prior approval of the central group of the Labor–Management Committee.

This was an explicit but verbal agreement between management and labor. At first blush it seems impossible that a misunderstanding could arise. But the project immediately hit a snag. The labor members insisted that the choice of a "janitor foreman" was in line with the other duties of the safety and health subcommittee. Management was indignant: its prerogatives were being encroached upon. But after several caucuses management agreed that if labor would have candidates submit their names, management might select the new janitor foreman from among them. The labor nominations were, with one exception, both workingmen and Irish. Management rejected all of them.

Several days later management posted notices that applications for "Sanitation Engineer" would be accepted and immediately chose Roundtree, who was Yankee and a plant guard.

The repercussions were violent, but the appointment "stuck." By changing the title of the new job from "foreman" to "engineer," management had removed the job from *supervision* to *administration*. It was clear that if the job could be placed under administration, it was entirely different from what labor had conceived it to be. Through the mechanism of a change of title, management had upset the social logic by which labor had concluded that the job was supervisory and should be secured for an Irishman. Labor's argument had lost its force.

B. DIFFERENCES IN PARTICIPATION RATES

The different characteristics, roles, and outlooks of an organization's members may produce two kinds of internal divergence: differences in participation in organizational affairs and factional disputes over the organization's aims and methods. Disputes occur not only because different factions exist but also because members are active. Whether members participate actively in organizational affairs is a problem distinct from the question of whether persons will become members. Chapter 3 of this book describes the social characteristics of the population that are associated with membership in voluntary associations; the present question is what social characteristics of members are associated with active participation.

Many research studies have identified the characteristics that distinguish the active citizens from the numerous other people who are inactive in politics.* Some have noted the same distinction in the membership of voluntary associations and of other private organizations: some members are active while many others are not.† The characteristics distinguishing activists and apathetics have been studied largely in politics and (among private associations) primarily in trade union memberships. In his selection, William Spinrad summarizes the work roles, trade union roles, and off-the-job statuses that affect participation in union affairs. Some of the determinants—particularly place of residence, personal associations, and non-work interests—may also govern membership participation in voluntary associations.

WHO JOINS TRADE UNIONS?‡

William Spinrad

The lack of widespread membership participation in most trade unions, a counterpart of the similar phenomenon in other large-scale organizations, is a commonplace observation of both theorists and investigators. Many persons are active members of their unions, however, whatever the proportion in specific unions. Research on American trade unions has produced a wealth of material which strives to answer the question: Which unionists are more likely to be active and why? This paper is a summary statement of an extensive analysis of approximately 35 published reports of studies in this area. The reports include case histories of specific union locals, comparisons of international unions and of locals, and comparisons of individuals and groups within single locals. The methods used range from impressionistic participant observation to statistical treatment of precisely formulated surveys.

We are primarily interested in analysis of participation in those situations where unions are well-established, where the problems of initial organization and recognition have been settled for some time. Indexes of participation vary, although holding a union office, serving on a committee, and attendance at meetings are commonly used; other criteria include voting in union elections, reading union literature, and using the grievance procedure. Some of these obviously imply more intense involvement than others,

but the findings reported here are generally unaffected by the indexes utilized. However, in some cases the official local leaders—unpaid officers and shop stewards—are singled out for special attention.

Before outlining what emerges from these studies it should be pointed out that many variables conceivably correlated with union participation are not treated because there is insufficient attention, lack of significant data, or grossly conflicting data. For instance, there are surprisingly few systematic inquiries into the effect of the special characteristics of the individual unions—local and international—on the participation patterns of individuals. There are numerous detailed narrative accounts of individual locals and a few about international unions, but such elements as the formal structure, the degree of internal democracy, the history of organization, and the position of the international within the organized labor movement, which *a priori,* seem to be related to the degree and kind of membership activity, are rarely sufficiently analyzed as factors affecting participation. . . .

Belief in "unionism" and in the general policies of the national and local union is of course a necessary condition for active participation. But it is not sufficient. Most of the members of a United Mine Workers local, for example, expressed unqualified loyalty to their union, but few attended meetings. There was little motivation for local union activity as almost all labor-management policies were decided at the national level. Participation also requires a belief that activity is functional, that it can achieve observable results. This is further borne out by the finding that, within several industrial plants, those departments with a record of *satisfied grievances* tended to have large numbers of active unionists.

The major variables associated with union participation, except for those already cited, can be grouped

* The American research is summarized in Robert E. Lane, *Political Life* (Glencoe: The Free Press, 1959).
† Bernard Barber, "Participation and Mass Apathy in Associations," in Alvin W. Gouldner (editor), *Studies in Leadership* (New York: Harper & Brothers, 1950), pp. 477-504.
‡ From William Spinrad, "Correlates of Trade Union Participation," *American Sociological Review*, Volume 25, Number 2 (April 1960), pp. 237-244. Reprinted with the permission of the author and the publisher, the American Sociological Association. The numerous bibliographical footnotes have been omitted.

under the headings of *objective features, personal associations,* and *personal orientations.*

OBJECTIVE FEATURES

JOB

The two most important types of objective factors appear to be those of the job and residence. The nature of the job, the studies strongly suggest, has important implications for personal relationships, income, and status.

(1) *Effect on interpersonal relations.* Small plant size seems to facilitate union participation for it establishes a more intimate work community, encouraging personal relations among work mates and facilitating more widespread involvement in decision making. Another possible correlate is a stable work force. However, studies have noted widespread participation among building trades workers, a very "casual" work group. This apparent discrepancy is readily explainable by the fact that both situations encourage the development of close personal ties over a period of time. Building trades workers have had numerous opportunities to work together in different jobs. In fact, the very instability of the industry demands that, in order to learn about jobs and conditions in the industry, it is necessary to attend union meetings, be informed of union affairs, be friendly with fellow workers and union officials, and appear frequently in the union hall. The "slack season," which brings large numbers of employees together at union headquarters, has had a similar effect on some garment workers.

Among typographers, two specific job features stimulate on and off the job personal contacts and resultant widespread union participation: the large proportion of night workers, and the unique substitute system by which a printer selects his replacement when going on leave.

Within specific *industrial* shops, those whose jobs permit mingling with many other workers, as is true of maintenance men, tend to be more active. In contrast, those whose jobs isolate them from other workers tend to be very apathetic. Work groups, the members of which work closely together and are relatively homogenous in pay, skill, and background tend to participate more in union affairs. The general conclusion is simply that those whose jobs facilitate and encourage frequent contact with fellow workers are more likely to be union activists.

(2) *Pay and status.* Union activity is typically associated with a relatively "higher" job. Thus, craft locals generally exhibit more participation than indus-

trial locals. Among needle trades workers, the high status cutters and pressers participate more than do the others. Within industrial locals, the evidence is also striking that union activists, especially local leaders, except for the period of initial organization and during faction fights in some unions, are disproportionately drawn from those of relatively higher pay and job status.

RESIDENCE

Where one lives (or has lived) appears to be the other type of objective variable associated with union participation. In terms of community of origin, those with rural backgrounds have been shown to be less involved in their unions than those brought up in an urban environment, while, at the opposite pole, the very active "ideological unionist" is mostly a product of politically-sophisticated metropolitan centers. As a result of both past and current influences, workers in industries that foster isolated geographic communities of fellow workers—for example, miners, fishermen, and, in a special sense, seamen—tend to have very strong pro-union attitudes throughout the world. If not always productive of intense local union activity, as in the case of United Mine Workers' groups, these sentiments do encourage such corollary forms of participation as heavy turnouts in voting for candidates considered pro-union.

This suggests the most common finding on residence-community factors, namely, that relative coincidence of geographic and occupational community facilitates union participation. Those who live in the town in which the plant is located are more likely to be active than workers who live "out of town," particularly residents of the "urban fringe." Work mates who live close together tend to be more active in their unions. Many unionists insist that the great distance between their homes and the union hall is at least a partial explanation for their inactivity.

Yet, this concurrence of geographic and occupational community can have very diverse effects. The result can be a local parochialism highly antithetical to the ideological unionism that grows up in the metropolis. Small industrial towns often reveal a close paternalistic bond between the workers and the owners and supervisors, which militates against union participation. When this bond is broken, however, the geographically cohesive worker community is likely to exhibit a high level of union activity.

PERSONAL ASSOCIATIONS

Some of the findings under this heading have already been implied by the data on objective conditions. Job situations leading to frequent and close associations with many fellow workers encourage union participation. Residential features which facilitate contact with worker colleagues, or with other "pro-union" people, stimulate union activity. Such interpersonal relations are intensified among typographers, with their many special printers' organizations and more informal leisure-time contacts, which is one of the reasons for their unusual involvement in union life. If not as extensive, the structure of the industries and the craft identifications create a guild-like occupational community among many building and garment workers. Leisure-time association seems also a concomitant of participation in industrial locals. Thus, one study of several industrial locals disclosed a statistical correlation between the extent of off-job contacts with fellow workers and attendance at union meetings.

Membership in two types of non-job social groups also seems to be associated with union participation. In accordance with common expectations, those with union family backgrounds tend to be more active. Secondly, union activists are disproportionately drawn from specific ethnic groups—Negroes, Mexicans, Jews, and Catholics—a finding also consistent with impressionistic observations. In general, these different groups may be classified as "deprived": minority ethnic status means some form of personal economic and social discrimination, or at least fears of such discrimination. These ethnics have thus been particularly responsive to the union's emphasis on collective efforts for improvement, frequently reflected in a greater degree of participation than is found among work colleagues from "dominant" ethnic groups. In some situations, however, the ethnic-occupational sub-community provides a clearly-defined setting for transmission of intense union loyalties which encourage participation, as among Jewish garment workers and Welsh and Scotch miners. Finally, work groups with common ethnic ties, whatever the minority ethnic group, tend to include more activists.

A few additional items have been reported of relevant interpersonal influences. Those workers related to or friendly with supervisors and owners are unlikely to be union activists. As already noted, a paternalistic atmosphere at least creates the illusion of intimacy, which can militate against union activity. Workers who are friendly with union leaders are more likely to be active. Contrariwise, those who know few union activists personally are less likely to participate themselves. . . .

These observations suggest a simple "differential association" model. The likelihood of union participation is enhanced by personal contact with pro-union work colleagues, union leaders, family members, ethnic associates; it is diminished by personal contacts with supervisors and non-union or anti-union friends, and as indicated in the material on residence, non-working-class neighbors.

ORIENTATIONS

JOB SATISFACTION

The most general observation here is that participation tends to increase with degree of job satisfaction. The craft gratification of many active skilled workers is one illustration. This relationship is also implicit in the findings that workers with higher pay and status within industrial locals tend to be "better unionists."

Studies of several industrial locals provide highly convincing evidence for this contention. Three of the reports, using observations of nine different unions, affirm that activists usually like their jobs more than non-activists. These findings, of course, seem to contradict the typical assessment of the union activist as motivated primarily by resentment over some feature of the work situation. Actually, if activists are more protesting it is probably because they are indignant about supervision, favoritism, and the like—about particular aspects of the job situation, not about the job itself. Such attitudes may characterize particularly the local leadership. Rank and file activists, however, may be no more critical of supervisors than other rank and filers.

Another aspect of job satisfaction may be involved —the relation to aspirations, particularly mobility strivings. Those more oriented towards occupational advance, particularly towards a supervisory or managerial position are less likely to be active in their unions. However, the actual potentiality for vertical mobility seems clearly unrelated to union participation. What seems to be more significant is the importance of mobility as a *goal*. For instance, one account describes local leaders as having more opportunities for appointment to supervisory positions but as being less interested in them. Those who feel thwarted in their aspirations, especially if they accuse the union of some responsibility for their situation, are very prone to union apathy.

Another element of job satisfaction is the role of the union in fostering such satisfaction. Even though the union's part in improving working conditions usually affects most members, those who verbally emphasize this fact are more likely to be activists.

Few union activists seem to be consciously motivated by a desire for a full-time union position. But union involvement can make the job situation much more pleasant and meaningful by providing an area for creativity and interpersonal influence and an avenue for status not found in the job itself. The union activists, particularly the local officials, apparently require such an outlet, for they are commonly found to be very "outgoing," "liking to deal with people," "possessing high activity levels" and "nervous tension."

NON-WORK INTERESTS

The active unionist thus has a positive orientation to his work situation as well as to his work group. This further steers him toward personal contacts with fellow-worker unionists, reinforcing pro-union values. As a counterpart, other values and commitments are de-emphasized: he spends less time with his family and shows less interest in fixing up his home. In contrast, a non-activist may exclaim that he has "too much work to do on my house."

With their positive orientation towards the work situation, it might be expected that activists would tend to be less interested in leisure activities than non-activists. Several studies, utilizing the personal remarks of a few non-activists or the comments of local officials, report that many workers prefer to have a "good time" rather than to be active in the union, or would rather "go to a ball game or a show" or "sit home and read a book" than attend a union meeting. But the evidence is not very substantial that activists are either less involved in or more oriented toward leisure pursuits. One study found that those who regularly attended union meetings were a little more likely to be regular card players and fishermen than the infrequent attenders. In a poll of a cross section of a community's industrial workers, union activists were shown actually to be a little more likely to "prefer leisure to work" than non-activists. The data at hand are thus, at best, uncertain. However, it would be necessary to know more about the nature of the leisure activity ("active" *versus* "passive," for example) and the type of leisure associates, as well as the activity level of the different unionists, before the notion implied in our earlier statements can be discounted—that union activity generally means sacrificing some leisure activity. As a final commentary, the union itself can become an area of leisure-type functions for many active unionists.

As indicated above, the union activists are less likely to find their close friends among non-occupational colleagues. At least in larger communities, their neighborhoods typically provide fewer close contacts; in fact, one study shows that union activists tend to have a lower estimate than non-activists of their neighborhoods and communities as places to live.

CLASS IDENTIFICATION

The active unionist, then, views his work group or the "working class" or both as a significant reference group. He emphasizes *collective* rather than *individual* efforts for improvement. According to several of the reports, many local leaders seem to be especially interested in helping the "working man" as an ethical or religious imperative. Whether he does or does not have a combative attitude towards management, the activist is "class conscious," that is, he sees himself as a *worker*, and tends to perceive industrial disputes from the vantage point of the "workers" rather than from the side of "management."

. . . There are unpaid activists in all union locals, whatever their number. Few students of the labor movement have included them in their theoretical expositions, despite the fact that they have been located in the several studies cited above. The union participant is a necessary ingredient without which most local unions could not operate. There must be personnel to fill posts, opinion leaders to inform and stimulate, a cadre to mobilize for the various modes of latent and overt combat.

To use the terminology of one study, the major institutional purposes of a union are *economic* (satisfying economic needs of workers) and *political* (serving as a rival power to management). These aims also define the core expectations of most union members. At the same time, however, the activists—those who feel part of a "movement," who speak of "we" rather than "they," who "enjoy playing the union game"—need, in addition, a *social* orientation. As a result of whatever influences and motivations, their union *tends* to take on, in the classic sociological language, a communal rather than a societal character. . . .

From this examination of the literature, the following conclusion emerges: participation in trade unions is enhanced by those factors which make for greater identification with one's occupational situation and occupational community, and diminished by those influences which foster contrary orientations. The nature of the job, the type of residence, the modes of interpersonal influences (past and present), and the orientation towards work life and work mates comprise the elements which determine that identification. Ultimately, union activity is a result of the acceptance of work, work place, work mates, and "working class" as somehow constituting a very meaningful part of the union member's life—not merely as instrumental features which are useful for the achievement of gratifications elsewhere.

C. THREE CASE STUDIES OF FACTIONAL CONFLICT

When people diverge in fundamental interests and outlooks, they may dispute over an organization's aims and methods. Political scientists have studied how political disputes result from the diverse economic, religious, regional, and other characteristics of the population.* Factional disputes, sometimes even bitter ones, can also occur in private organizations.

Some may be feuds between different factions of administrators. Some may be conflicts between higher and lower categories of personnel, such as the disputes between managers and workers. Others are factional disputes among the large constituency that may be the supreme governing authority of an organization; an example would be a proxy battle for control of a corporation. Disputes within such a large governing membership resemble the campaigns in the political electorate.

The course of a dispute depends on the sources of disagreement and the organization's mechanisms for coping with it. Some social structures have well-established channels for ventilating separate positions and for inducing communication and compromise between the sides: democracies have political parties and mass media to represent the different factions, and parliamentary institutions provide the means for testing relative power and adjusting rival views; industrial labor unions represent workers against management, and collective bargaining is the mechanism for producing compromises.

In many private associations, internal disputes never gain much headway because of membership apathy, solidarity between the leaders and most members, or organizational structures that strengthen the leadership and handicap dissenters. Several studies of the American Medical Association—the next selection is an example—have shown why rebellions against the leadership never progress very far: the bulk of the membership lets a minority run the county medical societies; the leadership usually takes action acceptable to the members; and indirect election and the leadership's control over information media strengthen the dominant minority and obstruct the plans of rebels.†

THE AMERICAN MEDICAL ASSOCIATION‡
The Editors of the Yale Law Journal

The American Medical Association consists of 53 state and territorial (constituent) societies and 1987 county (component) societies. Each county society sets its own qualifications for membership and its members automatically belong to the state association. Aside from racial barriers in most southern counties, all "reputable and ethical" licensed M.D.'s are eligible for membership. And in most areas virtually every practicing physician belongs to his local society.[1] Until recently, all members of county and state medical societies were also automatically members of the national association. But in 1950 payment of dues, previously assessed only by the county and state groups, became a prerequisite to AMA member-

* Some of this voluminous research is summarized by Robert E. Lane, *Political Life* (Glencoe: The Free Press, 1959), especially Part IV; Seymour M. Lipset et. al., "The Psychology of Voting: An Analysis of Political Behavior," in Gardner Lindzey (editor), *Handbook of Social Psychology* (Cambridge: Addison-Wesley Publishing Company, 1954), Ch. 30.

† The most detailed study (now somewhat out-of-date) is the book by Oliver Garceau cited in footnote 11 in the next selection. For a good study of factionalism in the American Library Association, see Oliver Garceau, *The Public Library in the Political Process* (New York: Columbia University Press, 1949), Ch. 4.

‡ Reprinted by permission of the copyright holder from the *Yale Law Journal*, Volume 63, Number 7, pp. 938-947. Single issues, as well as back issues, available at $2.50 from F. B. Rothman, 57 Leuning St., South Hackensack, New Jersey. Subscription $10.00 per volume available from Business Office, Yale Law Journal, 401-A Yale Station, New Haven, Conn. 06520. Copyright © 1952, by the Yale Law Journal Co.

1 Half of the societies report over 90 per cent membership among eligible, active physicians in their states. Only two states—Pennsylvania and Washington—report two-thirds membership or less. [These and other data are derived from questionnaires sent by the *Yale Law Journal* to all state medical societies and returned by twenty-four. —Eds.]

ship. Now some physicians belong only to their county and state societies, and are not members of the American Medical Association.[2] On the other hand, since belonging to a county society is a prerequisite to admission at all levels, membership in the AMA depends upon acceptance by the local organization.

REASONS FOR MEMBERSHIP

Many factors contribute to the high percentage of physician membership in organized medicine—a proportion unique among voluntary professional associations. With membership in the society, the doctor receives ready access to the social and professional contacts indispensable to the growth of his practice—contacts which may lead to patient referrals and consultations. Additionally, there is the all-important factor of association with men engaged in his own science, with opportunities for exchange of knowledge and acquisition of professional status. The medical societies disseminate the latest scientific information through professional journals which are available to members either at no cost or at reduced rates, and through lectures, exhibits, and medical libraries which the societies support. In addition to these professional services, the local and state societies aid members by providing group malpractice insurance, and by offering legal advice. Many of the larger societies maintain bill collection agencies. There may also be direct economic benefits incident to membership. Since the societies often contract to furnish medical care to indigents and veterans, participating physicians have a supplementary source of income from these programs. Membership can also be a conduit to such professional advancements as hospital staff appointments, teaching positions, and specialty ratings.

Beyond the advantages which accrue to the member physicians, there are services which the society renders to the profession as a whole. The AMA has improved curricula and facilities in American medical schools. It gives financial support to research projects and publicizes medical discoveries through its journals and meetings. Moreover, many doctors look to the American Medical Association to protect their interests against encroachment. Thus, the AMA spearheaded the drive against compulsory health insurance and other governmental inroads into private medical practice. And the Association has worked to rid the profession of quacks, as well as licensed physicians thought guilty of malpractice, and to limit the activities of nonmedical practitioners. Since the entire profession profits by these efforts of the AMA, physicians may feel obligated to join and give their material and moral support.

REASONS FOR NON-MEMBERSHIP

However, a substantial number of American doctors do not belong to the American Medical Association or its component units. Many of these are retired physicians who let their membership lapse, or young practitioners who have not yet fulfilled the residence requirements for their local society.[3] Doctors who do not conform to the code of medical ethics are not eligible for membership. And many southern societies exclude Negro physicians. Salaried doctors, such as those on the staffs of universities and research institutes, and civil servants often do not join medical societies; here professional advancement is available through channels other than medical society membership. In remote areas services which the society can render may be so negligible that doctors have little incentive to join. Some physicians may find the dues prohibitive; for example, in parts of California the total of county, state, and national dues runs as high as $190 annually.[4] Undoubtedly some doctors do not join because of apathy, while a small minority of physicians do not choose to belong because they disapprove of the policies of the AMA.

FORMAL STRUCTURE

The formal structure of the American Medical Association provides for the largest measure of direct democratic control in the county medical societies, and increasingly indirect representation at the state and national levels. Members vote directly for county officials and representatives to the state "legislature," usually known as the House of Delegates.[5] These delegates select their own state officers and elect the

---

[2] The AMA claims a membership of over 140,000 [at the time of writing. At this time, there are about 215,000 licensed physicians in the United States] . . . Although in one society—New Hampshire—less than 60 per cent of the state society members pay dues to the AMA, more typically 95 per cent to 99 per cent are AMA members . . . And in Illinois, the Society's constitution and bylaws require all members to pay AMA dues.

[3] Connecticut, for example, has a one-year residence requirement, and reports a corresponding lag in admitting physicians newly arrived in the state.

[4] . . . The range of county society dues within a state may be wide. E.g., Texas: $1 to $100; California: $5 to $125 . . . And state society dues vary from $15 to $55 a year; the average is about $25 . . . The AMA assesses its members $25 for annual dues . . . However, it grants exemptions for the following reasons: financial hardship, retirement from practice or reaching the age of 70, internship or residency with five years of graduation.

[5] Each county society is entitled to at least one delegate although representation in state Houses is generally proportional to membership in the local society. Apportionment ratios vary among the societies from one delegate for every ten members to one for every hundred; the average representation is one delegate for every twenty-five members . . . Densely populated areas tend to be underrepresented.

state representatives to the national House of Delegates. This body elects the President and other AMA officers and the nine-man Board of Trustees.[6]

In theory, the policy-making function of the American Medical Association is vested in the House of Delegates. However, since the House meets semi-annually, many administrative and policy decisions are necessarily left to the Board of Trustees. Although it is responsible to the House of Delegates, the Board functions with little supervision when the House is not in session. The members of the Board perform the typical role of corporate directors: they approve all AMA expenditures, and generally the Chiefs of the Association's operating bureaus are responsible to them. The Trustees also appoint the Secretary-General Manager and the Editor of the *Journal*. The President has little formal power in formulating AMA policy, although he enjoys tremendous prestige as chief spokesman for the organization.[7]

The AMA functions through standing committees or councils elected by the House of Delegates or appointed by the Board of Trustees. Each council directs the activities of the Association in a particular field with the assistance of a full-time staff. The 900 employees of the national organization are supervised by the Secretary-General Manager of the Association, who has chief responsibility for the day-to-day decisions of the organization between meetings of the Board of Trustees.

REAL POWER STRUCTURE

While democratic procedures exist at the county level, many members do not have sufficient interest in activities to attend meetings.[8] Doctors are ex-

tremely busy with their practice and have little time to devote to the problems of organized medicine. In New York, for example, 25 per cent attendance at a business meeting is considered good. Thus, the few doctors who are interested in medical politics can easily wield power and influence out of proportion to their numerical strength.

The nominating process for elections within the American Medical Association allows the officers in power to have the dominant influence in deciding who shall succeed them in office. At the county level, the President appoints a nominating committee which puts up a slate of officers and delegates for the state House of Delegates. The state President functions in the same way in the selection of national delegates. These elections are rarely contested. In at least one state, Alabama, the delegates are appointed by the President. The election of the official slate is made easier by the fact that the state and national organizations forbid electioneering and soliciting votes for office. Even where the official slate offers alternative nominees, basic differences between the candidates are unlikely.

The nominating process in combination with the apathy of the average doctor, assures domination by a single faction within the AMA. In New York—one of the few states where an organized opposition has developed—these challengers have had little success.[9] State societies report that reelection of delegates is common,[10] the same names appearing on the ballot year after year. Frequently officers progress steadily from county, to state, to national prominence as they acquire seniority.

One of the major obstacles to the formulation of

[6] An AMA delegate's term is two years. State societies are represented by one delegate for every thousand members or fraction thereof. A representative from the Army, Navy, Air Force, Veterans Administration and U. S. Public Health Service, and twenty representatives from the specialized medical fields within the AMA also serve in the House . . . The President, President-Elect, Vice-President, and other AMA officers are elected annually. The President and President-Elect serve on the Board of Trustees. The other Trustees are chosen for staggered five-year terms and may serve not more than two successive terms.

[7] The President's official duties consist largely of addressing the House of Delegates and nominating members for various committees, subject to confirmation by the House or Trustees . . . Prior to his term of office, the President serves as President-Elect for one year, during which time he presides over the General Sessions and Council of the Scientific Assembly . . . However, the President's Page in the *Journal* and his frequent appearances before Congressional Committees increase the President's importance as "chief spokesman for the Association on policy matters."

[8] The results of an AMA survey showed that urban county societies had the lowest average attendance at meetings. Sixty of 64 societies with more than 300 members report attendance of under 50 per cent, while only

48 of 581 societies having less than 100 members were in this category. And 111 of the smaller societies report 90-100 per cent attendance. *Activities of County Medical Societies* (Chicago: American Medical Association, 1951), p. 3 . . .

[9] The Physicians Forum was organized in 1941 by members of the Medical Society of the County of New York to defeat a proposed amendment to the state society constitution. This amendment provided that members "shall not initiate or participate in any activities outside the structure of the Medical Society of the State of New York, which are contrary to [its] policies . . ." Chapters have been formed in other cities and the group has promoted health insurance and other measures counter to "official AMA doctrine." Ernst P. Boas, letter to the editor, *New York Medicine*, Volume 12 (November 20, 1952), p. 13. Although the Forum was successful in defeating and in electing "several liberal minded physicians" to county officerships, its influence was of short duration. Richardson, "Freedom of Speech and Organized Medicine" (New York: Physicians Forum, undated manuscript), p. 16.

[10] Several societies report that all delegates are re-elected while others estimate that between one-third and one-half of the delegates are rechosen. One replied that "receptive delegates" are re-elected and another characterized the tenure of delegates as extending "until they choose to retire." Only three indicated that few or no delegates were "repeaters."

any opposition is the lack of an effective forum for dissident opinion. The *Journal of the American Medical Association*, which is the publication most widely read by members, rarely prints opinions in disagreement with positions taken by the House of Delegates or Board of Trustees. In response to criticism of this policy the American Medical Association asserts that members can present their views initially in their county societies; that if these views win approval, delegates will present them to the state society, and finally the members' opinions will be presented to the national House of Delegates for consideration. In practice, however, because of the indirect system of elections, such a procedure eliminates any dissident viewpoints above the county level unless they win majority support. And while a member can oppose official policy in his local society, the structure of organized medicine makes it almost impossible for him to effectuate his opinions within this framework.

One study of the American Medical Association has concluded that the physicians who rise to power within the medical societies are predominantly urban practitioners and specialists.[11] Although there is only a slightly larger number of specialists in the United States than general practitioners, usually over 90 per cent of the officers of the AMA are specialists.[12] Specialists, whose incomes are above those of the average practitioner, are probably better able to devote time to medical politics. Statistics also reveal that cities contribute a larger proportion of officers than rural areas.[13] And in the AMA House of Delegates those who have served long terms are primarily from urban localities, while the shorter term delegates tend to be from the rural areas.[14]

Although these officers are not "average" American doctors, it would not be accurate to say that their policies are unrepresentative. The support of the membership is clearly shown in the immediate response of most members to a voluntary assessment voted by the House of Delegates.[15] Most members also seem willing to distribute literature and advocate AMA policies. But perhaps the most indicative fact is that groups organized to oppose AMA policies regarding the economic and political aspects of medical practice have never gained widespread support among the doctors. No group of any significance that has been formed to modify or review AMA policy has offered itself as an alternative to the AMA. Doctors are free to join such organizations while retaining their AMA membership but few have enrolled. Even though the actively controlling group within the American Medical Association is a self-perpetuating minority, its viewpoint is readily accepted by the passive majority. This acquiescence assists that governing minority in excluding dissident opinion from organized medicine.

11 Oliver Garceau, *The Political Life of the American Medical Association* (Cambridge: Harvard University Press, 1941), pp. 55-58.
12 There were, in 1949, approximately 72,500 physicians exclusively in general practice, 55,000 exclusively practicing a specialty, and 23,000 general practitioners "giving attention" to a specialty. President's Commission on the Health Needs of the Nation, *Building America's Health* (Washington: United States Government Printing Office, 1953), Volume 3, p. 140. All but one of the present members of the Board of Trustees and all AMA Presidents, Vice-Presidents, and Speakers since 1947 have been specialists. [Calculations refer to the period between 1947 and original publication of this article in the *Yale Law Journal* in early 1954.—Eds.]
13 Only seven of 31 recent and present high officers and Trustees of the AMA practice in communities of 25,000 population or less.
14 Garceau, *op. cit.*, p. 50.
15 Only one state society indicated that less than 50 per cent of its membership paid the 1948 assessment. And 14 societies reported that from 60 per cent to 96 per cent of their members contributed.

Leaders may remain in power without challenges from an apathetic and acquiescent membership, provided that an organization is so successful that latent disagreements are not aroused. Organizational failure may trigger grass-roots revolts against the entrenched leadership. But if the structure and traditions of the organization cement the position of the leaders, the prompt and orderly replacement of people necessary for decisive policy changes may be impossible. An undercurrent of grumbling may beset the organization, adaptive changes in the leadership may occur slowly, and the organization may decline.

In the next selection, Joseph R. Gusfield describes such largely unre-

solved internal conflict in the Woman's Christian Temperance Union. The repeal of Prohibition in the 1930's created a policy crisis and split older from younger members. The older members and the entrenched leadership drawn from them wished to continue traditional policies; younger members believed that only new goals and means could enable the association to deal with its changed environment successfully. Some adaptive mechanisms have been employed to introduce new persons into the leadership, but the changes in personnel and in policy have not been fast enough to preserve the vigor, size, and public influence of the association. Gusfield's research provides a good example of how the structure of an organization can entrench an oligarchy in the face of grass-roots revolts and in the face of environmental changes that create a functional need for policy changes.

THE WOMAN'S CHRISTIAN TEMPERANCE UNION*

Joseph R. Gusfield

Conflicts of power and policy between age-groups are a common feature of many organizational structures. Factories, churches, labor unions, and political parties often distribute power, prestige, and income along an age-grade hierarchy. The existence of "old guard" and "young Turks" is found in many areas of society other than the specifically political. This paper examines some sources of age-graded power and their consequences for organizational stability in the Woman's Christian Temperance Union.

A depiction of the age-grade problem as one of culture conflict points to the difficulties age differences entail for organizational unity. Given such variables as rapid cultural change and competing cultural authorities, conflict between age-groups may be anticipated. Karl Mannheim has pointed out that the existence of generational differences leads to divergent political and social styles and modes of thought which greatly influence the character of public issues.[1] When two or more generations appear within the same organization we may consequently anticipate factional conflict.

In the Woman's Christian Temperance Union differences between generations have been most marked since repeal of the Eighteenth Amendment.[2] In the late nineteenth century—its early period of organization—the WCTU functioned as part of a general reform movement with humanitarian aims. Its major interests and activities manifested a concern

for the plight of lower-income groups. The central mission of the organization, total abstinence from use of all alcoholic beverages, was viewed as a solution to problems of poverty. In this period WCTU doctrine was the outlook of a socially secure Protestant middle class. Post-prohibition doctrine and activity of the WCTU has tended to express moral indignation toward contemporary American middle classes, rather than a concern for "uplifting the down trodden." Study of the socio-economic composition of WCTU local leadership revealed a decline in the socio-economic status of local leaders since repeal in 1933. The loss of prestige of WCTU membership has thus been a key problem within the WCTU.

RESPONSES TO ORGANIZATIONAL CRISIS

The repeal of the Eighteenth Amendment reflected a basic change in the reception of temperance doctrine by the American public. Temperance organizations now faced a more hostile public than at any time in their history. We are interested in the reaction of the organization's tactics to this crisis. Our general analysis of the generations problem leads us to see older generations as less willing than newer members to change tactics and past policy.

Within the WCTU two differing responses to the crisis of repeal were advocated at the time we studied the organization, 1952-1954.[3] One type of response we shall call "conviction-oriented." This type empha-

* From Joseph R. Gusfield, "The Problem of Generations in an Organizational Structure," *Social Forces,* Volume 35, Number 4 (May 1957), pp. 323-330. Reprinted with the permission of the author and the publisher, The University of North Carolina Press.

[1] Karl Mannheim, "The Problem of Generations," in *Essays on the Sociology of Knowledge* (London: Oxford University Press, 1952).

[2] Joseph R. Gusfield, "Social Structure and Moral Reform: A Study of the Woman's Christian Temperance Union," *American Journal of Sociology,* Volume LXI (November 1955), pp. 221-232.

[3] Forty-six interviews were held with National WCTU leaders and with local and county leaders in Chicago and in upstate New York. This article is based on these interviews plus the annual reports of the National WCTU and the issues of the WCTU weekly, *The Union Signal,* during the life of the WCTU, 1874-1953. For a detailed discussion of field and other methods used, see Gusfield, *Organizational Change: A Study of the Woman's Christian Temperance Union.* (Chicago: Unpublished dissertation for the Ph.D. at the University of Chicago, 1954).

sized the continuance of the tactics and goals of the prohibition period. Even though public accessibility is made more difficult, convictions must be maintained. The second type of response we shall call "public-oriented." Those who advocated this approach wished to substitute the primacy of educational and persuasional aims for those of less respectable legal and political measures to restrict the sale of liquor. The fact that this issue still existed indicates the unsettled nature of WCTU reaction after twenty years.

The conviction-oriented employed a tactic of rectitude. They refused to accept immediate organizational influence as justification for change in existent policy. This was especially stressed in their support of the prohibition doctrine and in the refusal to cooperate, in campaigns against alcoholism, with organizations not in sympathy with the WCTU stand of total abstinence. As one member put it:

> It makes no difference to me what others think as long as I think that I am in the right. As long as I'm on God's side, it doesn't matter how many think otherwise.

While conviction-oriented members were unconcerned about the impact of their actions on public acceptance and access, the public-oriented members advocated tact. These members argued that the prime strategy of the organization should be moral suasion They advocated a de-emphasis of the prohibition issue, which they saw as unworkable and a source of public antagonism. This type of adherent was fearful of the possible impression some WCTU members might have on public attitudes. Several told stories critical of individual members whose dress or eccentric behavior sustained the image of the temperance reformer as a "crackpot" or a "bluenose." As one national officer said:

> We have been inept in selling ourselves to others who think as we do. We've sort of shelved ourselves in. We will cooperate more with other groups in the future . . . We must act like ladies and be tolerant of other people's minds.

In concrete instances, of course, these two types overlapped frequently. Nevertheless, they gave tone and direction to specific policy that differed considerably. Conviction-orientation led to the maintenance of the prohibitionist cause and to an attitude of tactical rigidity. Public orientation led to tactical flexibility and a weakening of prohibitionist fervor. The two approaches, with their divergent emphases on the value of acceptance, were characterized by one local leader who said:

> The public thinks of us—let's face it—as a bunch of old women, as frowzy fanatics. This worries a good many in the WCTU. *They want to be accepted.*

X is a good woman and a good organizer, but she, too, has this point of view. She has remarked that we should always be well-dressed and have our hair marcelled. It's part of the movement to look smart. *That doesn't seem as important to me as making my position clear.*

In the twenty years between 1933 and 1953 the policies and activities of the WCTU have been closer to those of the conviction-oriented than to the policies and tactics of the public-oriented. Only with the ascension of a new president in 1953 has the WCTU seemed to be moving toward measures to enhance the organization's access to the public.

Within the WCTU, many persons interviewed spoke of the past administration as the "old guard" and of the conviction-oriented as the "diehards." Despite the changed environment resulting from Repeal, the WCTU maintained continuity with past doctrine. This cannot be explained by uniformity within the organization since, as we have seen, the outlines of factionalism existed. How were the "old-guard" able to keep control of the organization for a generation?

SOURCES OF GENERATIONAL POWER

The organizational power of the older generation may stem from the mechanisms which maintain the incumbent in positions of power. Given the rigid nature of a past commitment, the maintenance of incumbency power reduces the capacity of the organization for change. We can imagine a system in which older members respond to new situations by advocating organizational change as do younger members. Also, we can imagine a system in which older members resist organizational change, but the mechanisms of power distribution do not give them great opportunity to implement their commitments. Accordingly, our analysis of the WCTU's relative organizational rigidity focuses on the power and transformation of the office holders.

ORGANIZATIONAL OLIGARCHY

Like most American voluntary associations, the formal charter of the WCTU enunciates a system of representation and diffusion of power in which the rank and file possess great influence in making policy. As is often true in such a situation, the WCTU has developed an informal structure which places power in the hands of an "active minority" and acts to perpetuate incumbents in office.

One factor explaining the power of the incumbents on the national level is the scarcity of the skills and resources requisite for holding office in a woman's reform organization. Those who operate the organization in its day-to-day routine must be able to live near the national headquarters. In a woman's organization, availability of leaders is influenced by the husband's occupation. Where he is unable to leave a place of business, occupancy of a national office by the wife may entail a marital crisis. The constitution requires the president, corresponding secretary, and the treasurer to be in residence at headquarters. This restricts the offices to those who live nearby, are widows, or single, or have retired husbands. Both the costs of movement and the relatively low salaries ($3600 for the national president in 1952) further restrict the jobs to wealthy members. The general status of women and the relatively low level of personal commitment require that husband and wife both be able to take the position. This was shown during the study when the corresponding secretary resigned her position because her new husband's parish was not in the Chicago area.

Leadership in the day-to-day operation of an organization is of crucial importance in regulating control of policies. In the WCTU this fact makes the role of the national president immensely important. Through her control of the office at headquarters she leaves her "touch" on many avenues of WCTU activity. She reads the WCTU journal before it is printed each week and exercises considerable editorial power. The literature printed by the WCTU is chiefly made up at headquarters. Even the librarian pointed out that the library is run differently under different administrations. The "headquarters gang" thus has responsibility for the communications received by the local leaders and members. Further, the "headquarters people" travel among the local and state WCTUs very frequently, working as speakers at WCTU events. Consequently they are in communication with local areas. In these ways, the official positions are not nominal but really entail power.

OLIGARCHY AND SELF-SUCCESSION

One of the most significant ways in which the incumbent remains in power, however, is through the manipulation of the formal charter. This is most apparent in the incumbent's ability to be re-elected to office.

The nomination and election of officers takes place at the annual convention. Persons are nominated by write-in votes of delegates. If a majority is not achieved on the first ballot by any one candidate, a second ballot is held with candidacy limited to the two receiving the highest votes on the first ballot. This procedure might be expected to result in frequent turnovers of office and numerous second ballots. Indeed, it would seem that this procedure would make nomination and election very difficult and prevent the existence of a power-holding minority with lengthy tenure. The facts are otherwise. Since the organization of the WCTU in 1874 there have been 330 separate elections for various national offices. A second

ballot has been necessary in only 15 cases, approximately five per cent of the times.[4]

It seems highly unlikely that such unanimity could be obtained on the first ballot without some prior guidance to convention delegates. Indeed, the national officers and the executive board often functioned informally as a nominating committee. This was evident from the accounts of newly-elected national officers. One said that she had to decide in one month whether or not she wished to take the office, "when the committee asked me if I'd take it." Neither she nor the committee felt that this procedure was unusual or that there would be any difficulty in securing election. Another newly-elected officer explained that she got the position because someone on the executive board knew her and knew she had the needed skills for the job. "The former person in this office wasn't too satisfactory and they asked me." In this manner the group at the top manages to control the selection and succession of officers.

SUCCESSION RULES: THE "PIPELINE"

The issue of succession is a crucial question for any ongoing organization. Methods of life tenure and of hereditary succession have often been advocated as ways of solving the destabilizing effects of frequent change in officers and leaders. The "democratic mold" has been advocated as a means of insuring changes in policy and as a means to obtain both knowledge of the wishes of the rank and file and their loyal support of the leadership. While the democratic method operates to gain stability through obtaining assent, it leaves the organization open to frequent internal factionalism. Many American organizations have developed traditions which regulate succession in such fashion that the succession is decided by a set of norms which dictate the democratic selection.

One such tradition common in many American voluntary associations is that of the "pipeline." In this system, persons move up the ladder of offices in some regular order. In the WCTU, the presidency, when it becomes vacant, regularly goes to the vice-president. This system insures orderly succession. But such a system requires two things if it is also to insure flexibility of policy: (1) The office must be a "real" and not a nominal one; and (2) there must be some tradi-

---

4 This is based on the election returns, by ballot, reported in *Annual Report of the National Woman's Christian Temperance Union*, 1874-1953. The results of these elections may be compared with similar figures for labor unions in the period 1910-1940. Philip Taft found that in 17.2 per cent of the cases, officers were contested. This varied from 4.2 per cent for the Teamsters Union to 52.2 per cent for the Barbers Union. Philip Taft, "Opposition to Union Officers in Elections," *Quarterly Journal of Economics*, Volume 58 (1943-44), pp. 246-264.

tions which enforce vacancy and limit the tenure of the incumbent. The inconsistency in this system should be apparent. If an office is more than nominal, it creates power and necessitates experience in its work. Therefore, the second element is difficult to obtain. It is hard to get people out of office, because they have the power to stay there and because it takes time to learn the job . . .

In the WCTU the "pipeline" system operates to prevent policy changes. The existence of the powerful president who really runs the organization gives the presidency a lengthy tenure. Since the vice-president proceeds to the presidency, the effective choice of the president is made long before the situation in which she functions as president. Table I shows this. It indicates that in the past four presidencies the organization was being led, at the conclusion of the president's stay in office, by women whose selection had been effectively made approximately twenty years before. A consequence of this is to perpetuate older generations in power.

TABLE I

Age of WCTU presidents at vice-presidential and presidential accession and retirement

President	Age VP accession	Age Pres. accession	Retirement (or death)	Years between VP accession and presidential retirement
Stevens	47	50	66	21
Gordon	45	61	73	28
Boole	55	67	76	21
Smith	53	62	74	21
Colvin	51	61	71	20
Hays	55	58	—	—

Based on *Annual Reports of the Woman's Christian Temperance Union*, *Who's Who in America*, and *The Standard Encyclopedia of Alcohol Reform*, Ernest Cherrington (ed.) (Westerville, Ohio: The American Issue Press, 1920). The table includes only presidents since 1898. The vice-presidential office was established in 1895. The career pattern of the present president, Hays, appears to vary from the general pattern. The previous vice-president was elected in 1944 and retired in 1949, the first vice-president to retire from office. Her retirement does not appear to have been forced. She gave up the state presidency which she had held from 1939 and moved to Florida in 1949.

The impact of the "pipeline" on policy continuation is strikingly seen in the case of the last WCTU president. Early in her life, during her college days, she became deeply identified with the prohibition movement and the Prohibition Party. Her husband was one of the leading figures in the Prohibition Party, and once was its presidential nominee. She was a prominent leader in the WCTU and in 1933 was elected vice-president. In 1944, according to the traditional norms of succession, she was elected president. Her position epitomized the point of view of the conviction-oriented in the WCTU. It would have been extremely difficult for her to reverse the commitment of 40 years of agitation and assume a more flexible policy.

TENURE TRADITIONS

The modes of succession are not the only forces operating to keep older people in office. In general, it is difficult to get people out of office, once they have been installed.

We have analyzed the elections on the national level between 1947 and 1953. Of the 35 elections held in this period, only in 10 was there a contest, in the sense that one or more candidates, other than the electee, received 10 per cent or more of the total vote cast. Only in 3 of the 35 cases was a second ballot required. In only 4 cases did the winner receive less than 75 per cent of the vote.

Rejection of an incumbent is rare. Of the eight instances occurring in this time span, only two might be considered true rejections or turnovers. In two cases the incumbent moved up to a higher office, thus leaving a vacancy. The two higher offices were vacated because of poor health, a reason which was validated by interviews and by our knowledge of the hospitalization, in the previous year, of one of the officers. In another case, the officer had been the Washington lobbyist for WCTU for many years. The failure of her successor in this job forced her to return to it. In another instance, already mentioned, marriage necessitated resignation. Of the two cases of turnover, one resulted from executive committee action. The incumbent was not put up for re-election because she seemed to lack the skills necessary for the job. Nevertheless, she had held the post for six years. In the last case, the officer was not re-elected by the convention.

Why is it so difficult for the WCTU to change officers? Politics often witnesses the casting aside of the old leader when a change seems called for in the interests of party victory. While we have shown the existence of tenure and succession traditions, we have not indicated how these are maintained.

INCUMBENCY AND THE SENTIMENT AGAINST EGO-LOSS

Once established, a rule tends to be maintained by the power of the rule maker. It is also maintained by the sentiments which may be violated by breaking it. One of the most significant of these sentiments operative in the WCTU is the sentiment against inflicting aggression. Because a rule is stated in impersonal terms, applicable to all within its categories, departures from the rule have personal connotations. Thus, if the incumbent were to be turned out of office, the implication exists that she was so inept that, even given the tradition, the group could not accept her.

Erving Goffman has pointed out the difficult problem posed for social systems by the necessity to inflict defeat and failure on some persons.[5] In American culture, removal from office tends to be a blow to the ego of the officeholder. Consequently, the action of members to bring about such loss of ego is an aggressive act. Since the rules lead the officeholder to anticipate incumbency *as long as he is acceptable to the members,* turnover in office can hardly be kept from being a punishing action.

In organizations such as political parties, labor unions, or businesses, the pressures of financial commitment and career contingencies may act to balance the norms against inflicting ego-loss. The attitude that "business is business" implies the impersonality of the act and the consequent immunity of the power-holder from the imputation of aggressiveness. Even so, such organizations are often deeply troubled by the necessity for firing employees and officials.

In the WCTU, positions do not bring great tangible rewards for the officeholder. The salary is minimal and few have made a professional career out of the WCTU. This may be one factor in explaining the reluctance of members to break the norms of lengthy tenure. People feel guilt if they act to expel an incumbent from office or move ahead of her in the line of succession. The action is seen as one of hostility and as disturbing to "good feelings." One local president said:

> This is my third year as president. The woman who was vice-president wasn't too good. *I hated to take it ahead of her,* but we were down to ten or twelve members.

Efforts to utilize potential power to bring new persons into office are thus frustrated by the norm of kindness to the incumbent. As a result, officers can achieve long tenures in office. In one of the large states, WCTU members had suggested that the incumbent president retire. She had felt "very hurt" and the movement to defeat her was discontinued. One local leader put it:

> We have a tradition of keeping people in office a little too long. If you choose someone else, the incumbent would feel that there was something wrong with her.

The behavior contemplated in one state illustrates the lengths to which the group will go to maintain "good feelings." In this case, the state president had held office for more than thirty years. One of the national officers explained their current problem as follows:

> State X has not come along as well as it should. There's a lot of sentiment there but poor leadership.

[5] Erving Goffman, "On Cooling the Mark Out," *Psychiatry*, Volume XV (1952), pp. 451-461.

The president is jealous of anyone taking her place. She views all newcomers in terms of what it means for her place. . . . We are thinking of splitting it into two groups. There is a lot of territory there anyway. She could be president of one group and the other could do the major work.

In this fashion, the norm against aggression becomes a means for the maintenance of the incumbent and the continuance of tenure traditions. Once established, the rule is supported by the weight of the interests of the officeholder and the sentiment of the non-officeholder against disturbing the incumbent's ego.

ADAPTIVE STRUCTURES

The response types discussed earlier are not the only elements operative in structuring the approaches of the members and officers to WCTU policy. Certain consequences of these positions are not easily ignored. Other values than those encompassed in the response types are at work. The effort to realize contradictory values operates to produce what Talcott Parsons has called "adaptive structures." [6]

One of the imperatives of organizational existence is the continued recruitment of new personnel. As long as incumbent personnel are committed to organizational continuity they must face the problems of recruitment. "Adaptations," in the sense of changes in policy, are not a solution to the value conflict between the conviction-oriented and the public-oriented. This latter conflict is an argument about the ethics and strategy of "adaptation." Adaptive structures would rather be ways in which the value positions of the incumbents were not changed but the structure of the organization permitted new personnel in key posts.

Our previous analysis of the forces maintaining the structure suggests that two structural types might be solutions to the problem: (1) ways of ejecting incumbents which do not lead to loss of ego; and (2) ways of letting new persons into positions of power without disturbing incumbents. Such adaptive structures have appeared in the WCTU.

The tension between response types is also a tension between age groups. The power of the older group in the WCTU has been felt to repel younger members, people between 35 and 50. In the literature and in the interviews there was concern expressed that the WCTU was "top heavy" with old people. "We must do something to attract the younger member" was a common statement. In this manner recruitment becomes an "exigency" or constraint on the behavior of the incumbent and acts to develop adaptations such as the following:

[6] Talcott Parsons, *The Social System* (Glencoe: The Free Press, 1951), p. 168.

"EASING OFF" PROCESSES

Many sociologists and anthropologists have called attention to the important function played by ritual and ceremony in the transition from one role to another. Erving Goffman has shown the need for social devices to forestall the potential hostility of persons subjected to rejection, defeat, or failure. The WCTU has attempted to ease retirement from office by the development of fictional roles which enable the retiring incumbent to veil the rejective aspect of removal.

One such form is the office of Member or Officer Emeritus. This device, most prevalent in academic circles, is appearing more frequently in other organizations, such as churches and labor unions. In the WCTU, a member is eligible for the title if she has served on the executive board for 15 or more years. Such persons are listed in the annual convention report, written about in the WCTU journal, and introduced to the convention at annual meetings. In this way the guise of the "elder statesman" is maintained by a fiction which minimizes the finality of the rejection and enables the incumbent to preserve "face."

Another variant of this device is the practice of movement to an allied organization. This was used by several national presidents on retirement. The World Woman's Christian Temperance Union is an organization of prestige but little day-to-day work. WCTU presidents hold an office in it. Either through becoming president of that organization or by the mere official position they hold there, the national president can use this both as a tangible position of prestige and as an "excuse" for retirement which still minimizes ego-deprivation. Thus one local leader said of the retiring WCTU president:

> She said that she is going to retire next year. She has an office in the international office. Maybe she's going to concentrate on that.

"SEPARATE BUT EQUAL"

To some extent, conflict between groups is avoided by prevention of contact. In an effort to recruit younger people, give them some voice in the organization, and prevent tension between age groups, separate units of the WCTU were formed in 1933. These groups, known as Iota Sigma units, meet in the evenings rather than in the afternoons, as regular WCTUs do. Program materials speak of them as "open to business and professional women and to young matrons." The national corresponding secretary, who is in charge of recruitment, explicitly viewed the Iota Sigma as a way to meet the age-group conflict through separation:

> When we're gone the younger people will take our place. Well, there's just one thing. You know when

people are older they find it hard to give up their places. We're trying to organize the younger women into separate groups. They would rather be with the younger and not the older anyway.

Such efforts have not proved very successful in attracting membership. They must be limited to cities large enough to sustain two units. After twenty years, neither the total membership nor the annual increase in Iota Sigma units is reported in WCTU documents, although all other sub-units, such as children's and adolescent's branches, are reported.

"SEDUCTION OF THE INNOCENT"

The perfect mode of adaptation to this problem of transmission would be one which insured recruitment into positions of power for younger members and still did not lead to the rejection of older members. This is possible in one type of situation. When a new office is created or when, for some unique reason, there is no successor for a vacant office, an opportunity appears to place younger members in power. . . . Authority is given to the younger person, so as to insure greater representation. However, it is also given as a means to develop activities through which the new member or officer can develop a deeper commitment to the WCTU. For example, in upstate New York, county and state organizers initiated a unit in 1951. When they found a woman aged 35 interested in WCTU they offered her the first presidency, although there were other, older women there who had previous experience in WCTU in other towns. This coöptation was possible since there was no vested interest in the office dictated by any clear tradition. In another case, a local unit decided to organize a children's branch. The president chose a somewhat marginal member as the director. As the president explained it, "She's a woman in her forties, and we'd like to get her more in the WCTU."

THE NEUTRALITY OF RULES

In some state units, the WCTU is beginning to define the tenure of office by a rule which limits it to a specified term. In one state the term has been set at eight years. The rule is an impersonal form. Because it is stated in universalistic rather than in particularistic terms, rules limiting tenure are able to provide the ego protection necessary for the incumbent to accept gracefully removal from office. The limited use of this technique, however, suggests that it is not feasible to introduce it while offices are being filled. In one state it came into existence during an interregnum period with an acting president.

THE ADAPTIVE PROBLEM

In the long run, the WCTU is changing toward a more flexible organization bent on increasing its access to the general public within the framework of its present mission as a critic of deviation from older, middle-class standards. Newer and younger persons are succeeding to office. Death and illness, twin assistants to organizational change, are also constraints to which organizations are heir.

The problem of transmission, however, is a problem to which the entire organization is sensitive. As long as members and officers are committed to the perpetuation of the organizational mission, they are alive to this problem. Consequently, the tendencies toward incumbency power are somewhat reduced.

People who become committed to a cause and to a set of doctrines do not give up the fight easily. Like the cowboy hero, they prefer to "die with their boots on" rather than "hang up the spurs" and capitulate to the rustlers. The problems of organization, however, aggravate the conflicts created by generational diversities. The rules and traditions of succession may operate to accentuate the role of the older generation through maintaining the incumbent in power. The power of the opposition to remove the incumbent is limited by the norms against aggressive actions. Necessities of organizational transmission spring from the member's concern for its mission. These necessities leave the organization open to needs for recruitment of younger members and thus the needs to remove older persons from power. Some devices have arisen which permit graceful exits and which may as sure quicker entry into power positions. Nevertheless, the movement toward tactical and strategic change has taken a generation in the WCTU.

Like the WCTU, most private associations operate in a bureaucratic fashion despite the democratic principles in the official charter. Disagreements sometimes break out, but usually there are no permanent and organized mechanisms for expressing opposition. Instead, opposition at the most is intermittent and nonformalized; many organizations are dominated by their leaders; and rebellions are unusual.

Institutionalized opposition, regular contested elections, and rotation in office seem to depend on unusual conditions. Although trade unions are supposed to be run like political democracies, in practice they lack the prerequisite conditions in their structures and memberships. Most trade unions are oligarchic; differences in status and opinion exist among the membership but fail to result in an institutionalized opposition.* In one exceptional organization, the International Typographical Union, organized channels for different viewpoints exist, in the form of a democratic two-party system resembling a political democracy. In a book† and in the selection summarizing the book, Lipset describes the unique conditions that support the existence of such orderly mechanisms for expressing and controlling factional disagreements in the ITU. These conditions are absent in other unions. Many of them are absent in other private associations too, thus accounting for oligarchical tendencies in them. For democracy to exist in a voluntary association, more than a democratically-phrased charter would be necessary. As Lipset's work shows, the social structure of the association, the membership characteristics, and the social environment must meet certain criteria. The social requisites for democracy in voluntary associations can be identified only after research comparable to Lipset's studies of the social prerequisites of democracy in trade unions.

* Seymour M. Lipset, "The Political Process in Trade Unions," in Morroe Berger et al. (editors), *Freedom and Control in Modern Society* (New York: D. Van Nostrand Company, 1954), pp. 82-124.

† Seymour M. Lipset, Martin A. Trow, and James S. Coleman, *Union Democracy* (Glencoe: The Free Press, 1956).

THE INTERNATIONAL TYPOGRAPHICAL UNION*

Seymour M. Lipset

The problem of democracy in unions is a puzzling one: most unions are formally democratic, with regular elections, representative conventions, and other forms of democracy. Yet it is a fact that union elections seldom result in turnover in office; that a potent opposition to the incumbent seldom develops; and that union governments have taken on the aspect of stable bureaucracies rather than operating democracies in which the individual member has a real choice at election time. The average union member's choice is more like that in one-party totalitarian countries, where the citizen can do no more than approve or disapprove the party's candidate.

Here, then, is a discrepancy between formal edict and actual fact, a discrepancy which is all the more important since unions arose as the instrument by which a worker could express his will in management-labor problems; if this instrument is taken from the hands of the ordinary union member and put into the hands of a powerful hierarchy, it may stray far from serving the worker's interests.

Some observers have attempted to locate the source of this discrepancy in the malintentions of ambitious leaders. But the widespread existence of union bureaucracy, whether the ideology of the leaders be radical or conservative, suggests that the sources may lie in the social and economic structure of unions and the occupation in which they are located. Even attempts by existing leaders to encourage potential leaders who might succeed them have sometimes ended in failure.[1] In such a case, it appears that the failures of democracy lie deeper than the evil designs of ambitious men.

How can such a problem be approached? One method is to study a *deviant case*, in this instance a union which exhibits a strong democratic rather than the usual bureaucratic pattern. By an intensive analysis of such a deviant case, the dynamic patterns which—missing in other unions—tend to maintain a working democracy become evident. Such a deviant case study, an intensive analysis of the International Typographical Union, has been carried out specifically with this purpose in mind. By asking the question "What factors have created and maintained a functioning democracy in the ITU?" it becomes possible to answer why such democracy does not exist in most other unions.

The ITU, an old and powerful union, has had frequent turnover in office and continuing opposition parties since 1912 nationally, and even earlier locally. The study of the ITU took as its problem the examination of factors in the ITU which maintain its democracy. This "structural–functional" analysis, which attempts to show the functioning of parts in relation to one another at present, was supplemented by an historical analysis, which attempted to show the stages through which ITU democracy has passed. Thus the study focussed on the dynamic relations which *maintain* the present equilibrium state of democracy, together with a supplementary examination of the *establishment* of this equilibrium state.

METHODOLOGY

Procedurally, the [research team] spent about a year and a half studying the history and operation of the union and its party system through examination of historical records, qualitative interviews with members and leaders, and systematic observation of the union in action. Following this period, a number of hypotheses were advanced to account for the development and persistence of the democratic political system. In order to test some of these hypotheses, a survey study was planned involving interviews with a random sample of the members of the New York local of the ITU, plus interviews with a sample of chapel chairmen (the ITU's equivalent for shop stewards), and with a number of the leaders in the union and parties. In all about 540 men were interviewed in this phase of the study. In addition, voting records of all the locals in the international union, voting records of shops in the New York local, verbatim convention records and campaign statements as recorded in the monthly union magazine were also studied . . .

THE STRUCTURAL–FUNCTIONAL ANALYSIS

The analysis of elements presently operating to maintain democracy in the ITU showed the great importance of several factors in the union:

(1) The *social* involvement of printers with one another in leisure time, creating an "occupational community" which acts in many ways to facilitate the existence of an opposition group; this occupational community is far more pronounced than that of most other occupations. A number of factors are related to the existence of an "occupational community" among

---

* From Seymour M. Lipset, "Democracy in the International Typographical Union," *Year Book of the American Philosophical Society* (1955), pp. 211-218. Reprinted with the permission of the author and the American Philosophical Society.

1 For example, Dubinsky in the International Ladies Garment Workers Union has repeatedly attempted to generate leaders among the new ethnic groups, Negroes and Puerto Ricans, which are coming into the union; this has met with little success.

printers. Among these are (a) the high status of printing among manual occupations, which has the consequence of reducing printers' desires to associate with other manual workers who are lower in status, while at the same time, the fact that printers are manual workers lowers their chances to associate with middle-class individuals. Consequently, printers are "forced" on each other for leisure time associations; (b) the fact that printers like their work increases their desire to associate with each other; (c) a large proportion of printers work nights and weekends. This reduces their opportunities to associate with neighbors and other non-printers who work a more "normal" schedule; (d) most printers on entering the trade must serve a number of years as "substitutes," irregularly employed workers. In order to get employment during this period, printers must spend a great deal of their non-working time "downtown" near the printshops, and consequently associate with others in the same situation.

(2) The existence of clubs, associations, athletic leagues, veterans groups, and a multitude of other formal social organizations in the occupational community. These independent organizations found to such an extent in few other occupations, serve as the bases for prestige and power for potential oppositionists, and serve to communicate to all printers the point of view of the opposition.

(3) The shop organization, which is democratic at the "grass-roots" level, creates leaders with experience who are independent of the local or international officials. This, too, is an almost unique factor in unions, and is largely due to the decentralization of the printing industry. Its perpetuation must also be tied to the democratic system itself, for the shops are able to protect themselves against encroachments from the union by their power to defeat an administration.

(4) The autonomy of large locals which can themselves serve as sources of power in international politics, and can generate both leaders and the organizational facilities for an opposition party. This again is a function of the printing industry's decentralization, and the existence of a democratic system.

(5) The party system itself, once in operation, contains "self-maintaining" mechanisms, which perpetuate the forces which keep it in operation. For example, the norm of democracy is established, thus inhibiting any attempts by leaders to gain added power.

(6) The identification and involvement of printers with their craft and their union lead them to dampen divisive conflicts without accepting illegitimate encroachments by union officers upon their democratic privileges. It is paradoxically this same identification with the craft which leads them to repel encroachments upon their rights by the employer,

which makes them a strong militant union. To a large extent, the factors making for union democracy are the same ones making for strong and militant action against the employer.

THE HISTORICAL ANALYSIS

If the structural–functional analysis were more precise, it could state just how stable ITU's democracy is at present; just what changes in printing technology would be sufficient to undermine it, or whether the system is secure enough to prevent a brilliant and ambitious president from grasping larger and larger amounts of control. The analysis, if precise, could tell the points of weakness in ITU's democracy, points at which slight changes might bring about oligarchy. But the analysis still could not answer the questions posed earlier, the questions of whether or not democracy is a necessary result of structural factors in the ITU. It remains for the historical analysis to do this, to indicate which factors were favoring stability of ITU's democracy at each point in time, and the crucial juncture points at which one or another of these factors was changed. In this way we see that existence of democracy in ITU is largely the result of the convergence of a set of events, each of which contributes to or detracts from the continuing stability of the system. If some one event in early history had turned the other way, then present-day democracy in the union would have been less likely. The existence of democracy at present may thus be likened to a series of successive outcomes of a pair of dice, dice which are with each favorable outcome more loaded toward a favorable outcome on the next throw. Democracy is no necessary consequence, given the starting point and early history of the ITU, but one favored from the beginning by numerous factors and more favored as time went on and numerous events added to the system's stability.

The answer to our original question, then, could be found by using the structural–functional analysis and the historical analysis in conjunction to determine the system's stability at each point in time. This, together with some knowledge of how likely were events strong enough to upset a system with a certain stability, would give the probability at any time in ITU's history that its democracy would survive.

This, then, indicates our approach to the question with which we started, and the way in which the analysis carried out in the preceding chapters contributes to it. We shall employ this approach briefly in an examination of some of the crucial turning points in the union's early history.

Many of the factors which contribute to ITU's democracy were present as well when the union first was formed. The strong identification with the craft of printing, more pronounced then than now, meant that printers were fully involved in the affairs of their organization, not overcome with apathy. This same identification, together with other factors like the marginal status and irregular work hours of printing, also meant that a strong occupational community existed. This occupational community fostered grass-roots political participation from the beginning. The marginal status of printing, most fully exemplified by the existence of employer printers as well as employee printers in the union, insured the value cleavage which provided the content of politics and evenly split the union. The literacy and related organizational skills of printing meant that every printer was potentially an opposition leader; this factor helped promote opposition groups on convention floors and among small groups of printers. Perhaps most important of all at this formative period was the autonomy of locals, which first formed a loose federation, then a stronger international union which was nevertheless weaker, than the large locals. This autonomy insured that the international could not control the large locals and force through legislation reducing their power.[2]

These were factors not only making for early democracy in the union but also insuring that next "throws of the dice" would be loaded in favor of democracy and decentralization.

Probably the first important threat to democracy in the union was the existence of a powerful secret society, controlling both union offices and the foreman's jobs in the late nineteenth century. This clique might have further intrenched itself through legislation which progressively increased the power of the international. Yet it did not do so. Why? Here again it seems that the existence of autonomy in the large locals both prevented such centralizing legislation and abolished the secret society. The existence of local administrations which were anti-secret society gave the ordinary printers a nucleus of organization and exposed the activities of the secret society; without this, they might have been easy prey to the power of this clique. Of course, not to be overlooked as a factor contributing to the downfall of the secret society was the identification of printers with their craft, which made self-rule a matter of deep concern to them. Also important were the norms of "brotherhood" engendered by this identification, which made membership in an exclusive clique illegitimate in the eyes even of clique

2 Here a comparison with another union indicates the importance of this autonomy. Locals in the Pressman's union were largely organized by the International, thus scarcely independent of it to begin with; in later legislation their voting power was reduced by a kind of "county unit system"; this, with its succeeding ill consequences for democracy, could probably never have occurred if the Pressman locals had originally been as autonomous as the printers' locals.

members as soon as these cliques lost their early function of protecting the union.

Thus the stability of its democracy was tested even before the institutionalization of the party system, and found not wanting. The factors making for stability of the democratic equilibrium were quite strong at that time, at least strong enough to counteract the forces tending to destroy the equilibrium. How much greater a force they could have withstood is a question which cannot be answered; but it is easily conceivable that at this point some added chance element might have destroyed the democracy in its infancy.

The next crucial point in the political system's history occurred when a real central body was established (in the 1890's) with elected full time officers. Again the existence of autonomy showed itself (along with a sophisticated awareness of structural dangers to democracy) in making the election of officers a popular election rather than one by convention (which is usually controlled by the administration, even in ITU), and by reserving the decision on many important matters, including financial policy, to popular referenda.[3] Thus were instituted important legal elements which support the stability of ITU democracy today, and these, it is evident, were a consequence of existing elements which favored democracy. However, at this crucial turning point as in the one discussed previously, some element, perhaps a silver-tongued president of the union, might have so swayed the balance that these institutional safeguards of democracy might not have been enacted.

These two important points in the early history of the union indicate the pattern which numerous others followed. For example, passing a priority (seniority) law was due largely to the existence of the referendum; if events had turned otherwise when the referendum law was enacted, the priority law, another safeguard to democracy, might not exist now.

One other turning point in ITU's history deserves mention, because it represents the first coming to power of the opposition party. The 1919 New York vacationist strike provoked the incident; the incident was ITU President Scott's failure to support the strike and attempt to send the men back to work against the orders of their local leaders. Had this not led to a resounding defeat for Scott at the hands primarily of the New York local, the autonomy of large locals would have been seriously impaired. The international officers would have felt free to manipulate the large locals at will. As it was, this marked the first entry into office by the Progressives, and served at the

3 As a matter of fact, this tendency to reserve to the common printer decision on all important matters was great enough that by union law so many matters were referred to referendum that the locals were deluged, and quickly relegated some of these to the executive committee.

same time as a warning to future international officers not to treat lightly the wishes of large locals.[4]

It is important to note that much of the local autonomy which served as an exceedingly important factor early in union history is disappearing after having made major contributions to democracy. Institutional safeguards, such as referenda, popular elections, and other laws, which this local autonomy helped introduce, replace it as factors which preserve the democracy's stability. Whether such safeguards are strong enough to preserve democracy in the future as local autonomy and other factors such as identification with the craft begin to disappear is an open question. Probably no safeguards will be strong enough in the event that printers lose their identification with the craft of printing and involve themselves instead in activities unconnected with printing.

This study of the ITU makes evident one major point; the existence of democracy or its non-existence in a union can hardly be accounted for by the goodness or badness of men, but by structural factors inherent in the occupation and the union itself. Men are pretty much the same everywhere, but it is these structural factors which either allow ambitious leaders to have their way or allow the individual members to retain their autonomy and self-determination. An article in the *Reader's Digest*, which held the ITU up as an example of union democracy, asked why all unions cannot have such democracy, and by implication suggested that all that is needed is good intentions and will power. This intensive study of the ITU shows that the causes go much deeper. Democracy in the ITU exists as a consequence of certain structural factors in the present and past of printing, together with chance elements at crucial points in the union's history. Oligarchy in most other unions similarly exists as a consequence of structural factors in those unions together with chance elements at crucial points. If democracy is to be a possibility in an organization, these structural factors must be favorable. Some aid may come from an awareness of democratic and oligarchic processes on the part of members, but this will be of little avail if the structure does not itself favor democracy.

---

[4] Here again a comparison with the Pressman's union indicates the constraints induced by structural factors in the ITU. The Pressman president, George Berry, acted much more repressively against his New York pressmen (who were also striking) than did Scott, by sending in strikebreakers. Yet Berry was not defeated, and continued in office till his death.

Although organizations change over time, it is difficult to identify the specific organizational characteristics that change and the time at which they change. For the sociologist, a fundamental problem is to secure reliable evidence about the organizational dimensions at various time intervals.* John Tsouderos' selection is one of the few attempts to perform this ambitious task.

Some of Tsouderos' conclusions can be interpreted as advice to leaders of voluntary associations about what to expect when the initiating variables (such as membership) show changes that foreshadow the entry of an association into a new phase. It is not surprising to find that growth in membership is followed by an increase in income and in administrative overhead. But leaders of voluntary associations may not have anticipated some of Tsouderos' other findings and should keep them in mind as possible warnings in their own work: when membership declines, the association may experience an interval before income declines; the contraction of an organization does not simplify its administration: on the contrary, leaders and staff members may be tempted to make procedures more formal.

ORGANIZATIONAL GROWTH†

John E. Tsouderos

An attempt will be made in this paper to summarize some of the findings made in an empirical investigation of a number of quantitative variables related to the organizational growth of ten voluntary associations.[1] Theoretical considerations suggest that these variables are important in understanding the processes of organizational growth and formalization which constitute the topic of this paper.

In the course of conducting the field work,[2] three sources of information were used: (1) the financial statements of the associations; (2) the membership lists and statistics; (3) service statistics mostly con-

constructed from the documentary material taken from the files of the organization, i.e., minutes of board and committee meetings, pamphlets, publications, constitutions and by-laws, annual reports, letters and verbatim interviews with active key persons past and present. In gathering the data for these case histories an attempt was made to record as completely as possible all the successive changes in the manifest social structure of the association, such as formal membership criteria, specific functional positions of officers, the changes in board and committee structure, the changes in the administrative office procedure, the increases in physical property, personnel policies, size of paid regular staff workers, and the like. A consistent attempt was made to describe the life histories of the associations step by step in a temporal sequence. These ten associations were selected under the following conditions: (1) the officers of the association had to give approval to the research worker to have full access to all the records of the association; (2) the association had to have, for the purpose of this study, a fairly rich amount of documentary material; and (3) all ten belonged to a larger sample of voluntary associations. The observations and interpretations made in this paper seem to be corroborated by a more inclusive and representative sample of voluntary associations which have been treated statistically by this author. A random sample was drawn from a list of 535 voluntary associations. The sample consisted of 119 associations, 91 of which responded to the request for interviews. The president and executive secretary of each association were interviewed with a schedule. For detailed statistical analysis see [my] *Formalization Process of Voluntary Associations* (Minneapolis:

* Some social scientists have attempted to construct mathematical models of organizational processes; the interaction of changing structural variables is particularly convenient for formalization by differential equations or by some other technique. An example is Mason Haire (editor), *Modern Organization Theory* (New York: John Wiley, 1959), pp. 272-306.

† From John E. Tsouderos, "Organizational Change in Terms of a Series of Selected Variables," *American Sociological Review*, Volume 20, Number 2 (April 1955), pp. 206-210. Reprinted with the permission of the author and the publisher, the American Sociological Review.

[1] The study was based on ten case histories which were written by the present author for the purpose, and as a part of, an intensive and extensive study of the formalization process in small groups. These ten associations were: The Minneapolis League of Women Voters; The Ancient Order of United Workmen of Minnesota; Minnesota Council of Churches; Minnesota Nurses' Association; Alano Society of Minneapolis; Minnesota Association of Cooperatives; Lutheran Welfare Society; Minnesota Division American Cancer Society; Hennepin County League of Planned Parenthood; and the International Institute.

[2] The organizational histories of these associations were

piled by the administrative staffs on the volume of service activities discharged.

The variables subjected to time series analysis were: (1) total annual income; (2) total annual expenditures; (3) value of the property from year to year; (4) annual membership figures; and (5) the number of administrative employees from year to year.

It was seen in the case histories that the initial acquisition of property takes place when an association furnishes a meeting place for the membership and provides equipment to facilitate the discharge of administrative tasks. As the membership increases, a larger home is required by the association; more furniture is needed; real estate becomes desirable. Simultaneously, the growth of the membership group is accompanied by an increase in the volume of administrative tasks and expenditures; more office equipment is needed, especially after the first administrative worker has been hired.

Figure 1 is a graphic and composite representation of the relationship of these organizational variables, summarizing our findings. The key points of the findings are formulated here as tentative generalizations. As can be seen from the graph there is a definite functional relationship between the growth in membership of an association and other variables such as income, administrative expenditures, property and staff workers; that is, when one of these variables is modified in time the other undergoes a corresponding modification. However, certain qualifications should be made in terms of a general growth pattern of the organizational development: (1) The membership growth precedes the growth of income. Even though we find a positive relationship between the increase of membership and growth of income this relationship does not seem to be continuous. With a decline of the membership in an organization there is no immediate or actual decline in income. (2) There is a positive relationship between the growth in total income of an organization and its administrative expenditures. However, the administrative expenditures have a much lower rate of growth than income. It can be noted then that the administrative expenditures increase rapidly after the peak of total income has been passed. (3) Property and administrative office workers continue to accumulate while membership and total income begin to shrink. However, property increases more rapidly in periods of rapid rise in income. We find also a close correspondence between the growth of administrative expenditures and increases in the property of the association.

In general, the above findings demonstrate that there is a certain tendency for the process of formali-

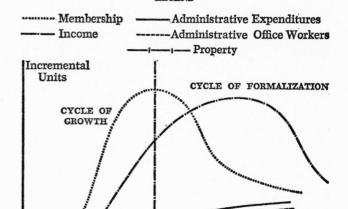

FIGURE 1. *Graphic representation of the relationship of certain organizational variables*

zation to continue in the period when the social group contracts. Evidence shows[3] that in this period of a contracting membership, the administrative staff expenditures, staff workers, and property rise cyclically. The association which in the past has learned to cope effectively with its many problems by formalization and rationalization of its structure, attempts to survive by continuing the process of formalization.

The question arises as to why there is a functional relationship between the growth of membership, income, administrative expenditures, property, and staff workers. Why do voluntary associations have a tendency to increase their membership to a certain point and then reach a point of maximum growth? Furthermore, why does membership decline after a period of time? Why is it that with a decline in membership there is no immediate or actual decline in income, and finally, why do property, administrative expenditures and office workers continue to accumulate while membership and total income begin to shrink? Before attempting to answer any of these questions we must clearly have in mind that the material presented above represents only an empirical study of a small selected group of voluntary associations and that the generalizations and interpretations might not fully conform to a more representative sample. It was attempted here merely to explore and suggest a possible method of observation, and, in addition, to present a set of hypotheses which would

3 These generalizations apply only to the ten case histories studied; this paper may be suggestive of an analytical approach to a method of studying the changing structure of a group.

guide and offer some insight for further research in this field.

In general, then, the above can be conceived as an *ideal type construct* for use as a comparative guide in research on the manifest structural differentiation of small groups. With these limitations in mind let us try to answer these questions in a series of interrelated and tentative propositions:

(1) The number of members and the continued growth of the membership group are the result of both the success of an association in coping with the internal functional problems posed by an expanding membership and the total adjustment or adaptation of an association as a functioning organizational unit to its social environment (including success in the enlistment of new members from this environment).

(2) The less specialized and segmental the role the members play in the association, the more pronounced is the tendency to regard participation in the association as an end in itself. This leads to a greater solidarity of the group and lessens the possibility of a decline in membership. The more specialized the role each member plays in the association, the more pronounced will be his tendency to regard participation as the means to an end. The loyalty of the members to their association can be stabilized when participation is regarded not merely as a means to the attainment of specified ends, but as the preservation of the association as an end in its own right. It is then to the advantage of the association to encourage primary group relations in the membership. However, a qualifying statement should be made here. We must not overlook on the other hand the stabilizing effect of the specialization and formalization of roles within an organization. That is to say, when the functional position or roles as such are abstracted from concrete persons and codified and defined by symbols, the organization acquires in general greater stability and flexibility than when it is under the personal authority of one or more charismatic leaders. However, the problem of formalization versus lack of it is this: the members most affected by the specialization and formalization of roles are those "who run the show," i.e., are actively engaged as leaders of the organization, and they are less likely to withdraw their membership. The greatest turnover of the membership is observed in the passive membership *after formalization,* whose roles have been the least specialized. The passivity of this non-specialized group might be due to the disparity that exists between it and the highly formalized segment of the association. Thus, a balance between sociability and formalization must be attained to prevent the disintegration of the association.

(3) Certain associations may serve very specific interests and it is precisely for this reason that their appeal is limited to certain types of individuals. This imposes a maximum size on any one organization in any given area.

(4) With the increasing need of a service rendered by a voluntary association there is a corresponding increase of membership, and with the fulfillment or partial fulfillment of such a service there is a corresponding decrease in membership.

(5) With an increased membership, however, there is a corresponding increase in the heterogeneity of the group in terms of sentiments, interests, dedication to the "cause," etc., and a corresponding decline in a feeling of intimacy and frequency of interaction. More specifically, there is a decline of membership in meetings and volunteer work. As a consequence, the membership becomes extremely passive and increasingly removed from the leadership of the association. As the membership expands, the group as a whole is likely to lose its primary character. This is not to say, however, that the primary group disappears; certain clusters of individuals are found to interact with one another more frequently than they do with the rest of the membership. Sub-groups appear which retain the primary character previously extending over the entire membership. These sub-group clusters are integrated into the manifest social structure and the membership is organized in membership units. At the same time the need for control arises out of the fact that some of these membership units tend to become relatively autonomous from the rest of the organization. In varying degrees loyalty of the members is diverted from the association to the membership units so that the basis for a conflict with the organization has been laid.

(6) The loss of membership in the organization might be due then to several reasons, such as increased secondary contacts, competing associations with similar functions, conflict within the association resulting from the heterogeneity of the group members, ineffectiveness of intracommunication, a decrease of the material or symbolic incentives offered by the association, a relative decrease in the need of a function or functions rendered by the association to its members or to the community and the extent to which the association is able to coordinate its formal and informal relationships.

(7) There is evidence that the formalization and contraction of the social group constitute a "vicious circle." In order to cope with its financial problems and declining membership, the association streamlines its structure and procedures according to modern organizational principles by introducing higher membership dues, professional help, and other means. These new organizational features alienate portions of the membership which had joined the association at an earlier and more informal stage, and lead to secession *en masse.* This mass separation

creates even greater problems with which the association attempts to cope by formalizing its organization even more.

(8) With a declining membership, efforts are made to control the drop by introducing new incentives, added services, professional and administrative staff in order to discharge and supervise such services. Special communicative devices appear with the declining frequency of face-to-face interaction, preceded by the increasing structural differentiation and the separation of various functional activities. Furthermore, the association is confronted with the problem of enforcing the pertinent features of its program through a relatively expensive outlay. Thus with an increase of controls there is a corresponding increase of staff and administrative expenditures. This phenomenon of increased controls, efforts to improve communication, and the use of additional profes-sional help can be found emerging not only when the membership declines, but also when the membership increases at a rapid rate.

(9) Increase of expenditures can also be explained in terms of increased capital outlay to improve facilities in order to maintain organizational prestige.

(10) With a decline in the membership of an organization, there is no immediate or actual decline in income. This phenomenon is due primarily to the greater efficiency of the organization in collecting dues and carrying out financial drives.

(11) Material property will increase over a period of time, and this increase is closely related to the expenditures for staff and upkeep. Unless the material property is withdrawn from use or permitted to deteriorate, these service expenditures cannot be reduced below a certain level.

Leaders often try to introduce changes into their organizations in order to improve work output and morale, reduce waste and costs, eliminate duplication and conflict, improve communications, and so on. Various techniques are available for changing organizations. Personnel may be sent to special training programs, such as leadership workshops. Staff members may be reassigned. New controls and rewards may be introduced.

After a change, the leader may have a feeling that matters have or have not improved, but such impressions are biased and fallible. His basic problems are to discover: whether desired changes in the organization's performance have actually occurred; whether these changes are a result of his planned reform or of something that he didn't manipulate (such as a coincidental improvement in the life of the community); in what ways changes have and have not occurred; and whether the planned reform produced undesirable and unanticipated changes that offset its desirable consequences. These are subtle questions that can be settled only by careful research, and the leader must beware of overestimating the effects of his reforms in complicated social situations.

Some behavioral scientists have studied the effects of planned social change in laboratory experiments with small groups and in real-life settings, such as factories. Several publications describe the research designs and results of these evaluation studies.* Until now, nearly all the evaluation studies of planned organizational change have been performed in

* For a summary of evaluation studies of some leadership training programs and some planned organizational changes, see Floyd C. Mann, "Studying and Creating Change," in Conrad Arensberg *et al., Research in Industrial Human Relations* (New York: Harper & Brothers, 1957), pp. 146-167. For an analysis of the effects of discussion workshops upon the leaders of organizations, see Robert Tannenbaum *et al., Leadership and Organization* (New York: McGraw-Hill Book Company, 1961), pp. 222-238. Facts and advice about planning change in groups and organizations, based on social research, appear in Ronald Lippitt *et al., The Dynamics of Planned Change* (New York: Harcourt, Brace and Company, 1958).

factories and in business firms, but similar research could be done in voluntary associations. Some results would be the same; others would be different.

Change in the structure of organizations is not identical with change in the attitudes and behavior of individual participants. Organizational changes can occur, while employees make only half-hearted adjustments. Since leaders and employees may have different perspectives and goals, leaders may desire changes in order to achieve greater efficiency or productivity, while employees may prefer to retain satisfactory social relationships and to avoid new arrangements that are unknown and that they cannot control. In the next selection, Paul R. Lawrence summarizes research about sources of resistance to change in some business organizations, and he advises leaders how to plan and initiate changes. His advice applies to voluntary associations, since analogous situations can be found in all organizations.

RESISTANCE TO CHANGE*

Paul R. Lawrence

One of the most baffling and recalcitrant of the problems which business executives face is employee resistance to change. Such resistance may take a number of forms—persistent reduction in output, increase in the number of "quits" and requests for transfer, chronic quarrels, sullen hostility, wildcat or slowdown strikes, and, of course, the expression of a lot of pseudo-logical reasons why the change will not work. Even the more petty forms of this resistance can be troublesome.

All too often when executives encounter resistance to change, they "explain" it by quoting the cliché that "people resist change" and never look further. Yet changes must continually occur in industry. This applies with particular force to the all-important "little" changes that constantly take place—changes in work methods, in routine office procedures, in the location of a machine or a desk, in personnel assignments and job titles. No one of these changes makes the headlines, but in total they account for much of our increase in productivity. They are not the spectacular once-in-a-lifetime technological revolutions, that involve mass layoffs or the obsolescence of traditional skills, but they are vital to business progress.

Does it follow, therefore, that business management is forever saddled with the onerous job of "forcing" change down the throats of resistant people? My answer is *no*. It is the thesis of this article that people do *not* resist technical change as such and that most of the resistance which does occur is unnecessary. I shall discuss these points, among others:

(1) A solution which has become increasingly popular for dealing with resistance to change is to get the people involved to "participate" in making the change. But as a practical matter "participation" as a device is not a good way for management to think about the problem. In fact, it may lead to trouble.

(2) The key to the problem is to understand the true nature of resistance. Actually, what employees resist is usually not technical change but social change—the change in their human relationships that generally accompanies technical change.

(3) Resistance is usually created because of certain blind spots and attitudes which staff specialists have as a result of their preoccupation with the technical aspects of new ideas.

(4) Management can take concrete steps to deal constructively with these staff attitudes. The steps include emphasizing new standards of performance for staff specialists and encouraging them to think in different ways, as well as making use of the fact that signs of resistance can serve as a practical warning signal in directing and timing technological changes.

(5) Top executives can also make their own efforts more effective at meetings of staff and operating groups where change is being discussed. They can do this by shifting their attention from the facts and so forth, to what the discussion of these items indicates about developing resistances and receptiveness to change.

Let us begin by taking a look at some recent research into the nature of resistance to change. There are two studies in particular that I should like to discuss. They highlight contrasting ways of interpreting resistance.

* From Paul R. Lawrence, "How to Deal with Resistance to Change," *Harvard Business Review*, Volume 32, Number 3 (May-June 1954), pp. 49-57. Reprinted with the permission of the author and the publisher.

IS PARTICIPATION ENOUGH?

The first study was conducted by Lester Coch and John R. P. French, Jr., in a clothing factory.[1] It deserves special comments because, it seems to me, it is the most systematic study of the phenomenon of resistance to change that has been made in a factory setting. To describe it briefly:

> The two researchers worked with four different groups of factory operators who were being paid on a modified piece-rate basis. For each of these four groups a minor change in the work procedure was installed by a different method, and the results were carefully recorded to see what, if any, problems of resistance occurred. The four experimental groups were roughly matched with respect to efficiency ratings and degree of cohesiveness; in each group the proposed change modified the established work procedure about the same degree.
>
> The work change was introduced to the first group by what the researchers called a "no-participation" method. This small group of operators was called into a room where some staff people told the members that there was a need for a minor methods change in their work procedures. The staff people then explained the change to the operators in detail, and gave them the reasons for the change. The operators were then sent back to the job with instructions to work in accordance with the new method.
>
> The second group of operators was introduced to the work change by a "participation-through-representation" method—a variation of the approach used with the third and fourth groups, which turned out to be of little significance.
>
> The third and fourth groups of operators were both introduced to the work change on a "total-participation" basis. All the operators in these groups met with the staff men concerned. The staff men dramatically demonstrated the need for cost reduction. A general agreement was reached that some savings could be effected. The groups then discussed how existing work methods could be improved and unnecessary operations eliminated. When the new work methods were agreed on, all the operators were trained in the new methods, and all were observed by the time-study men for purposes of establishing a new piece rate on the job.

RESEARCH FINDINGS

The researchers reported a marked contrast between the results achieved by the different methods of introducing this change.

No-participation group. The most striking difference was between Group #1, the no-participation group, and Groups #3 and #4, the total-participation groups. The output of Group #1 dropped immediately to about two thirds of its previous output rate. The output rate stayed at about this level throughout the period of 30 days after the change was introduced. The researchers further reported:

[1] "Overcoming Resistance to Change," *Human Relations,* Volume I, Number 4 (1948), pp. 512-532.

> Resistance developed almost immediately after the change occurred. Marked expressions of aggression against management occurred, such as conflicts with the methods engineer . . . hostility toward the supervisor, deliberate restriction of production, and lack of cooperation with the supervisor. There were 17% quits in the first 40 days. Grievances were filed about piece rates; but when the rate was checked, it was found to be a little 'loose.'

Total-participation groups. In contrast with this record, Groups #3 and #4 showed a smaller initial drop in output and a very rapid recovery not only to the previous production rate but to a rate that exceeded the previous rate. In these groups there were no signs of hostility toward the staff people or toward the supervisors, and there were no quits during the experimental period.

APPRAISAL OF RESULTS

Without going into all the researchers' decisions based on these experiments, it can be fairly stated that they concluded that resistance to methods changes could be overcome by *getting the people involved in the change to participate in making it.*

This was a very useful study, but the results are likely to leave the manager of a factory still bothered by the question, "Where do we go from here?" The trouble centers around that word "participation" . . .

Participation is a feeling on the part of people, not just the mechanical act of being called in to take part in discussions. Common sense would suggest that people are more likely to respond to the way they are customarily treated,—say, as people whose opinions are respected because they themselves are respected for their own worth—rather than by the stratagem of being called to a meeting or asked some carefully calculated questions. In fact, many supervisors and staff men have had some unhappy experiences with executives who have read about participation and have picked it up as a new psychological gimmick for getting other people to think they "want" to do as they are told—as a sure way to put the sugar coating on a bitter pill.

So there is the problem of how to get this thing called participation. And, as a matter of fact, the question remains whether participation was the determining factor in the Coch and French experiment or whether there was something of deeper significance underlying it.

RESISTANCE TO WHAT?

Now let us take a look at a second series of research findings about resistance to change. Recently, while making some research observations in a factory manufacturing electronic products, a colleague and I had an opportunity to observe a number of incidents that for us threw new light on this matter of resistance to change.[2] One incident was particularly illuminating:

> We were observing the work of one of the industrial engineers and a production operator who had been assigned to work with the engineer on assembling and testing an experimental product that the engineer was developing. The engineer and the operator were in almost constant daily contact in their work. It was a common occurrence for the engineer to suggest an idea for some modification in a part of the new product; he would then discuss his idea with the operator and ask her to try out the change to see how it worked. It was also a common occurrence for the operator to get an idea as she assembled parts, and to pass this idea on to the engineer, who would then consider it and, on occasion, ask the operator to try out the idea and see if it proved useful.

A typical exchange between these two people might run somewhat as follows:

> ENGINEER: "I got to thinking last night about that difficulty we've been having on assembling the x part in the last few days. It occurred to me that we might get around the trouble if we washed the part in a cleaning solution just prior to assembling it."
> OPERATOR: "Well, that sounds to me like it's worth trying."
> ENGINEER: "I'll get you some of the right kind of cleaning solution, and why don't you try doing that with about 50 parts and keep track of what happens."
> OPERATOR: "Sure, I'll keep track of it and let you know how it works."

With this episode in mind, let us take a look at a second episode involving the same production operator. One day we noticed another engineer approaching the production manager. We knew that this particular engineer had had no previous contact with the production operator. He had been asked to take a look at one specific problem on the new product because of his special technical qualifications. He had decided to make a change in one of the parts of the product to eliminate the problem, and he had prepared some of these parts using his new method. Here is what happened:

> He walked up to the production operator with the new parts in his hand and indicated to her by a gesture that he wanted her to try assembling some units using his new part. The operator picked up one of the parts and proceeded to assemble it. We noticed that she did not handle the part with her usual care. After she had assembled the product, she tested it and it failed to pass inspection. She turned to the new engineer and, with a triumphant air, said, "It doesn't work."
> The new engineer indicated that she should try another part. She did so, and again it did not work.

[2] For a complete report of the study, see Harriet O. Ronken and Paul R. Lawrence, *Administering Changes: A Case Study of Human Relations in a Factory* (Boston: Division of Research, Harvard Business School, 1952).

> She then proceeded to assemble units using all of the new parts that were available. She handled each of them in an unusually rough manner. None of them worked. Again she turned to the engineer and said that the new parts did not work.
> The engineer left, and later the operator, with evident satisfaction, commented to the original industrial engineer that the new engineer's ideas was just no good.

SOCIAL CHANGE

What can we learn from these episodes? To begin, it will be useful for our purposes to think of change as having both a technical and a social aspect. The *technical* aspect of the change is the making of a measurable modification in the physical routines of the job. The *social* aspect of the change refers to the way those affected by it think it will alter their established relationships in the organization.

We can clarify this distinction by referring to the two foregoing episodes. In both of them, the technical aspects of the changes introduced were virtually identical: the operator was asked to use a slightly changed part in assembling the finished product. By contrast, the social aspects of the changes were quite different.

In the first episode, the interaction between the industrial engineer and the operator tended to sustain the give-and-take kind of relationship that these two people were accustomed to. The operator was used to being treated as a person with some valuable skills and knowledge and some sense of responsibility about her work; when the engineer approached her with his idea, she felt she was being dealt with in the usual way. But in the second episode, the new engineer was introducing not only a technical change but also a change in the operator's customary way of relating herself to others in the organization. By his brusque manner and by his lack of any explanation, he led the operator to fear that her usual work relationships were being changed. And she just did not like the new way she was being treated.

The results of these two episodes were quite different also. In the first episode there were no symptoms of resistance to change, a very good chance that the experimental change would determine fairly whether a cleaning solution would improve product quality, and a willingness on the part of the operator to accept future changes when the industrial engineer suggested them. In the second episode, however, there were signs of resistance to change (the operator's careless handling of parts and her satisfaction in their failure to work), failure to prove whether the modified part was an improvement or not, and indications that the operator would resist any further changes by the engineer . . .

It is apparent from these two patterns that the variable that determines the result is the social aspect of the change. In other words, the operator did not resist the technical change as such but rather the accompanying change in her human relationships.

CONFIRMATION

This conclusion is based on more than one case. Many other cases in our research project substantiate it. Furthermore, we can find confirmation in the research experience of Coch and French, even though they came out with a different interpretation.

Coch and French tell us in their report that the procedure used with Group #1, the no-participation group, was the usual one in the factory for introducing work changes. And yet they also tell us something about the customary treatment of the operators in their work life. For example, the company's labor relations policies are progressive, the company and the supervisors place a high value on fair and open dealings with the employees, and the employees are encouraged to take up their problems and grievances with management. Also, the operators are accustomed to measuring the success and failure of themselves as operators against the company's standard output figures.

Now compare those *customary* work relationships with the way the Group #1 operators were treated when they were introduced to this particular work change. There is quite a difference. When the management called them into the room for indoctrination, they were treated as if they had no useful knowledge of their own jobs. In effect, they were told that they were not the skilled and efficient operators they had thought they were, that they were doing the job inefficiently, and that some "outsider" (the staff expert) would now tell them how to do it right. How could they construe this experience *except* as a threatening change in their usual working relationship? It is the story of the second episode in our research case all over again. The results were also the same, with signs of resistance, persistently low output, and so on.

Now consider experimental Groups #3 and #4, the total-participation groups. Coch and French referred to management's approach in their case as a "new" method of introducing change, but from the point of view of the *operators* it must not have seemed new at all. It was simply a continuation of the way they were ordinarily dealt with in the course of their regular work. And what happened? The results —reception to change, technical improvement, better performance—were much more like those reported in the first episode between the operator and the industrial engineer.

So the research data of Coch and French tend to confirm the conclusion that the nature and size of the technical aspect of the change does not determine the presence or absence of resistance nearly so much as does the social aspect of the change.

ROOTS OF TROUBLE

The significance of these research findings, from management's point of view, is that executives and staff experts need, not expertness in using the devices of participation, but a real understanding, in depth and detail, of the specific social arrangements that will be sustained or threatened by the change or by the way in which it is introduced.

These observations check with everyday management experience in industry. When we stop to think about it, we know that many changes occur in our factories without a bit of resistance. We know that people who are working closely with one another continually swap ideas about short cuts and minor changes in procedure that are adopted so easily and naturally that we seldom notice them or even think of them as change. The point is that because these people work so closely with one another, they intuitively understand and take account of the existing social arrangements for work and so feel no threat to themselves in such every day changes.

By contrast, management actions leading to what we commonly label "change" are usually initiated outside the small work group by staff people. These are the changes that we notice and the ones that most frequently bring on symptoms of resistance. By the very nature of their work, most of our staff specialists in industry do not have the intimate contact with operating groups that allows them to acquire an intuitive understanding of the complex social arrangements which their ideas may affect. Neither do our staff specialists always have the day-to-day dealings with operating people that lead them to develop a natural respect for the knowledge and skill of these people. As a result, all too often the staff men behave in a way that threatens and disrupts the established social relationships. And the tragedy is that so many of these upsets are inadvertent and unnecessary.

Yet industry must have its specialists—not only many kinds of engineering specialists (product, process, maintenance, quality, and safety engineers) but also cost accountants, production schedulers, purchasing agents, and personnel men. Must top management therefore reconcile itself to continual resistance to change, or can it take constructive action to meet the problem?

I believe that our research in various factory situations indicates why resistance to change occurs and what management can do about it. Let us take the "why" factors first.

SELF-PREOCCUPATION

All too frequently we see staff specialists who bring to their work certain blind spots that get them into trouble when they initiate change with operating people. One such blind spot is "self-preoccupation." The staff man gets so engrossed in the technology of the change he is interested in promoting that he becomes wholly oblivious to different kinds of things that may be bothering people. Here are two examples:

> In one situation the staff people introduced, with the best intentions, a technological change which inadvertently deprived a number of skilled operators of much of the satisfaction that they were finding in their work. Among other things, the change meant that whereas formerly the output of each operator had been placed beside his work position where it could be viewed and appreciated by him and by others, it was now being carried away immediately from the work position. The workmen did not like this.
>
> The sad part of it was that there was no compelling cost or technical reason why the output could not be placed beside the work position as it had been formerly. But the staff people who had introduced the change were so literal-minded about their ideas that when they heard complaints on the changes from the operators, they could not comprehend what the trouble was. Instead, they began repeating all the logical arguments why the change made sense from a cost standpoint. The final result here was a chronic restriction of output and persistent hostility on the part of the operators.
>
> An industrial engineer undertook to introduce some method changes in one department with the notion firmly in mind that this assignment presented him with an opportunity to "prove" to higher management the value of his function. He became so preoccupied with his personal desire to make a name for his particular techniques that he failed to pay any attention to some fairly obvious and practical considerations which the operating people were calling to his attention but which did not show up in his time-study techniques. As could be expected, resistance quickly developed to all his ideas, and the only "name" that he finally won for his techniques was a black one.

Obviously, in both of these situations the staff specialists involved did not take into account the social aspects of the change they were introducing. For different reasons they got so preoccupied with the technical aspects of the change that they literally could not see or understand what all the fuss was about.

We may sometimes wish that the validity of the technical aspect of the change were the sole determinant of its acceptability. But the fact remains that the social aspect is what determines the presence or absence of resistance. Just as ignoring this fact is the sure way to trouble, so taking advantage of it can lead to positive results. We must not forget that these same social arrangements that at times seem so bothersome are essential for the performance of work. Without a network of established social relationships a factory would be populated with a collection of people who had no idea of how to work with one another in an organized fashion. By working *with* this network instead of *against* it, management's staff representatives can give new technological ideas a better chance of acceptance.

OPERATORS' KNOW-HOW IS OVERLOOKED

Another blind spot of many staff specialists is to the strengths as well as to the weaknesses of firsthand production experience. They do not recognize that the production foreman and the production operator are in their own way specialists themselves—specialists in actual experience with production problems. This point should be obvious, but it is amazing how many staff specialists fail to appreciate the fact that even though they themselves may have a superior knowledge of the technology of the production process involved, the foreman or the operators may have a more practical understanding of how to get daily production out of a group of men and machines.

The experience of the operating people frequently equips them to be of real help to staff specialists on at least two counts: (1) The operating people are often able to spot practical production difficulties in the ideas of the specialists—and iron out those difficulties before it is too late. (2) The operating people are often able to take advantage of their intimate acquaintance with the existing social arrangements for getting work done. If given a change, they can use this kind of knowledge to help detect those parts of the change that will have undesirable social consequences. The staff experts can then go to work on ways to avoid the trouble area without materially affecting the technical worth of the change.

Further, some staff specialists have yet to learn the truth that, even after the plans for a change have been carefully made, it takes *time* to put the change successfully into production use. Time is necessary even though there may be no resistance to the change itself. The operators must develop the skill needed to use new methods and new equipment efficiently; there are always bugs to be taken out of a new method or piece of equipment even with the best of engineering. When a staff man begins to lose his patience with the amount of time that these steps take, the people he is working with will begin to feel that he is pushing them; *this* amounts to a change in their customary work relationships, and resistance will start building up where there was none before.

The situation is aggravated if the staff man mistakenly accuses the operators of resisting the idea of the change, for there are few things that irritate people more than to be blamed for resisting change when actually they are doing their best to learn a difficult new procedure.

MANAGEMENT ACTION

Many of the problems of resistance to change arise around certain kinds of *attitudes* that staff men are liable to develop about their jobs and their own ideas for introducing change. Fortunately, management can influence these attitudes and thus deal with the problems at their source.

BROADENING STAFF INTERESTS

It is fairly common for a staff man to work so hard on one of his ideas for change that he comes to identify himself with it. This is fine for the organization when he is working on the idea by himself or with his immediate colleagues; the idea becomes "his baby," and the company benefits from his complete devotion to his work.

But when he goes to some group of operating people to introduce a change, his very identification with his ideas tends to make him unreceptive to any suggestions for modification. He just does not feel like letting anyone else tamper with his pet ideas. It is easy to see, of course, how this attitude is interpreted by the operating people as a lack of respect for their suggestions.

This problem of the staff man's extreme identification with his work is one which, to some extent, can only be cured by time. But here are four suggestions for speeding up the process.

(1) The manager can often, with wise timing, encourage the staff man's interest in a different project that is just starting.

(2) The manager can also, by his "coaching" as well as by example, prod the staff man to develop a healthier respect for the contributions he can receive from operating people; success in this area would, of course, virtually solve the problem.

(3) It also helps if the staff man can be guided to recognize that the satisfaction he derives from being productive and creative is the same satisfaction he denies the operating people by his behavior toward them. Experience shows that staff people can sometimes be stimulated by the thought of finding satisfaction in sharing with others in the organization the pleasures of being creative.

(4) Sometimes, too, the staff man can be led to see that winning acceptance of his ideas through better understanding and handling of human beings is just as challenging and rewarding as giving birth to an idea.

USING UNDERSTANDABLE TERMS

One of the problems that must be overcome arises from the fact that the typical staff man is likely to have the attitude that the reasons why he is recommending any given change may be so complicated and specialized that it is impossible to explain them to operating people. It may be true that the operating people would find it next to impossible to understand some of the staff man's analytical techniques, but this does not keep them from coming to the conclusion that the staff specialist is trying to razzle-dazzle them with tricky figures and formulas—insulting their intelligence—if he does not strive to his utmost to translate his ideas into terms understandable to them. The following case illustrates the importance of this point:

> A staff specialist was temporarily successful in "selling" a change based on a complicated mathematical formula to a foreman who really did not understand it. The whole thing backfired, however, when the foreman tried to sell it to his operating people. They asked him a couple of sharp questions that he could not answer. His embarrassment about this led him to resent and resist the change so much that eventually the whole proposition fell through. This was unfortunate in terms not only of human relations but also of technological progress in the plant.

There are some very good reasons, both technical and social, why the staff man should be interested in working with the operating people until his recommendations make "sense." (This does not mean that the operating people need to understand the recommendations in quite the same way or in the same detail that the staff man does, but that they should be able to visualize the recommendations in terms of their job experiences.) Failure of the staff man to provide an adequate explanation is likely to mean that a job the operators had formerly performed with understanding and satisfaction will now be performed without understanding and with less satisfaction.

This loss of satisfaction not only concerns the individual involved but also is significant from the standpoint of the company which is trying to get maximum productivity from the operating people. A person who does not have a feeling of comprehension of what he is doing is denied the opportunity to exercise that uniquely human ability—the ability to use informed and intelligent judgment on what he does. If the staff man leaves the operating people with a sense of confusion, they will also be left unhappy and less productive.

Top line and staff executives responsible for the operation should make it a point, therefore, to know how the staff man goes about installing a change. They can do this by asking discerning questions when he reports to them, listening closely to reports of employee reaction and, if they have the opportunity, actually watching the staff man at work. At times they may have to take such drastic action as insisting that the time of installation of a proposed change be postponed until the operators are ready for it. But, for the most part, straightforward discussions with the staff man in terms of what they think of his approach should help him, over a period of time, to learn what is expected of him in his relationships with operating personnel.

NEW LOOK AT RESISTANCE

Another attitude that gets staff men into trouble is the *expectation* that all the people involved will resist the change. It is curious but true that the staff man who goes into his job with the conviction that people are going to resist any idea he presents with blind stubbornness is likely to find them responding just the way he thinks they will. The process is clear: whenever he treats the people who are supposed to buy his ideas as if they were bullheaded, he changes the way they are used to being treated; and they *will* be bullheaded in resisting *that* change!

I think that the staff man—and management in general—will do better to look at it this way: when resistance *does* appear, it should not be thought of as something to be *overcome*. Instead, it can best be thought of as a useful red flag—a signal that something is going wrong. To use a rough analogy, signs of resistance in a social organization are useful in the same way that pain is useful to the body as a signal that some bodily functions are getting out of adjustment.

The resistance, like the pain, does not tell what is wrong but only that something is wrong. And it makes no more sense to try to overcome such resistance than it does to take a pain killer without diagnosing the bodily ailment. Therefore, when resistance appears, it is time to listen carefully to find out what the trouble is. What is needed is not a long harangue on the logics of the new recommendations but a careful exploration of the difficulty.

It may happen that the problem is some technical imperfection in the change that can be readily corrected. More than likely, it will turn out that the change is threatening and upsetting some of the established social arrangements for doing work. Whether the trouble is easy or difficult to correct, management will at least know what it is dealing with.

NEW JOB DEFINITION

Finally, some staff specialists get themselves in trouble because they assume they have the answer in the thought that people will accept a change when they have participated in making it. For example:

> In one plant we visited, an engineer confided to us (obviously because we, as researchers on human relations, were interested in psychological gimmicks!) that he was going to put across a proposed production layout change of his by inserting in it a rather

obvious error, which others could then suggest should be corrected. We attended the meeting where this stunt was performed, and superficially it worked. Somebody caught the error, proposed that it be corrected, and our engineer immediately "bought" the suggestion as a very worthwhile one and made the change. The group then seemed to "buy" his entire layout proposal.

> It looked like an effective technique—oh, so easy —until later, when we became better acquainted with the people in the plant. Then we found out that many of the engineer's colleagues considered him a phony and did not trust him. The resistance they put up to his ideas was very subtle, yet even more real and difficult for management to deal with.

Participation will never work so long as it is treated as a device to get somebody else to do what you want him to. Real participation is based on respect. And respect is not acquired by just trying; it is acquired when the staff man faces the reality that he needs the contributions of the operating people.

If the staff man defines his job as not just generating ideas but also getting those ideas into practical operation, he will recognize his real dependence on the contributions of the operating people. He will ask them for ideas and suggestions, not in a backhanded way to get compliance, but in a straightforward way to get some good ideas and avoid some unnecessary mistakes. By this process he will be treating the operating people in such a way that his own behavior will not be perceived as a threat to their customary work relationships. It will be possible to discuss, and accept or reject, the ideas on their own merit.

The staff specialist who looks at the process of introducing change and at resistance to change in the manner outlined in the preceding pages may not be hailed as a genius, but he can be counted on in installing a steady flow of technical changes that will cut costs and improve quality without upsetting the organization.

ROLE OF THE ADMINISTRATOR

Now what about the way the top executive goes about his *own* job as it involves the introduction of change and problems of resistance?

One of the most important things he can do, of course, is to deal with staff people in much the same way that he wants them to deal with operators. He must realize that staff people resist social change, too. (This means, among other things, that he should not prescribe particular rules to them on the basis of this article!)

But most important, I think, is the way the administrator conceives of his job in coordinating the work of the different staff and line groups involved in a change. Does he think of his duties *primarily* as checking up, delegating and following through, applying pressure when performance fails to measure up?

Or does he think of them *primarily* as facilitating communication and understanding between people with different points of view—for example, between a staff engineering group and a production group who do not see eye to eye on a change they are both involved in? An analysis of management's actual experience—or, at least, that part of it which has been covered by our research—points to the latter as the more effective concept of administration.

I do not mean that the executive should spend his time with the different people concerned discussing the human problems of change as such. He *should* discuss schedules, technical details, work assignments, and so forth. But he should also be watching closely for the messages that are passing back and forth as people discuss these topics. He will find that

people—himself as well as others—are always implicitly asking and making answers to questions like: "How will he accept criticism?" "How much can I afford to tell him?" "Does he really get my point?" "Is he playing games?" The answers to such questions determine the degree of candor and the amount of understanding between the people involved.

When the administrator concerns himself with these problems and acts to facilitate understanding, there will be less logrolling and more sense of common purpose, fewer words and better understanding, less anxiety and more acceptance of criticism, less griping and more attention to specific problems—in short, better performance in putting new ideas for technological change into effect.

Organizational change occurs most harmoniously and results in the greatest efficiency if members make appropriate adaptations in attitudes and behavior. The inducement of change in the individual and his resistance to influence are extremely complicated subjects that have been subjects of considerable research by experimental psychologists and social psychologists. These research results have been summarized elsewhere.* Since the structure of an organization is a network of group relations, any changes of attitude and behavior among members must occur in group settings. The leader may find that group influences can be utilized to produce desired changes in individuals and ultimately in larger social patterns. In the final selection, Dorwin Cartwright provides some guidelines, based on the studies of the Research Center for Group Dynamics at the University of Michigan.

ACHIEVING CHANGE IN PEOPLE†

Dorwin Cartwright

"Group dynamics" refers to the forces operating in groups. The investigation of group dynamics consists of a study of these forces: what gives rise to them, what conditions modify them, what consequences they have, etc. The practical application of group dynamics (or the technology of group dynamics) consist of the utilization of knowledge about these forces for the achievement of some purpose. . . .

* Herbert C. Kelman, *Social Influence and Personal Belief* (New York: John Wiley and Sons, in press); Joseph T. Klapper, *The Effects of Mass Communication* (Glencoe: The Free Press, 1960); Milton J. Rosenberg et. al., *Attitude Organization and Change* (New Haven: Yale University Press, 1960).
† From Dorwin Cartwright, "Achieving Change in People," *Human Relations*, Volume 4, Number 4 (1951), pp. 381-392. Reprinted with the permission of the author and the publisher, Tavistock Publications.

Although interest in groups has a long and respectable history, the past fifteen years have witnessed a new flowering of activity in this field. Today, research centers in several countries are carrying out substantial programs of research designed to reveal the nature of groups and of their functioning. The phrase "group dynamics" has come into common usage during this time and intense efforts have been devoted to the development of the field, both as a branch of social science and as a form of social technology. . . .

LIMITATIONS OF INDIVIDUALIST EXPLANATIONS

For various reasons we have found that much of our work has been devoted to an attempt to gain a better understanding of the ways in which people change their behavior or resist efforts by others to have them do so. Whether we set for ourselves the practical goal of improving behavior or whether we take on the intellectual task of understanding why people do what they do, we have to investigate processes of communication, influence, social pressure—in short, problems of change.

In this work we have encountered great frustration. The problems have been most difficult to solve. Looking back over our experience, I have become convinced that no small part of the trouble has resulted from an irresistible tendency to conceive of our problems in terms of the individual. We live in an individualistic culture. We value the individual highly, and rightly so. But I am inclined to believe that our political and social concern for the individual has narrowed our thinking as social scientists so much that we have not been able to state our research problems properly. Perhaps we have taken the individual as the unit of observation and study when some larger unit would have been more appropriate. Let us look at a few examples.

Consider first some matters having to do with the mental health of an individual. We can all agree, I believe, that an important mark of a healthy personality is that the individual's self-esteem has not been undermined. But on what does self-esteem depend? From research on this problem we have discovered that among other things, repeated experiences of failure or traumatic failures on matters of central importance serve to undermine one's self-esteem. We also know that whether a person experiences success or failure as a result of some undertaking depends upon the level of aspiration which he has set for himself. Now, if we try to discover how the level of aspiration gets set, we are immediately involved in the person's relationships to groups. The groups to which he belongs set standards for his behavior which he must accept if he is to remain in the group. If his capacities do not allow him to reach these standards, he experiences failure, he withdraws or is rejected by the group and his self-esteem suffers a shock.

Suppose, then, that we accept a task of therapy, of rebuilding his self-esteem. It would appear plausible from our analysis of the problem that we should attempt to work with variables of the same sort that produced the difficulty, that is to work with him either in the groups to which he now belongs or to introduce him into new groups which are selected for the purpose and to work upon his relationships to groups as such. From the point of view of preventive mental health, we might even attempt to train the groups in our communities—classes in schools, work groups in business, families, unions, religious and cultural groups—to make use of practices better designed to protect the self-esteem of their members.

Consider a second example. A teacher finds that in her class she has a number of trouble-makers, full of aggression. She wants to know why these children are so aggressive and what can be done about it. A foreman in a factory has the same kind of problem with some of his workers. He wants the same kind of help. The solution most tempting to both the teacher and the foreman often is to transfer the worst trouble-makers to someone else, or if facilities are available, to refer them for counseling. But is the problem really of such a nature that it can be solved by removing the trouble-maker from the situation or by working on his individual motivations and emotional life? What leads does research give us? The evidence indicates, of course, that there are many causes of aggressiveness in people, but one aspect of the problem has become increasingly clear in recent years. If we observe carefully the amount of aggressive behavior and the number of trouble-makers to be found in a large collection of groups, we find that these characteristics can vary tremendously from group to group even when the different groups are composed essentially of the same kinds of people. In the now classic experiments of Lewin, Lippitt, and White[1] on the effects of different styles of leadership, it was found that the same group of children displayed markedly different levels of aggressive behavior when under different styles of leadership. Moreover, when individual children were transferred from one group to another, their levels of aggressiveness shifted to conform to the atmosphere of the new group. Efforts to account for one child's aggressiveness under one style of leadership merely in terms of his personality traits could hardly succeed under these conditions. This is not to say that a person's behavior is entirely to be accounted for by the atmosphere and structure of the immediate group, but it is remarkable to what an extent a strong, cohesive group can control aspects of a member's behavior traditionally thought to be expressive of enduring personality traits. Recognition of this fact rephrases the problem of how to change such behavior. It directs us to a study of the sources of the influence of the group on its members.

Let us take an example from a different field. What can we learn from efforts to change people by mass media and mass persuasion? In those rare instances when educators, propagandists, advertisers, and others who want to influence large numbers of people, have bothered to make an objective evaluation of the en-

[1] K. Lewin, R. Lippitt, and R. K. White, "Patterns of Aggressive Behavior in Experimentally Created 'Social Climates,'" *Journal of Social Psychology*, Volume 10 (1939), pp. 271-299.

during changes produced by their efforts, they have been able to demonstrate only the most negligible effects.[2] The inefficiency of attempts to influence the public by mass media would be scandalous if there were agreement that it was important or even desirable to have such influences strongly exerted. In fact, it is not exaggeration to say that all of the research and experience of generations has not improved the efficiency of lectures or other means of mass influence to any noticeable degree. Something must be wrong with our theories of learning, motivation, and social psychology.

Within very recent years some research data have been accumulating which may give us a clue to the solution of our problem. In one series of experiments directed by Lewin, it was found that a method of group decision, in which the group as a whole made a decision to have its members change their behavior, was from two to ten times as effective in producing actual change as was a lecture presenting exhortation to change.[3] We have yet to learn precisely what produces these differences of effectiveness, but it is clear that by introducing group forces into the situation a whole new level of influence has been achieved.

The experience has been essentially the same when people have attempted to increase the productivity of individuals in work settings. Traditional conceptions of how to increase the output of workers have stressed the individual: select the right man for the job; simplify the job for him; train him in the skills required; motivate him by economic incentives; make it clear to whom he reports; keep the lines of authority and responsibility simple and straight. But even when all these conditions are fully met we are finding that productivity is far below full potential. There is even good reason to conclude that this individualistic conception of the determinants of productivity actually fosters negative consequences. The individual, now isolated and subjected to the demands of the organization through the commands of his boss, finds that he must create with his fellow employees informal groups, not shown on any table of organization, in order to protect himself from arbitrary control of his life, from the boredom produced by the endless repetition of mechanically sanitary and routine operations, and from the impoverishment of his emotional and social life brought about by the frustration of his basic needs for social interaction, participation, and acceptance in a stable group. Recent experiments have demonstrated clearly that the productivity of

work groups can be greatly increased by methods of work organization and supervision which give more responsibility to work groups, which allow for fuller participation in important decisions, and which make stable groups the firm basis for support of the individual's social needs.[4] I am convinced that future research will also demonstrate that people working under such conditions become more mature and creative individuals in their homes, in community life, and as citizens.

As a final example, let us examine the experience of efforts to train people in workshops, institutes, and special training courses. Such efforts are common in various areas of social welfare, intergroup relations, political affairs, industry, and adult education generally. It is an unfortunate fact that objective evaluation of the effects of such training efforts has only rarely been undertaken, but there is evidence for those who will look that the actual change in behavior produced is most disappointing. A workshop not infrequently develops keen interest among the participants, high morale and enthusiasm, and a firm resolve on the part of many to apply all the wonderful insights back home. But what happens back home? The trainee discovers that his colleagues don't share his enthusiasm. He learns that the task of changing others' expectations and ways of doing things is discouragingly difficult. He senses, perhaps not very clearly, that it would make all the difference in the world if only there were a few other people sharing his enthusiasm and insights with whom he could plan activities, evaluate consequences of efforts, and from whom he could gain emotional and motivational support. The approach to training which conceives of its task as being merely that of changing the individual probably produces frustration, demoralization, and disillusionment in as large a measure as it accomplishes more positive results.

A few years ago the Research Center for Group Dynamics undertook to shed light on this problem by investigating the operation of a workshop for training leaders in intercultural relations.[5] In a project, directed by Lippitt, we set out to compare systematically the different effects of the workshop upon trainees who came as isolated individuals in contrast to those who came as teams. Since one of the problems in the field of intercultural relations is that of getting people of good will to be more active in community efforts to improve intergroup relations, one goal of the training workshop was to increase the activity of the trainees in such community affairs. We found that

2 D. Cartwright, "Some Principles of Mass Persuasion: Selected Findings of Research on the Sale of United States War Bonds," *Human Relations*, Volume 2, Number 3 (1949), pp. 253-267.
3 K. Lewin, *Field Theory in Social Science* (New York: Harper and Brothers, 1951), pp. 229-236.

4 L. Coch and J. R. P. French, Jr., "Overcoming Resistance to Change," *Human Relations*, Volume 1, Number 4 (1948), pp. 512-532.
5 R. Lippitt, *Training in Community Relations* (New York: Harper and Brothers, 1949).

before the workshop there was no difference in the activity level of the people who were to be trained as isolates and of those who were to be trained as teams. Six months after the workshop, however, those who had been trained as isolates were only slightly more active than before the workshop whereas those who had been members of strong training teams were now much more active. We do not have clear evidence on the point, but we would be quite certain that the maintenance of heightened activity over a long period of time would also be much better for members of teams. For the isolates the effect of the workshop had the characteristic of a "shot in the arm" while for the team member it produced a more enduring change because the team provided continuous support and reinforcement for its members.

SOME APPLICATIONS OF GROUP DYNAMICS

What conclusions may we draw from these examples? What principles of achieving change in people can we see emerging? To begin with the most general proposition, we may state that the behavior, attitudes, beliefs, and values of the individual are all firmly grounded in the groups to which he belongs. How aggressive or cooperative a person is, how much self-respect and self-confidence he has, how energetic and productive his work is, what he aspires to, what he believes to be true and good, whom he loves or hates, and what beliefs and prejudices he holds—all these characteristics are highly determined by the individual's group memberships. In a real sense, they are properties of groups and of the relationships between people. Whether they change or resist change will, therefore, be greatly influenced by the nature of these groups. Attempts to change them must be concerned with the dynamics of groups.

In examining more specifically how groups enter into the process of change, we find it useful to view groups in at least three different ways. In the first view, the group is seen as a source of influence over its members. Efforts to change behavior can be supported or blocked by pressures on members stemming from the group. To make constructive use of these pressures the group must be used *as a medium of change*. In the second view, the group itself becomes the *target of change*. To change the behavior of individuals it may be necessary to change the standards of the group, its style of leadership, its emotional atmosphere, or its stratification into cliques and hierarchies. Even though the goal may be to change the behavior of *individuals*, the target of change becomes the group. In the third view, it is recognized that many changes of behavior can be brought about only by the organized efforts of groups *as agents of*

change. A committee to combat intolerance, a labor union, an employers association, a citizens group to increase the pay of teachers—any action group will be more or less effective depending upon the way it is organized, the satisfactions it provides to its members, the degree to which its goals are clear, and a host of other properties of the group.

An adequate social technology of change, then requires at the very least a scientific understanding of groups viewed in each of these ways. We shall consider here only the first two aspects of the problem: the group as a medium of change and as a target of change.

THE GROUP AS A MEDIUM OF CHANGE

PRINCIPLE NO. 1

If the group is to be used effectively as a medium of change, those people who are to be changed and those who are to exert influence for change must have a strong sense of belonging to the same group.

Kurt Lewin described this principle well: "The normal gap between teacher and student, doctor and patient, social worker and public, can . . . be a real obstacle to acceptance of the advocated conduct." In other words, in spite of whatever status differences there might be between them, the teacher and the student have to feel as members of one group in matters involving their sense of values. The chances for re-education seem to be increased whenever a strong we-feeling is created.[6] Recent experiments by Preston and Heintz have demonstrated greater changes of opinions among members of discussion groups operating with participatory leadership than among those with supervisory leadership.[7] The implications of this principle for classroom teaching are far-reaching. The same may be said of supervision in the factory, army, or hospital.

PRINCIPLE NO. 2

The more attractive the group is to its members the greater is the influence that the group can exert on its members.

This principle has been extensively documented by Festinger and his co-workers.[8] They have been able to show in a variety of settings that in more cohesive groups there is a greater readiness of members to at-

6 K. Lewin, *Resolving Social Conflicts* (New York: Harper and Brothers, 1948), p. 67.
7 M. G. Preston and R. K. Heintz, "Effects of Participatory vs. Supervisory Leadership on Group Judgment," *Journal of Abnormal and Social Psychology*, Volume 44 (1949), pp. 345-355.
8 L. Festinger *et al.*, *Theory and Experiment in Social Communication* (Ann Arbor: Institute for Social Research, 1950).

tempt to influence others, a greater readiness to be influenced by others, and stronger pressures toward conformity when conformity is a relevant matter for the group. Important for the practitioner wanting to make use of this principle is, of course, the question of how to increase the attractiveness of groups. This is a question with many answers. Suffice it to say that a group is more attractive the more it satisfies the needs of its members. We have been able to demonstrate experimentally an increase in group cohesiveness by increasing the liking of members for each other as persons, by increasing the perceived importance of the group goal, and by increasing the prestige of the group among other groups. Experienced group workers could add many other ways to this list.

PRINCIPLE NO. 3

In attempts to change attitudes, values, or behavior the more relevant they are to the basis of attraction to the group, the greater will be the influence that the group can exert upon them.

I believe this principle gives a clue to some otherwise puzzling phenomena. How does it happen that a group, like a labor union, seems to be able to exert such strong discipline over its members in some matters (let us say in dealings with management), while it seems unable to exert nearly the same influence in other matters (let us say in political action)? If we examine why it is that members are attracted to the group, I believe we will find that a particular reason for belonging seems more related to some of the group's activities than to others. If a man joins a union mainly to keep his job and to improve his working conditions, he may be largely uninfluenced by the union's attempt to modify his attitudes toward national and international affairs. Groups differ tremendously in the range of matters that are relevant to them and hence over which they have influence. Much of the inefficiency of adult education could be reduced if more attention were paid to the need that influence attempts be appropriate to the groups in which they are made.

PRINCIPLE NO. 4

The greater the prestige of a group member in the eyes of the other members, the greater the influence he can exert.

Polansky, Lippitt, and Redl [9] have demonstrated this principle with great care and methodological ingenuity in a series of studies in children's summer camps. From a practical point of view it must be emphasized that the things giving prestige to a member may not be those characteristics most prized by the official management of the group. The most prestige-carrying member of a Sunday School class may not possess the characteristics most similar to the minister of the church. The teacher's pet may be a poor source of influence within a class. This principle is the basis for the common observation that the official leader and the actual leader of a group are often not the same individual.

PRINCIPLE NO. 5

Efforts to change individuals or subparts of a group which, if successful, would have the result of making them deviate from the norms of the group will encounter strong resistance.

During the past few years a great deal of evidence has been accumulated showing the tremendous pressures which groups can exert upon members to conform to the group's norms. The price of deviation in most groups is rejection or even expulsion. If the member really wants to belong and be accepted, he cannot withstand this type of pressure. It is for this reason that efforts to change people by taking them from the group and giving them special training so often have disappointing results. This principle also accounts for the finding that people thus trained sometimes display increased tension, aggressiveness toward the group, or a tendency to form cults or cliques with others who have shared their training.

These five principles concerning the group as a medium of change would appear to have readiest application to groups created for the purpose of producing changes in people. They provide certain specifications for building effective training or therapy groups. They also point, however, to a difficulty in producing change in people in that they show how resistant an individual is to changing in any way contrary to group pressures and expectations. In order to achieve many kinds of changes in people, therefore, it is necessary to deal with the group as a target of change.

THE GROUP AS A TARGET OF CHANGE

PRINCIPLE NO. 6

Strong pressure for changes in the group can be established by creating a shared perception by members of the need for change, thus making the source of pressure for change lie within the group.

Marrow and French [10] report a dramatic case-study which illustrates this principle quite well. A manufacturing concern had a policy against hiring women over thirty because it was believed that they were

---

9   N. Polansky, R. Lippitt, and F. Redl, "An Investigation of Behavioral Contagion in Groups," *Human Relations*, Volume 3, Number 4 (1950), pp. 319-348.

10   A. J. Marrow and J. R. P. French, Jr., "Changing a Stereotype in Industry," *Journal of Social Issues*, Volume 1, Number 3 (1945), pp. 33-37.

slower, more difficult to train, and more likely to be absent. The staff psychologist was able to present to management evidence that this belief was clearly unwarranted at least within their own company. The psychologist's facts, however, were rejected and ignored as a basis for action because they violated accepted beliefs. It was claimed that they went against the direct experience of the foremen. Then the psychologist hit upon a plan for achieving change which differed drastically from the usual one of argument, persuasion, and pressure. He proposed that management conduct its own analysis of the situation. With his help management collected all the facts which they believed were relevant to the problem. When the results were in they were now their own facts rather than those of some "outside" expert. Policy was immediately changed without further resistance. The important point here is that facts are not enough. The facts must be the accepted property of the group if they are to become an effective basis for change. There seems to be all the difference in the world in changes actually carried out between those cases in which a consulting firm is hired to do a study and present a report and those in which technical experts are asked to collaborate with the group in doing its own study.

PRINCIPLE NO. 7

Information relating to the need for change, plans for change, and consequences of change must be shared by all relevant people in the group.

Another way of stating this principle is to say that change of a group ordinarily requires the opening of communication channels. Newcomb[11] has shown how one of the first consequences of mistrust and hostility is the avoidance of communicating openly and freely about the things producing the tension. If you look closely at a pathological group (that is, one that has trouble making decisions or effecting coordinated efforts of its members), you will certainly find strong restraints in that group against communicating vital

11   T. M. Newcomb, "Autistic Hostility and Social Reality," *Human Relations,* Volume 1, Number 1 (1947), pp. 69-86.

information among its members. Until these restraints are removed there can be little hope for any real and lasting changes in the group's functioning. In passing it should be pointed out that the removal of barriers to communication will ordinarily be accompanied by a sudden increase in the communication of hostility. The group may appear to be falling apart, and it will certainly be a painful experience to many of the members. This pain and the fear that things are getting out of hand often stop the process of change once begun.

PRINCIPLE NO. 8

Changes in one part of a group produce strain in other related parts which can be reduced only by eliminating the change or by bringing about readjustments in the related parts.

It is a common practice to undertake improvements in group functioning by providing training programs for certain classes of people in the organization. A training program for foremen, for nurses, for teachers, or for group workers is established. If the content of the training is relevant for organizational change, it must of necessity deal with the relationships these people have with other subgroups. If nurses in a hospital change their behavior significantly, it will affect their relations both with the patients and with the doctors. It is unrealistic to assume that both these groups will remain indifferent to any significant changes in this respect. In hierarchical structures this process is most clear. Lippitt has proposed on the basis of research and experience that in such organizations attempts at change should always involve three levels, one being the major target of change and the other two being the one above and the one below.

These eight principles represent a few of the basic propositions emerging from research in group dynamics. Since research is constantly going on and since it is the very nature of research to revise and reformulate our conceptions, we may be sure that these principles will have to be modified and improved as time goes by.

INDEX OF NAMES AND ORGANIZATIONS

775103

DATE